Northern Ireland
Pages 258–289

North of the Liffey
Pages 88–97

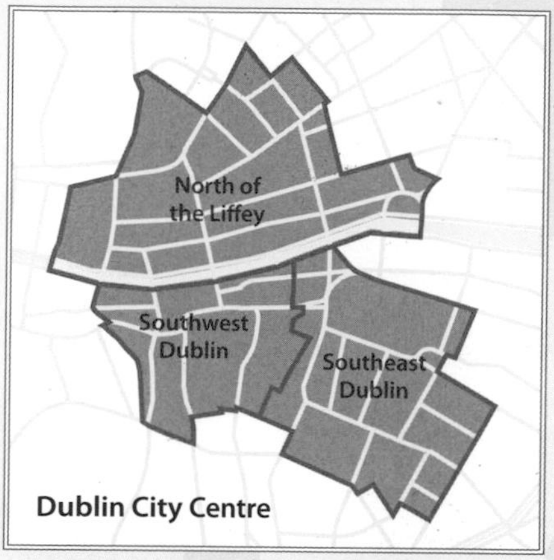

Southwest Dublin
Pages 76–87

Southeast Dublin
Pages 60–75

Southeast Ireland
Pages 128–155

The Midlands
Pages 240–257

EYEWITNESS TRAVEL

EYEWITNESS TRAVEL

IRELAND

Main Contributors **Lisa Gerard-Sharp and Tim Perry**

DK

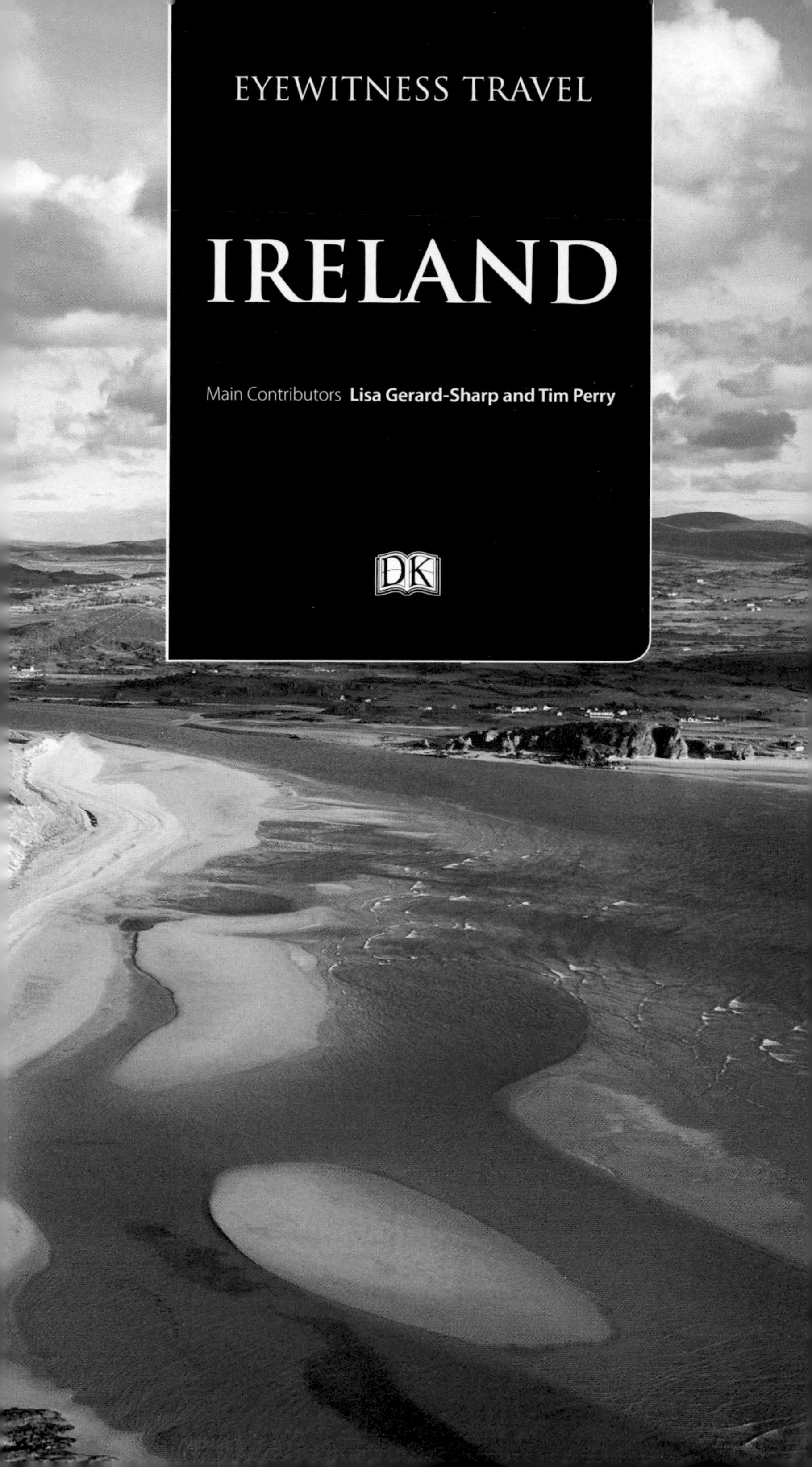

DK | Penguin Random House

Project Editor Ferdie McDonald

Art Editor Lisa Kosky

Editors Maggie Crowley, Simon Farbrother, Emily Hatchwell, Seán O'Connell, Jane Simmonds

Designers Joy Fitzsimmons, Jaki Grosvenor, Katie Peacock, Jan Richter

Researchers John Breslin, Andrea Holmes

Picture Researchers Sue Mennell, Christine Rista

DTP Designers Samantha Borland, Adam Moore

Contributors

Una Carlin, Polly Phillimore, Susan Poole, Martin Walters

Photographers

Joe Cornish, Tim Daly, Alan Williams

Illustrators

Draughtsman Maps, Maltings Partnership, Robbie Polley

Printed and bound in China

First published in the UK in 1995 by Dorling Kindersley Limited,
80 Strand, London WC2R 0RL, UK

16 17 18 19 10 9 8 7 6 5 4 3 2 1

Reprinted With Revisions 1996 (Twice), 1997, 1999, 2000, 2001, 2002, 2003, 2004, 2006, 2007, 2008, 2009, 2010, 2011, 2012, 2013, 2014, 2015, 2016

A CIP catalogue record is available from the British Library.

ISBN 978-0-24120-952-3

Front cover main image: Boyeeghter Bay, Rosguil, Co.Donegal, Ireland

◀ Inishowen Peninsula, Northwest Ireland

Contents

An evangelical symbol from the Book of Kells *(see p68)*

Introducing Ireland

Dublin Area by Area

Georgian doorway in Fitzwilliam Square, Dublin *(see p72)*

Detail of the Chorus Gate at Powerscourt *(see pp138–9)*

Ireland Region by Region

Grazing cows at Spanish Point near Mizen Head *(see p171)*

Travellers' Needs

Survival Guide

Façade of a pub in Dingle *(see p161)*

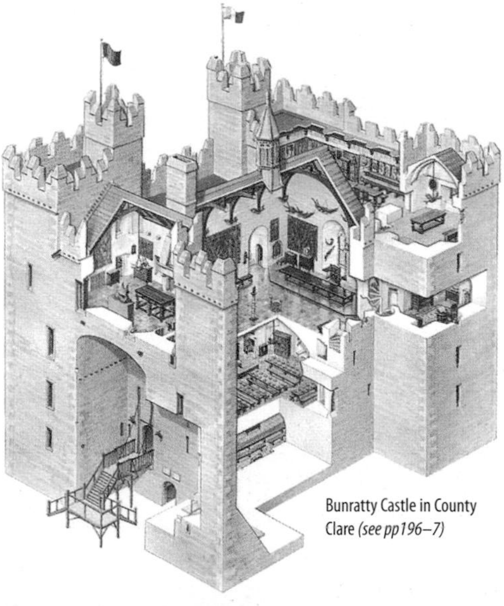

Bunratty Castle in County Clare *(see pp196–7)*

HOW TO USE THIS GUIDE

This guide helps you to get the most from your visit to Ireland. It provides both expert recommendations and detailed practical information. *Introducing Ireland* maps the country and sets it in its historical and cultural context. The seven regional chapters, plus *Dublin Area by Area*, contain descriptions of all the important sights, with maps, pictures and illustrations. Restaurant and hotel recommendations can be found in *Travellers' Needs*. The *Survival Guide* has tips on everything from the telephone system to transport both in the Republic and in Northern Ireland.

Dublin Area by Area

Central Dublin is divided into three sightseeing areas. Each has its own chapter, which opens with a list of the sights described. A fourth chapter, *Further Afield*, covers the suburbs and County Dublin. Sights are numbered and plotted on an *Area Map*. The descriptions of each sight follow the map's numerical order, making sights easy to locate within the chapter.

All pages relating to Dublin have *red* thumb tabs.

A locator map shows where you are in relation to other areas of the city centre.

1 Area Map For easy reference, the sights are numbered and located on a map. Sights in the city centre are also shown on the Dublin Street Finder on pages 122–3.

Sights at a Glance lists the chapter's sights by category: Churches, Museums and Galleries, Historic Buildings, Parks and Gardens.

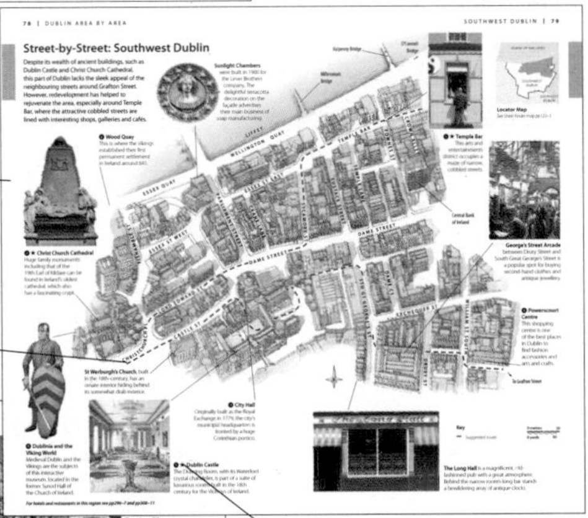

2 Street-by-Street Map This gives a bird's-eye view of the key area in each chapter.

A suggested route for a walk is shown in red.

Stars indicate the sights that no visitor should miss.

3 Detailed Information The sights in Dublin are described individually with addresses, telephone numbers and information on opening hours and admission charges.

Story boxes highlight noteworthy features of the sights.

Ireland Region by Region

Apart from Dublin, Ireland has been divided into seven regions, each of which has a separate chapter. The most interesting towns and places to visit in each area have been numbered on a *Regional Map*.

1 Introduction The landscape, history and character of each region is described here, showing how the area has developed over the centuries and what it offers to the visitor today.

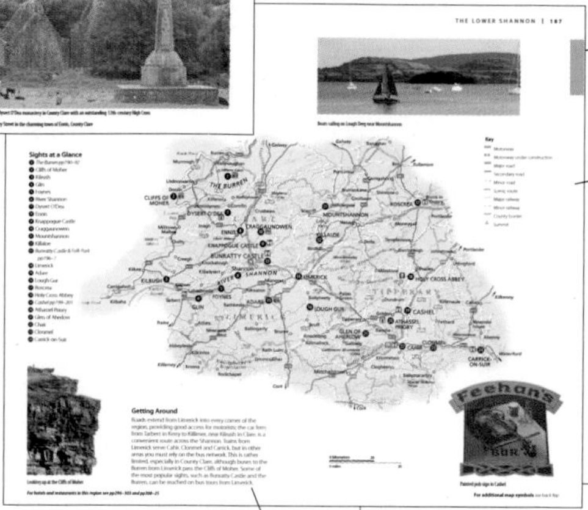

Each region of Ireland can be quickly identified by its colour coding, shown on the inside front cover.

2 Regional Map This shows the road network and gives an illustrated overview of the whole region. All interesting places to visit are numbered and there are also useful tips on getting around the region by car and train.

Getting Around gives tips on travel within the region.

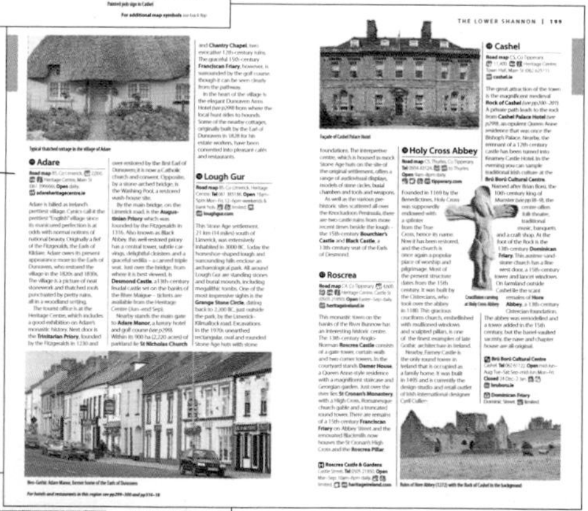

3 Detailed Information All the important towns and other places to visit are described individually. They are listed in order, following the numbering on the Regional Map. Within each town or city, there is detailed information on important buildings and other sights.

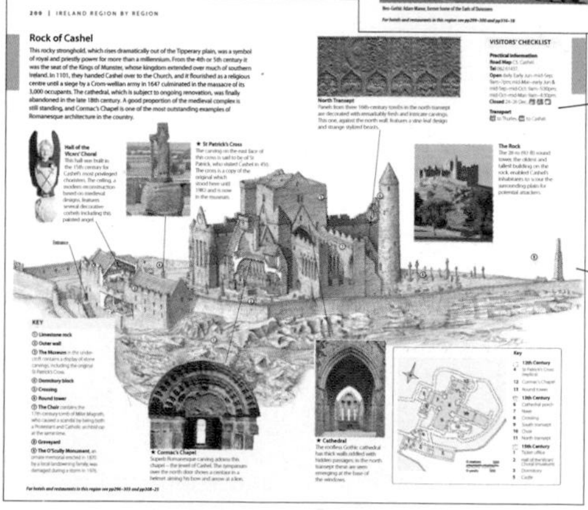

The Visitors' Checklist provides all the practical information you will need to plan your visit to all the top sights.

4 Ireland's Top Sights These are given two or more full pages. Historic buildings are dissected to reveal their interiors. The most interesting towns or city centres are shown in a bird's-eye view, with sights picked out and described.

INTRODUCING IRELAND

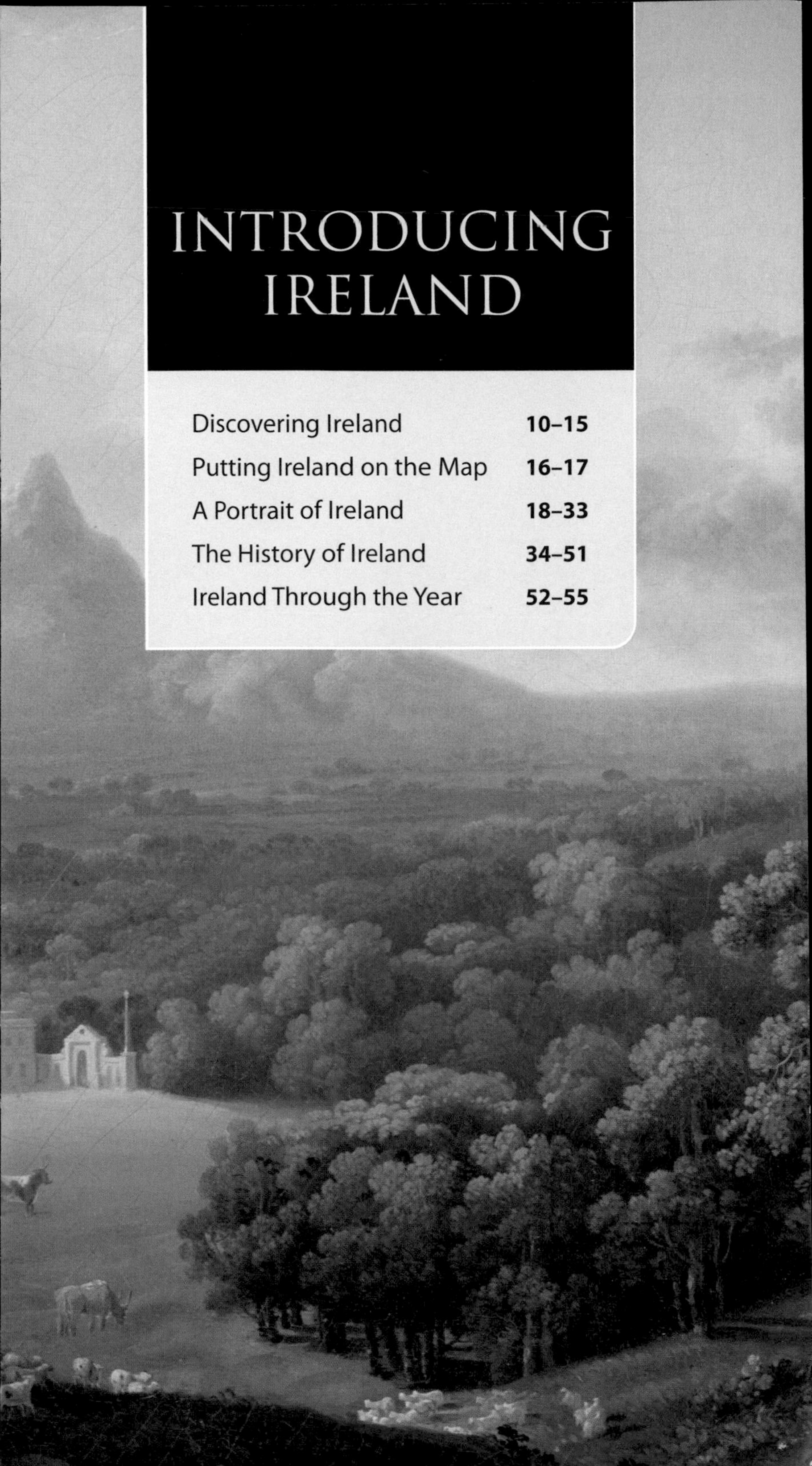

DISCOVERING IRELAND

The following itineraries have been designed to take in as many of Ireland's highlights as possible, while keeping long-distance travel manageable. First comes a two-day tour of the country's capital, Dublin. There is a three-day tour of Northern Ireland, with some time spent in the fascinating city of Belfast, as well as a trip to the beautiful Ards Peninsula and the Causeway Coast. A one-week tour of the whole country covers many of Ireland's must-see sights, stopping off at cities and areas of great natural beauty. Extra suggestions are provided for those who want to extend their trip to 10 days. Finally, there is a superb two-week tour of the whole country, which takes in all the sights of the one-week tour and more. Pick, combine and follow your favourite tours, or simply dip in and out and be inspired.

Carrick-a-rede Rope Bridge
Hanging 25 m (80 ft) above the sea, the Carrick-a-rede Rope Bridge spans a scary 20-m (65-ft) chasm across to a tiny rocky island.

One Week in Ireland

- Spend a day exploring the city of **Dublin**, Ireland's buzzing capital.
- Drive around the beautiful, **Ring of Kerry**, taking in sea views along the way.
- See the breathtaking **Cliffs of Moher** in the Burren, County Clare.
- Seek out great music in the vibrant city of **Galway**.
- Explore the **North Antrim Coastline**, stopping off at the beautiful sandy beach of **Benone Strand**.
- Stand in awe at the magnificent **Giant's Causeway** in County Antrim.
- Visit the passage tombs of **Newgrange** in the **Boyne Valley** to find out about Ireland's prehistoric past.

Key
One week in Ireland
Two weeks in Ireland

◀ *A View of Powerscourt* by George Barret the Elder (c. 1728–84)

Kilkenny
The picturesque city of Kilkenny sits on the banks of the River Nore.

Two Weeks in Ireland

- Get to know Ireland's vibrant capital, **Dublin**.
- Discover the wild **Wicklow Mountains**; spend some time shopping and eating in the lovely city of **Kilkenny**.
- Visit the oldest city in Ireland – **Waterford** – founded by the Vikings in 914.
- Take a tour of the scenic **Dingle Peninsula** and spend an evening in the laid-back town of **Dingle**.
- Walk in the beautiful **Connemara National Park**; end the day in **Westport**.
- Scramble over the weird and wonderful landscape of the **Giant's Causeway** in County Antrim.

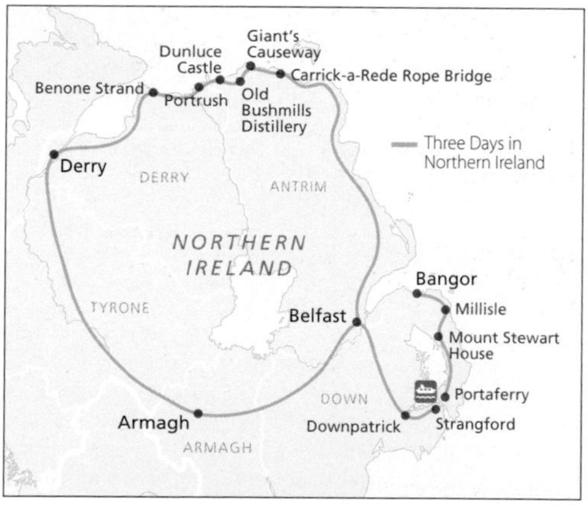

Three Days in Northern Ireland

- Head out from Belfast to explore the stunning **Ards Peninsula**; stop off to tour Mount Stewart House.
- Spend an evening in **Belfast's** historic drinking palace, the Crown Liquor Saloon.
- Wander the streets of one of Ireland's oldest cities, **Armagh**.
- Visit the walled city of **Londonderry** and learn about its history at the Tower Museum.
- See the atmospheric ruins of **Dunluce Castle** perched on a cliff on the Causeway Coastline.
- Explore the **Giant's Causeway** and walk the scary **Carrick-a-rede Rope Bridge**.

Two Days in Dublin

Ireland's vibrant capital is fairly small, but jam-packed with things to see and do.

- **Arriving** Dublin Airport is 12 km (7 miles) north of the city. The express coach, or a taxi, takes around 30 minutes to get to the city.

Day 1

Devote an hour to the magnificent **National Museum – Archaeology** *(pp70–71)*. Afterwards, visit **Trinity College** *(pp66–7)* to see the breathtaking Book of Kells Exhibition, and take a break in the college's lovely grounds. From here, it's a short walk to **Temple Bar** *(p82)*, a good place to stop off for lunch. Venture a little way out of the centre to visit the **Guinness Storehouse** *(p102)* to find out all there is to know about the nation's famous brew. Take a trip to the **National Museum of Ireland – Decorative Arts & History** *(p105)* where the rich history of Ireland is told through its crafts. In the evening see a play at the wonderful **Gate Theatre** *(p94)*.

Day 2

Begin your day with a visit to architecturally eclectic **Christ Church Cathedral** *(pp84–5)*. Just across the road is **Dublinia and the Viking World** *(p83)*, where the history of Viking Dublin is on display. Take the excellent tour of **Dublin Castle** *(pp80–81)* and visit the **Chester Beatty Library** *(p81)* to see the beautiful historic manuscripts. Pick up a picnic lunch and stroll down Grafton Street to the pretty, ancient park of **St Stephen's Green** *(pp64–5)*. Walk to **Fitzwilliam Square** *(p72)* and stop off at no. 29 for a fascinating insight into middle-class Georgian life. Visit the **National Gallery of Ireland** *(p74–5)* to see the small but significant collection of Irish and international art, and in the evening, enjoy the craic in one of the south side's lively pubs.

The grand façade of Trinity College's School of Law, Dublin

Three Days in Northern Ireland

- **Arriving** Arrive and depart from Belfast International or Belfast City Airport.
- **Transport** A car is essential for the Antrim Coast and the Ards Peninsula.
- **Booking ahead** In the height of the summer pre-booking a hire car is advisable. Pre-book a black cab tour of the Belfast murals.

Day 1: The Ards Peninsula

Start early and head east out of Belfast to explore a less-visited area, the **Ards Peninsula** *(p284)*, for its wonderful sights and beautiful scenery. Follow the coast road through Bangor and the pretty seaside town of Donaghadee to Millisle, where the fully functional Ballycopeland Windmill makes an interesting place to pause. Head westwards towards Strangford Lough and stop at **Mount Stewart House** *(pp286–7)* with its lovely gardens and excellent guided tours of the house. From here, follow the shores of the Lough southwards pausing to look at the ruins of Grey Abbey. Take the ferry from Portaferry and continue on to **Downpatrick** *(p285)* where the County Museum and Down Cathedral are both well worth a visit. From here, head back to **Belfast** *(pp280–83)* where you can admire the unspoiled Victoriana of the Crown Liquor Saloon. A drive around west Belfast reveals the city's dark history, told in its vivid murals. End the day with a trip to the outstanding **Titanic Quarter** *(p283)*. Visit the interactive Titanic Belfast attraction to learn about the construction and voyage of the ill-fated ship.

Day 2: Armagh and Londonderry

From Belfast, travel to **Armagh** *(p278)*, worth visiting for the planetarium set in picturesque gardens with good views over the city, and for the two St Patrick's Cathedrals facing each other across the city. The mall in the centre of the old town makes for a fine stroll. Continue on through Fermanagh to the walled city of **Londonderry** *(pp262–3)*. Visit the Tower Museum for an unbiased account of the city's history during the Troubles. Another exhibit, *An Armada Shipwreck*, focuses on the largest ship of the Spanish Armada.

Titanica, a sculpture by Rowan Gillespie, in front of Titanic Belfast

Day 3: The Causeway Coast

From Londonderry, the day's driving brings you to some of the finest unspoiled coastal scenery in the British Isles. The journey begins on the **North Antrim Coastline** *(p265)*. Head along the shores of Lough Foyle to **Benone Strand** *(p264)* to enjoy the fine, golden sandy beach. **Portrush** *(p264)* is the next stopping point, a busy but pretty seaside town. Moving on, admire the ruins of **Dunluce Castle** *(p265)* before stopping off at the **Old Bushmills Distillery** *(p270)* for a tour and

For practical information on travelling around Ireland, see pp365–73

a whiskey sampling session. The highlight of the day is the wonderful landscape of the **Giant's Causeway** *(pp266–7)*, made up of basalt columns. Continue on to the **Carrick-a-rede Rope Bridge** *(p265)* – it makes a fine adventure for those with a strong stomach. Relax for the rest of the day and enjoy the stunning views as the road follows the coast back towards Belfast.

One Week in Ireland

- **Arriving** Arrive and depart from Dublin Airport or by ferry from Liverpool or Holyhead.
- **Transport** A car is essential for this trip.

Day 1: Dublin
Pick a day from the city itinerary on p12.

Day 2: Kilkenny to Cashel
Visit **Kilkenny** *(pp146–8)* for some elegant architecture, the medieval St Canice's Cathedral, the beautifully restored Kilkenny Castle and some great shopping opportunities. Take a tour of the **Nicholas Mosse Pottery Factory** *(p333)*, in nearby Bennettsbridge. Next, visit **Cashel** *(p199)* with its imposing medieval abbey. Round the day off with a trip to the Brú Ború Cultural Centre, also in Cashel.

Day 3: Ring of Kerry
Start the day in the lively town of **Killarney** *(p163)*, where you can enjoy Irish tourism at its most flamboyant. Killarney has many attractive features, and it makes a good base, but it is the circular drive around the **Ring of Kerry** *(pp168–9)*, stopping at quaint villages and taking in the stunning seascapes, that really makes the trip worthwhile. End the tour in **Tralee** *(pp160–61)*, a working town steeped in traditional Irish culture. Pay a visit to the County Kerry Museum, and take in a performance of Siamsa Tíre – the National Folk Theatre of Ireland.

The Rock of Cashel, rising dramatically out over the Tipperary plain

To extend your trip...
Spend two days on the beautiful **Dingle Peninsula** *(pp162–3)* and stay a night in **Dingle** town *(p161)*.

Day 4: Tralee to Galway
From Tralee head towards **Limerick** *(p195)*. Here, visit the Hunt Museum, with its superb collection of antiquities, and the beautiful St Mary's Cathedral. Next stop is **Ennis** *(p193)*, a pretty, working town with some old-fashioned restaurants. Stop off for lunch in Ennis before heading towards the coast and the stunning **Cliffs of Moher** *(p188)*. From here you can follow winding coastal roads through Ballyvaughan in the Burren to **Galway** *(pp214–5)*. The city has lively nightlife with lots of options for traditional and not-so-traditional music.

The beautiful, dramatic landscape of Giant's Causeway, County Antrim

Day 5: Galway to Sligo
Head towards **Clifden** *(pp210–11)*, through stunning lakeland and mountain scenery. From here, head to **Westport** *(pp208)*, stopping off to visit Westport House. Next, travel to **Sligo** *(p238)* a busy rural town with a vibrant arts scene.

To extend your trip...
Visit beautiful **Achill Island** *(p208)* in County Mayo. It is easily reached by a road bridge.

Day 6: Northern Ireland
From Sligo, head towards Derry and spend a day exploring the **North Antrim Coastline** *(p265)*. Make the first stop at **Benone Strand** *(p264)*, an amazing stretch of sandy beach. Visit the seaside town of **Portrush** *(p264)* before moving on to the ruins of **Dunluce Castle** *(p265)*. The highlight is the **Giant's Causeway** a couple of hours wandering the bizarre, but beautiful landscape here. End the day with dinner in **Belfast** *(pp280–3)*.

Day 7: The Boyne Valley
The route back to Dublin lies through **Newgrange and the Boyne Valley** *(pp248–9)*. Here you will find passage graves, ancient ring forts and Neolithic artwork. Admission to the passage tombs are by tour only and cannot be booked in advance. Heading on, leave the M1 for Balbriggan and follow the coastal roads towards Dublin.

Two Weeks in Ireland

- **Airports** Arrive and depart from Dublin Airport or by ferry from Liverpool or Holyhead.
- **Transport** A car is essential for this trip.

Day 1: Dublin
Pick a day from the city itinerary on p12.

Day 2: Wicklow to Kilkenny
Head south out of the city towards Enniskerry, where there are fine gardens and a house to explore at **Powerscourt** *(pp138–9)*. From here you can follow part of the **Military Road** *(p142)* that winds through the windswept **Wicklow Mountains** *(p143)*. If the weather is fine, forgo the pleasures of the cafés at Powerscourt and take a picnic lunch. There are plenty of stunning beauty spots en route to take a break. Leave the circuit at Laragh and head towards **Kilkenny** *(pp146–7)* where there is excellent shopping, good restaurants and, if time allows, **Kilenny Castle** *(p148)* to explore.

Day 3: Kilkenny to Cork City
Head towards **Waterford** *(pp150–51)*, Ireland's oldest city. The three Waterfront Treasures museums tell the story of the city's rise and fall. Also take time to visit the Waterford Crystal Visitor Centre, where regular tours explain the process of creating the city's beautiful glassware. Follow the coast road to **Youghal** *(p183)* with its medieval town walls and imposing clock tower. From here, travel to Midleton to visit the 18th-century **Old Midleton Distillery** *(p183)* – it is Ireland's largest. Take a tour and sample some of the fine whiskey produced here. Finish your day in the city of **Cork** *(pp178–9)* and take a trip out to **Blarney Castle** *(p175)*. The pretty village of Blarney itself has some nice pubs in which to while away the evening.

Day 4: West Cork
Visit the **English Market** *(p180)* in Cork to admire the local cheeses and vegetables and perhaps pick up a picnic lunch. Next, head towards **Kinsale** *(pp176–7)* and spend a morning exploring this historic town. In the afternoon, travel along the coast through tiny villages and lovely seascapes towards Bantry. Look out for signposts to the **Drombeg Stone Circle** *(p174)* and, if there is time, take in the attractive seaside town of **Baltimore** *(p174)*. **Bantry** *(p171)* makes an excellent place to stop for the night – there are good restaurants and music here most nights in summer.

Day 5: Ring of Kerry via Kenmare
Take the stunning trip over the Caha mountains via Glengarriff to **Kenmare** *(p170)*, a great base for exploring the Ring of Kerry. Stop for lunch at one of the town's gourmet restaurants

Colourfully painted buildings lining a street in Dingle town

before driving around the Iveragh Peninsula, traditionally known as the **Ring of Kerry** *(pp168–9)*. Pause at one or two of the little villages along the way and enjoy the spectacular scenery. Spend the night in **Tralee** *(pp160–61)*, a workaday, but pretty town.

Day 6: Dingle Peninsula
Take a tour around the beautiful **Dingle Peninsula** *(pp162–3)*, and stop off in the town of **Dingle** *(p161)* for a seafood lunch in one of the bars in the bay. Spend a couple of hours enjoying the pleasures of this colourful town, then travel to the **Blasket Centre** *(p162)* to find out more about the islands. Now uninhabited, they once supported a strong Gaelic community and culture. Visit **Ballyferriter** *(p162)* to watch pots being made.

Day 7: Clare and the Burren
Making use of the Killimer-Tarbert ferry, follow the coast roads through Kilkee, Milltown Malbay, the **Cliffs of Moher** and **Doolin** *(p192)* for their elemental, windswept views and pleasant villages. Doolin is home to some excellent traditional music. Start your exploration of the **Burren** *(pp190–92)* in wild and beautiful **Mullaghmore** *(p192)*. The town of **Ennis** *(p193)* is an excellent place to stop for the night, not least for its musical pub life.

Powerscourt House and its beautiful gardens, Wicklow

For practical information on travelling around Ireland, see pp365–73

Day 8: Limerick to Galway
Turning south, spend the morning in **Limerick** *(p195)* admiring the amazing collection of antiquities in the Hunt Museum, and the austere St Mary's Cathedral. In the afternoon, visit the beautifully restored **Bunratty Castle & Folk Park** *(pp196–7)*. The Folk Park has meticulously recreated 19th-century rural life in Ireland and is well worth a visit. Next, move on to **Galway** city *(pp214–5)*, and spend the evening in one of the restaurants or bars lining Quay Street.

A calm sea inlet on the Sky Road, near Clifden, County Galway

Day 9: Connemara
From Galway, follow the coast roads through **Roundstone** and **Clifden** and the **Sky Road** *(pp10–11)*, a circular route with spectacular ocean views. Visit the organic farm of **Dan O'Hara's Homestead** *(p211)*, just east of Clifden, and the lovely lakeside castle of **Kylemore Abbey** *(p212)*. Walks in the beautiful **Connemara National Park** *(p212)* are accessible through the visitor centre. End your day in the smart little town of **Westport** *(p208)*.

Day 10: Mayo and Sligo
Start the day with a visit to the beautifully renovated 18th-century **Westport House** *(p208)*. Next, move on to **Achill Island** *(p208)*, and enjoy the seascapes of the Atlantic Coast Drive. Head to **Sligo** *(p238)* for lunch and check out the Model Arts & Niland Gallery in the town for wonderful paintings by Jack B Yeats. Look out for the statue of his brother, Ireland's most famous poet, W B Yeats, on Stephen Street. The Sligo County Museum on the same street houses a collection of Yeats memorabilia.

Day 11: Donegal
The coast of Donegal is one of the least visited and most beautiful areas of Ireland. Heading out from Sligo, journey towards the sleepy valley of **Glencolmcille** *(pp232–3)*. Take the narrow coastal roads –the traffic will be thin and the scenery is stunning. Drive through **The Rosses** *(p232)*, an area studded with lakes and inlets, and on to the **Bloody Foreland** *(p228)* named for the red hues of the rocks at sunset. For truly stunning views, make for **Horn Head** *(p229)*, and if the weather is fine, take a dip at the Killahoey Strand, the local beach. End the day's driving in Londonderry.

Day 12: Derry to Antrim
Spend the day on the North Antrim coastline. From Londonderry, head north towards **Benone Strand** *(p264)*. Look out for the Martello tower at the western end of this beautiful, sandy stretch of beach. Continue on to the atmospheric ruins of **Dunluce Castle** *(p265)*, perched on a crag on the Causeway coastline. Next stop is the **Old Bushmills Distillery** *(p270)*, where you can stop for a tour and a whiskey tasting. The highlight of the day, however, is a trip to the magnificent **Giant's Causeway** *(pp266–7)*. Made up of basalt columns stretching out into the sea, the causeway warrants a good hour's exploration.

Bronze statue of Sligo's favourite son, W B Yeats, Stephen Street, Sligo

Day 13: Belfast and Down
Head east towards Belfast and the scenic **Ards Peninsula** *(p284)*. From Belfast follow the coast road through Bangor, stopping off at the **Ulster Folk and Transport Museum** *(p284)* on the way. Further west is **Mount Stewart House** *(pp286–7)*. Break here for lunch and explore the lovely gardens. Continue on to Portaferry, where you can take the ferry across to **Downpatrick** *(p285)* to visit Down Cathedral and the interesting county museum. From here, drive back to Belfast for the evening.

Day 14: Boyne Valley and the Midlands
Travel south to **Newgrange and the Boyne Valley** *(pp248–9)*, the spiritual heartland of Ireland. Visit the mysterious passage tombs at **Newgrange** *(pp250–51)* and **Knowth** *(p249)* – both sites are accessed via tours run by the visitor centre near Newgrange. Be prepared for long queues. Next, head to the **Hill of Tara** *(p252)* for a tour of this important ancient site that takes in tombs and Iron Age hill forts. Drive back to Dublin for an evening meal and a drink in one of the city's lively pubs.

Putting Ireland on the Map

The island of Ireland covers an area of 84,430 sq km (32,598 sq miles). Lying in the Atlantic Ocean to the northwest of mainland Europe, it is separated from Great Britain by the Irish Sea. The Republic of Ireland takes up 85 per cent of the island, with a population of 4.6 million. Northern Ireland, part of the United Kingdom, has 1.8 million people. Dublin is the capital of the Republic and has good international communications.

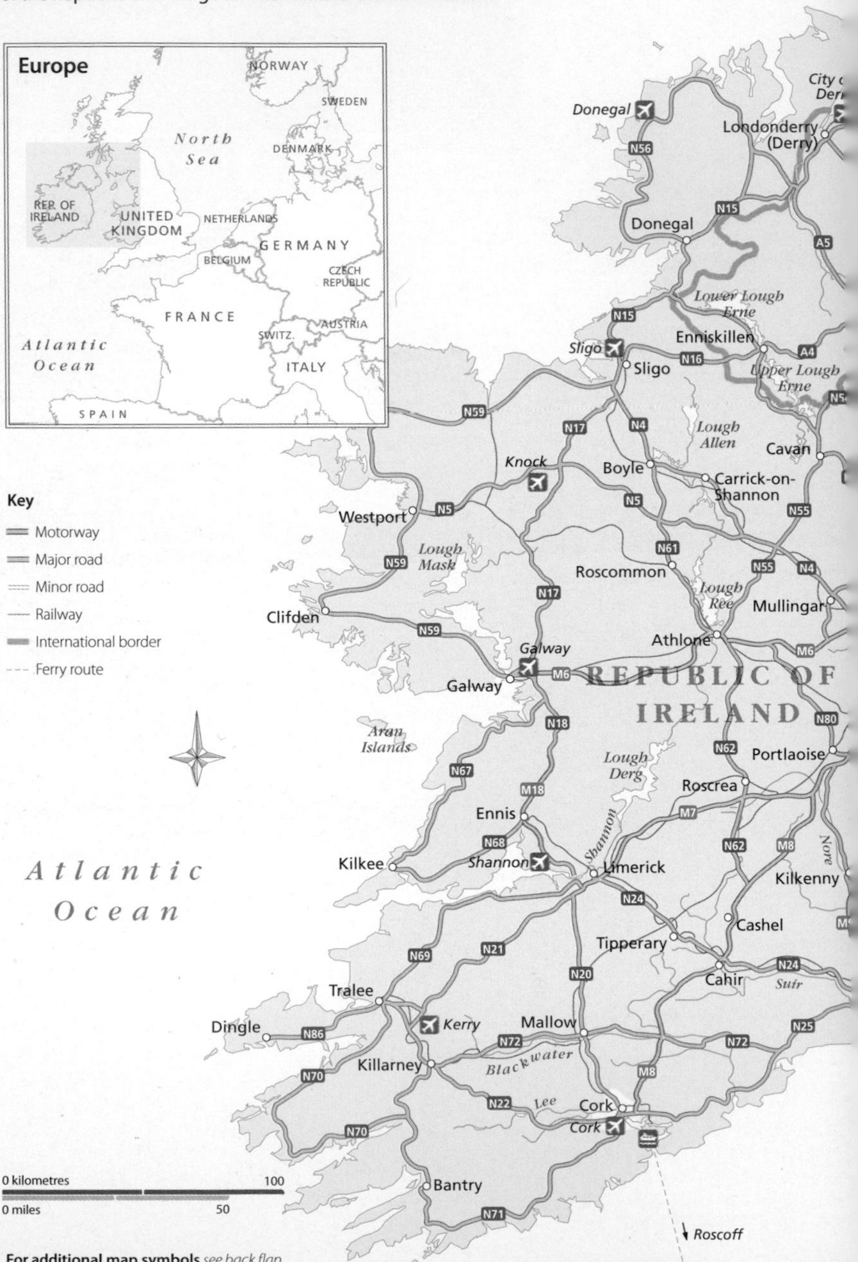

For additional map symbols *see back flap*

Greater Dublin
0 km 5
0 miles 5
Swords
Dublin Airport
Finglas
Royal Canal
Glasnevin
Marino
Howth
Liffey
DUBLIN
Lucan
Grand Canal
Kilmainham
Ballsbridge
Dublin Bay
Clondalkin
Rathmines
Tallaght
Dundrum
Dun Laoghaire
Mull
Jura
Islay
SCOTLAND
Greenock
Arran
Troon
Ayr
North Channel
Campbeltown
Ballycastle
Coleraine
Cairnryan
Stranraer
NORTHERN IRELAND
Larne
Antrim
Bangor
Belfast
Lough Neagh
Lisburn
Portaferry
Isle of Man
Douglas
Newry
Dundalk
Drogheda
Kells
Irish Sea
Dublin
DUBLIN
Dun Laoghaire
Kildare
Wicklow
Carlow
Slaney
Enniscorthy
Wexford
Rosslare
Waterford
St George's Channel
Roscoff, Cherbourg
Workington
Penrith
ENGLAND
Kendal
Heysham
Fleetwood
Blackpool
Preston
Bolton
Southport
Liverpool
Warrington
Holyhead
Chester
Wrexham
Shrewsbury
Aberystwyth
WALES
Hereford
Fishguard
Merthyr Tydfil
Newport
Pembroke
Swansea
Cardiff

DOWLING'S
GUINNESS

A PORTRAIT OF IRELAND

Many visitors see Ireland as a lush green island, full of thatched cottages, pubs, music, wit and poetry. Like all stereotypes, this image of the country has a basis in truth and the tourist industry helps sustain it. The political and economic reality is, of course, rather less ideal, but the relaxed good humour of the people still makes Ireland a most welcoming place to visit.

Ireland, at least for the time being, is a divided island. History and religion created a North–South divide, with two hostile communities in the North. The IRA ceasefire of 1997 and the Good Friday Agreement brought new hope, however. John Hume of the SDLP and David Trimble of the Ulster Unionist Party were jointly awarded the Nobel Prize for Peace for their work in the peace process, and the inaugural meeting of the Northern Ireland Assembly took place on 1 July 1998.

Ireland has had more than its fair share of wars and disasters, culminating in the Great Famine of 1845–8, since when emigration has been part of Irish life. More people of Irish descent live in the USA than in Ireland itself. Suffering and martyrdom in the cause of independence also play an important part in the Irish consciousness. The heroine of W B Yeats's play *Cathleen ní Houlihan* inspires young men to lay down their lives for Ireland. Her image appeared on the first banknote issued by the newly created Irish Free State in 1922.

Yet, the Irish retain their easy-going attitude to life, with a young, highly educated population working hard to make its way in today's European Union. In the Republic, 40 per cent of the population is under 30. Despite its high birth rate, rural Ireland is sparsely populated and emigration to the cities and abroad in recent years has taken its toll. The Industrial Revolution of the 19th century barely touched the South and for much of the 20th century

Trinity College, Dublin, the Republic's most prestigious university

◀ Mural on the side of a pub, Cashel

Mary Robinson, the first woman to be elected president in 1990

the Republic seemed an old-fashioned place, poorer than almost all its fellow members of the European Union.

Economic Development

Tax breaks and low inflation have attracted foreign investment to the Republic and many multinationals have subsidiaries here. Ireland joined the single European currency in 1999 and the economy boomed from the mid-1990s to 2007. The years since 2008 have been difficult. Unemployment fuelled emigration; property rates dropped and the national debt soared, but in September 2013, the Republic officially put the Recession behind it and the economy has slowly improved since.

An important industry for Ireland is tourism. The South receives over 6.5 million visitors a year and the North receives 1.7 million visitors.

Traditionally, Northern Ireland had far more industry than the South, but during the 25 years of the "Troubles", old heavy industries, such as shipbuilding, declined and new investors were scared away. However, the election of members to the new Northern Ireland Assembly in June 1998 ushered in a new political and economic era for the North. For both parts of Ireland, geography is still a barrier to prosperity. Located on the periphery of Europe, the island is isolated from its main markets and thus saddled with high transport costs. Subsidies from the EU have helped improve infrastructure in the Republic.

Religion and Politics

The influence of Catholicism is still felt but not to the extent that it once was. Irish Catholicism runs the gamut from missionary zeal to simple piety. In recent years, attendance at Mass has dropped off considerably and some estimates now place attendance at less than 50 per cent. Moral conservatism is, however, still most evident in attitudes to abortion.

The election of liberal lawyer Mary Robinson as President in 1990, the first woman to hold the post, was seen as a sign of more enlightened times by many people, an attitude reinforced by the election of Mary McAleese as her successor in 1998. A new political climate has favoured the quiet spread of feminism and challenged the old paternalism of Irish politics.

Pavement artist on O'Connell Street, Dublin

Irish horse racing, a popular national sport

Language and Culture

Ireland was a Gaelic-speaking nation until the 16th century, since when the language has steadily declined. Today, however, the Republic is officially bilingual. Knowledge of Irish is a requirement for a career in the public sector, and one in three people on the island as a whole has some degree of competency.

Irish culture, on the other hand, is in no danger of being eroded. The people have a genuine love of old folk legends and epic poetry and songs. Festivals, whether dedicated to St Patrick or James Joyce, pubs or oysters, salmon or sailing, are an important part of community life. Music is a national passion – from the rock of U2 and the indie of The Script to the folk music of Clannad, the Chieftains and Mary Black.

Another national passion is horse racing. Ireland's breeders and trainers are masters of their trade and enjoy astonishing international success for such a small country. Other sports are followed with equal intensity, including the traditional Irish pursuits of the Gaelic games and football.

Drinking also plays an important part in Irish culture: social life centres on the pub and the "craic" (convivial chat) to be enjoyed there. Unfortunately, the smoking ban and the recession have led to the closure of many pubs around the country, especially in rural areas. Although there is a concern that this may affect the traditional way of life, given the attachment to Guinness, gossip and music, this seems unlikely.

The Temple Bar, a famous cultural landmark in Dublin

The Landscape and Wildlife of Ireland

The landscape is one of Ireland's greatest attractions. It varies from bogs and lakes in the central lowlands to mountains and rocky islands in the west. Between these two extremes, the island has abundant lush, green pastureland, the result of plentiful rainfall, but little natural woodland. Parts of the far west, where the land is farmed by traditional methods, are havens for threatened wildlife, including the corncrake, which needs undisturbed hayfields in which to nest.

The Fauna of Ireland

Natterjack toad

Many animals (including snakes) did not make it to Ireland before the Irish Sea rose after the Ice Age. Other surprising absentees are the mole, weasel and common toad (the natterjack, however, can be seen). The wood mouse is the only small native rodent, but the once common red squirrel has now been virtually taken over by the grey.

Rocky Coasts

Chough

The Dingle Peninsula *(see pp162–3)* is part of a series of rocky promontories and inlets created when sea levels rose at the end of the Ice Age. Cliffs and islands offer many sites for sea birds, with some enormous colonies, such as the gannets of Little Skellig *(pp168–9)*. The chough still breeds on cliffs in the extreme west. Elsewhere in Europe, this rare species of crow is declining in numbers.

Thrift grows in cushion-like clumps, producing its papery pink flowerheads from spring right through to autumn.

Sea campion is a low-growing plant. Its large white flowers brighten up many a clifftop and seaside shingle bank.

Lakes, Rivers and Wetlands

Great crested grebe

This watery landscape around Lough Oughter is typical of the lakelands of the River Erne *(pp274–5)*. Rainfall is high throughout the year, which results in many wetlands, especially along the Shannon *(p189)* and the Erne. The elegant great crested grebe breeds mainly on the larger lakes in the north.

Water lobelia grows in the shallows of stony lakes. Its leaves remain below the water, while the pale lilac flowers are borne on leafless stems above the surface.

Fleabane, once used to repel fleas, thrives in wet meadows and marshes. It has yellow flowers like dandelions.

Red deer have been introduced into many areas, notably the hills of Connemara.

Grey seals are a common sight in the waters off the Atlantic coast, feeding on fish and occasionally on sea birds.

Pine martens, though mainly nocturnal, may be spotted in the Midlands and the east during daytime in summers.

Otters are more likely to be seen in the shallow seas off rocky coasts than in rivers and lakes, though they live in both habitats.

Mountain and Blanket Bog

Stonechat

As well as the raised bogs of the central lowlands *(p256)*, much of Ireland's mountainous ground, particularly in the west, is covered by blanket bog such as that seen here in Connemara *(pp210–13)*. On drier upland sites this grades into heather moor and poor grassland. The stonechat, which inhabits rocky scree and heathland, is a restless bird with an unmistakable white rump. It flits about, dipping and bobbing in pursuit of flies.

Bog myrtle is an aromatic shrub, common in Ireland's bogs. Its leaves can be used to flavour drinks.

Bogbean, a plant found in fens and wet bogland, has attractive white flowers splashed with pink. Its leaves were once used as a cure for boils.

Pastureland

Rook

Rolling pastureland with grazing livestock, as seen here in the foothills of the Wicklow Mountains *(pp142–3)*, is a very common sight throughout Ireland. The traditional farming methods employed in many parts of the island (particularly in the west) are of great benefit to wildlife. Rooks, for example, which feed on worms and insect larvae found in pasture, are very common.

Meadow vetchling uses its tendrils to clamber up grasses and other plants. It has clusters of pretty pale yellow flowers.

Marsh thistle is a common flower of wet meadows and damp woodland. It is a tall species with small, purple flowerheads.

Architecture in Ireland

Ireland's turbulent history has done incalculable damage to its architectural heritage. Cromwell's forces, in particular, destroyed scores of castles, monasteries and towns in their three-year campaign against the Irish in the mid-17th century. However, many fascinating buildings and sites remain, with Iron Age forts being the earliest surviving settlements. Christianity in Ireland gave rise to monasteries, churches and round towers; conflict between Anglo-Norman barons and Irish chieftains created castles and tower houses. The later landlord class built luxurious country mansions, while their labourers had to make do with basic, one-roomed cottages.

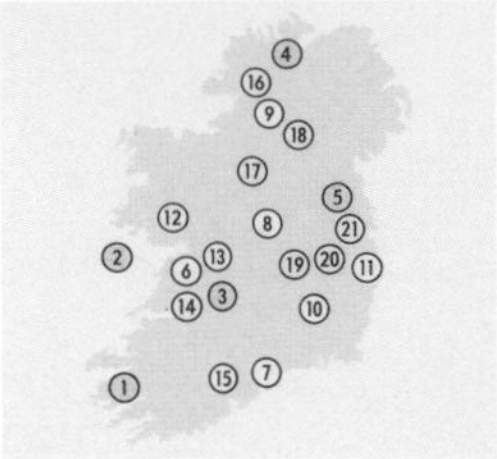

Locator Map

- Iron Age forts
- Round towers
- Tower houses
- Georgian country houses

Iron Age Forts

Ring forts (raths) were Iron Age farmsteads enclosed by an earth bank, a timber fence and a ditch to protect against cattle-raiders. Inside, people lived in huts with a souterrain (underground passage) for storage and refuge. Some were in use as late as the 17th century, but all you can usually see today are low circular mounds. In the west, stone was used for cahers (stone ring forts) and promontory forts (semi-circular forts built on clifftops using the sea as a natural defence).

Round Towers

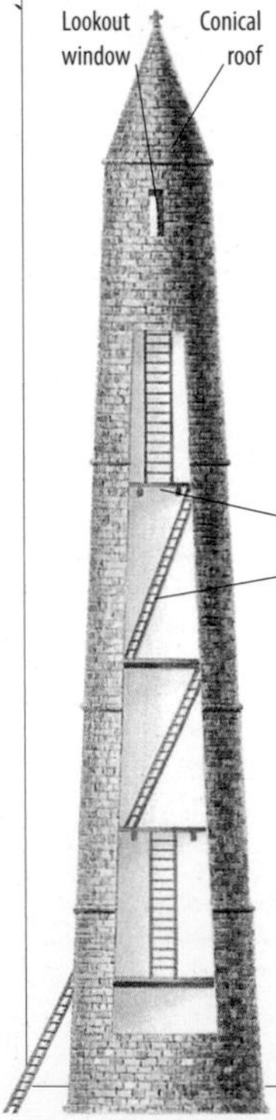

Round towers, often over 30 m (100 ft) tall, were built between the 10th and 12th centuries on monastic sites. They were bell towers, used as places of refuge and to store valuable manuscripts. The entrance, which could be as high as 4 m (13 ft) above ground, was reached by a ladder that was hauled up from the inside. Other moveable ladders connected the tower's wooden floors.

Tower Houses

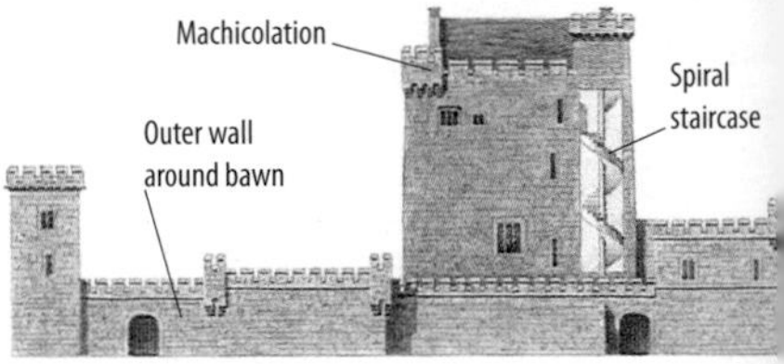

Tower houses were small castles or fortified residences built between the 15th and 17th centuries. The tall square house was often surrounded by a stone wall forming a bawn (enclosure), used for defence and as a cattle pen. Machicolations (projecting parapets from which to drop missiles) were sited at the top of the house.

Cottages

One-roomed cottages, thatched or slate-roofed, are still a common feature of the Irish landscape. Built of local stone with small windows to retain heat, the cottages were inhabited by farm workers or smallholders.

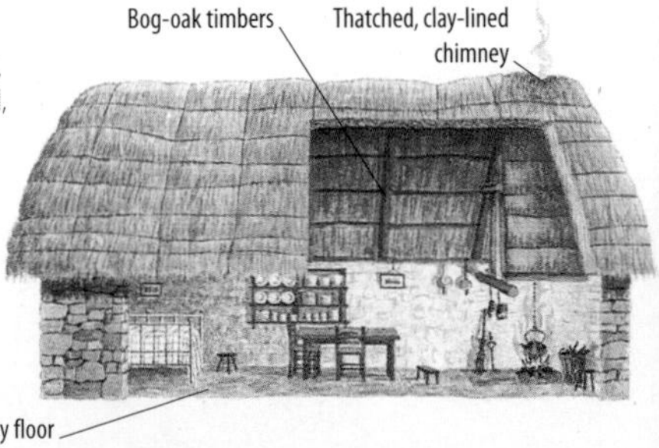

Iron Age Forts

1. Staigue Fort *p169*
2. Dún Aonghasa *p216*
3. Craggaunowen *p194*
4. Grianán Ailigh *pp230–31*
5. Hill of Tara *p252*

Round Tower

6. Kilmacduagh *p218*
7. Ardmore *p149*
8. Clonmacnoise *pp254–5*
9. Devenish Island *p275*
10. Kilkenny *p148*
11. Glendalough *pp144–5*

Tower Houses

12. Aughnanure Castle *p213*
13. Thoor Ballylee *pp218–19*
14. Knappogue Castle *p193*
15. Blarney Castle *p175*
16. Donegal Castle *p234*

Georgian Country Houses

17. Strokestown Park House *pp222–3*
18. Castle Coole *p276*
19. Emo Court *p257*
20. Russborough House *pp136–7*
21. Castletown House *pp132–3*

The well-preserved round tower at Ardmore

Georgian Country Houses

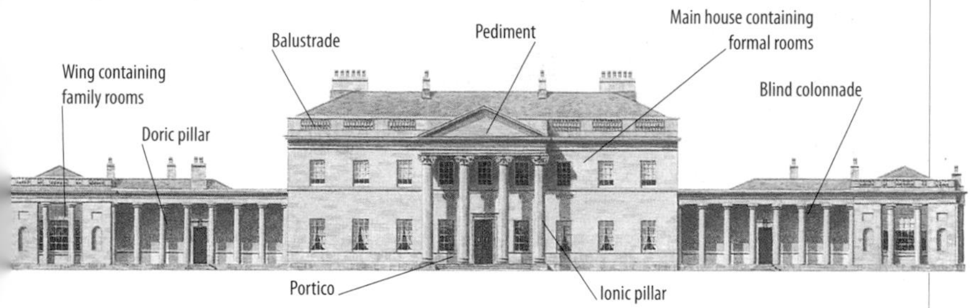

Between the 1720s and 1800, prosperous landlords commissioned palatial country mansions in the Palladian and Neo-Classical styles popular in England over that period. Castle Coole *(above)* has a Palladian layout, with the main house in the centre and a colonnade on either side leading to a small pavilion. The Neo-Classical influence can be seen in the unadorned façade and the Doric columns of the colonnades. Noted architects of Irish country houses include Richard Cassels (1690–1751) and James Wyatt (1746–1813).

Stucco

Stucco (decorative relief plasterwork), popular in the 18th century, is found in many Georgian country houses as well as town houses and public buildings. The Italian Lafrancini brothers were particularly sought after for their intricate stuccowork (notably at Castletown and Russborough) as was Irish craftsman Michael Stapleton (Trinity College, Dublin and Dublin Writers Museum).

Trompe l'oeil detail at Emo Court

Ceiling at Dublin Writers Museum

Stucco portrait at Castletown House

Stuccowork at Russborough House

Other Terms used in this Guide

Beehive hut: Circular stone building with a domed roof created by corbelling (laying a series of stones so that each projects beyond the one below).

Cashel: Stone ring fort.

Crannog: Defensive, partly artificial island on a lake. Huts were often built on crannogs *(see p37)*.

Curtain wall: Outer wall of a castle, usually incorporating towers at intervals.

Hiberno-Romanesque: Style of church architecture with rounded arches highly decorated with geometric designs and human and animal forms. Also called Irish-Romanesque.

Motte and bailey: Raised mound (motte) topped with a wooden tower, surrounded by a heavily fenced space (bailey). Built by the Normans in the 12th century, they were quickly erected in time of battle.

Tympanum: Decorated space over a door or window.

Literary Ireland

For a land the size of Ireland to have produced four Nobel Prize-winners in Shaw, Yeats, Beckett and Séamus Heaney is a considerable feat. Yet it is not easy to speak of an "Irish literary tradition" as the concept embraces rural and urban experiences, Protestant and Catholic traditions and the Gaelic and English languages. Irish fiction today, as in the past, is characterized by a sense of community and history, a love of storytelling and a zest for language.

W B Yeats – Ireland's most famous poet

The Blasket Islands, which provided inspiration for several writers

Gaelic Literature

Irish literature proclaims itself the oldest vernacular literature in Western Europe, dating back to early monastic times when Celtic folklore and sagas such as the epics of Cúchulainn *(see p30)* were written down for the first time. The disappearance of Gaelic literature followed the demise, in the 17th century, of the Irish aristocracy for whom it was written. Gaelic literature has had several revivals. Peig Sayers is famous for her accounts of the harsh life on the Blasket Islands *(see p162)* in the early 20th century.

Anglo-Irish Literature

The collapse of Gaelic culture and the Protestant Ascendancy led to English becoming the dominant language. Most literature was concerned with the privileged classes. An early Anglo-Irish writer was satirist Jonathan Swift *(see p86)*, author of *Gulliver's Travels*, who was born in Dublin in 1667 of English parents. Anglo-Irish literature was strong in drama, the entertainment of the cultured classes, and owed little to Irish settings or sensibilities. By the 1700s, Ireland was producing an inordinate number of leading playwrights, many of whom were more at home in London. These included Oliver Goldsmith, remembered for his comedy *She Stoops to Conquer*, and Richard Brinsley Sheridan, whose plays include *The School for Scandal*. Near the end of the century, Maria Edgeworth set a precedent with novels such as *Castle Rackrent*, based on the class divide in Irish society. The 19th century saw an exodus to England of Irish playwrights, including Oscar Wilde, who entered Oxford University in 1874 and later became the darling of London society with plays such as *The Importance of Being Earnest*. George Bernard Shaw *(see p104)*, writer of *St Joan* and *Pygmalion*, also made London his home. This dramatist, critic, socialist and pacifist continued to write until well into the 20th century.

Novelist Maria Edgeworth

20th-Century Writers

In 1898, W B Yeats and Lady Gregory founded Dublin's Abbey Theatre *(see p92)*. Its opening, in 1904, heralded the Irish Revival, which focused on national and local themes. Playwright John Millington Synge drew inspiration from a love of the Aran Islands and Irish folklore, but the "immoral language" of his *Playboy of the Western World* caused a riot when first performed at the Abbey Theatre. Along with contemporaries, like Sean O'Casey and W B Yeats, Synge influenced subsequent generations of Irish writers, including novelist Seán O'Faolain, writer and columnist Flann O'Brien, and hard-drinking, quarrelsome playwright Brendan Behan. The literary revival also produced many notable poets in the

Playwright George Bernard Shaw

mid-20th century such as the gifted Patrick Kavanagh and Belfast-born Louis MacNeice, often considered to be one of the finest poets of his generation.

Caricature of protesters at Dublin's Abbey Theatre in 1907

Three Literary Giants

From the mass of talent to emerge in Irish literature, three figures stand out as visionaries in their fields. W B Yeats *(see p237)* spent half his life outside Ireland but is forever linked to its rural west. A writer of wistful, melancholic poetry, he was at the forefront of the Irish Revival, helping forge a new national cultural identity. James Joyce *(see p94)* was another trailblazer – his complex narrative and stream of consciousness techniques influenced the development of the modern novel. *Ulysses* describes a day in the life of Joyce's beloved Dublin and shaped the work of generations of writers. Bloomsday, which is named after one of the novel's characters, Leopold Bloom, is still celebrated annually in the city. The last of the three literary giants, novelist and playwright Samuel Beckett *(see p67)*, was another of Dublin's sons, though he later emigrated to France. His themes of alienation, despair, and the futility of human existence pervade his best-known plays, *Waiting for Godot* and *Endgame*.

The writer Brendan Behan enjoying the company in a Dublin pub

The poet Patrick Kavanagh celebrating Bloomsday

Contemporary Writers

Ireland's proud literary tradition is today upheld by a stream of talented writers from both North and South. Among the finest are Cork-born William Trevor, regarded as a master of the short story. Anne Enright (2007) and John Banville (2005) are both Man Booker Prize-winners. Roddy Doyle is known for mining his working-class origins in novels such as *The Snapper* and *Paddy Clarke Ha Ha Ha*. Other established Irish writers are Joseph O'Connor, Cecelia Ahern, Colum McCann and Edna O'Brien. Among Ireland's contemporary poets, the Ulster-born writers the late Séamus Heaney and Derek Mahon are considered among the most outstanding.

Cast of *The Commitments*, written by Roddy Doyle

Ireland on Screen

Ireland has long been fertile ground for the world's film-makers, and its people have been the subjects of major films, notably *The Crying Game* (1992), *In the Name of the Father* (1994), *Michael Collins* (1996), *Once* (2007) and *The Guard* (2011). Another popular film was *The Commitments* (1991). Filmed in and around Dublin with an all-Irish cast, it was based on a novel by Roddy Doyle. More recently Ireland has become a top destination for big-budget television productions. TV shows such as *Ripper Street*, *Vikings* and *Game of Thrones* were all shot on location around the island.

The Music of Ireland

Ireland is the only country in the world to have a musical instrument – the harp – as its national emblem. In this land, famous for its love of music, modern forms such as country-and-western and rock flourish, but it is traditional music that captures the essence of the country. Whether you are listening to Gaelic love songs that date back to medieval times or 17th- and 18th-century folk songs with their English and Scottish influences, the music is unmistakably Irish. Dance is an equally important aspect of Irish traditional music, and some of the most popular airs are derived from centuries-old reels, jigs and hornpipes. Nowadays these are mainly performed at *fleadhs* (festivals) and *ceilís* (dances).

Turlough O'Carolan (1670–1738) is the most famous Irish harper. The blind musician travelled the country playing his songs to both rich and poor. Many of O'Carolan's melodies, such as *Lament for Owen Roe O'Neill*, still survive.

John F C McCormack (1884–1945) was an Irish tenor who toured America to great acclaim during the early part of the 20th century. His best-loved recordings were arias by Mozart. Another popular tenor was Derry-born Josef Locke. A singer of popular ballads in the 1940s and 1950s, he was the subject of the 1992 film *Hear My Song*.

The Current Music Scene

Ireland today is a melting pot of musical styles. Traditional Irish music has produced many respected musicians, such as pipe-players Liam Ó Floinn and Paddy Keenan from Dublin, while groups like the Chieftains and the Fureys have gained worldwide fame by melding old with new. Ireland is also firmly placed on the rock'n'roll map, thanks to singers such as Van Morrison in the 1970s and later bands like Thin Lizzy and the Boomtown Rats. The most famous rock band to come out of Ireland is Dublin's U2 who, in the 1980s, became one of the world's most popular groups. Other international successes include Enya, Sinéad O'Connor, Damien Rice; and bands like the Cranberries, the Corrs, Boyzone, Westlife and Snow Patrol. Today, the Irish music scene is dominated by acts such as Hozier and The Script.

Hozier

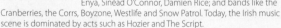

Snow Patrol

Traditional Instruments

There is no set line-up in traditional Irish bands. The fiddle is probably the most common instrument used. Like the music, some instruments, such as the uilleann pipes, have Celtic origins.

Traditional Irish dancing is currently enjoying renewed popularity. From the 17th century the social focus in rural areas was the village dance held every Sunday. From these gatherings, Irish dancing became popular.

The melodeon is a basic version of the button accordion. Both these instruments are better suited to Irish music than the piano accordion.

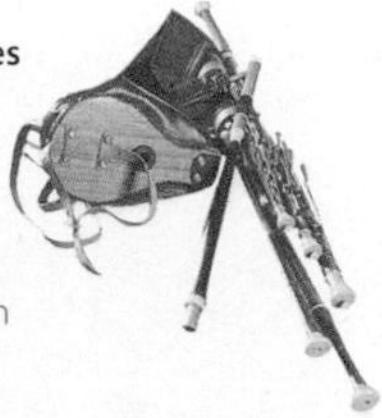

The uilleann pipes are similar to bagpipes and are generally considered to be one of the main instruments in Irish traditional music.

The harp has been played in Ireland since the 10th century. In recent years, there has been a keen revival of harp playing in Irish traditional music.

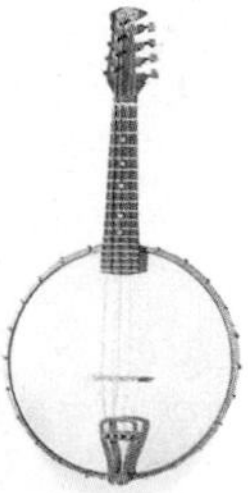

The banjo comes from the Deep South of the US and adds a new dimension to the sound of traditional bands.

Tin whistle

Flute

The flute and tin whistle are among the most common instruments used in traditional Irish music. The latter is often called the penny whistle.

The New National Song —

Erin Remember 1916

PRICE 2/- NET

Published by QUINN & COMPANY, 29 UPPER ABBEY ST., DUBLIN.

Irish folk songs, such as this one about the 1916 Easter Rising, tend to have a patriotic theme. But some of the most powerful songs have been written not just about the national struggle, but also about hardship, emigration and the longing for the homeland.

The violin is called a fiddle by most musicians. The style of playing and sound produced varies from region to region.

Ireland's Celtic Heritage

Ireland's rich tradition of storytelling embraces a folk heritage that abounds with myths and superstitions. Some stories have been in written form since the 8th century, but most originated over 2,000 years ago when druids passed on stories orally from one generation to the next. Like the Gaelic language itself, many of Ireland's legends have links with those of ancient Celtic races throughout Europe. As well as the heroic deeds and fearless warriors of mythology, Irish folklore is also rich in tales of fairies, leprechauns, banshees and other supernatural beings.

The formidable Queen Maeve of Connaught

Part of the 2,300-year-old Gundestrup Cauldron unearthed in Denmark, which depicts Cúchulainn's triumph in the Cattle Raid of Cooley

Cúchulainn

The most famous warrior in Irish mythology is Cúchulainn. At the age of seven, going by the name of Setanta, he killed the savage hound of Culainn the Smith by slaying it with a hurling stick (one of the first times the sport of hurling is mentioned in folklore). Culainn was upset at the loss so Setanta volunteered to guard the house, earning himself the new name of Cúchulainn, meaning the hound of Culainn.

Before he went into battle, Cúchulainn swelled to magnificent proportions, turned different colours and one of his eyes grew huge. His greatest victory was in the "Cattle Raid of Cooley" when Queen Maeve of Connaught sent her troops to capture the coveted prize bull of Ulster. Cúchulainn learned of the plot and defeated them single-handedly. However, Queen Maeve took revenge on Cúchulainn by using sorcerers to lure him to his death. Today, in Dublin's GPO *(see p93)*, a statue of Cúchulainn commemorates the heroes of the 1916 Easter Rising.

Finn McCool

The warrior Finn McCool is the most famous leader of the Fianna, an elite band of troops chosen for their strength and valour and who defended Ireland from foreign forces. Finn was not only strong and bold but also possessed the powers of a seer, and could obtain great wisdom by putting his thumb in his mouth and sucking on it. When they were not at war, the Fianna spent their time hunting. Finn had a hound called Bran which stood almost as high as himself and is said to be the original ancestor of the breed known today as the Irish wolfhound. Many of the Fianna possessed supernatural powers and often ventured into the life beyond, known as the

The diminutive figure of the leprechaun

Fairies, Leprechauns and Banshees

The existence of spirits, and in particular the "little people", plays a large part in Irish folklore. Centuries ago, it was believed that fairies lived under mounds of earth, or "fairy raths", and that touching one of these tiny figures brought bad luck. The most famous of the "little people" is the leprechaun. Legend has it that if you caught one of these, he would lead you to a crock of gold, but take your eyes off him and he would vanish into thin air. The banshee was a female spirit whose wailing presence outside a house was said to signal the imminent death of someone within.

A banshee with long flowing hair

Otherworld. Among these was Finn's son Ossian who was not only a formidable warrior, like his father, but was also renowned as a wise and knowledgeable poet. Through time, Finn has come to be commonly portrayed as a giant. Legend has it that he constructed the Giant's Causeway in County Antrim *(see pp266–7)*.

A 19th-century engraving of Finn McCool dressed for battle

The Children of Lir

One of the saddest tales in Irish folklore involves King Lir, who so adored his four children that their stepmother was driven wild with jealousy. One day she took the children to a lake and cast a spell on them, turning them into white swans confined to the waters of Ireland for 900 years. However, as soon as she had done the deed, she became racked with guilt and bestowed upon them the gift of exquisite song. The king then decreed that no swan in Ireland should be killed – an act which is still illegal

The children of King Lir being turned into white swans

today. The end of the children's 900-year ordeal coincided with the coming of Christianity. They regained human form but were wizened and weak. They died soon afterwards, but not before being baptized.

Saint Brendan

Brendan the Navigator, like many other 6th-century monks, travelled widely. It is known that although he lived in western Ireland he visited Wales, Scotland and France. It is likely, though, that his most famous journey is fictitious. This story tells of a shipload of monks who, after seven years of all kinds of strange encounters designed to test their faith, found the Land of Promise. It is essentially a Christian retelling of the common tales of the Celtic Otherworld. The Feast of St Brendan on 16 May is celebrated in Kerry by the climbing of Mount Brandon.

Engraving showing St Brendan and his monks encountering a siren

Origins of Irish Place Names

The names of many of Ireland's cities, towns and villages today are largely based on ancient Gaelic terms for prominent local landmarks, some of which no longer exist. Here are just a few elements of the place names the traveller may come across.

The fort on the Rock of Cashel that gives the town its name

Ar, ard – *high, height*
Ass, ess – *waterfall*
A, ah, ath – *ford*
Bal, bally – *town*
Beg – *small*
Ben – *peak, mountain*
Carrick, carrig – *rock*
Cashel – *stone fort*
Crock, knock – *hill*
Curra, curragh – *marsh*
Darry, derry – *oak tree*
Dun – *castle*
Eden – *hill brow*
Innis, inch – *island*
Inver – *river mouth*
Isk, iska – *water*
Glas, glass – *green*
Glen, glyn – *valley*
Kil, kill – *church*
Lough – *lake, sea inlet*
Mona, mone – *peat bog*
Mor – *great, large*
Mullen, mullin – *mill*
Rath, raha – *ring fort*
Slieve – *mountain*
Toom – *burial ground*
Tul, tulagh – *small hill*

St Canice's Cathedral in Kilkenny (the town's name means "church of Canice")

The Sporting Year

All major international team sports are played in Ireland, but the most popular games are the two uniquely native ones of Gaelic football and hurling. Most of the big games, plus soccer and rugby internationals, are sold out well in advance. However, if you can't get a ticket you'll find plenty of company with whom to watch the event in pubs. Horse racing, with over 240 days of racing a year, attracts fanatical support. For those keen on participatory sports, there are also Ireland's famous fishing waters and golf courses *(see pp342–7)*.

The North West 200 is the fastest motorcycle race in the world over public roads – held near Portstewart *(see p264)*.

The Irish Grand National is a gruelling steeplechase run at Fairyhouse in County Meath.

Four-day national hunt racing festival at Punchestown

Irish Football League Cup – Northern Ireland's final

Round-Ireland Yacht Race – held every two years

January	February	March	April	May	June

Irish Champion Hurdle, run at Leopardstown, County Dublin

Start of the salmon fishing season

The Six Nations Rugby Tournament, between Ireland, Scotland, Wales, England, France and Italy, runs until April. Ireland play their home games at the Aviva Stadium, Dublin.

The International Rally of the Lakes is a prestigious car rally around the Lakes of Killarney *(see pp166–7)*.

The Irish Open Golf Championship is held at a different course each year and attracts a world-class field to courses such as Ballybunion in County Kerry.

Key to Seasons

- Hurling
- Gaelic football
- Flat racing
- National Hunt racing
- Rugby
- Association football
- Salmon fishing
- Equestrianism

The Irish Derby, Ireland's premier flat race, attracts many of Europe's best three-year-olds to The Curragh *(see p135)*.

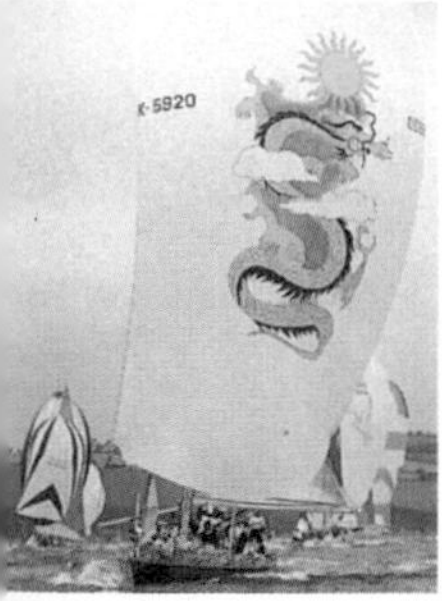

The All-Ireland Football Final is held at Croke Park in Dublin. The top two counties play for this Gaelic football championship. More people watch the game than any other event in Ireland.

Cork Week is a biennial regatta, organized by Royal Cork Yacht Club, where crews and boats of all classes meet and compete.

The Dublin Marathon is Ireland's foremost marathon event. It attracts a huge field including top-class athletes from around the world.

Greyhound Derby, run at Shelbourne Park, Dublin

Galway Race Week is one of Ireland's premier festival meetings and a popular social event.

July	August	September	October	November	December

Football Association of Ireland Cup – the Republic's football final

Millstreet Indoor International showjumping event

The Dublin Horse Show is Ireland's premier horse show and a major event in the social calendar.

All-Ireland Hurling Final at Croke Park, Dublin

The Gaelic Athletic Association

The GAA was founded in 1884 to promote indigenous Irish sport. Today, despite heavy competition from soccer, the most popular sport in Ireland remains Gaelic football. Its rules are somewhere between rugby and soccer, though it predates both games. In it, the ball can be carried and points scored over the goalpost. Another intriguing GAA game is hurling, a fast and physical field sport played with sticks and said to have originated in ancient Celtic times. Both games are played at parish and county level on a wholly amateur basis. The season ends with the All-Ireland finals, which draw large and passionate crowds to Dublin.

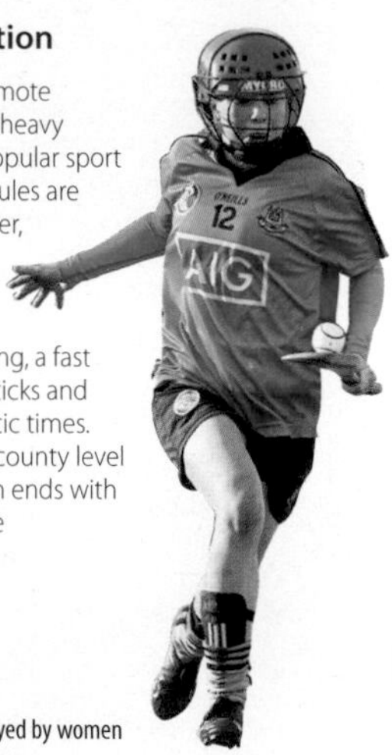

Camogie, a version of hurling played by women

THE HISTORY OF IRELAND

Ireland's relative isolation has cut it off from several of the major events of European history. Roman legions, for example, never invaded and the country's early history is shrouded in myths of warring gods and heroic High Kings. Nevertheless, the bellicose Celtic tribes were quick to embrace Christianity after the arrival of St Patrick on the island in AD 432.

Until the Viking invasions of the 9th century, Ireland enjoyed an era of relative peace. Huge monasteries like lonmacnoise and Glendalough were founded, where scholarship and art flourished. The Vikings failed to gain control of the island, but in 1169 the Anglo-Normans did. Many Irish chiefs submitted to Henry II of England, who declared himself Lord of Ireland. He left in 1172, and his knights shared out large baronies between themselves.

Matters changed when Henry VIII broke with the Catholic church in 1532. Ireland became a battleground between native Irish Catholics and the forces of the English Crown. Where the Irish were defeated, their lands were confiscated and granted to Protestants from England and Scotland. England's conquest was completed with the victory of William of Orange over James II at the Battle of the Boyne in 1690. Repressive Penal Laws were put into place, but opposition to English rule continued.

The Famine of 1845 to 1848 was one of the bleakest periods in Irish history. About 1.5 million people died, two million emigrated, and many who stayed were evicted by English landlords. A campaign for Home Rule gathered strength, but it was 1920 before the Government of Ireland Act divided the island. The South became the Irish Free State, gaining full independence in 1937, while the North became part of the UK. In the 1970s, 1980s and much of the 1990s, Northern Ireland was a battleground, with both Loyalist and Republican paramilitary groups waging bombing campaigns. In 1998, the Good Friday Agreement was signed, paving the way for a new Northern Ireland Assembly and hopes of peace.

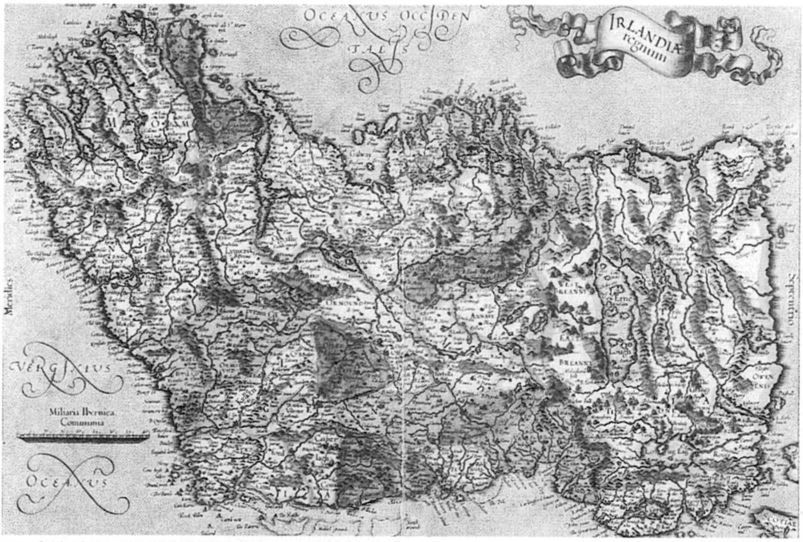

Map of Ireland, printed in 1592, showing the four traditional provinces

◀ *The Feast of St Kevin amid the Ruins of Glendalough* by Joseph Peacock (1813)

Prehistoric Ireland

Until about 9,500 years ago Ireland was uninhabited. The first people, who may have crossed by a land bridge from Scotland, were hunter-gatherers and left few traces of permanent settlement. The 4th millennium BC saw the arrival of Neolithic farmers and herdsmen who built stone field walls and monumental tombs such as Newgrange. Metalworking was brought from Europe around 2000 BC by the Bronze Age Beaker people, who also introduced new pottery skills. The Iron Age reached Ireland in the 3rd century BC along with the Celts, who migrated from Central Europe, via France and Britain, and soon established themselves as the dominant culture.

Ireland c. 8000 BC

Former Coastline

Present-day Coastline

Dolmens or Portal Tombs
These striking megalithic tombs date from around 2000 BC. Leganannny Dolmen in the Mountains of Mourne *(see p288)* is a fine example.

Gleninsheen Gorget

Many remarkable pieces of gold jewellery were created in the late Bronze Age. This gold collar dates from about 700 BC. The Iron Age Celts produced similarly fine metalwork and ornaments.

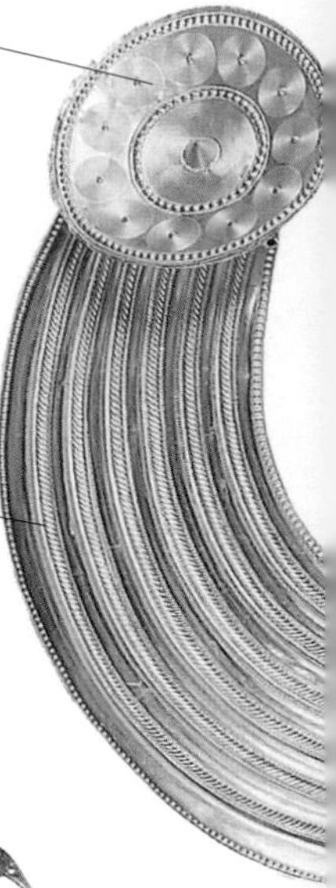

The terminal discs were worn on the shoulders.

Three strands of ropework

Wooden Idol
This Iron Age fetish would have played a role in pagan fertility rites.

Celtic Stone Idol
This mysterious three-faced head was found in County Cavan. In Celtic religion the number three has always had a special significance.

Bronze Bridle Bit
Celtic chiefs rode into battle on two-horse chariots with beautifully decorated harnesses.

Extinct giant deer or "Irish Elk"

c. 7500 BC First inhabitants of Ireland

5000–3000 Ireland covered by dense woodland dominated by oak and elm

2500 Building of Newgrange passage tomb *(see pp250–51)*

1500 Major advances in metalworking, especially gold

8000 BC | **6000** | **4000** | **2000** | **1000**

6000 Date of huts excavated at Mount-Sandel, Co Londonderry; oldest known dwellings in Europe

3700 Neolithic farmers reach Ireland; they clear woods to plant cereals

2050 Beaker people (so-called for their delicate pottery vessels) reach Ireland at the beginning of Bronze Age

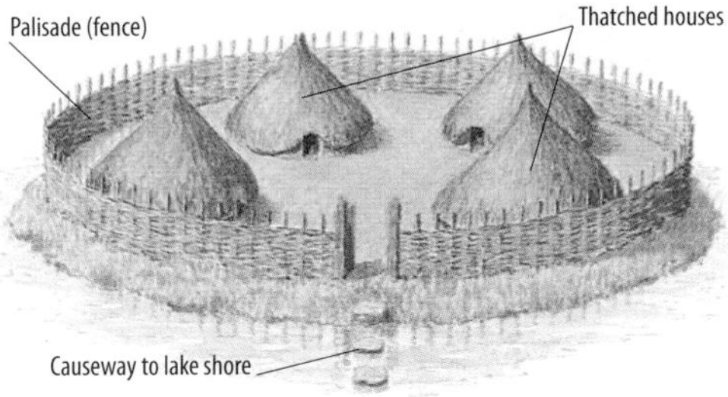

Reconstruction of a Crannog
Originating in the Bronze Age, crannogs were artificial islands built in lakes. At first used for fishing, they soon developed into well-protected homesteads. Some remained in use up to the 17th century.

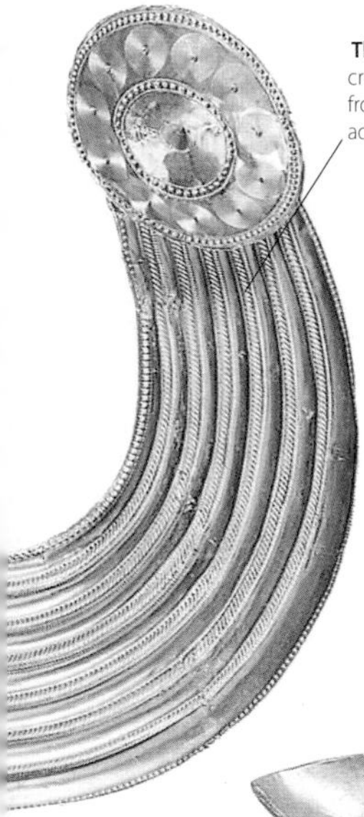

The raised bands on the collar were created by repoussé work, pushed through from the back. The delicate rope motifs were added from the front with a knife.

Bone Slip
(c. AD 50) This may have been used for divination or for gambling.

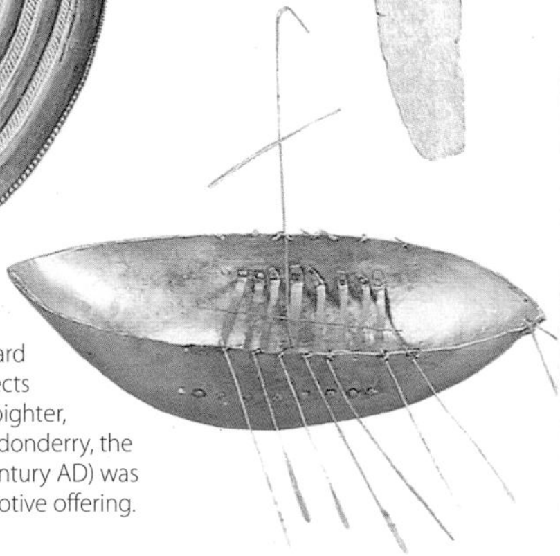

Gold Boat
Part of a hoard of gold objects found at Broighter, County Londonderry, the boat (1st century AD) was made as a votive offering.

Where to see Prehistoric Ireland

Prehistoric sites range from individual tombs such as Newgrange, Brownshill Dolmen *(see p145)* or Ossian's Grave to whole settlements, as at Céide Fields *(p208)* and Lough Gur *(p198)*. The largest Stone Age cemetery is at Carrowmore *(p238)*. Good reconstructions of prehistoric structures can be seen at Craggaunowen *(p194)*. The National Museum – Archaeology in Dublin *(pp70–71)* houses the finest collection of artifacts, including wonderful gold objects from the Bronze Age.

Newgrange *(pp250–51)* is Ireland's finest restored Neolithic tomb. At the entrance lie huge spiral-patterned boulders.

Ossian's Grave is a court grave, the earliest kind of Neolithic tomb *(p271)*. An open court stood before the burial mound.

600 First wave of Celtic invaders

500 Intertribal warfare; chieftains vie for title of *Ard Ri* (High King)

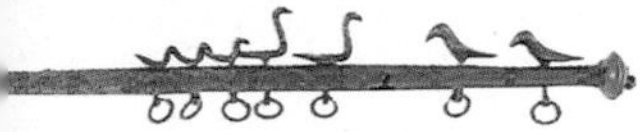

Bronze goad decorated with birds

500 | 250 | AD 1 | AD 250

250 Second wave of Celts, who bring La Tène style of pottery

AD 80 Roman general Agricola considers invasion of Ireland from Britain

c. 150 Greek geographer Ptolemy draws up map and account of Ireland

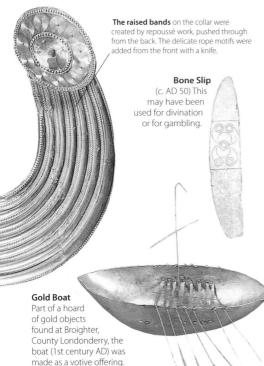

Bronze sword hilt imported from southern France

367 Roman Britain attacked by Irish, Picts and Saxons

Celtic Christianity

Celtic Ireland was divided into as many as 100 chiefdoms, though these often owed allegiance to kings of larger provinces such as Munster or Connaught. At times, there was also a titular High King based at Tara *(see p252)*. Ireland became Christian in the 5th century AD, heralding a golden age of scholarship centred on the new monasteries, while missionaries such as St Columba travelled abroad. At the end of the 8th century, Celtic Ireland was shattered by the arrival of the Vikings.

Ireland in 1000

Viking settlements

Traditional Irish provinces

Ogham Stone

The earliest Irish script, Ogham, dates from about AD 300. The notches correspond to Roman letters, like a form of Morse code.

Celtic Monastery

Monasteries were large centres of population. This reconstruction shows Glendalough (see pp144–5) *in about 1100. The tall round tower served as a lookout for Viking raiders.*

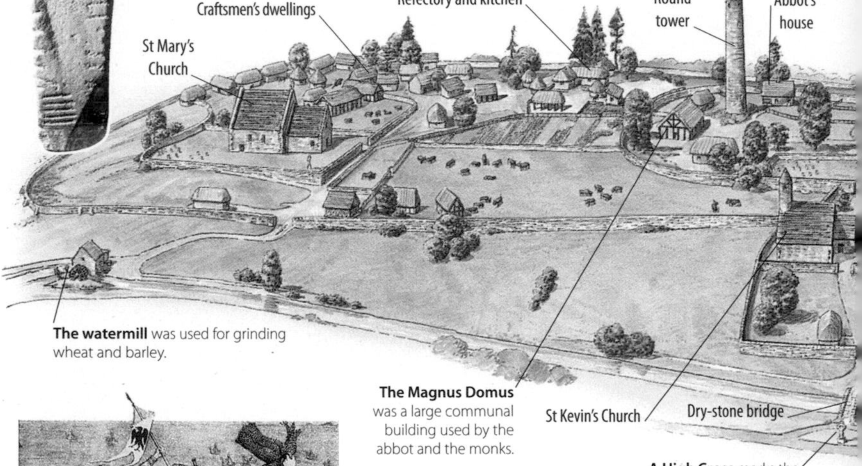

The watermill was used for grinding wheat and barley.

The Magnus Domus was a large communal building used by the abbot and the monks.

A High Cross marks the monastery boundary.

Battle of Clontarf

After their defeat by the Irish High King, BrianBorú, in 1014, the Vikings began to integrate more fully with the native population. BrianBorú himself was killed in the battle.

430 Pope sends first Christian missionary Palladius

432 Start of St Patrick's mission to Ireland

455 St Patrick founds church at Armagh

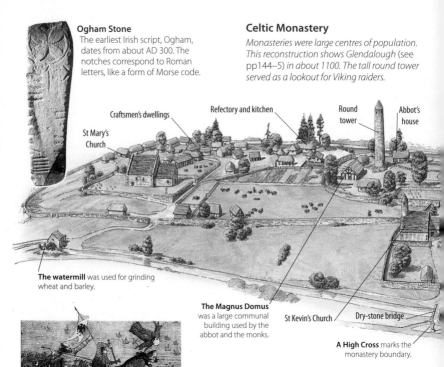

St Patrick

400

500

c. 550 Beginning of golden age of Celtic monasticism

563 St Columba (Colmcille), the first Irish missionary, founds monastery on Iona in the Hebrides

600

615 St Columbanus dies in Italy after founding many new monasteries on the Continent

664 Synod of Whitby decides that Irish Church should conform with Rome over date of Easter

700

c.690 *Book of Durrow* *(see p67)* completed

Viking Raids and Settlements
The first longships reached Ireland in 795. Though notorious for pillaging monasteries, the Vikings introduced new farming methods and coinage. They also founded walled cities such as Dublin, Waterford and Limerick.

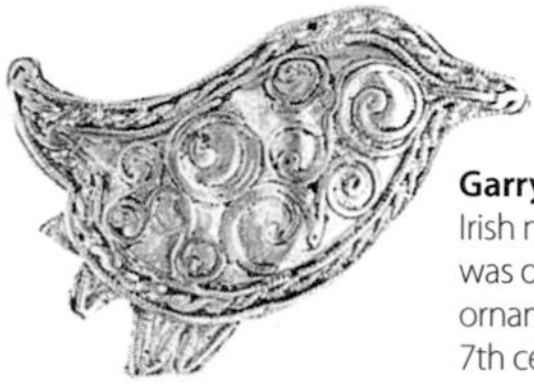

Garryduff Gold Bird
Irish metalwork in the early Christian era was of very high quality. See this gold ornament, a wren crafted around the 7th century, at the Cork public museum.

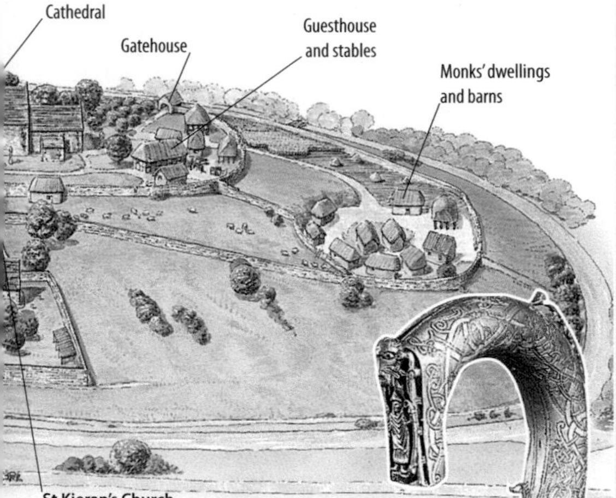

St Kieran's Church and other important churches were built of stone, but most buildings were wood.

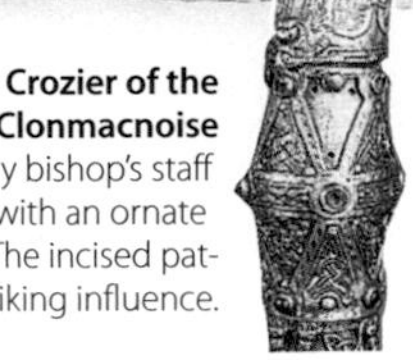

The Crozier of the Abbots of Clonmacnoise
This 11th-century bishop's staff is decorated with an ornate silver casing. The incised patterns show Viking influence.

Where to see Early Christian Ireland

Important early monastic sites besides Glendalough include Clonmacnoise and Devenish Island. Churches from this period can also be seen at Gallarus *(see p161)*, Clonfert *(p219)* and the Rock of Cashel *(pp200–201)*, while High Crosses *(p247)* and round towers *(p24)* survive all over Ireland. Dublin's National Museum – Archaeology *(pp70–71)* has excellent ecclesiastical (and Viking) artifacts and Trinity College *(pp66–8)* houses the finest illuminated manuscripts.

Devenish Island has a fine 12th-century round tower and enjoys a peaceful setting on Lower Lough Erne *(p275)*.

Clonmacnoise *(pp254–5)* lies on the east bank of the Shannon. This Romanesque doorway is part of the ruined Nuns' Church.

Viking silver brooch

795 First Viking invasion of coastal monasteries

800

807 Work starts on Kells Monastery *(see p245)*

841 A large Viking fleet spends the winter at Dublin

900

967 Irish warriors sack Limerick and begin military campaign against Viking overlords

999 Sitric Silkenbeard, the Viking king of Dublin, surrenders to Brian Ború

1000

1014 High King Brian Ború of Munster defeats joint army of Vikings and the King of Leinster at Clontarf

Viking coin

1100

1134 Cormac's Chapel is built at Cashel *(see pp200–201)*

1142 Ireland's first Cistercian house founded at Mellifont *(see p249)*

1166 Dermot McMurrough, King of Leinster, flees overseas

Anglo-Norman Ireland

Anglo-Norman nobles, led by Richard de Clare (nicknamed Strongbow), were invited to Ireland by the King of Leinster in 1169. They took control of the major towns and Henry II of England proclaimed himself overlord of Ireland. In succeeding centuries, however, English power declined and the Crown controlled just a small area around Dublin known as the Pale (see p136). Many of the Anglo-Norman barons living outside the Pale opposed English rule just as strongly as did the native Irish clans.

Ireland in 1488
Extent of the Pale

Carrickfergus Castle

The first Anglo-Norman forts were wooden structures, but they soon started to build massive stone castles. Carrickfergus (see p279) was begun in the 1180s and by 1250 had acquired a keep and a gatehouse.

The keep contained a hall on the first floor and, above that, the lord's private apartments.

Guardroom

Storeroom

Stables

Bakery

The Marriage of Strongbow and Aoife
The King of Leinster gave his daughter to Strongbow for helping him regain his lands. Daniel Maclise's painting (1854) emphasizes Anglo-Norman power over the Irish.

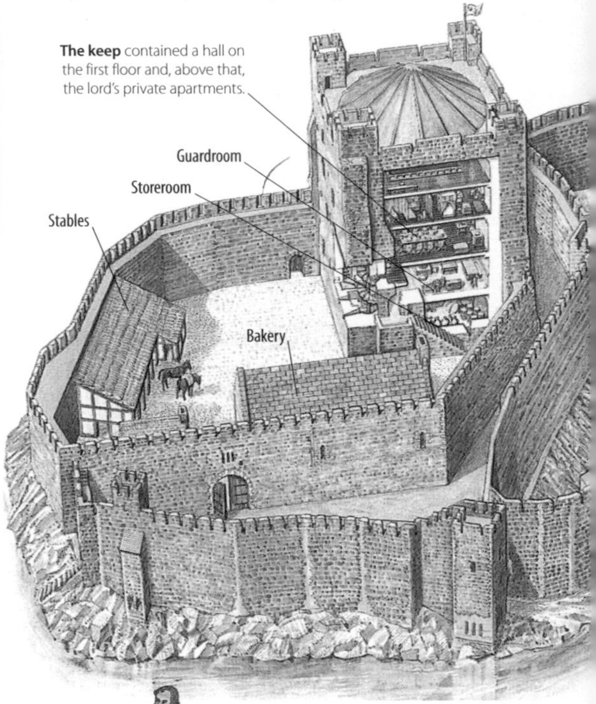

Norman Weapons
These bows and arrows, unearthed at Waterford, may be relics of Strongbow's assault on the city in 1170.

1172 Pope affirms King Henry II of England's lordship over Ireland

1177 John de Courcy's forces invade Ulster

Dermot McMurrough, King of Leinster, who invited Strongbow to come to his aid

1260 Powerful Irish chieftain Brian O'Neill killed at the Battle of Down

1318 Bruce killed in battle

1315 Scots invade Ireland; Edward Bruce crowned king

1200

1250

1300

1169 Strongbow's Anglo-Normans arrive at invitation of exiled King of Leinster, Dermot McMurrough

1224 Dominican order enters Ireland and constructs friaries

1297 First Irish Parliament meets in Dublin

Richard II's Fleet Returning to England in 1399
Richard made two trips to Ireland – in 1394 and 1399. On the first he defeated Art McMurrough, King of Leinster, and other Irish chiefs, but the second was inconclusive.

Where to see Anglo-Norman Ireland

The strength of Norman fortifications is best seen in the castles at Carrickfergus, Limerick *(see p195)* and Trim *(p252)* and in Waterford's city walls. Gothic cathedrals that survive include Dublin's Christ Church *(pp84–5)* and St Patrick's *(pp86–7)* and St Canice's *(p148)* in Kilkenny. There are impressive ruins of medieval Cistercian abbeys at Jerpoint and Boyle *(p223)*.

The gatehouse was the last addition made in the 13th century. The two towers have arrow loops for longbowmen.

Kitchen

Drawbridge

Chapel

The hall was where the lord of the castle held public court and decided cases brought before him.

Éamonn Burke
The 14th-century Lord of Mayo was a typically independent chieftain of Anglo-Norman descent.

Jerpoint Abbey *(p149)* has a 15th-century cloister containing carvings of elongated figures.

Waterford's Anglo-Norman city walls include this sturdy watchtower *(pp150–51)*.

Great Charter Roll of Waterford (1372) showing portraits of the mayors of four medieval cities

1394 King Richard II lands with army to reassert control; returns five years later but with inconclusive results

1471 8th Earl of Kildare made Lord Deputy of Ireland

1496 Kildare regains Lord Deputy position

1491 Kildare supports Perkin Warbeck, pretender to the English throne

1350

1400

1450

1366 Statutes of Kilkenny forbid marriage between Anglo-Normans and Irish

English force (left) confront Irish horsemen on Richard II's return expedition

1487 Kildare crowns Lambert Simnel "Edward VI" in Dublin

1494 Lord Deputy Edward Poynings forbids Irish Parliament to meet without royal consent

1348 The Black Death: one third of population killed in three years

Protestant Conquest

England's break with the Catholic Church, the dissolution of the monasteries and Henry VIII's assumption of the title King of Ireland incensed both the old Anglo-Norman dynasties and resurgent Irish clans such as the O'Neills. Resistance to foreign rule was fierce and it took over 150 years of war to establish the English Protestant Ascendancy. Tudor and Stuart monarchs adopted a policy of military persuasion, then Plantation. Oliver Cromwell was even more forceful. Irish hopes were raised when the Catholic James II ascended to the English throne, but he was deposed and fled to Ireland, where he was defeated by William of Orange (William III) in 1690.

Ireland in 1625

Main areas of Plantation in the reign of James I

Battle of the Boyne
This tapestry, from the Bank of Ireland (*see p64*), shows William of Orange leading his troops against the army of James II in 1690. His victory is still celebrated by Orangemen in Northern Ireland.

The first relief ship to reach Londonderry was the *Phoenix*. For three months English ships had been prevented from sailing up the Foyle by a wooden barricade across the river.

James II's army on the east bank of the Foyle attacks the ship.

The artist's depiction of 17th-century weapons and uniforms is far from accurate.

Silken Thomas Fitzgerald
Silken Thomas, head of the powerful Kildares, renounced his allegiance to Henry VIII in 1534. He was hanged along with his five uncles in 1537.

Henry VIII

1504 8th Earl of Kildare becomes master of Ireland after victory at Knocktoe

1500 | 1525 | 1550 | 1575 | 1

1534 Silken Thomas rebels against Henry VIII

1539 Henry VIII dissolves monasteries

1541 Henry VIII declared King of Ireland by Irish Parliament

Sir Thomas Lee, an officer in Elizabeth I's army, dressed in Irish fashion

1557 Mary I orders first plantations in Offaly and Laois

1582 Desmond rebellion in Munster

1585 Ireland is mapped and divided into 32 counties

1588 Spanish Armada wrecked off west coast

1592 Trinity College, Dublin founded

1603 Earl o Tyrone ends eight years o war by signing the Treaty of Mellifon

1607 Flig the Ear Irish leade to the Cont Plantat

The Siege of Drogheda (1649)
Between 1649 and 1652 Cromwell's army avenged attacks on Protestant settlers with ruthless efficiency. Here Cromwell himself directs the gunners bombarding Drogheda.

Plantation Ireland

James I realized that force alone could not stabilize Ireland. The Plantation programme uprooted the native Irish and gave their land to Protestant settlers from England and Scotland. London livery companies organized many of the new settlements. The policy created loyal garrisons who supported the Crown.

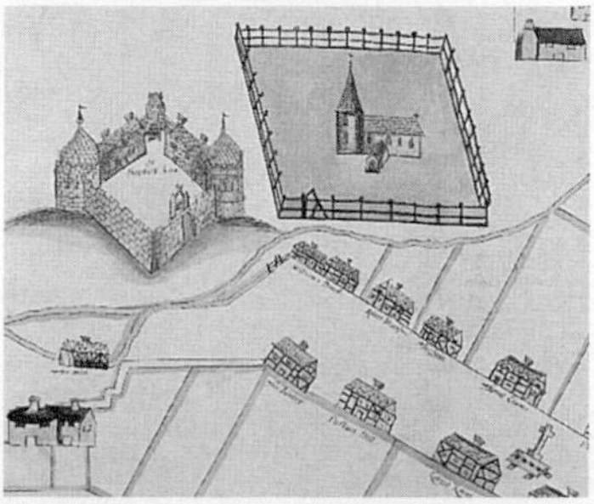

Bellaghy in County Londonderry was settled by the Vintners Company. This map of the neatly planned town dates from 1622.

The Walls of Derry have never been breached by any attacker and many of the original 17th-century gates and bastions that withstood the siege of 1689 are still in place *(see pp262–3)*.
St George's flag
Ship Quay
Protestants emerge from the besieged city to greet the English relieving force and to engage the enemy.

The Siege of Derry (1689)

Some 20,000 Protestants were besieged for 105 days in Londonderry by James II's forces. Thousands died from starvation, until relief finally came from English warships. This 18th-century painting by William Sadler II gives a rather fanciful picture of the ending of the siege.

Loftus Cup
Adam Loftus, Chancellor of Ireland, used his position to enrich his family. In 1593 he had the Great Seal of Ireland melted down and made into this silver-gilt cup.

1625

1632 Important Irish history, *The Annals of the Four Masters*, written by four Franciscan friars from Donegal

1641 Armed rebellion in Ulster opposes Plantation

1650

1649 Cromwell lands in Dublin; razes Drogheda and Wexford; Catholic landowners transplanted to far west

Protestant apprentice boys closing the gates of Derry before the siege of 1689

1675

1688 James II, deposed Catholic king of England, flees to Ireland and raises army

1689 Siege of Derry

1690 William of Orange defeats James II at Battle of the Boyne; James's army surrenders the following year in Limerick

1700

1695 Penal code severely reduces rights of Roman Catholics

Georgian Ireland

The Protestant Ascendancy was a period of great prosperity for the landed gentry, who built grand country houses and furnished them luxuriously. Catholics, meanwhile, were denied even the right to buy land. Towards the end of the 18th century, radicals, influenced by events in America and France, started to demand independence from the English Crown. Prime Minister Henry Grattan tried a parliamentary route; Wolfe Tone and the United Irishmen opted for armed insurrection. Both approaches ultimately failed.

Ireland in 1703

Counties where Protestants owned over 75 per cent of land

The Irish House of Commons
This painting shows Irish leader Henry Grattan addressing the house *(see p64)*. The "Grattan Parliament" lasted from 1782 to 1800, but was then abolished by the Act of Union.

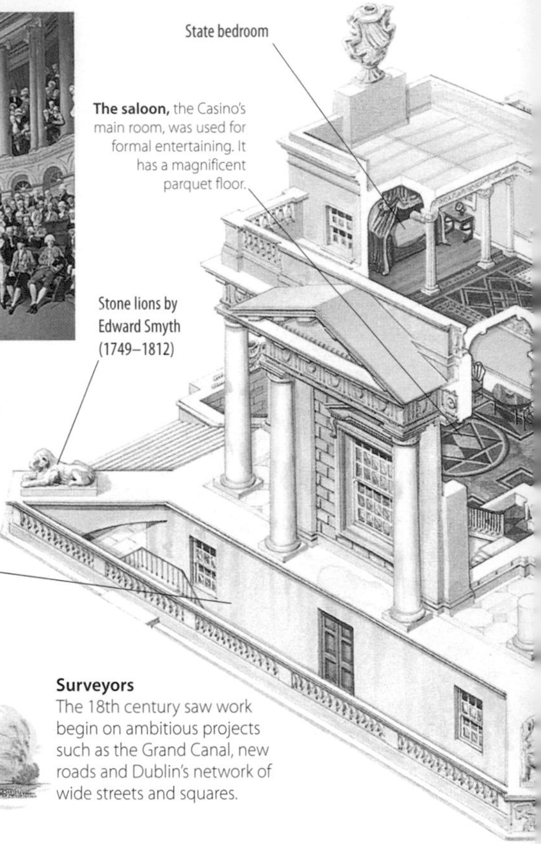

State bedroom
The saloon, the Casino's main room, was used for formal entertaining. It has a magnificent parquet floor.
Stone lions by Edward Smyth (1749–1812)
The basement contains the servants' hall, the kitchen, pantry and wine cellar.

Surveyors
The 18th century saw work begin on ambitious projects such as the Grand Canal, new roads and Dublin's network of wide streets and squares.

Jonathan Swift (1667–1745)

1710 | 1720 | 1730 | 1740 | 1750

1713 Jonathan Swift appointed Dean of St Patrick's Cathedral *(see p86)*

1724 Swift attacks Ireland's penal code in *A Modest Proposal*

1731 Royal Dublin Society founded to encourage agriculture, art and crafts

1731 First issue of the *Belfast News-letter*, the world's oldest continually running newspaper

1738 Death of Ireland's most famous harper, Turlough O'Carolan *(see p28)*

1742 First performance of Handel's *Messiah* given in Dublin

1751 Dublin's Rotunda Lying-In Hospital is first maternity hospital in the British Isles

Linen Bleaching
Ulster's linen industry flourished thanks to the expertise of Huguenot weavers from France. The woven cloth was spread out in fields or on river banks to bleach it *(see p272)*.

Irish Painting
Aristocratic patronage encouraged the development of an Irish school of painting. This picture, by an unknown artist, shows Leixlip Castle in an idealized rural setting.

The Classical urns on the roof conceal chimneys.
The china closet was originally designed as a bedroom.
The hall ends in a semi-circular apse leading to the saloon.
Entrance

Casino Marino

This frivolous summer house was built in the 1760s for the first Earl of Charlemont on his estate just north of Dublin (see p104). *Palladian architecture of this kind was popular among the Irish aristocracy, who followed 18th-century English fashions.*

Where to see Georgian Ireland

Dublin preserves many fine Georgian terraces and public buildings such as the Custom House *(see p92)* and the Four Courts *(p96)*. Around Dublin, the grand houses at Castletown *(pp132–3)*, Russborough and Powerscourt *(pp138–9)* are fascinating reminders of the lifestyle of the gentry. Other 18th-century country seats open to the public include Emo Court, Westport House *(pp208–9)* and Castle Coole *(p276)*.

Emo Court's façade, with its plain Ionic portico, is by James Gandon, architect of many of Dublin's public buildings *(p257)*.

Russborough House *(p136)* was built in 1741 by Richard Castle. Elegant niches with Classical busts flank the grand fireplace in the entrance hall.

Guinness Brewery Gate

1782 Parliament gains greater degree of independence from Westminster

The Irish Volunteers, a local militia which pressed Parliament for reform

1798 Rebellion of Wolfe Tone's United Irishmen quashed

1760 | 1770 | 1780 | 1790

1759 Arthur Guinness buys the St James's Gate Brewery in Dublin

Custom House

1791 James Gandon's Custom House built in Dublin

1795 Orange Order formed by Ulster Protestants

1793 Limited emancipation for Irish Catholics

Famine and Emigration

The history of 19th-century Ireland is dominated by the Great Famine of 1845–48, which was caused by the total failure of the potato crop. Although Irish grain was still being exported to England, more than one million people died from hunger or disease, with even more fleeing to North America. By 1900, the pre-famine population of eight million had fallen by half. Rural hardship fuelled a campaign for tenants' rights which evolved into demands for independence from Britain. Great strides towards "Home Rule" were made in Parliament by the charismatic politician Charles Stewart Parnell.

Ireland in 1851

Areas where population fell by over 25 per cent during the Famine

Daniel O'Connell
Known as "The Liberator", O'Connell organized peaceful "monster rallies" of up to a million people in pursuit of Catholic emancipation. He was elected MP for Clare in 1828.

The ships that brought the Irish to America were overcrowded and fever-ridden, and known as "coffin ships".

Castle Clinton was used for processing new arrivals to New York prior to the construction of the huge depot on Ellis Island.

The Boycotting of Landlords
In 1880, troops guarded the crops of Captain Boycott, the first notable victim of a campaign to ostracize landlords guilty of evicting tenants. His name later passed into the English language.

Charles Bianconi's coach service, 1836

1815 First coach service begins in Ireland

1817 Royal Canal is completed

1838 Father Mathew founds temperance crusade – five million Irish take abstinence pledge and whiskey production is reduced by half

1845 Great F which l fou

1800 | 1810 | 1820 | 1830 | 1840

1803 Uprising, led by Robert Emmet, is crushed after feared Napoleonic invasion of England fails to materialize

1800 Act of Union: Ireland legally becomes part of Britain

1829 After a five-year campaign by Daniel O'Connell, Catholic Emancipation Act is passed, giving a limited number of Catholics the right to vote

Fathe Math

Eviction of Irish Farmers
In the late 1870s, agricultural prices plummeted. Starving tenant farmers fell into arrears and were mercilessly evicted. Their plight spawned the Land League, which lobbied successfully for reform.

The Irish Abroad

One result of the Famine was the growth of a strong Irish community in the USA. From the lowest rung of American society, the immigrants rose up the social scale and became rich by Irish Catholic standards. They sent money to causes back home, and as a well-organized lobby group put pressure on the American government to influence British policies in Ireland. A more militant group, Clan na Gael, sent veterans of the American Civil War to fight in the Fenian risings of 1865 and 1867.

New Yorkers stage a huge St Patrick's Day parade, 17 March 1870.

The Irish were widely perceived as illiterate peasants in the USA and often met with a hostile reception.

Immigrants Arrive In New York

The Irish who survived the journey to America landed at Castle Garden in New York, seen here in a painting by Samuel Waugh (1855). Although mainly country people, most new arrivals settled in Manhattan, often enduring horrific living conditions.

Charles Stewart Parnell
A campaigner for the Land League and Home Rule, Parnell saw his political career ruined in 1890, when he was cited as co-respondent in a divorce case.

1850 | 1860 | 1870 | 1880 | 1890

848 Failure of the oung Ireland Uprising – spontaneous response insurrections lsewhere in Europe

1853 Dublin Exhibition is opened by Queen Victoria

1867 Irish-Americans return home to fight in a rising led by the Irish Republican Brotherhood, also known as the Fenians

1877 Parnell becomes leader of the new Home Rule Party

1879–82 Land War, led by Michael Davitt's Land League, campaigns for the reform of tenancy laws

1881 Parnell is jailed in Kilmainham Gaol, Dublin

1884 Founding of Gaelic Athletic Association, first group to promote Irish traditions

1886 British PM Gladstone sponsors first Home Rule Bill but is defeated by Parliament

1892 Second Home Rule Bill is defeated

War and Independence

Plans for Irish home rule were shelved because of World War I; however, the abortive Easter Rising of 1916 inspired new support for the Republican cause. In 1919 an unofficial Irish Parliament was established and a war began against the "occupying" British forces. The Anglo-Irish Treaty of 1921 divided the island in two, granting independence to the Irish Free State, while Northern Ireland remained in the United Kingdom. There followed a civil war between pro-Treaty and anti-Treaty factions in the South.

Ireland in 1922

- Northern Ireland
- Irish Free State

The Unionist Party
Leader of the campaign against Home Rule was Dublin barrister Edward Carson. In 1913 the Ulster Volunteer Force was formed to demand that six counties in Ulster remain part of the UK.

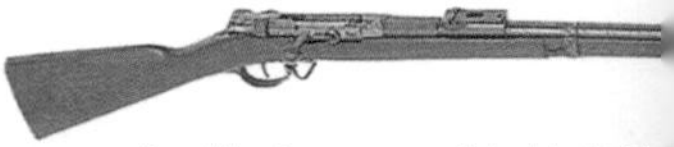

Patrick Pearse, a poet, read the Proclamation of the Republic from the steps of the GPO or Easter Monday.

The 1916 Service Medal, issued to all who fought in the Easter Rising, depicts, on one side, the mythical Irish warrior Cúchulainn.

The Black and Tans
Named for their makeshift uniforms, these British troops – mostly demobbed World War I soldiers – carried out savage reprisals against the Irish in 1920–21.

The Titanic

1904 Dublin's Abbey Theatre opens

1905 Sinn Féin (We Ourselves) party founded

1905

1910

1912 Belfast-built *Titanic* sinks on her maiden voyage

1912 Edward Carson rallies Ulster Protestants; solemn covenant to defeat Home Rule signed by 471,414 people

1913 General strike in Dublin

Despatch bag carried by Constance Markievicz during Easter Rising

1915

1916 Easter Rising quashed

1918 Sinn Féin wins 73 seats at Westminster; Constance Markievicz elected first woman MP

1919 Firs meeting indepen parliame *(Dáil Éirea*

1920 Government of Ireland Act proposes partition of the island

1921 Anglo-Irish Treaty signe Valera resigns; southern Ire plunged into civi

The General Post Office, Easter 1916
What was supposed to be a national uprising was confined to 2,500 armed insurgents in Dublin. They managed to hold the GPO and other public buildings for five days.

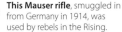

This Mauser rifle, smuggled in from Germany in 1914, was used by rebels in the Rising.

Eamon De Valera (1882–1975)

After escaping execution for his part in the Easter Rising, American-born de Valera went on to dominate Irish politics for almost 60 years. The opposition of his party, Sinn Féin, to the Anglo-Irish Treaty of 1921 plunged the new Irish Free State into civil war. After forming a new party, Fianna Fáil, he became Prime Minister *(Taoiseach)* in 1932. De Valera remained in office until 1948, with further terms in the 1950s. Between 1959 and 1973 he was President of Ireland.

Leaders of the 1916 Rising

This collage portrait shows 14 leaders of the Easter Rising, who were all court-martialled and shot at Kilmainham Gaol. The brutality of their executions (the badly injured James Connolly was tied to a chair before being shot) changed public opinion of the Rising and guaranteed their status as martyrs.

Mementos of the Rising at Dublin's Kilmainham Gaol *(see p101)* include this crucifix made by a British soldier from rifle bullets.

Election Poster
Cumann na nGaedheal, the pro-Treaty party in the Civil War, won the Free State's first general election in 1923. It merged with other parties in 1933 to form Fine Gael.

22 Irish Free State augurated; Michael ollins shot dead in nbush in Co Cork

Michael Collins (1890–1922), hero of the War of Independence, became chairman of the Irish Free State and Commander-in-Chief of the Army

1932 Fianna Fáil sweeps to victory in general election, and de Valera begins 16-year term as *Taoiseach* (Prime Minister)

1936 IRA proscribed by Free State Government

1939 Éire declares neutrality during World War II

1925 | 1930 | 1935

1923 W B Yeats wins Nobel Prize in literature

1926 De Valera quits Sinn Féin; sets up Fianna Fáil (Soldiers of Destiny) party

1925 G B Shaw also receives Nobel Prize

1929 Work starts on River Shannon hydro-electric power scheme

1933 Fine Gael (United Ireland) party formed to oppose Fianna Fáil

1937 New constitution declares complete independence from Britain; country's name changes to Éire

Modern Ireland

Since joining the European Economic Community (now the EU) in 1973, the Irish Republic has done much to modernize its traditional rural-based economy. There have been social changes too and divorce has become legalized. Meanwhile, Northern Ireland has lived through more than 25 years of unrest. But recent peace agreements have brought new hope, especially since the inauguration in 1998 of the Northern Ireland Assembly. The power-sharing Sinn Féin and DUP government is addressing the final stumbling blocks of policing and justice.

1949 New government under John A Costello. Country changes name from Éire to Republic of Ireland and leaves British Commonwealth

1956 IRA launches a terrorism campaign along the border with Northern Ireland which lasts until 1962

1967 Northern Ireland Civil Rights Association is set up to fight discrimination against Catholics

1969 Violent clashes between the police and demonstrators in Belfast and Derry. British troops sent to restore order

1972 Bloody Sunday – British soldiers shoot dead 13 demonstrators in Derry. Northern Ireland Parliament is suspended and direct rule from Westminster imposed

1976 Organizers of the Ulster Peace Movement, Mairead Corrigan and Betty Williams, are awarded the Nobel Peace Prize in Oslo

1982 Rising debt and unemployment lead to economic crisis and instability. Three elections are held in two years

NORTHERN IRELAND

1940 | **1950** | **1960** | **1970** | **1980**

REPUBLIC OF IRELAND

1955 Republic of Ireland joins United Nations

1959 Eamon de Valera resigns as *Taoiseach* (Prime Minister) and is later elected President

1973 The Republic joins the European Economic Community. Membership has given the country access to much-needed development grants

1979 Pope John Paul II visits Ireland and celebrates Mass in Dublin's Phoenix Park, in front of more than a million people

1947 Statue of Queen Victoria is removed from the courtyard in front of the Irish Parliament in Dublin

1963 John F Kennedy, the first American President of Irish Catholic descent, visits Ireland. He is pictured here with President Eamon de Valera

1969 Samuel Beckett, seen here rehearsing one of his own plays, is awarded the Nobel Prize in literature, but does not go to Stockholm to receive it

35 Barry McGuigan beats the
amanian, Eusebio Pedroza, for
rld featherweight boxing title

1986 Bitter Loyalist opposition follows the previous year's signing by the British and Irish governments of the Anglo-Irish Agreement

1987 IRA bomb explodes during Enniskillen's Remembrance Day parade, killing 11 people

1994 IRA and Unionist cease fires. Gerry Adams, Sinn Féin leader, allowed to speak on British radio and television

1998 The Good Friday Agreement sets out proposed framework for self-government in Northern Ireland

2001 David Trimble resigns as first minister, but is later re-elected. The beginning of a tortuous period of suspended talks and return to Westminster's direct rule

2005 The IRA announces an end to its armed campaign, saying it will follow an exclusively democratic path

2008 Padraig Harrington wins both the Open Championship and the PGA Championship

2010 The Democratic Unionist Party and Sinn Féin reach agreement to allow full transfer of police and justice powers from London to Belfast

2011 Queen Elizabeth makes a historic state visit to Ireland, the first such visit by a British monarch

NORTHERN IRELAND

1990 **2000** **2010** **2020**

REPUBLIC OF IRELAND

2002 The single European currency, the euro, replaces Irish punt notes and coins

1995 For the first time in 25 years, there are no troops on daylight patrols in Northern Ireland

1994 Republic of Ireland football team reaches quarter finals of World Cup in the USA. Here, Ray Houghton is congratulated on scoring the winning goal against Italy

1991 Mary Robinson becomes first female President of the Republic, succeeded by Mary McAleese in 1998

1988 Dublin's millennium is celebrated, boosting the city's image

1987 Dubliner Stephen Roche wins the Tour de France, Giro d'Italia and World Championship in one incredible season

2005 Foreign ministers of the European Union unanimously agree to make Irish an official language of the EU

2014 President Michael D Higgins makes a historic state visit to Britain, the first Irish Head of State to do so

2013 President Obama visits Northern Ireland

2012 Katie Taylor wins a gold medal in boxing at the London Olympics

2011 Michael D Higgins inaugurated as 9th President of Ireland

2011 US President Obama visits the Republic of Ireland

IRELAND THROUGH THE YEAR

Popular months for visiting Ireland are July and August, and Belfast no longer closes down in July for the marching season. June and September can be pleasant but never count on the weather, for Ireland's lush beauty is the product of a wet climate. Most tourist sights are open from Easter to September but have restricted opening hours or close in the low season. During spring and summer, festivals are held in honour of everything from food to religion. A common thread is music, and few festivities are complete without musical accompaniment. Ireland is at its best during celebrations, so is an inspired choice for Christmas and New Year. Look out for the word *fleadh* (festival) but remember that the Irish are spontaneous: festivities can spring from the air, or from a tune on a fiddle. Festival dates may vary.

Dublin's annual parade to celebrate St Patrick's Day (17 March)

Spring

St Patrick's Day is often said to mark the beginning of the tourist season. Later, the spring bank holiday weekend in May, when accommodation is in short supply, is celebrated with music in most places. After the quiet winter months, festivals and events start to become more common.

March

St Patrick's Festival *(17 Mar)*. Five days of parades, concerts, céilí dances and fireworks in Dublin, and parades in all major towns around the country.

Horse Ploughing Match and Heavy Horse Show, Ballycastle *(17 Mar, see p270)*. A popular annual competition.

DLR Poetry Now Festival *(end Mar)*. Dun Laoghaire. Four-day celebration of Irish poetry.

A St Patrick's Day float advertising Guinness

Feis Ceoil, Dublin *(end Mar)*. A classical music festival held at many different venues throughout the city.

April

Pan Celtic Festival, location changes annually. A lively celebration of Celtic culture, with music, dance and song.

Cork Choral Festival *(late Apr)*.

May

Belfast Civic Festival and Lord Mayor's Show *(mid-May, see pp280–81)*. Street parade with bands and floats.

Balmoral Show, Belfast *(mid-May)*. A three-day show with a diverse range of events including sheep-shearing competitions, dancing dogs and fashion shows.

"A Taste of Baltimore" Shellfish Festival *(end May, see p174)*.

Fleadh Nua, Ennis, *end May, see p193)*. Four days of traditional Irish music, songs and dance.

Summer

For the visitor, summer represents the height of the festive calendar. This is the busiest time of year for organized events, from music and arts festivals to lively local race meetings, summer schools and matchmaking festivals. Book accommodation if your plans include a popular festival.

Beach races at Laytown

June

Kilkenny Cat Laughs *(end May–early Jun)*. Internationally renowned comedy festival.

County Wicklow Garden Festival *(May–Jul)*. Held at private and public gardens around the county, including Powerscourt *(see pp138–9)*.

Dublin Docklands Maritime Festival *(early Jun)*. Tall ships, street theatre, outdoor markets, concerts and events for all ages.

Women's Mini Marathon, Dublin City *(early Jun)*.

Bloomsday, Dublin *(16 Jun)*. Lectures, talks, readings and walks to celebrate James Joyce's greatest novel, *Ulysses*.

Scurlogstown Olympiad Celtic Festival, Trim *(early Jun, see p252)*. Traditional Irish music and selection of a festival queen.

Average Daily Hours of Sunshine

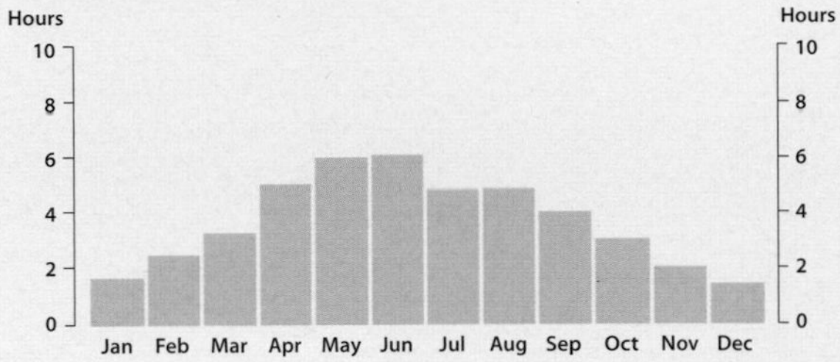

Sunshine Chart
The chart gives figures for Dublin, though conditions are similar around the country. The Southeast enjoys more sunshine hours than any other part of Ireland, while Northern Ireland receives marginally fewer hours of sun than the Republic.

Great Music in Great Irish Houses *(mid-Jun)*. Classical music recitals in grand settings at various venues.
Castleward Opera, Strangford *(all month, see p288)*. Opera festival in the grounds of 18th-century stately home.
County Wexford Strawberry Festival, Enniscorthy *(end Jun–early Jul, see p153)*. Craft fair, music, street theatre and, of course, strawberries.
Dublin Pride, Dublin *(end Jun)*. A week-long celebration for the capital's LGBT community, culminating in a street parade.

July
Twelfth of July *(12 Jul, see p248)*. Members of the Orange Order march in towns across Northern Ireland to celebrate the Protestants' landmark victory over King James II's Catholic army in 1690.
Galway Arts Festival *(third & fourth weeks, see pp214–15)*. Processions, concerts, street theatre, children's shows and other events in the medieval city centre. Followed by Galway's popular five-day race meeting.

Traditional sailing craft in the Cruinniú na mBád at Kinvara (August)

Mary from Dungloe International Festival, Dungloe *(last week, see p232)*. Dancing, music and selection of "Mary", the beauty queen.
Lughnasa Fair, Carrickfergus Castle *(end Jul, see p279)*. A popular medieval-style fair.
Ballyshannon International Folk Festival *(end Jul or early Aug, see p235)*. Three days of traditional Irish music.
O'Carolan Harp and Traditional Music Festival, Keadue, Co Roscommon *(end Jul or early Aug)*. Traditional music and dance celebrations.

Orangemen parading on the Twelfth of July

Steam-engine at Stradbally Rally (August)

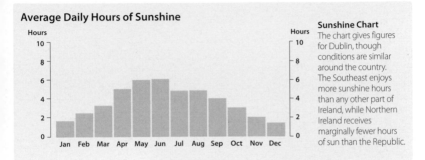

August
Stradbally Steam-engine Rally, Co Laois *(early Aug)*. Many types of steam-engine join this rally.
Galway Race Week, Co Galway *(early Aug)*. World renowned horse racing.
Dublin Horse Show *(first or second week)*. A premier showjumping competition and social event.
Puck Fair, Killorglin, Co Kerry *(mid-Aug, see p169)*. A wild goat is crowned "king" at this two-day-long traditional festival.
Blessing of the Sea *(second or third Sunday)*. Held in seaside towns all over Ireland.
Oul' Lammas Fair, Ballycastle *(mid–end Aug, see p270)*. A popular fair that is particularly famous for its edible seaweed.
Kilkenny Arts Festival *(middle of the month, see pp146–7)*. A major arts festival including poetry, film and crafts.
Rose of Tralee Festival, *(end Aug, see p160)*. Bands, processions, dancing and selection of the "Rose".
Cruinniú na mBád, Kinvara *(mid-Aug, see pp215 & 218)*. Various types of traditional sailing craft take part in this "gathering of the boats".

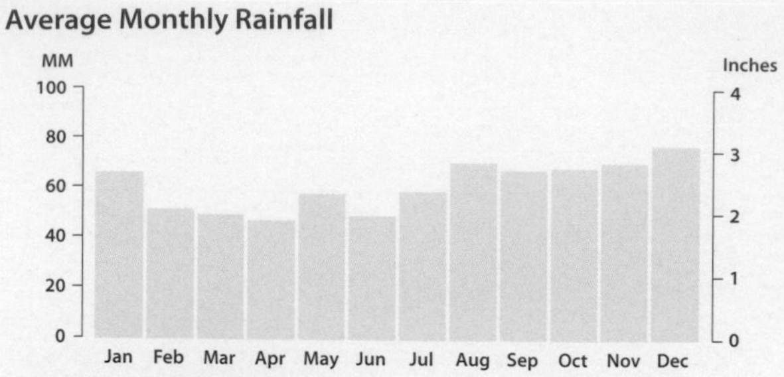

Rainfall Chart
Ireland is one of the wettest countries in Europe, with rainfall distributed evenly through the year – the figures displayed here are for Dublin. The West has the heaviest annual rainfall, while the Southeast receives marginally less rain than other regions.

Galway Oyster Festival (September)

Autumn

Oysters and opera are the two big events in autumn. There are also festivals devoted to jazz, film and music. The October bank holiday weekend is celebrated with music in many towns.

September
Heritage Week *(late Aug–early Sep)*. Events countrywide.
Laytown Beach Races, Co Meath *(first week of Sep)*. Horse races on the sand.
All-Ireland Hurling Final, Croke Park, Dublin *(first or second Sunday, see p33)*.
Dublin Fringe Festival *(two weeks mid-Sep)*. The country's biggest performing arts festival features music, dance and street theatre.
Lisdoonvarna Matchmaking Festival *(all month and first week of Oct, see p192)*. Singles gather for traditional music and dance.
All-Ireland Football Final, Croke Park, Dublin *(3rd Sunday, see p33)*. Gaelic football final.
Galway Oyster Festival *(end Sep, see pp214–15)*. Oyster tastings at different venues.

All-Ireland Hurling at Croke Park, Dublin

October
Oktoberfest, Londonderry *(all month, see pp262–3)*. Dancing, poetry, film, comedy, theatre and music.
Cork Film Festival *(early Oct, see pp178–9)*. Irish and international film screenings.
Kinsale International Festival of Fine Food *(early Oct, see pp176–7)*. Superb food served in restaurants, hotels and pubs of Kinsale.
Ballinasloe Fair, Co Galway *(first week)*. One of Europe's oldest horse fairs, staged amid lively street entertainment.
Dublin Theatre Festival *(first two weeks)*. Features works by both Irish and foreign playwrights.
Wexford Festival Opera *(last two weeks in Oct, see p339)*. A festival of lesser-known operas.
Hallowe'en (Samhain) *(31 Oct)*. An occasion celebrated all over the country.
Cork Jazz Festival *(end Oct, see pp178–9)*. An extremely popular festival, with music throughout the city.

Horse and trap at Lisdoonvarna fair

November
Belfast Festival at Queen's, Queen's University *(last two weeks Oct, see pp282–3)*. Arts festival featuring drama, ballet, cinema and all types of music from classical to jazz.
Éigse Sliabh Rua, Slieverue, Co Kilkenny *(mid-Nov)*. Festival of local history and music with guests and interesting talks.
Sligo International Choral Festival *(mid-Nov, see p238)*. Choirs from around the world in concert and competition.

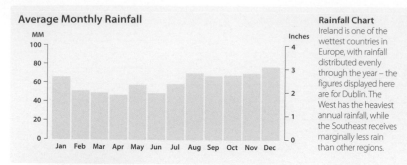

A procession as part of Dublin Theatre Festival (October)

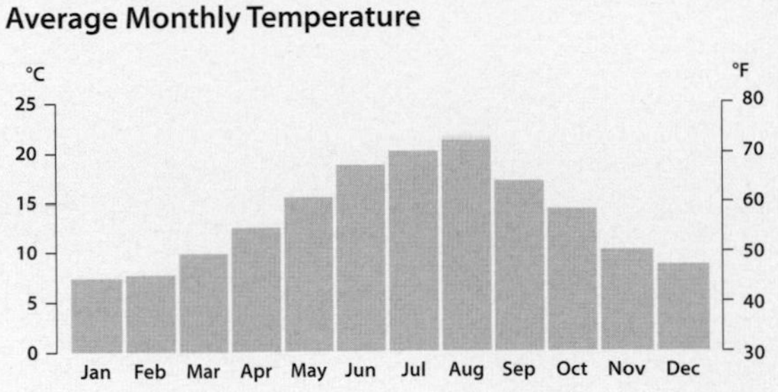

Temperature Chart
This chart gives the average minimum and maximum temperatures for the city of Dublin. Winter is mild throughout Ireland, except in the high mountain ranges, while the warmest summer temperatures are in the Southeast.

Winter

Although a quiet time for festivals, there's a range of entertainment including musical and theatrical events. Christmas is the busiest social period and there are plenty of informal celebrations. There is also a wide choice of National Hunt race meetings *(see p32)*.

Young boys dressed up as Wren boys on St Stephen's Day

December

Twelve Days of Christmas *(Dec)*. Dublin. A Christmas market with a vibrant festival atmosphere.

Leopardstown Races *(26 Dec, see p135)*. The biggest meeting held on this traditional day for racing. There are other fixtures at Limerick and Down Royal.

St Stephen's Day *(26 Dec)*. Catholic boys traditionally dress up as Wren boys (chimney sweeps with blackened faces) and sing hymns to raise money for charitable causes.

January

Salmon and Sea Trout Season *(17 Jan–end Sep, see pp342–3)*. Season begins for one of Ireland's most popular pastimes.

February

Jameson Dublin International Film Festival *(end Feb–early Mar)*. Films at various venues.

Belfast Musical Festival *(end Feb–mid-Mar)*. For over 100 years, young people have taken part in music (and speech and drama) competitions.

Six Nations Rugby Tournament, Aviva Stadium, Dublin *(varying Saturdays and Sundays Feb–Apr, see p32)*.

Glendalough *(see pp144–5)* in the snow

Public Holidays

New Year's Day (1 Jan)
St Patrick's Day (17 Mar)
Good Friday
Easter Monday
May Day (first Mon in May)
Spring Bank Holiday (Northern Ireland: last Mon in May)
June Bank Holiday (Republic: first Mon in Jun)
Twelfth of July (Northern Ireland: 12 Jul)
August Bank Holiday (Republic: first Mon in Aug).
Summer Bank Holiday (Northern Ireland: last Mon in Aug)
October Bank Holiday (Republic: last Mon in Oct)
Christmas Day (25 Dec)
St Stephen's Day (Republic: 26 Dec)
Boxing Day (Northern Ireland: 26 Dec)

DUBLIN AREA BY AREA

Dublin at a Glance

Ireland's capital has a wealth of attractions, most within walking distance of each other. For the purpose of this guide, central Dublin has been divided into three sections: *Southeast Dublin*, heart of the modern city and home to the prestigious Trinity College; *Southwest Dublin*, site of the old city around Dublin Castle; and *North of the Liffey*, the area around the imposing O'Connell Street. The map references given for sights in the city refer to the *Dublin Street Finder* on pages 122–3.

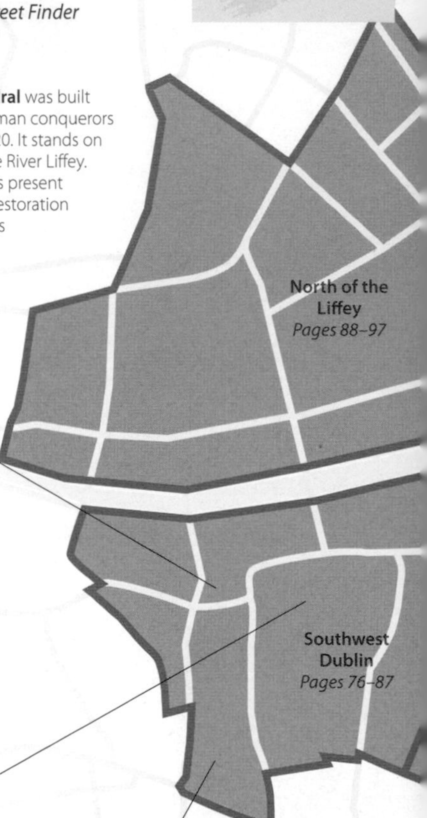

Christ Church Cathedral was built by Dublin's Anglo-Norman conquerors between 1172 and 1220. It stands on high ground above the River Liffey. Much of the cathedral's present appearance is due to restoration carried out in the 1870s *(see pp84–5)*.

0 metres 400

0 yards 400

Dublin Castle stands in the heart of old Dublin. St Patrick's Hall is part of the suite of luxury State Apartments housed on the upper floors on the south side of the castle. Today, these rooms are used for functions of national importance such as presidential inaugurations *(see pp80–81)*.

Saint Patrick's Cathedral has a spectacular choir featuring banners and stalls decorated with the insignia of the Knights of St Patrick. The cathedral also holds one of the world's finest organs of the late Romantic period, as well as memorials to Dean Jonathan Swift and prominent Anglo-Irish families *(see pp86–7)*.

◀ The Old Library at Trinity College, Dublin

O'Connell Street, Dublin's busiest thoroughfare, has a fine mix of architectural styles and a grand central mall punctuated with statues of famous Irish citizens and the 120-m (394-ft) Monument of Light spire. Just off O'Connell Street, on Moore Street, is a lively market *(see pp92–3)*.

The Custom House, a classic Georgian public building by James Gandon, was built between 1781 and 1791. The sculpted heads on the keystones are personifications of the rivers of Ireland; the one shown above represents the River Foyle *(see p92)*.

Trinity College is home to the Old Library which contains priceless illuminated manuscripts. These include the *Book of Kells* which dates back to the 9th century *(see pp66–8)*.

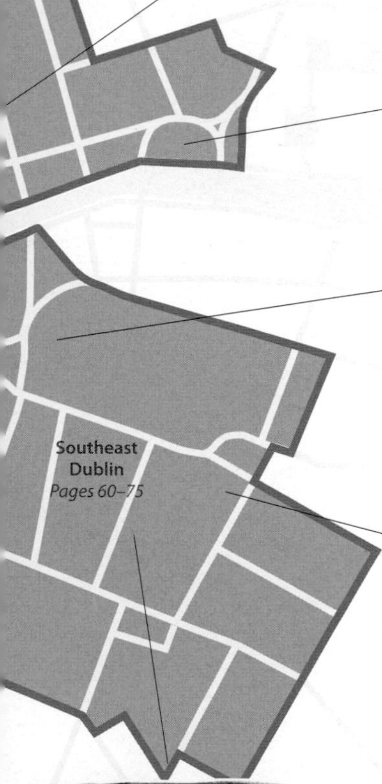

The National Gallery was opened in 1864. Housed on two floors, it holds an eclectic collection, particularly strong on Irish and Italian works. The gallery's most prized painting is Caravaggio's *The Taking of Christ*. The Millennium Wing has over 500 works on display *(see pp74–5)*.

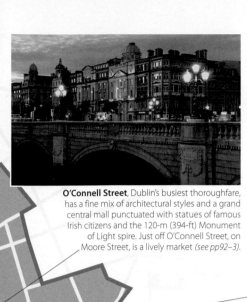

National Museum of Ireland – Archaeology has an impressive collection of artifacts dating from the Stone Age to the 20th century. The Ardagh Chalice (c.AD 800) is one of the many Celtic Christian treasures on display *(see pp70–71)*.

SOUTHEAST DUBLIN

Despite its location close to the old walled city, this part of Dublin remained virtually undeveloped until the founding of Trinity College in 1592. Even then, it was almost a hundred years before the ancient common land further south was enclosed to create St Stephen's Green, a spacious city park.

The mid-18th century saw the beginning of a construction boom in the area. During this time, magnificent public buildings such as the Old Library at Trinity College, Leinster House and the Bank of Ireland were built. However, the most conspicuous reminders of Georgian Dublin are the beautiful squares and terraces around Merrion Square. Many of these buildings still have their original features, including doorknockers, fanlights and wrought-iron balconies.

Today, Southeast Dublin is very much the tourist heart of the city: few visitors can resist the lively atmosphere and attractive shops of Grafton Street. The area is also home to much of Ireland's cultural heritage. The National Gallery has a good collection of Irish and European paintings while the National Museum – Archaeology has superb displays of Irish Bronze Age gold and early Christian treasures.

Sights at a Glance

Museums, Libraries and Galleries

7 The Little Museum of Dublin
8 *National Museum of Ireland – Archaeology pp70–71*
9 National Library
11 National Wax Museum Plus
12 National Museum of Ireland – Natural History
13 *National Gallery of Ireland pp74–5*
15 Royal Hibernian Academy

Historic Buildings

1 Bank of Ireland
2 *Trinity College pp66–7*
5 Mansion House
10 Leinster House

Historic Streets

3 Grafton Street
14 Merrion Square
16 Fitzwilliam Square

Churches

6 St Ann's Church

Parks and Gardens

4 St Stephen's Green

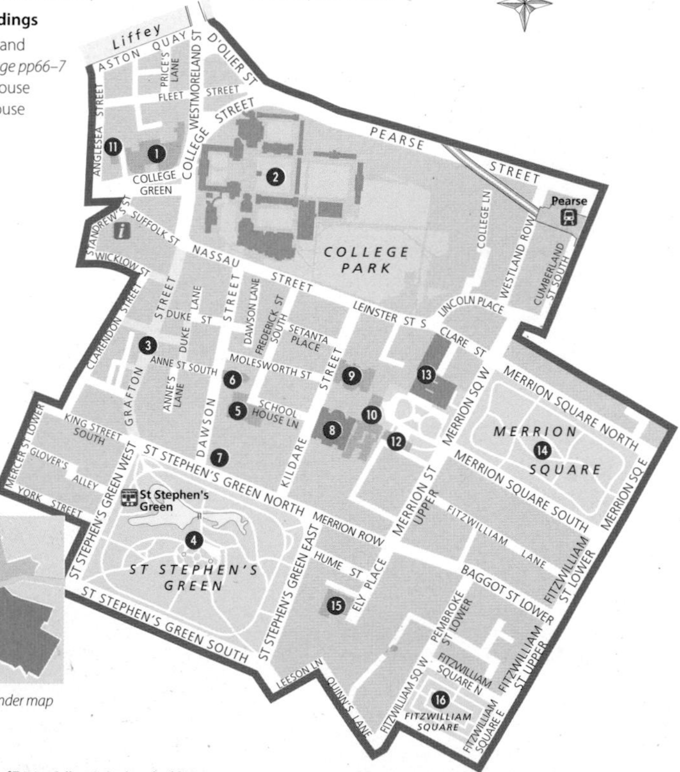

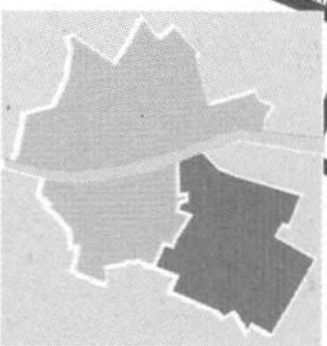

See also Street Finder map pp122–3

◀ The interior of Trinity College's Geology building

Street-by-Street: Southeast Dublin

The area around College Green, dominated by the façades of the Bank of Ireland and Trinity College, is very much the heart of Dublin. The alleys and malls cutting across busy pedestrianized Grafton Street boast many of Dublin's better shops, hotels and restaurants. Just off Kildare Street are the Irish Parliament, the National Library and the National Museum – Archaeology. To escape the city bustle many head for sanctuary in St Stephen's Green, which is overlooked by fine Georgian buildings.

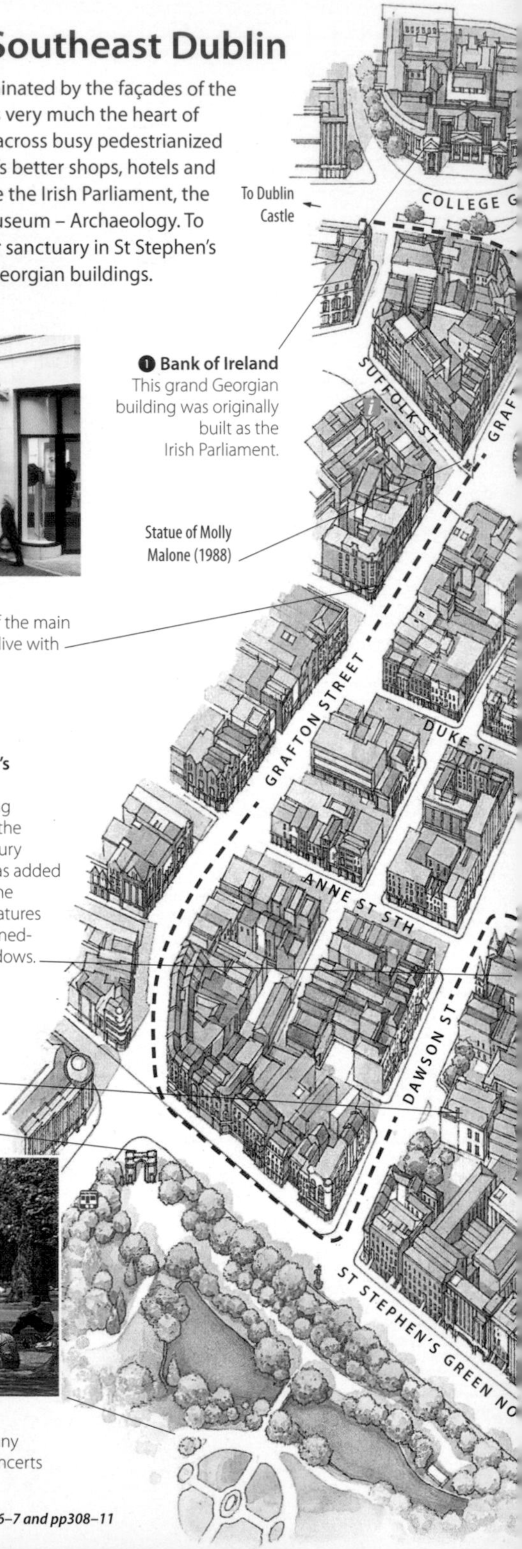

❶ Bank of Ireland
This grand Georgian building was originally built as the Irish Parliament.

❸ Grafton Street
Brown Thomas department store is one of the main attractions on this pedestrianized street, alive with buskers and pavement artists.

❻ St Ann's Church
The striking façade of the 18th-century church was added in 1868. The interior features lovely stained-glass windows.

❺ Mansion House
This has been the official residence of Dublin's Lord Mayor since 1715.

❹ ★ St Stephen's Green
The relaxing city park is surrounded by many grand buildings. In summer, lunchtime concerts attract tourists and workers alike.

For hotels and restaurants in this region see pp296–7 and pp308–11

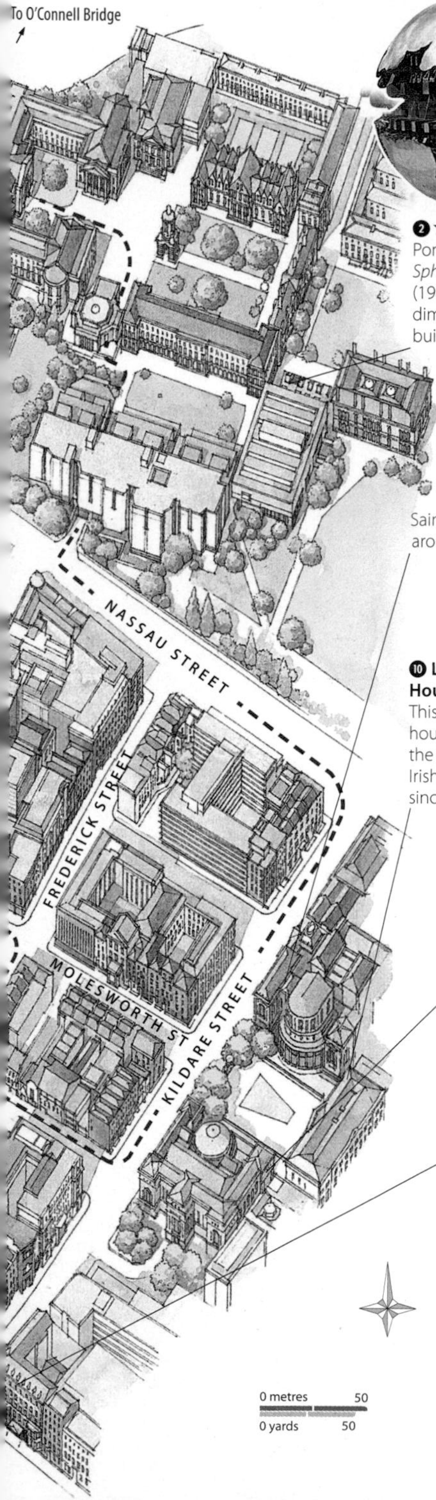

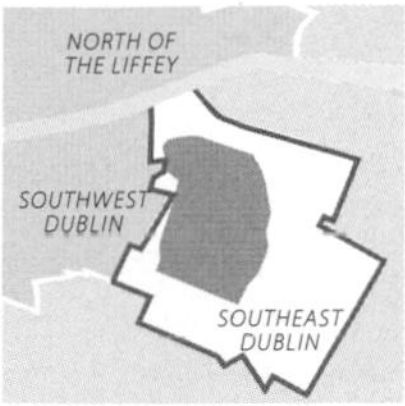

Locator Map

See Street Finder map pp122–3

❷ ★ Trinity College
Pomodoro's sculpture, *Sphere within Sphere* (1982), adds a modern dimension to the grand buildings of the campus.

❾ National Library
Saintly cherubs appear on the frieze around the library's magnificent old reading room, once a haunt of novelist James Joyce .

❿ Leinster House
This grand house has been the home of the Irish Parliament since 1922.

❽ ★ National Museum of Ireland – Archaeology
The museum's collection of Irish antiquities includes a bronze object known as the Petrie Crown (2nd century AD).

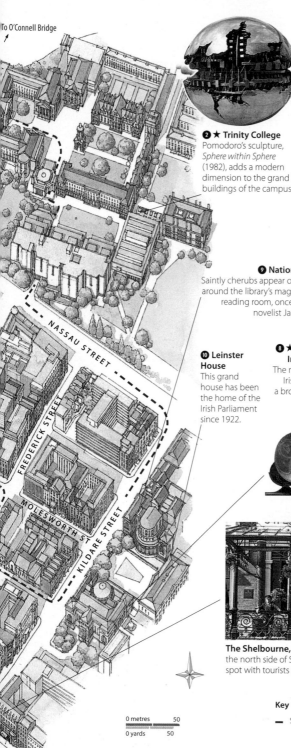

The Shelbourne, established in 1824, overlooks the north side of St Stephen's Green. It is a popular spot with tourists and locals for afternoon tea.

Key

— Suggested route

For key to symbols *see back flap*

Original chamber of the Irish House of Lords at the Bank of Ireland

❶ Bank of Ireland

2 College Green. **Map** D3. **Tel** 677 6801. **Open** 10am–4pm Mon, Tue & Fri, 10am–4pm Wed, 10am–5pm Thu. **Closed** Sat, Sun & public hols. House of Lords 10:30am, 11:30am & 1:45pm Tue.

The prestigious offices of the Bank of Ireland began life as the first purpose-built parliament house in Europe. The original central section was started by Irish architect Edward Lovett Pearce and completed in 1739 after his death. Sadly, Pearce's masterpiece, the great octagonal chamber of the House of Commons *(see p44)*, was removed at the behest of the British government in 1802. The House of Lords, however, remains gloriously intact, especially its coffered ceiling and oak panelling. There are also huge tapestries of the *Battle of the Boyne* and the *Siege of Londonderry*, and a splendid 1,233-piece crystal chandelier dating from 1788.

The east portico was added by architect James Gandon in 1785, with further additions around 1797. After the dissolution of the Irish Parliament in 1800, the Bank of Ireland bought the building. The present structure was then completed in 1808 with the transformation of the former lobby of the House of Commons into a magnificent cash office and the addition of a curving screen wall and the Foster Place annexe.

At the front of the bank on College Green is a statue (1876) by John Foley of Henry Grattan *(see p44)*, the most formidable leader of the old parliament.

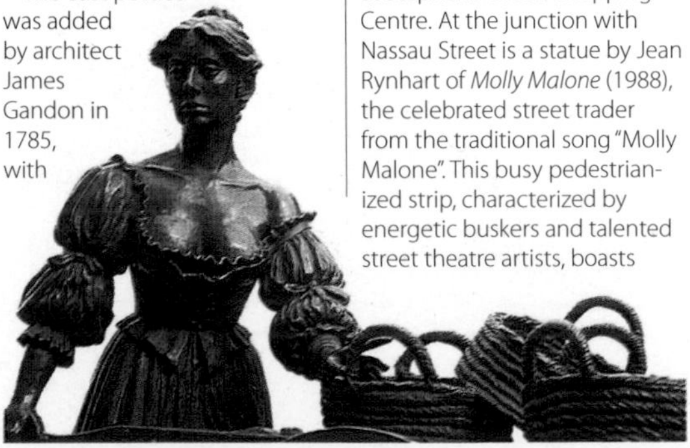

Bronze statue of *Molly Malone* at the bottom of Grafton Street

❷ Trinity College

See pp66–7.

❸ Grafton Street

Map D4.

The spine of Dublin's most popular and stylish shopping district *(see pp108–9)* runs south from Trinity College to the glass St Stephen's Green Shopping Centre. At the junction with Nassau Street is a statue by Jean Rynhart of *Molly Malone* (1988), the celebrated street trader from the traditional song "Molly Malone". This busy pedestrianized strip, characterized by energetic buskers and talented street theatre artists, boasts Brown Thomas, one of Dublin's finest department stores *(see p108)*. In addition, there are plenty of recognizable high-street retailers to tempt shoppers, including Tommy Hilfiger and River Island. There are also many excellent jewellers in Grafton Street. Number 78 stands on the site of Samuel Whyte's school, whose illustrious roll included Robert Emmet *(see p81)*, leader of the 1803 Rebellion, and the Duke of Wellington.

Hidden along many of the side streets are quaint, traditional Irish pubs, catering to the weary shopper's need for a refreshment break.

Royal College of Surgeons, which overlooks St Stephen's Green

❹ St Stephen's Green

Map D5. **Open** daylight hours.
St Stephen's Green, Dublin 2.
Tel 475 7816. **Open** all year round
Closed 25 Dec; phone for closing details
tours on request.

Originally one of three ancient commons in the old city, St Stephen's Green was enclosed in 1664. The 9-ha (22-acre) green was laid out in its present form in 1880, using a grant given by Lord Ardilaun, a member of the Guinness family. Landscaped with flowerbeds, trees, a fountain and a lake, the green is dotted with memorials to eminent Dubliners, including Ardilaun himself. There is a bust of James Joyce *(see p94)*, and a memorial by Henry Moore (1967) dedicated to W B Yeats

Beautifully manicured grounds of St Stephen's Green

(see pp236–7). At the Merrion Row corner stands a massive monument (1967) by Edward Delaney to 18th-century nationalist leader Wolfe Tone – it is known locally as "Tonehenge". The 1887 bandstand is still the focal point for free daytime concerts in summer.

The imposing Royal College of Surgeons stands on the west side. Built in 1806, it was commandeered by rebel troops under Countess Constance Markievicz in the 1916 Rising *(see pp48–9)* and its columns still bear the marks of bullets from the fighting.

The busiest side of the Green is the north, known during the 19th century as the Beaux'Walk and still home to gentlemen's clubs. The most prominent building is the refurbished venerable hotel, Shelbourne. Dating back to 1824, its entrance is adorned by statues of Nubian princesses and attendant slaves. It is well worth popping in for a look at the chandeliered foyer and for afternoon tea in the Lord Mayor's Lounge.

Situated on the south side is Newman House, home of the Catholic University of Ireland (now part of University College). Opened in 1856, its first rector was English theologian John Henry Newman. Famous past pupils include the poet Gerald Manley Hopkins, former Taoiseach Eamon de Valera *(see p49)* and author James Joyce. Tours reveal some of the best Georgian interior decor to survive in the city. The walls and ceilings of the Apollo Room and Saloon at No. 85 are festooned with intricate Baroque stuccowork (1739) by the Swiss brothers Paolo and Filippo Lafrancini. The Bishops' Room at No. 86 is decorated with heavy 19th-century furniture.

The small University Church (1856) next door has a colourful, richly marbled Byzantine interior. Also on the south side of St Stephen's Green is Iveagh House, a town house once owned by the Guinness family and now the Department of Foreign Affairs.

❺ Mansion House

Dawson St. **Map** E4.
Closed to the public.

Set back from Dawson Street by a neat cobbled forecourt, the Mansion House is an attractive Queen Anne-style building. It was built in 1710 for the aristocrat Joshua Dawson, after whom the street is named. The Dublin Corporation bought it from him five years later as the official residence of the city's Lord Mayor. The Round Room adjacent to the main building was built in 1821 for the visit of King George IV. The Dáil Éireann *(see p69)*, which adopted the Declaration of Independence, first met here on 21 January 1919.

❻ St Ann's Church

Dawson St. **Map** E4. **Tel** 676 7727.
Open 10am–4pm Mon–Fri (also for Sun service at 11:15am).

St Ann's, founded in 1707, has a striking Romanesque façade, which was added in 1868. Inside are colourful stained-glass windows, dating from the mid-19th century. The church has a long tradition of charity work: in 1723 Lord Newton left a bequest to buy bread for the poor. The original shelf for the bread still stands next to the altar.

Famous past parishioners include Wolfe Tone *(see p45)*, who was married here in 1785, Douglas Hyde *(see p87)* and Bram Stoker (1847–1912), author of *Dracula*.

Detail of window depicting Faith, Hope and Charity, St Ann's Church

❼ The Little Museum of Dublin

15 Stephen's Green. **Map** D4.
Tel 661 1000. **Open** 9:30am–5pm daily (until 8pm Thu).

Described as "Dublin's best museum experience" by *The Irish Times*, The Little Museum of Dublin is housed in a beautiful Georgian building on St Stephen's Green. The museum charts the cultural, social and political history of the capital through a collection of over 5,000 items, including art, photography, letters and postcards, donated by the public. Admission includes a 10 percent discount in Hatch & Sons, the acclaimed restaurant in the basement of the museum.

❷ Trinity College

Trinity College was founded in 1592 by Queen Elizabeth I on the site of an Augustinian monastery. Originally a Protestant college, it was not until 1793 that Catholics started entering the university, although certain restrictions were applied until the 1970s. Among Trinity's many famous students were playwrights Oliver Goldsmith and Samuel Beckett, and political writer Edmund Burke. The college's lawns and cobbled quads provide a pleasant haven in the heart of the city. The major attractions are the Long Room and the Book of Kells Exhibition, housed in the Old Library.

★ Campanile
The 30-m (98-ft) bell tower, erected in 1853, was designed by Sir Charles Lanyon, architect of Queen's University, Belfast *(see p282)*.

Chapel (1798)
This was the first university chapel in the Republic to accept all denominations. The painted window above the altar is from 1867.

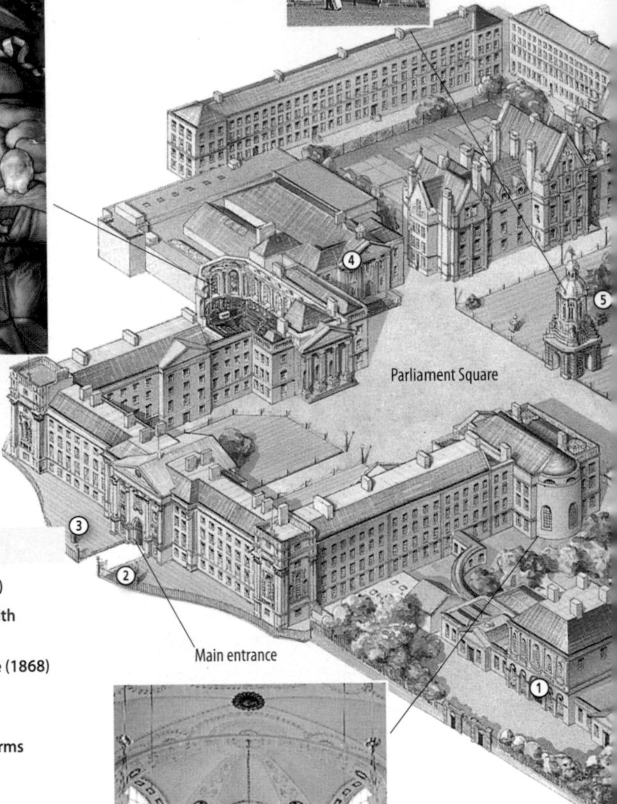

KEY

① **Provost's House (c. 1760)**

② **Statue of Oliver Goldsmith (1864) by John Foley**

③ **Statue of Edmund Burke (1868) by John Foley**

④ **Dining Hall (1761)**

⑤ **Reclining Connected Forms (1969) by Henry Moore**

⑥ **The Museum Building**, completed in 1857, is noted for its Venetian exterior, and the domed roof made of blue, red and yellow enamelled bricks.

⑦ **Sphere within Sphere**, (1982) was given to the college by its sculptor Arnaldo Pomodoro.

⑧ **Berkeley Library Building by Paul Koralek (1967)**

⑨ **The Douglas Hyde Gallery**, was built in the 1970s to house temporary art exhibitions.

Examination Hall
Completed in 1791 to a design by Sir William Chambers, the hall features a gilded oak chandelier and ornate ceilings by Michael Stapleton.

Library Square
The red-brick building (known as the Rubrics) on the east side of Library Square was built around 1700 and is the oldest surviving part of the college.

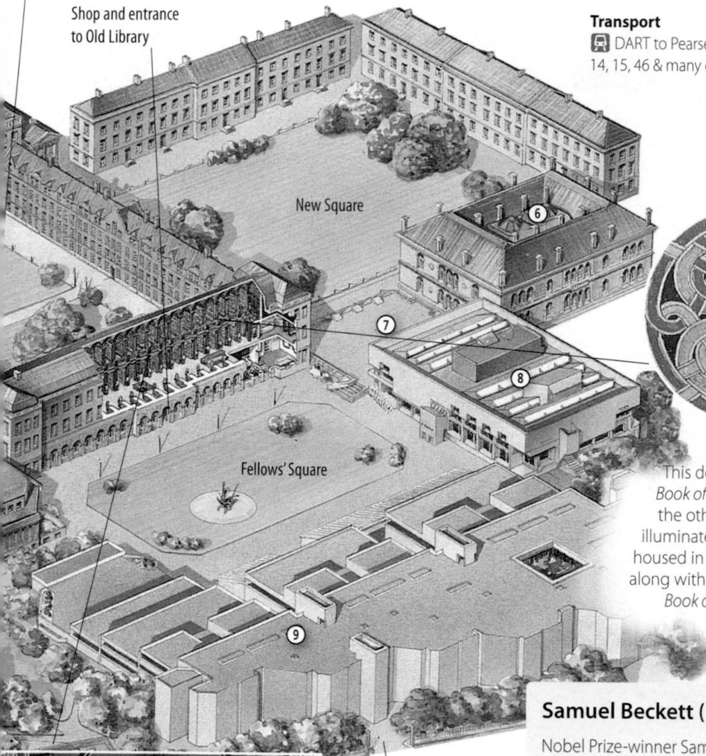

★ Old Library
This detail is from the *Book of Durrow*, one of the other magnificent illuminated manuscripts housed in the Old Library along with the celebrated *Book of Kells* *(see p68)*.

★ Long Room (1732)
The spectacular Long Room measures 64 m (210 ft) from end to end. It houses 200,000 antiquarian texts, marble busts of scholars and the oldest surviving harp in Ireland.

VISITORS' CHECKLIST

Practical Information
College Green.
Map D3.
Tel 896 1000.
W tcd.ie/library
Long Room and Old Library:
Open 9:30am–5pm Mon–Sat, 9:30am–4:30pm Sun (May–Sep), noon–4:30pm Sun (Oct–Apr).
Closed 10 days at Christmas.
by arrangement.
Chapel: **Open** by appt.
Douglas Hyde Gallery:
Open for exhibitions.

Transport
DART to Pearse Street. 10, 14, 15, 46 & many other routes.

Samuel Beckett (1906–89)

Nobel Prize-winner Samuel Beckett was born at Foxrock, south of Dublin. In 1923 he entered Trinity, and later graduated with a first in modern languages and a gold medal. He was also a keen member of the college cricket team. Forsaking Ireland, Beckett moved to France in the early 1930s. Many of his major works such as *Waiting for Godot* (1951) were written first in French, and later translated, by Beckett, into English.

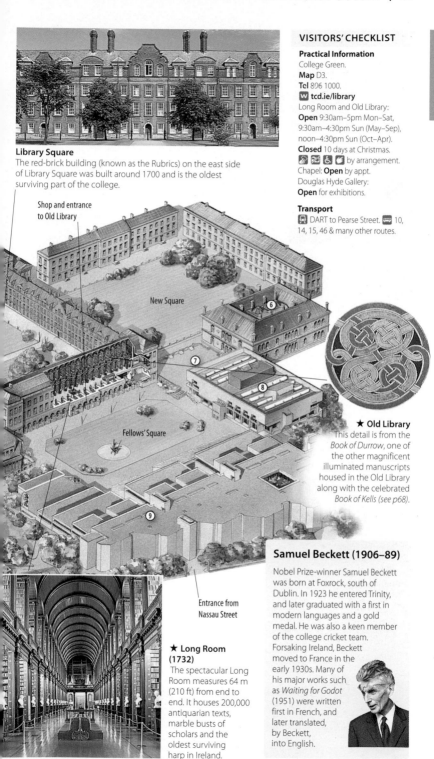

The Book of Kells

The most richly decorated of Ireland's medieval illuminated manuscripts, the *Book of Kells* may have been the work of monks from Iona, who fled to Kells *(see p245)* in AD 806 after a Viking raid. The book, which was moved to Trinity College *(see pp66–7)* in the 17th century, contains the four gospels in Latin. The scribes who copied the texts also embellished their calligraphy with intricate interlacing spirals as well as human figures and animals. Some of the dyes used were imported from as far as the Middle East.

Pair of moths

Stylized angel

The Greek letter "X"

The symbols of the four evangelists are used as decoration throughout the book. The figure of the man symbolizes St Matthew.

The letter that looks like a "P" is a Greek "R".

The letter "I"

Interlacing motifs

Cat watching rats

Rats eating bread could be a reference to sinners taking Holy Communion. The symbolism of the animals and people decorating the manuscript is often hard to interpret.

A full-page portrait of St Matthew, shown standing barefoot in front of a throne, precedes the opening words of his gospel.

Monogram Page

The most elaborate page of the book, this contains the first three words of St Matthew's account of the birth of Christ. The first word "XRI" is an abbreviation of "Christi".

The text is in a beautifully rounded Celtic script with brightly ornamented initial letters. Animal and human forms are often used to decorate the end of a line.

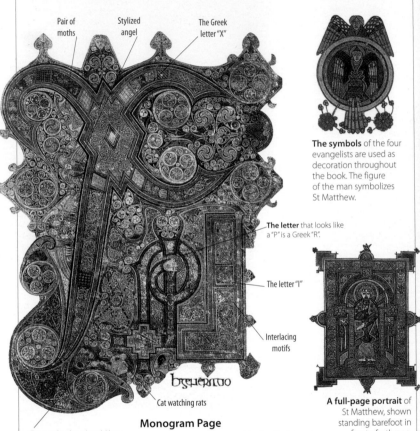

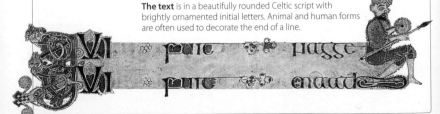

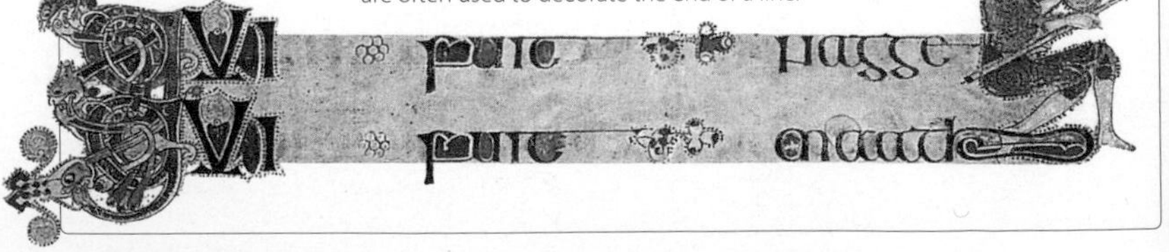

The magnificent domed Reading Room on the first floor of the National Library

❽ National Museum of Ireland – Archaeology

See pp70–71.

❾ National Library

Kildare St. **Map** E4. **Tel** 603 0213. **Open** 9:30am–7:45pm Mon–Wed, 9:30am–4:45pm Thu & Fri, 9:30am–4:30pm Sat (Reading Room closes 12:45pm). **Closed** public hols. **nli.ie**

Designed by Sir Thomas Deane, the National Library opened in 1890. It now contains first editions of every major Irish writer and a copy of almost every book ever published in Ireland. Its holdings also include manuscripts, prints, drawings, maps, photographs, newspapers, music, ephemera and genealogical material, all of which comprise the most outstanding collection of Irish documentary heritage in the world.

Visitors can view the famous Reading Room where distinguished Irish writers have studied, or explore the award-winning exhibitions.

For anyone interested in family history, the Genealogy Advisory Service is available for free to all personal callers.

The library also hosts an ongoing programme of events, including public lectures, poetry and music recitals, theatre, children's storytelling, public tours of exhibitions, creative workshops and a lot more. Admission is free.

❿ Leinster House

Kildare St. **Map** E4. **Tel** 618 3000. **Open** for tours 10:30am & 2:30pm daily; email events.desk@oireachtas.ie to book in advance. **oireachtas.ie**

This stately mansion houses the Dáil and the Seanad – the two chambers of the Irish Parliament. It was originally built for the Duke of Leinster in 1745. Designed by German-born architect Richard Cassels, the Kildare Street façade resembles that of a large town house. However, the rear, looking on to Merrion Square, has the air of a country estate complete with sweeping lawns. The Royal Dublin Society bought the building in 1815. The government obtained a part of it in 1922 for parliamentary use and bought the entire building two years later.

Email ahead to book a place on the two daily tours of the rooms, including the Seanad chamber with its heavily ornamented ceiling.

The Irish Parliament

The Irish Free State, forerunner of the Republic of Ireland, was inaugurated in 1922 *(see p48)*, although an unofficial Irish parliament, the Dáil, had already been in existence since 1919. Today, parliament is made up of two houses: Dáil Éireann (House of Representatives) and Seanad Éireann (the Senate). The Prime Minister is the Taoiseach and the deputy, the Tánaiste. The Dáil's 166 representatives – Teachtaí Dála, known as TDs – are elected by proportional representation. The 60-strong Seanad is appointed by various individuals and authorities, including the Taoiseach and the University of Dublin.

Opening of the first parliament of the Irish Free State in 1922

❽ National Museum of Ireland – Archaeology

Opened in 1890, the National Museum of Ireland – Archaeology has a domed rotunda featuring marble pillars and a mosaic floor. The Treasury houses priceless items such as the Broighter gold boat *(see p37)*, while *Ór – Ireland's Gold*, an exhibition of Ireland's Bronze Age gold, has jewellery such as the Gleninsheen Gorget *(see pp36–7)*. The National Museum of Ireland consists of three other sites: Decorative Arts and History at Collins Barracks *(see p105)*, Country Life and Natural History *(see p72)*.

Egyptian Mummy
This mummy of the lady Tentdinebu is thought to date back to c.945–716 BC. Covered in brilliant colours, it is part of the stunning Egyptian collection.

★ Ór – Ireland's Gold
This is one of the most extensive collections of Bronze Age gold in Western Europe. This gold lunula (c.1800 BC), found in Athlone, is one of many pieces of ancient jewellery in this exhibition.

Key to Floorplan

- Kingship and Sacrifice
- Ór – Ireland's Gold
- The Treasury
- Prehistoric Ireland
- Medieval Ireland
- Viking Ireland
- Ancient Egypt
- Ceramics and Glass from Ancient Cyprus
- Life and Death in the Roman World
- Temporary exhibition space
- Non-exhibition space

★ Bog Bodies
This preserved hand (c.600 BC) is one of the pieces in this fascinating exhibition of Iron Age bodies discovered in 2003.

The domed rotunda, based on the design of the Altes Museum in Berlin, makes an impressive entrance hall.

The Treasury houses masterpieces of Irish crafts such as the Ardagh Chalice *(see p59)*.

Gallery Guide

The ground floor holds The Treasury, Ór – Ireland's Gold exhibition, the Kingship and Sacrifice and the Prehistoric Ireland display. On the first floor is the Medieval Ireland exhibition, which illustrates many aspects of life in later medieval Ireland. Also on the first floor are artifacts from Ancient Egypt and from the Viking settlement of Dublin.

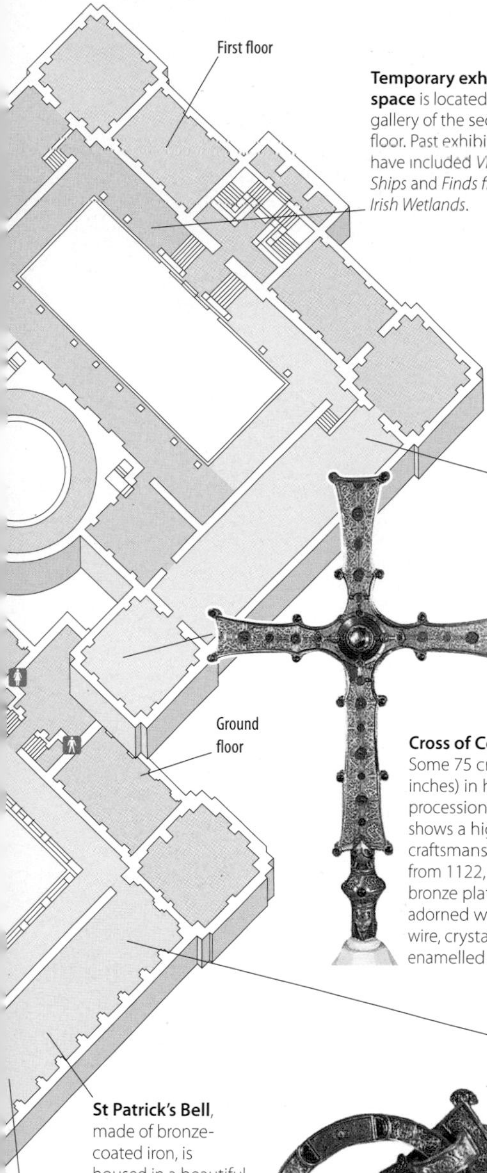

Temporary exhibition space is located in the gallery of the second floor. Past exhibitions have included *Viking Ships* and *Finds from Irish Wetlands*.

VISITORS' CHECKLIST

Practical Information
Kildare St.
Map E4.
Tel 677 7444.
museum.ie
Open 10am–5pm Tue–Sat, 2–5pm Sun.
Closed Good Fri & 25 Dec.
ground floor only.

Transport
DART to Pearse Station, LUAS Green Line to St Stephen's Green. 10, 11, 13 and many other routes.

Wooden Object
The Viking exhibition houses many items, including coins, pottery and swords, uncovered in the 1970s from the Viking settlement discovered beside the Liffey at Wood Quay *(see p82)*.

Cross of Cong
Some 75 cm (30 inches) in height, this processional cross shows a high level of craftsmanship. Dating from 1122, its gilt-bronze plating is adorned with silver wire, crystals and enamelled studs.

St Patrick's Bell, made of bronze-coated iron, is housed in a beautiful 12th-century shrine.

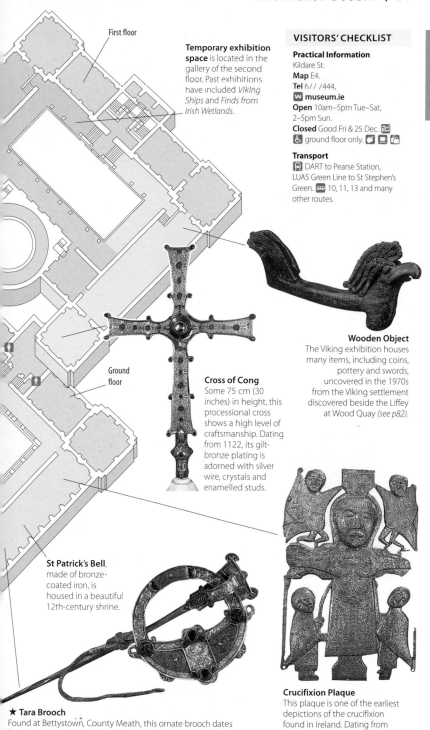

Crucifixion Plaque
This plaque is one of the earliest depictions of the crucifixion found in Ireland. Dating from the late 7th century, it may have been decoration for a manuscript cover.

★ Tara Brooch
Found at Bettystown, County Meath, this ornate brooch dates from the 8th century AD. It is decorated on the front and rear with a filigree of gold wire entwined around settings of amber and enamel.

⓫ National Wax Museum Plus

4 Foster Place, Temple Bar, Dublin 2. **Map** D3. **Tel** 671 8373. **Open** 10am–7pm daily. **Closed** 24–26 Dec.
W **waxmuseumplus.ie**

This museum offers a modern take on the traditional wax-works museum, with displays over four floors that provide an interactive experience.

Visitors are taken on a journey through time with wax models of figures from Irish history, literature, music, film, science, politics and more. The Grand Hall is dedicated to stars of Irish rock music and film, such as U2 and Liam Neeson. International stars such as Madonna and Elvis also feature. In the Recording Studio, you can use the latest technology to make a music video.

A children's cinema and characters such as Harry Potter are the attractions in the Children's Fantasy World. The basement Chamber of Horrors is not for the faint-hearted.

The Wax Museum, located in the historical Armoury building

⓬ National Museum of Ireland – Natural History

Merrion St. **Map** E4. **Tel** 677 7444. **Open** 10am–5pm Tue–Sat, 2–5pm Sun. **Closed** Mon, Good Fri, 25 Dec. limited. **W** **museum.ie**

This museum was opened in 1857 with an inaugural lecture by Scottish explorer Dr David Livingstone. Inside the front door are three skeletons of extinct giant deer known as the "Irish elk". The ground floor houses the Irish Room, which is devoted to local wildlife. The upper floor illustrates the range of mammals inhabiting our planet. Among the most fascinating exhibits are the primates, a Bengal tiger and skeletons of whales hanging from the ceiling.

Georgian town houses overlooking Merrion Square gardens

⓭ National Gallery of Ireland

See pp74–5.

⓮ Merrion Square

Map F4. **W** **merrionsquare.ie**

Merrion Square, one of Dublin's largest and grandest Georgian squares, was laid out by John Ensor around 1762.

On the west side are the impressive façades of the Natural History Museum, the National Gallery and the front garden of Leinster House *(see p69)*. There are lovely Georgian town houses on the other three sides of the square.

Many of the houses – now predominantly used as office space – have plaques detailing the rich and famous who once lived in them. These include the poet W B Yeats *(see pp236–7)*, who lived at No. 82. The playwright Oscar Wilde *(see p26)* spent his childhood at No. 1.

The attractive central park once served as an emergency soup kitchen, feeding the hungry during the Great Famine in the 1840s *(see p223)*. On the northwest side of the park stands the restored Rutland Fountain. It was originally erected in 1791 for the sole use of Dublin's poor.

⓯ Royal Hibernian Academy

15 Ely Place. **Map** E5. **Tel** 661 2558. **Open** 11am–5pm Mon–Sat (to 8pm Wed); noon–5pm Sun. **Closed** Christmas hols.
W **rhagallery.ie**

The academy is one of the largest exhibition spaces in the city. Through its touring exhibitions of painting, sculpture and other works, the institution challenges the public's understanding of the visual arts. This modern building, does, however, look out of place at the end of Ely Place, an attractive Georgian cul-de-sac.

⓰ Fitzwilliam Square

No. 29 Fitzwilliam St Lower **Map** E5. **Tel** 702 6165. **Open** 10am– 5pm Tue–Sat, noon–5pm Sun & public hols. **Closed** Mon, Good Fri & mid-Dec–mid-Feb.
limited, call in advance.
W **esb.ie/numbertwentynine**

This square, which dates from the 1790s, was one of the last Georgian squares to be laid out in central Dublin. Much smaller than Merrion Square, it is a popular location for medical practices.

In the 1960s, 16 town houses on Fitzwilliam Street Lower were torn down to make way for the headquarters of the Electricity Supply Board. The company has since tried to appease public indignation by renovating No. 29 as a Georgian showpiece home.

Dublin's Georgian Terraces

The 18th century was Dublin's Age of Elegance, a time of relative prosperity when the Irish gentry, keen not to appear as the poor relations of Britain, set about remodelling Dublin into one of the most elegant cities in Europe. Terraced town houses were built, forming handsome new streets and squares. During the 19th century the city's wealth declined, forcing some middle-class families to divide their homes into tenements. Many of Dublin's once grand streets slowly deteriorated. A century later the property boom of the 1960s threatened to rip out what was left of Georgian Dublin. Fortunately, much has survived and some of the city's finest architecture can be seen in Merrion Square and Fitzwilliam Square.

Wrought-iron balconies gave added prestige to the Georgian house. Those still in place today are mostly later Victorian additions.

The bedrooms were usually on the second floor, while the upper floors contained the servants' quarters and children's rooms.

Lavish stuccowork was an important way of showing an owner's wealth during the 18th century.

The drawing room was always on the first floor. The high ceiling was decorated with the finest plasterwork.

The dining room was normally on the ground floor.

The kitchen contained a huge cooking range which was fired by either coal or wood. The adjoining pantry was used to store the household's groceries.

The doorway was usually crowned with a segmented fanlight. The principal decoration on the door itself was a heavy brass knocker.

Georgian Terraced House

While Georgian streetscapes may appear uniform, closer inspection reveals a diversity of styles in terms of details such as fanlights, architraves and balconies. The hallways usually had stone floors and, facing the hall door, a staircase rising to the upper floors. Many of the town houses did not have gardens – the railed-off parks in the centre of the squares were reserved for residents only and served as such.

⓭ National Gallery of Ireland

This purpose-built gallery was opened to the public in 1864. It houses many excellent exhibits, largely due to generous bequests, such as the Milltown collection of works of art from Russborough House *(see p136)*. Playwright George Bernard Shaw was also a benefactor, leaving a third of his estate to the gallery. Although the emphasis is on Irish art, the major schools of European painting are well represented. During the current major refurbishment of the historic Dargan and Milltown wings, the location of exhibits is subject to change.

★ Pierrot
This Cubist-style work, by Spanish-born artist Juan Gris, is one of many variations he painted on the theme of Pierrot and Harlequin. This particular one dates from 1921.

Gallery Guide

The main entrance is through the lofty Millennium Wing on Clare Street. The gallery is undergoing major refurbishments until 2016, and this will result in changes to the presentation of the collection. Visitors are advised to call or email in advance to confirm whether and where specific exhibits will be displayed.

★ A Landscape
This work, by Irish landscape painter Thomas Roberts (1748–77), does not depict a particular place, but illustrates the artist's preference for the classical landscape.

Key to Floorplan

- Irish School
- European Sculpture and Decorative Arts
- Print Gallery
- Italian School
- Spanish School
- Northern European and French Schools
- Yeats Museum
- Temporary exhibitions
- Closed for refurbishment until 2016
- Non-exhibition space

★ **The Taking of Christ**
Rediscovered in a Dublin Jesuit house in 1990, this 1602 composition by Caravaggio has enhanced the gallery's reputation.

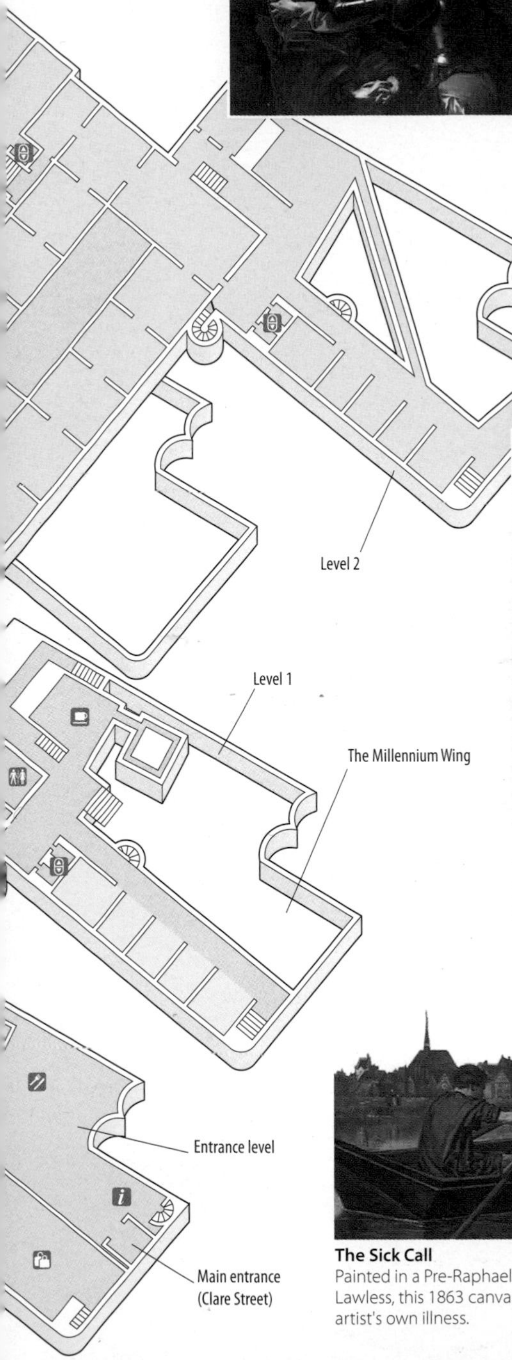

VISITORS' CHECKLIST

Practical Information
Clare Street, Merrion Square West.
Map E4. **Tel** 661 5133.
Open 9:30am–5:30pm Mon–Sat, 9:30am–8:30pm Thu; noon–5:30pm Sun; 10am–5:30pm public hols. **Closed** Good Fri & 24–26 Dec. for special exhibitions.
nationalgallery.ie

Transport
DART to Pearse. 4, 7, 8, 26, 44, 46A, 61, 66A/B, 67, 120.
LUAS to St Stephen's Green.

Judith with the Head of Holofernes
This monochrome image by Andrea Mantegna (c.1431–1506) depicts the decapitation of an Assyrian chief.

The Sick Call
Painted in a Pre-Raphaelite style by Matthew James Lawless, this 1863 canvas is said to be inspired by the artist's own illness.

ADAM

SOUTHWEST DUBLIN

The area around Dublin Castle was first settled in prehistoric times, and it was from here that the city grew. Dublin gets its name from the dark pool (Dubh Linn) which formed at the confluence of the Liffey and the Poddle, a river which once ran through the site of Dublin Castle. It is now channelled underground and trickles out into the Liffey by Grattan Bridge. Archaeological excavations behind Wood Quay, on the banks of the Liffey, reveal that the Vikings established a trading settlement here around 841.

Following Strongbow's invasion of 1170, a medieval city began to emerge; the Anglo-Normans built strong defensive walls around the castle. A small reconstructed section of these old city walls can be seen at St Audoen's Church. More conspicuous reminders of the Anglo Normans are provided by the grand medieval Christ Church Cathedral and Ireland's largest church, Saint Patrick's Cathedral. When the city expanded to the north and east during the Georgian era, the narrow cobbled streets of Temple Bar became a quarter of skilled craftsmen and merchants. Today this lively area of town bustles with tourists, and is home to a variety of "alternative" shops and cafés. The Powerscourt Centre, an elegant 18th-century mansion, has been converted into one of the city's best shopping centres.

Sights at a Glance

Museums and Libraries

2 Chester Beatty Library
8 Dublinia and the Viking World
12 Marsh's Library

Historic Buildings

1 *Dublin Castle pp80–81*
3 City Hall
4 Powerscourt Centre
10 Tailors' Hall

Historic Streets

5 Temple Bar
6 Wood Quay

Churches

7 *Christ Church Cathedral pp84–5*
9 St Audoen's Church
11 Saint Patrick's Cathedral
13 Whitefriar Street Carmelite Church

See also Street Finder map pp122–3

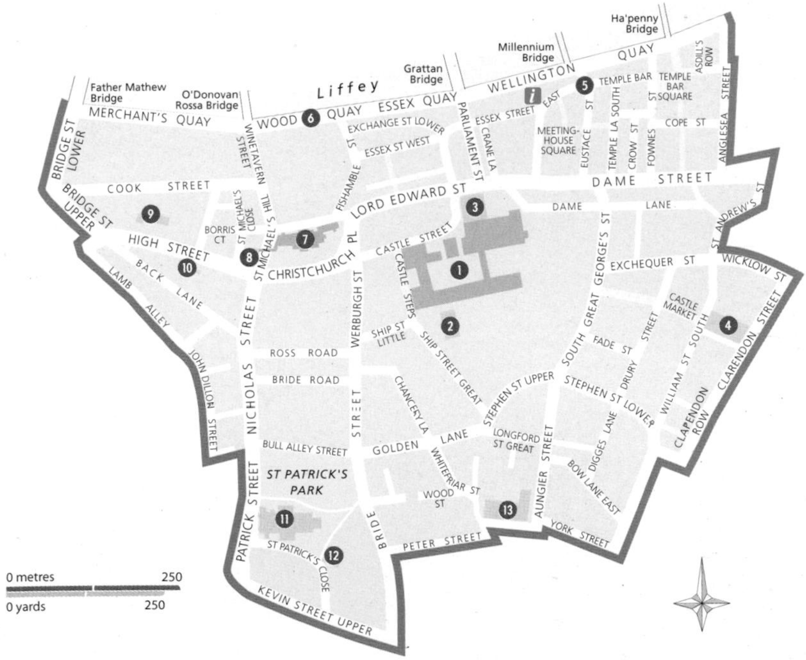

◀ A stunning stained-glass window in Christ Church Cathedral

Street-by-Street: Southwest Dublin

Despite its wealth of ancient buildings, such as Dublin Castle and Christ Church Cathedral, this part of Dublin lacks the sleek appeal of the neighbouring streets around Grafton Street. However, redevelopment has helped to rejuvenate the area, especially around Temple Bar, where the attractive cobbled streets are lined with interesting shops, galleries and cafés.

Sunlight Chambers were built in 1900 for the Lever Brothers company. The delightful terracotta decoration on the façade advertises their main business of soap manufacturing.

❻ Wood Quay
This is where the Vikings established their first permanent settlement in Ireland around 841.

❼ ★ Christ Church Cathedral
Huge family monuments including that of the 19th Earl of Kildare can be found in Ireland's oldest cathedral, which also has a fascinating crypt.

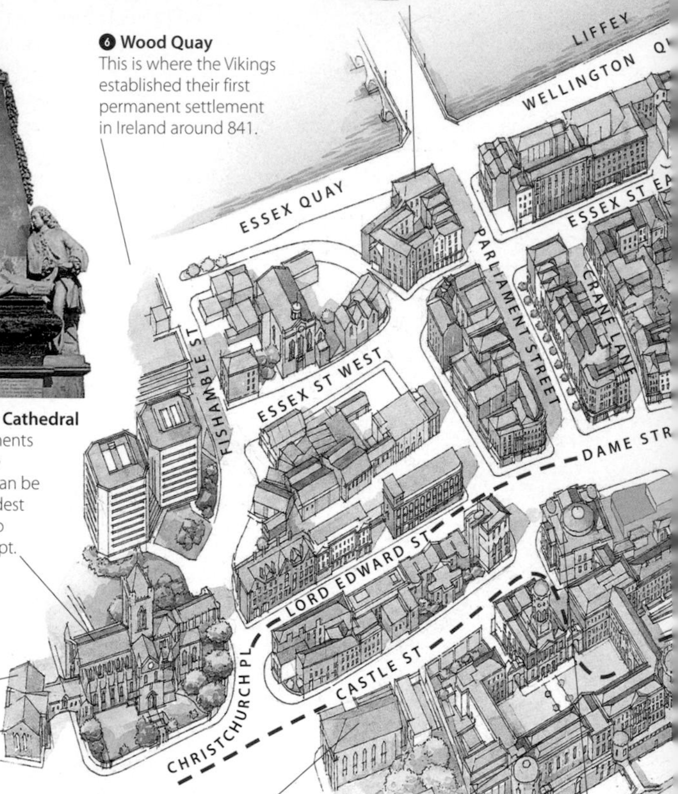

St Werburgh's Church, built in the 18th-century, has an ornate interior hiding behind its somewhat drab exterior.

❽ Dublinia and the Viking World
Medieval Dublin and the Vikings are the subjects of this interactive museum, located in the former Synod Hall of the Church of Ireland.

❸ City Hall
Originally built as the Royal Exchange in 1779, the city's municipal headquarters is fronted by a huge Corinthian portico.

❶ ★ Dublin Castle
The Drawing Room, with its Waterford crystal chandelier, is part of a suite of luxurious rooms built in the 18th century for the Viceroys of Ireland.

For hotels and restaurants in this region see pp296–7 and pp308–11

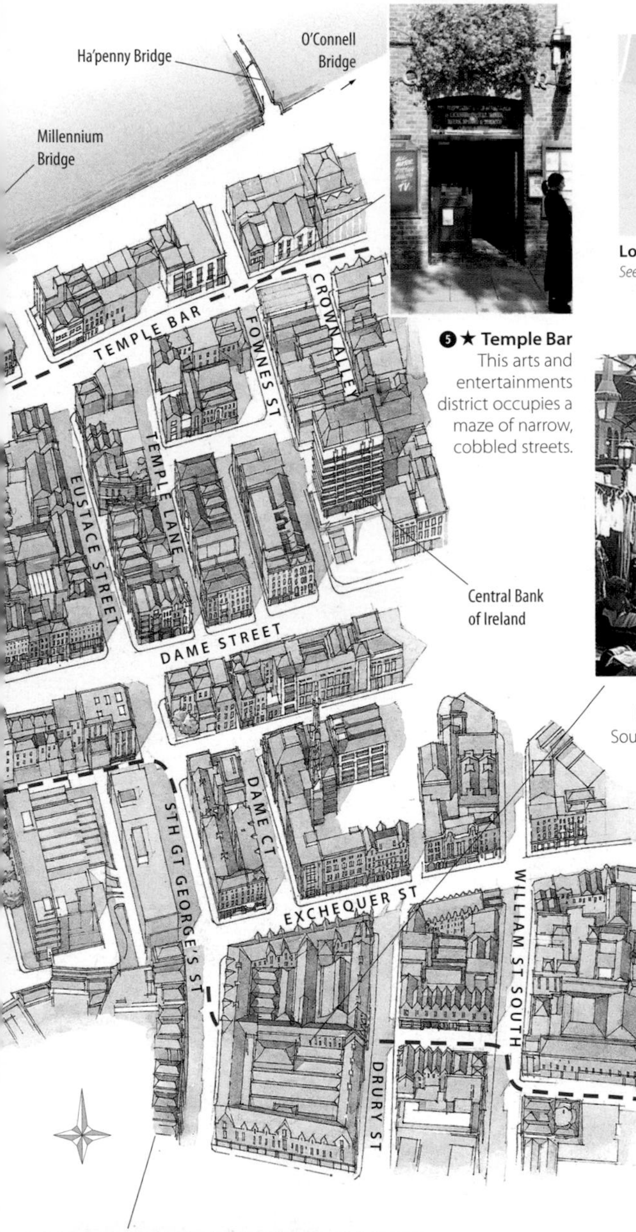

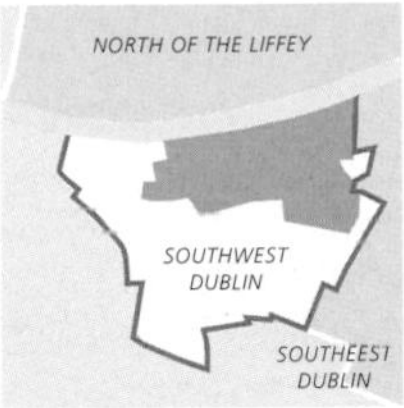

Locator Map

See Street Finder map pp122–3

5 ★ Temple Bar
This arts and entertainments district occupies a maze of narrow, cobbled streets.

George's Street Arcade between Drury Street and South Great George's Street is a popular spot for buying second-hand clothes and antique jewellery.

4 Powerscourt Centre
This shopping centre is one of the best places in Dublin to find fashion accessories and arts and crafts.

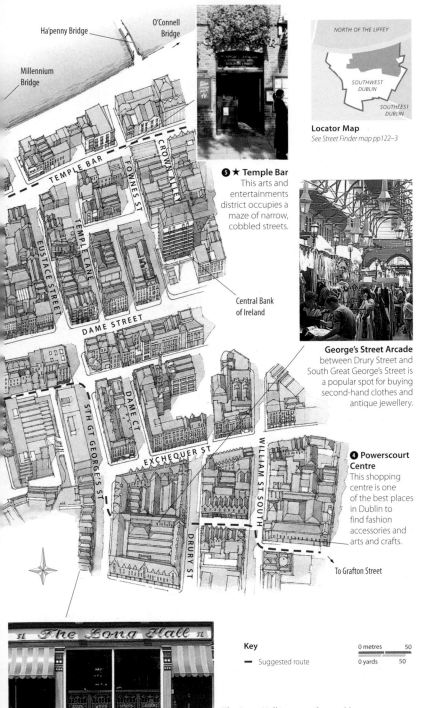

Key

— Suggested route

0 metres 50
0 yards 50

The Long Hall is a magnificent, old-fashioned pub with a great atmosphere. Behind the narrow room's long bar stands a bewildering array of antique clocks.

❶ Dublin Castle

For seven centuries Dublin Castle was the seat of English rule, ever since the Anglo-Normans built a fortress here in the 13th century. All that remains of the original structure is the southeastern tower, now called the Record Tower. Following a fire in 1684, the Surveyor-General, Sir William Robinson, laid down the plans for the Upper and Lower Castle Yards in their present form. On the first floor of the south side of the Upper Yard are the luxury State Apartments, including St Patrick's Hall. These magnificent rooms served as home to the British-appointed Viceroys of Ireland.

Figure of Justice
Facing the Upper Yard above the main entrance from Cork Hill, this statue aroused much cynicism among Dubliners, who felt she was turning her back on the city.

★ Throne Room
This room is one of the grandest of the state apartments and contains a throne first installed for the visit of King George IV in 1821.

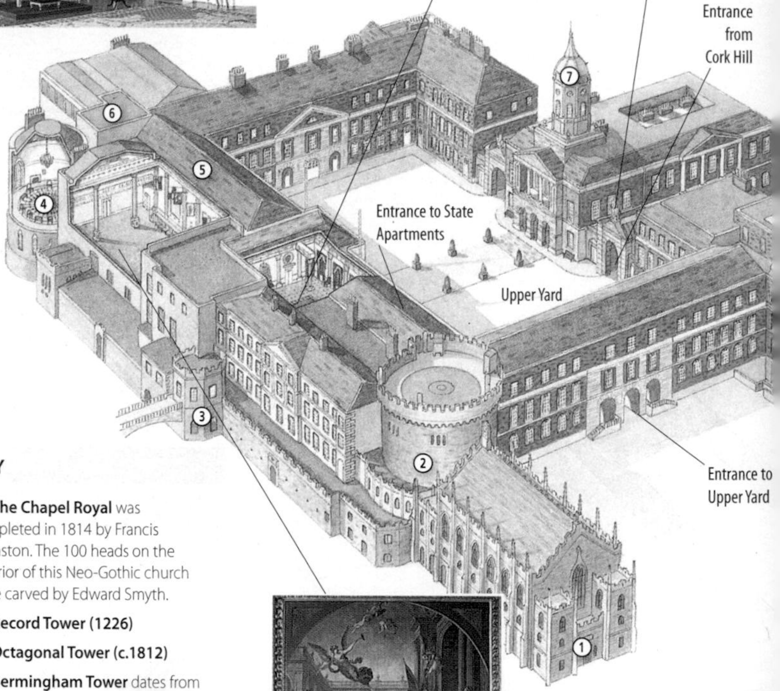

KEY

① **The Chapel Royal** was completed in 1814 by Francis Johnston. The 100 heads on the exterior of this Neo-Gothic church were carved by Edward Smyth.

② **Record Tower (1226)**

③ **Octagonal Tower (c.1812)**

④ **Bermingham Tower** dates from the 13th century. It was turned into an elegant supper room around 1777.

⑤ **Portrait Gallery**

⑥ **Wedgwood Room**

⑦ **Bedford Tower**

⑧ **The treasury building**, constructed in 1717, is the oldest dedicated office block in Dublin.

⑨ **Government offices**

★ St Patrick's Hall
This hall, with its banners of the now-defunct Knights of St Patrick, has ceiling paintings by Vincenzo Valdré (late 1780s), symbolizing the relationship between Britain and Ireland.

VISITORS' CHECKLIST

Practical Information
Off Dame St. **Map** C3.
Tel 645 8813. **W** **dublincastle.ie**
State Apartments: **Open** 10am–4:45pm Mon–Sat, noon–4:45pm Sun & public hols.
Closed 1 Jan, Good Fri, 24–27 Dec.

Transport
49, 56A, 77, 77A, 123.

Robert Emmet

Robert Emmet (1778–1803), leader of the abortive 1803 rebellion, is remembered as a heroic champion of Irish liberty. His plan was to capture Dublin Castle as a signal for the country to rise up against the Act of Union *(see p46)*. Emmet was detained in the Kilmainham Gaol and hanged, but the defiant, patriotic speech he made from the dock helped to inspire future generations of Irish freedom fighters.

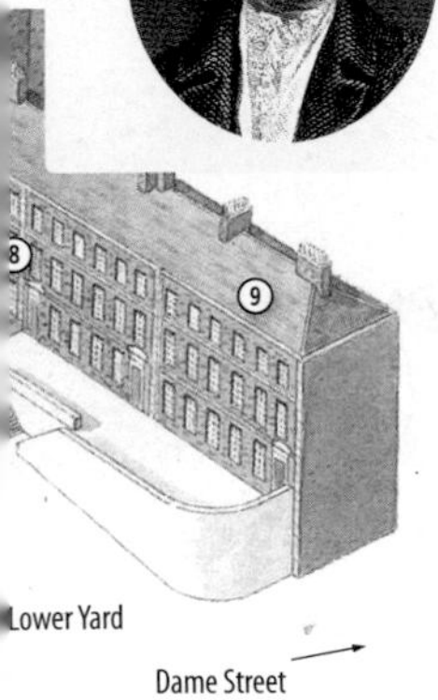

The bright exterior of the state apartments seen from outside the walls of Dublin Castle

Manuscript (1874) from the Holy Koran written by calligrapher Ahmad Shaikh in Kashmir, on display at Chester Beatty Library

❷ Chester Beatty Library

Dublin Castle. **Tel** 407 0750. **Open** 10am–5pm Mon–Fri (Tue–Fri Nov–Feb), 11am–5pm Sat, 1–5pm Sun. **Closed** 1 Jan, Good Fri, 24–26 Dec & public holidays. **W** **cbl.ie**

This world-renowned collection was named European Museum of the Year in 2002. It was bequeathed to Ireland by the American mining magnate and art collector Sir Alfred Chester Beatty, who died in 1968. This generous act no doubt led to his selection as Ireland's first honorary citizen in 1957.

During his lifetime, Beatty accumulated almost 300 copies of the Koran, representing the works of master calligraphers. Also on display are 6,000-year-old Babylonian stone tablets, Greek papyri and biblical material written in Coptic, the ancient language of Egypt.

Treasures from the Far East include a collection of Chinese jade books – each leaf is made from thinly cut jade, engraved with Chinese characters which are then filled with gold. Burmese and Siamese art is represented by the collection of 18th- and 19th-century *Parabaiks*, books of folk tales with colourful illustrations on mulberry leaf paper. The Japanese collection includes paintings, woodblock prints and books and scrolls from the 16th to 19th centuries. One of the most beautiful manuscripts in the western European collection is the *Coëtivy Book of Hours*, an illuminated 15th-century French prayer book.

❸ City Hall

Cork Hill, Dame St. **Map** C3. **Tel** 222 2204. **Open** 10am–5:15pm Mon–Sat. **Closed** 1 Jan, Good Fri & 24–26 Dec. **W** **dublincity.ie/dublincityhall**

Designed by Thomas Cooley, this Corinthian-style building was erected between 1769 and 1779 as the Royal Exchange. It was bought by Dublin Corporation in 1851 as a meeting place for the city council.

The building has been restored to its original condition and a permanent multimedia exhibition, Dublin City Hall – *The Story of the Capital*, traces the evolution of Dublin, from before the Anglo-Norman invasion of 1170 to the present day.

City Hall from Parliament Street

Central courtyard of Powerscourt Townhouse Shopping Centre

❹ Powerscourt Centre

South William St. **Map** D4. **Tel** 679 4144. **Open** 10am–6pm Mon–Fri (8pm Thu), 9am–6pm Sat, noon–6pm Sun. *See also Shopping in Ireland pp332–3.* **powerscourtcentre.ie**

Completed in 1774 by Robert Mack, this grand mansion was built as the city home of Viscount Powerscourt, who also had a country estate at Enniskerry *(see pp138–9)*. Granite from the Powerscourt estate was used in its construction. Today the building houses one of Dublin's best shopping centres. Inside it still features the original grand mahogany staircase, and detailed plasterwork by Michael Stapleton.

The building became a drapery warehouse in the 1830s, and major restoration during the 1960s turned it into a centre of specialist galleries, antique shops, jewellery stalls, cafés and other shop units. The enclosed central courtyard, topped by a glass dome, is a popular meeting place with Dubliners. The centre can also be reached from Grafton Street down the Johnson Court alley.

❺ Temple Bar

Map C3. Temple Bar Information **Tel** 677 2255. *See also Entertainment in Dublin p118.* Project Arts Centre: 39 East Essex Street. **Tel** 881 9613. Irish Film Institute: 6 Eustace Street. **Tel** 679 5744. Diversions, (May–Sep). **templebar.ie**

These narrow, cobbled streets running between the Bank of Ireland *(see p64)* and Christ Church Cathedral are now home to some of the city's best galleries and arts spaces, as well as the most raucous night spots. In the 18th century the area was home to many insalubrious characters – Fownes Street was noted for its brothels. It was also the birthplace of parliamentarian Henry Grattan *(see p44)*. Skilled craftsmen and artisans, such as clockmakers and printers, lived and worked around Temple Bar until post-war industrialization led to a decline in the area's fortunes.

In the 1970s, the CIE (the national transport authority) bought up parcels of land in this area to build a major bus depot. Before building, the CIE rented out, on cheap leases, some of the old retail and warehouse premises to young artists and to record, clothing and book shops. The area developed an "alternative" identity, and when the development plans were scrapped the artists and retailers stayed on. Described by some cynics as the city's "officially designated arts zone", Temple Bar today is is an odd mix of excellent galleries and theatres alongside kitsch tourist pubs, souvenir shops, fast-food restaurants and nightclubs popular with visiting stag and hen parties.

Highlights include the **Project Arts Centre**, a highly respected venue for avant-garde performance art; and the **Irish Film Institute**, which shows art-house and independent films, and has a popular restaurant/ bar and shop.

Nearby Meeting House Square, with its retractable canopy, hosts a diverse programme of outdoor concerts, film screenings and theatre performances. The National Photographic Archive and Gallery of Photography are also on the square and there is an excellent organic food market here on Saturdays, where you can sample oysters, salmon, cheese and other local produce.

The Temple Bar pub, established in 1840, located on Temple Bar

Strolling through the streets of Temple Bar

❻ Wood Quay

Map B3.

Named after the timber supports used to reclaim the land, Wood Quay has undergone excavations revealing the remains of one of the earliest Viking villages in Ireland *(see p83)*. The excavated area opened to public view in 2008.

Valuable and informative Viking artifacts that were discovered can be seen at the Dublinia exhibition *(see p83)* and at the National Museum *(see pp70–71)*.

Former Synod Hall, now home to the Dublinia exhibition

7 Christ Church Cathedral

See pp84–5.

8 Dublinia and the Viking World

St Michael's Hill. **Map** B3. **Tel** 679 4611. **Open** Apr–Sep: 10am–6:30pm (last entry 5:30pm); Oct–Mar: 10am–5:30pm. **Closed** 17 Mar & 23–26 Dec. charge to enter Christ Church Cathedral via bridge. **dublinia.ie**

The Dublinia exhibition covers the formative period of Dublin's history from the arrival of the Anglo-Normans in 1170 to the closure of the monasteries in the 1540s *(see p42)*. The exhibition is housed in the Neo-Gothic Synod Hall, which, up until 1983, was home to the ruling body of the Church of Ireland. The building and the hump-backed bridge linking it to Christ Church Cathedral date from the 1870s. Before Dublinia was established in 1993, the Synod Hall was used as a nightclub.

The exhibition is interactive, encouraging the visitor to become an investigator of Dublin's past. For instance, in the Medieval Dublin exhibition, the city's sights and sounds are brought to life. Crime and punishment, death and disease and even toothache remedies from 700 years ago are all part of the interesting experience. Major events in Dublin's history, such as the Black Death and the rebellion of Silken Thomas *(p42)* are also portrayed here as well as a large-scale model of Dublin circa 1500. An interactive archaeology room highlights excavations at nearby Wood Quay *(see p82)*.

The 60-m (200-ft) high St Michael's Tower offers one of the best vantage points for views across the city.

The Vikings in Dublin

Viking raiders arrived in Ireland in the late 8th century and founded Dublin in 841. They built a fort where the River Poddle met the Liffey at a black pool (Dubh Linn), on the site of Dublin Castle. They also established a settlement along the banks of the Liffey at Wood Quay *(see p82)*. Much of their trade was based on silver, slaves and piracy.

Following their defeat by Brian Ború at the Battle of Clontarf in 1014 *(see p38)*, the Vikings integrated fully with the local Irish, adopting Christian beliefs. After Strongbow's Anglo-Norman invasion in 1169 *(see p40)*, the flourishing Hiberno-Viking trading community declined, and many were banished to a separate colony called Oxmanstown, just north of the river.

Artist's impression of a Viking ship in Dublin Bay

Tower of St Audoen's Church

9 St Audoen's Church

High St, Cornmarket. **Map** B3. **Tel** 677 0088. **Open** May–Oct 9:30am–5:30pm.

Designated a national monument and open for visitors throughout the summer months, St Audoen's is the earliest surviving medieval church in Dublin.

The 15th-century nave remains intact and the three bells date from 1423. The building stands in an attractive churchyard with well-kept lawns and shrubs. To the rear of the churchyard, steps lead down to St Audoen's Arch, the only remaining gateway of the old city. Flanking the gate are restored sections of the 13th-century city walls.

Next door stands St Audoen's Roman Catholic Church, which was built in the 1840s. The two Pacific clam shells by the front door hold holy water.

❼ Christ Church Cathedral

Christ Church Cathedral was established by the Hiberno-Norse king of Dublin, Sitric "Silkbeard", and the first bishop of Dublin, Dunan. It was rebuilt by the Anglo-Norman archbishop, John Cumin in 1186. It is the cathedral for the Church of Ireland (Anglican) diocese of Dublin and Glendalough. By the 19th century it was in a bad state of repair, but was remodelled by architect George Street in the 1870s. The vast 12th-century crypt was restored in 2000.

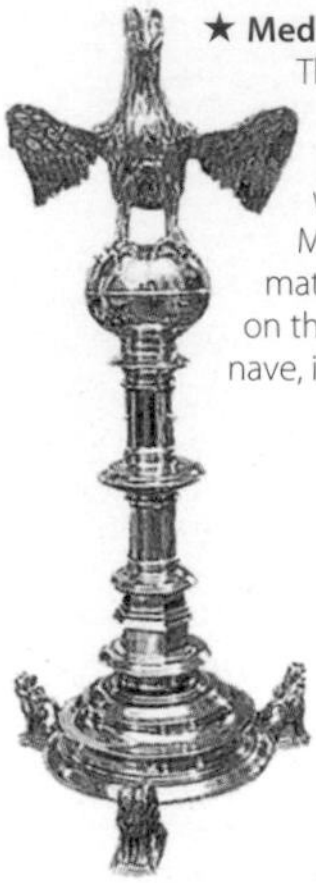

★ Medieval Lectern
This beautiful brass lectern in the crypt's treasury was hand-wrought during the Middle Ages. A matching lectern stands on the north side of the nave, in front of the pulpit.

Great Nave
The 25-m (68-ft) high nave has some fine early Gothic arches. On the north side, the original 13th-century wall leans out by as much as 50 cm (18 in) due to the weight of the roof.

KEY

① **The bridge** to the Synod Hall was added when the cathedral was being rebuilt in the 1870s.

② **Crypt**

③ **Medieval stone carvings** are on display in the north transept. Dating from about 1200, these exquisite Romanesque capitals feature a troupe of musicians and two human faces enveloped by legendary griffons.

④ **The Lady Chapel** is used to celebrate the daily Eucharist.

⑤ **Stairs to crypt**

⑥ **The foundations** of the original Chapter House date back to the early 13th century.

★ Strongbow Monument
The large effigy in chain armour is probably not Strongbow. However, his remains are buried in the cathedral and the curious half-figure may be part of his original tomb.

The Cat and the Rat
A mummified cat and rat are displayed in the Crypt. Found in an organ pipe, they grew to literary fame after James Joyce wrote of their chase.

VISITORS' CHECKLIST

Practical Information
Christchurch Place.
Map B3.
Tel 677 8099.
W christchurchdublin.ie
Open check website for details.
Closed 26 Dec.
12:45pm Mon–Fri, 11am & 3:30pm Sun. limited.

Transport
50, 66, 77 & other routes.

★ Crypt
This decorated plate by Francis Garthorne is part of a collection presented to Christ Church Cathedral in 1690 by King William III to mark his victory at the Battle of the Boyne in 1690.

Romanesque Doorway
Leading to the south transept, this ornately carved doorway is one of the finest examples of 12th-century Irish stonework.

1038 Construction of original wooden Viking cathedral

1186 The first Anglo-Norman archbishop, John Cumin, begins work on the new cathedral.

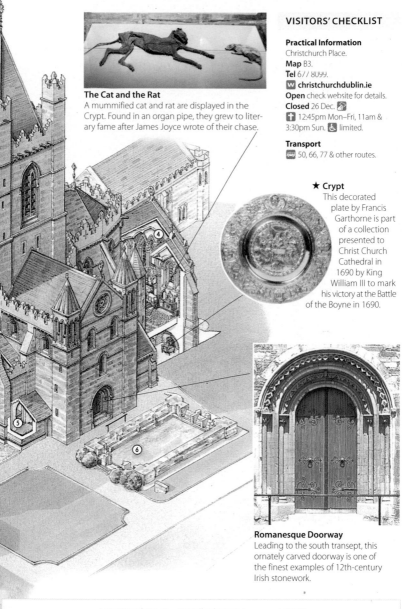

Meeting between Lambert Simnel and the Earl of Kildare (see p41)

1240 Completion of stone cathedral

1487 Coronation of 10-year-old Lambert Simnel as King of England

1541 King Henry VIII alters constitution of cathedral

1600 Shopkeepers rent crypt space

1689 King James II of England worships in cathedral

1742 Choir participates in first performance of Handel's *Messiah*

1871 Major rebuilding of the cathedral begins, including Synod Hall and Bridge

1983 Cathedral ceases using Synod Hall

1000 | 1200 | 1400 | 1600 | 1800

⑩ Tailors' Hall

Back Lane. **Map** B4. **Tel** 707 7076.
Open 9am–5pm Mon–Fri.
W antaisce.org

Dublin's only surviving guildhall preserves a delightful corner of old Dublin in an otherwise busy redevelopment zone. Built in 1706, it stands behind a limestone arch in a quiet cobbled yard. The building is the oldest guildhall in Ireland and was used by various trade groups including hosiers, saddlers and barber-surgeons as well as tailors. It also hosted political meetings – Wolfe Tone addressed a public United Irishmen rally here before the 1798 rebellion *(see p45)*. The building closed in the early 1960s due to neglect, but an appeal by Desmond Guinness saw it refurbished. It now houses An Taisce (the Irish National Trust).

Façade of Tailors' Hall, home of the Irish National Trust

Saint Patrick's Cathedral with Minot's Tower and spire

⑪ Saint Patrick's Cathedral

Saint Patrick's Close. **Map** B4. **Tel** 453 9472. **Open** 9:30am–5pm Mon–Fri, 9am–6pm Sat (to 5pm Nov–Feb), 9–10:30am, 12:30–2:30pm, 4:30–6pm Sun (to 2:30pm Nov–Feb). Visiting restricted during service times (9am & 5:30pm). **W stpatrickscathedral.ie**

Ireland's largest church was founded beside a sacred well where St Patrick is said to have baptized converts circa AD 450. A stone slab bearing a Celtic cross and covering the well was unearthed over a century ago. It is now preserved in the west end of the cathedral's nave. The original building was just a wooden chapel and remained so until 1192 when Archbishop John Cumin rebuilt the cathedral in stone.

Over the centuries, Saint Patrick's came to be seen as the people's church, while the older Christ Church Cathedral *(see pp84–5)* nearby was more associated with the British establishment. In the mid-17th century, Huguenot refugees from France arrived in Dublin, and were given the Lady Chapel by the Dean and Chapter as their place of worship. The chapel was separated from the rest of the cathedral and used by the Huguenots until the late 18th century. Today Saint Patrick's Cathedral is the Anglican/Episcopalian Church of Ireland's national cathedral.

Much of the present building dates back to work completed between 1254 and 1270. The cathedral suffered over the centuries from desecration, fire and neglect but, thanks to the generosity of Sir Benjamin Guinness, it underwent extensive restoration during the 1860s. The building is 91 m (300 ft) long; at the western end is a 43-m (141-ft) tower, restored by Archbishop Minot in 1370 and now known as Minot's Tower. The spire was added in the 18th century.

The interior is dotted with busts, brasses and monuments. A leaflet available at the front desk helps identify them. The largest, most colourful and elaborate tomb was dedicated to the Boyle family in the 17th century. Erected by Richard Boyle, Earl of Cork, in memory of his second wife Catherine, it is decorated with painted figures

Jonathan Swift (1667–1745)

Jonathan Swift was born in Dublin and educated at Trinity College *(see pp66–7)*. He left for England in 1689, but returned in 1694 when his political career failed. Back in Ireland he began a life in the church, becoming Dean of St Patrick's in 1713. In addition to his clerical duties, Swift was a prolific political commentator – his best-known work, *Gulliver's Travels*, contains a bitter satire on Anglo-Irish relations. Swift's personal life, particularly his friendship with two younger women, Esther Johnson, better known as Stella, and Esther Vanhomrigh, attracted criticism. In his final years, Swift suffered from Ménière's disease – an illness of the ear which led many to believe him insane.

of his family, including his wife's parents. Other famous citizens remembered in the church include the harpist Turlough O'Carolan (1670–1738) *(see p28)* and Douglas Hyde (1860–1949), the first president of Ireland.

Many visitors come to see the memorials associated with Jonathan Swift, the satirical writer and Dean of Saint Patrick's. In the south aisle is "Swift's Corner", containing various memorabilia such as an altar table and a bookcase holding his death mask. A self-penned epitaph can be found on the wall on the southwest side of the nave. A few steps away, two brass plates mark his grave and that of his beloved Stella, who died before him in 1728.

At the west end of the nave is an old door with a hole in it – a relic from a feud which took place between the Lords Kildare and Ormonde in 1492. The latter took refuge in the Chapter House, but a truce was soon made and a hole was cut in the door by Lord Kildare so the two could shake hands in friendship.

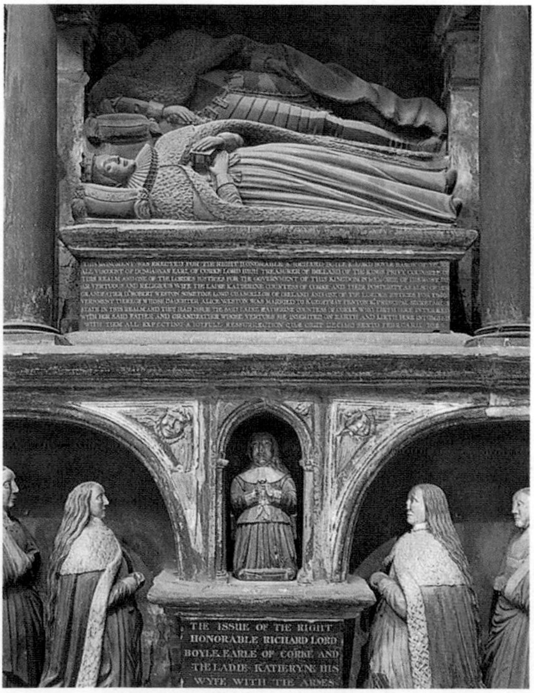

Carved monument (1632) to the Boyle family in St Patrick's Cathedral

⓬ Marsh's Library

St Patrick's Close. **Map** B4. **Tel** 454 3511. **Open** 9:30am–5pm Mon & Wed–Fri, 10am–5pm Sat. **Closed** Tue & Sun, 10 days at Christmas & public hols. **W** **marshlibrary.ie**

The oldest public library in Ireland was built in 1701 for the Archbishop of Dublin, Narcissus Marsh. It was designed by Sir William Robinson, architect of much of Dublin Castle *(see pp80–81)* and the Royal Hospital Kilmainham *(see p101)*.

Inside, the bookcases are topped by a mitre and feature carved gables with lettering in gold leaf. To the rear of the library are wired alcoves (or "cages") where readers were locked in with rare books. The collection, from the 16th, 17th and early 18th centuries, includes irreplaceable volumes, such as Bishop Bedell's 1685 translation of the Old Testament into Irish, and Clarendon's *History of the Rebellion*, complete with anti-Scottish margin notes by Jonathan Swift.

Statue of Virgin and Child in Whitefriar Street Carmelite Church

⓭ Whitefriar Street Carmelite Church

56 Aungier St. **Map** C4. **Tel** 475 8821. **Open** 7:45am–6pm Mon & Wed–Sat; 8am–7:30pm Tue; 9:30am–7pm Sun & public hols. **W** **whitefriarstreetchurch.ie**

Designed by George Papworth, this Catholic church was built in 1827. It stands alongside the site of a medieval Carmelite foundation of which nothing remains.

In contrast to the two Church of Ireland cathedrals, St Patrick's and Christ Church, which are usually full of tourists, this church is frequented by city worshippers. Every day they come to light candles to various saints, including St Valentine – the patron saint of lovers. His remains, previously buried in the cemetery of St Hippolytus in Rome, were offered to the church as a gift from Pope Gregory XVI in 1836. Today they rest beneath the commemorative statue of St Valentine, which stands in the northeast corner of the church beside the high altar.

Nearby is a Flemish oak statue of the Virgin and Child, dating from the late 15th or early 16th century. It may have belonged to St Mary's Abbey *(see p97)* and is believed to be the only wooden statue of its kind to escape destruction when Ireland's monasteries were sacked at the time of the Reformation *(see p42)*.

NORTH OF THE LIFFEY

Dublin's northside was the last part of the city to be developed during the 18th century. The city authorities envisioned an area of wide, leafy avenues, but the reality of today's heavy traffic has rather spoiled their original plans. Nonetheless, O'Connell Street, lined with fine statues and monuments, is an impressive thoroughfare. This is where Dubliners come to shop and some of the adjacent streets, particularly Moore Street, have a colourful parade of stalls and street vendors offering cut-price tobacco.

Some public buildings, such as James Gandon's glorious Custom House and majestic Four Courts, together with the historic General Post Office *(see p93)*, add grace to the area. The Rotunda Hospital, Europe's first purpose-built maternity hospital, is another fine building. Dublin's two most celebrated theatres, the Abbey and the Gate, act as a cultural magnet, as do the Dublin Writers Museum and the James Joyce Cultural Centre, two museums dedicated to writers who lived in the city.

Some of the city's finest Georgian streetscapes are found in the north of the city. Many have been neglected for decades, but, thankfully, some areas, most notably North Great George's Street, are undergoing restoration.

Sights at a Glance

Museums and Libraries
5 James Joyce Centre
9 Dublin Writers Museum
10 Hugh Lane Gallery
13 Old Jameson Distillery
17 National Leprechaun Museum

Historic Buildings
1 Custom House
7 Rotunda Hospital
11 King's Inns
15 Four Courts

Historic Streets
3 O'Connell Street
12 Smithfield
18 Ha'penny Bridge

Theatres
2 Abbey Theatre
6 Gate Theatre

Churches
4 St Mary's Pro-Cathedral
14 St Michan's Church
16 St Mary's Abbey

Parks and Gardens
8 Garden of Remembrance

See also Street Finder map pp122–3

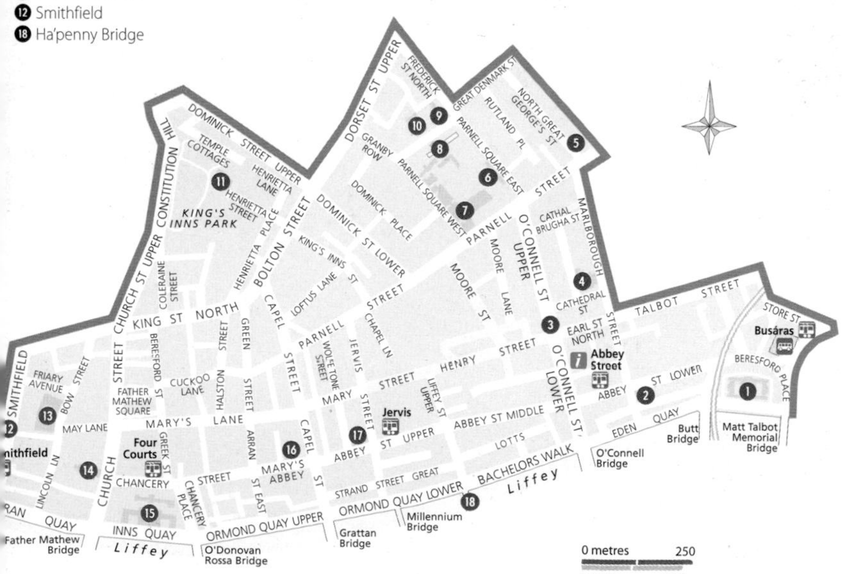

◀ The central dome and the portico of Custom House

For map symbols *see back flap*

Street-by-Street: Around O'Connell Street

Throughout the Georgian era, O'Connell Street was very much the fashionable part of Dublin to live in. However, the 1916 Easter Rising destroyed many of the fine buildings along the street, including much of the General Post Office – only its original façade still stands. Today, this main thoroughfare is lined with shops and businesses. Other attractions nearby include St Mary's Pro-Cathedral and James Gandon's Custom House, overlooking the Liffey.

5 James Joyce Centre
This well-restored Georgian town house contains a small Joyce museum.

6 Gate Theatre
Founded in 1928, the Gate is renowned for its productions of contemporary drama.

7 Rotunda Hospital
Housed in the Rotunda Hospital is a chapel built in the 1750s to a design by Richard Cassels. It features lovely stained-glass windows, fluted columns, panelling and intricate iron balustrades.

Moore Street Market is the busiest of the streets off O'Connell. Be prepared for the shrill cries of the stall holders offering an enormous variety of fresh fruit, vegetables and cut flowers.

The Spire, an elegant stainless steel landmark rising to 120 m (394 ft).

The General Post Office, the grandest building on O'Connell Street, was the centre of the 1916 Rising.

Key

— Suggested route

0 metres 50
0 yards 50

For key to symbols *see back flap*

❹ St Mary's Pro-Cathedral
Built around 1825, this is Dublin's main place of worship for Catholics. The plaster relief above the altar in the sanctuary depicts *The Ascension*.

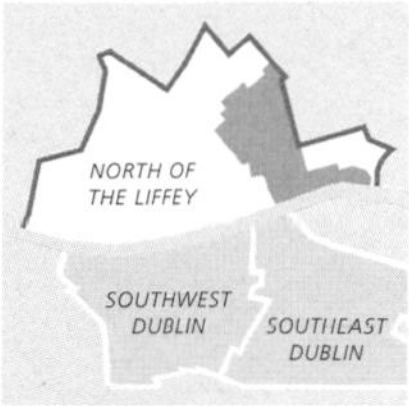

Locator Map
See Street Finder map pp122–3

The statue of James Joyce (1990) by Marjorie Fitzgibbon commemorates one of Ireland's most famous novelists. Born in Dublin in 1882, he catalogued the people and streets of Dublin in *Dubliners* and in his most celebrated work, *Ulysses*.

❶ ★ Custom House
This Classical grotesque head, by Edward Smyth, symbolizes the River Liffey. It is one of 14 carved keystones that adorn the building.

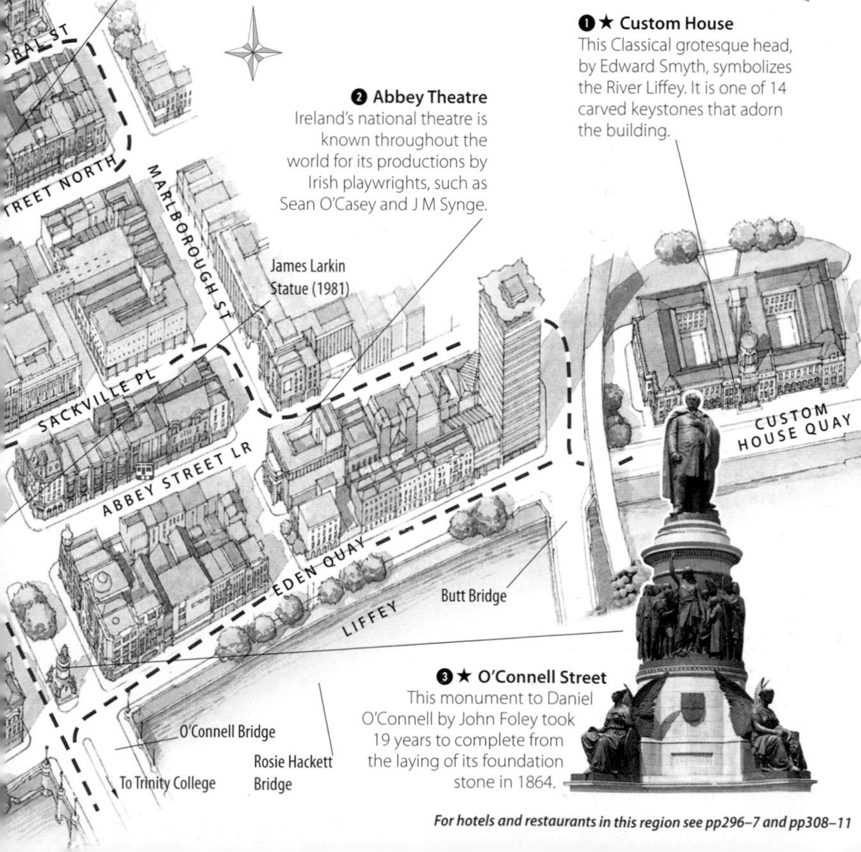

❷ Abbey Theatre
Ireland's national theatre is known throughout the world for its productions by Irish playwrights, such as Sean O'Casey and J M Synge.

❸ ★ O'Connell Street
This monument to Daniel O'Connell by John Foley took 19 years to complete from the laying of its foundation stone in 1864.

For hotels and restaurants in this region see pp296–7 and pp308–11

Façade of the Custom House reflected in the Liffey

❶ Custom House

Custom House Quay. **Map** E2
Tel 888 2000. **Closed** to the public.

This majestic building was designed as the Custom House by the English architect James Gandon. However, just nine years after its completion, the 1800 Act of Union *(see p46)* transferred the customs and excise business to London, rendering the building practically obsolete. In 1921, supporters of Sinn Féin celebrated their election victory by setting light to what they saw as a symbol of British imperialism. The fire blazed for five days causing extensive damage. Reconstruction took place in 1926, although further deterioration meant that the building was not completely restored until 1991, when it reopened as government offices.

The main façade is made up of pavilions at each end with a Doric portico in its centre. The arms of Ireland crown the two pavilions and a series of 14 allegorical heads, by Dublin sculptor Edward Smyth, form the keystones of arches and entrances. These heads depict Ireland's main rivers and the Atlantic Ocean. Topping the central copper dome is a statue of Commerce, while the north façade is decorated with figures representing Europe, Africa, America and Asia. The best view of the building is from the south of the Liffey beyond Matt Talbot Bridge.

Sculpture symbolizing Ireland's rivers, by Edward Smyth

❷ Abbey Theatre

26 Lower Abbey St. **Map** E2. **Tel** 878 7222. **Open** for performances only. Box office: **Open** 10:30am–7pm Mon–Sat. *See also Entertainment in Dublin p112.* **W abbeytheatre.ie**

The Abbey staged its first play in 1904 with W B Yeats and Lady Gregory as co-directors. The early years of this much-lauded national theatre witnessed works by W B Yeats, J M Synge and Sean O'Casey. Many were controversial: nationalist sensitivities were severely tested in 1926 during the premiere of O'Casey's *The Plough and the Stars* when the flag of the Irish Free State appeared on stage in a scene which featured a pub frequented by prostitutes.

Logo of the Abbey Theatre

Today, the Abbey is supported by the Arts Council of Ireland/ An Chomhairle Ealaíon and its function is to nurture new Irish writing and artistic talent and produce an annual programme of diverse, engaging, innovative Irish and international theatre.

Productions have included work by Wilde, Beckett, Shakespeare and Brecht, as well as plays by Marina Carr, Tom MacIntyre, Billy Roche and Sam Shepard.

❸ O'Connell Street

Map D1–D2.

O'Connell Street is very different from the original plans of Irish aristocrat Luke Gardiner. When he bought the land in the mid-18th century, Gardiner envisioned a grand residential parade with an elegant mall running along its centre. Such plans were short-lived. The construction of Carlisle (now O'Connell) Bridge around 1790 transformed the street into the city's main north–south route. Also, several buildings were destroyed during the 1916 Easter

Rising and the Irish Civil War. Since the 1960s many of the old buildings have been replaced by the plate glass and neon of fast-food joints, amusement arcades and chain stores.

A few venerable buildings remain, such as the General Post Office (1818), Gresham Hotel (1817), the former Clery's department store (1822) and the Royal Dublin Hotel, part of which occupies the street's only original town house.

A walk down the central mall is the most enjoyable way to see the street's mix of architectural styles and take a close look at the series of monuments lining the route. At the south end stands a massive monument to Daniel O'Connell *(see p46)*, unveiled in 1882. The street, which throughout the 19th century had been called Sackville Street, was renamed after O'Connell in 1922. Higher up, almost facing the General Post Office, is an animated statue of James Larkin, leader of the Dublin general strike in 1913. The next statue is of Father Theobald Mathew (1790–1856), founder of the Pioneer Total Abstinence Movement. At the north end of the street is the obelisk-shaped monument to Charles Stewart Parnell (1846–91), who was leader of the Home Rule Party and known as the "uncrowned King of Ireland" *(see p47)*. The Dublin Spire sits on the site where Nelson's column used to be. It is a stainless steel, conical spire which tapers from a 3-m (10-ft) diameter base to a 10-cm (4-in) pointed tip of optical glass at a height of 120 m (394 ft), making it the city's tallest structure.

The busy thoroughfare of O'Connell Street

Statue of James Larkin (1981) in O'Connell Street

The General Post Office (GPO)

Irish Life magazine cover showing the 1916 Easter Rising

Built in 1818 halfway along O'Connell Street, the GPO became a symbol of the 1916 Irish Rising. Members of the Irish Volunteers and Irish Citizen Army seized the building on Easter Monday, and Patrick Pearse *(see p48)* read out the Proclamation of the Irish Republic from its steps. The rebels remained inside for a week, but shelling from the British eventually forced them out. At first, many viewed the Rising unfavourably. However, as W B Yeats wrote, matters "changed utterly" and a "terrible beauty was born" when, during the following weeks, 14 of the leaders were caught and shot at Kilmainham Gaol *(see p101)*. A museum has a copy of the 1916 Proclamation and accounts from the staff who were working that day. It also explores the influence of the post office in Ireland, and has a beautiful stamp collection.

❹ St Mary's Pro-Cathedral

83 Marlborough St. **Map** D2. **Tel** 874 5441. **Open** 7:30am–6:45pm Mon–Fri (to 7:15pm Sat), 9am–1:45pm & 5:30–7:45pm Sun, 10am–1:30pm public hols. **W procathedral.ie**

Dedicated in 1825 before Catholic emancipation *(see p46)*, St Mary's backstreet site was the best the city's Anglo-Irish leaders would allow a Catholic cathedral.

The façade is based on a Greek temple. Doric columns support a pediment with statues of St Mary, St Patrick and St Laurence O'Toole, 12th-century Archbishop of Dublin and patron saint of the city. Inside, one striking feature is the intricately carved high altar.

St Mary's is home to the famous Palestrina Choir, with which the great tenor John McCormack *(see p28)* began his career in 1904. The choir still sings on Sundays at 11am.

Austere Neo-Classical interior of St Mary's Pro-Cathedral

❺ James Joyce Centre

35 North Great George's St. **Map** D1. **Tel** 878 8547. **Open** 10am–5pm Tue–Sat, noon–5pm Sun. **Closed** Good Fri, 21 Dec–3 Jan & public hols.
W **jamesjoyce.ie**

This agreeable stop on the literary tourist trail is primarily a meeting place for Joyce enthusiasts, but is also worth visiting for its Georgian interior. The centre is in a 1784 town house which was built for the Earl of Kenmare. Michael Stapleton, one of the greatest stuccoers of his time, contributed to the plasterwork, of which the friezes are particularly noteworthy.

The centre's permanent and temporary exhibitions interpret and illuminate aspects of Joyce's life and work. Among the displays are biographies of real people on whom Joyce based his characters. Professor Dennis J Maginni, a peripheral character in *Ulysses*, ran a dancing school from this town house. Leopold and Molly Bloom, the central characters of *Ulysses*, lived a short walk away at No. 7 Eccles Street. The centre also organizes walking tours of Joyce's Dublin.

At the top of the road, on Great Denmark Street, is the Jesuit-run Belvedere College attended by Joyce between 1893 and 1898. He recalls his unhappy schooldays there in *A Portrait of the Artist as a Young Man*. The college's interior contains some of Stapleton's best and most colourful plasterwork (1785).

James Joyce (1882–1941)

Born in Dublin, Joyce spent most of his adult life in Europe. He used the city of Dublin as the setting for all his major works including *Dubliners*, *A Portrait of the Artist as a Young Man* and *Ulysses*. Joyce claimed that if the city was ever destroyed it could be recreated through the pages of *Ulysses*. However, the Irish branded the book pornographic and banned it until the 1960s.

The Gate Theatre, where new and classic plays are staged

❻ Gate Theatre

1 Cavendish Row. **Map** D1. **Open** for performances only. Box office: **Tel** 874 4045. **Open** 10am–7pm Mon–Sat. *See also Entertainment in Dublin p112.*
W **gatetheatre.ie**

Renowned for its staging of contemporary international drama in Dublin, the Gate Theatre was founded in 1928 by Hilton Edwards and Mícheál Mac Liammóir. The latter is now best remembered for *The Importance of Being Oscar*, his long-running one-man show about the writer Oscar Wilde *(see p26)*. An early success was Denis Johnston's *The Old Lady Says No*, so-called because of the margin notes made on one of his scripts by Lady Gregory, founding director of the Abbey Theatre *(see p92)*. Although still noted for staging new plays, the Gate's current output often includes classic Irish plays. Among the young talent to get their first break here were James Mason and a teenage Orson Welles.

❼ Rotunda Hospital

Parnell Square West. **Map** D1. **Tel** 817 1700. **W** **rotunda.ie**

Standing in the middle of Parnell Square is Europe's first purpose-built maternity hospital. Founded in 1745 by Dr Bartholomew Mosse, the design of the hospital is similar to that of Leinster House *(see p69)*. German-born architect Richard Cassels designed both buildings, as well as Powerscourt Centre *(see p82)* and Russborough House *(see pp136–7)*.

On the first floor is a beautiful chapel featuring striking stained-glass windows and exuberant Rococo plasterwork and ceiling (1755) by the German stuccoer Bartholomew Cramillion. The ceiling portrays the symbol of fertility and the virtues of faith, hope and charity.

Nowadays, over 8,000 babies are born in the Rotunda Hospital every year.

Stained-glass Venetian window (c.1863) in Rotunda Hospital's chapel

❽ Garden of Remembrance

Parnell Square. **Map** C1. **Tel** 821 3021. **Open** Apr–Sep: 8:30am–6pm daily; Oct–Mar: 9:30am–4pm daily. **W heritageireland.ie**

At the northern end of Parnell Square is a park dedicated to the men and women who have died in the pursuit of Irish freedom. The Garden of Remembrance marks the spot where several leaders of the 1916 Easter Rising were held overnight before being taken to Kilmainham Gaol *(see p101)*. The Irish Volunteers movement was formed here in 1913.

Designed by Daithí Hanly, the garden was opened by President Eamon de Valera *(see p49)* in 1966, to mark the 50th anniversary of the Easter Rising. In the centre is a cruciform pool. A mosaic on the pool floor depicts abandoned weapons and shields, symbolizing peace. The focal point at one end of the garden is a bronze sculpture by Oisín Kelly of the *Children of Lir* (1971), who were changed into swans by their step-mother *(see p31)*. Queen Elizabeth laid a commemorative wreath in the gardens during her historic state visit to Ireland in 2011.

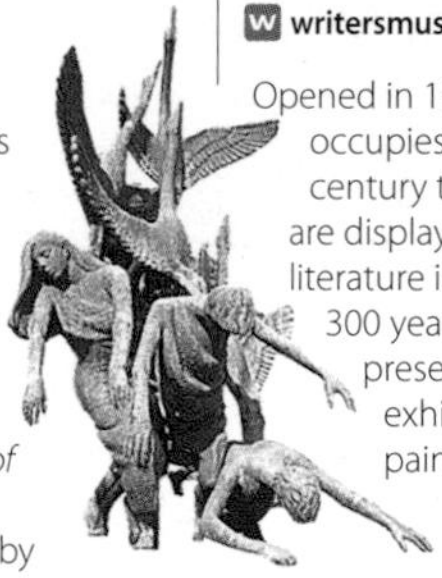

Children of Lir in the Garden of Remembrance

Gallery of Writers at Dublin Writers Museum

❾ Dublin Writers Museum

18 Parnell Sq North. **Map** C1. **Tel** 872 2077. **Open** 10am–5pm Mon–Sat; 11am–5pm Sun & public hols (last adm: 45 mins before closing). **Closed** 25 & 26 Dec. **W writersmuseum.com**

Opened in 1991, the museum occupies a tasteful 18th-century town house. There are displays relating to Irish literature in all its forms from 300 years ago to the present day. The exhibits include paintings, manuscripts, letters, rare editions and mementos of many of Ireland's finest authors. There are a number of temporary exhibits and a sumptuously decorated Gallery of Writers upstairs. The museum also hosts frequent poetry readings and lectures. A specialist bookstore, providing an out-of-print search service, adds to the relaxed, friendly ambience.

❿ Hugh Lane Gallery

Charlemont House, Parnell Square North. **Map** C1. **Tel** 222 5550. **Open** 10am–6pm Tue–Thu, 10am–5pm Fri & Sat, 11am–5pm Sun. **Closed** 24–28 Dec. **W hughlane.ie**

Art collector Sir Hugh Lane donated his collection of Impressionist paintings to the Dublin Corporation in 1908, but the lack of a suitable location for them prompted Lane to begin transferring his gift to the National Gallery in London. The Corporation then proposed Charlemont House and Lane relented. However, before Lane's revised will could be witnessed, he died on board the *Lusitania (see p182)*. This led to a 50-year dispute which has been resolved by the Corporation and the National Gallery swapping the collection every five years.

Besides the Lane bequest of paintings by Degas, Renoir and Monet, the gallery has an extensive collection of modern Irish paintings and a sculpture hall with work by Rodin and others. An exciting addition is a bequest by John Edwards of the contents of Francis Bacon's renowned London studio. In 2009, the gallery celebrated Francis Bacon's centenary.

Beach Scene (c.1876) by Edgar Degas, Hugh Lane Gallery

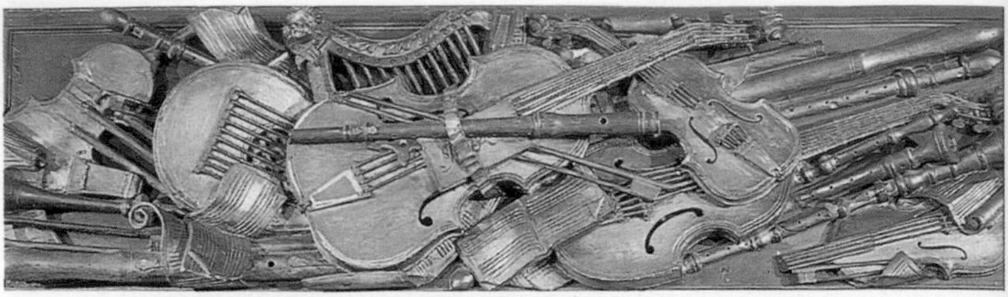

Detail of woodcarving (c.1724) at St Michan's Church

⓫ King's Inns

Henrietta St/Constitution Hill. **Map** B1. **Closed** to the public. **W kingsinns.ie**

This classically proportioned public building was founded in 1800 as a place of residence and study for barristers. To build it, James Gandon chose to seal off the end of Henrietta Street, which at the time was one of Dublin's most fashionable addresses. Francis Johnston added the graceful cupola in 1813, and the building was finally completed in 1817. Inside is a fine Dining Hall, and the Registry of Deeds (formerly the Prerogative Court). The west façade has two doorways flanked by Classical caryatids carved by Edward Smyth. The male figure, with book and quill, represents the law.

Sadly, much of the area around Constitution Hill is less attractive than it was in Georgian times. However, the gardens, which are open to the public, are still pleasing.

The west façade of King's Inns, with its caryatids and two doorways

⓬ Smithfield

Map A2.

Laid out in the mid-17th century as a marketplace, Smithfield used to be one of Dublin's oldest residential areas. However the 2.5- acre space received a £3.5 million makeover with a well-designed pedestrian cobbled plaza. It is used as a venue for outdoor civic events. The traditional horse fair is still held here on the first Sunday of the month. The Lighthouse cultural cinema is a welcome addition to the area.

⓭ Old Jameson Distillery

Bow St. **Map** A2. **Tel** 807 2355. **Open** 9am–6pm daily (from 10am Sun). Last tour: 5:30pm. **Closed** Good Fri, 24–26 Dec. **W jamesonwhiskey.com**

Proof of investment in the emerging Smithfield area is this large exhibition in a restored part of John Jameson's distillery, which produced whiskey from 1780 until 1971. A visit here starts with a video and further whiskey-related facts are then explained on a 40-minute tour. This takes you around displays set out as a working distillery, with different rooms devoted to the various stages of production.

The tour guides show how the Irish process differs from that of Scotch whisky: here the barley is dried with clean air, while in Scotland it is smoked over peat. The claim is that the Irish product is a smoother, less smoky tipple. After the tour, visitors can sample this in the bar.

⓮ St Michan's Church

Church St. **Map** B3. **Tel** 872 4154. **Open** mid-Mar–Oct: 10am–12:45pm & 2–4:45pm Mon–Fri, 10am–12:45pm Sat; Nov–mid-Mar: 12:30–3:30pm Mon–Fri, 10am–12:45pm Sat. limited. **W stmichans.com**

Largely rebuilt in 1685 on the site of an 11th-century Hiberno-Viking church, the dull façade of St Michan's hides a more exciting interior. Deep in its vaults lie a number of bodies preserved because of the dry atmosphere created by the church's magnesian limestone walls. Their wooden caskets, however, have cracked open, revealing the intact bodies, complete with skin and strands of hair. Among those thought to lie here are the brothers Henry and John Sheares, leaders of the 1798 rebellion *(see p45)*, who were executed that year.

Other less gory attractions include an organ (1724) on which Handel is said to have played. It is thought that the churchyard contains the unmarked grave of United Irishman Robert Emmet *(see p81)*, leader of the abortive 1803 Rising.

⓯ Four Courts

Inn's Quay (public entrance: Morgan Place). **Map** B3. **Tel** 888 6000. **Open** 9:30am–12:30pm, 2–4:30pm Mon–Fri (when courts in session).

Completed in 1802 by James Gandon, this majestic public building was virtually gutted 120 years later during the Irish Civil War *(see pp48–9)*. The Public Records Office, with its irreplaceable collection of documents dating back to the 12th century, was also destroyed by fire. By 1932, the main buildings were sympathetically restored using Gandon's original design. An imposing copper-covered lantern dome rises above the six-columned Corinthian portico, which is crowned with the figures of Moses, Justice, Mercy, Wisdom and Authority. This central section is flanked by two wings containing the four original courts. An information panel gives details about the building's history.

⑯ St Mary's Abbey

Meetinghouse Lane. **Map** C2. **Tel** 833 1618. **Closed** until further notice; check website in advance

heritageireland.ie

Founded by Benedictines in 1139, but transferred to the Cistercian order in 1147, this was one of the largest and most important monasteries in medieval Ireland. As well as controlling extensive estates, the abbey acted as state treasury and meeting place for the Council of Ireland. It was during a council meeting in St Mary's that "Silken Thomas" Fitzgerald *(see p42)* renounced his allegiance to Henry VIII and marched out to raise the short-lived rebellion of 1534. The monastery was dissolved in 1539 and during the 17th century the site served as a quarry.

The Ha'penny Bridge connecting Temple Bar to Liffey Street

All that remains today is the vaulted chamber of the Chapter House containing a model of how it would have looked 800 years ago.

⑰ National Leprechaun Museum

Twilfit House, Jervis St. **Map** C2. **Tel** 873 3899. **Open** 10am–6:30pm daily (last adm 5:45pm), evening tours 7:30pm & 8pm Fri & Sat.

This charming museum focuses on Irish myths and folklore, taking visitors inside Celtic culture to learn about leprechauns, fairies, banshees and other mythological creatures. Children will enjoy the lively storytelling by expert guides, but there is plenty to keep adults amused too.

⑱ Ha'penny Bridge

Map D3.

Linking the Temple Bar area *(see p82)* and Liffey Street, this high-arched cast-iron foot-bridge is used by thousands of people every day. It was built by John Windsor, an ironworker from Shropshire, England. One of Dublin's most photographed sights, it was originally named the Wellington Bridge. It is now officially called the Liffey Bridge, but is also known as the Ha'penny Bridge. Opened in 1816, the bridge got its better-known nickname from the halfpenny toll that was levied on it up until 1919. Restoration work, which included the installation of period lanterns, has made the bridge even more attractive.

James Gandon's Four Courts overlooking the River Liffey

FURTHER AFIELD

There are many interesting sights just outside the city centre. The best part of a day can be spent exploring the western suburbs taking in the Museum of Modern Art housed in the splendid Royal Kilmainham Hospital and the eerie Kilmainham Gaol. Phoenix Park, Europe's largest city park, is a good place for a stroll and also has a zoo. Further north are the National Botanic Gardens, with over 20,000 plant species from around the world. Nearby is Casino Marino, one of Ireland's finest examples of Palladian architecture. The magnificent coastline with its stunning views of Dublin Bay is easily reached by the DART rail network. It encompasses the towering promontory of Howth, while the highlights of the southern stretch are around Dalkey village and Killiney Bay. One of many Martello towers built as defences along this coast is known as the James Joyce Tower and houses a collection of Joyce memorabilia. To the northeast, a bit further from the city centre, is Malahide Castle, former home of the Talbot family.

Sights at a Glance

Museums and Galleries

- 2 Kilmainham Gaol
- 3 Irish Museum of Modern Art–Royal Hospital Kilmainham
- 4 Guinness Storehouse®
- 6 National Print Museum
- 9 National Museum of Ireland – Decorative Arts & History
- 14 James Joyce Tower

Parks and Gardens

- 1 Phoenix Park
- 5 National Botanic Gardens
- 10 Glasnevin Cemetery

Historic Buildings

- 7 Casino Marino
- 8 Dublin Docklands
- 11 Malahide Castle

Towns and Villages

- 12 Howth
- 13 Dun Laoghaire
- 15 Dalkey
- 16 Killiney

Key

- Main sightseeing areas
- Motorway
- Major road
- Minor road
- Railway

0 kilometres 4

0 miles 2

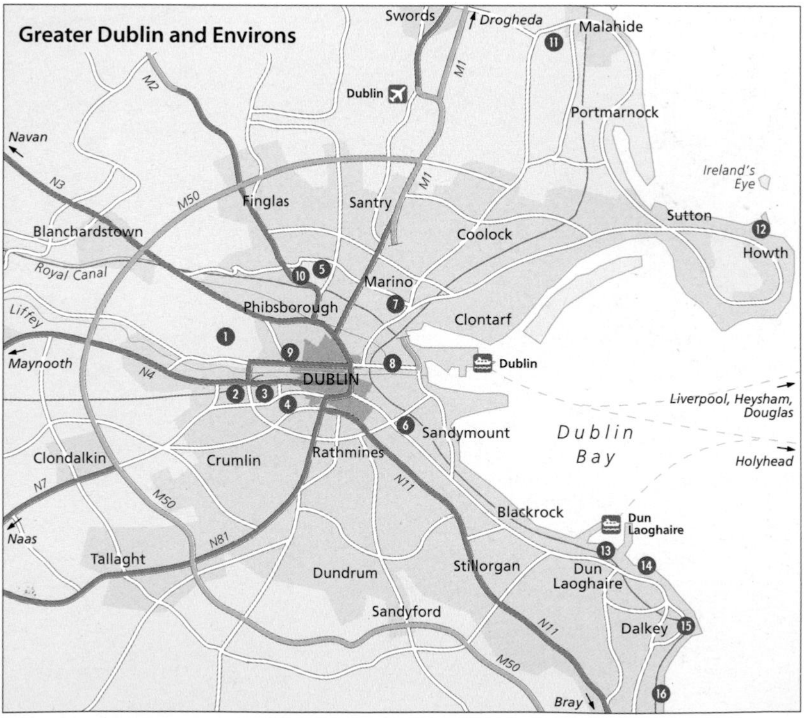

A greenhouse in the National Botanic Gardens, Dublin

For map symbols *see back flap*

1 Phoenix Park

Park Gate, Conyngham Rd, Dublin 8. 🚌 10, 25, 26, 37, 38, 39 & many other routes. **Open** daily. Phoenix Park Visitor Centre: **Tel** 677 0095. **Open** Apr–Oct: 10am–6pm daily; Nov–Mar: 9:30am–5:30pm Wed–Sun. ground floor only. **W phoenixpark.ie**
Zoo: **Tel** 474 8900. **Open** Mar–Sep: 9:30am– 6pm daily; Oct: 9:30am–5:30pm daily; Nov–Dec: 9:30am–4pm daily; Jan: 9:30am–4:30pm daily; Feb: 9:30am–5pm daily. (last adm: 1 hr before closing). **W dublinzoo.ie**

The Phoenix Column in Dublin, erected by the fourth Earl of Chesterfield in 1747

Just to the west of the city centre, ringed by an 11-km (7-mile) wall, is Europe's largest enclosed city park. The name "Phoenix" is said to be a corruption of the Gaelic *Fionn Uisce*, or "clear water". The **Phoenix Column** is crowned by a statue of the mythical bird. Phoenix Park originated in 1662, when the Duke of Ormonde turned the land into a deer park. In 1745 it was landscaped and opened to the public.

Near Park Gate is the lakeside **People's Garden** – the only part of the park which has been cultivated. A little further on is **Dublin Zoo**, established in 1831, making it the third oldest zoo in the world. The zoo is renowned for the successful breeding of lions, including the one that appears at the beginning of MGM movies. The African Plains Savanna houses the larger residents.

In addition to the Phoenix Column, the park has two other conspicuous monuments. The **Wellington Testimonial**, a 63-m (206-ft) obelisk, was begun in 1817 and completed in 1861. Its bronze bas-reliefs were made from captured French cannons. The 27-m (90-ft) steel **Papal Cross** marks the spot where the pope celebrated Mass in front of over one million people in 1979. Buildings within the park include two 18th-century houses: **Áras an Uachtaráin**, the Irish President's official residence, for which 525 tickets are issued every Saturday for a free guided tour, and Deerfield, home of the US Ambassador. **Ashtown Castle** is a restored 17th-century tower house, now home to the Phoenix Park Visitor Centre.

Restored central hall at Kilmainham Gaol

❷ Kilmainham Gaol

Inchicore Rd, Kilmainham, Dublin 8. **Tel** 453 5984. 51B, 51C, 69, 73, 78A, 79. **Open** Apr–Sep: 9:30am–6pm daily; Oct–Mar: 9:30am–5:30pm Mon–Sat, 10am–6pm Sun & public hols (last adm: 1 hr before closing). **Closed** 24, 25 & 26 Dec. advanced booking for groups. limited. **heritageireland.ie**

A long tree-lined avenue runs from the Royal Hospital Kilmainham to the grim, grey bulk of Kilmainham Gaol. The building was opened in 1796, but was restored in the 1960s. During its 130 years as a prison, it housed many of those involved in the fight for Irish independence, including Robert Emmet *(see p81)* and Charles Stewart Parnell *(p47)*. The last prisoner held was Eamon de Valera *(p49)*, who was transferred from Kilmainham in April 1924 before being finally released on 16 July.

The tour includes the chapel, where Joseph Plunkett married Grace Gifford a few hours before he faced the firing squad for his part in the 1916 Rising *(see pp48–9)*. The tours end in the prison yard where Plunkett's badly wounded colleague James Connolly, unable to stand up, was strapped into a chair before being shot. You also pass the dank cells of those involved in the 1798, 1803, 1848 and 1867 uprisings, as well as the punishment cells and hanging room. Among the exhibits are personal mementos of some of the former inmates and depictions of various events which took place in the Gaol until it closed down in 1924.

Part of the tour takes place outside so dress accordingly.

❸ Irish Museum of Modern Art – Royal Hospital Kilmainham

Military Road, Kilmainham, Dublin 8. **Tel** 612 9900. Heuston Station. 51, 51B, 78A, 79, 79a, 90, 123. Irish Museum of Modern Art: **Open** 10am–5:30pm Tue–Sat, 10:30am–5:30pm Wed, noon–5:30pm Sun & public hols (last adm: 5:15pm). **Closed** Good Fri & 24–27, 31 Dec. 1:15pm Wed, 2:30pm Sat & Sun. limited. Gardens open all year. **imma.ie**

Ireland's finest surviving 17th-century building was laid out in 1684, styled on Les Invalides in Paris. It was built by Sir William Robinson as a home for 300 wounded soldiers – a role it kept until 1927. When it was completed, people were so impressed by its Classical symmetry that it was suggested it would be better used as a campus for Trinity College. The Baroque chapel has fine carvings and intricate stained glass. The Formal Gardens, restored using many of the 17th-century designs, are now open to the public.

The hospital's former residential quarters became the Irish Museum of Modern Art. The collection includes a cross-section of Irish and international modern and contemporary art. The museum was refurbished in 2013 and houses over 3,500 artworks by Irish and international artists, which are displayed on a rotating basis and include special visiting exhibitions.

The Royal Hospital Kilmainham designed by Sir William Robinson in the 1680s

Guinness Storehouse's rooftop Gravity Bar

❹ Guinness Storehouse®

St James's Gate, Dublin 8.
Tel 408 4800. 78A, 51B, 123.
Open 9:30am–5pm (to 7pm Jul & Aug) daily. **Closed** Good Fri, 24–26 Dec.
W **guinness-storehouse.com**

The Guinness Storehouse® is a development based in St James's Gate Brewery, the original house of Guinness, now completely remodelled. This 1904 listed building covers nearly four acres of floor space over seven floors built around a huge glass atrium. The first impression the visitor has is of walking into a large glass pint, with light spilling down from above; there's a copy of the original lease signed by Arthur Guinness enshrined on the floor. The Ingredients section is next, where visitors can touch, smell and feel the ingredients through interactive displays. The tour continues into an authentic Georgian anteroom to "meet" Arthur Guinness and see him at work. The Brewing Exhibition is a noisy, steamy and "hoppy" area, which creates the impression of brewing all around and provides a full explanation of the process. The historical development of Guinness cooperage is accompanied by video footage of the craft. Models and displays tell the story of Guinness transportation, the appeal of Guinness world-wide, and the company's popular advertising campaigns. The tour ends with a free pint of draught Guinness in the traditional Brewery Bar and the rooftop Gravity Bar.

The Brewing of Guinness

Guinness is a black beer, known as "stout", renowned for its distinctive malty flavour and smooth creamy head. From its humble beginnings over 200 years ago, the Guinness brewery site at St James's Gate now sprawls across 26 ha (65 acres). It is the largest brewery in Europe and exports beers to more than 120 countries throughout the world. Other famous brands owned by Guinness include Harp Lager and Smithwick's Ale.

How Guinness is Made

The four main ingredients used to brew Guinness are barley, hops, yeast and water which, contrary to popular belief, comes from the Wicklow Mountains rather than the River Liffey.

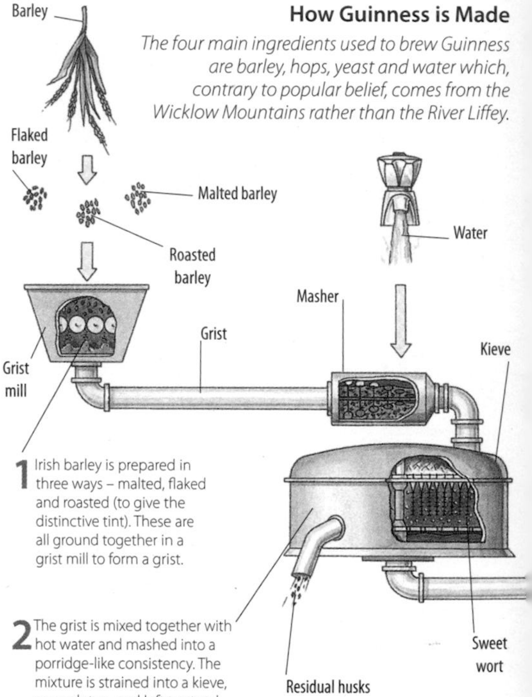

1 Irish barley is prepared in three ways – malted, flaked and roasted (to give the distinctive tint). These are all ground together in a grist mill to form a grist.

2 The grist is mixed together with hot water and mashed into a porridge-like consistency. The mixture is strained into a kieve, or mash tun, and left to stand for an hour. Here starches are turned into sugars, producing a dark, sweet wort.

Guinness advertising has become almost as famous as the product itself. Since 1929, when the first advertisement announced that "Guinness is Good for You", poster and television advertising campaigns have employed many amusing images of both animals and people.

Arthur Guinness

Arthur Guinness

In December 1759, 34-year-old Arthur Guinness signed a 9,000-year lease at an annual rent of £45 to take over St James's Gate Brewery, which had lain vacant for almost ten years. At the time the brewing industry in Dublin was at a low ebb – the standard of ale was much criticized and in rural Ireland beer was virtually unknown, as whiskey, gin and poteen were the more favoured drinks. Furthermore, Irish beer was under threat from imports. Guinness started brewing ale, but was also aware of a black ale called porter, produced in London. This new beer was so called because of its popularity with porters at Billingsgate and Covent Garden markets. Guinness decided to stop making ales and develop his own recipe for porter (the word "stout" was not used until the 1920s). So successful was the switch that he made his first export shipment in 1769.

Engraving (c.1794) of a satisfied customer

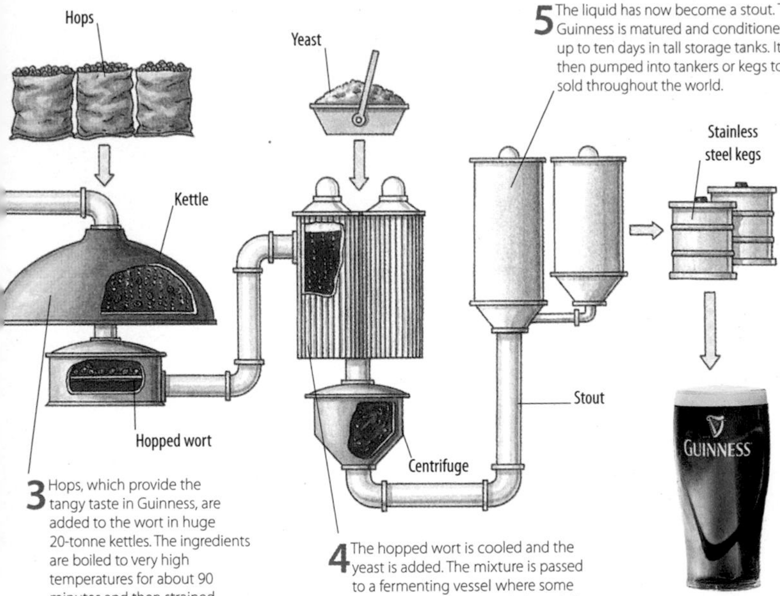

3 Hops, which provide the tangy taste in Guinness, are added to the wort in huge 20-tonne kettles. The ingredients are boiled to very high temperatures for about 90 minutes and then strained.

4 The hopped wort is cooled and the yeast is added. The mixture is passed to a fermenting vessel where some sugars are turned to alcohol. It is left to ferment for 48 hours and the yeast is removed by centrifuge.

5 The liquid has now become a stout. The Guinness is matured and conditioned for up to ten days in tall storage tanks. It is then pumped into tankers or kegs to be sold throughout the world.

A draught of Guinness beer

The Guinness brewery has relied heavily on water transport since its first export was shipped to England in 1769. The barges, which up until 1961 made the short trip with their cargo up the Liffey to Dublin Port, were a familiar sight on the river. Once at port, the stout would be loaded on to huge tanker ships for worldwide distribution.

Bottles on display at the Guinness Academy Bar

A lake at the National Botanic Gardens, Dublin

❺ National Botanic Gardens

Botanic Ave, Glasnevin, Dublin 9. **Tel** 804 0300. 4, 13, 19, 19A, 83. **Open** Oct–Feb: 9am–4:30pm Mon–Fri, 10am–4:30pm Sat & Sun; Mar–Sep: 9am–5pm Mon–Fri, 10am–6pm Sat & Sun. **Closed** 25 Dec. noon & 2:30pm Sun. **botanicgardens.ie**

Opened in 1795, the National Botanic Gardens are Ireland's foremost centre of botany and horticulture. They still possess an old-world feel, thanks to the beautiful Palm House and architect Richard Turner's curvilinear glasshouses. Turner was also responsible for the Palm House at Kew Gardens, London, and the glasshouses at Belfast's Botanic Gardens *(see p282)*.

The 20-ha (49-acre) park contains over 16,000 different plant species. Particularly attractive are the colourful old-fashioned Victorian carpet bedding, the rich collections of cacti and orchids, renowned rose garden, and 30-m (100-ft) high redwood tree.

The visitor centre houses a restaurant, a display area with exhibits relating to the history and purpose of the gardens and a lecture hall, which hosts a programme of regular talks and workshops. The National Botanic Gardens back onto the huge Glasnevin or Prospect Cemetery *(see p105)*; the gate between the two is open to the public.

Built by local craftsmen using traditional building materials and techniques, the new Viking House is a faithful replica of a typical Dublin house and garden of one thousand years ago, similar to buildings excavated in the city centre in the late 1980s.

❻ National Print Museum

Garrison Chapel, Beggar's Bush Barracks, Haddington Road, Dublin 4. **Tel** 660 3770. DART to Landsdowne or Grand Canal Dock 4, 7. **Open** 9am–5pm Mon–Fri, 2–5pm Sat & Sun. **Closed** Bank holiday weekends. limited **nationalprintmuseum.ie**

Opened in 1996, in the former chapel of Beggar's Bush Barracks, the National Print Museum has an extensive collection which depicts the history of print in Ireland. The collection includes functional printing machinery, printing blocks, pamphlets, periodicals and books. Along with regular exhibitions and tours, the museum has a variety of art and crafts workshops on calligraphy, letterpress printing, traditional bookbinding, origami and card making.

Printing blocks at National Print Museum

❼ Casino Marino

Cherrymount Crescent. **Tel** 833 1618. DART to Clontarf. 20A, 20B, 27A, 42, 42C, 123. **Open** mid-Mar–Oct: 10am–5pm daily. obligatory (last tour 45 mins before closing). **heritageireland.ie**

This delightful little villa *(see pp44–5)*, designed by Sir William Chambers in the 1760s for Lord Charlemont, now sits in its own grounds at Marino. Originally built as a summer house for the Marino Estate, the villa survives although the main house was pulled down in 1921. The Casino is acknowledged to be one of the finest examples of Neo-Classical architecture in Ireland. Some innovative features were used in its construction, including chimneys disguised as urns and hollow columns that accommodate drains. Outside, four carved stone lions, thought to be by English sculptor Joseph Wilton, stand guard at each of the corners.

Carved stone lion at Casino Marino

The building's squat, compact exterior conceals 16 rooms built on three floors around a central staircase. The ground floor comprises a spacious hall and a saloon, with beautiful silk hangings, elaborate flooring and a coffered ceiling. On the first floor is the ostentatious State Room and servant rooms.

A gilded chair on display at the National Museum of Ireland

8 Dublin Docklands

dublindocklands.ie

Over three hundred years ago, most of the Docklands was underwater, with the exception of the small fishing hamlet of Ringsend. The area was redeveloped during the 1990s and 2000s and is one of the city's most exciting districts. Theatres, museums, numerous cafés and restaurants, water sports and a memorial to those who died in the Great Famine are all draws to Dublin Docklands. The Docklands span both sides of the Liffey to the east of the city centre and are joined by the Samuel Beckett Bridge.

9 National Museum of Ireland – Decorative Arts & History

Collins Barracks, Benburb St, Dublin 7. **Tel** 677 7444. 25, 25A, 66, 67, 90. **Open** 10am–5pm Tue–Sat, 2–5pm Sun. **Closed** Good Fri & 25 Dec. **museum.ie**

Close to Phoenix Park and just across the Liffey from the Guinness Brewery stands the wonderful decorative arts and history annexe of the National Museum *(see pp70–71)*. Its setting in the historic Collins Barracks is an inspired move. The massive complex was commissioned by King William III in 1700, just ten years after victory at the Battle of the Boyne, and was the largest barracks in his domain, with accommodation for over 5,000 people. It was in use right up to the 1990s. After Irish independence the barracks was named for Michael Collins, the first commander-in-chief of the Irish Army.

The large central courtyard, measured at one hundred marching paces, is an object lesson in simplicity. In marked contrast to the grey institutional exterior, the museum's interior presents the exhibits in an innovative way using the latest technology, with interactive multimedia displays.

Furniture, silver, glassware, ceramics and scientific instrument collections form the bulk of items on show in the South Block. In the West Block, however, visitors get an insight into the history, work and development of the National Museum. The Out of Storage exhibit brings together a wide array of artifacts from around the world, comple- mented by banks of interactive multimedia computers. One of the highlights of the museum is the Curator's Choice section where 25 unusual exhibits – such as an early hurling stick and ball – are displayed with the story of their cultural significance.

The North Block holds a permanent exhibition, Soldiers and Chiefs, which explores Irish military history through the eyes of the average Irish soldier from 1550 to the late 1990s.

10 Glasnevin Cemetery

Finglas Rd. **Tel** 882 6500. 13, 19, 19A, 40, 40A from Parnell St. **Open** 9am–6pm daily. 2:30pm daily (lasts 90 minutes). Museum: **Tel** 882 6550. **Open** 10am–5pm Mon–Fri, 11am–5pm Sat & Sun. **glasnevinmuseum.ie**

The largest cemetery in Ireland, Glasnevin covers more than 50 ha (124 acres) and contains over one million graves. Originally called Prospect Cemetery, Glasnevin was founded in 1828 after Daniel O'Connell *(see p46)* campaigned for a burial ground in which both Irish Catholics and Protestants could bury their dead with dignity.

The main part features high walls and watchtowers, intended to keep out body snatchers in the early 19th century. The St Paul's area across the road was added when more burial space was needed. The burial plots of both communities have a huge variety of monuments, from the austere high stones used until the 1860s, to the elaborate Celtic crosses of the nationalist revival from the 1860s to the 1960s, to the plain marble of the late 20th century.

Glasnevin is a national monument and has a museum detailing its history and the people who are buried there. There are also daily walking tours offering interesting insights into the people ≠whose final resting place it is, including Daniel O'Connell, Michael Collins, Éamon de Valera, Constance Markiewicz and Brendan Behan.

Glasnevin Cemetery, Dublin's largest cemetery

A view of Malahide Castle from the extensive surrounding grounds

⓫ Malahide Castle

Malahide, Co Dublin. and DART to Malahide. 42 from Beresford Place, near Busáras. **Tel** 816 9538. **Open** 9:30am–5:30pm daily. obligatory. Last tours: 4:30pm (3:30pm Nov–Mar).
malahidecastle andgardens.ie

Near the seaside dormitory town of Malahide stands a huge castle set in 100 ha (250 acres) of grounds. The castle's core dates from the 12th century but later additions, such as its rounded towers, have given it a classic fairy-tale appearance. The building served as a stately home for the Talbot family until 1973. They were staunch supporters of James II: on the day of the Battle of the Boyne in 1690 *(see p248)*, 14 members of the family breakfasted here; none came back for supper.

Guided tours take you round the castle's collection of 18th-century Irish furniture, the oak-beamed Great Hall and the impressively carved Oak Room. Part of the Portrait Collection, on loan from the National Gallery *(see pp74–5)*, can be seen here. It includes portraits of the Talbot family and other figures such as Wolfe Tone *(see p45)*.

A visitor centre in the courtyard has an interactive exhibition on the fascinating history of the Talbot family. The ornamental walled gardens, covering about 22 acres, are also worth exploring. They were largely created by the last member of the family to live in the castle, Lord Milo Talbot, an enthusiastic plant collector who is also believed to have been a Soviet spy.

⓬ Howth

Co Dublin. DART. Howth Castle grounds **Open** 8am–sunset daily.
howthcastle.ie

The commercial fishing town of Howth is the northern limit of Dublin Bay. Howth Head, a huge rocky mass, has lovely views of the bay. A footpath runs around its tip, which is known as the "Nose". Nearby is Baily Lighthouse (1814). Sadly, this area has suffered from building development.

To the west of the town is Howth Castle, which dates back to Norman times. The **National Transport Museum** in the grounds is worth a visit.

Ireland's Eye, an islet and bird sanctuary where puffins nest, can be reached by a short boat trip from Howth.

National Transport Museum
Tel 01 832 0427. **Open** 2–5pm Sat, Sun & public hols. **Closed** Mon–Fri.
nationaltransportmuseum.org

⓭ Dun Laoghaire

Co Dublin. DART. National Maritime Museum: **Tel** 280 0969. **Open** 11am–5pm daily. Comhaltas Ceoltóirí Éireann: **Tel** 280 0295. **Open** for music Wed & Sat; Céilí Fri. **comhaltas.ie**

Ireland's major passenger ferry port and yachting centre, with its brightly painted villas, parks and palm trees, can sometimes

Baily Lighthouse on the southeastern tip of Howth Head

Yachts anchored in Dun Laoghaire harbour

exude a decidedly continental feel. Many visitors head straight out of Dun Laoghaire (pronounced Dunleary) but the town offers some magnificent walks around the harbour and to the lighthouse along the east pier. The villages of Sandycove and Dalkey can be reached via "The Metals" footpath which runs alongside the railway line.

The 1837 Mariners' Church is housed in the National Maritime Museum. Exhibits include a longboat used by French officers during Wolfe Tone's unsuccessful invasion at Bantry in 1796 *(see pp172–3)*.

Up the road in Monkstown's Belgrave Square is the Comhaltas Ceoltóirí Éireann, Ireland's main centre for traditional music and dance, with music sessions and *céilís* (dances).

⓮ James Joyce Tower

Sandycove, Co Dublin. **Tel** 280 9265. DART to Sandycove. 59, 7/A. **Open** 10am–6pm daily.
W **jamesjoycetower.com**

This Martello tower stands on a rocky promontory above the village of Sandycove. It is one of 15 defensive towers erected between Dublin and Bray in 1804 to withstand a threatened invasion by Napoleon. One hundred years later James Joyce *(see p94)* stayed here for a week as the guest of Oliver St John Gogarty, poet and model for the *Ulysses* character Buck Mulligan. Gogarty rented the tower for a mere £8 per year. Inside the squat 12-m (40-ft) tower's granite walls is a small museum run by a group of local volunteers, containing some of Joyce's correspondence, personal belongings, such as his guitar, cigar case and walking stick, and his death mask. There are also photographs and first editions of his works, including a deluxe edition (1935) of *Ulysses* illustrated by Henri Matisse. The roof, originally a gun platform but later used as a sunbathing deck by Gogarty, affords marvellous views of Dublin Bay. Below the tower is Forty Foot Pool, traditionally an all-male nude bathing spot, but now open to all.

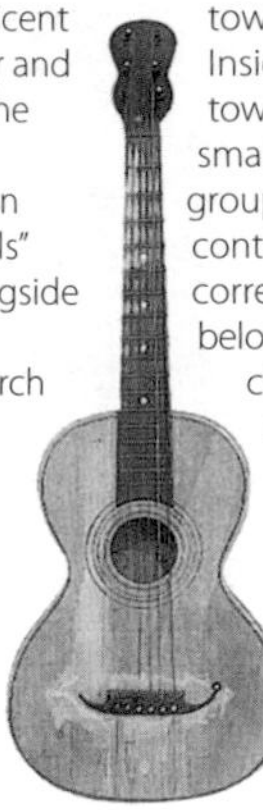

Guitar at James Joyce Tower

⓯ Dalkey

Co Dublin. DART.
W **ilovedalkey.com**

Dalkey was once known as the "Town of Seven Castles", but only two of these now remain. They are both on the main street of this attractive village whose tight, winding roads and charming villas give it a Mediterranean feel.

A little way offshore is tiny Dalkey Island, a rocky bird sanctuary with a Martello tower and a medieval Benedictine church, both now in a poor state of repair. In summer the island can be reached by a boat ride from the town's Coliemore Harbour.

⓰ Killiney

Co Dublin. DART to Dalkey or Killiney.

South of Dalkey, the coastal road climbs uphill before tumbling down into the village of Killiney. The route offers one of the most scenic vistas on this stretch of the east coast, with views often compared to those across the Bay of Naples. Howth Head is clearly visible to the north, with Bray Head *(see p137)* and the foothills of the Wicklow Mountains *(see pp142–3)* to the south. There is another exhilarating view from the top of Killiney Hill Park, off Victoria Road – well worth tackling the short steep trail for. Down below is the popular pebbly beach, Killiney Strand.

Dalkey Castle and Heritage Centre on Castle Street

SHOPPING IN DUBLIN

Dublin has two main shopping thoroughfares, each on either side of the River Liffey. On the north side, the area around Henry Street is where swanky department stores and small specialty shops beckon. The south side, especially trendy Grafton Street with its upmarket boutiques and shops, is reputed for its glamour and style. Yet, despite the wide choice of internationally known brands and retail chains found throughout the city, the spirit of Dublin shines in the cheerful cacophony of its street markets, many of which stock a cornucopia of highly original Irish crafts and gifts. Dublin is also a haven for those searching for bargains and second-hand deals on everything from books and CDs to clothes and trinkets. There is something for everyone in this lively city, and the following pages will tell you where to start looking.

Where to Shop

Temple Bar has become a staple tourist destination. While the area is frequented by revellers at night, it's a treasure trove of funky craft, design and souvenir outlets during the day, and several second-hand boutiques offer everything from vintage shoes to designer handbags.

Bustling Henry Street on the north side of the Liffey is lined with high-street shops and department stores, as well as the flagship Primark outlet Penney's, famous for its cheap fashions.

Those who prefer a more relaxed and upmarket shopping experience should head for Grafton Street on the city's south side, which is home to the Brown Thomas department store and designer outlets. The area to the west of here, especially along South William Street and Wicklow Street, is packed with small boutiques and homeware stores. The Powerscourt Centre, housed in a Georgian town house, has an array of designer outlets and antique jewellery stores.

When to Shop

Shopping hours are generally from 9am to 6pm, Monday to Saturday, and from 11am or noon to 6pm on Sundays. Many shops stay open until 9pm on Thursdays.

How to Pay

Major credit cards such as Visa and MasterCard are accepted in almost all outlets. Sales tax or VAT is usually 23 per cent, which non-EU visitors can redeem at airports and ports. Redemption forms are available at points of purchase.

Department Stores

The best-known department stores in Dublin are **Arnott's**, the city's oldest and largest, and **Debenhams**, both

Brown Thomas department store

on Henry Street. One of Dublin's most popular shops, **Avoca** on Suffolk Street, stocks everything from women's and kids' wear to vintage furniture. It also houses one of the best cafés in the city. Prominent Irish retailer **Brown Thomas** is known for its upmarket wares, with goods from the world's top designers.

There are also numerous Marks & Spencer shops, including branches on Grafton Street and Mary Street.

Grafton Street, a popular shopping destination

Shopping Centres

There are four main shopping centres in Dublin – three on the south side and one on the north. South of the Liffey are **Stephen's Green Centre** and the **Powerscourt Centre**. Stephen's Green Centre is one of the largest enclosed shopping areas, with scores of shops under its roof. These include

The colourful George's Street Arcade

many craft and gift stores, clothing outlets and several fast-food restaurants.

Set in an enclosed four-storey Georgian courtyard, the Powerscourt Centre is more upmarket and plush. It is home to many fine boutiques, restaurants and lovely antique shops. Also on the south side of the city is the **Dundrum Centre**.

On the north side of the river is the **Jervis Centre**, which houses many British chain stores as well as a number of popular Irish retailers.

Markets

On Dublin's north side, just off Henry Street, the famous and still-evolving Moore Street Market hosts a daily fruit and vegetable bazaar, replete with very vocal street vendors. The area has also become a hive of ethnic shops, where you can source anything from Iranian dance music CDs to tinned bok choi.

The wonderful **Temple Bar Food Market**, where you will find a wide range of organically produced items, is held every Saturday. A particularly popular stall sells delicious fresh oysters and wine by the glass – a great stop-off point for the weary shopper.

Quirky, quaint and unique, **George's Street Arcade** is open seven days a week and has many second-hand shops. It is a good place for records, books, Irish memorabilia and bric-a-brac, as well as funky clothing and accessories.

Souvenirs and Gifts

A popular destination for souvenirs in Dublin is at the **Guinness Storehouse®** *(see pp102–103)*. The interactive tours of the storehouse are best rounded off with a visit to the gift shop, where a multitude of Guinness branded souvenirs and clothing can be bought.

Finely crafted pottery

Nassau Street has a concentration of fine tourist gift shops, such as **Heraldic Artists**, which assists visitors in tracing their ancestry. On the same street, the **Kilkenny Shop** stocks uniquely Irish ceramic wares, the famous Waterford crystal and many other handcrafted products.

Across the road, the gift shop at Trinity College sells university memorabilia and mementos of the *Book of Kells*, as well as many other souvenirs.

Rua, a boutique-style shop on the historic Capel Street, has an array of unique and interesting treasures, from handmade homewares to jewellery and accessories. Across the river, **Scout**, on Essex Street, has carefully selected Irish and international clothing and footwear labels as well as vintage accessories. The tiny **Irish Design Shop** on Drury Street offers a small but charming range of Irish crafts, jewellery, prints and home furnishings. **Industry**, also on Drury Street, has an eclectic collection of vintage, upcycled and new furniture and homewares.

Food and Wine

Connoisseurs of fine wines and whiskies have many choices in Dublin. **Mitchell & Son** boasts a large shop in the financial services centre and an online delivery facility. The **Celtic Whiskey Shop** stocks a variety of Irish and Scotch whiskies, and the staff are very knowledgeable.

A number of gourmet food retailers add culinary character to the city. **Sheridan's Cheesemongers** specializes in Irish farmhouse cheeses but stocks a wide array of other cheeses and foods too. **Butler's Irish Chocolate** tempts with exquisite handmade chocolates. For those craving freshly caught Irish salmon, **Fallon & Byrne** on Exchequer Street is a good bet. They also sell an extensive range of organic and imported produce, alongside a fine selection of wines, cheeses and charcuterie. Dublin's growing multi-culturalism has led to the proliferation of ethnic food stores, many of which can be found on Parnell Street and Moore Street on the north side, or around George's Street on the south side.

Sheridan's Cheesemongers' tempting display

Fashion

Although there are many elegant boutiques in Dublin, the most fashionable are clustered close to Dublin's "Fifth Avenue" – the smart Grafton Street area. **Costume**, with its wide range of Irish and international designer labels, is a popular destination for women's haute couture. You'll also find designers such as Roland Mouret, Temperley and Jonathan Saunders here.

Bargain hunters should head for the Temple Bar's Designer Mart on Cow's Lane (10am–5pm every Sunday), where there are stalls selling handmade Irish crafts and design.

For classic menswear, **Louis Copeland** is Dublin's most famous tailor. For traditional clothing, stop at the Kilkenny Shop *(see p109)* or **Kevin & Howlin**. Both stock tweeds, Arans and other typically Irish clothing.

Books

Given its rich literary heritage, it is not surprising that there are several specialist and interesting bookstores peppering Dublin's streets. Dawson Street is the top draw for book lovers, with the vast **Hodges Figgis**. **Eason** on O'Connell Street and **Dubray Books** on Grafton Street have comprehensive collections, while **The Gutter Bookshop** in Temple Bar is an independent shop, which hosts regular events and readings. **The Secret Book and Record Store** has a small, but quality selection of books dedicated to Irish literature, history and philosophy. Antiquarian bookseller, **Cathach Books**, is Dublin's specialist provider of old Irish titles. The shop stocks an impressive selection of first editions and rarities. **Chapters** is the city's biggest bookstore, with an excellent second-hand and bargain section.

Music

The most concentrated area for record shops is in Temple Bar, where small stores stock everything from obscure electronica to indie and reggae. Many independent music stores have closed in recent years, but **Tower Records** is a popular haunt that is bucking the trend with live gigs and a newly opened café. For the best in hip-hop culture and dance music, pay a visit to **All City Records**.

Most record shops in Dublin stock traditional Irish music, but **Celtic Note** on Nassau Street has one of the largest selections. The staff will gladly make recommendations.

McCullough Piggot and **Waltons**, both on the south side of the city, are best for sheet music and traditional Irish instruments including accordions, uilleann pipes and *bodhráns*.

Antiques

One of Dublin's oldest antique retailers, **Oman Antique Galleries**, specializes in quality Georgian, Victorian and Edwardian furniture. **Clifford Antiques** offers both original and reproduction antique furniture, as well as decorative fireplaces. Its collection of bronze fountains and figures is unrivalled in the city. The eclectic collection at **Christy Bird** includes an array of salvaged and recycled furniture and pub fittings.

The Powerscourt Centre is also home to many antique dealers. Of these, **Delphi** is a specialist in Victorian and Edwardian period jewellery, and also stocks fragile Belleek porcelain antiques. **Courtville Antiques** specializes in Art Deco and antique jewellery, including diamond engagement rings, Victorian brooches and Edwardian enamel jewellery. For silver antiques, including Irish and English portrait miniatures from the 18th to the 20th century, visit **The Silver Shop**.

For antique maps and prints, the Grafton Street area is a good hunting ground, with the **Neptune Gallery** nearby.

Located near the historical Coombe, Francis Street offers a mish-mash of antique stores. Old clocks, second-hand furniture and loads of bric-a-brac line the streets, inviting visitors into shops that are almost antiques themselves. Outside the city centre, **Beaufield Mews** specializes in porcelain and early 20th-century pictures, while **Q Antiques** in Dun Laoghaire stocks an interesting range of period lighting and furniture.

Those who wish to further explore vintage Irish treasures should consult the website and local listings for the **Antiques Fairs** that are held in the city at different times and locations throughout the year.

Galleries

The abundance of galleries and artists' workshops in Dublin make it a favourite destination of art lovers and collectors. Many galleries are located on Dawson Street, which runs parallel to Grafton Street.

On Westland Row, the **Oisín Gallery** sells the work of some of Ireland's best young artists in its split-level exhibition space, while the **Doorway Gallery** on South Frederick Street specializes in Irish art for larger spaces. Visitors may also visit **Whyte's Auction Rooms** to bid on international and Irish art. The catalogues, which are published online should be consulted by those seriously interested in Irish painting.

On Sundays, an outdoor art market is held at Merrion Square close to the museum quarter. Works of vastly varying quality are hung from the square's perimeter black railing, and in good weather, the colourful, impromptu exhibition makes for very enjoyable browsing.

The Temple Bar area is also home to many of the city's galleries, including the **Temple Bar Gallery and Studios**. It is one of the more cutting-edge venues, housing the eclectic work of more than 30 Irish artists working in several mediums. Nearby, in the heart of Dublin's Left Bank, is the **Original Print Gallery** and the **Gallery of Photography**, which stocks an impressive collection of glossy art books. Despite its association with partying and drunken misconduct, the area is still deserving of its "cultural quarter" status.

DIRECTORY

Department Stores

Arnott's
12 Henry St. **Map** D2. **Tel** 01 805 0400. **W** arnotts.ie

Avoca Store and Café
11–13 Suffolk St. **Map** D2. **Tel** 01 677 4215. **W** avoca.com

Brown Thomas
88–95 Grafton St. **Map** D4. **Tel** 01 605 6666. **W** brownthomas.com

Debenhams
54–62 Henry St. **Map** D2. **Tel** 01 814 7200. **W** debenhams.com

Shopping Centres

Dundrum Centre
Dundrum. **Tel** 01 299 1700. **W** dundrum.ie

Jervis Centre
125 Upper Abbey St. **Map** C2. **Tel** 01 878 1323. **W** jervis.ie

Powerscourt Centre
59 S William St. **Map** D4. **Tel** 01 679 4144. **W** powerscourtcentre.com

Stephen's Green Centre
St Stephen's Green West. **Map** D4. **Tel** 01 478 0888. **W** stephensgreen.com

Markets

George's Street Arcade
George's St. **Map** C4. **Tel** 01 283 6077. **W** georgesstreetarcade.ie

Temple Bar Food Market
Meeting House Sq, Temple Bar. **Map** D3. **Tel** 01 677 2255. **W** templebar.ie

Souvenirs & Gifts

Guinness Storehouse®
St James's Gate. **Map** A3. **Tel** 01 408 4800. **W** guinness-storehouse.com

Heraldic Artists
3 Nassau St. **Map** A3. **Tel** 01 679 7020. **W** roots.ie

Industry
41a/b Drury St. **Map** D4. **Tel** 01 613 9111. **W** industrydesign.ie

Irish Design Shop
41 Drury St. **Map** D4. **Tel** 01 679 8871. **W** irishdesignshop.com

Kilkenny Shop
6–10 Nassau St. **Map** E4. **Tel** 01 677 7066. **W** kilkennyshop.com

Rua
55 Capel St. **Map** C2. **Tel** 01 874 8051. **W** ruaboutique.ie

Food and Wine

Butler's Irish Chocolate
24 Wicklow St. **Map** D4. **Tel** 01 671 0591. **W** butlerschocolates.com

Celtic Whiskey Shop
27–28 Dawson St. **Map** D4. **Tel** 01 675 9744. **W** celticwhiskeyshop.com

Fallon & Byrne
11–17 Exchequer St. **Map** D4. **Tel** 01 472 1010. **W** fallonandbyrne.com

Mitchell & Son
Chq Building, IFSC. **Map** D2. **Tel** 01 612 5540. **W** mitchellandson.com

Sheridan's Cheesemongers
11 South Anne St. **Map** D4. **Tel** 01 679 3143. **W** sheridanscheesemongers.com

Fashion

Costume
10 Castle Market. **Map** D4. **Tel** 01 679 4188. **W** costumedublin.ie

Kevin & Howlin
31 Nassau St. **Map** E4. **Tel** 01 633 4576. **W** kevinandhowlin.com

Louis Copeland
39–41 Capel St. **Map** C2. **Tel** 01 872 1600.

Scout
5 Smock Alley Court, Essex St West. **Map** C3. **Tel** 01 677 8846. **W** scoutdublin.com

Books

Cathach Books
10 Duke St. **Map** D4. **Tel** 01 671 8676. **W** rarebooks.ie

Chapters
Ivy Exchange, Parnell St. **Map** D2. **Tel** 01 872 3297. **W** chapters.ie

Dubray Books
24 Grafton St. **Map** D4. **Tel** 01 677 5568. **W** dubraybooks.ie

Eason
40 Lower O'Connell St. **Map** D2. **Tel** 01 858 3800. **W** easons.com

The Gutter Bookshop
Cow's Lane. **Map** C3. **Tel** 01 679 9206. **W** gutterbookshop.com

Hodges Figgis
56–58 Dawson St. **Map** D4. **Tel** 01 677 4754.

The Secret Book and Record Store
15a Wicklow St, Dublin 2. **Map** D3. **Tel** 01 679 7272.

Music

All City Records
4 Crow St, Temple Bar. **Map** C3. **Tel** 01 677 2994.

Celtic Note
12 Nassau St. **Map** E4. **Tel** 01 670 4157. **W** celticnote.com

Claddagh Records
2 Cecilia St, Temple Bar. **Map** D3. **Tel** 01 677 0262. **W** claddaghrecords.com

McCullough Piggot
11 S William St. **Map** D4. **Tel** 01 677 3138. **W** mcculloughpiggot.com

Tower Records
7 Dawson St. **Map** D4. **Tel** 01 671 3250. **W** towerrecords.ie

Waltons
69 S Great George's St. **Map** D1. **Tel** 01 475 0661. **W** waltons.ie

Antiques

Antiques Fairs
W vintageireland.eu

Beaufield Mews
Woodlands Ave, Stillorgan, Co Dublin. **Road map** D4. **Tel** 01 288 0375. **W** beaufieldmews.com

Christy Bird
32 S Richmond St. **Tel** 01 475 4049.

Clifford Antiques
7/8 Parnell St. **Map** D1. **Tel** 01 872 6062. **W** cliffordantiques.ie

Courtville Antiques
Powerscourt Centre. **Map** D4. **Tel** 01 679 4042. **W** courtvilleantiques.com

Delphi
Powerscourt Centre. **Map** D4. **Tel** 01 679 0331. **W** delphiantiques.com

Neptune Gallery
41 S William St. **Map** D4. **Tel** 01 671 5021.

Oman Antique Galleries
20/21 S William St. **Map** D4. **Tel** 01 616 8991.

Q Antiques
76 York Rd, Dun Laoghaire, Co Dublin. **Map** D4. **Tel** 01 280 2895.

The Silver Shop
Powerscourt Centre. **Map** D4. **Tel** 01 679 4147. **W** silvershopdublin.com

Galleries

Doorway Gallery
24 South Frederick St. **Map** E4. **Tel** 01 764 5895. **W** thedoorwaygallery.com

Gallery of Photography
Meeting House Sq, Temple Bar. **Map** C3. **Tel** 01 671 4654. **W** galleryofphotography.ie

Oisín Gallery
44 Westland Row. **Map** F3. **Tel** 087 254 9370. **W** oisingallery.com

Original Print Gallery
4 Temple Bar. **Map** D3. **Tel** 01 677 3657.

Temple Bar Gallery and Studios
5–9 Temple Bar. **Map** D3. **Tel** 01 671 0073. **W** templebargallery.com

Whyte's Auction Rooms
38 Molesworth St. **Map** D2. **Tel** 01 676 2888. **W** whytes.ie

ENTERTAINMENT IN DUBLIN

Although Dublin is well served by theatres, cinemas, nightclubs and rock venues, what sets the city apart from other European capitals is its pubs. Lively banter, impromptu music sessions and great Guinness are the essential ingredients for an enjoyable night in any of the dozens of atmospheric hostelries here.

One of the most popular entertainment districts is the rejuvenated Temple Bar area. Along this narrow network of cobbled streets, you can find everything from traditional music in grand old pubs to the latest dance tracks in a post-industrial setting. The many pubs and venues around this area make the city centre south of the Liffey the place to be at night. The north side does, however, boast the two most illustrious theatres, the largest cinemas and the impressive 3Arena, a converted 19th-century rail terminal beside the docks. It is now the venue for all major rock concerts and stage musicals, as well as a number of classical music performances.

The outside of the Gate Theatre, located on the north side of Dublin

Entertainment Listings

Listings for clubs, cinemas, theatre and other entertainment can be found in most newspapers, such as the *Irish Times* and the *Irish Independent*, particularly on weekends. *Hot Press*, a national bimonthly newspaper covering both rock and traditional music, has comprehensive listings for Dublin. *The Herald* is also a sound source of information for the latest concerts, movies and gigs. For bar and restaurant reviews, try the *The Ticket*, a free supplement that comes with Friday's Irish Times. Look out for *Totally Dublin*, a free listings magazine found in most pubs and cafés.

Booking Tickets

Tickets for many events are available on the night, but it is usually safer to book in advance. All the major venues take credit card payment over the telephone. **Ticketmaster** accepts phone bookings by credit card only for many of the major shows and events in and around Dublin, while **Dublin Tourism** (Suffolk Street) sell tickets for most of the top theatres and major rock gigs.

Theatre

Ireland's national theatre, the **Abbey** *(see p92)*, is the city's most popular venue, concentrating on major new productions as well as revivals of works by Irish playwrights such as Brendan Behan, Sean O'Casey, J M Synge and W B Yeats. The smaller Peacock Theatre downstairs features experimental works. Also on the north side, the **Gate Theatre** *(see p94)* is noted for its interpretations of well-known international plays, and the **Bord Gáis Energy Theatre** hosts West End musicals, ballet, opera and theatre productions. The **Samuel Beckett Theatre** is renowned for its sparse yet powerful productions. The main venue south of the Liffey, the **Gaiety Theatre**, stages a mainstream mix of plays, often by Irish playwrights. Some of the best fringe theatre and modern dance in Dublin can be seen at the **Project Arts Centre** in Temple Bar. **Smock Alley Theatre** hosts guest productions by experimental theatre groups, as well as student productions. **Bewley's Café Theatre** offers intimate lunchtime drama. The **Olympia Theatre** specializes in comedy and popular drama, and occasionally stages rock and Irish music concerts. Most theatres are closed on Sunday.

Every October, the **Dublin Theatre Festival** takes over all the city venues with mainstream, fringe and international plays.

Record shop and ticket office in Crown Alley, Temple Bar

Façade of the Hugh Lane Gallery

Cinema

The city's cinemas had a boost in the 1990s with the success of Dublin-based films such as *My Left Foot* (1989). Huge growth in the country's movie production industry followed, and hits like *Intermission* (2004), *The Guard* (2011) and *Calvary* (2014) keep Ireland in the spotlight.

The **Irish Film Institute** showcases mostly foreign and independent films, along with a programme of lectures. It boasts two screens, as well as a bar and restaurant. **Screen**, close to Trinity College, and **The Lighthouse Cinema** in Smithfield have a repertoire of art-house films.

The large first-run cinemas are all located on the north side. They usually offer tickets at reduced prices for afternoon screenings, and show late-night films on the weekend. The summer-long **Temple Bar Cultural Events** include open-air screenings, mainly in Meeting House Square.

Classical Music, Opera and Dance

The **National Concert Hall** is served well by its resident orchestra, the RTÉ National Symphony Orchestra, which gives weekly performances. There are also impressive visiting international orchestras, such as the Berlin Philharmonic Orchestra. The popular venue caters for a wide range of musical tastes, with performances covering opera, jazz, dance, musicals, Irish folk and popular music among others.

The **Hugh Lane Gallery** *(see p95)*, which boasts an exceptional collection of paintings including works by Renas, Renoir and Monet, has regular and free Sunday lunchtime concerts. Other venues include the Irish Museum of Modern Art at the **Royal Hospital Kilmainham** *(see p101)*, which houses over 3,500 artworks by Irish and inter-national artists, such as the **Royal Dublin Society (RDS)**. International opera is staged in the **3Arena**. Opera Ireland performs every April and November at the Gaiety Theatre. The programme at the **Bord Gáis Energy Theatre** on the city's south side includes opera and ballet productions.

Rock, Jazz, Blues and Country

Dublin has had a thriving rock scene ever since local band Thin Lizzy made it big in the early 1970s. U2's success acted as a further catalyst for local bands, and each night there's usually an interesting gig somewhere in the city. **Whelan's** is probably the most popular live venue. Since 1989, many famous names have performed on its stage. Temple Bar venue, **The Mezz**, hosts live reggae, funk and rock music most nights of the week. Set on two floors, this place is always packed with students and tourists. Get there early if you want to find a good seat by the stage.

The Workman's Club is another of Dublin's live music venues, with several bars and stages spread across two floors. DJs keep the tunes pumping late into the night, with indie, hillbilly, rock and ska sounds.

The upstairs room at the likeable **International Bar** plays host to an acoustic session on Wednesday nights where singer/songwriters come to test themselves in public. There is also a Sunday afternoon traditional Irish music session that takes place between 1pm and 4pm. The **Ha'penny Bridge Inn** has folk and blues on Friday and Saturday nights.

Big names play at either the 3Arena or, in summer, at the local sports stadia. The **Olympia**, a Victorian theatre, hosts memorable concerts in extraordinary surroundings. Outside Dublin, Slane Castle hosts a big rock event most summers *(see p249)*.

Button Factory and **The Sugar Club** offer jazz, salsa, Latin and blues all year, and **The Academy** has live bands and DJs over four floors. Country music is popular in Ireland, and plays at several Dublin pubs. Check entertainment listings for details.

Live rock band performing at the Sugar Club

Traditional Music and Dance

To many Irish people, the standard of music in a pub is just as important as the quality of the Guinness. Central Dublin has a host of pubs reverberating to the sound of *bodhráns*, fiddles and uilleann pipes. One of the most famous is **O'Donoghue's**, where the legendary Dubliners started out in the early 1960s. The **Cobblestone** and the **Auld Dubliner** are also renowned venues. **Legends** at the Arlington Hotel combines Irish cuisine with nightly dance shows. **Johnnie Fox's**, in the Dublin mountains, is about 35 minutes by car from the city centre and has live music nightly.

Pubs and Bars

Dublin's pubs are a slice of living history. These are the places where some of the best-known scenes in Irish literature have been set, where rebellious politicians have met, and where world-famous music acts have made their debuts. Today, it's the singing, dancing, talk and laughter that make a pub tour of Dublin an absolute must.

There are nearly 1,000 pubs inside the city limits. Among the best of the traditional bars are **Neary's**, popular with actors and featuring a gorgeous marble bar, the atmospheric **Long Hall**, and the friendly and chic **Stag's Head** dating from 1770.

Cosy snugs, where drinkers could lock themselves away for private conversation, were an important feature of 19th-century bars. A few remain, notably at the tiny, journalists' haunt of **Doheny & Nesbitt** and intimate **Kehoe's**.

The **Brazen Head** claims to be the city's oldest pub, dating back to 1198. The present pub, built in the 1750s, is lined with old photographs and dark wood panelling, and showcases traditional music sessions nightly. Every pub prides itself on the quality of its Guinness, though most locals acknowledge that **Mulligan's**, founded in 1782, serves the best pint in the city. **The Bull and Castle** serves a great variety of craft beers and is also known for good food.

The Grave Diggers is situated on the northern outskirts of the city in Phibsborough. Located next to a graveyard, this bar has more character than most, and it's worth the taxi ride just to see what a Dublin bar would have looked like hundreds of years ago. On summer weekends, the green outside fills with drinkers enjoying pints and chatting.

Grogan's bar, on South William Street, is frequented by many of Dublin's bohemian characters. Part bar, part art gallery, it exhibits an array of paintings by local artists.

Café en Seine is influenced by a *belle époque* Parisian bar. Its interior is huge and cavernous, and the decor rich and alluring.

A Guinness advertisement at a Dublin pub

At weekends, this bar heaves with Dublin's single thirty-somethings. Situated next door is **37 Dawson St**, a newly opened bar and eatery that is already a hit with the hipsters. Pull up a seat at their whiskey bar and enjoy a snifter of *usice beatha*.

Grand Central is one of the very few bars on the city's main thoroughfare, O'Connell Street. It's housed in a former bank, and many of the original features have been retained.

Dakota is a large and lively tapas and wine bar that draws a trendy young crowd. **Cassidy's** on Westmoreland Street is one of the city's most popular hipster hangouts, with graffitied walls and a dazzling array of Irish and international craft beers sold on tap and by the bottle.

Dice Bar is a pseudo-dive bar with a dark interior of clashing blacks and reds. The music policy is a combination of rare rock 'n' roll and blues records.

Urban and cosmopolitan, **The Globe** is as popular during the day for coffee as it is at night. The crowd is a cool mix of musicians and city hipsters. Not unlike the Globe, but with a modern twist, **4 Dame Lane** is a slickly designed bar. At night it fills with a young crowd that loves the eclectic music. Two flaming torches mark the entrance.

Part of the sleek Morgan Hotel in Temple Bar, the beautifully designed **Morgan Bar** prides itself on serving outstanding cocktails. **The Market Bar** is one of the city's favourite gastro-pubs. Set in an old factory, it has high ceilings and red-brick walls that lend this place a certain retro-industrial charm. Superb food is served throughout the day.

Small, comfy **Peter's Pub** has a reputation for quality pints and is considered by many to be the quintessential Dublin boozer.

French-style interior of the Café en Seine

Traditional façade of Doheny & Nesbitt

A Literary Pub Crawl

Pubs with strong literary associations abound in Dublin, particularly around Grafton Street. **McDaid's**, an old pub with an Art Deco interior, still retains some of its bohemian air from the time when writers such as Patrick Kavanagh and Brendan Behan were regulars.

Davy Byrne's has a plusher decor than it did when Leopold Bloom dropped in for a gorgonzola and mustard sandwich in *Ulysses*, but it is still well worth paying a visit. These pubs, and others frequented by Ireland's most famous authors and playwrights, are featured on the excellent **Dublin Literary Pub Crawl**. The two-and-a-half-hour tours, which are led by actors, start with a beer in **The Duke**, and are by far the most entertaining way to get a real feel for the city's booze-fuelled literary heritage. Tours take place daily in summer, but are usually held only at weekends in winter.

Nightclubs

Dublin's clubs are continually revamping and relaunching, and variety remains the key in clubland, with plenty of massive superclubs and more intimate, laid-back venues. The scene is somewhat curtailed, however, by the city's licensing laws. A nightclub licence allows a club to remain open until 2:30am – early by many major cities' standards. So Dublin clubbers start their night early, often beginning at a pub. Describing itself as a "drinking pub with a music problem", **Sweeney's** on Dame Street heaves every Thursday to Saturday night with a mass of bodies moving to an eclectic mix of hip-hop, rockabilly, soul, funk and house, across three floors. Tucked away in the basement of the super-stylish Powerscourt Centre, **Pygmalion** is a café-bar by day and a pumping club by night, particularly popular with the city's young hipster folk. The tiny dance floor heats up when international DJs come to visit.

Copper Face Jacks is the most profitable nightclub of its size in Europe, notorious for its sweaty dance floors, pop music and groups of single men and women looking for a good time. If the queues are too long you'll find several similar venues nearby, mostly located along Harcourt Street.

Formerly Spirit, **The Academy** is a vibrant music mecca with weekly gigs. It plays music on four floors and is attempting to rival Whelans as a live music centre with a predilection for rock and pop acts as well as a range of DJs from all over the world.

Those looking for good dance music might prefer **Mother**, a popular gay club, which opened in 2010. Its known for hosting the best parties in the city, however the club is open only on Saturday nights.

Krystle, on Harcourt Street, running down St Stephen's Green, is the coolest nightclub in town. The large gastro pub and club sits on the north side of the River Liffey and its links with Irish rugby players and glamorous models have made it the place to be seen.

Occupying two Georgian town houses on nearby Leeson Street, **House** caters for a similar clientele, but in more relaxed surroundings. Lounge in front of a log fire in the front parlour, among the olive and citrus trees in the garden, or dance the night away in the opulent Red Room, which is open late on Friday and Saturday.

Ri-Ra, Irish for uproar, is one of Dublin's longest running nightclubs and has a different theme every night, from hip-hop and house to funk, soul and reggae.

Touted as Dublin's most presti-gious night club, **Lillie's Bordello** has a luxurious, decadent atmosphere. The legendary VIP room has long been a favourite of Dublin's rich and famous, and regulars often rub shoulders with the entertainment elite.

Howl at the Moon is a smart club close to Merrion Square. It is spread across three floors and has outdoor areas, including a heated, covered smoking area. The door policy is smart-casual and over 23. Entry on Thursday and Friday nights is free and there are usually special promotions available on drinks prices.

At **The Grand Social**, on the north side of the Liffey, in-house and guest DJs spin funky disco, indie, classic rock and electro at the weekends. There's also a popular jazz club every Monday night.

The George is Dublin's premier gay venue, with club nights, karaoke and nightly drinks specials. Don't miss the infamous transvestite bingo night on Sundays.

The Front Lounge has a more relaxed, gay-friendly vibe, with comfy chairs and great food. It is liveliest on Tuesday nights, when there is karaoke from 10pm.

DIRECTORY

Booking Agents

Dublin Tourism
Tourism Centre, Suffolk St. **Map** D3
Tel 01 605 7700.
W visitdublin.ie

Ticketmaster
Tel 0818 719300.
W ticketmaster.ie

Theatre

Abbey Theatre
Abbey St Lower.
Map E2.
Tel 01 878 7222.
W abbeytheatre.ie

Bewley's Café Theatre
Bewley's Café, 78 Grafton St.
Map D4.
Tel 01 679 5720.
W bewleyscafe theatre.com

Bord Gáis Energy Theatre
Grand Canal Square, Docklands.
Tel 01 677 7999.
W bordgaisenergy theatre.ie

Dublin Theatre Festival
44 Essex St East.
Map C3.
Tel 01 677 8439.
W dublintheatre festival.com

Gaiety Theatre
King St South.
Map D4.
Tel 0818 719 388.
W gaietytheatre.com

Gate Theatre
Cavendish Row, Parnell Sq.
Map D1.
Tel 01 874 4045.
W gate-theatre.ie

Olympia Theatre
Dame St.
Map C3.
Tel 01 679 3323.
W olympia.ie

Project Arts Centre
39 East Essex St.
Map C3.
Tel 01 881 9613.
W projectartscentre.ie

Samuel Beckett Theatre
Trinity College.
Map E3.
Tel 01 896 1334.
W tcd.ie

Smock Alley Theatre
6/7 Exchange St Lower, Temple Bar.
Map C3.
Tel 01 677 0014.
W smockalley.com

Cinema

Cineworld Cinemas
Parnell St.
Map C2.
Tel 1520 880 444.
W cineworld.ie

Irish Film Institute
6 Eustace St, Temple Bar.
Map C3.
Tel 01 679 5744.
W ifi.ie

The Lighthouse Cinema
Market Square, Smithfield.
Map B2.
Tel 01 872 8006.
W lighthousecinema.ie

Screen
D'Olier St. **Map** D3.
Tel 01 671 4034.
W screencinema.ie

Temple Bar Cultural Events
W templebar.ie

Classical Music, Opera and Dance

3Arena
East Link Bridge, North Wall Quay.
Map D1.
Tel 01 819 8888.
W 3arena.ie

Bord Gáis Energy Theatre
See Theatre section.

Hugh Lane Gallery
Charlemont House, Parnell Sq North.
Map C1.
Tel 01 222 5550.
W hughlane.ie

National Concert Hall
Earlsfort Terrace.
Map D5.
Tel 01 417 0000.
W nch.ie

Royal Dublin Society (RDS)
Ballsbridge.
Tel 01 668 0866.
W rds.ie

Royal Hospital Kilmainham
Military Lane, Kilmainham, Dublin 18.
Tel 01 612 9900.
W rhk.ie

Rock, Jazz, Blues and Country

The Academy
57 Abbey St.
Map C2.
Tel 01 877 9999.
W theacademy dublin.com

Button Factory
Curved St, Temple Bar.
Map E4.
Tel 01 670 9202.
W buttonfactory.ie

Ha'penny Bridge Inn
42 Wellington Quay.
Map C3.
Tel 01 677 0616.

International Bar
23 Wicklow St.
Map D3.
Tel 01 677 9250.
W international-bar.com

The Mezz
Eustace St, Temple Bar, Dublin 2.
Map C3.
Tel 01 670 7655.
W mezz.ie

Slane Castle
Slane, Co Meath.
Tel 041 982 0643.
W slanecastle.ie

The Sugar Club
8 Lower Leeson St.
Map E5.
Tel 01 678 7188.
W thesugarclub.com

Whelan's
25 Wexford St.
Map E4 C5.
Tel 01 478 0766.
W whelanslive.com

The Workman's Club
10 Wellington Quay, Dublin 2.
Map C3.
Tel 01 670 6692.
W theworkmans club.com

Traditional Music and Dance

Auld Dubliner
Auld Dubliner, 24–25 Temple Bar.
Map D3.
Tel 01 677 0527.
W thesmithgroup.ie

Cobblestone
77 King St North.
Map A2.
Tel 01 872 1799.
W cobblestonepub.ie

Johnnie Fox's
Glencullen, Co Dublin.
Tel 01 295 5647.
W jfp.ie

Legends
Arlington Hotel, Temple Bar, 16–18 Lord Edward St.
Map C3.
Tel 01 670 8777.
W arlingtonhotel templebar.com

O'Donoghue's
15 Merrion Row.
Map E5.
Tel 01 660 7194.
W odonoghues.ie

The Temple Bar
48 Temple Bar, Dublin 2.
Map C3.
Tel 01 672 5287.
W thetemplebar pub.com

DIRECTORY

Pubs and Bars

4 Dame Lane
4 Dame Lane, Dublin 2.
Map C3.
Tel 01 679 0291.
W 4damelane.ie

37 Dawson St
37 Dawson St.
Map D4.
Tel 01 902 2908.
W 37dawsonstreet.ie

Brazen Head
20 Bridge St Lower.
Map A3.
Tel 01 677 9549.
W brazenhead.com

The Bull and Castle
5–7 Lord Edward St.
Map C3.
Tel 01 475 1122.
W bull-and-castle.fxbuckley.ie

Café en Seine
40 Dawson St, Dublin 2.
Map D4.
Tel 01 677 4567.
W cafeenseine.ie

Cassidy's
27 Westmoreland St.
Map D3.
Tel 670 8604.

Dakota
9 S William St, Dublin 2.
Map D4.
Tel 01 672 7696.
W dakotabar.ie

Davy Byrne's
21 Duke St.
Map D4.
Tel 01 677 5217.
W davybyrnes.com

Dice Bar
79 Queen St, Dublin 7.
Map A2.
Tel 01 633 3936.
W thatsitdublin.com

Doheny & Nesbitt
5 Lower Baggot St.
Map E5.
Tel 01 676 2945.
W dohenyandnesbitts.ie

Dublin Literary Pub Crawl
9 Duke St.
Map D3.
Tel 01 670 5602.
W dublinpubcrawl.com

The Duke
9 Duke St.
Map D4.
Tel 01 679 9553.
W thedukedublin.com

The Globe
11 S Great George's St, Dublin 2.
Map C4.
Tel 01 671 1220.
W theglobe.ie

Grand Central
10–11 O'Connell St, Dublin 1.
Map D2.
Tel 01 872 8658.
W grandcentral.ie

The Grave Diggers
Prospect Sq, Glasnevin.
Map D1.
Tel 01 830 7978.

Grogan's
15 S William St, Dublin 2.
Map D4.
Tel 01 677 9320.
W groganspub.ie

Kehoe's
9 S Anne St.
Map D4.
Tel 01 677 8312
W louisfitzgerald.com/kehoes.

Long Hall
51 S Great George's St.
Map C4.
Tel 01 475 1590.

The Market Bar
14a Fade St, Dublin 2.
Map D4.
Tel 01 613 9094.
W marketbar.ie

McDaid's
3 Harry St.
Map D4.
Tel 01 679 4395.

Morgan Bar
The Morgan Hotel, 10 Fleet St, Dublin 2.
Map D3.
Tel 01 643 7000.
W themorgan.com

Mulligan's
8 Poolbeg St.
Map E3.
Tel 01 677 5582.
W mulligans.ie

Neary's
1 Chatham St.
Map D4.
Tel 01 677 8596.

Peter's Pub
1 Johnson's Place, Dublin 2.
Map D4.
Tel 01 679 3347.
W peterspub.ie

Stag's Head
1 Dame Court, off Dame Lane.
Map D3.
Tel 01 679 3687.
W stagshead.ie

Nightclubs

The Academy
57 Abbey St, Dublin 1.
Map C2.
Tel 01 877 9999.

Copper Face Jacks
29–30 Harcourt St.
Map D5.
Tel 01 475 8777.
W copperfacejacks.ie

The Front Lounge
33–34 Parliament St.
Map C3.
Tel 01 670 4112.
W thefrontlounge.ie

The George
89 Sth Great George's St.
Map C4.
Tel 01 478 2983.
W thegeorge.ie

The Grand Social
35 Lower Liffey St, Dublin 1.
Map D3.
Tel 01 873 4332.
W thegrandsocial.ie

House
27 Lower Leeson St.
Map E5.
Tel 01 905 9090.
W housedublin.ie

Howl at the Moon
7 Lower Mount St.
Map F4.
Tel 01 634 5460.
W howlatthemoon.ie

Krystle
Harcourt St, Dublin 2.
Map D5.
Tel 087 674 5393.
W krystlenightclub.com

Lillie's Bordello
Adam Court, off Grafton St. **Map** E4–D4.
Tel 01 679 9204.
W lilliesbordello.ie

Mother
Copper Alley, Exchange St, Temple Bar, Dublin 2.
Map C3. **Tel** 01 675 5025.
W motherclub.ie

Pygmalion
South William St.
Map D5. **Tel** 01 633 4479.
W pyg.ie

Ri-Ra
South Great George's St, Dublin 2. **Map** E3.
Tel 01 671 1220.
W riraclub.ie

Sweeneys
32 Dame St. **Map** E3.
Tel 01 635 0056.
W sweeneysdublin.ie

Dublin's Best: Entertainment

It's easy to pack a lot into a night out in Dublin. Most of the best nightspots are situated close to each other and, in the Temple Bar area alone, there are plenty of exciting haunts to try out. The city offers something to suit every taste and pocket: choose from world-class theatre, excellent concert venues, designer café-bars and lively or laid-back clubs hosting nights of traditional, country, jazz or rock music. Even when there is no specific event that appeals, you can simply enjoy Dublin's inexhaustible supply of great traditional pubs.

Gate Theatre
The Gate puts on both foreign plays and Irish classics such as Sea O'Casey's *Juno and the Paycock* *(see p94)*.

Stag's Head
This gorgeous Victorian pub has a long, mahogany bar and has retained its original mirrors and stained glass. Located down an out-of-the-way alley, this atmospheric pub is well worth seeking out *(see p114)*.

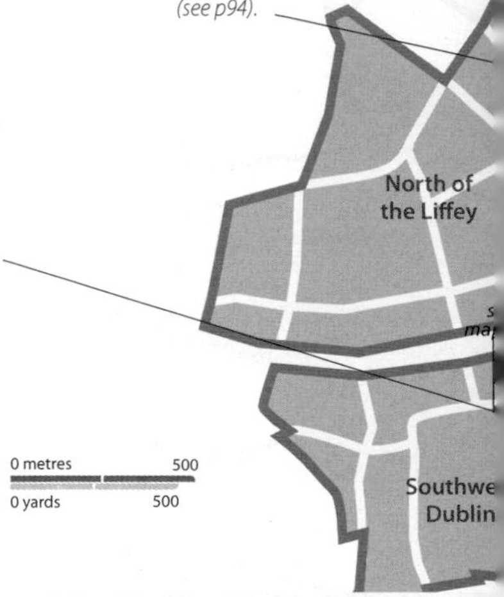

The Temple Bar Area

It will take more than a couple of evenings to explore fully all that these narrow streets have to offer. Many of Dublin's best mid-priced restaurants are here, while modern bars sit next to traditional pubs hosting fiddle sessions. There are also theatres and the Irish Film Institute. Later, clubs play music ranging from country to the latest dance sounds.

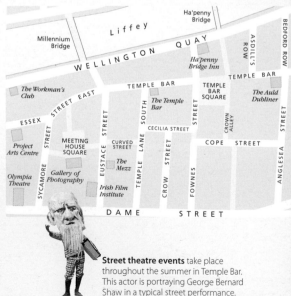

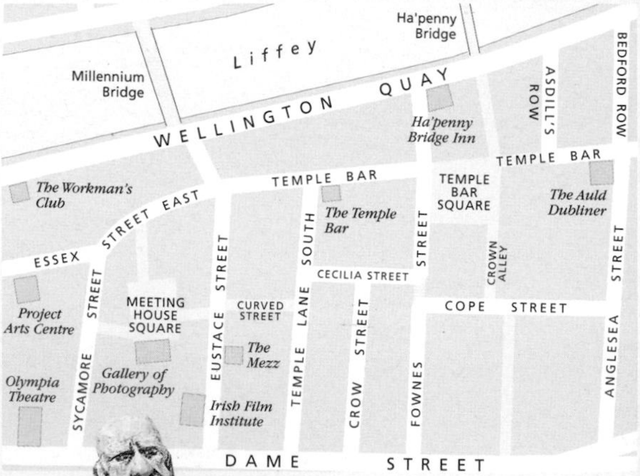

Street theatre events take place throughout the summer in Temple Bar. This actor is portraying George Bernard Shaw in a typical street performance.

Abbey Theatre
Despite recurring financial problems, Ireland's prestigious national theatre still manages to stage compelling drama, such as *An Ideal Husband* by Oscar Wilde *(see p92)*.

The 3Arena
Built in 1878 as a goods depot for the Great Southern and Western Railway Company, the 3Arena (formerly known as the O2 or Point Depot) is Ireland's top music venue. It offers perfect sightlines and crystal-clear acoustics that make every performance here special *(see p113)*.

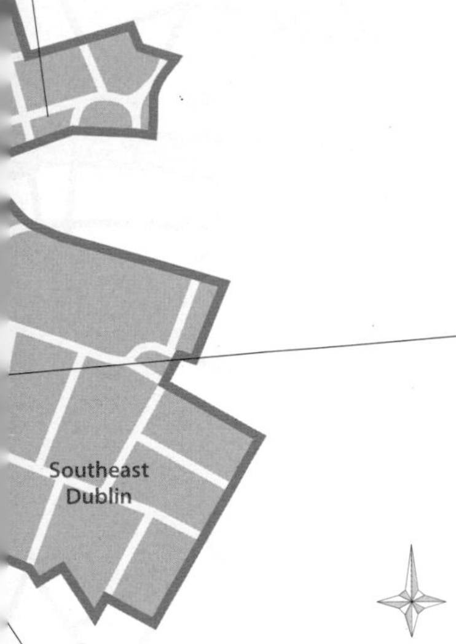

McDaid's
Playwright Brendan Behan *(see p26)* downed many a pint in this pub, which dates from 1779. Though firmly on the tourist trail, McDaid's retains its bohemian charm, and bars upstairs and downstairs provide space for a leisurely drink *(see p117)*.

National Concert Hall
As Ireland's premier music venue, the National Concert Hall boasts a thrilling line up of national and international musicians in a broad range of events from traditional to opera, classical to jazz and weekly concerts by resident RTE National Symphony Orchestra *(see p113)*.

Street Finder Index

Key to the Street Finder

- Major sight
- Place of interest
- Railway station
- Bus station
- DART station
- Luas stop
- Tourist information office
- Hospital with casualty unit
- Police station
- Church
- Railway line
- Pedestrian street

Scale of Map Pages

0 metres 200
0 yards 200
1:11,500

Key to Street Finder Abbreviations

Ave	Avenue	**E**	East	**Pde**	Parade	**Sth**	South
Br	Bridge	**La**	Lane	**Pl**	Place	**Tce**	Terrace
Cl	Close	**Lr**	Lower	**Rd**	Road	**Up**	Upper
Ct	Court	**Nth**	North	**St**	Street/Saint	**W**	West

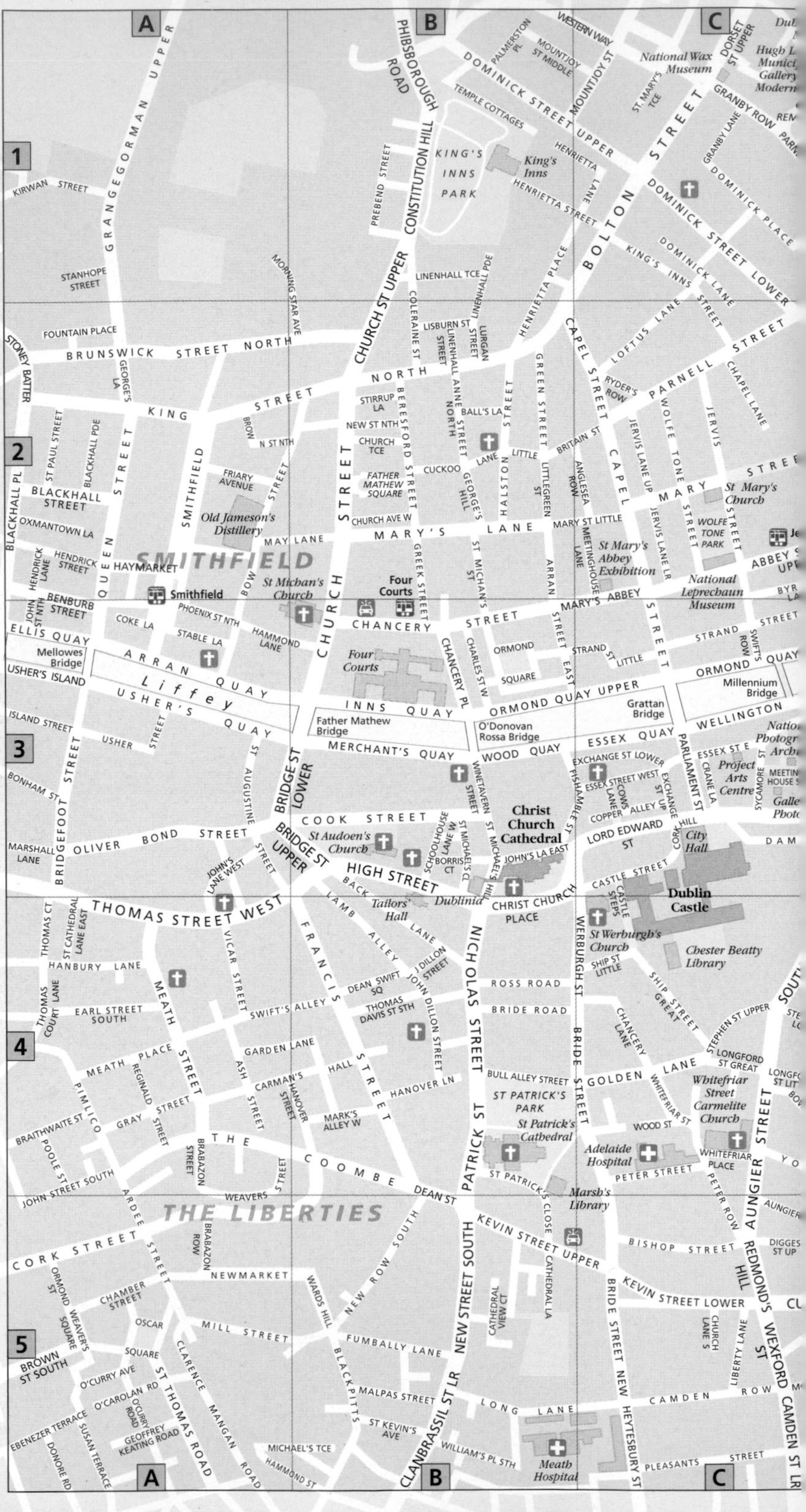
A
B
C
1
2
3
4
5
SMITHFIELD
THE LIBERTIES
Liffey
GRANGEGORMAN UPPER
KIRWAN STREET
STANHOPE STREET
FOUNTAIN PLACE
STONEY BATTER
BRUNSWICK STREET NORTH
GEORGE'S LA
KING STREET NORTH
PHIBSBOROUGH ROAD
CONSTITUTION HILL
PREBEND STREET
CHURCH ST UPPER
MORNING STAR AVE
COLERAINE ST
LINENHALL TCE
LINENHALL PDE
LISBURN ST
LINENHALL ST
LURGAN STREET
KING'S INNS PARK
King's Inns
TEMPLE COTTAGES
DOMINICK STREET UPPER
PALMERSTON PL
MOUNTJOY ST MIDDLE
WESTERN WAY
MOUNTJOY ST
HENRIETTA LANE
HENRIETTA STREET
HENRIETTA PLACE
BOLTON STREET
National Wax Museum
ST. MARY'S TCE
DORSET ST UPPER
GRANBY ROW
GRANBY LANE
DOMINICK PLACE
DOMINICK STREET LOWER
KING'S INNS STREET
DOMINICK LANE
LOFTUS LANE
PARNELL STREET
CHAPEL LANE
CAPEL STREET
RYDER'S ROW
Hugh Lane Municipal Gallery of Modern Art
BLACKHALL PL
ST PAUL STREET
BLACKHALL PDE
QUEEN STREET
BLACKHALL STREET
OXMANTOWN LA
HENDRICK LANE
HENDRICK STREET
HAYMARKET
JOHN ST NTH
BENBURB STREET
SMITHFIELD
FRIARY AVENUE
Old Jameson's Distillery
BOW STREET
BOW LANE
BROW
N ST NTH
MAY LANE
Smithfield
St Michan's Church
CHURCH STREET
STIRRUP LA
NEW ST NTH
CHURCH TCE
FATHER MATHEW SQUARE
CHURCH AVE W
BERESFORD STREET
GREEK STREET
Four Courts
ANNE STREET NORTH
BALL'S LA
CUCKOO LANE
GEORGE'S HILL
HALSTON STREET
LITTLE GREEN ST
GREEN STREET
BRITAIN ST
ANGLESEA ROW
MARY'S LANE
ST MICHAN'S ST
MARY ST LITTLE
ARRAN STREET EAST
MEETINGHOUSE LANE
St Mary's Abbey Exhibition
JERVIS LANE UP
JERVIS LANE LR
WOLFE TONE STREET
WOLFE TONE PARK
JERVIS
MARY STREET
St Mary's Church
ABBEY ST UPPER
National Leprechaun Museum
MARY'S ABBEY
PHOENIX ST NTH
COKE LA
STABLE LA
HAMMOND LANE
CHANCERY STREET
ELLIS QUAY
Mellowes Bridge
USHER'S ISLAND
ARRAN QUAY
USHER'S QUAY
INNS QUAY
Four Courts
CHANCERY PL
CHARLES ST W
ORMOND SQUARE
STRAND ST LITTLE
STRAND STREET
SWIFT'S ROW
ORMOND QUAY
ORMOND QUAY UPPER
Millennium Bridge
Grattan Bridge
O'Donovan Rossa Bridge
Father Mathew Bridge
WELLINGTON QUAY
ISLAND STREET
USHER STREET
ST AUGUSTINE STREET
BRIDGE ST LOWER
MERCHANT'S QUAY
WOOD QUAY
ESSEX QUAY
WINETAVERN STREET
National Photographic Archive
EXCHANGE ST LOWER
ESSEX ST E
FISHAMBLE ST
ESSEX STREET WEST
COWS LANE
EXCHANGE ST UP
PARLIAMENT ST
CRANE LA
Project Arts Centre
SYCAMORE ST
MEETING HOUSE SQ
Gallery of Photography
BONHAM ST
BRIDGEFOOT STREET
COOK STREET
COPPER ALLEY
Christ Church Cathedral
CORK HILL
LORD EDWARD ST
City Hall
DAME
MARSHALL LANE
OLIVER BOND STREET
St Audoen's Church
SCHOOLHOUSE LANE W
ST MICHAEL'S CL
ST MICHAEL'S HILL
JOHN'S LA EAST
JOHN'S LANE WEST
BRIDGE ST UPPER
BORRIS CT
HIGH STREET
CASTLE STREET
Dublin Castle
BACK LANE
Tailors' Hall
Dublinia
CHRIST CHURCH PLACE
CASTLE STEPS
THOMAS STREET WEST
THOMAS CT
ST CATHEDRAL LANE EAST
HANBURY LANE
THOMAS COURT LANE
EARL STREET SOUTH
MEATH STREET
VICAR STREET
FRANCIS STREET
LAMB ALLEY
J DILLON STREET
DEAN SWIFT SQ
SWIFT'S ALLEY
THOMAS DAVIS ST STH
JOHN DILLON STREET
NICHOLAS STREET
ROSS ROAD
BRIDE ROAD
WERBURGH ST
St Werburgh's Church
SHIP ST LITTLE
Chester Beatty Library
SHIP STREET GREAT
CHANCERY LANE
STEPHEN ST UPPER
MEATH PLACE
REGINALD STREET
GARDEN LANE
ASH STREET
CARMAN'S HALL
HANOVER STREET
HANOVER LN
BULL ALLEY STREET
ST PATRICK'S PARK
GOLDEN LANE
BRIDE STREET
WHITEFRIAR ST
LONGFORD ST GREAT
LONGFORD ST LITTLE
Whitefriar Street Carmelite Church
PIMLICO
BRAITHWAITE ST
GRAY STREET
MARK'S ALLEY W
St Patrick's Cathedral
WOOD ST
Adelaide Hospital
WHITEFRIAR PLACE
AUNGIER STREET
POOLE ST
BRABAZON STREET
THE COOMBE
DEAN ST
PATRICK ST
ST PATRICK'S CLOSE
Marsh's Library
PETER STREET
PETER ROW
AUNGIER
JOHN STREET SOUTH
WEAVERS STREET
ARDEE STREET
BRABAZON ROW
NEW ROW SOUTH
NEW STREET SOUTH
KEVIN STREET UPPER
BISHOP STREET
DIGGES ST UP
REDMOND'S HILL
CORK STREET
ORMOND ST
NEWMARKET
WARDS HILL
CATHEDRAL VIEW CT
CATHEDRAL LA
KEVIN STREET LOWER
CHAMBER STREET
WEAVER'S SQUARE
OSCAR SQUARE
MILL STREET
FUMBALLY LANE
BLACKPITTS
BRIDE STREET NEW
CHURCH LANE S
LIBERTY LANE
WEXFORD ST
BROWN ST SOUTH
O'CURRY AVE
O'CAROLAN RD
O'CURRY ROAD
CLARENCE MANGAN ROAD
ST THOMAS ROAD
MALPAS STREET
LONG LANE
CAMDEN ROW
CLANBRASSIL ST LR
HEYTESBURY ST
CAMDEN ST LR
EBENEZER TERRACE
SUSAN TERRACE
GEOFFREY KEATING ROAD
DONORE RD
MICHAEL'S TCE
HAMMOND ST
ST KEVIN'S AVE
WILLIAM'S PL STH
Meath Hospital
PLEASANTS STREET

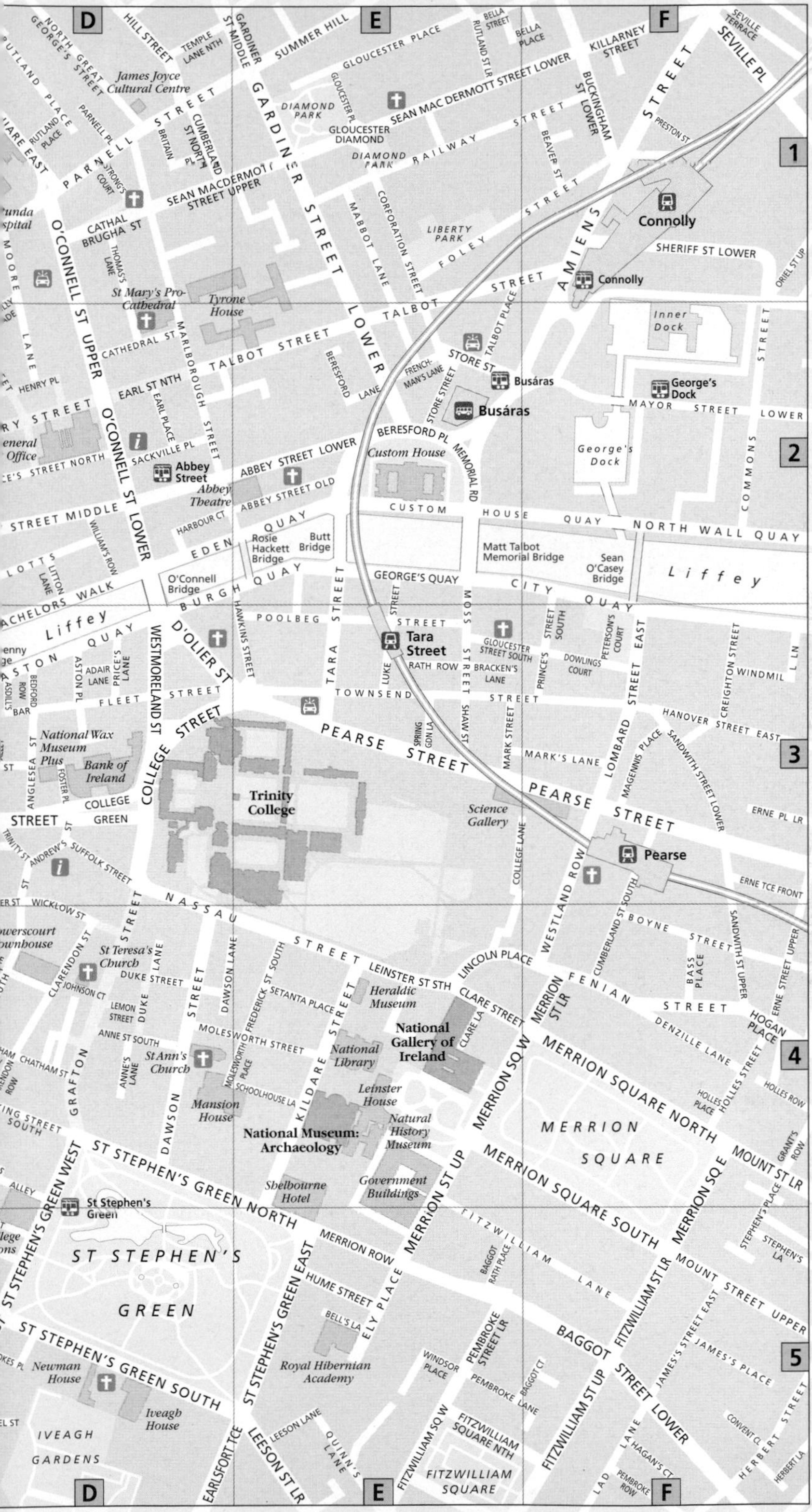
D
E
F
1
2
3
4
5
Connolly
Busáras
George's Dock
Abbey Street
Tara Street
Pearse
St Stephen's Green
James Joyce Cultural Centre
St Mary's Pro-Cathedral
Tyrone House
Custom House
Abbey Theatre
Inner Dock
George's Dock
Liffey
Rosie Hackett Bridge
Butt Bridge
O'Connell Bridge
Matt Talbot Memorial Bridge
Sean O'Casey Bridge
National Wax Museum Plus
Bank of Ireland
Trinity College
Science Gallery
Powerscourt Townhouse
St Teresa's Church
Heraldic Museum
National Gallery of Ireland
National Library
St Ann's Church
Mansion House
Leinster House
Natural History Museum
National Museum: Archaeology
Shelbourne Hotel
Government Buildings
MERRION SQUARE
ST STEPHEN'S GREEN
Newman House
Iveagh House
IVEAGH GARDENS
Royal Hibernian Academy
FITZWILLIAM SQUARE
DIAMOND PARK
LIBERTY PARK
GLOUCESTER DIAMOND
HILL STREET
SUMMER HILL
GARDINER ST MIDDLE
GARDINER STREET LOWER
GLOUCESTER PLACE
SEAN MAC DERMOTT STREET LOWER
SEAN MACDERMOTT STREET UPPER
KILLARNEY STREET
SEVILLE PL
SEVILLE TERRACE
BUCKINGHAM ST LOWER
RAILWAY STREET
FOLEY STREET
AMIENS STREET
SHERIFF ST LOWER
ORIEL ST UP
PARNELL STREET
O'CONNELL ST UPPER
O'CONNELL ST LOWER
CATHAL BRUGHA ST
MARLBOROUGH STREET
CATHEDRAL ST
TALBOT STREET
EARL ST NTH
HENRY PL
HENRY STREET
SACKVILLE PL
ABBEY STREET LOWER
ABBEY STREET OLD
ABBEY STREET MIDDLE
BERESFORD PL
MEMORIAL RD
STORE ST
MAYOR STREET LOWER
COMMONS STREET
CUSTOM HOUSE QUAY
NORTH WALL QUAY
EDEN QUAY
BURGH QUAY
GEORGE'S QUAY
CITY QUAY
BACHELORS WALK
ASTON QUAY
D'OLIER ST
WESTMORELAND ST
HAWKINS STREET
POOLBEG STREET
TARA STREET
TOWNSEND STREET
PEARSE STREET
FLEET STREET
COLLEGE STREET
COLLEGE GREEN
LOMBARD STREET EAST
HANOVER STREET EAST
WINDMILL LN
ERNE PL LR
ERNE TCE FRONT
WESTLAND ROW
NASSAU STREET
SUFFOLK STREET
GRAFTON STREET
DAWSON STREET
DUKE STREET
MOLESWORTH STREET
KILDARE STREET
LEINSTER ST STH
CLARE STREET
LINCOLN PLACE
MERRION SQ W
MERRION SQUARE NORTH
MERRION SQUARE SOUTH
MERRION SQ E
FENIAN STREET
BOYNE STREET
HOLLES STREET
MOUNT ST LR
MOUNT STREET UPPER
ST STEPHEN'S GREEN NORTH
ST STEPHEN'S GREEN EAST
ST STEPHEN'S GREEN SOUTH
ST STEPHEN'S GREEN WEST
MERRION ROW
MERRION ST UP
HUME STREET
ELY PLACE
FITZWILLIAM LANE
BAGGOT STREET LOWER
FITZWILLIAM ST LR
FITZWILLIAM ST UP
PEMBROKE STREET LR
JAMES'S PLACE
HERBERT STREET
EARLSFORT TCE
LEESON ST LR
LEESON LANE
FITZWILLIAM SQ W

IRELAND REGION BY REGION

Ireland at a Glance

The lure of Ireland's much-vaunted Atlantic shores, from the wild coastline of Cork and Kerry to the remote peninsulas of the Northwest, is strong. However, to neglect the interior would be to miss out on Ireland's equally characteristic landscapes of lush valleys, dark peatlands and unruffled loughs. Most regions are rich in historic sights: from world-famous Neolithic sites in the Midlands to imposing Norman castles in the North and Palladian mansions in the Southeast.

Yeats Country is a charming part of County Sligo closely associated with WB Yeats. The poet was born here and is buried within sight of Ben Bulben's ridge *(see pp236–7)*.

Connemara National Park in County Galway boasts stunning landscapes in which mountains and lakes are combined with a dramatic Atlantic coastline. The extensive blanket bogs and moorland are rich in wildlife and unusual plants *(see p212)*.

The Rock of Cashel, a fortified medieval abbey, perches on a limestone outcrop in the heart of County Tipperary. It boasts some of Ireland's finest Romanesque sculpture *(see pp200–201)*.

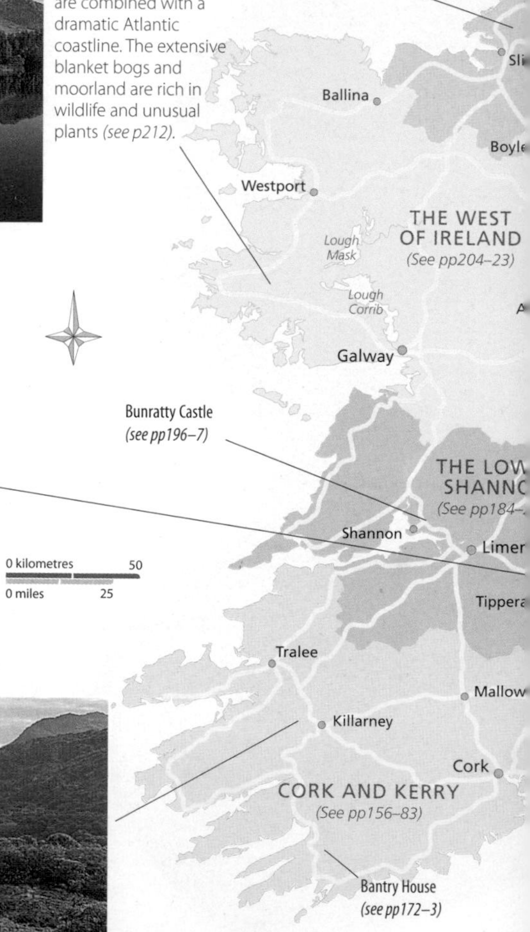

The Lakes of Killarney, flanked by the lush, wooden slopes of some of the country's highest mountains, are the principal attraction in the southwest of Ireland *(see pp166–7)*.

◀ Quaint waterfront Irish cottage at sunset

The Giant's Causeway, where ancient lava flows have been eroded to reveal columns of unnatural regularity, is Northern Ireland's most curious sight. According to local mythology, the rocks were placed here by a giant called Finn MacCool to enable him to walk across the sea to Scotland *(see pp266–7)*.

Newgrange *(see pp250–51)*

Mount Stewart House, a 19th-century mansion, is most renowned for its magnificent gardens. These were created as recently as the 1920s, and a colourful array of exotic plants has since thrived in the warm microclimate of this part of County Down *(see pp286–7)*.

Powerscourt is a large estate in superb countryside on the edge of the Wicklow Mountains. Its grounds rank among the last great formal gardens of Europe. Originally planted in the 1730s, they were restored and embellished in the 19th century *(see pp138–9)*.

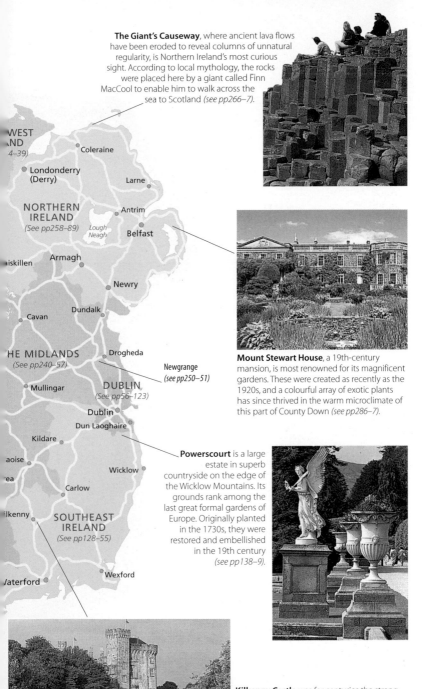

Kilkenny Castle was for centuries the stronghold of the Butler dynasty, which controlled much of southeast Ireland in the Middle Ages. The vast Norman fortress was remodelled during the Victorian period and still dominates Kilkenny – one of the country's most historic and pleasant towns *(see pp146–8)*.

SOUTHEAST IRELAND

Kildare · Wicklow · Carlow · Kilkenny · Waterford · Wexford

Blessed with the warmest climate in Ireland, the Southeast has always presented an attractive prospect for settlers. Landscapes of gently rolling hills have been tamed by centuries of cultivation, with lush farmland, imposing medieval castles and great houses enhancing the region's atmosphere of prosperity.

The Southeast's proximity to Britain meant that it was often the first port of call for foreign invaders. Viking raiders arrived here in the 9th century and founded some of Ireland's earliest towns, including Waterford and Wexford. They were followed in 1169 by the Anglo-Normans *(see pp40–41)*, who shaped the region's subsequent development.

Given its strategic importance, the Southeast was heavily protected, mostly by Anglo-Norman lords loyal to the English Crown. Remains of impressive castles attest to the power of the Fitzgeralds of Kildare and the Butlers of Kilkenny, who between them virtually controlled the Southeast throughout the Middle Ages. English influence was stronger here than in any other part of the island. From the 18th century, wealthy Anglo-Irish families were drawn to what they saw as a stable zone, and felt confident enough to build fine mansions like the Palladian masterpieces of Russborough and Castletown. English rule was not universally accepted, however. The Wicklow Mountains became a popular refuge for opponents to the Crown, including the rebels who fled the town of Enniscorthy after a bloody battle during the uprising against the English in 1798 *(see p45)*.

This mountainous region is still the only real wilderness in the Southeast, in contrast to the flat grasslands that spread across Kildare to the west. To the east, sandy beaches stretch almost unbroken along the shore between Dublin and Rosslare in Wexford.

Traditional thatched cottages in Dunmore East, County Waterford

◀ A 12th-century Norman castle in Kilkenny, County Kilkenny

Exploring Southeast Ireland

The southeast has something for everyone, from busy seaside resorts to quaint canalside villages, Norman abbeys and bird sanctuaries. The Wicklow Mountains, the location of several major sights such as the monastic complex of Glendalough and the magnificent gardens of Powerscourt, provide perfect touring and walking territory. Further south, the most scenic routes cut through the valleys of the Slaney, Barrow and Nore rivers, flanked by historic ports such as New Ross, from where you can explore local waterways by boat. Along the south coast, which is more varied than the region's eastern shore, beaches are interspersed with rocky headlands, and quiet coastal villages provide good alternative bases to the busy towns of Waterford and Wexford. Further inland, the best places to stay include Lismore and Kilkenny, which is one of the finest historic towns in Ireland.

Graiguenamanagh, on the Barrow north of New Ross

Sights at a Glance

1. *Castletown House pp132–3*
2. Robertstown
3. Bog of Allen Nature Centre
4. Monasterevin
5. Kildare
6. Russborough House
7. *Powerscourt pp138–9*
8. Bray
9. Killruddery House
11. Wicklow Mountains
12. Mount Usher Gardens
13. Glendalough
14. Avondale House
15. Brownshill Dolmen
16. *Kilkenny pp146–8*
17. Jerpoint Abbey
18. Lismore
19. Ardmore
20. *Waterford pp150–51*
21. Dunmore East
22. Hook Peninsula
23. New Ross
24. Enniscorthy
25. Irish National Heritage Park
26. Wexford
27. Johnstown Castle
28. Saltee Islands
29. Rosslare

Tours

10. Military Road

For hotels and restaurants in this region see pp297–8 and pp311–13

A 19th-century winged horse at Powerscourt

Getting Around

Routes M11, M9 and M7 fan out from Dublin, serving Wexford, Waterford and Kildare respectively. Rail lines follow a similar course: the eastern coastal towns are served by the Dublin Rosslare railway, and there are good train services to Kildare, Kilkenny and Waterford. You will need a car to explore the south coast; the Passage East–Ballyhack ferry is a useful shortcut between Waterford and Wexford across the River Suir.

Key

- Motorway
- Major road
- Secondary road
- Minor road
- Scenic route
- Main railway
- Minor railway
- International border
- County border
- △ Summit

Imposing façade of Killruddery House and Gardens

For additional map symbols *see back flap*

❶ Castletown House

Built in 1722–29 for William Conolly, Speaker of the Irish Parliament, the façade of Castletown was the work of Florentine architect Alessandro Galilei and gave Ireland its first taste of Palladianism. The magnificent interiors date from the second half of the 18th century. They were commissioned by Lady Louisa Lennox, wife of William Conolly's great-nephew, Tom, who lived here from 1759. Castletown remained in the family until 1965, when it was taken over by the Irish Georgian Society. The state now owns the house and it is open to the public.

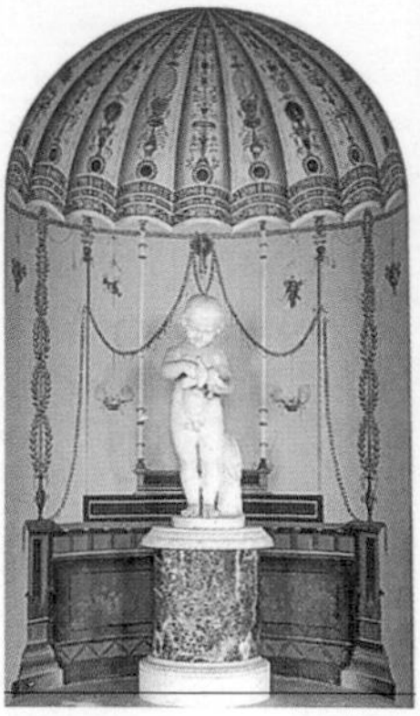

★ Long Gallery
The heavy ceiling sections and friezes date from the 1720s and the walls were decorated in the Pompeiian manner in the 1770s.

Red Drawing Room
The red damask covering the walls of this room is probably French and dates from the 19th century. This exquisite mahogany bureau was made for Lady Louisa in the 1760s.

Boudoir Wall Paintings
The boudoir's decorative panels, moved here from the Long Gallery, were inspired by the Raphael Loggia in the Vatican.

KEY

① **West wing** with kitchen and visitor's café.

② **The Dining Room**, with a compartmentalized ceiling, was designed by Isaac Ware.

③ **Green Drawing Room**

④ **The Entrance Hall** is an austere Neo-Classical room. Its most decorative feature is the delicate carving on the pilasters of the upper gallery.

⑤ ***The Boar Hunt*****,** painted by Paul de Vos (1596–1678).

⑥ **The east wing** houses the renovated stables, conference centre and audio-visual room.

Conolly's Folly

This folly, which lies just beyond the grounds of Castletown House, provides the focus of the view from the Long Gallery. Speaker Conolly's widow, Katherine, commissioned it in 1740 as a memorial to her late husband, and to provide employment after a harsh winter. The unusual structure of superimposed arches crowned by an obelisk is from designs by Richard Cassels, architect of Russborough House *(see p136)*.

VISITORS' CHECKLIST

Practical Information
Road map D4.
Celbridge, Co Kildare.
Tel 01 628 8252.
castletown.ie
Open mid-Mar–end-Oct: daily). limited.
obligatory.
Summer: concerts.

Transport
67, 67A from Dublin.

★ Staircase Hall
This portrait of Lady Louisa is part of the superb Rococo stuccowork by the Lafrancini brothers which decorates the staircase.

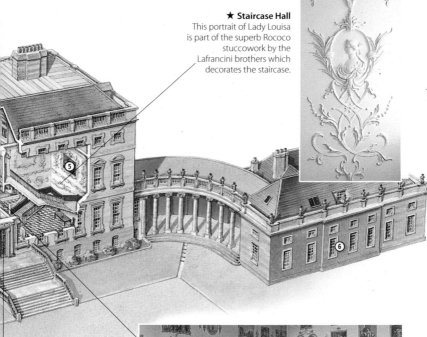

★ Print Room
In this, the only intact 18th-century print room in Ireland, Lady Louisa indulged her taste for Italian engravings. It was fashionable at that time for ladies to paste prints directly on to the wall and frame them with elaborate festoons.

❷ Robertstown

Road map D4. Co Kildare. 650.

Ten locks west along the Grand Canal from Dublin, Robertstown is a characteristic 19th-century canalside village, with warehouses and cottages flanking the waterfront. Freight barges plied the route until about 1960, but pleasure boats have since replaced them. Visitors can take barge cruises from the quay and the Robertstown Hotel, built in 1801 for canal passengers, is now used for banquets.

Near Sallins, about 8 km (5 miles) east of Robertstown, the canal is carried over the River Liffey along the **Leinster Aqueduct**, an impressive structure built in 1783.

The Robertstown Hotel in Robertstown

❸ Bog of Allen Nature Centre

Road map D4. Lullymore, Co Kildare. **Tel** 045 860133. to Newbridge. to Allenwood. **Open** 9am–5pm Mon–Fri, special weekends May–Sep. limited. **ipcc.ie**

Housed in an old farmhouse at Lullymore, 9 km (6 miles) northeast of Rathangan, the Nature Centre lies at the heart of the Bog of Allen, a vast expanse of raised bogland *(see p256)* that extends across the counties of Offaly, Meath, Westmeath, Laois and Kildare. An exhibition of flora, fauna and archaeological finds explores the history and ecology of the bog, while pre-booked guided walks across the peatlands introduce visitors to the bog's delicate ecosystem.

Stacking peat for use as fuel

❹ Monasterevin

Road map D4. Co Kildare. 3,000.

This Georgian market town lies west of Kildare, where the Grand Canal crosses the River Barrow. Waterborne trade brought prosperity to Monasterevin in the 18th century, but the locks now see little traffic. However, you can still admire the aqueduct, which is a superb example of canal engineering.

Moore Abbey, next to the church, was built in the 18th century on the site of a monastic foundation, but the grand Gothic mansion owes much to Victorian remodelling. Once the ancestral seat of the Earls of Drogheda, in the 1920s Moore Abbey became the home of the celebrated tenor, John McCormack *(see p28)*. It is now a hospital.

❺ Kildare

Road map D4. Co Kildare. 7,500. Market House 045 521240. Thu. **kildare.ie**

The charming and tidy town of Kildare is dominated by **St Brigid's Cathedral**, which commemorates the saint who founded a religious community on this site in 480. Unusually, monks and nuns lived here under the same roof, but this was not the only unorthodox practice associated with the community. Curious pagan rituals, including the burning of a perpetual fire, continued until the 16th century. The fire pit is still visible, as is the highest round tower that can be climbed in Ireland, which was probably built in the 12th century and has a Romanesque doorway. The cathedral was rebuilt in the Victorian era,

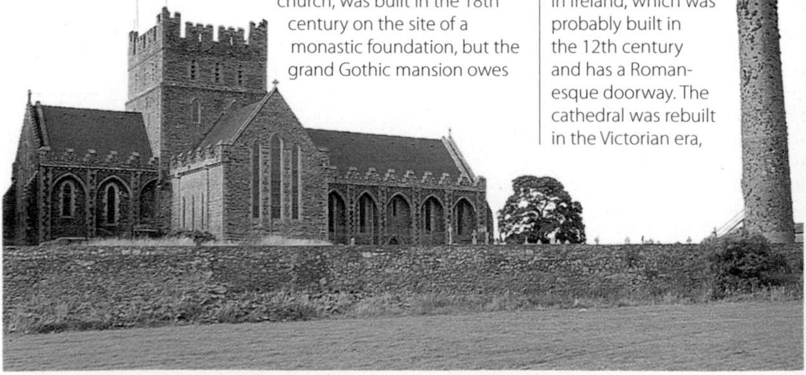

St Brigid's Cathedral and roofless round tower in Kildare town

Japanese Gardens at Tully near Kildare

but the restorers largely adhered to the 13th-century design.

St Brigid's Cathedral
Market Square. **Tel** 085 120 5920.
Open May–Sep: daily. **Donation**.

Environs

Kildare lies at the heart of racing country: the Curragh racecourse is nearby, stables are scattered all around and bloodstock sales take place at Kill, northeast of town.

The **National Stud** is a semi-state-run bloodstock farm at Tully, just south of Kildare. It was founded in 1900 by an eccentric Anglo-Irish colonel called William Hall-Walker. He sold his foals on the basis of their astrological charts, and put skylights in the stables to allow the horses to be "touched" by sunlight and moonbeams. Hall-Walker received the title Lord Wavertree in reward for bequeathing the farm to the British Crown in 1917.

Visitors can explore the 400-ha (1,000-acre) grounds and watch the horses being exercised. Mares are generally kept in a separate paddock from the stallions. Breeding stallions wait in the covering shed: each one is expected to cover 100 mares per season. There is a special foaling unit where the mare and foal can remain undisturbed after the birth.

The farm has its own forge and saddlery, and also a Horse Museum. Housed in an old stable block, this illustrates the importance of horses in Irish life. Exhibits include the frail skeleton of Arkle, a famous champion steeplechaser in the 1960s.

Sharing the same estate as the National Stud are the **Japanese Gardens** and **St Fiachra's Garden**. The Japanese Gardens were laid out in 1906–10 by Japanese landscape gardener Tassa Eida, with the help of his son Minoru and 40 assistants. The impressive array of trees and shrubs includes maple, bonsai, mulberry, magnolia, sacred bamboo and cherry. The gardens take the form of an allegorical journey through life, beginning with the Gate of Oblivion and leading to the Gateway of Eternity, a contemplative Zen rock garden.

St Fiachra's Garden covers 1.6 ha (4 acres) of woodland, wetland, lakes and islands, and features a Waterford Crystal Garden within the monastic cells.

National Stud and Japanese and St Fiachra's Gardens
Tully. **Tel** 045 521617. **Open** mid-Feb–Nov: 9am–6pm. **Closed** Dec–mid-Feb.
National Stud only.
irishnationalstud.ie

Horse Racing in Ireland

Ireland has a strong racing culture and, thanks to its non-elitist image, the sport is enjoyed by all. Much of the thoroughbred industry centres around the Curragh, a grassy plain in County Kildare stretching unfenced for more than 2,000 ha (5,000 acres). This area is home to many of the country's studs and training yards, and every morning horses are put through their paces on the gallops. Most of the major flat races, including the Irish Derby, take place at the Curragh racecourse just east of Kildare. Other fixtures are held at nearby Punchestown – most famously the steeplechase festival in April/May – at Leopardstown, which also hosts major National Hunt races *(see pp32–3)* and Fairyhouse, home to the Irish Grand National.

Finishing straight at the Curragh racecourse

Saloon in Russborough House with original fireplace and stuccowork

❻ Russborough House

Road map D4. Blessington, Co Wicklow. **Tel** 045 865239. 🚌 65 from Dublin. **Open** 10am–5pm daily. obligatory. **W** **russboroughhouse.ie**

This Palladian mansion, built in the 1740s for Joseph Leeson, Earl of Milltown, is one of Ireland's finest houses. Its architect, Richard Cassels, also designed Powerscourt House *(see pp138–9)* and is credited with introducing the Palladian style to Ireland.

Unlike many grand estates in the Pale, Russborough has survived magnificently, both inside and out. The house claims the longest frontage in Ireland, with a façade adorned by heraldic lions and curved colonnades. The interior is even more impressive. Many rooms feature superb stucco decoration, which was done largely by the Italian Lafrancini brothers, who also worked on Castletown House *(see pp132–3)*. The best examples are found in the music room, saloon and library, which are embellished with exuberant foliage and cherubs. Around the main staircase, a riot of Rococo plasterwork depicts a hunt, with hounds clasping garlands of flowers. The stucco mouldings in the drawing room were designed especially to enclose marine scenes by the French artist, Joseph Vernet (1714–89). The paintings were sold in 1926, but recovered over 40 years later and returned to the house.

Vernet seascape in the drawing room

Russborough has many other treasures, including finely worked fireplaces of Italian marble, imposing mahogany doorways and priceless collections of silver, porcelain and Gobelin tapestries.

Such riches aside, one of the principal reasons to visit Russborough is to see the **Beit Art Collection**, famous for its Flemish, Dutch and Spanish Old Master paintings. Sir Alfred Beit, who bought the house in 1952, inherited the pictures from his uncle – also named Alfred Beit and co-founder of the de Beers diamond mining empire in South Africa. In 1974, 1986 and 2000 several masterpieces were stolen from the house. Most were later retrieved. More disappeared in another robbery in 2001, but were recovered. Only a selection of paintings is on view in the house at any one time, while others are on permanent loan to the National Gallery in Dublin

The History of the Pale

The term "Pale" refers to an area around Dublin which marked the limits of English influence from Norman to Tudor times. The frontier fluctuated, but at its largest the Pale stretched from Dundalk in County Louth to Waterford town. Gaelic chieftains outside the area could keep their lands provided they agreed to bring up their heirs within the Pale.

The Palesmen supported their rulers' interests and considered themselves the upholders of English values. This widened the gap between the Gaelic majority and the Anglo-Irish, a foretaste of England's doomed involvement in the country. Long after its fortifications were dismantled, the idea of the Pale lived on as a state of mind. The expression "beyond the pale" survives as a definition of those outside the bounds of civilized society.

An 18th-century family enjoying the privileged lifestyle typical within the Pale

Bray's beachfront esplanade, with Bray Head in the background

(see pp74–5). A self-guided interactive exhibition in the basement includes 3-D photographs taken by Sir Alfred Beit in the 1920s and 1930s, as well as a selection of vinyl records and sheet music from the 1920s.

The west wing of the building was fully restored following a fire in 2010, and eight double bedrooms are now available to rent. Bookings can be made through the Irish Landmark Trust (www.irishlandmark.com).

Environs

The **Poulaphouca Reservoir**, which was formed by the damming of the River Liffey, extends south from Blessington. It is popular with water sports enthusiasts, while others enjoy the mountain views.

7 Powerscourt

See pp138–9.

8 Bray

Road map D4. Co Wicklow. 33,000. DART. Old Court House, Main St (01 286 7128). **bray.ie**

Once a refined Victorian resort, Bray is nowadays a brash holiday town, with amusement arcades and fish and chip shops lining the seafront. Its beach attracts large crowds in summer, including many young families. A more peaceful alternative is nearby Bray Head, where there is scope for bracing cliffside walks. Bray also makes a good base from which to explore Powerscourt Gardens, the Wicklow Mountains and the coastal villages of Killiney and Dalkey in Dublin *(see p107)*.

9 Killruddery House and Gardens

Road map D4. Bray, Co Wicklow. **Tel** 01 286 3405. House: **Open** Jul–Sep: 1–4pm daily. Gardens: **Open** 1 May–30 Sep: 9:30am–6pm daily; Oct & Apr: 9:30am–6pm Sat & Sun. Farmer's Market: **Open** 10am–4pm Sat. outside main opening times, groups of 20–50 by appt only. limited. **killruddery.com**

Killruddery House lies just to the south of Bray, in the shadow of Little Sugar Loaf Mountain. Built in 1651, it has been the family seat of the Earls of Meath ever since, although the original mansion was remodelled in an Elizabethan Revival style in the early 19th century. The house contains some good carving and stuccowork, but the real charm of Killruddery lies in the 17th-century formal gardens, regarded as the finest French Classical gardens in the country. They were laid out in the 1680s by a French gardener named Bonet, who also worked at Versailles.

The gardens, planted with great precision, feature romantic parterres, hedges and many fine trees and shrubs. The sylvan theatre, a small enclosure surrounded by a bay hedge, is the only known example of its kind in Ireland.

The Long Ponds, a pair of canals which extend 165 m (542 ft), once stocked fish. Beyond, a pool enclosed by two circular hedges leads to a Victorian arrangement of paths flanked by statues and hedges of yew, beech and lime.

View across the Long Ponds to Killruddery House

❼ Powerscourt

The gardens at Powerscourt are probably the finest in Ireland, both for their design and their dramatic setting at the foot of Great Sugar Loaf Mountain. The house and grounds were commissioned in the 1730s by Richard Wingfield, the 1st Viscount Powerscourt. New ornamental gardens were completed in 1875 by the 7th Viscount, who added gates, urns and statues collected during his travels in Europe. The house was gutted by an accidental fire in 1974, but the ground floor has been beautifully renovated and now accommodates an upmarket shopping centre with an excellent restaurant and café.

Bamberg Gate
Made in Vienna in the 1770s, this gilded wrought-iron gate was brought to Powerscourt by the 7th Viscount from Bamberg Church in Bavaria.

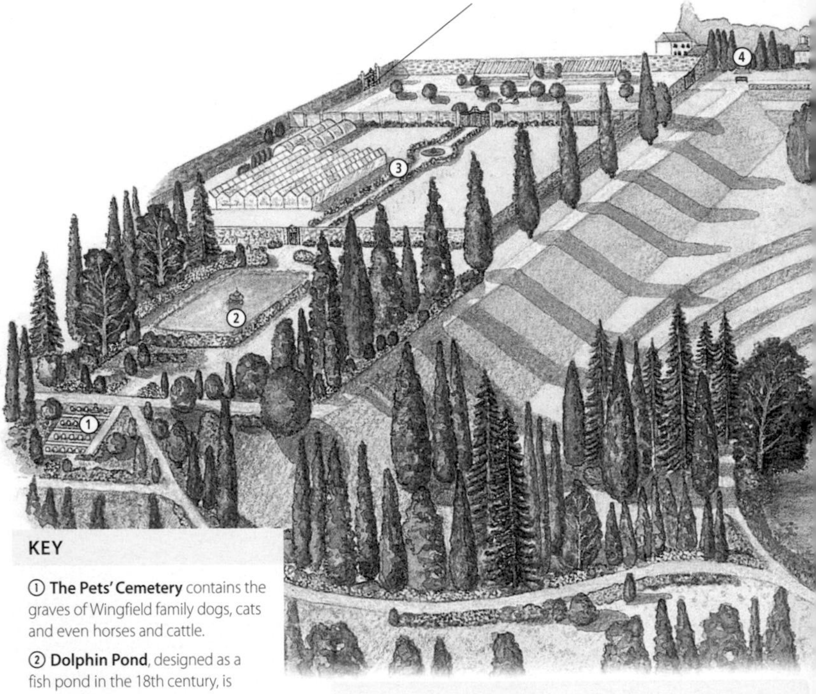

KEY

① **The Pets' Cemetery** contains the graves of Wingfield family dogs, cats and even horses and cattle.

② **Dolphin Pond**, designed as a fish pond in the 18th century, is enclosed by exotic conifers in a lovely secluded garden.

③ **The Walled Gardens** include a formal arrangement of clipped laurel trees.

④ **Statue of Laocoön**

⑤ **The Italian Garden** is laid out on terraces which were first cut into the steep hillside in the 1730s.

⑥ **The Pebble Mosaic** was made using many tonnes of pebbles, which were gathered from Bray beach to construct the Perron.

⑦ **The Pepper Pot Tower** was built in 1911.

Powerscourt House

Originally built in 1731 on the site of a Norman castle, the Palladian mansion at Powerscourt was designed by Richard Cassels, who was also the architect of Russborough House *(see p136)*. In 1974 a fire left the fine building a burnt-out, roofless shell. The Slazenger family, who now own the estate, have restored part of the house. It now includes a terrace café, speciality shops and audiovisual displays covering the history of the estate.

Powerscourt ablaze in 1974

★ The Perron
Leading down to Triton Lake is the Perron, a beautiful Italianate stairway added in 1874. Beside the lake, it is guarded by two statues of Pegasus – the mythical winged horse and emblem of the Wingfield family.

VISITORS' CHECKLIST

Practical Information
Road map D4.
Enniskerry, Co Wicklow.
Tel 01 204 6000.
W powerscourt.ie
Open 9:30am–5:30pm (dusk Oct–Mar) daily. **Closed** 25 & 26 Dec.

Transport
185 from Bray DART station, 44 from Enniskerry.

★ Triton Lake
Made for the first garden, the lake takes its name from its central fountain, which is modelled on a 17th-century work by Bernini in Rome.

★ Japanese Gardens
These enchanting Edwardian gardens, created out of bogland, contain Chinese conifers and bamboo trees.

View of Lower Lake, Glendalough ▶

⑩ A Tour of the Military Road

The British built the Military Road through the heart of the Wicklow Mountains during a campaign to flush out Irish rebels after an uprising in 1798 *(see p153)*. Now known as the R115, this road takes you through the emptiest and most rugged landscapes of County Wicklow. Fine countryside, in which deer and other wildlife flourish, is characteristic of the whole of this tour.

① Glencree
The former British barracks in Glencree are among several found along the Military Road.

② Sally Gap
This remote pass is surrounded by a vast expanse of blanket bog dotted with pools and streams.

③ Glenmacnass
After Sally Gap, the road drops into a deep glen where a waterfall spills dramatically over rocks.

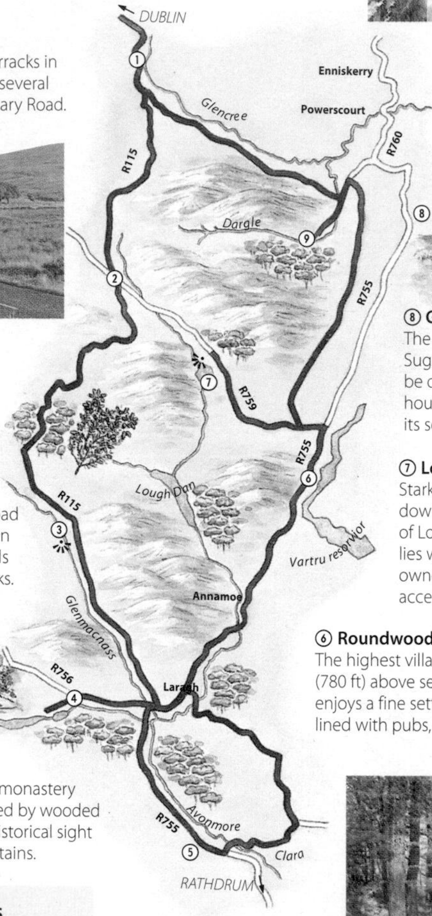

④ Glendalough
This ancient lakeside monastery *(see pp144–5)*, enclosed by wooded slopes, is the prime historical sight in the Wicklow Mountains.

⑨ Powerscourt Waterfall
The River Dargle cascades 130 m (425 ft) over a granite escarpment to form Ireland's highest waterfall.

⑧ Great Sugar Loaf
The granite cone of Great Sugar Loaf Mountain can be climbed in under an hour from the car park on its southern side.

⑦ Lough Tay
Stark, rocky slopes plunge down to the dark waters of Lough Tay. Though it lies within a Guinness-owned estate, the lake is accessible to walkers.

⑥ Roundwood
The highest village in Ireland at 238 m (780 ft) above sea level, Roundwood enjoys a fine setting. Its main street is lined with pubs, cafés and craft shops.

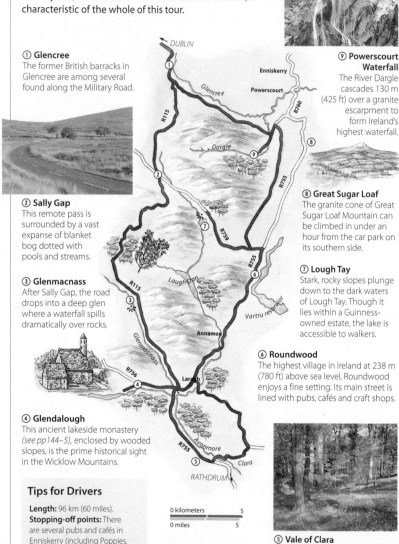

⑤ Vale of Clara
This picturesque wooded valley follows the River Avonmore. It contains the tiny village of Clara, which consists of two houses, a church and a school.

Tips for Drivers

Length: 96 km (60 miles).
Stopping-off points: There are several pubs and cafés in Enniskerry (including Poppies, an old-fashioned tearoom), and also in Roundwood, but this area is better for picnics. There are several marked picnic spots south of Enniskerry.

0 kilometers 5
0 miles 5

Key

Tour route
Other roads
Viewpoint

⓫ Wicklow Mountains

Road map D1. 🚉 to Rathdrum & Wicklow. 🚌 to Enniskerry, Wicklow, Glendalough, Rathdrum & Avoca. ℹ Rialto House, Fitzwilliam Square, Wicklow (0404 69117).
W discoverireland.ie/eastcoast

Standing amid the rugged wilderness of the Wicklow Mountains, it can be hard to believe that Dublin is under an hour's drive away. The inaccessibility of the mountains meant that they once provided a safe hideout for opponents of English rule. When much of the southeast was obedient to the English Crown, within an area known as the Pale *(see p136)*, warlords such as the O'Tooles ruled in the Wicklow Mountains. Rebels who took part in the 1798 uprising *(see p45)* sought refuge here too. One of their leaders, Michael Dwyer, remained at liberty in the hills around Sally Gap until 1803.

The building of the **Military Road**, started in 1800, made the area more accessible, but the mountains are still thinly populated. There is little traffic to disturb enjoyment of the beautiful rock-strewn glens, lush forest and bogland where heather gives a purple sheen to the land. Turf-cutting is still a thriving cottage industry, and you often see peat stacked up by the road. Among the numerous walking trails here is **Wicklow Way**, the oldest established walking route in Ireland, which extends 132 km (82 miles) from Marlay Park in Dublin to Clonegal in County Carlow. It is marked but not always easy to follow, so do not set out without a decent map. Although no peak exceeds 915 m (3,000 ft), the Wicklow Mountains can be dangerous in bad weather.

Hiking apart, there is plenty to see and do in this region. A good starting point for exploring the northern area is the estate village of **Enniskerry**. In summer, it is busy with tourists who come to visit the gardens at Powerscourt *(see pp138–9)*. From Laragh, to the south, you can reach Glendalough *(see pp144–5)* and the **Vale of Avoca**, where cherry trees are laden with blossom in the spring. The beauty of this gentle valley was captured in the poetry of Thomas Moore (1779–1852): "There is not in the wide world a valley so sweet as that vale in whose bosom the bright waters meet" – a reference to the confluence of the Avonbeg and Avonmore rivers, the so-called **Meeting of the Waters** beyond Avondale House *(see p145)*. Nestled among wooded hills at the heart of the valley is the hamlet of Avoca, where the **Avoca Handweavers** produce colourful tweeds in the oldest hand-weaving mill in Ireland, in operation since 1723.

Road sign in the Wicklow Mountains

Colourful moorland around Sally Gap in the Wicklow Mountains

Mount Usher Gardens, on the banks of the River Vartry

Further north, towards the coast near Ashford, the River Vartry rushes through the deep chasm of the **Devil's Glen**. On entering the valley, the river falls 30 m (100 ft) into a pool known as the Devil's Punchbowl. There are good walks around here, with fine views of the coast.

Avoca Handweavers
Avoca. **Tel** 0402 35105. **Open** 9am–6pm daily. **Closed** 25 & 26 Dec.
W avoca.ie

⓬ Mount Usher Gardens

Road map D4. Ashford, Co Wicklow. **Tel** 0404 40205. 🚌 to Ashford. **Open** Feb–Oct: 10am–6pm. open all year. limited. call to book. **W mountushergardens.ie**

Set beside the River Vartry just east of Ashford are the Mount Usher Gardens. They were designed in 1868 by a Dubliner, Edward Walpole, who imbued them with his strong sense of romanticism.

The gardens contain more than 5,000 species of shrubs and trees, from Chinese conifers and bamboos to Mexican pines. The Maple Walk is glorious in autumn. The river provides the main focus, and amid the vegetation you can glimpse herons.

⑬ Glendalough

Road map D4. Co Wicklow.
St Kevin's Bus from Dublin. Ruins **Open** 9:30am–5pm (to 6pm mid-Mar–mid-Oct) daily. in summer.
Visitor Centre **Tel** 0404 45325/45352.
Open daily. **Closed** 23–30 Dec.
glendalough.ie

The steep, wooded slopes of Glendalough, the "valley of the two lakes", harbour one of Ireland's most atmospheric monastic sites. Established by St Kevin in the 6th century, the settlement was sacked time and again by the Vikings but nevertheless flourished for over 600 years. Decline set in only after English forces partially razed the site in 1398, though it functioned as a monastic centre until the Dissolution of the Monasteries in 1539 *(see p42)*. Pilgrims kept on coming to Glendalough even after that, particularly on St Kevin's Feast Day, 3 June, which was often a riotous event *(see p34)*.

The age of the buildings is uncertain, but most date from

Remains of the Gatehouse, the original entrance to Glendalough

View along the Upper Lake at Glendalough

the 10th to 12th centuries. Many were restored during the 1870s. The main group of ruins lies east of the Lower Lake, but other buildings associated with St Kevin are by the Upper Lake. Here, where the scenery is much wilder, you are better able to enjoy the tranquillity of Glendalough and to escape the crowds which inevitably descend on the site. Try to arrive as early as possible in the day, particularly during the peak tourist season. You enter the monastery through the double stone arch of the **Gatehouse**, the only surviving example in Ireland of a gateway into a monastic enclosure.

St Kevin's Kitchen

A short walk leads to a graveyard with a **Round Tower** in one corner. Reaching 30 m (100 ft) in height, this is one of the finest of its kind in the country. Its cap was rebuilt in the 1870s using stones found inside the tower. The roofless **Cathedral** nearby dates mainly from the 10th and 13th centuries and is the valley's largest ruin. At the centre of the churchyard stands the tiny **Priests' House**, whose name derives from the fact that it was a burial place for local clergy. The worn carving of a robed figure above the door is possibly of St Kevin, flanked by two disciples. East of here, is **St Kevin's Cross**, which dates from the 8th century. Made of granite it is one of the best preserved of Glendalough's High Crosses. Below, nestled in the lush valley, a minuscule oratory with a steeply pitched stone roof is a charming sight. Erected in the 11th century or even earlier, it is popularly known as **St Kevin's Kitchen;** this is perhaps because its belfry, thought to be a later addition, resembles a chimney. One of the earliest churches at Glendalough, **St Mary's**, lies

Plan of Glendalough

The Visitor Centre explains the history of the monastery and is the best place to start a tour. You can see both groups of ruins, which lie less than 1.5 km (1 mile) apart, in about two hours, but to make the most of the site allow a full day.

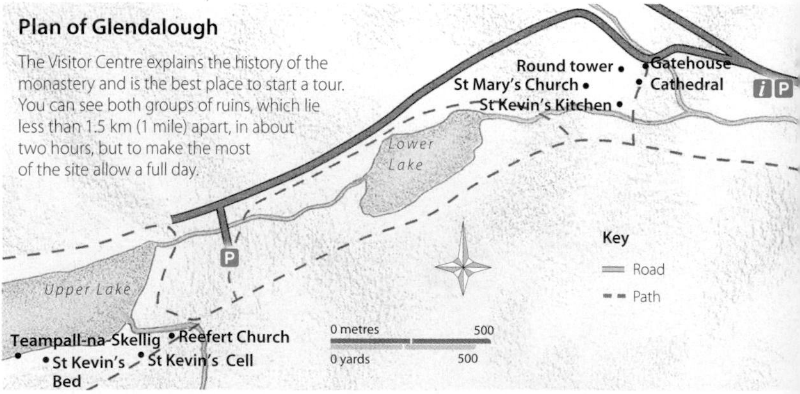

For key to symbols *see back flap*

Round tower at Glendalough

across a field to the west. Some traces of moulding are visible outside the east window. Following the path along the south bank of the river, you reach the Upper Lake. This is the site of more monastic ruins and is also the chief starting point for walks through the valley and to a number of disused lead and zinc mines.

Situated in a grove not far from the Poulanass waterfall are the ruins of the **Reefert Church**, a simple nave-and-chancel building. Its unusual name is a corruption of *Righ Fearta*, meaning "burial place of the kings"; the church may mark the site of an ancient cemetery. Near here, on a rocky spur overlooking the Upper Lake, stands **St Kevin's Cell**, the ruins of a beehive-shaped structure which is thought to have been the hermit's home.

There are two sites on the south side of the lake which cannot be reached on foot but are visible from the opposite shore. **Teampall-na-Skellig**, or the "church of the rock", was supposedly built on the site of the first church that St Kevin founded at Glendalough. To the east of it, carved into the cliff, is **St Kevin's Bed**. This small cave, in reality little more than a rocky ledge above the upper lake, was apparently used as a retreat by St Kevin. It was from here that the saint allegedly rejected the advances of a woman by tossing her into the lake.

St Kevin at Glendalough

St Kevin was born in 498, a descendant of the royal house of Leinster. He rejected his life of privilege, however, choosing to live instead as a hermit in a cave at Glendalough. He later founded a monastery here, and went on to create a notable centre of learning devoted to the care of the sick and the copying and illumination of manuscripts. St Kevin attracted many disciples to Glendalough during his lifetime, but the monastery became more celebrated as a place of pilgrimage after his death in around 618.

Colourful legends about the saint make up for the dearth of facts about him. That he lived to the age of 120 is just one of the stories told about him. Another tale claims that one day, when St Kevin was at prayer, a blackbird laid an egg in one of his outstretched hands. The saint remained in the same position until it was hatched.

⓮ Avondale House

Road map D4. Co Wicklow. **Tel** 0404 46111. to Rathdrum. House: **Open** Jun–Aug: 11am–5pm daily; Apr–May & Sep–Oct: 11am–4pm Tue–Sun. **Closed** Good Fri & 23–28 Dec. limited. Grounds: **Open** 8:30am–8:30pm daily. **heritageisland.com**

Lying just south of Rathdrum, Avondale House is the birthplace of the 19th-century politician and patriot, Charles Stewart Parnell *(see p47)*. The Georgian mansion is now a museum dedicated to Parnell and the fight for Home Rule.

The grounds are open to the public. Known as **Avondale Forest Park**, they include an impressive arboretum planted in the 18th century and much added to since 1900. There are some lovely walks through the woods, with pleasant views along the River Avonmore.

⓯ Brownshill Dolmen

Road map D4. Co Carlow. to Carlow. **Open** daily.

In a field 3 km (2 miles) east of Carlow, along the R726, stands a dolmen boasting the biggest capstone in Ireland. Weighing a reputed 100 tonnes, this massive stone is embedded in the earth at one end and supported at the other by three much smaller stones. Dating back to 2000 BC, Brownshill Dolmen is thought to mark the tomb of a local chieftain. A path leads to it from the road.

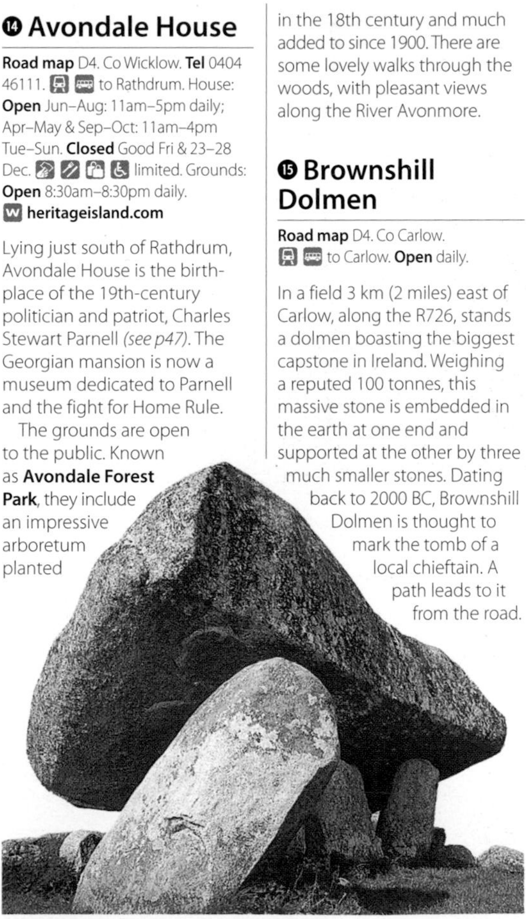

Brownshill Dolmen, famous for its enormous capstone

⓰ Street-by-Street: Kilkenny

Kilkenny is undoubtedly Ireland's loveliest inland city. It rose to prominence in the 13th century and became the medieval capital of Ireland. The Anglo-Norman Butler family came to power in the 1390s and held sway over the city for 500 years. Their power has gone but their legacy is visible in the city's historic buildings, many of which have been restored. Kilkenny is proud of its heritage and every August hosts the Republic's top arts festival and the Catslaugh Comedy Festival.

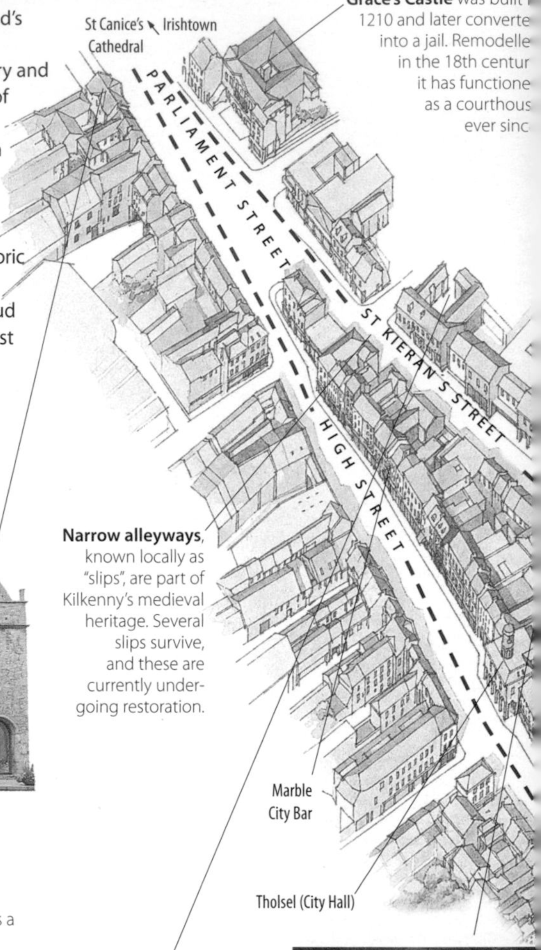

Grace's Castle was built i 1210 and later converte into a jail. Remodelle in the 18th centur it has functione as a courthous ever sinc

Narrow alleyways, known locally as "slips", are part of Kilkenny's medieval heritage. Several slips survive, and these are currently undergoing restoration.

★ Rothe House
This fine Tudor merchant's house, built around two courtyards, is fronted by arcades once typical of Kilkenny's main streets. A small museum inside the house contains a display of local archaeological artifacts and a costume collection.

Kyteler's Inn
This medieval coaching inn *(see p326)* is named after Dame Alice Kyteler, a 14th-century witch who once lived in the building. Like most of the pubs in the city, Kyteler's Inn sells Smithwick's beer, which has been brewed in Kilkenny since 1710.

Key

▬ Suggested route

Butter Slip
The alley is named after the butter stalls that once lined this small marketplace.

View of the High Street
The 18th-century Tholsel, with its distinctive clock tower and arcade, is the main landmark on the High Street. Its elegant Georgian chamber is used by city councillors to this day.

VISITORS' CHECKLIST

Practical Information
Road map C4. Co Kilkenny.
26,000.
Shee Alms House, Rose Inn St (056 775 1500).
Rothe House: **Tel** 056 772 2893.
Open Apr–Oct: 10:30am–5pm Mon–Sat, 3–5pm Sun; Nov–Mar: 10:30am–4:30pm Mon–Sat.
Closed 1–2pm Sat.

Transport
Dublin Rd (056 772 2024).
Bus Eireann (051 317 864).

★ Kilkenny Castle
Set in a commanding position overlooking the River Nore, this Norman fortress is one of Ireland's most famous castles. The Long Gallery, the finest room in the house, has a striking 19th-century hammer-beam and glass roof.

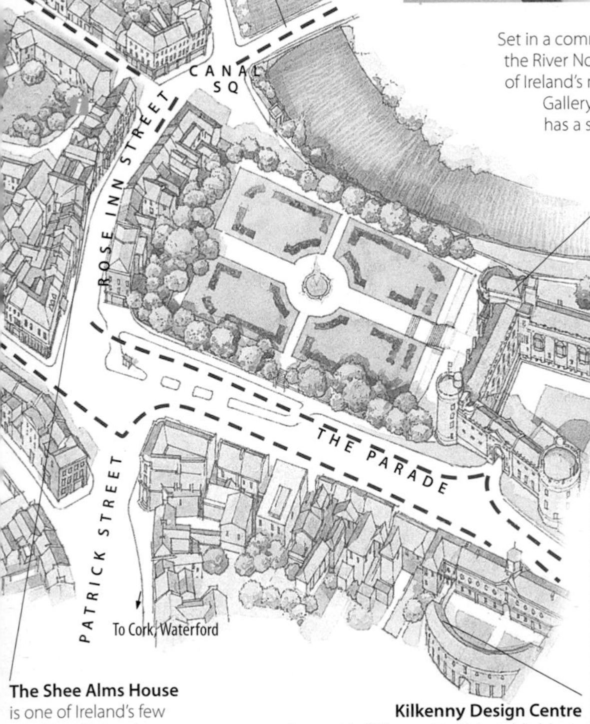

The Shee Alms House is one of Ireland's few surviving Tudor alms-houses and is now the city's tourist information office.

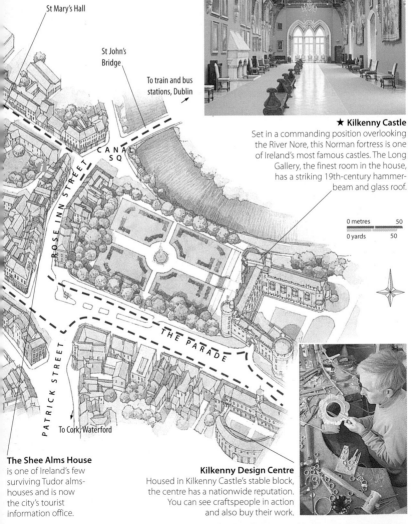

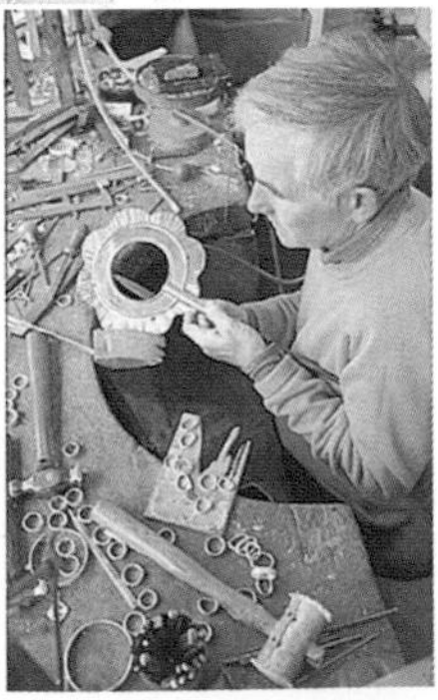

Kilkenny Design Centre
Housed in Kilkenny Castle's stable block, the centre has a nationwide reputation. You can see craftspeople in action and also buy their work.

For hotels and restaurants in this region see pp297–8 and pp311–13

Exploring Kilkenny

Set in a lovely spot beside a kink in the River Nore, Kilkenny is of great architectural interest, with much use made of the distinctive local black limestone, known as Kilkenny marble. A tour of the town also reveals many unexpected treasures: a Georgian façade often seems to conceal a Tudor chimney, a Classical interior or some other surprise.

The survival of the Irishtown district, now dominated by St Canice's Cathedral, recalls past segregation in Kilkenny. The area once known as Englishtown still boasts the city's grandest public buildings.

As a brewery city, Kilkenny is a paradise for keen drinkers, with at least 60 pubs to choose from.

North side of Kilkenny Castle showing Victorian crenellations

Sign of the Marble City Bar on Kilkenny's High Street

Kilkenny Castle

The Parade. **Tel** 056 770 4100.
Open daily (check website for details). **Closed** Good Fri & Christmas. obligatory. limited. Queues are likely during the summer.
kilkennycastle.ie

Built in the 1190s, Kilkenny Castle was occupied right up until 1935. The powerful Butler family *(see p146)* lived in it from the late 14th century. Their descendants eventually donated Kilkenny Castle to the nation in 1967. With its drum towers and solid walls, the castle retains its medieval form, but has undergone many alterations. The Victorian changes made in Gothic Revival style have had the most enduring impact.

Two wings of the castle have been restored to their 19th-century splendour and include a library, drawing room and the magnificent Long Gallery with its restored picture collection. The final phase of restoration includes a state-of-the-art conference centre, which is situated in one of the castle's beautiful 12th-century towers.

The castle grounds have diminished considerably over the centuries, but the French Classical gardens remain, with terraces opening onto a woodland walk and pleasant rolling parkland.

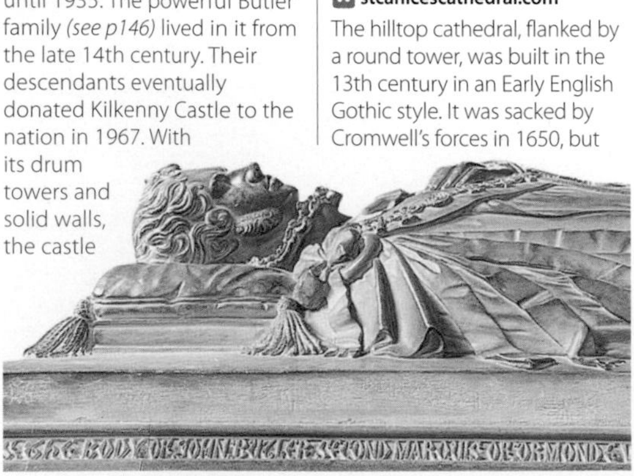

Tomb of 2nd Marquess of Ormonde in St Canice's Cathedral

St Canice's Cathedral

Irishtown. **Tel** 056 776 4971.
Open daily.
stcanicescathedral.com

The hilltop cathedral, flanked by a round tower, was built in the 13th century in an Early English Gothic style. It was sacked by Cromwell's forces in 1650, but has survived as one of Ireland's medieval treasures. Walls of the local Kilkenny limestone and pillars of pale limestone combine to create an interior of simple grandeur. An array of splendid 16th-century tombs includes the beautiful effigies of the Butler family in the south transept. It is worth climbing the tower for a fine view over Kilkenny.

Black Abbey

Abbey St. **Tel** 056 772 1279.
Open daily. **kilkenny.ie**

Lying just west of Parliament Street, this Dominican abbey was founded in 1225. Part of it was turned into a courthouse in the 16th century, but is once again a working monastery. The church has a fine vaulted undercroft, distinctive stonework, some beautiful stained-glass windows, and a 14th-century alabaster statue of the holy trinity.

Environs

Just north of the town lies **Dunmore Cave**, a limestone cavern with an impressive series of chambers, noted for its curious rock formations.

Bennettsbridge, on the Nore 8 km (5 miles) south of Kilkenny, is famous for its ceramics. The Nicholas Mosse Pottery *(see p337)* specializes in colourful earthenware made from the local clay.

Dunmore Cave

Ballyfoyle. **Tel** 056 776 7726.
Open Mar–Oct: 9:30am–5pm daily (to 6:30pm mid-Jun–mid-Sep); Nov–Feb: 9:30am–5pm Wed–Sun. obligatory. **heritageireland.ie**

For hotels and restaurants in this region see pp297–8 and pp311–13

⓱ Jerpoint Abbey

Road map D5. Thomastown, Co Kilkenny. **Tel** 056 772 4623. to Thomastown. **Open** Mar–Sep: 9am–5:30pm daily; Oct: 9am–5pm daily; Nov: 9:30am–4pm daily; Dec–Feb: by appt only. **Closed** 25 Dec. Dec–Mar: pre-booked tours only **heritageireland.ie**

On the banks of the Little Arrigle, just south of Thomastown, is Jerpoint Abbey, one of the finest Cistercian ruins in Ireland. Founded in 1160, the fortified medieval complex rivalled Duiske Abbey *(see p153)* in prestige. Jerpoint flourished until the Dissolution of the Monasteries *(see pp42–3)*, when it passed to the Earl of Ormonde.

The 15th-century cloisters have not survived as well as some earlier parts of the abbey. Despite this, they are the highlight, with their amusing sculptures of knights, courtly ladies, bishops and dragons. The church itself is well preserved. The Irish-Romanesque transepts date back to the earliest period of the Abbey's development and contain16th-century tombs with exquisite stylized carvings. The north side of the nave has a rich array of decorated Romanesque capitals and throughout the abbey are tombs and effigies of bishops. The battlemented crossing tower was added during the 1400s.

Stylized carving of saints on 16th-century tomb in Jerpoint Abbey

⓲ Lismore

Road map C5. Co Waterford. 1,500. Lismore Heritage Centre, Main St (058 54975). craft shop. **discoverlismore.com**

This genteel riverside town is dwarfed by **Lismore Castle**, perched above the River Blackwater. Built in 1185 but remodelled in the 19th century, the castle is the Irish seat of the Duke of Devonshire and is closed to the public. However, you can visit the sumptuous gardens, which include a lovely riverside walk. **Lismore Heritage Centre** tells the story of St Carthage, who founded a monastic centre here in the 7th century. The town has two cathedrals dedicated to him. The Protestant **Cathedral of St Carthage** is the more interesting. It dates from 1633 but incorporates older elements and was later altered to suit the Neo-Gothic tastes of the Victorians. It has fine Gothic vaulting, and a stained-glass window by the Pre-Raphaelite artist, Sir Edward Burne-Jones.

Burne-Jones window in St Carthage's Cathedral, Lismore

Lismore Castle
Gardens: **Tel** 058 54061. **Open** mid-Apr–mid-Oct: 10:30am–5:30pm daily. **lismorecastlegardens.com**

Environs
From Lismore you can follow a picturesque route through the **Blackwater Valley** *(see p181)*. This runs from Cappoquin, in an idyllic woodland setting east of Lismore, to the estuary at Youghal *(see p183)*.

St Declan's Cathedral at Ardmore, with its near-perfect round tower

⓳ Ardmore

Road map C5. Co Waterford. 450. 024 94444.

Ardmore is a popular seaside resort with a splendid beach, lively pubs, good cliff walks and some interesting architecture. The hill beside the village is the site of a monastery established in the 5th century by St Declan, the first missionary to bring Christianity to this area.

Most of the buildings, including the ruined **St Declan's Cathedral**, one of Ireland's earliest ecclesiastical sites, date from the 12th century. The cathedral's west wall has fine Romanesque sculptures, arranged in a series of arcades. The scenes include The Archangel Michael Weighing Souls in the upper row, and below this The Adoration of the Magi and The Judgment of Solomon.

The adjacent round tower is one of the best-preserved examples in Ireland, and rises to a height of 30 m (98 ft). An oratory nearby is said to mark the site of St Declan's grave.

20 Waterford

Waterford, Ireland's oldest city, was founded by Vikings in 914. Set in a commanding position by the estuary of the River Suir, it became southeast Ireland's main seaport. From the 18th century, the city's prosperity was consolidated by local industries, including the glassworks for which Waterford is famous. The strong commercial tradition persists today and Waterford's port is still one of Ireland's busiest. Following extensive archaeological excavations in the city centre, a new heart and atmosphere has been put into the old city with the creation of pedestrian precincts in the historic quarter and along the quays.

Ardmore Castle Watch Tower and signal station, Co Waterford

Exploring Waterford

The extensive remains of the city walls clearly define the area originally fortified by the Vikings. The best-preserved section runs northwest from the **Watch Tower** on Castle Street, although Reginald's Tower, overlooking the river, is the largest structure in the old defences. In The Reginald Bar you can see the arches through which boats sailed forth down the river; these sallyports are one of several Viking sections of the largely Norman fortifications.

Although Waterford retains its medieval layout, most of the city's finest buildings are Georgian. Some of the best examples can be seen on the Mall, which runs southwest from Reginald's Tower, and in the lovely Cathedral Square. The latter takes its name from **Christchurch Cathedral**, which was built in the 1770s to a design by John Roberts, a local architect who contributed much to the city's Georgian heritage. It is fronted by a fine Corinthian colonnade. A grim 15th-century effigy of a rotting corpse is an unexpected sight inside. Heading down towards the river, you pass the 13th-century ruins of **Grey Friars**, often known as the French Church after it became a Huguenot chapel in 1693.

West along the waterfront is a Victorian clock tower, which stands at the top of Barronstrand Street. Rising above the busy shops is **Holy Trinity Cathedral**, which has a rich Neo-Classical interior. George's Street, which runs west from here, is dotted with period houses and cosy pubs. It leads to O'Connell Street, whose partially restored warehouses contrast with the shabbier buildings on the quay. In the summer, you can enjoy another view of the waterfront by taking a cruise on the river.

Reginald's Tower on the quayside

Reginald's Tower

The Quay. **Tel** 051 304220.
Open Jun–Aug: 9:30am–6pm Mon–Sat, 11am– 6pm Sun; Sep–May: 9:30am–5pm Mon–Sat, 11am–5pm Sun.

In 1185, the Anglo-Normans built the stone structure seen here today. With walls 3-m (10-ft) thick, it is said to be the first Irish building to use mortar, a primitive concoction of blood, lime, fur and mud. It is the oldest civic urban building in Ireland.

Medieval Museum

The Granary, Merchants Quay.
Tel 051 304500. **Open** Jun–Aug: 9:30am–6pm Mon–Sat, 11am–6pm Sun; Sep–May: 9:30am–5pm Mon–Sat, 11am–5pm Sun.

The 13th-century Chorister's Hall building on Merchant's Quay houses the Medieval Museum, showcasing treasures from the Middle Ages.

View of the city of Waterford across the River Suir

For hotels and restaurants in this region see pp297–8 and pp311–13

Waterford Crystal Visitor Centre

The Mall. **Tel** 051 317000.
Open Nov–Mar: 9:30am–3:15pm Mon–Fri; Apr–Oct: 9am–4:15pm daily.
Closed 24–27 Dec.
waterfordvisitorcentre.com

A visit to the Waterford Crystal Visitor Centre is highly recommended to learn about and observe the process of crystal-making.

The original glass factory was founded in 1783 by two brothers, George and William Penrose, who chose Waterford

Craftsman engraving a vase at the Waterford Crystal Visitor Centre

because of its port. For many decades their crystal enjoyed an unrivalled reputation, but draconian taxes caused the firm to close in 1851. A new factory and visitor centre was opened in 1947, just south of the city, and master blowers and engravers were brought from the Continent to train local apprentices. Competition from Tipperary and Galway Crystal had an effect in the early 1990s, but sales revived.

Following the closure in 2009 of the factories and visitor centre, a deal was brokered to secure the future of the glass in Waterford. While much of the glass manufacture now happens elsewhere, visitors can still observe the making of prestige pieces in a custom-built facility on the site of the grand old ESB building on the Mall. The centre offers tours that cover more than 225 years of glass-making and take in master craftsmen at work on individual pieces. A shop with the world's largest display of Waterford Crystal sells fine pieces engraved with the famous Waterford signature.

VISITORS' CHECKLIST

Practical Information
Road map D5. Co Waterford.
49,000. 120 Parade Quay (051 875823).
discoverireland.ie/southeast
Waterford Spraoi (Aug).

Transport
10 km (6 miles) S. Plunkett Station, The Bridge (051 873401).
The Quay (051 879000).

Ballyhack Port, across Waterford Harbour from Passage East

Environs

The small port of **Passage East**, 12 km (7 miles) east of Waterford, witnessed the landing of the Normans in 1170 *(see p40)*, but little has happened since. A car ferry links the village to Ballyhack in County Wexford, providing a scenic shortcut across Waterford Harbour as well as an excellent entry point to the Hook Peninsula *(see p152)*.

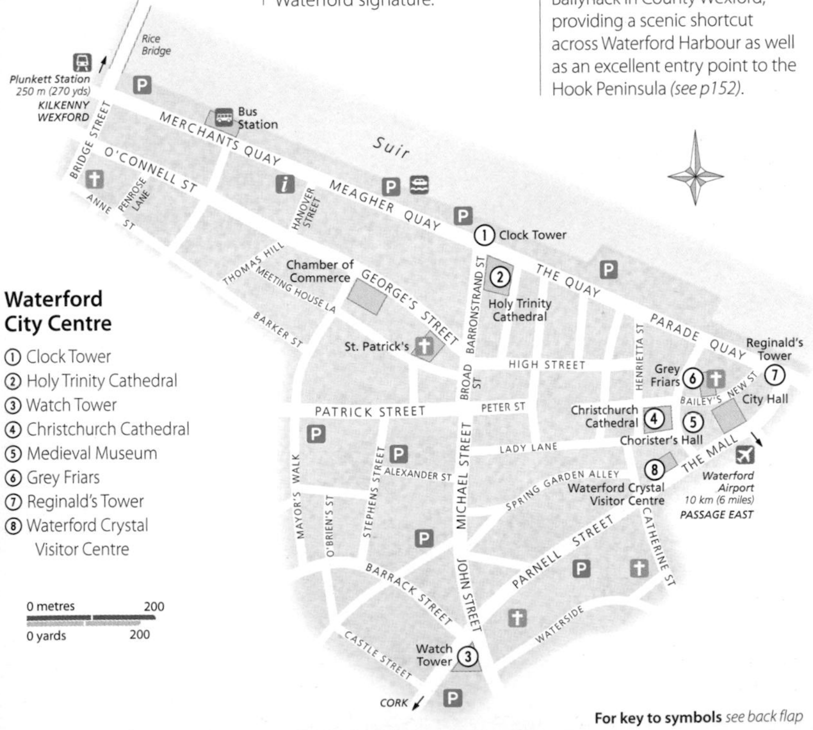

For key to symbols *see back flap*

㉑ Dunmore East

Road map D5. Co Waterford.
1,600.

The appeal of Dunmore East, Waterford's most charming fishing village, lies chiefly in its red sandstone cliffs and bustling harbour. Paths run along the foot of the cliffs, but for the best views take the road that winds uphill from the beach, past tidy cottages and the ivy-clad Azzurro to the Haven Hotel. A gate nearby leads to delightful gardens overlooking the fishing boats below. Climbing further, up steps cut into the rock, you are rewarded by views of the cliffs and noisy kittiwake colonies.

Busy fishing harbour at Dunmore East

㉒ Hook Peninsula

Road map D5. Co Wexford. to Duncannon. from Passage East to Ballyhack (051 382480). Fethard-on-Sea (051 397502).
hooktourism.com

This tapering headland of gentle landscapes scattered with ancient ruins and quiet villages is perfect for a circular tour. The "Ring of Hook" route begins south of New Ross at **Dunbrody Abbey**, the ruins of a 12th-century Cistercian church, but **Ballyhack** is another good place to start. Once a fortified crossing point into County Waterford, the town still has a ferry service to neighbouring Passage East *(see p151)*. **Ballyhack Castle**, built by the Knights Templar in about 1450, contains a small museum. About 4 km (2.5 miles) beyond is the small resort of **Duncannon**, with a broad sandy beach and a star-shaped fort, which was built in 1588 in expectation of an attack by the Spanish Armada.

The coast road continues south to **Hook Head**. Here is the world's oldest working lighthouse, dating from 1172 and now with its own visitor centre. Paths skirt the coast famous for its fossils, seals and a variety of sea birds.

Just 2 km (1.5 miles) east is the village of **Slade**. A ruined 15th-century tower house, **Slade Castle**, presides over the harbour where fishing boats cluster around the slipways. The road proceeds along the rugged coastline, past the resort of Fethard-on-Sea and Saltmills to the dramatic ruin of **Tintern Abbey**. This 13th-century Cistercian foundation was built by William Marshall, Earl of Pembroke. Fields lead to an old stone bridge and views over **Bannow Bay**, where it is thought the Normans made their first landing in 1169.

Dunbrody Abbey
Campile. **Tel** 051 388603. **Open** May–Sep: 11am–6pm daily.

Ballyhack Castle
Ballyhack. **Tel** 051 389468. **Open** end-Jun–Aug: 10:30am–5pm Sat–Wed.

Tintern Abbey
Tel 051 562 650. **Open** 10am–5pm daily. mid-May–Sep: daily.

Norman lighthouse at Hook Head, on the tip of the Hook Peninsula

Castle ruins and harbour at Slade on the Hook Peninsula

㉓ New Ross

Road map D5. Co Wexford. 6,000. South Quay (051 421857). Tue. **experiencenewross.com**
Galley Cruising Restaurants: The Quay (051 421723). **Open** Apr–Oct.

Lying on the banks of the River Barrow, New Ross is one of the oldest towns in the county. Its importance, now as in the past, stems from its status as a port. In summer there is much activity on the river, with cruises plying the Barrow, Nore and Suir rivers. Docked at South Quay is **The Dunbrody Famine Ship**, a full-scale reconstruction of a cargo ship that carried emigrants to the US and Canada during the famine. Traditional shopfronts line the streets, which rise steeply from the quayside. The **Tholsel**, now the town hall but originally a tollhouse, was occupied by the British during the 1798 rebellion *(see pp44–5)*. Opposite, a monument to a Wexford pikeman commemorates the bravery of the Irish rebels who faced the British.

Nearby is **St Mary's** which, when founded in the 13th century, was the largest parish church in Ireland. A modern church occupies the site, but the original (now roofless) south transept remains, as do many medieval tombstones.

▥ The Dunbrody Famine Ship
South Quay. **Tel** 051 425239.
Open Apr–Sep: 9am–6pm; Oct–Mar: 9am–5pm. ☒ ⓦ **dunbrody.com**

Environs
A popular trip up the meandering Barrow goes 16 km (10 miles) north to **Graiguena-managh**. The main attraction of this market town is **Duiske Abbey**, the largest Cistercian church in Ireland. Founded in 1207, it has been extensively restored and now acts as the parish church. The most striking features include a Romanesque door in the south transept, the great oak roof and traces of a medieval pavement below floor level. There is also a cross-legged statue of the Knight of Duiske, which is one of the finest medieval effigies in Ireland.

Trips along the Nore River take you to **Inistioge**. Lying in a deep, wooded valley, this is an idyllic village, with neat 18th-century houses, a square planted with lime trees and a ten-arched bridge spanning the Nore.

View over Enniscorthy and St Aidan's Cathedral from Vinegar Hill

Near to Inistioge you can visit the **Woodstock Gardens and Aboretum**. Overlooking the River Nore, the gardens offer a relaxing environment in which to spend a few hours.

On a hill 12 km (7.5 miles) south of New Ross, a large area of woodland is enclosed within the **JFK Memorial Park**. Founded in 1968, near the late president's ancestral home in Dunganstown (now **The Kennedy Homestead**), the 400-acre park boasts more , than 4,500 types of tree and provides splendid panoramic views. There are marked paths and nature trails.

⌂ Duiske Abbey
Graiguenamanagh, Co Kilkenny.
Tel 059 972 4238. **Open** Mon–Fri. ♿

♣ The JFK Memorial Park
New Ross, Co Wexford. **Tel** 051 388171. **Open** daily. **Closed** Good Fri & 25 Dec. ☒ ♿ ▯ May–end Sep. ⓦ **heritageireland.ie**

㉔ Enniscorthy

Road map D5. Co Wexford. ▨ 5,000. ▦ ▤ ⓘ The 1798 visitor centre (053 923 7596).

The streets of Enniscorthy, on the banks of the River Slaney,

are full of character and redolent of the town's turbulent past. In 1798, Enniscorthy witnessed the last stand of the Wexford pikemen, when a fierce battle was fought against a British force of 20,000 on nearby **Vinegar Hill**. The events of that year are told in depth at the multimedia **National 1798 Visitor Centre**. Enniscorthy's other main sight is the Neo-Gothic **St Aidan's Cathedral**, designed in the 1840s by A W N Pugin (1812–52), better known for his work on London's Houses of Parliament.

Granaries, mills and potteries overlook the Slaney, including Carley's Bridge, founded in 1654 and still operational. Enniscorthy's historic pubs are another attraction. They include The Antique Tavern *(see p326)*, which is hung with pikes used during the Battle of Vinegar Hill in 1798.

▥ National 1798 Visitor Centre
Millpark Road. **Tel** 053 923 7596.
Open Apr–Sep: 9:30am–5pm Mon–Fri; Oct–Mar: 10am–4pm Mon–Fri; Sat & Sun: 12pm–5pm. ☒ ▯ ⌂
ⓦ **1798centre.ie**

⌂ St Aidan's Cathedral
Main St. **Tel** 053 923 5777.
Open 9am–6pm daily. ♿

The inland port of New Ross seen from the west bank of the River Barrow

View across the harbour to Wexford town

㉕ Irish National Heritage Park

Road map D5. Ferrycarrig, Co Wexford. **Tel** 053 912 0733. **Open** May–Aug: 9:30am–6:30pm (to 5:30pm Sep–Apr). **Closed** week at Christmas. Mar–Oct. **inhp.com**

Built on former marshland near Ferrycarrig, north of Wexford, the Irish National Heritage Park is a bold open-air museum. Trails lead through woods to replicas of homesteads, places of worship and burial sites, providing a fascinating lesson on the country's ancient history *(see pp36–7)*.

Highlights include the Viking boatyard, complete with raiding ship, and a 7th-century horizontal watermill.

㉖ Wexford

Road map D5. Co Wexford. 17,000. Quay Front (053 912 3111). **discoverireland.ie/southeast**

Wexford's name derives from *Waesfjord*, a Norse word meaning "estuary of the mud flats". It thrived as a port for centuries but the silting of the harbour in the Victorian era put an end to most sea traffic. Wexford's quays, from where ships once sailed to Bristol, Tenby and Liverpool, are now used mainly by a fleet of humble mussel dredgers.

Wexford is a vibrant place, packed with fine pubs and boasting a varied arts scene. The town's singular style is often linked to its linguistic heritage. The *yola* dialect, which was spoken by early settlers, survives in the local pronunciation of certain words.

Wexford retains few traces of its past, but the Viking fishbone street pattern still exists, with narrow alleys fanning off the meandering Main Street. Keyser's Lane, linking South Main Street with The Crescent, is a tiny tunnel-like Viking alley which once led to the Norse waterfront. The Normans were responsible for Wexford's town walls, remnants of which include one of the original gateways. Behind it lies **Selskar Abbey**, the ruin of a 12th-century Augustinian monastery. King Henry II is said to have done penance here for the murder of Thomas à Becket in 1170.

Sign of a popular Wexford pub

Wexford also has several handsome buildings dating from a later period, including the 18th-century market house (now an arts centre), known as the **Cornmarket**, on Main Street. The nearby square, the **Bull Ring**, is of historic note: it was used for bull-baiting in Norman times and was the scene of a cruel massacre by Cromwell's men in 1649.

Wexford Opera Festival, held in October, is the leading operatic event in the country. It takes place at the state-of-the-art **Wexford Opera House** on the site of the old Theatre Royal. Aficionados praise the festival for its intimate atmosphere – both during performances and afterwards, when artists and audience mingle together in the pubs; the Centenary Stores off Main Street is a favourite.

Environs

Skirting the shore just east of the town is **Wexford Wildfowl Reserve**. It covers 100 ha (250 acres) of reclaimed land and is noted for its geese: over a third of the world's entire population of Greenland white-fronted geese winter here between October and April.

The mudflats also attract large numbers of swans and waders. The birds can be viewed from hides and an observation tower. Another way to enjoy the region's wildlife is to take a boat trip up the Slaney River to **Raven Point** to see the seal colony.

Wexford Opera House
High Street. **Tel** 053 912 2400. **wexfordoperahouse.ie**

Wexford Wildfowl Reserve
Wexford. **Tel** 053 912 3406. **Open** daily. at weekends.

Boat Trips
Harbour Thrills, Seaview, Murrintown. **Tel** 085 732 9787.

㉗ Johnstown Castle

Road map D5. Co Wexford. **Tel** 053 914 2888. to Wexford. Gardens: **Open** 9am–4:30pm daily (till 5:30pm in summer). **Closed** 24 & 25 Dec.

Johnstown Castle, a splendid Gothic Revival mansion, lies amid gardens and woodland 6 km (4 miles) southwest of Wexford. In state hands since 1945, the castle is closed to the

Façade of Johnstown Castle

Vast crescent of sand and shingle beach at Rosslare

public. However, it is possible to visit the **Irish Agriculture Museum**, housed in the castle's farm buildings. Reconstructions illustrate traditional trades and there is an excellent exhibition on the Famine. There are also interesting exhibitions on traditional village crafts and country kitchens.

The real glory are the beautiful castle grounds, from the Italian garden to the lakes. Azaleas and camellias flourish alongside an array of trees including Japanese cedars and redwoods. The lakes are home to a wide range of waterfowl – mute swans, water hens, little grebes and heron.

Hidden among the dense woods west of the house lurk the ruins of **Rathlannon Castle**, a medieval tower house.

Irish Agriculture Museum
Johnstown Castle. **Tel** 053 918 4671. **Open** Apr–Oct: 9am–5pm daily (till 4pm Nov–Mar). limited.
irishagrimuseum.ie

28 Saltee Islands

Road map D5. Co Wexford. from Wexford to Kilmore Quay: Wed & Sat. from Kilmore Quay: Apr–Sep (weather permitting). **Tel** 053 91 29637. **salteeislands.info**

These islands off the south coast of Wexford are a haven for sea birds. Great and Little Saltee together form Ireland's largest bird sanctuary, nurturing an impressive array, from gannets and gulls to puffins and Manx shearwaters. Great Saltee particularly is famous for its colonies of cormorants. It also has more than 1,000 pairs of guillemots and is a popular stopping-off place for spring and autumn migrations. A bird-monitoring programme is in progress, and a close watch is also kept on the colony of more than 100 grey seals.

The two uninhabited islands are privately owned, but visitors are welcome. Boat trips are run in fine weather from **Kilmore Quay**. These leave in late morning and return mid-afternoon. Kilmore Quay is a fishing village built on Precambrian gneiss rock – the oldest rock in Ireland. Pretty thatched cottages nestle above a fine sandy beach and the harbour.

29 Rosslare

Road map D5. Co Wexford. 2,000. (053 912 3111).
rosslareharbour.ie

Rosslare replaced Wexford as the area's main port after the decline of the original Viking city harbour. The port is so active today that people tend to asso-ciate the name Rosslare more with the ferry terminal for France and Wales than with the town lying 8 km (5 miles) further north.

Rosslare town prides itself on being the sunniest place in Ireland and draws many holiday-makers. It boasts a fine beach stretching the length of the southern peninsula, some 9.5 km (6 miles). There are a few lively pubs and an excellent golf course fringed by sand dunes plus some great trails and walks north to Rosslare Point. **Rosslare Watersports Centre** rents kayaks and windsurfing equipment, and runs summer camps for children in July and August.

Rosslare Watersports Centre
Tagoat. **Tel** 053 913 2202.
rosslareholidayresort.ie

Colony of gannets nesting on the cliffs of Great Saltee Island

CORK AND KERRY

Cork · Kerry

Magnificent scenery has attracted visitors to this region since Victorian times. Rocky headlands jut out into the Atlantic and colourful fishing villages nestle in the shelter of the bays. County Kerry offers dramatic landscapes and a wealth of prehistoric and early Christian sites, whereas County Cork's gentle charm has enticed many a casual visitor into becoming a permanent resident.

Killarney and its romantic lakes are a powerful magnet for tourists, and so are Cork's attractive coastal towns and villages. Yet the region remains remarkably unspoiled, with a friendly atmosphere and authentic culture still alive in Irish-speaking pockets. There is also a long tradition of arts and crafts in the area.

This corner of Ireland used to be the main point of contact with the Continent. In the 17th century, in response to the threat of invasions from France and Spain, the English built a line of forts along the Cork coast, including the massive Charles Fort at Kinsale.

In the 19th century, the city of Cork was an important departure point for people fleeing from the Famine *(see p223)*, with Cobh the main port for emigrants to the New World. Cork's importance as a port has diminished, but it is still the Republic's second city with a lively cultural scene.

Poverty and temperament helped foster a powerful Republican spirit in the southwest. The region saw much guerrilla action in the War of Independence and the subsequent Civil War. In 1920, the centre of Cork city was burned in an uncontrolled act of reprisal by the notorious Black and Tans *(see pp48–9)*.

Kerry is known as "the Kingdom" on account of its tradition of independence and disregard for Dublin rule. The Irish recognize a distinctive Kerry character, with a boisterous sense of living life to the full. They also make Kerrymen the butt of countless jokes.

As well as the friendliest people in Ireland, the region has some of the finest scenery. Cork has lush valleys and a beautiful coast while Kerry is wilder and more mountainous. The islands off the Kerry coast appear bleak and inhospitable, but many were once inhabited. Remote, rocky Skellig Michael, for example, was the site of a 6th-century Christian monastery.

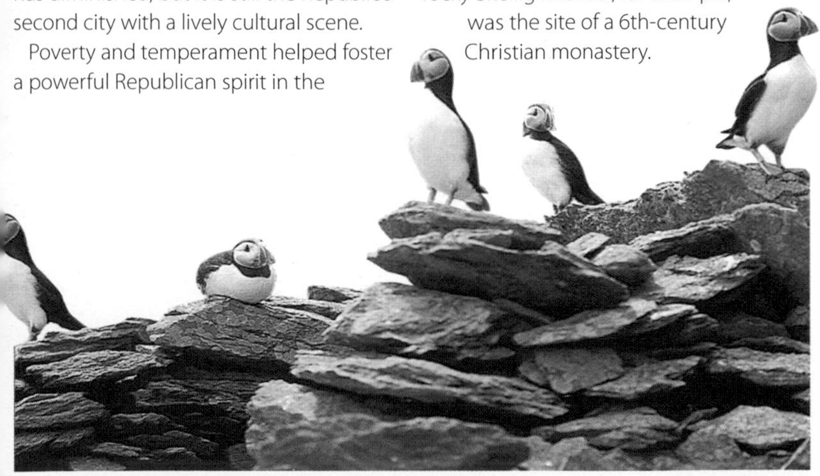

Puffins on the island of Skellig Michael off the coast of Kerry

◀ Flight of stone steps leading to the monastry on Skellig Michael, County Kerry

Exploring Cork and Kerry

Killarney is a popular base with tourists for exploring Cork and Kerry, especially for touring the Ring of Kerry and the archaeological remains on the Dingle Peninsula. Despite the changeable weather, the region attracts many visitors who come to see its dramatic scenery and lush vegetation. As you pass through quiet fishing villages and genteel towns, such as Kenmare, you will always encounter a friendly welcome from the locals. For the adventurous there are plenty of opportunities to go riding, hiking or cycling. Cork city offers a more cosmopolitan atmosphere, with its art galleries and craft shops.

Kissing the Blarney Stone at Blarney Castle near Cork

Getting Around

To explore the region a car is essential. The N22 connects Cork, Killarney and Tralee while the N71 follows the coastline via Clonakilty, Bantry and on to Killarney. In the more remote parts the road signs may only be written in Irish. Killarney is the base for organized coach tours of the area. The train service from Cork to Dublin is efficient, and trains also connect Killarney with Dublin and Cork, but you may have to change trains en route. Buses run throughout the region, but services to the smaller sights may be infrequent.

For hotels and restaurants in this region see pp298–9 and pp313–16

Cattle grazing near Ardfert Cathedral

Sights at a Glance

1. Carrigafoyle Castle
2. Ardfert Cathedral
3. Tralee
4. Dingle (An Daingean)
5. Gallarus Oratory
7. Killarney
8. *Lakes of Killarney pp166–7*
9. Valentia Island
10. The Skellig Islands
12. Kenmare
13. Beara Peninsula
14. Garnish Island
15. *Bantry House pp172–3*
16. Bantry Bay
17. Mizen Head
18. Baltimore
19. Drombeg Stone Circle
20. Clonakilty
21. Timoleague Abbey
22. River Lee
23. Blarney Castle
24. *Kinsale pp176–7*
25. *Cork pp178–80*
26. River Blackwater
27. Cobh
28. Old Midleton Distillery
29. Youghal

Tours

6. Dingle Peninsula
11. Ring of Kerry

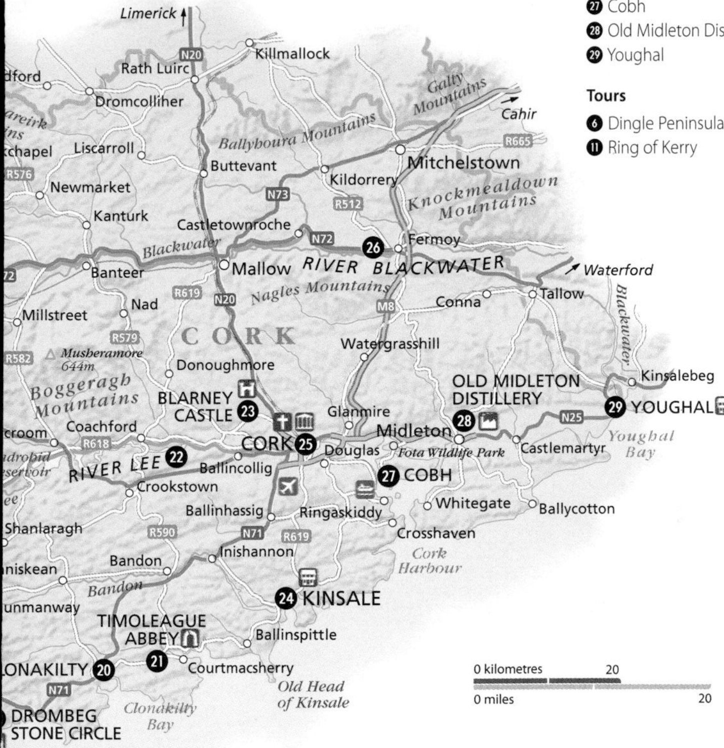

Key

- Motorway
- Major road
- Secondary road
- Minor road
- Scenic route
- Main railway
- Minor railway
- County border
- Summit

Newman's Mall in the quaint village of Kinsale

For additional map symbols *see back flap*

Ardfert Cathedral and the ruins of Teampall na Hoe and Teampall na Griffin

❶ Carrigafoyle Castle

Road map B5. Co Kerry. 🚌 to Listowel.

High above the Shannon estuary, 3 km (2 miles) from Ballylongford, this 15th-century castle belonged to the O'Connor clan, who ruled much of northern Kerry. The English besieged or sacked it repeatedly but the body blow was delivered in 1649 by Cromwellian forces *(see p43)*. The ruins include a keep and walled bawn, with romantic views of the estuary from the top of the tower.

Ruined keep of Carrigafoyle Castle

❷ Ardfert Cathedral

Road map A5. Co Kerry. **Tel** 066 713 4711. **Open** Easter–Sep: daily; rest of year on request.
W heritageireland.ie

This complex of churches is linked to the cult of St. Brendan the Navigator *(see p219)*, who was born nearby in 484 and founded a monastery here in the 6th century. The ruined cathedral dates back to the 12th century and retains a delicate Romanesque doorway and blind arcading. The battlements were added in the 15th century. The south transept houses an exhibition of the history of the site. In the graveyard stand the remains of a Romanesque nave-and-chancel church, Teampall na Hoe, and a late Gothic chapel, Teampall na Griffin. The latter is named after the curious griffins carved beside an interior window.

A short walk away are the ruins of a Franciscan friary. It was founded by Thomas Fitzmaurice in 1253, but the cloisters and south chapel date from the 15th century.

Environs

Just northwest of Ardfert is **Banna Strand**. Irish patriot Roger Casement landed here in 1916 on a German U-boat, bringing in rifles for the Easter Rising *(see pp48–9)*. He was arrested as soon as he landed and a memorial stands on the site of his capture. A 20-minute drive north of Ardfert, in the village of Ballyduff, stands the 28-m (92-ft) high **Ratoo Round Tower**. Dating from the 10th or 11th century, it was built as a lookout to warn of Viking attack. The tower contains a sheela-na-gig, a carving used as a protective symbol and the only one in a round tower in Ireland.

❸ Tralee

Road map B5. Co Kerry. 203,000. 🚉 🚌 ℹ Ashe Memorial Hall, Denny St (066 712 1288). Fri.
W discoverireland.ie/southwest

Host to the renowned Rose of Tralee International Festival *(see p53)*, Tralee has made great strides in promoting its cultural and leisure facilities. The town's main attraction is **Kerry County Museum**. Its theme park, "Kerry the Kingdom", offers a show on Kerry scenery and a display of archaeological finds. The "Geraldine Experience" brings one back to medieval times.

The **Siamsa Tíre** National Folk Theatre of Ireland is a great ambassador for Irish culture. Traditional song and dance performances take place here throughout the summer. Just

Steam train on the narrow-gauge railway between Tralee and Blennerville

outside Tralee is the authentic **Blennerville Windmill**. Opposite the windmill is the Lee Valley Park, where a wetlands centre and eco-park opened in 2012. The Steam Railway connects the park with Tralee along a narrow gauge track. The train also runs from Ballyard Station to the windmill.

Kerry County Museum
Ashe Memorial Hall, Denny St. **Tel** 066 712 7777. **Open** Jan–May & Sep–Dec: 9:30am–6pm Tue–Sat; Jun–Aug: 9am–5:30pm daily; 10am–5pm Sun & bank hol Mon. **Closed** 1 week at Christmas.

Siamsa Tíre
Town Park, Denny St. **Tel** 066 712 3055. **Open** for performances May–Sep.

Blennerville Windmill Lane
Tel 066 712 1064. **Open** Apr–Oct: daily.

Steam Railway
Ballyard Station. **Tel** 066 712 1064. **Open** May–Sep: daily.

Gallarus Oratory, a dry-stone early Christian church

4 Dingle

Road map A5. Co Kerry. 2,000. Apr–Oct. Strand St (066 915 1188). Fri. **discoverireland.ie/southwest**

This once remote Irish-speaking town is today a thriving fishing port and an increasingly popular tourist centre. Brightly painted craft shops and cafés abound, often with slightly hippy overtones.

Dingle Bay is attractive, with a ramshackle harbour lined with fishing trawlers. Along the quayside are lively bars offering music and seafood. The harbour is home to Dingle's biggest star: Fungi, the dolphin, who has been a permanent resident since 1984 and can be visited by boat or on swimming trips. Other sea creatures can be seen at Ocean World, a great attraction with breathtaking underwater tunnels that bring visitors face to face with the local sea life.

5 Gallarus Oratory

Road map A5. Co Kerry. to Dingle. **Tel** 064 663 2402. **Open** May–Aug: 10am–6pm. (Apr–Sep)

Shaped like an upturned boat, this miniature church overlooks Smerwick Harbour. It was built some time between the 6th and 9th centuries and is the best-preserved early Christian church in Ireland. It represents the apogee of dry-stone corbelling, using techniques first developed by Neolithic tomb-makers. The stones were laid at a slight angle, allowing water to run off.

Fishing trawlers moored alongside the quay at Dingle

❻ A Tour of the Dingle Peninsula

The Dingle Peninsula offers some of Ireland's most beautiful scenery. To the north rises the towering Brandon Mountain, while the west coast has some spectacular seascapes. A drive around the area, which takes at least half a day, reveals fascinating antiquities ranging from Iron Age stone forts to inscribed stones, early Christian oratories and beehive huts. These are sometimes found on private land, so you may be asked for a small fee by the farmer to see them. Some parts of the peninsula – especially the more remote areas – are still Gaelic speaking, so many road signs are written only in Irish.

View from Clogher Head

⑦ Riasc *(An Riasc)*
This excavated monastic settlement dates from the 6th century. The enclosure contains the remains of an oratory, several cross-inscribed slabs and an inscribed pillar stone *(see p247)*.

⑥ Ballyferriter *(Baile an Fheirtéaraigh)*
The attractions of this friendly village include the pastel-coloured cottages, Louis Mulcahy's pottery and a museum featuring the cultural heritage of the area.

⑤ Blasket Centre *(Ionad an Bhlascaoid)*
Overlooking Blasket Sound, the centre explains the literature, language and way of life of the inhabitants of the Blasket Islands. The islanders moved to the mainland in 1953.

④ Dunmore Head *(Ceann an Dúin Mhoir)*
Mainland Ireland's most westerly point offers dramatic views of the Blaskets.

③ Slea Head *(Ceann Sléibe)*
As you round the Slea Head promontory, the Blasket Islands come into full view. The sculpture of the Crucifixion beside the road is known locally as the Cross *(An Cros)*.

Key

- Tour route
- Other roads
- Viewpoint

0 kilometres 2
0 miles 1

⑨ **Kilmalkedar *(Cill Maolchéadair)***
Once a pagan centre of worship, Kilmalkedar is home to a ruined Irish Romanesque church with stone carvings. The graveyard still contains primitive pagan stones, a cross and a sundial.

⑧ **Gallarus Oratory *(Séipéilín Ghallrois)***
This tiny, dry-stone church *(see p161)* is a relic of early Irish Christianity.

① **Dingle *(An Daingean)***
Dingle, famous for local resident Fungi the dolphin, is a good place to eat, drink or stay the night *(see p161)*.

Dunbeg Fort *(An Dún Beag)*
:ing from the Iron Age, this is one he best-preserved promontory ts in Ireland. Just beyond are the ian beehive huts, early Christian :s thought to have been built for grims visiting the area.

Tips for Drivers

Length: 40 km (25 miles).
Stopping-off points: Most villages on the route, such as Dunquin and Ballyferriter, have friendly bars offering pub meals. There are also many opportunities to stop for a picnic. On the winding coast road around Slea Head stop only at the safe and clearly marked coastal viewing points *(see also pp365–7)*.

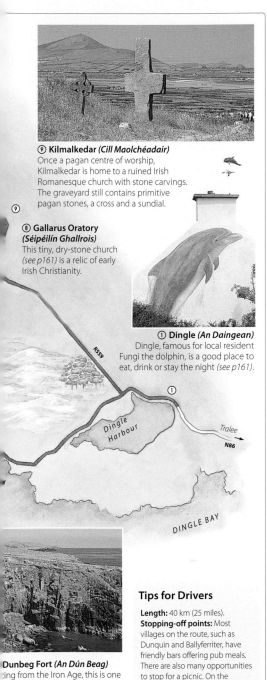

Jaunting cars waiting to take visitors to sights around Killarney

❼ Killarney

Road map B5. Co Kerry. 15,000. Beech Rd (064 663 1633). Fri. **killarney.ie**

Killarney is often derided as "a tourist town" but this has not dented its cheerful atmosphere. The infectious Kerry humour is personified by the wise-cracking jarveys whose families have run jaunting cars (pony and trap rides) here for generations. The town gets busy in summer but still has much to offer then, with shops open until 10pm, several excellent restaurants, and a few prestigious hotels around the lakes. From the town visitors can explore the sights around the Lakes of Killarney *(see pp166–7)* and the surrounding heather-covered hills.

Environs
Overlooking the lakes and a short drive from Killarney is **Muckross House**, an imposing mansion built in 1843 in Elizabethan style. Inside, the elegant rooms are decorated with period furnishings. The mansion is also home to the Museum of Kerry Folklife. Next to the house is the Walled Garden Centre; the landscaped gardens are particularly beautiful in spring when the rhododendrons and azaleas are in bloom. The nearby Muckross Traditional Farms portray rural life in the 1930s and 1940s.

Muckross House
Footer 6 km (3.5 miles), The National Park, S of Killarney. **Tel** 064 667 0144.
Open Jul–Aug: 9am– 7pm daily; Sep–Jun: 9am–5:30pm daily.
Closed 26 Dec–2 Jan.
muckross-house.ie

Stunning view of the Sneem River on the Ring of Kerry ▶

❽ Lakes of Killarney

Renowned for its splendid scenery, the area is one of Ireland's most popular tourist attractions. The three lakes are contained within Killarney National Park. Although the landscape is dotted with ruined castles and abbeys, the lakes are the focus of attention: the moody water scenery is subject to subtle shifts of light and colour. The area has entranced many artists and writers including Thackeray, who praised "a precipice covered with a thousand trees … and other mountains rising as far as we could see". In autumn, the bright red fruits of the strawberry tree colour the shores of the lakes.

★ Muckross House
The 19th-century manor *(see p163)* enjoys a lovely location overlooking the lakes. Visit the wildlife centre for an introduction to the flora and fauna of the National Park.

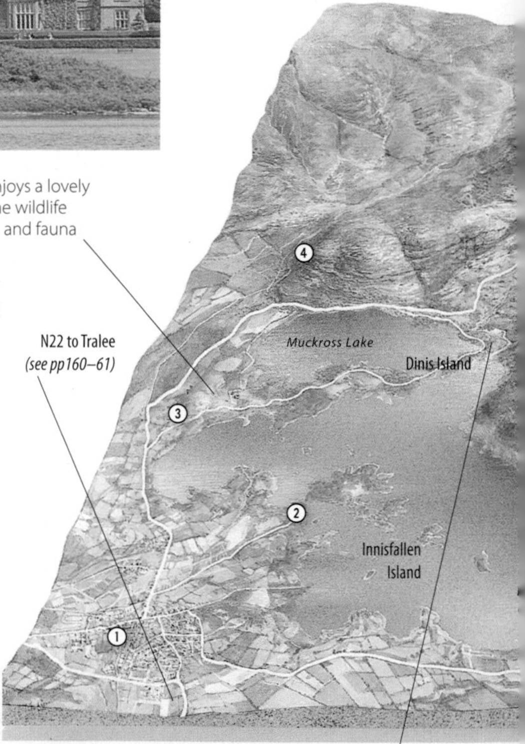

KEY

① **Killarney** *(see p163)* is the main town from which tourists visit the sights around the lakes.

② **Ross Castle**, built in the 15th century, was the last stronghold under Irish control to be taken by Cromwellian forces in 1653.

③ **Muckross Abbey** was founded by the Franciscans in 1448, but was burnt down by Cromwellian forces in 1653.

④ **Torc Waterfall**, an 18-m (60-ft) high waterfall, cascades through the wooded Friars' Glen into Muckross Lake. A pretty path winds up to the top revealing views of Torc Mountain.

⑤ **Long Range River**

⑥ **Ladies' View** gets its name from the delight it gave Queen Victoria's ladies-in-waiting when they visited the spot in 1861.

⑦ **Purple Mountain, 832 m (2,730 ft)**

⑧ **Tomies Mountain, 735 m (2,411 ft)**

⑨ **Kate Kearney's Cottage** was home to a local beauty who ran an illegal drinking house for passing travellers in the mid-19th century. It is still a pub today.

Meeting of the Waters
This beauty spot, best seen from Dinis Island, is where the waters from the Upper Lake meet Muckross Lake and Lough Leane. At the Old Weir Bridge, boats shoot the rapids.

For hotels and restaurants in this region see pp298–9 and pp313–16

Upper Lake
This narrow lake is the smallest of the three lakes. It flows into the Long Range River to the Meeting of the Waters.

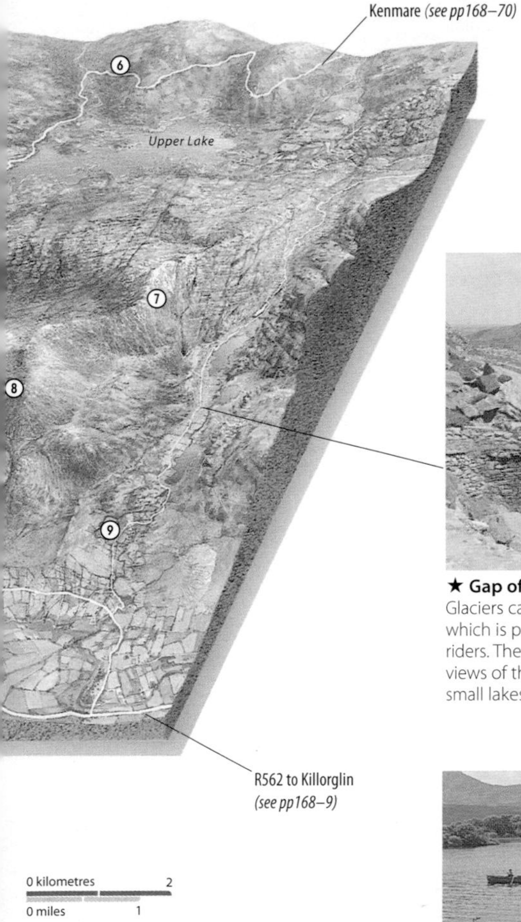

VISITORS' CHECKLIST

Practical Information
Road map B5. Killarney, Co Kerry. Killarney (064 663 1633). National Park: **Tel** 064 663 1440. **Open** pedestrian access at all times; 8am–6pm (7pm Jun–Aug) for car access. **killarney nationalpark.ie** Muckross House: **Tel** 064 667 0144. **Open** 9am–5:30pm (7pm Jul–Aug) daily. **muckross-house.ie** Ross Castle: **Tel** 064 663 5851. **Open** mid-Mar–mid-Oct: daily. obligatory. The Lily of Killarney: (064 663 3358): May–Oct. Kate Kearney's Cottage: **Tel** 064 664 4146. **Open** Easter–Oct: 9am–midnight daily; Nov–Easter: 11am–10pm. **katekearneyscottage.com**

Transport
Kerry (066 976 4644). from Ross Castle: MV Pride of the Lakes (064 662 7737): Apr–Oct (weather permitting).

★ Gap of Dunloe
Glaciers carved this dramatic mountain pass which is popular with walkers, cyclists and horse riders. The route through the gap offers fabulous views of the boulder-strewn gorge and three small lakes.

Lough Leane
The largest lake is dotted with uninhabited islands and fringed with wooded slopes. Boat trips run between Ross Castle and Innisfallen.

9 Valentia Island

Road map A5. Co Kerry. to Cahirciveen. May–Sep: Cahirciveen (066 947 2589). **visitvalentiaisland.ie**

Although it feels like the mainland, Valentia is an island, albeit linked by a causeway to Portmagee. It is 11 km (7 miles) long and noted for its seascapes, water sports and archaeological sites. Valentia is also popular for its proximity to the Skellig Islands.

The **Skellig Experience Centre**, near the causeway, houses an audiovisual display about the monastery on Skellig Michael, the largest of the Skellig Islands. Other subjects include the marine life around the islands, a reminder that the Skellig cliffs lie underwater for a depth of 50- m (165- ft). The centre also operates cruises around the islands. The main village, **Knightstown**, has varied accommodation, pubs and superb views. The island's highest point, **Geokaun Mountain and Fogher Cliffs**, offers 360-degree views. It's perfect for picnics and accessible for cars and walkers of all abilities.

Stairway leading to Skellig Michael monastery

Geokaun Mountain & Fogher Cliffs
Valentia Island. **Tel** 087 649 3728.
Open 6am–11pm daily.
geokaun.com

Skellig Experience Centre
Valentia Island. **Tel** 066 947 6306.
Open May–Sep: daily; Mar, Apr, Oct & Nov: varying days (call ahead).
skelligexperience.com

10 The Skellig Islands

Road map A6. Co Kerry. mid-Mar–Oct: from Valentia Island.
Tel 066 947 6306.

Skellig Michael, also known as Great Skellig, is a UNESCO World Heritage Site. This inhospitable rock rising out of the Atlantic covers an area of 17 ha (44 acres). Perched on a ledge almost 218-m (714-ft) above sea level and reached by a 1,000-year-old stairway is an isolated early Christian monastery. Monks

11 A Tour of the Ring of Kerry

This long-established route around the Iveragh Peninsula, which can be taken in either direction, is always referred to as the Ring of Kerry. Allow a day to see its captivating mountain and coastal scenery, dotted with slate-roofed fishing villages. Set out early to avoid the mass of coach tours which converge on the towns for lunch and tea. There are interesting detours across the spine of the peninsula.

③ **Glenbeigh**
Stop here to visit the Kerry Bog Village, a cluster of reconstructed cottages dating from the 1800s.

④ **Cahirciveen**
The main town on the peninsula is home to a unique heritage centre.

Beach at Ballinskelligs

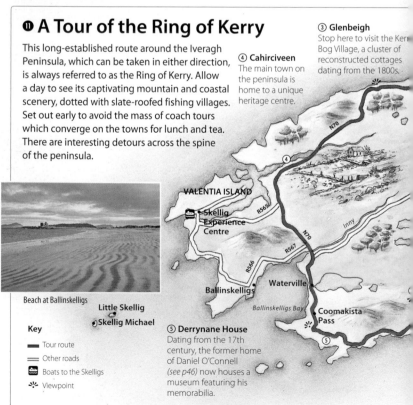

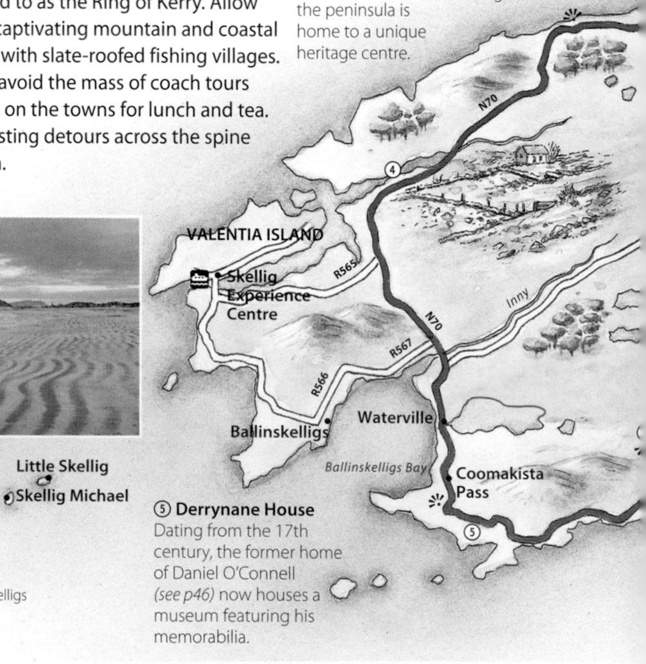

⑤ **Derrynane House**
Dating from the 17th century, the former home of Daniel O'Connell *(see p46)* now houses a museum featuring his memorabilia.

settled for solitude on Skellig Michael during the 6th century, building a cluster of six corbelled beehive cells and two boat-shaped oratories. These dry-stone structures are still standing. The monks were self-sufficient, trading eggs, feathers and seal meat with passing boats in return for cereals, tools and animal skins. The skins were needed to produce the vellum on which the monks copied their religious manuscripts. They remained on this bleak island until the 12th century, when they retreated to the Augustinian priory at Ballinskelligs on the mainland.

Today the only residents on Skellig Michael are the thousands of sea birds which nest and breed on the high cliffs, including storm petrels, puffins and Manx shearwaters. The breeding colonies are protected from predators by the sea and rocky shores.

Gannets flying around the precipitous cliffs of Little Skellig

Closer to the mainland is Little Skellig. Covering an area of 7 ha (17 acres), the island has steep cliffs. Home to a variety of sea birds, it has one of the largest colonies of gannets (about 22,000 breeding pairs) in the world. Giant basking sharks, dolphins and turtles can also be seen here. Except for a pier on Skellig Michael, there are no landing stages on the islands. This is to discourage visitors from disturbing the wildlife, plant cover and archaeological remains. Atlantic gales permitting, there are boat tours around the islands. Private operators also run unofficial trips to the islands from Portmagee or Ballinskelligs during the summertime.

Despite objections from conservationists, the island was used as a filming location for *Star Wars: The Force Awakens*, released in December 2015 and *Star Wars: Episode VIII*, which will appear in theatres in 2017.

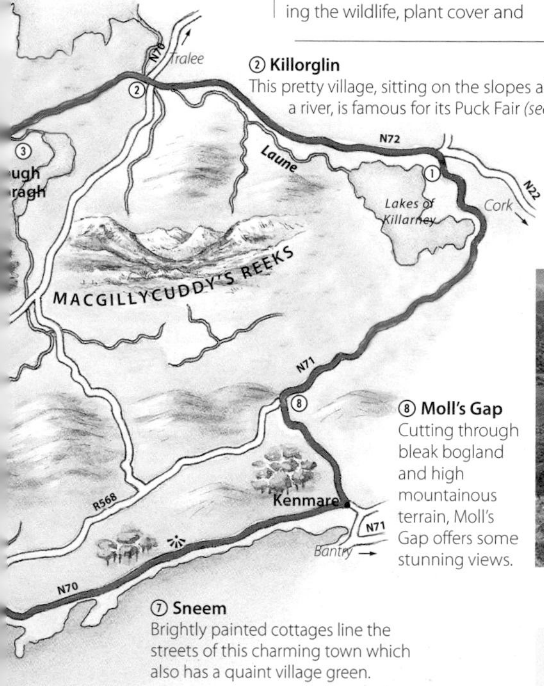

② Killorglin
This pretty village, sitting on the slopes above a river, is famous for its Puck Fair *(see p53)*.

① Killarney
Visitors touring the Ring of Kerry usually start and finish here. The route passes lovely views of the Lakes of Killarney *(see pp166–7)*.

⑧ Moll's Gap
Cutting through bleak bogland and high mountainous terrain, Moll's Gap offers some stunning views.

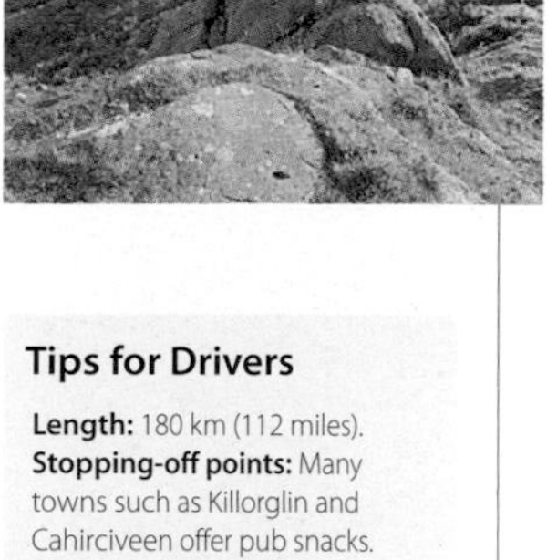

⑦ Sneem
Brightly painted cottages line the streets of this charming town which also has a quaint village green.

⑥ Staigue Fort
Set on a hill up a narrow track, this Iron Age, dry-stone fort *(caher)* is the best preserved in Ireland.

0 kilometres 10
0 miles 5

Tips for Drivers

Length: 180 km (112 miles).
Stopping-off points: Many towns such as Killorglin and Cahirciveen offer pub snacks. Finish the day in one of the excellent gourmet restaurants in Kenmare *(see also pp365–7)*.

Sign for a bed-and-breakfast in Kenmare

⑫ Kenmare

Road map B5. Co Kerry. 1,700. May–Sep: The Square (064 664 1233). Wed. **discoverireland.ie**

This town, on the mouth of the River Sheen, was founded in 1670 by Sir William Petty, Cromwell's surveyor general. However, Kenmare's appearance owes more to his descendant, the first Marquess of Lansdowne who, in 1775, made it a model landlord's town of neat stone façades with decorative plasterwork.

Today Kenmare is renowned for its traditional lace. During the famine years, local nuns introduced lace-making to create work for the women and girls. Other attractions include the fine hotels *(see p298–9)* and gourmet restaurants *(see p315)*. The town is also an excellent base for exploring the Beara Peninsula and the Ring of Kerry *(see pp168–9)*.

Set in a riverside glade off Market Street is the **Druid's Circle**, a prehistoric ring of 15 stones associated with human sacrifice.

⑬ Beara Peninsula

Road map A6. Co Cork & Co Kerry. to Glengarriff (daily) & Castletownbere (Mon, Wed, Fri & Sun). Kenmare (064 664 1233).

Dotted with sparsely populated fishing villages surrounded by bleak moorland, this peninsula is remote. It used to be a refuge for smugglers, with the Irish exchanging pilchards for contraband French brandy.

The peninsula offers some spectacular scenery and wonderful walking country. From the **Healy Pass**, which cuts a jagged path across the spine of the Caha Mountains, there are some fine views of Bantry Bay and the rugged landscape of West Cork. To the west of the pass is **Hungry Hill**, the highest mountain in the Caha range and popular with hill walkers.

Encircled by the Caha and Slieve Miskish Mountains is **Castletownbere**, the main town on the peninsula. This sheltered port was once a haven for smugglers, but is now awash with foreign fishing trawlers. McCarthy's Bar on Town Square features an authentic matchmaking booth, where families used to agree marriage terms until a generation ago.

West of Castletownbere stands the shell of **Puxley Mansion**, home of the Puxley family who owned the mines at nearby **Allihies**. Centre of the copper-mining district until the 1930s, it is an interesting place, with tall Cornish-style chimneys and piles of ochre-coloured spoil and is home to the **Allihies Copper Mine Museum**.

From the tip of the peninsula a cable car travels across to **Dursey Island**, with its ruined castle and colonies of sea birds. Licensed to carry six passengers or one large animal at a time, the cable car offers views of Bull, Cow and Calf islands.

From the headland the R757 road back to Kenmare passes through the pretty villages of **Eyeries**, noted for its brightly painted cottages and crafts, and **Ardgroom**, a base for exploring the scenic glacial valley around **Glenbeg Lough**.

Allihies Copper Mine Museum
Allihies. **Tel** 027 73218. **Open** 10am–5:30pm daily.
acmm.ie

⑭ Garnish Island

Road map B6. Co Cork. from Glengarriff (027 63116). Gardens **Tel** 027 63040. **Open** Apr–Oct: daily. limited. **garnishisland.com**

Also known as Ilnacullin, this small island was turned into an

View of Caha Mountains from the Healy Pass, Beara Peninsula

talianate garden with lily pool and folly on Garnish Island

exotic garden in 1910 by Harold Peto for Annan Bryce, a Belfast businessman. Framed by views of Bantry Bay, the gardens are landscaped with Neo-Classical follies and planted with subtropical flora. The micro-climate and peaty soil provide the damp, warm conditions needed for these ornamental plants to flourish.

Exotic shrubberies abound especially during the summer. In May and June, there are beautiful displays of camellias, azaleas and rhododendrons. There is also a New Zealand fernery, a Japanese rockery, and a rare collection of Bonsai trees. A Martello tower, thought to be the first ever built, crowns the island and among the follies are a clock tower and a Grecian temple.

The centrepiece is a colonnaded Italianate garden, with a Classical folly and ornamental lily pool. Much of its charm resides in the contrast between the cultivated lushness of the garden and the glimpses of wild seascape and barren mountains beyond. An added attraction of the boat trip across to this Gulf Stream paradise is the chance to see cavorting seals in Bantry Bay.

⓯ Bantry House

See pp172–3.

⓰ Bantry Bay

Road map A6. Co Cork. 🚌 to Bantry and Glengarriff. ℹ Mar–Oct: The Square, Bantry (027 50229). **W bantry.ie** Bamboo Park: **Tel** 027 63007. **W bamboo-park.com**

Bantry Bay encompasses the resorts of **Bantry** and **Glengarriff**. It is also a springboard for trips to Mizen Head and the Beara Peninsula.

Bantry nestles beneath the hills which run down to the bay. Just offshore you can see **Whiddy Island**, the original home of the White family, who moved to Bantry House in the early 18th century. Further along is **Bere Island**, a British base until World War II.

Glengarriff, at the head of the bay, exudes an air of Victorian gentility with its neatly painted shopfronts and craft shops. On the coast is the Eccles Hotel, a haunt of Queen Victoria and where George Bernard Shaw supposedly wrote *Saint Joan*.

Bamboo Park in Glengarriff is a unique, exotic garden with 30 different species as well as other tropical plants.

⓱ Mizen Head

Road map A6. Co Cork.
🚌 to Goleen.
ℹ Town Hall, North St, Skibbereen (028 21766).

Mizen Head, the most south-westerly tip of Ireland, has steep cliffs, often lashed by storms. In a lighthouse, **Mizen Head Visitors' Centre** is reached by a bridge. From the car park, a headland walk takes in views of cliffs and Atlantic breakers. The sandy beaches of nearby **Barley Cove** attract bathers and walkers; to the east is **Crookhaven**, a pretty yachting harbour. From here, a walk to Brow Head offers views of the lighthouse.

Mizen Head can be reached either from Bantry via Durrus or from the market town of **Skibbereen**, on the R592, via the charming crafts centre of **Ballydehob** and the village of **Schull**. Trips to Cape Clear Island *(see p174)* leave from Schull in the summer months.

Visitors' Centre
Mizen Head. **Tel** 028 35115.
Open Mar–Oct: daily; Nov–mid-Mar: Sat & Sun. limited.
W mizenhead.net

Rocky cliffs at Mizen Head

⑮ Bantry House

Bantry House has been the home of the White family, formerly Earls of Bantry, since 1739. The original Queen Anne house was built around 1700, but the north façade overlooking the bay was a later addition. Inside is an eclectic collection of art and furnishings brought from Europe by the 2nd Earl of Bantry. Highlights include the Aubusson tapestries made for Marie Antoinette on her marriage to the future Louis XVI. Guestrooms are available here on a bed and breakfast basis.

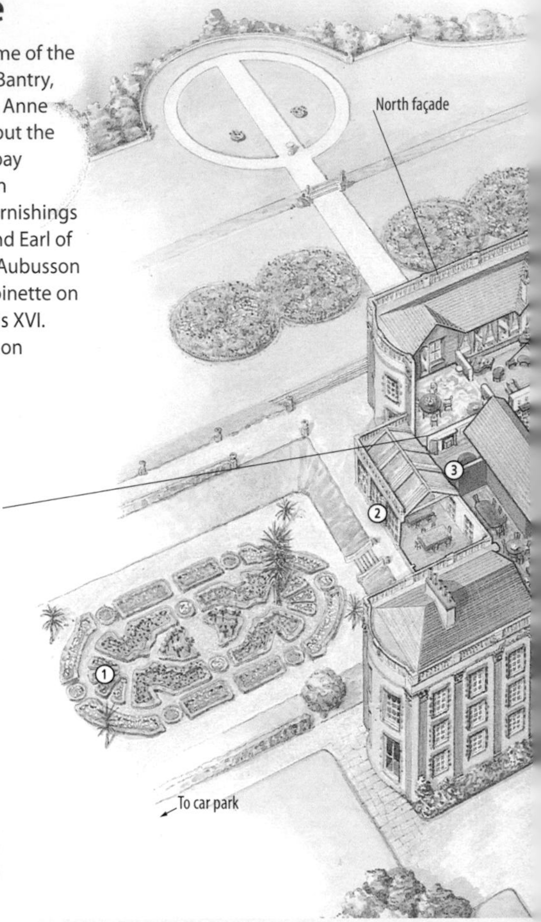

Gobelin Drawing Room
The subject of this 18th-century Gobelin tapestry is *The Bath of Cupid and Psyche*. The room also contains an early 19th-century piano.

KEY

① **The Rose Garden**, laid out in the early 18th century, is, in the words of the 1st Earl of Bantry, "a parterre after the English manner".

② **Loggia**

③ **The anteroom** contains family mementos, china and a collection of 18th-century prints.

④ **Statue of Diana (1840)**

⑤ **Library**

⑥ **The steps**, known as the "Staircase to the Sky", lead to a series of terraces with fabulous views over the house and across the bay.

1st Earl of Bantry (1767–1851)

Richard White, 1st Earl of Bantry, played a leading role in defending Ireland against an attempted invasion by Wolfe Tone and the United Irishmen *(see pp44–5)*. On 16 December 1796, Tone sailed from Brest in Brittany with a fleet of 43 French ships bound for Ireland. White chose strategic spots around Bantry Bay and mustered volunteers to fight. His efforts proved unnecessary as the French fleet was forced back by bad weather. Nonetheless, White was rewarded with a peerage by George III for his "spirited conduct and important services". In 1800 he was made Viscount Bantry, becoming Earl of Bantry in 1816.

★ Rose Drawing Room
The rose-coloured tapestries (c.1770) hanging in this room are thought to have been made for Marie Antoinette on her marriage to the Dauphin of France.

VISITORS' CHECKLIST

Practical Information
Road map B6. Bantry, Co Cork.
Tel 027 50047.
bantryhouse.com
Open Apr–Oct: 10am–5pm daily.
Closed 25 Dec. limited.
Concerts: monthly & 2 summer music festivals.
Tel 027 52788.
westcorkmusic.ie.
See also Hotels p298.

Transport
from Cork to Bantry daily.

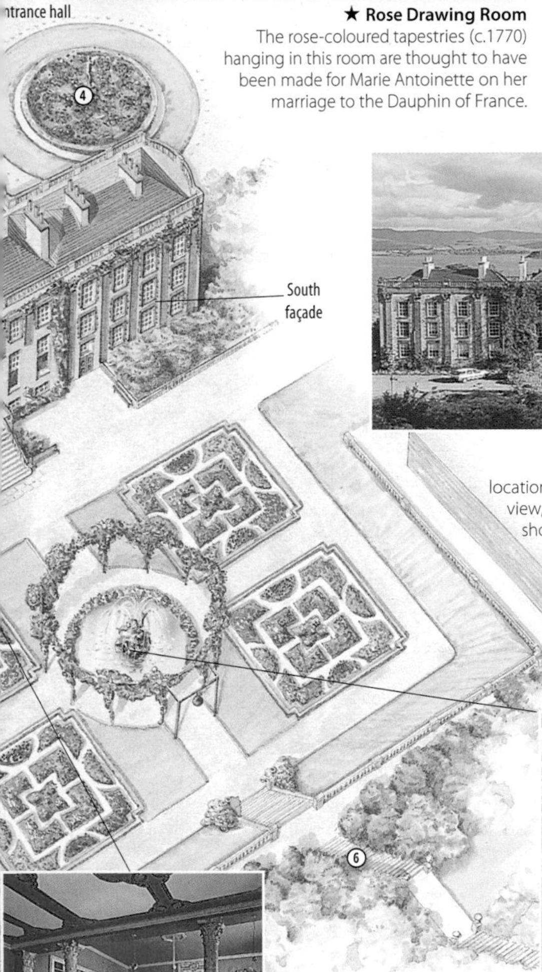

★ View of House and Bantry Bay
Bantry House enjoys a magnificent location overlooking Bantry Bay. This lovely view, from the terraces above the house, shows the harbour with Whiddy Island and the Caha Mountains beyond.

★ Blue Dining Room
This room is dominated by portraits of King George III and Queen Charlotte by court painter Allan Ramsay. The Spanish chandelier is decorated with Meissen china flowers.

Italian Garden
Inspired by the Boboli Gardens in Florence, this garden encircles a pool decorated in Classical Grotesque style. It was designed in the early 1850s by the 2nd Earl.

⓲ Baltimore

Road map B6. Co Cork. 300. to Sherkin Island (087 911 7377) **sherkinisland.ie/eu**; to Cape Clear Island (028 39159). **cailinoir.com**

Baltimore's most bizarre claim to fame dates back to 1631 when more than 100 citizens were carried off as slaves by Algerian pirates. Now that the threat of being kidnapped has gone, this village appeals to the yachting fraternity and island-hoppers. Like neighbouring Schull, the town bustles with summer festivals.

Overlooking the harbour is a ruined 15th-century castle, once the stronghold of the O'Driscoll clan. Also worth a visit are the seafood pubs, including Bushe's Bar, an atmospheric inn hung with nautical memorabilia. Behind the village, cliff walks lead to splendid views of Carbery's Hundred Isles – mere specks on Roaringwater Bay. Baltimore Beacon is an important marker for boats in the bay.

A short ferry ride away is **Sherkin Island** with its sandy beaches in the west, ruined 15th-century abbey, marine station and pubs. The ferry ride to **Cape Clear Island** is more dramatic, as the boat weaves between sharp black rocks to this remote, Irish-speaking island, noted for its bird observatory in the North Harbour. There are spectacular views of the mainland.

Distinctive white beacon for boats approaching Baltimore

Drombeg Stone Circle, erected around the 2nd century BC

⓳ Drombeg Stone Circle

Road map B6. Co Cork. to Skibbereen or Clonakilty.

On the Glandore road 16 km (10 miles) west of Clonakilty, Drombeg is the finest of the many stone circles in County Cork. Dating back to about 150 BC, this circle of 17 standing stones is 9.5- m (31- ft) in diameter. At the winter solstice, the rays of the setting sun fall on the flat altar stone which faces the entrance to the circle, marked by two upright stones.

Nearby is a small stream with a Stone Age cooking pit *(fulacht fiadh)*, similar to one at Craggaunowen *(see p194)*. A fire was made in the hearth and hot stones from the fire were dropped into the cooking pit to heat the water. Once the water boiled, the meat, usually venison, was added.

⓴ Clonakilty

Road map B6. Co Cork. 4,000. 25 Ashe Street (023 883 3226). **clonakilty.ie**

Founded as an English outpost around 1588, this market town has a typically hearty West Cork atmosphere. The **West Cork Regional Museum**, housed in an old schoolhouse, remembers the town's industrial heritage. A number of quayside buildings, linked to the town's industrial past, have been restored. Particularly pleasant is the Georgian nucleus of Emmet Square.

Until the 19th century Clonakilty was a noted linen producer. Today, it is renowned for its rich black puddings, hand-painted Irish signs and traditional music pubs. Near the town centre is a model village, depicting the town as it was in the 1940s. Just east of town is the reconstructed **Lios-na-gCon Ring Fort**, with earthworks, huts and souterrains *(see p24)*. A causeway links Clonakilty to **Inchydoney** beach.

Sign for Clonakilty black pudding

West Cork Regional Museum
Western Rd. **Tel** 023 883 3115.
Open May–Oct (call for timings).

Lios-na-gCon Ring Fort
Tel 086 059 1854. **Open** by appt only; call ahead. **liosnagcon.com**

㉑ Timoleague Abbey

Road map B6. Co Cork. to Clonakilty or Courtmacsherry. **Open** daily. **timoleague.ie**

Timoleague Abbey enjoys a waterside setting overlooking an inlet where the Argideen estuary opens into Courtmacsherry Bay. The abbey, founded around the late 13th century, is a ruined Franciscan friary. The buildings have been extended at various times. The earliest section is the chancel of the Gothic church. The most recent ddition, the 16th-century ɔwer, was added by the ranciscan Bishop of Ross. The iary was ransacked by the nglish in 1642 but much of ignificance remains, ıcluding the church, ıfirmary, fine ancet windows, efectory and a valled courtyard. here are also ections of loisters and wine ellars. In keeping vith Franciscan radition, the omplex is plain o the point of austerity. Yet such restraint belied the friars' penchant for high living: the friary prospered on trade in smuggled Spanish wines, easily delivered thanks to its position on the then navigable creek.

Lancet window in ruined church at Timoleague Abbey

22 River Lee

Road Map B6. Co Cork. to Cork. Cork (021 425 5100).

Carving a course through farm- and woodland to Cork city *(see pp178–80)*, the River Lee begins its journey in the lake of the enchanting **Gougane Barra Park**. The shores of the lake are linked by a causeway to **Holy Island,** where St Finbarr, the patron saint of Cork, founded a monastery. The Feast of St Fin Barre, on 25 September, signals celebrations that climax in a pilgrimage to the island on the following Sunday.

The Lee flows through many Irish-speaking market towns and villages. Some, such as **Ballingeary**, with its fine lakeside views, have good angling. The town is also noted for its Irish language college. Further east, near the town of Inchigeela, stand the ruins of **Carrig-nacurra Castle**. Further downstream lies the Gearagh, an alluvial stretch of marsh and woods which has been designated a wildlife sanctuary.

The river then passes through the Sullane valley, home of the thriving market town of **Macroom**. The hulk of a medieval castle, with its restored entrance, lies just off the main square. In 1654, Cromwell granted the castle to Sir William Penn. His son, who was to found the American state of Pennsylvania, also lived here for a time.

Between Macroom and Cork, the Lee Valley passes through a hydroelectric power scheme surrounded by artificial lakes, water meadows and wooded banks. Just outside Cork, on the south bank of the river is **Ballincollig**, home to the fascinating former Royal Gunpowder Mills.

23 Blarney Castle

Road Map B5. Blarney, Co Cork. **Tel** 021 438 5252. to Cork. **Open** daily. **Closed** 24 & 25 Dec. grounds only, no charge. **blarneycastle.ie**

Visitors from all over the world flock to this ruined castle to see the legendary Blarney Stone. Kissing the stone is a long-standing tradition, intended to confer a magical eloquence. It is set in the wall below the castle battlements and, in order to kiss it, the visitor is grasped by the feet and suspended backwards under the parapet.

Little remains of the castle today except the keep, built in 1446 by Dermot McCarthy. Its design is typical of a 15th-century tower house *(see p24)*. The vaulted first floor was once the Great Hall. To reach the battlements you need to climb the 127 steps to the top of the keep.

The castle grounds offer some attractive walks, including a grove of ancient yew trees and limestone rock formations at Rock Close. **Blarney House**, a Scottish baronial mansion and the residence of the Colthurst family since the 18th century, is only open to the public from April to mid-June.

A short walk from the castle, Blarney has a pretty village green with welcoming pubs and some craft shops. The **Blarney Woollen Mills** sells garments and souvenirs.

Battlemented keep and ruined towers of Blarney Castle

㉔ Street-by-Street: Kinsale

For many visitors to Ireland, Kinsale heads the list of places to see. One of the prettiest small towns in Ireland, it has had a long and chequered history. The defeat of the Irish forces and their Spanish allies in the Battle of Kinsale in 1601 signified the end of the old Gaelic order. An important naval base in the 17th and 18th centuries, Kinsale today is a popular yachting centre. It is also famous for the quality of its cuisine – the town's annual Festival of Fine Food attracts food lovers from far and wide. As well as its many wonderful restaurants, the town has pubs and wine bars to cater for all tastes.

Desmond Castle was built around 1500. It is known locally as the "French Prison".

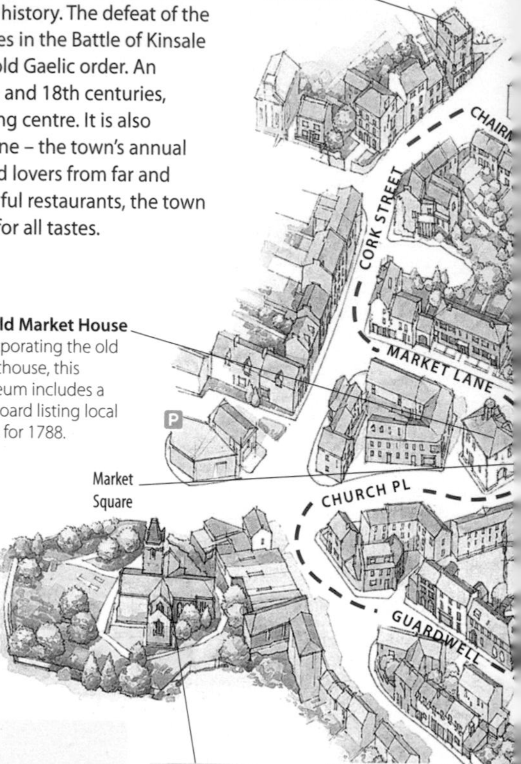

★ Old Market House
Incorporating the old courthouse, this museum includes a toll board listing local taxes for 1788.

Market Square

★ St Multose Church
This much-altered Norman church is named after an obscure 6th-century saint and marks the centre of the medieval town.

Charles Fort

The star-shaped fort is 3 km (2 miles) east of town in Summercove, but can be reached by taking the signposted coastal walk from the quayside, past the village of Scilly. The fort was built in the 1670s by the English to protect Kinsale harbour against foreign naval forces but, because of its vulnerability to land attack, was taken during the siege of 1690 by William of Orange's army. Nonetheless, it remained in service until 1922 when the British forces left the town and handed it over to the Irish Government. Charles Fort remains one of the finest remaining examples of a star-shaped bastion fort in Europe.

Walls and bastions of Charles Fort

Key

— Suggested route

For key to symbols *see back flap*

VISITORS' CHECKLIST

Practical Information
Road map B6. Co Cork. 3,413. Pier Road (021 477 2234). **kinsale.ie** Arts Week (Jul); Annual Regatta (Aug); Kinsale Fringe Jazz Festival (Oct); International Festival of Fine Food (Oct). Old Court House: **Tel** 021 477 7930. **Open** Mar–Oct. St Multose Church: **Tel** 021 477 2220. **Open** daily. Desmond Castle and International Museum of Wine: **Tel** 021 477 4855. **Open** Apr–Sep: 10am–6pm daily. Charles Fort: **Tel** 021 477 2263. **Open** daily.

Transport
from Cork city.

Kinsale Harbour
Situated on the estuary of the Bandon River, this is one of Ireland's most scenic harbours. Kinsale is host to a number of international sailing events throughout the year.

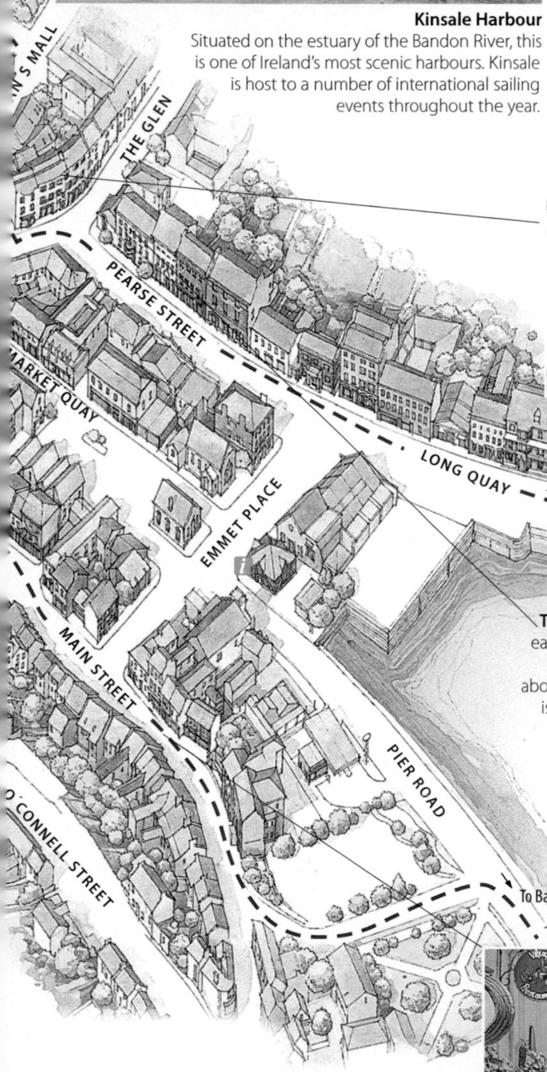

Mother Hubbard's, one of Kinsale's most popular cafés, is situated in the heart of town on Market Street.

The Blue Haven, easily identified by the ornate clock above the entrance, is one of Kinsale's finest seafood restaurants.

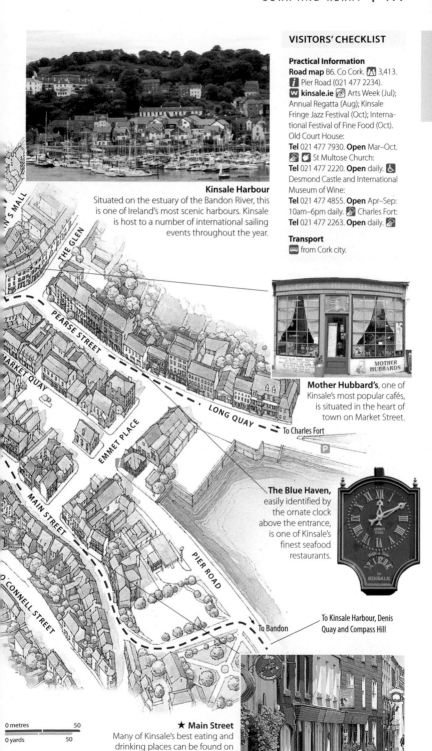

★ Main Street
Many of Kinsale's best eating and drinking places can be found on this picturesque street.

㉕ Cork

Cork city derives its name from the marshy land on the banks of the River Lee – its Irish name *Corcaigh* means marsh – on which St Finbarr founded a monastery around AD 650. The narrow alleys, waterways and Georgian architecture give the city a Continental feel. Since the 19th century, when Cork was a base for the National Fenian movement *(see p47)*, the city has had a reputation for political rebelliousness. Today this mood is reflected in the city's attitude to the arts and its bohemian spirit, much in evidence at the lively October jazz festival.

Clock tower and weather vane of St Anne's Shandon

St Anne's Shandon

Church St. **Tel** 021 450 5906. **Open** daily. **Closed** 2 weeks at Christmas. limited. **shandonbells.ie**

This famous Cork landmark stands on the hilly slopes of the city, north of the River Lee. Built in 1722, the church has a façade made of limestone on two sides, and of red sandstone on the other two. The steeple is topped by a weather vane in the shape of a salmon. The clock face is known by the locals as the "four-faced liar" because, up until 1986 when it was repaired, each face showed slightly different times. Visitors can climb the tower and, for a small fee, ring the famous Shandon bells.

Cork Butter Museum

O'Connell Square. **Tel** 021 430 0600. **Open** Mar–Oct: 10am–5pm daily (to 6pm Jul–Aug), Nov–Feb: 10am–3:30pm Sat & Sun. **corkbutter.museum**

This museum tells the story of Ireland's most important food export and the world's largest butter market. The exchange opened in 1770 and was where butter was graded before it was exported to the rest of the world. By 1892 it was exporting around 500,000 casks of butter a year. The exchange shut in 1924. Next door is the Shandon Craft Centre where visitors can watch craft workers, such as crystal cutters and weavers, at work.

Crawford Art Gallery

Emmet Place. **Tel** 021 480 5042. **Open** 10am–5pm Mon–Sat (to 8pm Thu). **Closed** public hols. **crawfordartgallery.ie**

The red-brick and limestone building that houses Cork's major art gallery dates back to 1724. Built as the city's original custom house, it became a school of design in 1850. In 1884, a well-known art patron, William Horatio Crawford, extended the building to accommodate studios and sculpture and picture galleries.

The gallery houses some fine examples of late 19th- and

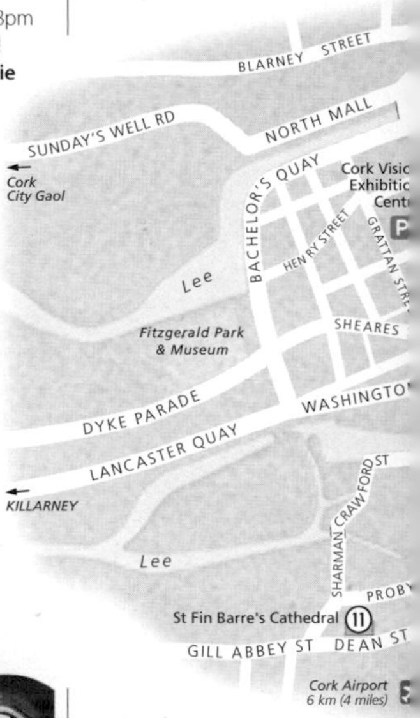

Detail of stained-glass window *The Meeting of St Brendan and the Unhappy Judas* (1911) by Harry Clarke, Crawford Art Gallery

Sights at a Glance

1. St Anne's Shandon
2. Cork Butter Museum
3. St Mary's Dominican Church
4. Crawford Art Gallery
5. Father Mathew Statue
6. English Market
7. National Monument
8. Parliament Bridge
9. Red Abbey
10. Elizabeth Fort
11. St Fin Barre Cathedral

early 20th-century Irish art including paintings by Jack Yeats. There are also three fine windows by Ireland's foremost stained-glass artist, Harry Clarke (1889–1931).

Another attraction is the small collection by British artists and international works by artists such as Joán Miró and Georges Rouault.

The gallery is well known for its excellent café, which serves lunches and delicious teas. The room is decorated with works of art from the collection.

Richly decorated apse ceiling of St Fin Barre's Cathedral

St Fin Barre's Cathedral

Bishop Street. **Tel** 021 496 3387. **Open** May–Oct: daily; Nov–Apr: Mon–Sat. **Closed** 24 Dec–2 Jan (except services).
cathedral.cork.anglican.org

Situated in a quiet part of town, this cathedral is dedicated to the founder and patron saint of the city. Completed in 1870 to the design of William Burges, it is an exuberant triple-spired edifice built in Gothic Revival style. Inside, the painted and gilded apse ceiling shows Christ in Glory surrounded by angels. The stained-glass windows below tell the story of Christ's life.

VISITORS' CHECKLIST

Practical Information
Road map C5. Co Cork.
119,000. Tourist House, Grand Parade (021 425 5100).
discoverireland.ie
Cork Jazz Festival (Oct); Cork Film Festival (Oct/Nov).

Transport
6 km (4 miles) S of Cork (021 431 3131). Kent Station (021 450 6766). Parnell Place (021 450 8188).

Cork City Gaol

Convent Avenue, Sunday's Well. **Tel** 021 430 5022. **Open** daily. **Closed** 25 & 26 Dec.
corkcitygaol.com

A pretty, 20-minute walk west of the city centre leads to the restored City Gaol, complete with its furnished cells. An exhibition traces the lives of individual inmates imprisoned here during the 19th and 20th centuries. Conditions were miserable and, for punishment, prisoners were made to run on a human treadmill that would normally be used to grind grain.

The Radio Museum Experience is also housed in this building and chronicles the development of radio in Ireland and across the world.

South Channel of the River Lee, looking towards Parliament Bridge

For map symbols *see back flap*

Exploring Cork

One of Cork's great attractions is that it is a city built on water. Its heart lies on an island between two arms of the River Lee, and many of today's streets were in fact once waterways lined with warehouses and merchants' residences. Although the Dutch canalside appearance has faded, picturesque quays and bridges remain. Steep lanes rise to the north and south of the central island to the city's 19th-century suburbs, offering wonderful views of the city and its fine buildings.

Selling fruit and vegetables at the English Market

The Quays

Although the river now plays only a minor part in the city's economy, much of Cork's commercial activity still takes place around the Quays (pronounced "kays" in the Cork accent). The South Mall, which covers an arm of the River Lee, was a waterway until the late 18th century. Boats were once moored at the foot of a series of stone steps, some of which are still intact today. These led to merchants' domestic quarters above. The arches below led to warehouses where goods were unloaded.

Near South Mall is **Parliament Bridge**, built in 1806 to commemorate the Act of Union *(see p46)*. It is an elegant, single-arched bridge which is made mainly from limestone. Designed by William Hargrave, it replaced a bridge on the same site which was damaged by a flood in 1804. A short walk away, on Sullivan's Quay, is the Quay Co-Op, a popular vegetarian restaurant and meeting place. From Sullivan's Quay an elegant footbridge, built in 1985, crosses the river to the south end of Grand Parade.

Grand Parade and St Patrick's Street

National Monument, Grand Parade

On Grand Parade, also once a waterway, stands the grandiose **National Monument**, recalling the Irish patriots who died between 1798 and 1867. Bishop Lucey Park, off Grand Parade, has a section of city walls and a fine gateway from the old cornmarket. Between St Patrick's Street and Grand Parade is the **English Market**, a covered fruit and vegetable market established in 1610. Bustling St Patrick's Street, the backbone of the city, was a waterway until 1800 when boats were moored under the steps of gracious houses such as the Chateau Bar *(see p327)*. At the top of the street, near Patrick Bridge, is the **Father Mathew Statue**, a monument to the founder of the Temperance Movement.

St Patrick's Quay on the north channel of River Lee

Paul Street

Noted for its ethnic restaurants, chic bars, bookshops and trendy boutiques, Paul Street is the hub of the liveliest district in town. Just off Paul Street are the busy backstreets of Carey's Lane and French Church Street. In the early 18th century, Huguenots (French Protestants) settled in these streets and set themselves up as butter exporters, brewers and wholesale merchants. This area is Cork's equivalent to Dublin's Temple Bar *(see p82)*.

Shandon Quarter

Crossing the Christy Ring Bridge to Pope's Quay, you will see on your left **St Mary's Dominican Church**, with its portico of Ionic columns topped by a huge pediment. John Redmond Street leads to the northern slopes of Cork, dominated by the spire of St Anne's Shandon *(see p178)* with its fine views of the city. To the northeast lies the lofty Montenotte district, once the epitome of Victorian gentility.

St Fin Barre's Quarter

South of the river, rising above the city, this area's distinctive landmark is St Fin Barre's Cathedral *(see p179)*. Nearby is the ivy-clad **Elizabeth Fort**, a 16th-century structure which was converted into a prison in 1835 and later a Garda (police) station. A short walk to the east lies the **Red Abbey**, a 13th-century relic from an Augustinian abbey – the oldest building in Cork.

Environs

Some beautiful countryside surrounds the city of Cork, especially along the lush valley of the River Lee *(see p175)*. The landscape of East Cork is much gentler than the wild, rocky coastline of West Cork and County Kerry, and the land is much more fertile. Many local attractions make good day trips and there are also plenty of opportunities for outdoor activities such as walking, riding and fishing.

Blackrock Castle Observatory

Blackrock. **Tel** 021 435 7917. **Open** 10am–5pm Mon–Fri; 11am–5pm Sat & Sun. **Closed** 1 Jan & 24–26 Dec. **bco.ie**

On the banks of the River Lee, 1.5 km (1 mile) downstream from the city centre, stands Blackrock Castle. Built in 1582 by Lord Mountjoy as a harbour fortification, the castle was destroyed by fire in 1827 and rebuilt in 1829. Welcoming schools and groups, it houses an exhibition on the cosmos. Further south at Carrigtwohill, near Fota Wildlife Park *(see pp182–3)*, is Barryscourt Castle.

Blackrock Castle standing on the banks of the River Lee

Barryscourt Castle

Carrigtwohill, Co Cork. **Tel** 021 488 2218. **Open** Jun–Sep: 10am–6pm daily. obligatory. **heritageireland.ie**

This castle was the 16th-century seat of the Barry family. The building has been restored and has period fittings and furniture. It is a fine example of a 15th-century tower house with 16th-century additions and alterations. It is roughly rectangular with a four-storey tower house occupying the southwest corner. What makes Barryscourt stand out from most other tower-house complexes is the 50-m- (164-ft-) long hall, which occupies the western section of the castle. Both the Great Hall and the Main Hall are open to the public and the keep houses an exhibition on the arts in Ireland from 1100 to 1600. The orchard has also been restored to an original 16th-century design and has a herb garden by the castle walls.

The 15th-century tower house of Barryscourt Castle

Desmond Castle

Kinsale. **Tel** 021 477 4855. **Open** Apr–Sep: 10am–6pm daily (last adm: 5pm). **heritageireland.ie**

Situated some 16 km (10 miles) south of Cork City, Desmond Castle was built by Maurice Bacach Fitzgerald, the ninth Earl of Desmond, in around 1500. A good example of an urban tower house, the castle consists of a keep with storehouses to the rear. It has spent time as an ordnance store, workhouse, customs house and prison. In 1938 it was declared a national monument.

The castle also houses the **International Museum of Wine**, which tells the story of wine in Ireland and has wine-related artifacts and antique wine bottles.

26 River Blackwater

Road Map B5. Co Cork. to Mallow. to Fermoy, Mallow or Kanturk.

The second-longest river in Ireland after the Shannon *(see p189)*, the Blackwater rises in high bogland in County Kerry. It then flows eastwards through County Cork until it reaches Cappoquin, County Waterford, where it changes course south through wooded sandstone gorges to the sea at Youghal *(see p183)*. Much of the valley is wooded, a reminder that the entire area was forested until the 17th century. The river passes some magnificent country houses and pastoral views. However, the region is best known for its fishing – the Blackwater's tributaries are filled with fine brown trout.

The best way to see the valley is to take the scenic Blackwater Valley Drive from Youghal to Mallow. The route passes through **Fermoy**, a town founded by Scottish merchant John Anderson in 1789. Angling is the town's main appeal, especially for roach, rudd, perch and pike. Further west is **Mallow**, a prosperous town noted for its fishing, golf and horse racing, and a good base for tours of the area. Detours along the tributaries include **Kanturk**, a pleasant market town with a castle, on the River Allow.

Weirs and bridge at Fermoy on the River Blackwater

27 Cobh

Road map C6. Co Cork. 13,000. Old Yacht Club (021 481 3612). **visitcobh.com**

Cobh (pronounced "cove") lies on Great Island, one of the three islands in Cork Harbour which are now linked by causeways. The Victorian seafront has rows of steeply terraced houses overlooked by the Gothic Revival **St Colman's Cathedral**.

Following a visit by Queen Victoria in 1849, Cobh was renamed Queenstown but reverted to its original name in 1922. The town has one of the world's largest natural harbours, hence its rise to prominence as a naval base in the 18th century. It was also a major port for merchant ships and the main port from which Irish emigrants left for America.

Cobh was also a port of call for luxury passenger liners. In 1838, the *Sirius* made the first transatlantic crossing under steam power from here. Cobh was also the last stop for the *Titanic*, before its doomed Atlantic crossing in 1912. Three years later, the *Lusitania* was torpedoed and sunk by a German submarine just off Kinsale *(see pp176–7)*, southwest of Cobh. A memorial on the promenade is dedicated to all those who died in the attack.

Irish Emigration

Between 1848 and 1950 more than six million people emigrated from Ireland – two and a half million of them leaving from Cobh. The famine years of 1844–8 *(see p223)* triggered mass emigration as the impoverished made horrific transatlantic journeys in cramped, insanitary conditions. Many headed for the United States and Canada, and a few risked the long journey to Australia. Up until the early 20th century, emigrants waiting to board the ships were a familiar sight in Cobh. However, by the 1930s world recession and immigration restrictions in the United States and Canada led to a fall in the numbers leaving Ireland.

19th-century engraving of emigrants gathering in Cobh Harbour

The Queenstown Story

Cobh Heritage Centre. **Tel** 021 481 3591. **Open** daily. **Closed** 22 Dec–5 Jan.
cobhheritage.com

Housed in a Victorian railway station, *The Queenstown Story* is an exhibition detailing the town's marine history. Exhibits and audiovisual displays recall the part Cobh played in Irish emigration and the transportation of convicts. Between 1791 and 1853, 40,000 convicts were sent to Australian penal colonies in notorious "coffin ships". The exhibition also documents Cobh's role as a port of call for transatlantic liners.

Environs

North of Cobh is Fota Island, with **Fota House and Gardens**. This glorious Regency mansion, surrounded by landscaped gardens, has a 19th-century arboretum with rare trees and shrubs.

Also on the island is the **Fota Wildlife Park**, which concentrates on breeding and reintroducing

Cobh Harbour with the steeple of St Colman's Cathedral rising above the town

nimals to their natural habitat. he white-tailed sea eagle is ne native species that has een saved from extinction in eland. The park boasts over 0 species, including giraffe, amingo, and zebra. A train nks the sections of the park.

Fota House and Gardens
ota Island. **Tel** 021 481 5543.
)pen Apr–Sep: daily. house only.
fotahouse.com

Fota Wildlife Park
ota Island. **Tel** 021 481 2678.
)pen daily. **Closed** 25 & 26 Dec.
fotawildlife.ie

Old Midleton Distillery

Road map C5. Distillery Walk, Aidleton, Co Cork. **Tel** 021 461 3594. to Midleton. **Open** 9am–6pm daily. **Closed** Good Fri & 24 & 25 Dec. in summer only.
jamesonwhiskey.com

A sensitively restored 18th-century distillery, Old Midleton Distillery is part of the vast Irish Distillers group at Midleton. Bushmills *(see p270)* s the oldest distillery in Ireland but Midleton is the largest, with a series of distilleries each producing a different whiskey, including Jameson.

The story of Irish whiskey is presented through audiovisual displays, working models and authentic machinery. A tour of the old distillery takes in the mills, maltings, still-houses, kilns, granaries and warehouses. Visitors can take part in whiskey tasting and try to distinguish between various brands of Irish, Scotch and bourbon whiskies. Highlights of the visit include the world's largest pot still, with a capacity of over 30,000 gallons, and the working waterwheel.

Fishing boats moored in the harbour, Youghal

29 Youghal

Road map C5. Co Cork. 7,500. Market Place (024 92447).
youghal.ie

Youghal (pronounced "yawl") is a historic walled town and thriving fishing port. The town was granted to Sir Walter Raleigh by Queen Elizabeth I but later sold to the Earl of Cork. In Cromwellian times, Youghal became a closed borough – an English Protestant garrison town. The picturesque, four-storey **Clock tower** was originally the city gate, but was recast as a prison. Steep steps beside the tower lead up to a well-preserved section of the medieval town wall and fine views across the Blackwater estuary. Through the tower, in the sombre North Main Street, is the **Red House**, a Dutch mansion built in 1710. Virtually next door are some grim Elizabethan almshouses and, on the far side of the road, a 15th-century tower, known as **Tynte's Castle**.

Nestling in the town walls opposite is **Myrtle Grove** (closed to the public), one of the few unfortified Tudor manor houses to survive in Ireland. It has a triple-gabled façade and exquisite interior oak panelling. Just uphill is the Gothic **Church of St Mary**. Inside are tomb effigies and stained-glass windows depicting the coats of arms of local families.

Grain truck (c.1940) at the Jameson Heritage Centre

The QUEENS
BAR

THE LOWER SHANNON

Clare · Limerick · Tipperary

In the three counties which flank the lower reaches of the Shannon, Ireland's longest river, the scenery ranges from the rolling farmland of Tipperary to the eerie limestone plateau of the Burren. The Shannon's bustling riverside resorts draw many visitors, and there are medieval strongholds and atmospheric towns of great historic interest. The region also boasts a vibrant music scene.

The River Shannon has long made this area an attractive prospect for settlers. There are several important Stone Age sites, including a major settlement by Lough Gur. From the 5th century, the region lay at the heart of Munster, one of Ireland's four Celtic provinces. The Rock of Cashel, a remarkable fortified abbey in county Tipperary, was the seat of the Kings of Munster for more than 700 years.

The Vikings penetrated the Shannon in the 10th century, but Gaelic clans put up stern resistance. During the Norman period, the chieftains of these clans built Bunratty Castle and other fortresses that were impressive enough to rival the strongholds erected by the Anglo-Irish dynasties. Foremost among the latter families were the Butlers, the Earls of Ormonde, who held much land in Tipperary, and the Fitzgeralds, the main landowners in the Limerick area. From the Middle Ages, Limerick was often at the centre of events in the Lower Shannon. In 1691, the army of William of Orange laid siege to the town, heralding the Treaty of Limerick that triggered the Catholic nobility's departure for Europe – the so-called "Flight of the Wild Geese".

Lush grassland, which has turned the Lower Shannon into prime dairy country, is typical of the region. In places this gives way to picturesque glens and mountains, such as the Galty range in southern Tipperary. The region's most dramatic scenery, however, is found along the coast of Clare, a county otherwise best known for its thriving traditional music scene.

Ruins of Dysert O'Dea monastery in County Clare with an outstanding 12th-century High Cross

◀ Abbey Street in the charming town of Ennis, County Clare

Exploring the Lower Shannon

The central location of Limerick city makes it a natural focus for visitors to the region. However, there are many charming towns that make pleasanter bases, such as Adare, Cashel and also Killaloe, which is well placed for exploring the River Shannon. Most places of interest in Tipperary lie in the southern part of the county, where historic towns such as Clonmel and Cahir overlook the River Suir. County Clare's small villages are full of character and some, such as Doolin, are renowned for traditional music. The county is also home to Bunratty Castle and the Burren.

Sights at a Glance

1. *The Burren pp190–92*
2. Cliffs of Moher
3. Kilrush
4. Glin
5. Foynes
6. River Shannon
7. Dysert O'Dea
8. Ennis
9. Knappogue Castle
10. Craggaunowen
11. Mountshannon
12. Killaloe
13. *Bunratty Castle & Folk Park pp196–7*
14. Limerick
15. Adare
16. Lough Gur
17. Roscrea
18. Holy Cross Abbey
19. *Cashel pp199–201*
20. Athassel Priory
21. Glen of Aherlow
22. Cahir
23. Clonmel
24. Carrick-on-Suir

Looking up at the Cliffs of Moher

Getting Around

Roads extend from Limerick into every corner of the region, providing good access for motorists; the car ferry from Tarbert in Kerry to Killimer, near Kilrush in Clare, is a convenient route across the Shannon. Trains from Limerick serve Cahir, Clonmel and Carrick, but in other areas you must rely on the bus network. This is rather limited, especially in County Clare, although buses to the Burren from Limerick pass the Cliffs of Moher. Some of the most popular sights, such as Bunratty Castle and the Burren, can be reached on bus tours from Limerick.

For hotels and restaurants in this region see pp299–300 and pp316–18

Boats sailing on Lough Derg near Mountshannon

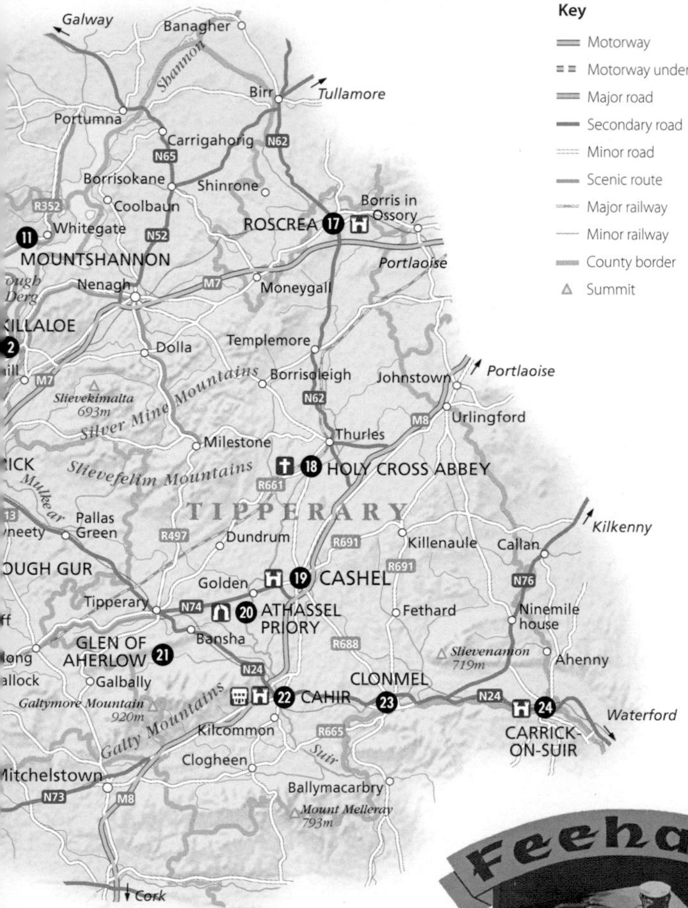

Key

- Motorway
- Motorway under construction
- Major road
- Secondary road
- Minor road
- Scenic route
- Major railway
- Minor railway
- County border
- Summit

Painted pub sign in Cashel

For additional map symbols *see back flap*

Looking south along the Cliffs of Moher, one of the most dramatic stretches of Ireland's west coast

❶ The Burren

See pp190–92.

❷ Cliffs of Moher

Road map B4. Co Clare. from Ennis, Galway & Limerick. Visitors' Centre: **Tel** 065 708 6141. **Open** daily. **Closed** 24–26 Dec.
cliffsofmoher.ie

Even when shrouded in mist or buffeted by Atlantic gales, the Cliffs of Moher are breathtaking, rising to a height of 214- m (690- ft) out of the sea and extending for 8 km (5 miles). The sheer rock face, with its layers of black shale and sandstone, provides sheltered ledges where guillemots and other sea birds nest.

Well-worn paths lead along the cliffs. From the **Visitors' Centre**, northwest of Liscannor, you can walk south to **Hag's Head** in an hour. To the north, there is a three-hour coastal walk between **O'Brien's Tower** – a viewing point built for Victorian tourists – and Fisherstreet near **Doolin** *(see p192)*.

❸ Kilrush

Road map B4. Co Clare. 2,800. Francis St (065 905 1577). **Open** Jun–Sep. **kilrush.ie**

With the addition of a marina and the promotion of Kilrush as a heritage town, the fortunes of this 18th-century estate town have been greatly revived.

Follow the well-marked walking trail starting from Market Square, which highlights the town's historic sights.

Environs

From Kilrush Marina, boats take visitors dolphin-spotting – the chances of seeing one of the 100 bottle-nosed dolphins identified in the estuary are high. Boats also run to uninhabited **Scattery Island**, site of a medieval monastery. The ruins include five churches and one of the tallest round towers in the country.

The **Loop Head Drive** is a 27 km (17 mile) route which begins at the resort of Kilkee, west of Kilrush. It winds south past dramatic coastal scenery to Loop Head, from where you can enjoy superb views.

❹ Glin

Road map B5. Co Limerick. 600. from Limerick.

This village on the banks of the Shannon is the seat of the Knights of Glin, a branch of the Fitzgeralds who have lived in the district for seven centuries. Their first medieval castle is a ruin, but west of the village stands their newer home, **Glin Castle**. Built in 1780, the manor succumbed to the vogue for Gothic romance in the 1820s, when it acquired battlements and gingerbread lodges. The castle is currently home to the 29th Knight of Glin.

Glin Castle, designed in the Gothic romance style, was built in 1780

❺ Foynes

Road map B5. Co Limerick. 650. from Limerick.

Foynes enjoyed short-lived fame in the 1930s and 1940s as the eastern terminus of the first airline passenger route across the Atlantic. **Foynes Flying Boat and Maritime Museum** presents a detailed history of the seaplane service. The original Radio and Weather Rooms have transmitters, receivers and Morse code equipment. There is also a 1940s-style tea room and a full-sized replica of a B314 flying boat.

Foynes Flying Boat and Maritime Museum
Aras Ide, Foynes. **Tel** 069 65416.
Open mid-Mar–mid-Nov: daily. **flyingboatmuseum.com**

Environs

The historic town of **Askeaton**, 11 km (7 miles) east of Foynes, has a castle and Franciscan friary. The friary is particularly interesting, with a 15th-century cloister of black marble. In Rathkeale, 8 km (5 miles) south, is **Castle Matrix**, restored15th-century tower house renowned for the library in the Great Hall.

Castle Matrix
Rathkeale. **Tel** 085 730 7760.
Open by appointment only.

Fishing on Lough Derg, the largest of the lakes on the Shannon

Exploring the Shannon

Carrick-on-Shannon is the main centre for boating on the upper reaches of the river, while Portumna and the atmospheric ports of Mountshannon and Killaloe are the principal bases for exploring Lough Derg.

Cruiser on the Shannon

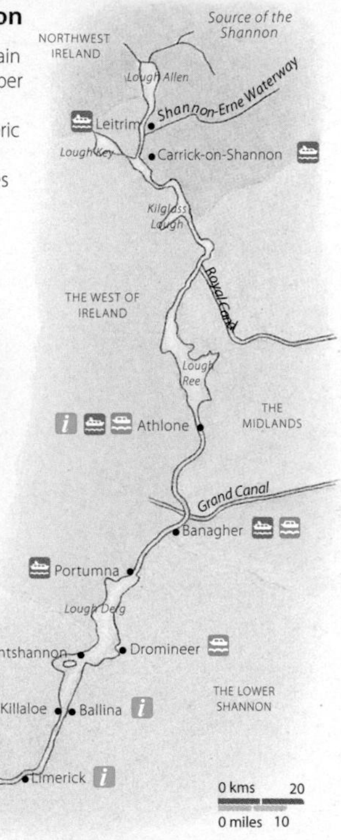

❻ River Shannon

Road map B4, C4, C3. 🚌 to Limerick or Athlone. 🚌 to Carrick-on-Shannon, Athlone or Limerick. *i* Arthur's Quay, Limerick (061 317522).
W discoverireland.ie

The Shannon is the longest river in Ireland, rising in County Cavan and meandering down to the Atlantic. Flowing through the heart of the island, it has traditionally marked the border between the provinces of Leinster and Connaught. In medieval times, castles guarded the major fords from Limerick to Portumna, and numerous monasteries were built along the riverbanks, including the celebrated Clonmacnoise *(see pp254–5)*. Work began on the Shannon navigation system in the 1750s, but it fell into disuse with the advent of the railways. It has since been revived, with the Shannon–Erne Waterway the latest stretch to be restored *(see p239)*.

There are subtle changes of landscape along the length of the river. South of **Lough Allen**, the countryside is covered with the drumlins or low hills typical of the northern Midlands. Towards **Lough Ree**, islands stud the river in an area of ecological importance which is home to otters, geese, grey herons and whooper swans. Continuing south beyond **Athlone** *(see p253)*, the river flows through flood plains and bog before reaching **Lough Derg**, the biggest of the lakes on the Shannon. The scenery is more dramatic here, with the lough's southern end edged by wooded mountains. From **Killaloe** *(see p194)*, the river gains speed on its rush towards **Limerick** *(see p195)* and the sea. The mudflats of the Shannon estuary attract a great variety of birdlife. The port of **Carrick-on-Shannon** *(see p239)* is the cruising centre of Ireland, but there are bases all along the river – especially around Lough Derg, which is the lake most geared to boating. Water-buses connect most ports south of Athlone. If you hire a cruiser, enquire about the weather conditions before setting out, particularly on Loughs Ree and Derg, which are very exposed. The calm stretch from **Portumna** *(see p219)* to Athlone is easier for inexperienced sailors.

Walkers can enjoy the Lough Derg Way, a sign-posted route around the lake. The woods by **Lough Key** *(see p223)* also provide good walking territory.

Grey heron on the Shannon

Athlone and the southern reaches of Lough Ree

❶ The Burren

The word Burren derives from *boireann*, which means "rocky land" in Gaelic – an apt name for this vast limestone plateau in northwest County Clare. In the 1640s, Cromwell's surveyor described it as "a savage land, yielding neither water enough to drown a man, nor tree to hang him, nor soil enough to bury". Few trees manage to grow in this desolate place, yet other plants thrive. The Burren is a unique botanical environment in which Mediterranean and alpine plants rare to Ireland grow side by side. From May to August, an astonishing array of flowers adds splashes of colour to the austere landscape. These plants grow most abundantly around the region's shallow lakes and pastures, but they also take root in the crevices of the limestone pavements which are the most striking geological feature of the rocky plateau. In the southern part of the Burren, limestone gives way to the black shale and sandstone that form the dramatic Cliffs of Moher *(see p188)*.

Grazing in the Burren
A quirk in the local climate means that, in winter, the hills are warmer than the valleys – hence the unusual practice in the Burren of letting cattle graze on high ground in winter.

Limestone pavement
Glaciation and wind and rain erosion have formed limestone pavements with deep crevices known as "grykes". The porous rock is easily penetrated by rainwater, which has gouged out an extensive cave system beneath the rocky plateau.

KEY

① **Spring gentian**

② **Turloughs** are shallow lakes which are dry in summer but flood in winter, when they attract wildfowl and waders.

③ **Exposed layers of limestone**

④ **Hawthorn** is one of the few trees which manages to grow in the Burren, although the plants are usually twisted and stunted.

⑤ **Stone-built Burren cottage**

⑥ **Dry-stone wall**

⑦ **Limestone slabs, or "clints"**

⑧ **Maidenhair fern** thrives in the damp crevices of the Burren.

⑨ **Holly trees** can gain a foothold in the pavement, but grazing and wind restrict their growth.

⑩ **The hoary rock rose** is one of several rare plants to grow abundantly in the Burren.

Bloody Cranesbill
This striking plant, common in the Burren, is a member of the geranium family. It flowers in June.

Fauna of the Burren

The Burren is one of the best places in Ireland for butterflies, with 28 species found in the area. The birdlife is also varied. Skylarks and cuckoos are common on the hills and in the meadows, while the coast is a good place for razorbills, guillemots, puffins and other sea birds. Mammals are harder to spot. Badgers, foxes and stoats live here, but you are much more likely to see a herd of shaggy-coated wild goats or an Irish hare.

The pearl-bordered fritillary, one of a number of fritillaries found in the Burren, can be seen in no other part of Ireland.

An Irish hare's white and brown winter coat turns to reddish-brown in the summer.

Whooper swans from Iceland flock to the wetlands of the Burren in winter.

The hooded crow is easily identified by its grey and black plumage.

Mountain Avens
Normally a mountain plant, this flower grows here at sea level.

Exploring the Burren

If you are interested in the unique geology and natural history of the Burren, head for **Mullaghmore**, to the southeast of the area. This is one of the wildest parts of the plateau and reaches a height of 191- m (626- ft), with some of the best limestone pavements in the area.

A good place to begin a tour of the more accessible parts of the Burren is at the **Cliffs of Moher** *(see p188)*. From here it is a short drive north to **Doolin**, near the port for the Aran Islands *(see pp216–17)*. One of the world's largest free hanging stalactites is in Doolin Cave. The village is renowned for its traditional music; Gus O'Connor's pub *(see p328)* acts as a focus for music lovers in the area. The coastal road runs north from Doolin to a desolate limestone outcrop at **Black Head**, while turning inland will take you to **Lisdoonvarna**. The Victorians developed the town as a spa, but it is now most renowned for its colourful pubs and its matchmaking festival *(see p54)*. To the north along the N67 lies **Ballyvaughan**, a fishing village dotted with slate-roofed cottages and busy with tourists in summer. It is well placed for reaching a number of sights. Nearby **Bishop's Quarter** has a sheltered beach with glorious views across a lagoon towards Galway Bay. **Aillwee Cave**, to the south, is just one of thousands of caves in the Burren. In the first, known as Bear Haven, the remains of hibernation pits used by bears are still visible.

Poulnabrone Dolmen in the heart of the Burren's limestone plateau

Music shop in Doolin

Ruined forts and castles and numerous prehistoric sites dot the landscape. Just west of Aillwee Cave is **Cahermore Stone Fort**, which has a lintelled doorway, and to the south is **Gleninsheen Wedge Tomb**, a style of grave which marks the transition between Stone and Bronze Age cultures. The more famous **Poulnabrone Dolmen** nearby is a striking portal tomb dating back to 2500–2000 BC. Continuing south you reach the ghostly shell of **Leamaneagh Castle**, a 17th-century mansion that incorporates an earlier tower house built by the O'Briens.

On the southern fringe of the Burren lies **Kilfenora**, a Catholic diocese which, by a historical quirk, has the Pope for its bishop. The village's modest cathedral, one of many 12th-century churches in the Burren, has a roofless chancel with finely sculpted capitals. Kilfenora, however, is more famous for its High Crosses: there are several in the graveyard. Best preserved is the Doorty Cross, with a carving of a bishop and two other clerics on the east face. Next door, the **Burren Centre** offers an excellent multidimensional exhibition giving information on the geology and fauna of the area and man's impact on the landscape.

Carved capital in Kilfenora Cathedral

Aillwee Cave
Ballyvaughan. **Tel** 065 707 7036.
Open daily.

Burren Centre
Kilfenora. **Tel** 065 708 8030.
Open Mar–Oct: daily.
theburrencentre.ie

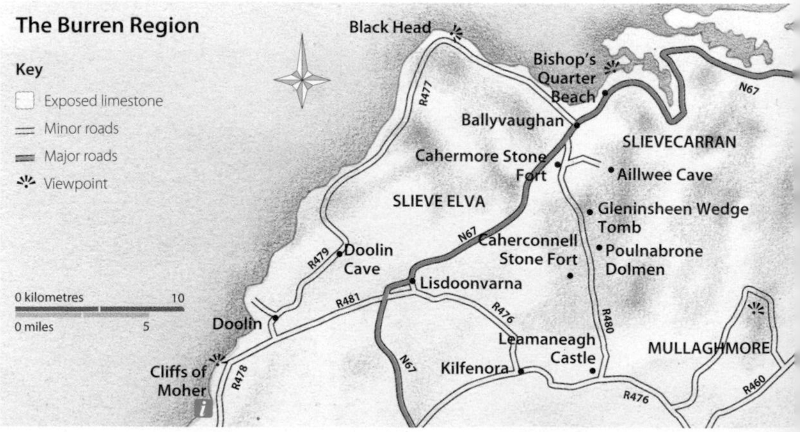

7 Dysert O'Dea

Road map 4 B. Corrofin, Co Clare. from Ennis. **Tel** 065 683 7401. **Open** May–Sep: daily.

Dysert O'Dea Castle stands on a rocky outcrop 9 km (6 miles) north of Ennis. This tower house, erected in the 15th century, is home to the **Archaeology Centre**, which includes a small museum and also marks the start of a trail around nearby historic sights. A map of the path, designed for both walkers and cyclists, is available in the castle.

Across a field from the castle is a monastic site said to have been founded by the obscure St Tola in the 8th century. The ruins are overgrown and rather worn, but the Romanesque carving above one doorway is still clear, and there is also an impressive 12th-century High Cross, with a bishop sculpted on the east side *(see p247)*.

Further south, the trail leads past the remains of two stone forts, a ruined castle and the site of a 14th-century battle.

8 Ennis

Road map 4B. Co Clare. 25,000. Arthur's Row (065 6828366). **ennis.ie**

Clare's county town, on the banks of the River Fergus, is a charming place with winding lanes that recall Ennis's medieval beginnings. The town is also renowned for its painted shop-fronts and folk music festivals (known as *fleadh* in Gaelic). It abounds in "singing" pubs and traditional music shops.

15th-century Knappogue Castle, County Clare

Ennis can trace its origins to the 13th century and to the O'Briens, Kings of Thomond, who were the area's feudal overlords in the Middle Ages. The Franciscan friary that they founded here in the 1240s is now the town's main attraction. Dating from the 14th and 15th centuries, the ruined **Ennis Friary** is famous for its rich carvings and decorated tombs in the chancel – above all the 15th-century MacMahon tomb with its finely carved alabaster panels. Extensive conservation work is ongoing here.

Next door to the friary is a delightful 17th-century house, now Cruise's restaurant, and on the corner of nearby Francis Street stands the Queen's Hotel – featured in James Joyce's *Ulysses*. To the south, O'Connell Square has a monument to Daniel O'Connell *(see p46)*, who was elected MP for Clare in 1828. He also gave his name to the town's main street, where, among the pubs and shops, you can spot a medieval tower, a Jacobean chimney stack and an 18th-century arch.

Finely carved Romanesque doorway at Dysert O'Dea

Ennis Friary
Abbey St. **Tel** 065 682 9100.
Open Easter–Oct: daily.

Environs
The area around Ennis is rich in monastic ruins. Just 3 km (2 miles) south of the town is **Clare Abbey**, an Augustinian foundation set up by the O'Briens in 1189 but dating mainly from the 1400s.

Quin Franciscan Friary, set in meadows 13 km (8 miles) southeast of Ennis, was also built in the 15th century, and incorporates the romantic ruins of a Norman castle. The well-preserved cloister is one of the finest of its kind in Ireland.

9 Knappogue Castle

Road map 4B. Quin, Co Clare. **Tel** 061 360788. **Open** May–Sep: daily. limited. **shannonheritage.com**

A powerful local clan called the MacNamaras erected Knappogue Castle in 1467. Apart from a ten-year spell in Cromwellian times, it stayed in their hands until 1815. During the War of Independence *(see pp48–9)*, the castle was used by the revolutionary forces.

Knappogue is one of Ireland's most charmingly furnished castles. The central tower house is original, but the rest is Neo-Gothic. Inside are fine Elizabethan fireplaces and linenfold wood panelling.

Medieval banquets are staged in the castle from April to October *(see p340)*, with storytelling and singing.

⑩ Craggaunowen

Road map B4. Kilmurry, Co Clare.
Tel 061 360788. **Open** Apr–Sep: daily.
limited.
shannonheritage.com

The Craggaunowen Project, known as "Craggaunowen: the Living Past" and designed to bring Bronze Age and Celtic culture to life, is a shining example of a recreated prehistoric site. The centre was created in the grounds of Craggaunowen Castle in the 1960s by John Hunt, a noted archaeologist who had been inspired by his excavations at Lough Gur *(see p198)*. The "Living Past" experience is about the arrival of the Celts in Ireland and their farming and hunting methods.

In summer, people in costume sometimes act out particular trades, such as spinning or potting, or serve as guides. In addition there is a description of how communities lived in the ring fort, a typical early Christian homestead. You can also see a *fulacht fiadh*, a traditional hunter's cooking hole where meat was prepared.

The complex includes part of a *togher*, an original Iron Age timber road that was discovered in Longford. The most eye-catching sight, however, is the crannog *(see p37)*, a man-made island enclosing wattle and daub houses – a style of defensive homestead that survived to the early 1600s.

Another exhibit is a leather-hulled boat built in the 1970s by Tim Severin. He used it to retrace the route which legend says St Brendan took in a similar vessel across the Atlantic in the 6th century *(see p31)*.

A woman in peasant costume spinning wool at Craggaunowen

⑪ Mountshannon

Road map C4. Co Clare. 240.
East Clare Heritage. **Tel** 061 921351. **mountshannon.com**

This village on the banks of Lough Derg *(see p189)* seems to have its back turned to the lake but is nevertheless a major angling centre. Solid 18th-century stone houses and churches cluster around the harbour, along with some pubs.

Mountshannon is well placed for exploring the lake's western shores, with plenty of scope for walks and bicycle rides. Fishing boats are available for hire, and in summer you can go by boat to **Holy Island**, the site of a monastery founded in the 7th century. The ruins include four chapels and a graveyard of medieval tombs.

Bicycle hire and boat trips at Mountshannon

⑫ Killaloe

Road map C4. Co Clare. 950.
May–Oct: Brian Ború Heritage Centre, The Bridge (061 370788).
discoverkillaloe.com

Killaloe, birthplace of Brian Ború (940–1014), High King of Ireland *(see p38)*, lies close to where the Shannon emerges from Lough Derg, and is the lake's most prosperous pleasure port. A 17th-century bridge separates Killaloe from its twin town of Ballina on the opposite bank. Ballina has better pubs, such as Goosers on the waterfront *(see p329)*, but Killaloe is the main boating centre *(see p345)* and offers more of historical interest.

Killaloe's grandest building is **St Flannan's Cathedral**, built around 1182. Its richly carved Romanesque doorway was once part of an earlier chapel. The church also has an ancient Ogham Stone *(see p38)*, unusual because the inscription is carved in both Nordic runes and Ogham. Outside stands St Flannan's Oratory, built around the same time as the cathedral.

The Brian Ború Heritage Centre, on the bridge, has an interesting exhibition on the history of Brian Ború and from here you can walk along a small section of the old Killaloe Canal. You can also arrange for local fishermen to take you out on the lake.

⑬ Bunratty Castle

See pp196–7.

14 Limerick

Road map B4. Co Limerick. 90,000. Shannon. Arthur's Quay (061 317522). Sat. **limerick.ie**

The third-largest city in the Republic, Limerick was founded by the Vikings. Given its strategic point on the River Shannon, it thrived under the Normans, but later bore the brunt of English oppression. After the Battle of the Boyne *(see p248)*, the rump of the defeated Jacobite army withdrew here. The siege which followed has entered Irish folklore as a heroic defeat, sealed by the Treaty of Limerick in 1691. English treachery in reneging on most of the terms of the treaty still rankles. It is no coincidence that Catholicism and nationalism are strong in the city.

Limerick has a reputation for high unemployment, crime and general neglect. However, it is fast acquiring a new image as a commercial city, revitalized by new industries and restoration projects. Even so, visitors may still have to dig a little to appreciate its charm.

Carved misericord in St Mary's Cathedral

The city centre consists of three historic districts. King's Island was the first area to be settled by the Vikings and was later the heart of the medieval city, when it was known as Englishtown. It boasts Limerick's two main landmarks, King John's Castle and St Mary's Cathedral. The old Irishtown, south of the Abbey River, has its fair share of drab houses and shops, but also has its own historic buildings and a pocket of Georgian elegance in St John's Square. Near here is Limerick's most conspicuous sight, St John's Cathedral, built in 1861. Its 85-m (280-ft) spire is the tallest in the country.

The most pleasant part of Limerick in which to stroll is Newtown Pery – a grid of gracious Georgian terraces focused on O'Connell Street.

King John's Castle

Nicholas St. **Tel** 061 360788. **Open** daily. **Closed** 23–26 Dec. limited. **shannonheritage.com**

Founded by King John in 1200, not long after the Normans arrived, this imposing castle has five drum towers and solid curtain walls. Inside, the castle is less interesting architecturally, but it houses a good audio-visual exhibition on the history of the city. Ongoing excavations have unearthed pots and jewellery, and you can also see Viking houses and later fortifications.

Across the nearby Thomond Bridge, the Treaty Stone marks the spot where the Treaty of Limerick was signed in 1691.

St Mary's Cathedral

Bridge Street. **Tel** 061 310293. **Open** 9:30am–4:30pm Mon–Fri, 9:30am–2pm Sat, for services only Sun. **cathedral.limerick.anglican.org**

Built in 1172, this is the oldest structure in the city. Except for a fine Romanesque door-way and the nave, however, little remains of the early church. The 15th-century misericords in the choir stalls are the pride of St Mary's, with superb carvings in black oak of angels, griffins and other creatures both real and imaginary.

Characteristic Georgian doorway in St John's Square

Nearby, George's Quay is a pleasant street with restaurants, outdoor cafés and good views across the river.

Hunt Museum

Rutland St. **Tel** 061 312833. **Open** 10am–5pm Mon–Sat, 2pm–5pm Sun & bank hols. free on Sun **Closed** 1 Jan, Good Fri, 25 & 26 Dec. **huntmuseum.com**

Located in the Old Customs House, this fine museum has one of the greatest collections of antiquities in Ireland, gathered by the archaeologist John Hunt. The best exhibits, dating from the Bronze Age, include gold jewellery and a magnificent shield. Among the other artifacts are Celtic brooches and the 9th-century Antrim Cross.

Limerick Museum

Istabraaq Hall, City Hall, Merchants Quay. **Tel** 061 417 826. **Open** 10am–1pm, 2:15–5pm Mon–Fri. **Closed** for lunch, public hols & 7 days at Christmas. **museum.limerick.ie**

Limerick's history and traditions from lace- and silver-making to rugby are on display.

View of Limerick showing Thomond Bridge across the Shannon and King John's Castle

⑬ Bunratty Castle & Folk Park

This formidable castle was built in the 15th century by the MacNamaras. Its most important residents were the O'Briens, Earls of Thomond, who lived here from the early 16th century until the 1640s. The present interior looks much as it did under the so-called "Great Earl", who died in 1624. Abandoned in the 19th century, the castle was derelict when Lord Gort bought it in the 1950s, but it has been beautifully restored to its original state. The adjacent Folk Park reflects 19th-century Irish rural and village life. Bunratty is also famous for its splendid medieval banquets.

★ North Solar
This 17th-century German chandelier is the most curious feature in the Great Earl's private apartments. The term "solar" was used during the Middle Ages to describe an upper chamber.

Entrance

KEY

① **The basement** with walls 3-m (10-ft) thick, was probably used for storage or as a stable.

② **The Murder Hole** was designed for pouring boiling water or pitch on to the heads of attackers.

③ **The chimney** is a replica in wood of the stone original. It provided a vent for the smoke given off by the fire in the centre of the Great Hall.

④ **The Robing Room** was where the earls put on their gowns before an audience in the Great Hall. They also used it for private interviews.

⑤ **A spiral staircase** is found in each of the four towers.

★ Main Guard
Now used for medieval-style banquets, this was the room where Bunratty's soldiers ate, slept and relaxed. Music was played to them from the Minstrels' Gallery, and a gate in one corner gave instant access to the dungeons.

For hotels and restaurants in this region see pp299–300 and pp316–18

North Front
Bunratty Castle is unusual for the high arches on both the north and south sides of the keep. However, the first-floor entrance, designed to deter invaders, was typical of castles of the period.

VISITORS' CHECKLIST

Practical Information
Road map B4. Bunratty, Co Clare.
Tel 061 360788.
W shannonheritage.com
Open 9:30am–5:30pm daily (last admission 4pm).
Closed 24–26 Dec.
to Folk Park. Banquets *see p340.*

Transport
Shannon. from Ennis, Limerick, Shannon. Castle & Folk Park.

South Solar
The South Solar houses guest apartments. The elaborately decorated carved ceiling is partly a reconstruction in the late Tudor style.

Bunratty Folk Park

A meticulous recreation of rural life in Ireland at the end of the 19th century, this Folk Park began with the reconstruction of a farmhouse which was saved during the building of nearby Shannon Airport. It now consists of a complete village, incorporating shops and a whole range of domestic architecture from a labourer's cottage to an elegant Georgian house. Other buildings in the park include a farmhouse typical of the Moher region in the Burren *(see p188)* and a working corn mill. During the main summer season, visitors can meet with various costumed characters from the period.

Main street of Bunratty Folk Park village

★ Great Hall
This Tudor standard was among the many furnishings that Lord Gort brought to the castle. It stands in the Great Hall, once the banqueting hall and audience chamber, and still Bunratty's grandest room.

Typical thatched cottage in the village of Adare

⓯ Adare

Road map B5. Co Limerick. 2,000. Heritage Centre, Main St (061 396666). **Open** daily. **adareheritagecentre.ie**

Adare is billed as Ireland's prettiest village. Cynics call it the prettiest "English" village since its manicured perfection is at odds with normal notions of national beauty. Originally a fief of the Fitzgeralds, the Earls of Kildare, Adare owes its present appearance more to the Earls of Dunraven, who restored the village in the 1820s and 1830s. The village is a picture of neat stonework and thatched roofs punctuated by pretty ruins, all in a woodland setting.

The tourist office is at the Heritage Centre, which includes a good exhibition on Adare's monastic history. Next door is the **Trinitarian Priory**, founded by the Fitzgeralds in 1230 and over-restored by the first Earl of Dunraven; it is now a Catholic church and convent. Opposite, by a stone-arched bridge, is the Washing Pool, a restored wash-house site.

By the main bridge, on the Limerick road, is the **Augustinian Priory** which was founded by the Fitzgeralds in 1316. Also known as Black Abbey, this well-restored priory has a central tower, subtle carvings, delightful cloisters and a graceful sedilia – a carved triple seat. Just over the bridge, from where it is best viewed, is **Desmond Castle**, a13th-century feudal castle set on the banks of the River Maigue – tickets are available from the Heritage Centre (Jun–end Sep).

Nearby stands the main gate to **Adare Manor**, a luxury hotel and golf course *(see p299)*. Within its 900 ha (2,220 acres) of parkland lie **St Nicholas Church** and **Chantry Chapel**, two evocative 12th-century ruins. The graceful 15th-century **Franciscan Friary**, however, is surrounded by the golf course, though it can be seen clearly from the pathway.

In the heart of the village is the elegant Dunraven Arms Hotel *(see p299)* from where the local hunt rides to hounds. Some of the nearby cottages, originally built by the Earl of Dunraven in 1828 for his estate workers, have been converted into pleasant cafés and restaurants.

⓰ Lough Gur

Road map B5. Co Limerick. Heritage Centre: **Tel** 061 385186. **Open** 10am–5pm Mon–Fri; 12–6pm weekends & bank hols. limited. **loughgur.com**

This Stone Age settlement, 21 km (14 miles) south of Limerick, was extensively inhabited in 3000 BC. Today the horseshoe-shaped lough and surrounding hills enclose an archaeological park. All around Lough Gur are standing stones and burial mounds, including megalithic tombs. One of the most impressive sights is the **Grange Stone Circle**, dating back to 2,200 BC, just outside the park, by the Limerick–Kilmallock road. Excavations in the 1970s unearthed rectangular, oval and rounded Stone Age huts with stone

Neo-Gothic Adare Manor, former home of the Earls of Dunraven

Façade of Cashel Palace Hotel

foundations. The interpretive centre, which is housed in mock Stone Age huts on the site of the original settlement, offers a range of audiovisual displays, models of stone circles, burial chambers and tools and weapons.

As well as the various prehistoric sites scattered all over the Knockadoon Peninsula, there are two castle ruins from more recent times beside the lough – the 15th-century **Bourchier's Castle** and **Black Castle**, a 13th-century seat of the Earls of Desmond.

⑰ Roscrea

Road map C4. Co Tipperary. 4,600. Heritage Centre, Castle St (0505 21850). **Open** Easter–Sep: daily. **heritageireland.ie**

This monastic town on the banks of the River Bunnow has an interesting historic centre. The 13th-century Anglo-Norman **Roscrea Castle** consists of a gate tower, curtain walls and two corner towers. In the courtyard stands **Damer House**, a Queen Anne-style residence with a magnificent staircase and Georgian garden. Just over the river lies **St Cronan's Monastery**, with a High Cross, Romanesque church gable and a truncated round tower. There are remains of a 15th-century **Franciscan Friary** on Abbey Street and the renovated Blackmills now houses the St Cronan's High Cross and the **Roscrea Pillar**.

Roscrea Castle & Gardens
Castle Street. **Tel** 0505 21850. **Open** Mar–Sep: 10am–6pm daily. limited. **heritageireland.com**

⑱ Holy Cross Abbey

Road map C5. Thurles, Co Tipperary. **Tel** 0504 43124. to Thurles. **Open** 9am–8pm daily. **tipperary.com**

Founded in 1169 by the Benedictines, Holy Cross was supposedly endowed with a splinter from the True Cross, hence its name. Now it has been restored, and the church is once again a popular place of worship and pilgrimage. Most of the present structure dates from the 15th century. It was built by the Cistercians, who took over the abbey in 1180. This gracious cruciform church, embellished with mullioned windows and sculpted pillars, is one of the finest examples of late Gothic architecture in Ireland.

Nearby, Farney Castle is the only round tower in Ireland that is occupied as a family home. It was built in 1495 and is currently the design studio and retail outlet of Irish international designer Cyril Cullen.

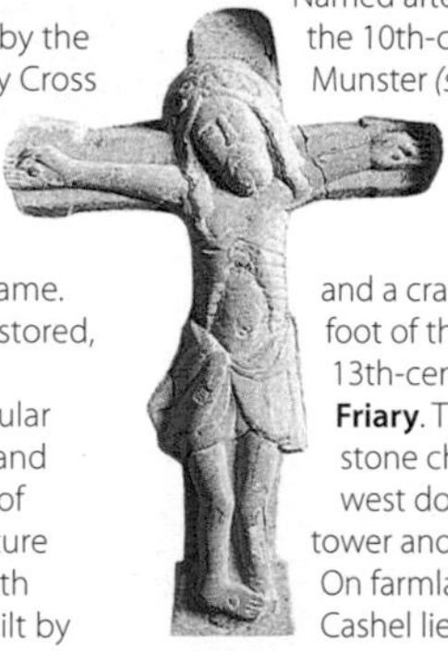

Crucifixion carving at Holy Cross Abbey

⑲ Cashel

Road map C5. Co Tipperary. 11,400. Heritage Centre, Town Hall, Main St (062 62511). **cashel.ie**

The great attraction of the town is the magnificent medieval **Rock of Cashel** *(see pp200–201)*. A private path leads to the rock from **Cashel Palace Hotel** *(see p299)*, an opulent Queen Anne residence that was once the Bishop's Palace. Nearby, the remnant of a 12th-century castle has been turned into Kearney Castle Hotel. In the evening you can sample traditional Irish culture at the **Brú Ború Cultural Centre**. Named after Brian Ború, the 10th-century king of Munster *(see pp38–9)*, the centre offers folk theatre, traditional music, banquets, and a craft shop. At the foot of the Rock is the 13th-century **Dominican Friary**. This austere sandstone church has a fine west door, a 15th-century tower and lancet windows.

On farmland outside Cashel lie the scant remains of **Hore Abbey**, a 13th-century Cistercian foundation. The abbey was remodelled and a tower added in the 15th century, but the barrel-vaulted sacristy, the nave and chapter house are all original.

Brú Ború Cultural Centre
Cashel. **Tel** 062 61122. **Open** mid-Jun–Aug: Tue–Sat; Sep–mid-Jun: Mon–Fri. **Closed** 24 Dec–2 Jan. **bruboru.ie**

Dominican Friary
Dominic Street. limited.

Ruins of Hore Abbey (1272) with the Rock of Cashel in the background

Rock of Cashel

This rocky stronghold, which rises dramatically out of the Tipperary plain, was a symbol of royal and priestly power for more than a millennium. From the 4th or 5th century it was the seat of the Kings of Munster, whose kingdom extended over much of southern Ireland. In 1101, they handed Cashel over to the Church, and it flourished as a religious centre until a siege by a Crom-wellian army in 1647 culminated in the massacre of its 3,000 occupants. The cathedral, which is subject to ongoing renovation, was finally abandoned in the late 18th century. A good proportion of the medieval complex is still standing, and Cormac's Chapel is one of the most outstanding examples of Romanesque architecture in the country.

Hall of the Vicars' Choral
This hall was built in the 15th century for Cashel's most privileged choristers. The ceiling, a modern reconstruction based on medieval designs, features several decorative corbels including this painted angel.

★ St Patrick's Cross
The carving on the east face of this cross is said to be of St Patrick, who visited Cashel in 450. The cross is a copy of the original which stood here until 1982 and is now in the museum.

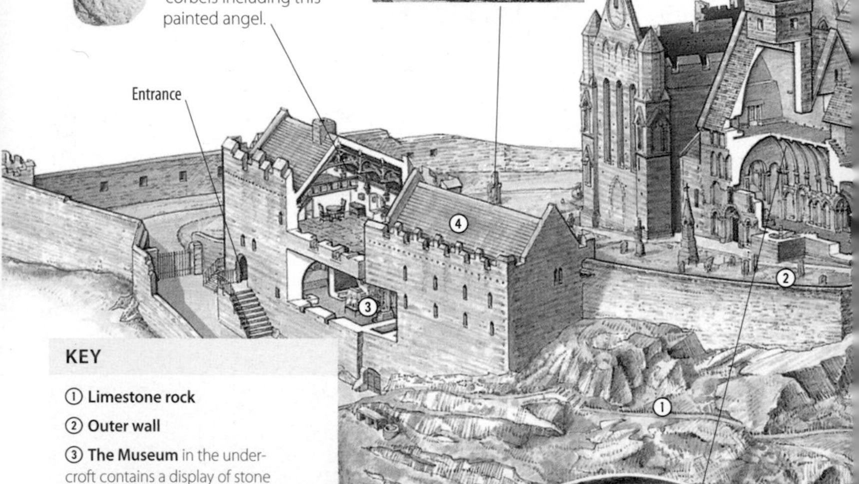

KEY

① **Limestone rock**

② **Outer wall**

③ **The Museum** in the undercroft contains a display of stone carvings, including the original St Patrick's Cross.

④ **Dormitory block**

⑤ **Crossing**

⑥ **Round tower**

⑦ **The Choir** contains the 17th-century tomb of Miler Magrath, who caused a scandal by being both a Protestant and Catholic archbishop at the same time.

⑧ **Graveyard**

⑨ **The O'Scully Monument**, an ornate memorial erected in 1870 by a local landowning family, was damaged during a storm in 1976.

★ Cormac's Chapel
Superb Romanesque carving adorns this chapel – the jewel of Cashel. The tympanum over the north door shows a centaur in a helmet aiming his bow and arrow at a lion.

North Transept
Panels from three 16th-century tombs in the north transept are decorated with remarkably fresh and intricate carvings. This one, against the north wall, features a vine-leaf design and strange stylized beasts.

VISITORS' CHECKLIST

Practical information
Road Map C5. Cashel.
Tel 062 61437.
Open daily. Early Jun–mid-Sep: 9am–7pm; mid-Mar–early Jun & mid-Sep–mid-Oct: 9am–5:30pm; mid-Oct–mid-Mar: 9am–4:30pm.
Closed 24–26 Dec.

Transport
to Thurles. to Cashel.

The Rock
The 28-m (92-ft) round tower, the oldest and tallest building on the rock, enabled Cashel's inhabitants to scour the surrounding plain for potential attackers.

★ Cathedral
The roofless Gothic cathedral has thick walls riddled with hidden passages; in the north transept these are seen emerging at the base of the windows.

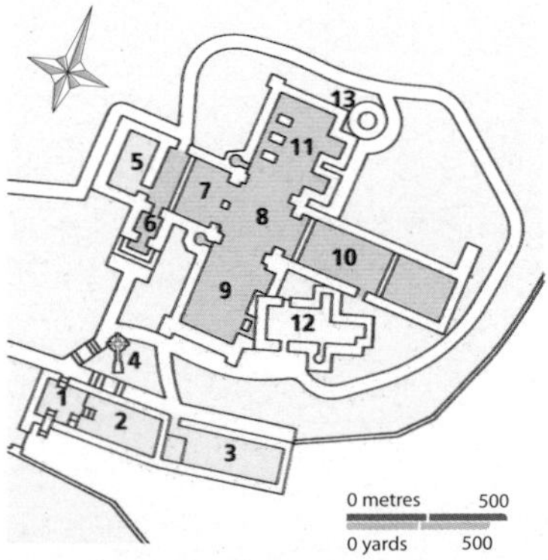

Key

12th Century
4 St Patrick's Cross (replica)
12 Cormac's Chapel
13 Round tower

13th Century
6 Cathedral porch
7 Nave
8 Crossing
9 South transept
10 Choir
11 North transept

15th Century
1 Ticket office
2 Hall of the Vicars' Choral (museum)
3 Dormitory
5 Castle

⑳ Athassel Priory

Road map C5. 8 km (5 miles) W of Cashel, Co Tipperary. 🚌 to Tipperary. **Open** daily. **W** **cashel.ie**

This ruined Augustinian priory is situated on the west bank of the River Suir. The tomb of William de Burgh, the Norman founder of the priory, lies in the church. Established in 1192, Athassel is believed to have been the largest medieval priory in Ireland until it burned down in 1447. The scattered monastic site conveys a tranquil atmosphere, from the gatehouse and church to the remains of the cloisters and chapter house. The church has a fine west doorway, nave and chancel walls, as well as a 15th-century central tower.

The ruins of Athassel Priory, on the banks of the River Suir

㉑ Glen of Aherlow

Road map C5. Co Tipperary. 🚌 to Bansha or Tipperary. **i** Coach Rd, on R663 8 km (5 miles) E of Galbally (062 56331). **W** **aherlow.com**

The lush valley of the River Aherlow runs between the Galty Mountains and the wooded ridge of Slievenamuck. Bounded by the villages of **Galbally** and **Bansha**, the glen was historically an important pass between Limerick and Tipperary and a notorious hideout for outlaws.

Today there are opportunities for riding, cycling, rambling and fishing. Lowland walks follow the trout-filled river along the valley floor. More adventurous walkers will be tempted by the Galty range, which offers more rugged hill walking, past wooded foothills, mountain streams, tiny corrie lakes and splendid sandstone peaks.

View across the unspoilt Glen of Aherlow

㉒ Cahir

Road map C5. Co Tipperary. 2,100. 🚉 🚌 **i** Apr–Oct: Castle Street (052 744 1453). **W** **discoverireland.ie/southeast**

Once a garrison and mill town, Cahir is today a busy market town. The pub-lined Castle Street is the most appealing area. It leads to the Suir River, Cahir Castle and the walk to the Swiss Cottage.

On the edge of town lies the ruined **Cahir Abbey**, a 13th-century Augustinian priory. Its fine windows are decorated with carved heads.

Cahir Castle

Castle Street. **Tel** 052 744 1011. **Open** daily. **Closed** 24–30 Dec. ♿ limited. **W** **heritageireland.ie**

Built on a rocky island in the River Suir, Cahir is one of the most formidable castles in Ireland and a popular film set. This well-preserved fortress dates from the 13th century but is inextricably linked to its later owners, the Butlers. A powerful family in Ireland since the Anglo-Norman invasion, they were considered trusty lieges of the English crown and were granted the Cahir barony in 1375. Under their command, the castle was renovated and extended throughout the 15th and 16th centuries. It remained in the Butler family until 1964.

The castle is divided into outer, middle and inner wards, with a barbican at the outer entrance. The inner ward is on the site of the original Norman castle; the foundations are 13th-century, as are the curtain walls and keep. The restored interior includes the striking great hall, which dates largely from the 1840s, though two of the walls are original and the windows are 15th-century. From the ramparts there are views of the river and millrace.

Swiss Cottage

Kilcommon, Cahir. **Tel** 052 744 1144. **Open** Apr–Oct: daily. obligatory.

The Swiss Cottage is a superb example of a *cottage orné,* a rustic folly. It was designed for the Butlers by the Regency architect John Nash in 1810. Here, Lord and Lady Cahir played at bucolic bliss, enjoying picnics dressed as peasants.

Fashion dictated that a *cottage orné* should blend in with the countryside and all designs should be drawn from nature with nothing matching, so the windows and sloping eaves are all different. The beautifully restored cottage contains a tea room, gracious music room and two bedrooms.

The Swiss Cottage at Cahir, beautifully restored to its original state

㉓ Clonmel

Road map C5. Co Tipperary. 17,000. The Main Guard (052 612 2960). **discoverireland.ie**

Set on the River Suir, Clonmel is Tipperary's main town. This Anglo-Norman stronghold was a fief of the Desmonds and eventually of the Butlers. Its prosperity was founded on milling and brewing. Today, Clonmel is a bustling, brash town with quirky architecture and lively nightlife.

The **Franciscan Friary** by the quays was remodelled in Early English style in Victorian times but retains a 15th-century tower and houses 16th-century Butler tomb effigies. Nearby is O'Connell Street, Clonmel's main shopping street, which is straddled by the West Gate, built in 1831. Visitors to **Hearn's Hotel** on Parnell Street can see memorabilia of Charles Bianconi (1786–1875), including pictures of the horse-drawn coach service he established between Clonmel and Cahir. Eventually this developed into a nationwide passenger service.

Clonmel's mock Tudor West Gate, spanning O'Connell Street

㉔ Carrick-on-Suir

Road map C5. Co Tipperary. 5,500. Heritage Centre, Main St (051 640200).

This small market town has a distinctly old-fashioned air. In the 15th century, it was a strategic site commanding access west to Clonmel and southeast to Waterford, but after Tudor times the town sank into oblivion. Apart from Ormond Castle, there are few specific sights. However, you can stroll by the old waterside warehouses or shop in Blarney Woollen Mills *(see p334)*.

Ormond Castle

Castle Park. **Tel** 051 640787.
Open Apr–mid-Sep: daily.
obligatory. limited.
heritageireland.ie

Although once a fortress, Ormond Castle is the finest surviving Tudor manor house in Ireland. It was built by the powerful Butler family, the Earls of Ormonde, who were given their title by the English crown in 1328. The castle has a gracious Elizabethan façade overlaying the medieval original; the battlemented towers on the south side sit oddly with the gabled façade and its mullioned and oriel windows.

The state rooms contain some of the finest decorative plasterwork in Ireland, while the Long Gallery extends to 30 m (100 ft). The Elizabethan part of the castle was added by Black Tom Butler, the 10th Earl of Ormonde. On his death, the Ormondes abandoned Carrick for Kilkenny *(see pp146–7)*.

Environs

In the churchyard at **Ahenny**, about 10 km (6 miles) north of Carrick, stand two magnificent High Crosses *(see p247)*. Both are crowned by "caps" or "bishops' mitres" and have intricate cable, spiral and fret patterns.

At **Kilkieran**, 5 km (3 miles) north of Carrick, are three other interesting High Crosses, dating from the 9th century. The Plain Cross is unadorned but capped; the West Cross is profusely ornamented though weathered; the Long Shaft Cross has an odd design of stumpy arms on a long shaft.

Intricate wood carving on a four-poster bed at Ormond Castle

THE WEST OF IRELAND

Mayo · Galway · Roscommon

This is the heart of Connaught, Ireland's historic western province. The West lives up to its image as a traditional, rural, sparsely populated land, with windswept mountains and countryside speckled with low stone walls and peat bogs. Yet it also encompasses Galway, a vibrant university town whose youthful population brings life to the medieval streets and snug pubs.

The rugged Atlantic coastline of the West has been occupied for over 5,000 years. It is rich in prehistoric sites such as the land enclosures of Céide Fields and the ring forts on the Aran Islands. Evidence of the monastic period can be seen in the mysterious and beautiful remains at Kilmacduagh and Clonfert; and the region's religious associations still exert an influence, apparent in the pilgrimages to Knock and Croagh Patrick in County Mayo.

In medieval times, the city of Galway was an Anglo-Norman stronghold, surrounded by warring Gaelic clans. After the Cromwellian victories of the 1640s, many Irish were dispossessed of their fertile lands and dispatched "to hell or to Connaught". Landlords made their mark in the 17th and 18th centuries, building impressive country houses at Clonalis, Strokestown Park and Westport. During the Great Famine, the West – especially County Mayo – suffered most from emigration. In spite of this, strong Gaelic traditions have survived in County Galway, which is home to the country's largest Gaeltacht *(see p233)*, where almost half the population speaks Irish as a first language.

The bracken browns and soft violets of Connemara in the west of Galway and the fertile farmland, extensive bogs and placid lakes of County Roscommon are in striking contrast to the magnificent cliff scenery of the remote islands off the coast. This region is often shrouded in a misty drizzle or else battered by Atlantic winds and accompanying heavy downpours.

Summer is a time for festivities, such as the Galway Races in July and August, the Galway Arts Festival in July, traditional sailing boat races off Kinvara in August and the Galway Oyster Festival in September.

Swans by the quayside of the Claddagh area of Galway

◀ The scenic coastline of Keem Bay, Achill Island

Exploring the West of Ireland

Galway city, Clifden and Westport make the best bases for exploring the region, with cosy pubs, good walks and access to the scenic islands. Connemara and the wilds of County Mayo attract nature lovers, while the islands of Achill, Aran, Clare and Inishbofin appeal to water-sports enthusiasts and ramblers. The lakes of counties Roscommon, Mayo and Galway are popular with anglers, and Lough Corrib and Lough Key offer relaxing cruises.

Colourful shopfronts lining a Galway street

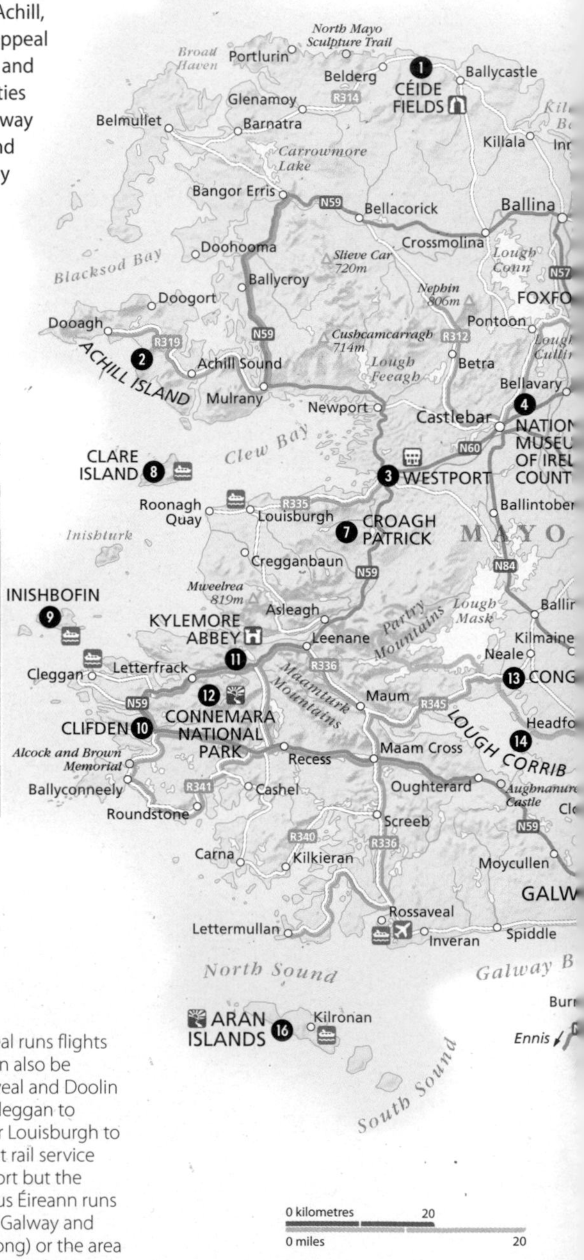

Getting Around

The tiny airport near Rossaveal runs flights to the Aran Islands, which can also be reached by ferry from Rossaveal and Doolin (Co Clare). Ferries run from Cleggan to Inishbofin and Roonagh near Louisburgh to Clare Island. There is no direct rail service between Galway and Westport but the towns are linked by buses. Bus Éireann runs services to Connemara from Galway and Clifden (via Oughterard or Cong) or the area can be explored on day-long coach tours from Galway or Clifden.

For hotels and restaurants in this region see pp300–301 and pp318–20

River valley at Delphi in northern Connemara

Sights at a Glance

1. Céide Fields
2. Achill Island
3. Westport
4. National Museum of Ireland – Country Life
5. Foxford
6. Knock
7. Croagh Patrick
8. Clare Island
9. Inishbofin
10. Clifden
11. Kylemore Abbey
12. Connemara National Park
13. Cong
14. Lough Corrib
15. *Galway pp214–15*
16. *Aran Islands pp216–17*
17. Kinvara
18. Kilmacduagh
19. Thoor Ballylee
20. Portumna
21. Clonfert Cathedral
22. Turoe Stone
23. Roscommon
24. Clonalis House
25. Strokestown Park
26. Boyle

Decorative stuccowork in Westport

Key

- Motorway
- Motorway under construction
- Major road
- Secondary road
- Minor road
- Scenic route
- Major railway
- Minor railway
- County border
- △ Summit

For additional map symbols *see back flap*

❶ Céide Fields

Road map B2. 8 km (5 miles) W of Ballycastle, Co Mayo. **Tel** 096 43325. **Open** Apr–end Oct: daily. **W** **heritageireland.ie**

Surrounded by heather-clad moorlands and mountains along a bleak, dramatic stretch of north Mayo coastline is Europe's largest Stone Age monument. Over 10 sq km (4 sq miles) were enclosed by walls to make fields suitable for growing wheat and barley, and grazing cattle. Remains of farm buildings indicate that it was an extensive community. The fields were slowly buried below the creeping bog formation, where they have been preserved for over 5,000 years.

Part of the bog has been cut away to reveal the collapsed stone walls of the ancient fields. The remains are simple but guides help visitors to find and recognize key features. Stone Age pottery and a primitive plough have been found in excavations. The striking, pyramid-shaped interpretative centre has a viewing platform overlooking the site, audiovisual presentations and displays on local geology and botany.

Environs

Scattered around the wilderness of the spectacular north Mayo coast from Ballina to the end of the Mullet peninsula is a series of sculptures forming the **North Mayo Sculpture Trail**. Created by 12 sculptors from three continents, the 14 works, often on a huge scale, are made from earth, stone and other natural materials, complementing their surroundings. They aim to highlight the coast's grandeur and enduring nature. Temporary exhibits also feature.

❷ Achill Island

Road map A3. Co Mayo. 3,000. from Westport. 098 20705. **W** **achilltourism.com**

Ireland's largest island, 22 km (13.5 miles) long and 19 km (12 miles) wide, is reached by a road bridge that can be raised for boats to pass. Achill offers moorland, mountains, rugged cliffs and long beaches, and is a popular spot for angling and water sports. There is evidence that the island was inhabited as many as 5,000 years ago.

For motorists, the best introduction is the **Atlantic Coast Drive**, a circular, signposted route from Achill Sound, by the bridge. The road goes to the island's southern tip, then north around the rest. Between Doeega and Keel in the southwest run the dramatic Minaun Cliffs and Cathedral Rocks. In the north a mountain overlooks Slievemore, abandoned during the Great Famine *(see p223)*.

❸ Westport

Road map B3. Co Mayo. 6,000. Bridge St (098 25711). Thu. **W** **westporttourism.com**

Westport is a neat town and has a bustling, prosperous air. In the 1770s, architect James Wyatt laid out the wide, tree-lined streets, including the North and South Mall on either side of Carrowbeg River. The town originally traded in yarn, cloth, beer and slate, but industrialization and the Great Famine *(see p223)* brought a dramatic decline until the 1950s when new industry and visitors were attracted to the area.

Beyond the South Mall is Bridge Street, lined with cafés and pubs; the most appealing is Matt Molloy's *(see p330)*, named after and owned by the flautist from The Chieftains.

The *Angel of Welcome* above the marble staircase at Westport House

Bog oak and silver bowl from Westport House

Westport House

Westport. **Tel** 098 27766. **Open** mid-Mar–Sep: daily; Oct–Dec: weekends. **W** **westporthouse.ie**

Just west of the town is the Carrowbeg estuary and Clew Bay. At the head of the bay stands Westport House, the seat of the Earls of Altamont, descendants of the Browne family, who were Tudor settlers. The town of Westport itself was started in the 1750s by John Browne, first Lord Altamont, to complement the house. Designed in 1732 by Richard Cassels, and completed by James Wyatt in 1778, the limestone mansion stands on the site of an O'Malley castle. The mansion is privately owned by the Browne family, who are direct descendents of pirate Grace O'Malley. Its imposing interior is adorned with family portraits. There is also a boating lake, miniature railway, museum and a Pirate Adventure Park for children.

Bogwood centrepiece in Céide Fields interpretative centre

tatue of St Patrick at the foot of Croagh Patrick, looking out to Clew Bay

4 National Museum of Ireland – Country Life

Turlough Park, Turlough, off the N5, 3 km (5 miles) east of Castlebar, Co Mayo. **Tel** 094 903 1755. **Open** 10am–5pm Tue–Sat, 2–5pm Sun. museum.ie

Explore rural life in Ireland in this award-winning museum set in the grounds of Turlough Park. The collection focuses on the period from 1850–1950, when tenant farmers were struggling to become owners of the land they worked. The museum's exhibits illustrate the traditional way of country life while providing historical context of this difficult time. Four floors display fascinating artifacts, such as handcrafted harvest knots and wickerwork; spinning wheels and boats, and hand-operated machinery.

5 Foxford

Road map B3. Co Mayo. 1,000. from Galway. Westport (098 25711).

This tranquil market town is known for good angling in nearby Lough Conn and for its woven rugs and tweeds. In the town centre is **Foxford Woollen Mills**, founded in 1892 by an Irish nun, Mother Arsenius (originally named Agnes). The thriving mill now supplies top fashion houses. An audiovisual tour traces the mill's history, and visitors can see craftspeople at work.

Foxford Woollen Mills and Visitor Centre
Providence Rd. **Tel** 094 925 6104. **Open** daily. **Closed** 1 Jan, 16 Mar, Good Fri & 24–26 Dec. Exhibition Centre.
foxfordwoollenmills.com

6 Knock

Road map B3. Co Mayo. 575. 15 km (9 miles) N of Knock. May–Sep: Knock (094 938 8193). **discoverireland.ie**

In 1879, two local women saw an apparition of the Virgin, St Joseph and St John the Evangelist by the gable of the Church of St John the Baptist. It was witnessed by 13 more onlookers and validated by the Catholic Church amid claims of miracle cures. Every year, over 1.5 million believers make the pilgrimage to the shrine, including Pope John Paul II in 1979 and Mother Teresa in 1993. Its focal point is the gable where the apparition was seen, which is now covered over to form a chapel. Nearby is the Basilica of Our Lady, a modern basilica and Marian shrine. **Knock Museum**, beside the basilica, portrays life in 19th-century rural Ireland. An Apparition section covers the background to the miracle.

Croagh Patrick

Knock Shrine and Museum
Tel 094 938 8100. **Open** daily. **Closed** 25 & 26 Dec. museum **knock-shrine.ie**

7 Croagh Patrick

Road map B3. Murrisk, Co Mayo. from Westport. Westport (098 25711). **croagh-patrick.com**

Ireland's holy mountain, named after the national saint *(see p285)*, is one of Mayo's best-known landmarks. From the bottom it seems cone-shaped, an impression dispelled by climbing to its flat peak. This quartzite, scree-clad mountain has a history of pagan worship from 3000 BC. However, in AD 441, St Patrick is said to have spent 40 days on the mountain fasting and praying for the Irish.

Since then, penitents, often barefoot, have made the pilgrimage to the summit in his honour, especially on Garland Friday and Reek Sunday in July. From the start of the trail at Campbell's Pub in Murrisk, where there is a huge statue of the saint, it is a two-hour climb to the top, at 765 m (2,510 ft). On Reek Sunday mass is celebrated on the peak in a modern chapel. A visitor centre has amenities for exhausted hikers.

❽ Clare Island

Road map A3. Co Mayo. 130. from Roonagh Quay, 6.5 km (4 miles) W of Louisburgh. **Tel** 098 23737 or 086 851 5003 (ferry services). Westport (098 25711). **clareisland.ie**

Clare Island is dominated by two hills, and a square 15th-century castle commands the headland and harbour. In the 16th century the island was the stronghold of Grace O'Malley, pirate queen and patriot, who held sway over the western coast. Although, according to Tudor state papers, she was received at Queen Elizabeth I's court, she stood out against English rule until her death in her seventies in 1603. She is buried here in a tiny Cistercian abbey decorated with medieval murals and inscribed with her motto: "Invincible on land and on sea".

The island is dotted with Iron Age huts and field systems as well as promontory forts and Bronze Age cooking sites. Clare Island is rich in bog flora and fauna, making it popular with walkers. Animal lovers come to see the seals, dolphins, falcons and otters.

Environs

The mainland coastal town of **Louisburgh** offers rugged Atlantic landscape, sheltered coves and sea angling. The **Granuaile Centre** tells the story of Grace O'Malley (*Granuaile* in Gaelic) and has displays on Mayo folklore and archaeology.

The ferry to Inishbofin leaving Cleggan Harbour

Granuaile Visitor Centre
St Catherine's Church, Louisburgh. **Tel** 098 66341. **Open** Mon–Fri, weekends by appt only.

❾ Inishbofin

Road map A3. Co Galway. 200. from Cleggan (095 45819). Clifden (095 21163).

The name Inishbofin means "island of the white cow". This mysterious, often mist-swathed island was chosen for its remoteness by the exiled 7th-century St Colman, English Abbot of Lindisfarne. On the site of his original monastery is a late medieval church, graveyard and holy well. At the sheltered harbour entrance lies a ruined castle, occupied in the 16th century by Spanish pirate Don Bosco in alliance with Grace O'Malley. In 1653 it was captured by Cromwellian forces and used as a prison for Catholic priests. Inishbofin was later owned by a succession of absentee landlords and now survives on farming and lobster fishing.

Surrounded by reefs and islets, the island's landscape is characterized by stone walls, reed-fringed lakes and hay meadows, where the corncrake *(see p22)* can be seen, or heard. Inishbofin's beaches offer bracing walks.

❿ Clifden

Road map A3. Co Galway. 920. Mar–end Sep: Galway Road (095 21163). Tue & Fri. **discoverireland.ie/west**

Framed by the grandeur of the Twelve Bens mountain range and with a striking skyline dominated by two church spires, this early 19th-century market town passes for the capital of the Connemara region and is a good base for exploring. Clifden was founded in 1812 by John d'Arcy, a local landowner and High Sheriff of Galway, to create a pocket of respectability within the lawlessness of Connemara. The family eventually went bankrupt trying to bring prosperity and order to the town. The Protestant church contains a copy of the Cross of Cong *(see p71)*.

Today craft shops have taken over much of the town. In the centre is the Square, a place for lively pubs such as E J Kings *(see p329)*. Connemara is noted for its *sean nós* (unaccompanied singing), but in Clifden, generally traditional music is more common.

Clifden against a backdrop of the Twelve Bens mountains

Connemara

This wild region in the west of Galway encompasses bogs, mountains and a rugged coastline. Major sights include the Connemara National Park and Kylemore Abbey *(see p212)*. For those without a car, coach tours are available from Galway *(see p370)*.

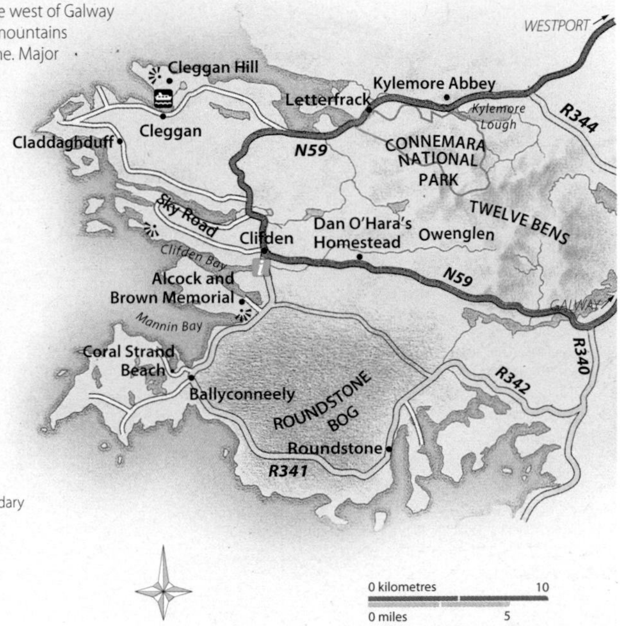

utting out into **Clifden Bay** s a sand spit and beach, sign-posted from Clifden Square. South of Clifden, at the start of the Roundstone Road, is Owenglen Cascade where, in May, salmon leap on their way to spawn upstream.

Environs

The **Sky Road** is an 11-km (7-mile) circular route with stunning ocean views. The road goes northwest from Clifden and passes desolate scenery and the narrow inlet of Clifden Bay. Clifden Castle, John d'Arcy's Gothic Revival ruin, lies just off the Sky Road, as do several inlets.

The coastal road north from Clifden to **Cleggan**, via Claddaghduff, is spectacular, passing former smuggling coves. Cleggan, a pretty fishing village, nestles into the head of Cleggan Bay. From here boats leave for Inishbofin and Inishturk. **Cleggan Hill** has a ruined Napoleonic Martello tower and a megalithic tomb.

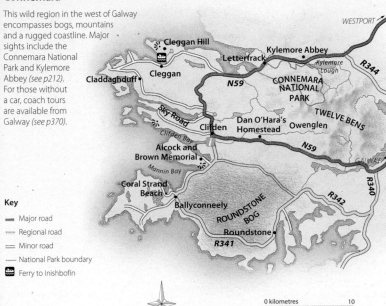

View of the coast from the Sky Road

To the south of Clifden, the coastal route to Roundstone skirts a mass of bogland pitted with tiny lakes. The **Alcock and Brown Memorial** overlooks the bog landing site of the first transatlantic flight made by Alcock and Brown in 1919. Nearby is Marconi's wireless station, which exchanged the first transatlantic radio messages with Nova Scotia in 1907. The **Ballyconneely** area has craggy islands and the beautiful **Coral Strand Beach**. The village of **Roundstone** is best seen during the summer regatta of traditional Galway hookers *(see p215)*.

A short drive to the east of Clifden is **Dan O'Hara's Homestead**. In a rocky setting, this organic farm recreates the tough conditions of life in Connemara before the 1840s. There is an audiovisual display on the history of Connemara.

Dan O'Hara's Homestead
Connemara Heritage & History Centre, Lettershea, off N59. **Tel** 095 21246.
Open Apr–Oct: 9am–6pm.
connemaraheritage.com

For additional map symbols *see back flap*

The imposing Kylemore Abbey on the shores of Kylemore Lough

⓫ Kylemore Abbey

Road map A3. Connemara, Co Galway. **Tel** 095 52001. from Galway. **Open** daily. **Closed** Christmas. groups call to book. Walled garden: **Open** daily. limited. **kylemore abbeytourism.ie**

Sheltered by the slopes of the Twelve Bens, this lakeside castle is a romantic, battlemented Gothic Revival fantasy. It was built as a present for his wife by Mitchell Henry (1826–1911), who was a Manchester tycoon and later Galway MP. The Henrys also purchased a huge area of moorland, drained the boggy hillside and planted thousands of trees as a windbreak for their new orchards and exotic walled gardens. After the sudden deaths of his wife and daughter, Henry left Kylemore and the castle was sold.

It became an abbey when Benedictine nuns, fleeing from Ypres in Belgium during World War I, sought refuge here. For many years it was run by the nuns as a girls' school. Visitors can view restored rooms in the abbey, as well as explore the grounds, a restaurant, craft shop, pottery studio and soap factory.

There is also a restored Victorian walled garden in the grounds, featuring the longest double herbaceous borders in Ireland, a nuttery and a meandering streamside walk.

⓬ Connemara National Park

Road map A3. Letterfrack, Connemara, Co Galway. **Tel** 095 41054. Park: **Open** daily. Visitors' Centre: **Tel** 095 41054. **Open** Mar–Oct: daily. **connemaranationalpark.ie**

A combination of bogland, lakes and mountains makes up this National Park in the heart of Connemara. Within its more than 2,000 ha (5,000 acres) are four of the Twelve Bens, including Benbaun, the highest mountain in the range at 730 m (2,400 ft), and the peak of Diamond Hill. At the centre is the valley of Glanmore and the Polladirk River. Visitors come for the spectacular landscape and to glimpse the famous Connemara ponies.

Part of the land originally belonged to the Kylemore Abbey estate. In 1980 it became a National Park. There are traces of the land's previous uses all over the park: megalithic tombs, up to 4,000 years old, can be seen as well as old ridges marking former grazing areas and arable fields.

The park is open all year, while the Visitors' Centre near the entrance, just outside Letterfrack, is open only from March to mid-October. It features displays on local flora and fauna and on how the landscape developed and was used. There is also an indoor picnic area. Three signposted walks start from the Visitors' Centre. In summer there are guided walks, some led by botanists, and various children's activities. Climbing the Twelve Bens should be attempted only by experienced walkers equipped for all weather conditions.

Connemara Wildlife

The blanket bogs and moorlands of Connemara are a botanist's paradise, especially for unusual bog and heathland plants. Birdlife is also varied: there are hooded crows, which can be recognized by their grey and black plumage, stonechats, peregrines and merlins – the smallest falcons in the British Isles. Red deer have been successfully reintroduced into the area and a herd can be seen in the National Park. Badgers, foxes, stoats and otters may also be spotted, as well as grey seals along the rocky coast.

The merlin nests in old clumps of heather and feeds mainly on small birds.

St Dabeoc's heath, a pretty heather, grows nowhere else in Ireland or Great Britain.

For hotels and restaurants in this region see pp300–301 and pp318–20

13 Cong

oad map B3. Co Mayo. 350.
Old Courthouse (094 954 6542).
pen Mar–Oct: daily.
congtourism.com

his picturesque village lies on ne shores of Lough Corrib, just vithin County Mayo. Cong neans isthmus – the village lies n the strip of land between ough Corrib and Lough Mask.)uring the 1840s, as a famine elief project, a canal was built nking the two lakes, but the vater drained through the orous limestone bed. Stone ridges and stone-clad locks are till in place along the dry canal.

Cong Abbey lies close to the nain street. The Augustinian bbey was founded in the early 2th century by Turlough)'Connor, King of Connaught nd High King of Ireland. he abbey has doorvays in a style ransitional between omanesque and othic, stone carvngs and restored loisters. The Cross f Cong, an ornate rocessional cross ntended for the bbey, is in the lational Museum of eland in Dublin, ollowing a successful xhibition in the Museum of ountry Life in Turlough. The nost fascinating remains are ne Gothic chapter house, stone ridges and the monks' fishingouse that overhangs the river the monks had a system where a bell rang in the kitchen when a fish took the bait.

Just south of Cong is **Ashford Castle**, rebuilt in Gothic Revival style in 1870 by Lord Ardilaun of the Guinness family. One of Ireland's best hotels *(see p300)*, its grounds can be visited by boat from Galway and Oughterard. Cong was the setting for *The Quiet Man*, the 1950s' film starring John Wayne.

Carved 12th-century doorway of Cong Abbey

14 Lough Corrib

Road map B3. Co Galway. from Galway and Cong. from Oughterard, Cong and Wood Quay, Galway.

An angler's paradise, Lough Corrib offers the chance to fish with local fishermen for brown trout, salmon, pike, perch and eels. Despite its proximity to Galway, the lake is tranquil, dotted with uninhabited islands and framed by meadows, reedbeds and wooded shores. The waterside is home to swans and coots. On **Inchagoill**, one of the largest islands, stand the ruins of an early Christian monastic settlement and a Romanesque church.

The lake's atmosphere is best appreciated on a cruise. From Galway, the standard short cruise winds through the marshes to the site of an Iron Age fort, limestone quarries and the battlemented Menlo Castle. Longer cruises continue to Cong or include picnics on the islands.

View over Lough Corrib from the shore northwest of Oughterard

Environs

On the banks of Lough Corrib, **Oughterard** is known as "the gateway to Connemara". The village has craft shops, thatched cottages and friendly pubs. It is also an important centre for golf, angling, hiking and pony trekking. Towards Galway City, **Brigit's Garden** in Roscahill has 4.45 ha (11 acres) of themed gardens.

About 4 km (2.5 miles) southeast of Oughterard (off the N59) is **Aughnanure Castle**. This well-restored six-storey tower house clings to a rocky island on the River Drimneen. The present castle, built by the O'Flaherty clan, is on the site of one dating from 1256. The clan controlled West Connaught from Lough Corrib to Galway and the coast in the 13th to 16th centuries. From this castle the feuding O'Flaherty chieftains held out against the British in the 16th century. In 1545 Donal O'Flaherty married the pirate Grace O'Malley *(see p210)*. The tower house has an unusual double bawn *(see p24)* and a murder hole from which missiles could be dropped on invaders.

Aughnanure Castle
Oughterard. **Tel** 091 552214.
Open Apr–Oct: daily.
limited. **heritageireland.ie**

onnemara ponies roam semivild and are fabled to be from rab stock that came ashore rom Spanish Armada wrecks.

Fuchsias grow profusely in the hedgerows of Connemara, thriving in the mild climate.

⑮ Galway

Galway is both the centre for the Irish-speaking regions in the West and a lively university city. Under the Anglo-Normans, it flourished as a trading post. In 1396 it gained a Royal Charter and, for the next two centuries, was controlled by 14 merchant families, or "tribes". The city prospered under English influence, but this allegiance to the Crown cost Galway dear when, in 1652, Cromwell's forces wreaked havoc. After the Battle of the Boyne *(see p248)*, Galway fell into decline, unable to compete with east-coast trade. However, the city's profile has been revived as a developing centre for high-tech industry.

Inside The Quays seafood restaurant and pu

Houses on the banks of the Corrib

Exploring Galway

The centre of the city lies on the banks of the River Corrib, which flows down from Lough Corrib *(see p213)* widening out as it reaches Galway Bay. Urban renewal since the 1970s has led to extensive restoration of the narrow, winding streets of this once-walled city. Due to its compact size, Galway is easy to explore on foot, and a leisurely pace provides plenty of opportunity to stop off at its shops, pubs and historic sights.

Eyre Square

The redeveloped square encloses a pleasant plaza and park lined with imposing, mainly 19th-century, buildings. On the northwest of the square is the **Browne Doorway**, a 17th-century entrance from a mansion in Abbeygate Street Lower. Beside it is a fountain adorned with a sculpture of a Galway hooker boat. The **Eyre Square Centre**, overlooking the park, is a modern shopping mall built to incorporate sections of the historic city walls. Walkways link Shoemakers and Penrice towers, two of the 14 wall towers that used to ring the city in the 17th century.

Latin Quarter

From Eyre Square, William Street and Shop Street are the main routes into the bustling "Latin Quarter". On the corner of Abbeygate Street Upper and Shop Street stands **Lynch's Castle**, now a bank, bu still the grandest 16th-century town house in Galway. It was owned by the Lynch family, one of the 14 "tribes".

A side street leads to the **Collegiate Church of St Nicholas**, Galway's finest medieval building. The church, founded in 1320, was extendec in the 15th and 16th centuries, but then damaged by the Cromwellians, who used it to stable horses. The west porch is from the 15th century and there are some finely carved gargoyles under the parapet.

Quay Street is lined with restaurants and pubs, includin **The Quays** *(see p329)*. Tígh Neachtain is a town house which belonged to "Humanity Dick", an 18th-century MP whc promoted laws against cruelty to animals. Today, it too is a restaurant and pub *(see p330)*. Nearby are the Taibhdhearc ar Druid theatres *(see p338)*.

North Galway

The **Cathedral of St Nicholas** (1965), built of local limestone and Connemara marble, stand on the west bank. From here you can see Wood Quay, wher Lough Corrib cruises start in th summer *(see p213)*. **National University of Ireland Galway**, further west, is a large campus with a 1849 Gothic Revival quad. Salmon Weir Bridge links the two banks. Shoals of salmo rest under the bridge on their way upstream to spawn.

Colourfully painted shopfronts in the historic city of Galway

Galway Hookers

Galway's traditional wooden sailing boats, featured on the city's coat of arms, were known as *pucans* and *gleotogs* – hookers in English. They have broad black hulls, thick masts and white or rust-coloured sails. Once common in the Claddagh district, they were also used along the Atlantic coast to ferry peat, cattle and beer. Hookers can be seen in action at the Cruinniú na mBád festival in Kinvara *(see p218)*.

Small Galway hooker sailing by the old quays and Spanish Arch

The Old Quays

The **Spanish Arch**, where the river opens out, was built in 1584 to protect the harbour, then outside the city walls. Here, Spanish traders unloaded their ships. Behind the arch is the **Galway City Museum** with exhibits on the city's history.

The Claddagh

Beyond the Spanish Arch, on the west bank of the Corrib, lies the Claddagh. The name comes from *An Cladach*, meaning "flat, stony shore". From medieval times, this fiercely independent fishing community beyond the city walls was governed by a "king", the last of whom died in 1954. The only remnants of this once close-knit, Gaelic-speaking community are Claddagh rings, betrothal rings traditionally handed down from mother to daughter *(see p336)*.

Environs

Just west of the city is **Salthill**, Galway's seaside resort. The beaches at Palmer's Rock and Grattan Road are particularly popular with families in summer. A bracing walk along the promenade is still a Galway tradition.

VISITORS' CHECKLIST

Practical Information
Road map B4. Co Galway. 60,000. The Fairgreen, Foster St (091 537 700). Sat & Sun. Galway Arts Festival (mid-Jul); Galway Races (late Jul–Aug).

Transport
Carnmore, 11 km (7 miles) NE of Galway. Ceannt Station (091 561444). Ceannt Station (091 562000).

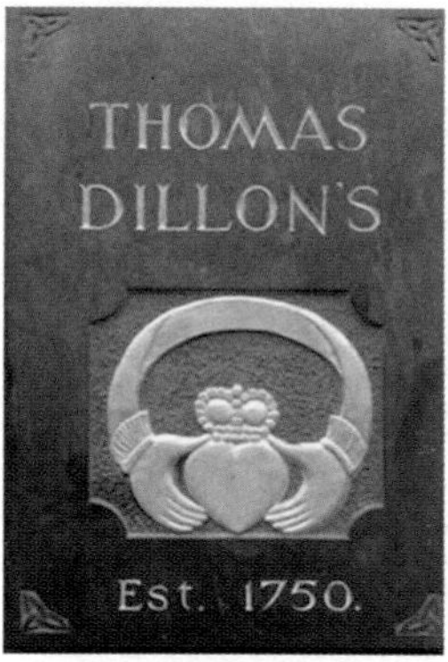

Plaque outside Dillon's Shop, the first makers of Claddagh rings

Galway City Centre

1. Cathedral of St Nicholas
2. Collegiate Church of St Nicholas
3. Lynch's Castle
4. Browne Doorway
5. The Quays Pub
6. Spanish Arch
7. Galway City Museum
8. The Claddagh

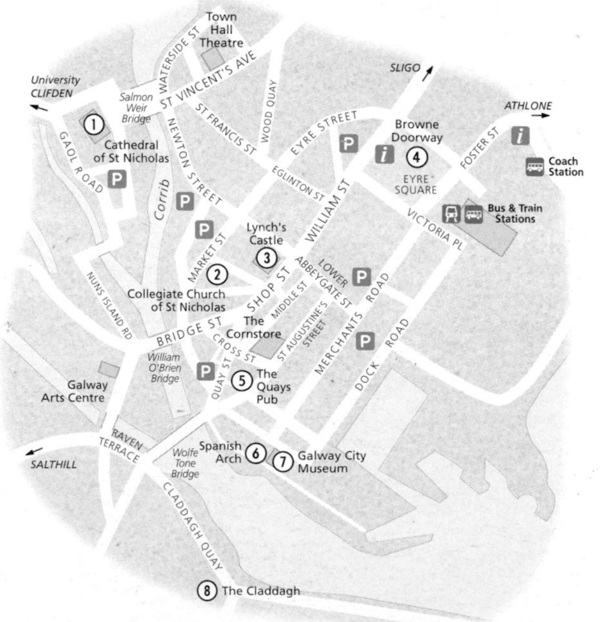

0 metres 200
0 yards 200

⓰ Aran Islands

Inishmore (Inis Mōr), Inishmaan (Inis Meāin) and Inisheer (Inis Oírr), the three Aran Islands, are formed from a limestone ridge. The largest, Inishmore, is 13 km (8 miles) long and 3 km (2 miles) wide. The attractions of these islands include the austere landscape crisscrossed with dry-stone walls, stunning coastal views and several large prehistoric stone forts. In the 5th century, St Enda brought Christianity to the islands, starting a long monastic tradition. Protected for centuries by their isolated position, the islands today are a bastion of traditional Irish culture. Farming, fishing and tourism are the main occupations of the islanders.

Looking over the cliff edge at Dún Aonghasa

Kilmurvey Beach
The attractive sandy beach east of Kilmurvy offers safe swimming in a sheltered cove. The town itself is a quiet place to stay near a number of the island's most important sights.

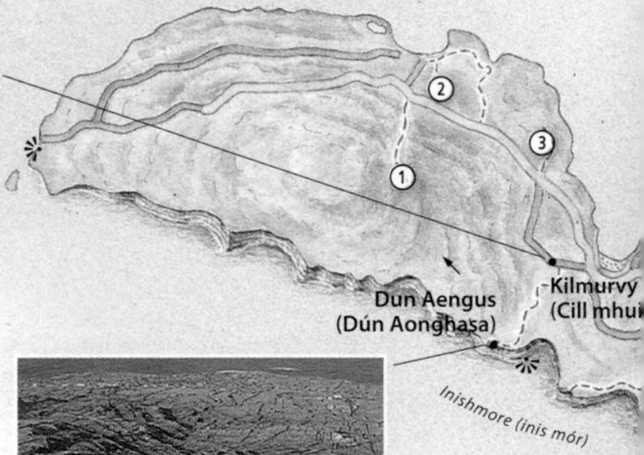

★ Dún Aonghasa
This Iron or Bronze Age promontory fort *(see p24)* has four concentric stone walls. It is also protected by a *chevaux de frise*, a ring of razor-sharp, pointed stone stakes.

KEY

① **Dún Eoghanachta** is a circular stone fort dating back to the Iron Age, with a single wall terraced on the inside.

② **Na Seacht Teampaill**, the so-called Seven Churches, make up a monastic settlement dedicated to St Brecan. Built between the 9th and 15th centuries, some are probably domestic buildings.

③ **Clochán na Carraige** is a large, well-preserved beehive hut *(see p25)*, probably built by early Christian settlers on the islands.

④ **Teampall Chiaráin**, dedicated to St Ciaran, is a ruined 12th-century church with striking doorways. Nearby are several stones inscribed with crosses.

⑤ **Dún Eochla** is a circular Bronze Age fort standing close to the highest point on Inishmore.

Aran Traditions

The islands are famous for their knitwear *(see p334)* and for the traditional Aran costume that was still worn by some of the older generation not long ago: for women, a red flannel skirt and crocheted shawl; for men a sleeveless tweed jacket and a colourful knitted belt. From time to time you may still see a *currach* or low rowing boat, the principal form of transport for centuries. Land-making, the ancient and arduous process of creating soil by covering bare rock with sand and seaweed, continues to this day.

Currach made from canvas coated in tar

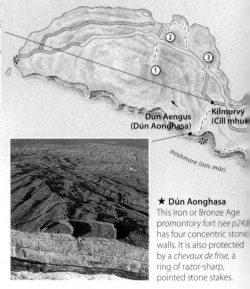

For hotels and restaurants in this region see pp300–301 and pp318–20

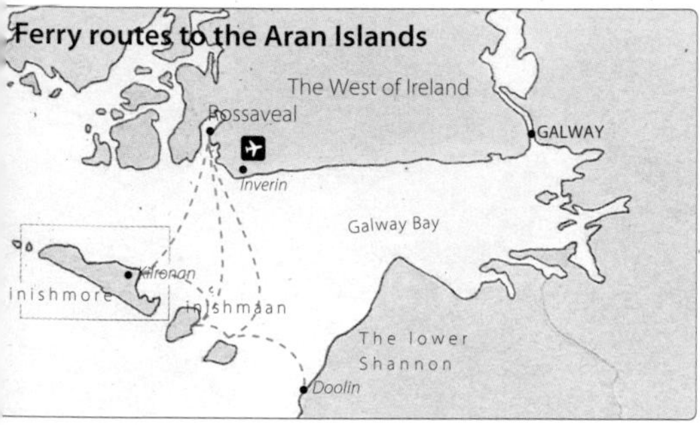

VISITORS' CHECKLIST

Practical Information
Road map A4, B4. Co Galway.
1,200.
Kilronan, Inishmore (099 61263).
aranislands.ie

Transport
from Connemara Airport, Inverin (**aerarann islands.ie**; 091 593034). from Rossaveal: **Island Ferries** (**aranisland ferries.com**; 091 568903); from Doolin: **Doolin Ferry Company** (**doolinferries.com**; Mar–Oct only; 065 707 5949). *Ferries sail throughout the year; some go to all three main islands. Phone for details. Cars cannot be taken to the islands. From Kilronan, you can hire bicycles and jaunting cars, or go on minibus tours (087 253 2030).*

0 kilometres 2
0 miles 1

Key
Main road
Minor road
Track
Beach
Viewpoint

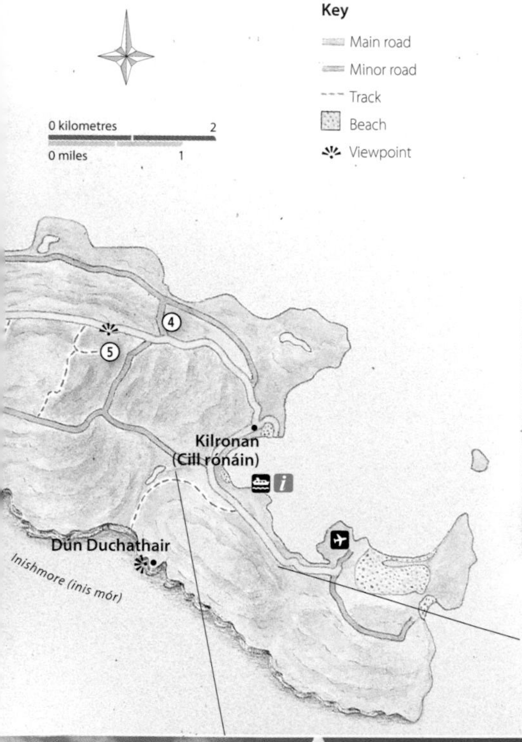

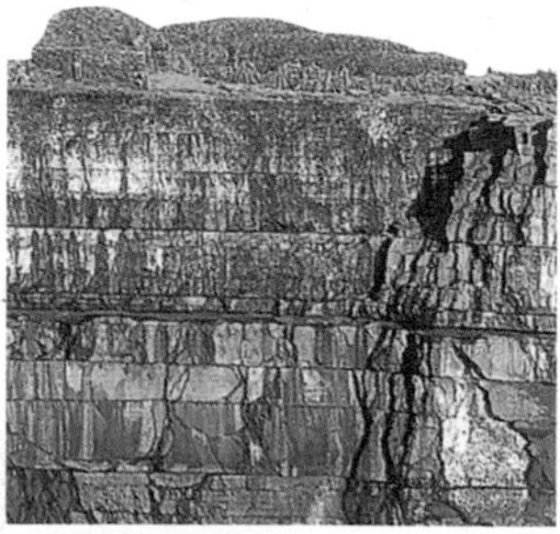

★ Dún Duchathair
Built on a headland, this Iron Age construction is known as the Black Fort. It has dry-stone ramparts.

★ Kilronan
The Aran Islands' main port is a busy place, with jaunting cars (ponies and traps) and minibuses waiting by the pier to give island tours; bicycles can also be hired. Nearby, the fascinating Aran Heritage Centre is dedicated to the disappearing Aran way of life.

Mural in the centre of Kinvara depicting a shopfront

⑰ Kinvara

Road map B4. Co Galway. 550.
Galway (091 537700).

One of the most charming fishing villages on Galway Bay, Kinvara's appeal lies in its sheltered, seaweed-clad harbour and traditional sea-faring atmosphere. From medieval times, its fortunes were closely linked to Kilmacduagh, the powerful monastery and bishopric upon which the village depended.

The pier is bordered by a row of fishermen's cottages. Kinvara remains a popular port of call for sailors of traditional Galway hookers *(see p215)* and is known for the Cruinniú na mBád (gathering of the boats) festival in August. Rambles include historical and nature trails. Bird-watchers may spot teal, curlews and oystercatchers by the shore.

Environs
North of Kinvara, on a promontory on the shore of Galway Bay, lies **Dunguaire Castle**. It is perched just beyond some quaint thatched cottages and a stone bridge. The castle is named after the 7th-century King Guaire of Connaught, whose court here was renowned as the haunt of bards and balladeers. Although the medieval earth-works survive, the present castle was built in the 16th century, a quintessential tower house *(see p24)* with sophis-ticated machicolations. The banqueting hall is still used for "medieval banquets" with Celtic harp music and the recital of Irish poetry.

Dunguaire Castle
Tel 061 360788. **Open** May–Sep: daily.
shannonheritage.com

⑱ Kilmacduagh

Road map B4. Outside Gort on Corofin Rd, Co Galway. to Gort.
Open daily.

This monastic settlement is in a remote location on the borders of Counties Clare and Galway, roughly 5 km (3 miles) southwest of Gort. The sense of isolation is accentuated by the stony moonscape of the Burren to the west *(see pp190–91)*. Reputedly foundec by St Colman MacDuagh in the early 7th century, Kilmacduagh owes more to the monastic revival which led to rebuilding from the 11th century onwards.

The centrepiece of the extensive site is a large, slightl leaning 11th- or 12th-century round tower and a roofless church, known as the cathedra or Teampall. The cathedral is a pre-Norman structure, which was later remodelled in Gothic style, with flamboyant tracery and fine tomb carvings. In the surrounding fields lie the remains of several other churches that once depended on the monastery. To the northeast of the Teampall is the late medieval Glebe or Abbot's House, a variant of a 14th- or 15th-century tower house *(see p24)*.

⑲ Thoor Ballylee

Road map B4. Gort, Co Galway.
Ballylee Castle: to Gort.
Closed due to flood damage; call Galway Tourist Office on 091 537700 to check if open. limited.

For much of the 1920s, this beguiling tower house was a summer home to the poet W B Yeats *(see pp26–7)*. Yeats was a regular visitor to nearby Coole Park, the home of his friend Lady Gregory (1852–1932), whc was a cofounder of the Abbey Theatre *(see p92)*.

On one visit Yeats came upor Ballylee Castle, a 14th-century de Burgo tower adjoining a cos cottage with a walled garden and stream. In 1902, both the tower and the cottage became part of the Gregory estate and

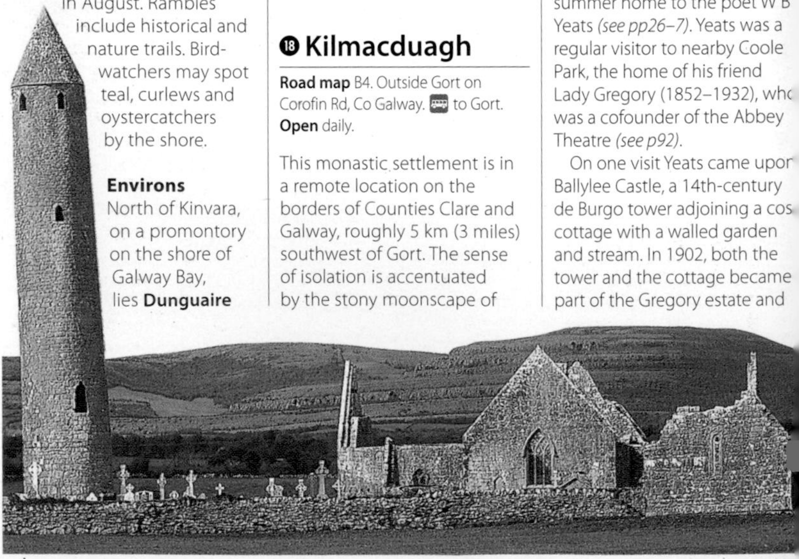
Round tower and cathedral, the most impressive monastic remains at Kilmacduagh

Yeats bought them in 1916. From 1919 onwards, his family divided their time between Dublin and their Galway tower. Yeats used the name Thoor Ballylee as the address, using the Irish word for tower to "keep people from suspecting us of modern gothic and a deer park". His collection, *The Tower* (1928), includes several poems inspired by the house.

An audiovisual tour includes readings from Yeats's poetry, but the charm of a visit lies in the tower itself, with its spiral stone steps and views from the battlements over forest and farmland.

Environs

Just to the north of Gort is **Coole Park**, once the home of Lady Gregory. Although the house was demolished in 1941, the estate farm has been restored and the fine gardens survive. In particular, there is the "autograph tree", a spreading copper beech carved with the initials of George Bernard Shaw, W B Yeats, J M Synge *(see pp26–7)* and Jack Yeats . In the farm buildings is an audiovisual display. The emphasis of the visitors' centre is on the life of Lady Gregory: it is the start of two sign-posted walks, one around the gardens and the other through beech, hazel, birch and ash woodland to Coole Lake.

Coole Park
3 km (2 miles) NE of Gort. **Tel** 091 631804. Visitors' centre: **Open** Easter–Sep: daily; park open all year. limited. **coolepark.ie**

Thoor Ballylee tower house, the summer home of W B Yeats

Gentle hills and woodland by Coole Lake in Coole Park

⑳ Portumna

Road map C4. Co Galway. 1,200. Galway (091 537700). Fri.

Portumna is a historic market town with scattered sights, many of which have been restored. Situated on Lough Derg, it is a convenient base for cruising the River Shannon *(see p189)* and has a modern marina. **Portumna Castle**, built in the early 17th century, was the main seat of the de Burgo family. It boasts some elaborate interior stonework. Nearby is **Portumna Priory**. Most of the remains date from 1414 when it was founded by the Dominicans, but traces can also be found of the Cistercian abbey that was previously on the site. The de Burgo estate to the west of the town now forms **Portumna Forest Park**, with picnic sites and signposted woodland trails leading to Lough Derg.

Portumna Castle
Tel 090 974 1658. **Open** Apr–Sep and weekends in Oct.

㉑ Clonfert Cathedral

Road map C4. Clonfert, Co Galway. **Open** daily.

Situated near a bleak stretch of the Shannon bordering the boglands of the Midlands, Clonfert is one of the jewels of Irish-Romanesque architecture. The tiny cathedral occupies the site of a monastery, which was founded by St Brendan in AD 563, and is believed to be the burial place of the saint.

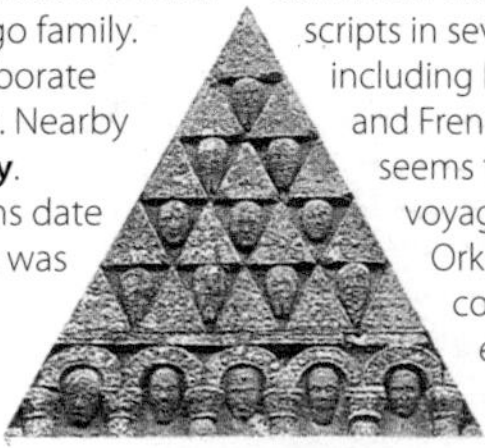

Human heads carved on the tympanum at Clonfert Cathedral

Although a great scholar and enthusiastic founder of monasteries, St Brendan is best known as the "great navigator". His journeys are recounted in *Navigatio Sancti Brendani*, written in about 1050, which survives in medieval manuscripts in several languages including Flemish, Norse and French. The text seems to describe a voyage to Wales, the Orkneys, Iceland and conceivably the east coast of North America. His voyage and his boat *(see p194)* have been recreated by modern explorers in an attempt to prove that St Brendan may have preceded Columbus by about 900 years.

The highlight of Clonfert is its intricately sculpted sandstone doorway. The round arch above the door is decorated with animal and human heads, foliage and symbolic motifs. The carvings on the triangular tympanum above the arch are of strange human heads. In the chancel, the 13th-century east windows are fine examples of late Irish-Romanesque art. The 15th-century chancel arch is adorned with sculptures of angels and a mermaid. Although Clonfert was built over several centuries, the church has a profound sense of unity.

Winding stone walls on Inishmore, the largest of the Aran Islands ▶

East wall and gatehouse at Roscommon Castle

㉒ Turoe Stone

Road map B4. Turoe, Bullaun, Loughrea, Co Galway. **Tel** 091 841580. **Open** mid-May–Aug: daily; Sep–mid-May: Sat & Sun only.
W **turoepetfarm.com**

The Turoe Stone stands at the centre of the Turoe Pet Farm and Leisure Park, near the village of Bullaun (on the R350). The white granite boulder, which stands about 1 m (3 ft) high, dates back to the 3rd or 2nd century BC. Its top half is carved with curvilinear designs in a graceful Celtic style, known as La Tène, also found in Celtic parts of Europe, particularly Brittany. The lower half has a smooth section and a band of step-pattern carving. The stone was originally found at an Iron Age ring fort nearby, and is thought to have been used there in fertility rituals. Efforts at preservation sometimes hamper viewing, so call ahead.

The park around the Turoe Stone is designed mainly for children. The Pet Farm has some small fields containing farm animals and a pond. There is also a wooded riverside walk with a nature trail, outdoor and indoor picnic areas, a playground and two supervised indoor play areas.

The Celtic Turoe Stone carved with graceful swirling patterns

㉓ Roscommon

Road map C3. Co Roscommon. 3,500. Jun–Sep: Harrison Hall (090 662 6342). Fri.
W **discoverireland.ie**

The county capital is a busy market town. In Main Street is the former gaol, which had a woman as its last executioner. "Lady Betty", as she was known, was sentenced to death for the murder of her son in 1780, but negotiated a pardon by agreeing to become a hangwoman.

South of the town centre, just off Abbey Street, is the **Dominican Friary**, founded in 1253 by Felim O'Conor, Lord of Connaught. Set in the north wall of the choir is a late 13th-century effigy of the founder.

Roscommon Castle, an Anglo-Norman fortress north of the town, was built in 1269 by Robert d'Ufford, Lord Justice of Ireland on land seized from the Dominican Friary, and rebuilt 11 years later after being destroyed by the Irish led by Hugh O'Conor, King of Connaught.

㉔ Clonalis House

Road map B3. Castlerea, Co Roscommon. **Tel** 094 962 0014. **Open** Jun–end Aug: 11am–5pm Mon–Sat. limited.
W **clonalis.com**

This Victorian manor just outside Castlerea is the ancestral home of the O'Conors, the last High Kings of Ireland and Kings of Connaught. This old Gaelic family can trace its heritage back 1,500 years. The ruins of their gabled 17th-century home are visible in the grounds. On the lawn lies the O'Conor coronation stone, which dates from 90 BC.

The interior includes a library of many books and documents recording Irish history, a tiny private chapel and a gallery of family portraits spanning 500 years. In the billiard room is the harp once played by Turlough O'Carolan (1670–1738), blind harpist and last of the Gaelic bards *(see p28)*.

㉕ Strokestown Park

Road map C3. Strokestown, Co Roscommon. House, Pleasure Gardens and Museum: **Tel** 071 963 3013. **Open** daily. **Closed** 1 week at Christmas.
W **strokestownpark.ie**

Strokestown Park, the greatest Palladian mansion in County Roscommon, was built in the 1730s for Thomas Mahon, an MP whose family was granted the lands by Charles II after the Restoration. It incorporates an earlier 17th-century tower house *(see p24)*. The design of the new house owes most to Richard Cassels, architect of Russborough *(see p136)*. The galleried kitchen, panelled stairwell and groin-vaulted stables are undoubtedly his work, tailoring Palladian principles to the requirements of the Anglo-Irish gentry.

The house stayed in the family's hands until 1979, when major restoration began. In its heyday, the estate included ornamental parkland, a deer park, folly, mausoleum and the illage of Strokestown itself. y 1979, the estate's original 2,000 ha (30,000 acres) had windled to 120 ha (300 acres), ut the recreation of the leasure Gardens and the Fruit nd Vegetable Garden have reatly increased the area.

Set in the stable yards, the **amine Museum** uses the trokestown archives to tell the tory of tenants and landlords luring the 1840s Famine. During the crisis, landlords livided into two camps: the haritable, some of whom tarted up Famine Relief chemes, and the callous, like he Mahons of Strokestown. Major Denis Mahon was nurdered after forcing two-thirds of the starving peasantry off his land by a combination of eviction and passages in "coffin ships" to North America. A section of the exhibition deals with continuing famine and malnutrition worldwide.

The Great Famine

The failure of the Irish potato crop in 1845, 1846 and 1848, due to potato blight, had disastrous consequences for the people of Ireland, many of whom relied on this staple crop. More than a million died of starvation and disease, and by 1856 over two and a half million had been forced to emigrate. The crisis was worsened by unsympathetic landlords who often continued collecting rents. The Famine had far-reaching effects: mass emigration became a way of life *(see pp46–7)* and many rural communities, particularly in the far west, were decimated.

Peasants queuing for soup during the Famine (1847)

26 Boyle

Road map C3. Co Roscommon. 2,200. Jun–Sep: King House (071 966 3247). Fri. **discoverireland.ie**

Boyle, County Roscommon's most charming town, is blessed with fine Georgian and medieval architecture. **Boyle Abbey** is a well-preserved Cistercian abbey founded in 1161 as a sister house to Mellifont in County Louth *(see p249)*. It survived raids by Anglo-Norman barons and Irish chieftains, as well as the 1539 suppression of the monasteries. In 1659 it was turned into a castle. The abbey is still remarkably intact, with a church, cloisters, cellars, sacristy and even kitchens. The nave of the church has both Romanesque and Gothic arches and there are well-preserved 12th-century capitals. Major renovations were completed on the building in 2011. The visitors' centre has exhibits on the abbey's history.

King House, a Palladian mansion, is the ancestral home of the Anglo-Irish King family, later Earls of Kingston. Inside is a contemporary art gallery, and displays on such subjects as Georgian architecture, the history of the surrounding area and the Connaught chieftains.

Carved capital in the nave at Boyle Abbey

The gatehouse and remains of the nave at Boyle Abbey

Boyle Abbey
Tel 071 966 2604. **Open** Easter–mid-Sep: 10am–6pm.

King House
Main St. **Tel** 071 966 3242. **Open** Apr–Sep: Tue–Sat & public hols. on request. **kinghouse.ie**

Environs

Lough Key is often called the loveliest lake in Ireland. The island-studded lake and surrounding woodland make a glorious setting for the **Lough Key Forest Park**. The 320-ha (790-acre) park formed part of the Rockingham estate until 1957, when Rockingham House, a John Nash design, burned down. The woods were added by 18th-century landlords.

The **Lough Key Experience** takes visitors on an audio journey through the 19th-century underground tunnels, up to the Moylurg viewing tower and along Ireland's first Tree Canopy Trail.

There are also several ring forts *(see p24)*, a river jetty and an adventure playground providing entertainment for children of all ages.

Lough Key Forest Park
N4 8 km (5 miles) E of Boyle. **Tel** 071 967 3122. **Open** Easter–Oct: daily; Nov–Mar: Fri–Sun.

NORTHWEST IRELAND

Donegal · Sligo · Leitrim

Towering cliffs, deserted golden beaches and rocky headlands abound along the rugged coast of Donegal, which incorporates some of Ireland's wildest scenery. To the south, Sligo is steeped in prehistory and Celtic myth, with its legacy of ancient monuments and natural beauty enriched by associations with the poet, W B Yeats. By contrast, Leitrim is a quiet county of unruffled lakes and waterways.

In Celtic mythology Sligo was the power base of the warrior Queen Maeve of Connaught *(see p30)*, and the county's legacy of prehistoric sites shows that the area was heavily populated in Celtic times. Later, however, both County Sligo and neighbouring County Leitrim often seemed to be little affected by events taking place in the rest of Ireland. The Normans, for example, barely disturbed the rule of local Gaelic clans.

Donegal, on the other hand, is part of Ulster and has played an active role in the history of the north. The O'Donnells held sway over most of Donegal in the Middle Ages, but they fled to Europe in 1607 following their ill-fated stand against the English alongside the O'Neills *(see p259)*. Protestant settlers moved on to land confiscated from the two clans, but they left much of Donegal and its poor soil to the native Irish, who lived there in isolation from the rest of Ulster. County Donegal remains one of the most remote parts of Ireland, and it is no coincidence that it boasts the country's largest number of Gaelic speakers. There is a wealth of traditions and culture to be found around the county and on islands such as Tory Island *(see p228)*.

While the beauty of Donegal lies mainly along the coast, Sligo's finest landscapes are found inland, around Lough Gill and among the sparsely populated Bricklieve Mountains.

The 19th-century interior of Hargadon's bar in Sligo town, with its original counter and stout jars

◀ Fanad Head Lighthouse, County Donegal

Exploring Northwest Ireland

The supreme appeal of Donegal lies in the natural beauty of its coast, with windswept peninsulas, precipitous cliffs and a host of golden beaches. There is a scattering of small seaside resorts which make good bases, and Donegal town is well placed for exploring the southern part of the county. The cultural heartland of the Northwest lies in and around Sligo, the only sizeable town in the region, from where you can reach several prehistoric remains and other historic sights. Further south, lovely scenery surrounds Lough Gill and the more remote Lough Arrow. In Leitrim, a county of lakes and rivers, the main centre of activity is the lively boating resort of Carrick-on-Shannon.

Beautiful Lough Eske in the county of Donegal

Key

- Major road
- Secondary road
- Minor road
- Scenic route
- Main railway
- Minor railway
- International border
- County border
- △ Summit

For additional map symbols *see back flap*

Getting Around

The N56, linking Letterkenny and Donegal, provides access to much of the Northwest's best scenery, with minor roads branching off it around the coast's rocky peninsulas. A few buses serve this route, but travelling around without a car is easier further south, with buses running daily from Donegal along the N15 to Sligo. The rail network barely reaches the Northwest, though there are daily trains between Sligo and Carrick-on-Shannon.

Thatched cottage near Malin Head on Inishowen Peninsula

Sights at a Glance

1 Tory Island
2 Bloody Foreland
3 Derryveagh Mountains
4 Horn Head
5 Rosguill Peninsula
6 Fanad Peninsula
8 Grianán Ailigh
9 Letterkenny
10 The Rosses
11 Ardara
12 Glencolmcille
13 Slieve League
14 Killybegs
15 Donegal
16 Lough Derg
17 Rossnowlagh
18 Ballyshannon
19 Lissadell House
21 Parke's Castle
22 Sligo
23 Lough Arrow
24 Carrick-on-Shannon
25 The Organic Centre

Tours

7 Inishowen Peninsula
20 Yeats Country

View from Carrowkeel Bronze Age cemetery above Lough Arrow

For hotels and restaurants in this region see pp301–2 and pp320–21

Quartzite cone of Errigal, the highest of the Derryveagh Mountains

❶ Tory Island

Road map C1. Co Donegal. 100. from Magheraroarty Pier near Gortahork and Bunbeg (daily in summer: 074 953 5061; weather permitting in winter: 074 953 1340). **toryislandferry.com**

The turbulent Tory Sound separates this windswept island from the northwestern corner of mainland Donegal. Given that rough weather can cut off the tiny island for days, it is not surprising that Tory's inhabitants have developed a strong sense of independence. Most of the islanders speak Gaelic and they even have their own monarch: the powers of this non-hereditary position are minimal, but the current incumbent is heavily involved in promoting the interests of his "subjects" and in attracting visitors to the island.

During the 1970s, the Irish government tried to resettle most of the islanders on the mainland, but they refused to move. Their campaign of resistance was led by Tory's school of Primitive artists. This emerged after 1968, inspired by a local man called James Dixon who claimed he could do better than a visiting English painter, Derek Hill. Since then, the school of artists has drawn a growing number of tourists; the **Dixon Gallery** opened in 1992 in the main village of West Town.

There are ruins of a monastery founded by St Columba *(see p38)* nearby, or else you can explore the island's dramatic cliffs and sea bird rookeries.

Dixon Gallery
West Town. **Tel** 074 913 5011.
Open Easter–Sep: daily.

❷ Bloody Foreland

Road map C1. Co Donegal. to Letterkenny.

Bloody Foreland, which gets its name from the rubescent glow of the rocks at sunset, boasts magnificent scenery. The R257 road skirts the coast around the headland, providing lovely views. The most scenic viewpoint is on the north coast and looks across to the cliffs of nearby offshore islands, including Tory. A short distance further south, the tiny village of **Bunbeg** has a pretty harbour, but elsewhere the rocky landscape is spoiled by a blanket of holiday bungalows.

❸ Derryveagh Mountains

Road map C1. Co Donegal.

The wild beauty of these mountains provides one of the high spots of a visit to Donegal. Errigal Mountain, the range's tallest peak at 751 m (2,466 ft), attracts keen hikers, but the cream of the mountain scenery lies within **Glenveagh National Park**. Covering nearly 16,000 ha (40,000 acres), this takes in the beautiful valley occupied by Lough Veagh, and Poisoned Glen, a marshy valley enclosed by dramatic cliffs. The park also protects the largest herd of red deer in the country.

Fountain at Glenveagh

Glenveagh Castle stands on the southern shores of Lough Veagh, near the visitors' centre. This splendid granite building was constructed in 1870 by John Adair, notorious for his eviction of many families from the area after the Famine *(see p223)*. The castle was given to the nation in the 1970s by its last owner, a wealthy art dealer from Pennsylvania.

Shuttle buses whisk you up the private road to the castle from the visitors' centre.

Glenveagh Castle overlooking Lough Veagh

Looking across to Dunfanaghy, gateway to the Horn Head peninsula

You can go on a guided tour of the sumptuous interior or just stroll through the formal gardens and rhododendron woods. Trails weave all around the castle grounds; one path climbs steeply to reward you with a lovely view over Lough Veagh.

Glebe House and Gallery overlooks Lough Gartan, 6 km (4 miles) south of the visitors' centre. This modest Regency mansion was the home of the painter, Derek Hill, who was also a keen collector. The house reveals his varied tastes, with William Morris wallpapers, Islamic ceramics and paintings by Tory Island artists. The gallery contains works by Picasso, Renoir and Jack B Yeats among others.

The **Colmcille Heritage Centre**, less than a kilometre south, uses stained glass and illuminated manuscripts to trace the life of St Columba (Colmcille in Gaelic), who was born in nearby Church Hill in AD 521 *(see p38)*. A flagstone in Lacknacoo is said to mark the site of the saint's birthplace.

Glenveagh National Park and Castle
Off R251, 16 km (10 miles) N of Churchill. **Tel** 076 100 2537. Park & Castle: **Open** daily. ltd. **glenveaghnationalpark.ie**

Glebe House and Gallery
Tel 074 913 7071. **Open** Easter & May–Sep: Sat–Thu. limited.

Colmcille Heritage Centre
Tel 074 913 7306. **Open** Easter & May–Sep: daily.
colmcilleheritagecentre.ie

4 Horn Head

Road map C1. Co Donegal. to Dunfanaghy from Letterkenny. The Workhouse, Dunfanaghy (074 913 6540). Jul & Aug: daily, Sep–Jun: Mon–Sat. **dunfanaghy workhouse.ie**

Carpeted in heather and rich in birdlife, this is the most scenic of the northern Donegal headlands, with lovely views of the sea and mountains. The appeal of the area is enhanced by **Dunfanaghy**, a delightful town with an air of affluence and Presbyterianism unusual in this area. The local beach, **Killahoey Strand**, offers excellent swimming.

5 Rosguill Peninsula

Road map C1. Co Donegal.

Rosguill Peninsula juts out into the Atlantic Ocean between Sheephaven and Mulroy bays. The simplest way to see it is to follow the 11-km (7-mile) Atlantic Drive, a circular route which skirts the clifftops at the tip of the headland. Doe Castle, 5 km (3 miles) north of Creeslough village, is worth a visit as much for its setting on a promontory overlooking Sheephaven Bay as for its architectural or historical interest. It has been restored from the remains of a castle erected in the 16th century by the MacSweeneys, a family of Scottish mercenaries.

6 Fanad Peninsula

Road map C1. Co Donegal. to Rathmelton & Portsalon from Letterkenny.

A panoramic route winds between the hilly spine and rugged coast of this tranquil peninsula. The eastern side is by far the most enjoyable and begins at **Rathmelton**, a charming Plantation town founded in the 17th century. Elegant Georgian homes and handsome old warehouses flank its tree-lined Main Street.

Further north, **Portsalon** offers safe bathing and great views from nearby Saldanha Head. Near **Doagh Beg**, on the way to Fanad Head in the far north, the cliffs have been eroded into arches and other dramatic shapes.

Doe Castle on Rosguill Peninsula, with its 16th-century battlements

7 A Tour of the Inishowen Peninsula

Inishowen, the largest of Donegal's northern peninsulas, is an area laden with history, from early Christian relics to strategically positioned castles and forts. The most rugged scenery lies in the west and north, around the the steep rockstrewn landscape of the Gap of Mamore and the spectacular cape of Malin Head, the northernmost point in Ireland. Numerous beaches dot the coastline and cater for all tastes, from the remote Isle of Doagh to the busy family resort of Buncrana. From the shores, there are views to Donegal's Derryveagh Mountains to the west and the Northern Ireland coast in the east. The Inishowen Peninsula can be explored by car as a leisurely day trip.

Tower on Banba's Crown, Malin Head

④ Carndonagh Cr
This 7th-cent
early Christian cr
is carved w
human figures a
interlacing lir

③ Gap of Mamore
The road between Mamore Hill and the Urris Hills is 250 m (820 ft) above sea level and offers panoramic views.

② Dunree Head
On the headland, Dunree Fort overlooks Lough Swilly. It was built in 1798 to counter the threat of French invasion. Since 1986, it has been a military museum.

① Buncrana
Buncrana has 5 km (3 miles) of sandy beaches and two castles. Buncrana Castle was rebuilt in 1718 and the intact keep of O'Doherty Castle dates from Norman times.

Shores of Lough Swilly near Dunree Fort

⑦ Grianán Ailigh
At the neck of the Inishowen Peninsula, perched on a hilltop, stands this formidable circular stone fort. The solid structure that can be seen today is the result of extensive restoration in the 1870s.

For hotels and restaurants in this region see pp301–2 and pp320–21

ips for Drivers

'our length: 157 km (98 miles).
topping-off points: Malin, ireencastle and Carndonagh all ave pubs and eating places; icnic sites are dotted around the oast. The Guns of Dunree Military Museum has a café. There s a 3- km (1.8- mile) scenic walk etween Moville and Greencastle *see also pp365–7).*

⑤ **Malin Head**
This part of the peninsula is a good stop for enjoying the superb Atlantic views from Malin Head. At the highest point, Banba's Crown, stands a tower built in 1805 to monitor shipping.

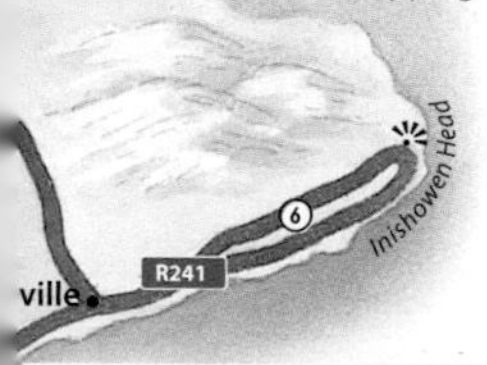

⑥ **Greencastle**
A resort and fishing port, Greencastle is named after the overgrown castle ruins just outside town. Built in 1305 by Richard de Burgo, Earl of Ulster, the castle guarded the entrance to Lough Foyle.

0 kilometres 5
0 miles 5

Enjoying the views from the ramparts of the Grianán Ailigh

❽ Grianán Ailigh

Road map C1. Co Donegal.
from Letterkenny or Londonderry.
Open 10am–4pm daily.
Letterkenny (074 912 1160).

Donegal's most impressive and intriguing ancient monument stands just 10 km (6 miles) west of the city of Londonderry *(see pp262–3)* at the entrance to the lovely Inishowen Peninsula.

Overlooking Lough Swilly and Lough Foyle, the circular stone structure, measuring 23 m (77 ft) in diameter, is believed to have been built as a pagan temple around the 5th century BC, although the site was probably a place of worship before this date. Later, Christians adopted the fort: St Patrick is said to have baptized Eoghan, founder of the O'Neill dynasty, here in AD 450. It became the royal residence of the O'Neills, but was damaged in the 12th century by the army of Murtagh O'Brien, King of Munster.

The fort was restored in the 1870s. Two doorways lead from the outside into a grassy arena ringed by three terraces. The most memorable feature of the fort, however, is its magnificent vantage point, which affords stunning views in every direction.

At the foot of the hill stands an attractive church, dedicated to St Aengus and built in 1967. Its circular design echoes that of the Grianán.

❾ Letterkenny

Road map C1. Co Donegal. 19,500. Neil T Blaney Rd (074 912 1160). **discoverireland.ie**

Straddling the River Swilly, with the Sperrin Mountains to the east and the Derryveagh Mountains *(see pp228–9)* to the west, Letterkenny is Donegal's largest town. It is also the region's main business centre, a role it took over from Londonderry after partition in 1921. The likeable town makes a good base from which to explore the northern coast of Donegal and, for anglers, is well placed for access to the waters of Lough Swilly.

Letterkenny has one of the longest main streets in Ireland, which is dominated by the 65-m (215-ft) steeple of **St Eunan's Cathedral**. A Neo-Gothic creation built in the late 19th century, it looks particularly impressive when floodlit at night. It contains Celtic-style stonework, a rich marble altar and vivid stained-glass windows. **Donegal County Museum** is located in a former workhouse building. It offers informative displays on local history from the Stone Age to the 20th century. It also has a collection of archaeological artifacts found in Donegal, some of them dating from the Iron Age.

Donegal County Museum
High Rd. **Tel** 074 912 4613.
Open Mon–Sat (pm only Sat).
Closed Christmas and public hols.

The imposing spire of St Eunan's Cathedral in Letterkenny

Isolated cottage near Burtonport in the Rosses

⑩ The Rosses

Road map C1. Co Donegal. to Dungloe or Burtonport from Letterkenny. seasonal: Dungloe (074 952 1297). to Arranmore from Burtonport (074 952 0532).

A rocky headland dotted with more than 100 lakes, the Rosses is one of the most picturesque and unspoilt corners of Donegal. It is also a strong Gaeltacht area, with many people speaking Gaelic.

The hub of the Rosses, at the southern end of the headland, is **Dungloe**, a bustling market town and major angling centre.

Environs

There is a glorious sheltered beach 8 km (5 miles) west of Dungloe at **Maghery Bay**. From here you can also walk to nearby **Crohy Head**, an area known for its caves, arches and unusual cliff formations. From the small fishing village of Burtonport, 8 km (5 miles) north of Dungloe, car ferries sail daily to Donegal's largest island, **Arranmore**. The rugged northwest coast here is ideal for clifftop walks, and from the south coast you can enjoy fine views across to the Rosses. Most of Arranmore's population of 500 lives in Leabgarrow, where the harbour is located.

⑪ Ardara

Road map C2. Co Donegal. 700. from Killybegs or Donegal. Donegal (074 972 1148). **ardara.ie**

Ardara, the weaving capital of Donegal, abounds shops selling locally made tweeds and hand-knitted sweaters. Some larger stores put on displays of hand-loom weaving. Ardara is also worth a stop for its pubs, much loved for their fiddle sessions.

Environs

A drive along the narrow peninsula to **Loughros Point**, 10 km (6 miles) west of town, provides dramatic coastal views. Another picturesque route runs southwest from Ardara to Glencolmcille, going over **Glengesh Pass**, a series of bends through a wild, deserted landscape.

Hand-loom worker in Ardara

⑫ Glencolmcille

Road map B2. Co Donegal. 260. from Killybegs. Donegal (074 972 1148). **glencolmcille.ie**

Glencolmcille, a quiet, grassy valley scattered with brightly coloured cottages, feels very much like a backwater, in spite of the sizeable number of visitors who come here.

The "Glen of St Colmcille" is a popular place of pilgrimage due to its associations with the saint more commonly known as St Columba. Just north of the village of Cashel, on the way to Glen Head, is the church where St Columba worshipped: it is said that between prayers the saint slept on the two stone slabs still visible in one corner.

Another attraction here is the **Folk Village Museum**, which depicts rural Donegal lifestyles through the ages. It was started in the 1950s by a local priest called Father James McDyer. Concerned about the high rate

Old irons at the Folk Village Museum in Glencolmcille

For hotels and restaurants in this region see pp301–2 and pp320–21

Slieve League, one of the highest sea cliffs in Europe

of emigration from this poor region, he sought to provide jobs and a sense of regional pride, partly by encouraging people to set up craft cooperatives. There are regular craft demonstrations – such as spinning – at the museum and the folk village shop sells local wares.

There is plenty to explore in the valley, which is littered with cairns, dolmens and other ancient monuments. The nearby coast is lovely too, the best walks taking you west across the grassy foreland of **Malinbeg**. Beyond the small resort of Malin More, steps drop down to an idyllic sandy cove hemmed in by cliffs.

Folk Village Museum
Dooey. **Tel** 074 973 0017. **Open** Easter–Sep: daily.

⓭ Slieve League

Road map B2. Co Donegal. to Carrick from Donegal or Killybegs.

One of the highest cliff faces in Europe, Slieve League is spectacular not just for its sheer elevation but also for its colour: at sunset the rock is streaked with changing shades of red, amber and ochre. The 8-km (5-mile) drive to the eastern end of Slieve League from **Carrick** is bumpy but well worth enduring. Beyond Teelin, the road becomes a series of alarming switchbacks before reaching **Bunglass Point** and Amharc Mor, the "good view". From here, you can see the whole of Slieve League, its sheer cliffs rising dramatically out of the ocean.

Only experienced hikers should attempt the treacherous ledges of **One Man's Pass**. This is part of a trail which climbs westwards out of Teelin and up to the highest point of Slieve League – from where you can admire the Atlantic Ocean shimmering 598 m (1,962 ft) below. The path then continues on to Malinbeg, 16 km (10 miles) west. During the summer, for a less strenuous but safer and equally rewarding excursion, pay a boat-owner from Teelin to take you out to see Slieve League from the sea.

⓮ Killybegs

Road map C2. Co Donegal. 3,000. from Donegal. Donegal (074 972 1148). **killybegs.ie**

Narrow winding streets give Killybegs a timeless feel, which contrasts sharply with the industriousness of this small town. The sense of prosperity stems in part from the manufacture of the Donegal carpets for which the town is famous, and which adorn Dublin Castle *(see pp80–81)* and other palaces around the world.

Killybegs is one of Ireland's busiest fishing ports and the quays are well worth seeing when the trawlers arrive to offload their catch: gulls squawk overhead and the smell of fish fills the air. Trawlermen come from far and wide – so do not be surprised if you hear Eastern European voices as you wander around the town.

Trawler crew in Killybegs relaxing after unloading their catch

The Irish Gaeltachts

The term "Gaeltacht" refers to Gaelic-speaking areas of Ireland. Up to the 16th century, virtually the entire population spoke the native tongue. British rule, however, undermined Irish culture, and the Famine *(see p223)* drained the country of many of its Gaelic-speakers. The use of the local language has fallen steadily since. Even so, in the Gaeltachts 75 per cent of the people still speak it, and road signs are exclusively in Irish – unlike in most other parts of Ireland.

Irish road sign in Gaeltacht region

The Donegal Gaeltacht stretches almost unbroken along the coast from Fanad Head to Slieve League and boasts the largest number of Irish-speakers in the country. Ireland's other principal Gaeltachts are in Galway and Kerry.

The imposing 15th-century Donegal Castle

⓯ Donegal

Road map C2. Co Donegal. 2,300. The Quay (074 972 1148). **donegaltown.ie**

Donegal means "Fort of the Foreigners", after the Vikings who built a garrison here. However, it was under the O'Donnells that the town began to take shape. The restored **Donegal Castle** in the town centre incorporates the gabled tower of a fortified house built by the family in the 15th century. The adjoining house and most other features are Jacobean – added by Sir Basil Brooke, who moved in after the O'Donnells were ousted by the English in 1607 *(see pp42–3)*.

Brooke was also responsible for laying out the market square, which is known as the **Diamond**. An obelisk in the centre commemorates four Franciscan monks who wrote the *Annals of the Four Masters* in the 1630s, tracing the history of the Gaelic people from 40 days before the Great Flood up until the end of the 16th century. Part of it was written at **Donegal Abbey**, south of the market square along the River Eske. Built in 1474, little now remains of the abbey but a few Gothic windows and cloister arches. About 1.5 km (1 mile) further on is **Donegal Craft Village**, a showcase for the work of local craftspeople.

The town has some nice hotels *(see p301)* and makes a good base for exploring the southern part of the county.

Donegal Castle
Tirchonaill St. **Tel** 074 972 2405.
Open Easter–mid-Sep: daily; mid-Sep–Easter: Thu–Mon. limited.

Donegal Craft Village
Ballyshannon Rd. **Tel** 074 972 2225.
Open Apr–Sep: Mon–Sat; Oct–Mar: Tue–Sat. limited.

⓰ Lough Derg

Road map C2. Co Donegal. Jun–mid-Aug (pilgrims only). to Pettigo from Donegal. **loughderg.org**

Pilgrims have made their way to Lough Derg ever since St Patrick spent 40 days praying on one of the lake's islands in an attempt to rid Ireland of all evil spirits. The Pilgrimage of St Patrick's Purgatory began in around 1150 and still attracts thousands of Catholics every summer. Their destination is the tiny **Station Island**, close to Lough Derg's southern shore and reached by boat from a jetty 8 km (5 miles) north of the border village of Pettigo. The island is completely covered by a religious complex, which includes a basilica, built in 1921, and hostels for pilgrims.

The pilgrimage season runs from April to September. People spend three days on the island, eating just one meal of dry bread and black tea per day. Although only pilgrims can visit Station Island, it is interesting to go to the jetty to savour the atmosphere and get a good view of the basilica near the shore.

Holiday-makers enjoying the fine sandy beach at Rossnowlagh

⓱ Rossnowlagh

Road map C2. Co Donegal. 55. from Bundoran & Donegal. May–Sep: The Bridge, Bundoran (071 984 1350).

At Rossnowlagh, Atlantic waves break on to one of Ireland's finest beaches, drawing crowds of both bathers and surfers to this tiny place. Even so, the village remains far more peaceful than the resort of Bundoran, 14 km (9 miles) south. In addition, the cliffs at Rossnowlagh provide scope for exhilarating coastal walks. Away from the sea, you can visit the **Donegal Historical Society Museum**, housed in a striking Franciscan friary built in the 1950s. The tiny but

Basilica on Station Island viewed from the shores of Lough Derg

Lissadell House dining room with Gore-Booth family portraits

fascinating collection includes displays of Stone Age flints, Irish musical instruments and other local artifacts.

Rossnowlagh never fails to make the news in July, when it hosts the only parade to take place in the Republic by the Protestant organization, the Orange Order *(see p53)*.

Donegal Historical Society Museum
Tel 071 985 1726. **Open** daily.

⑱ Ballyshannon

Road map C2. Co Donegal. 2,600. from Bundoran & Donegal.

In Ballyshannon, well-kept Georgian homes jostle for space along hilly streets on the banks of the River Erne, near where it flows into Donegal Bay. This is a bustling town, full of character and off the main tourist track – though it gets packed during July's festival of traditional music, which is one of the best of its kind in the country.

The festival apart, Ballyshannon is most famous as the birthplace of poet William Allingham (1824–89), who recalled his home town in the lines "Adieu to Ballyshanny and the winding banks of the Erne". He lies buried in the graveyard of St Anne's Church, off Main Street. There is a fine view over the river from here: you can see the small island of **Inis Saimer** where, according to legend, Greeks founded the first colony in Ireland after the Great Flood. Beyond, you can glimpse a large Irish Army base: Ballyshannon's position on a steeply rising bluff overlooking the River Erne has always made the town a strategic military site.

About 1.5 km (1 mile) northwest of town lie the scant ruins of **Assaroe Abbey**, founded by Cistercians in 1184. A graveyard with some ancient burial slabs and headstones is all that remains. Nearby, two water wheels installed by the monks have been restored. **The Water Wheels** has a small heritage centre as well as a café.

The Water Wheels
Assaroe Abbey. **Tel** 071 985 1580.
Open Easter–end Oct: Sun only.

⑲ Lissadell House

Road map B2. Carney, Co Sligo.
Tel 071 916 3150. or to Sligo.
Open Jun–mid-Sep: 10:30am–6pm.
lissadellhouse.com

A Greek Revival mansion built in the 1830s, Lissadell is famous more for its occupants than its architecture. It used to be the home of the Gore-Booths who, unlike some of the Anglo-Irish gentry, have contributed much to the region over the four centuries they have been in County Sligo. During the Famine *(see p223)*, Sir Robert charitably mortgaged the house to help feed his employees.

The most famous member of the Gore-Booth family is Sir Robert's granddaughter, Constance Markievicz (1868–1927), a leading nationalist who took part in the 1916 Rising *(see pp48–9)*. She was the first woman to be elected to the British House of Commons and later became Minister for Labour in the first Dáil. W B Yeats, who first visited the house in 1894, immortalized Constance and her sister, Eva, in one of his poems, describing them as "Two girls in silk kimonos, both beautiful, one a gazelle".

Mural of the family dog in Lissadell's dining room

Built in grey limestone, the exterior of Lissadell House is rather austere. The interior, on the other hand, has an appealing atmosphere of faded grandeur, with copious memorabilia of the building's former occupants. The finest rooms are the gallery and the dining room, decorated with extraordinary full-length murals of the Gore-Booth family, their famous butler Thomas Kilgallon, the gamekeeper, head woodman and a dog.

Lissadell House, now a private home, has been renovated by its owners and is open to the public at certain times only. Check the website for details. You can also explore the paths skirting the seashore, and the beach itself is a lovely spot, with spectacular views across the bay.

⑳ A Tour of Yeats Country

Even for people unfamiliar with the poetry of W B Yeats, Sligo's engaging landscapes are reason enough to make a pilgrimage. This tour follows a varied route, taking you past sandy bays and dramatic limestone ridges, through forest and alongside rivers and lakes. Lough Gill lies at the heart of Yeats country, enclosed by wooded hills crisscrossed by walking trails. In summer, boats ply the length of the lough, or you can head to one of the northwest's best beaches, at Rosses Point.

⑤ Ben Bulben
The eerie silhouette of Ben Bulben rises abruptly out of the plain. You can climb to the top, but go with great care.

④ Lissadell House
Yeats was a close friend of the Gore-Booth sisters who lived at Lissadell. The house is closed to the public *(see p235)*.

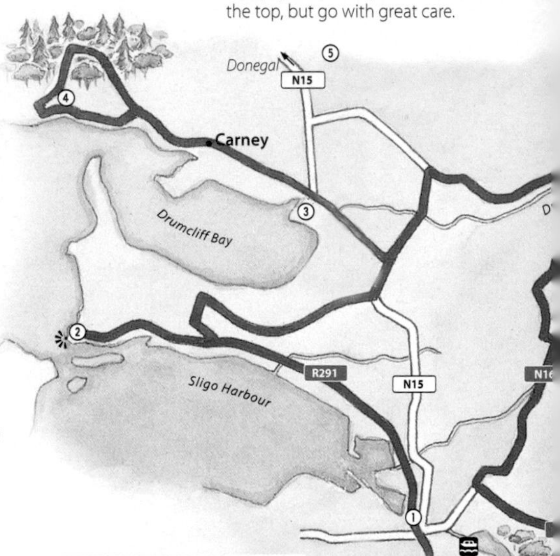

③ Drumcliff
Although he died in France, in 1948 Yeats's body was laid to rest in Drumcliff churchyard. The ruins of an old monastic site include a fine High Cross.

Key

- Tour route
- Other roads
- Boat trips
- Viewpoint

Tips for Drivers

Length: 88 km (55 miles).
Stopping-off points: North of Sligo, the best choice of eating places is at Rosses Point, although there are good pubs in Drumcliff and Dromahair. Lough Gill provides most choice in terms of picnic spots.
Boat trips: visit www.sligoboatcharters.com or www.roseofinnisfree.com *(see also pp365–7)*.

② Rosses Point
Yeats and his brother used to spend their summers at this pretty resort. It stands at the entrance to Sligo Bay, and a steady flow of boats passes by.

① Sligo
This town is a good place to begin a tour of Yeats country. It has many connections with the poet and his family, whose literary and artistic legacy has helped to inspire Sligo's thriving arts scene *(see p238)*.

W B Yeats and Sligo

W B Yeats (1865–1939)

As a schoolboy in London, Yeats *(see p27)* longed for his native Sligo, and as an adult he often returned here. He lovingly describes the county in his *Reveries over Childhood and Youth*, and the lake-studded landscape haunts his poetry. "In a sense", Yeats said, "Sligo has always been my home", and it is here that he wished to be buried. His gravestone in Drumcliff bears an epitaph he penned himself: "Cast a cold eye on life, on death. Horseman pass by."

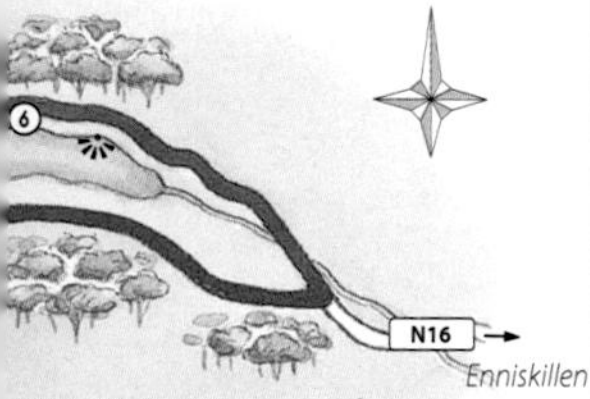

⑦ Parke's Castle
This 17th-century fortified manor house commands a splendid view over the tranquil waters of Lough Gill. It is a starting point for boat trips around the lough.

⑥ Glencar Lough
"There is a waterfall … that all my childhood counted dear", wrote Yeats of the cataract which tumbles into Glencar Lough. A path leads down to it from the road.

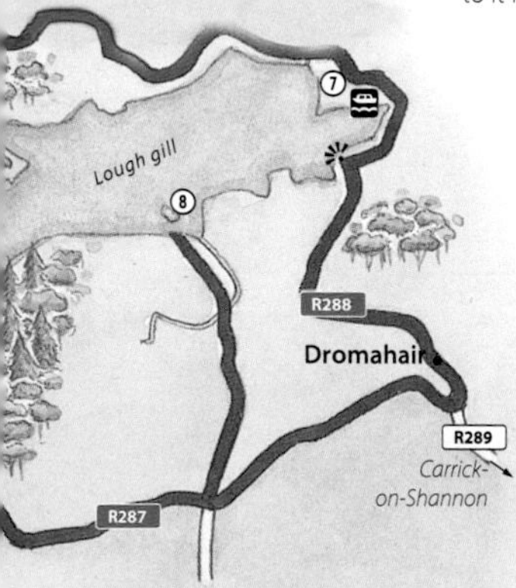

⑧ Isle of Innisfree
"There midnight's all a glimmer, and noon a purple glow", is how Yeats once described Innisfree. There is not much to see on this tiny island but it is a romantic spot. In summer, a boatman ferries visitors here.

⑨ Dooney Rock
A steep path leads from the road to Dooney Rock, from where glorious views extend over the lough to Ben Bulben. Trails weave through the surrounding woods and by the lake.

Parke's Castle viewed from across the calm waters of Lough Gill

㉑ Parke's Castle

Road map C2. 6 km (4 miles) N of Dromahair, Co Leitrim. **Tel** 071 916 4149. or to Sligo. **Open** Apr–end Oct: 10am–6pm daily (last adm 5:15pm). limited.
heritageireland.ie

This fortified manor house dominates the eastern end of Lough Gill. It was built in 1609 by Captain Robert Parke, an English settler who later became MP for Leitrim. It has been beautifully restored by the Office of Public Works using 17th-century building methods and native Irish oak.

Parke's Castle was erected on the site of a 16th-century tower house belonging to the O'Rourkes, a powerful local clan, and stones from this earlier structure were used in the new building. The original foundations and part of the moat were incorporated, but otherwise Parke's Castle is the epitome of a Plantation manor house *(see p43)*. It is protected by a large enclosure or bawn, whose sturdy wall includes a gatehouse and turrets as well as the house itself.

Among the most distinctive architectural features of Parke's Castle are the diamond-shaped chimneys, mullioned windows and the parapets. There is also a curious stone hut, known as the "sweathouse", which was an early Irish sauna. Inside, an exhibition and audiovisual display cover Parke's Castle and various historic and prehistoric sites in the area. There is also a working forge.

Boat trips around sights on Lough Gill that are associated with the poet, W B Yeats, leave from outside the castle walls.

Hargadon's bar *(see p330)*, one of Sligo town's most famous watering holes

22 Sligo

Road map C2. Co Sligo. 20,000. 071 916 8280. Old Bank Building, O'Connell St (071 916 1201). Fri. **sligotown.net**

The port of Sligo sits at the mouth of the River Garavogue, sandwiched between the Atlantic and Lough Gill. The largest town in the Northwest, it rose to prominence under the Normans, being well placed as a gateway between the provinces of Ulster and Connaught. The appearance of Sligo today is mainly the result of growth during the late 18th and 19th centuries.

Sligo is perfectly situated for touring the ravishing countryside nearby, and it is also a good centre for traditional music. While at first sight it can seem a bit sombre, the town is thriving as the arts capital of Northwest Ireland.

Sligo's link with the Yeats family is the main source of the town's appeal. W B Yeats *(see pp236–7)*, Ireland's best-known poet, was born into a prominent local family. The Pollexfen warehouse, at the western end of Wine Street, has a rooftop turret from which the poet's grandfather would observe his merchant fleet moored in the docks.

The town's sole surviving medieval building is **Sligo Abbey**, founded in 1253. Some original features remain, such as the delicate lancet windows in the choir, but this ruined Dominican friary dates mainly from the 15th century. The best features are a beautifully carved altar and the cloisters. A short distance west from the abbey is O'Connell Street, with the town's main shops and Hargadon's bar – an old Sligo institution complete with a dark, wooden interior, snugs and a grocery counter. Near the junction with Wine Street, overlooking Hyde Bridge, is the Yeats Memorial Building. This houses the Yeats Society, who are dedicated to commemorating the life of the poet. The Yeats International Summer School is held here too: a renowned annual festival of readings and lectures on the poet's life and work.

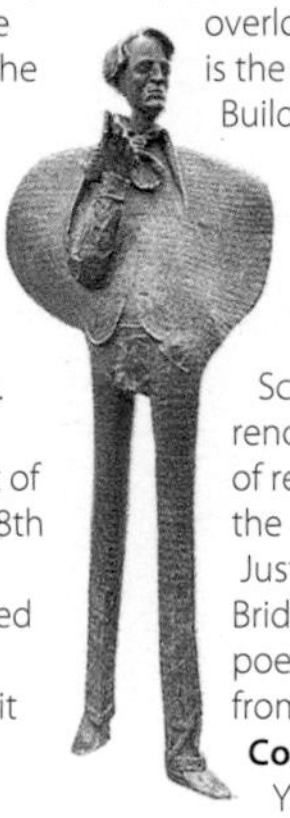

Bronze statue of W B Yeats

Just the other side of Hyde Bridge is a statue of the poet, engraved with lines from his own verse. **Sligo County Museum** has Yeatsian memorabilia and local artifacts but the entire Niland Collection including the paintings by Jack B Yeats is in the **Model Arts & Niland Gallery** in The Mall. This outstanding centre also puts on temporary exhibitions of major Irish and international contemporary art.

Sligo Abbey
Abbey St. **Tel** 071 914 6406. **Open** mid-Apr–mid-Oct: daily; mid-Oct–early Nov: Fri–Sun.

Sligo County Museum
Stephen St. **Tel** 071 911 1679. **Open** Tue–Sat (Oct–Apr: am only).

Model Arts & Niland Gallery
The Mall. **Tel** 071 914 1405. **Open** Tue–Sun. **themodel.ie**

Environs

Improbably set in the suburbs of Sligo, **Carrowmore Megalithic Cemetery** once held the country's largest collection of Stone Age tombs. Quarrying destroyed much, but about 40 passage tombs *(see pp250–51)* and dolmens *(see p36)* survive among the abandoned gravel pits, with some in private gardens and cottages.

The huge unexcavated cairn atop **Knocknarea** mountain dates back 5,000 years and is said to contain the tomb of the legendary Queen Maeve of Connaught *(see p30)*. It is an hour's climb starting 4 km (2.5 miles) west of Carrowmore.

Tobernalt Holy Well, by Lough Gill 5 km (3 miles) south of Sligo, means "cliff well", after a nearby spring with alleged curative powers. It was a holy site in Celtic times and later became a Christian shrine. Priests came here to celebrate Mass in secret during the 18th century, when Catholic worship was illegal. The Mass rock, next to an altar erected around 1900, remains a place of pilgrimage.

Carrowmore Cemetery
Tel 071 916 1534. **Open** Easter–Oct. **heritageireland.ie**

Altar by the holy well at Tobernalt, overlooking Lough Gill in Sligo

㉓ Lough Arrow

Road map C3. Co Sligo. to Ballinafad. Jun–Sep: Boyle (071 966 2145). **discoverireland.ie**

People go to Lough Arrow to sail and fish for the local trout, and also simply to enjoy the glorious countryside. You can explore the lake by boat, but the views from the shore are the real joy of Lough Arrow. A full circuit of the lake is recommended, but for the most breathtaking views head for the southern end around **Ballinafad**. This small town lies in a gorgeous spot, enclosed to the north and south by the Bricklieve and Curlew Mountains.

The **Carrowkeel Passage Tomb Cemetery** occupies a remote and eerie spot in the Bricklieve Mountains to the north of Ballinafad. The best approach is up the single track road from Castlebaldwin, 5 km (3 miles) northeast of the site.

The 14 Neolithic passage graves, which are scattered around a hilltop overlooking Lough Arrow, are elaborate corbelled structures. One is comparable with Newgrange *(see pp250–51)*, except that the burial chamber inside this cairn is lit by the sun on the day of the summer solstice (21 June) as opposed to the winter solstice. On a nearby ridge are the remains of Stone Age huts, presumably those occupied by the farmers who buried their dead in the Carrowkeel passage graves.

Passage tomb in Carrowkeel cemetery above Lough Arrow

㉔ Carrick-on-Shannon

Road map C3. Co Leitrim. 3,000. May–Sep: The Old Barrel Store (071 962 0170). **leitrimtourism.com**

The tiny capital of Leitrim, one of the least populated counties in Ireland (although this is changing), stands in a lovely spot on a tight bend of the River Shannon.

The town's river location and its proximity to the Grand Canal were crucial to Carrick's development. They are also the main reasons for its now thriving tourist industry. There is a colourful, modern marina, where private boats can moor in summer and boats are available for hire.

Already a major boating centre, Carrick has benefited from the reopening of the Shannon-Erne Waterway, one end of which begins 6 km (4 miles) north at Leitrim. The channel was restored in a cross-border joint venture billed as a symbol of peaceful cooperation between Northern Ireland and the Republic.

Away from the bustle of the marina, Carrick is an old-fashioned place, with 19th-century churches and convents, refined Georgian houses and shopfronts. The town's most curious building is the quaint **Costello Chapel** on Bridge Street, one of the smallest in the world. It was built in 1877 by local businessman Edward Costello, to house the tombs of himself and his wife.

㉕ The Organic Centre

Road map C3. Rossinver, Co Leitrim. **Tel** 071 985 4338. **Open** 10am–5pm Tue–Sun (closed weekends Nov–Feb). **theorganiccentre.ie**

Situated about 3.2 kilometres (2 miles) from Rossinver on the Kinlough Road, The Organic Centre is a non-profit-making company that provides training, information and demonstrations of organic gardening, cultivation and farming.

The centre is located on a 7.7-ha (19-acre) site at Rossinver in the unspoilt countryside of sparsely populated north Leitrim. There are display gardens for visitors including a children's garden, a taste garden and a heritage garden. The Eco Shop sells seeds, cuttings and vegetables, as well as books and kitchen equipment. Some items can also be bought online.

Shannon-Erne Waterway

This labyrinthine system of rivers and lakes passes through unspoiled border country, linking Leitrim on the Shannon and Upper Lough Erne in Fermanagh. It follows the course of a canal which was completed and then abandoned in the 1860s. The channel was reopened in 1993, enabling the public to enjoy both the Victorian stonework (including 34 bridges) and the state-of-the-art technology used to operate the 16 locks.

Cruiser negotiating a lock on the Shannon-Erne Waterway

THE MIDLANDS

Cavan · Monaghan · Louth · Longford · Westmeath
Meath · Offaly · Laois

The cradle of Irish civilization and the Celts' spiritual home, he Midlands encompass some of Ireland's most sacred ind symbolic sites. Much of the region is ignored, but he ragged landscapes of lush pastures, lakes and bogland eveal ancient Celtic crosses, gracious Norman abbeys ind Gothic Revival castles.

The fertile Boyne Valley in County Meath was ettled during the Stone Age and became he most important centre of habitation in he country. The remains of ancient sites rom this early civilization fill the area and nclude Newgrange, the finest Neolithic omb in the country. In Celtic times, the ocus shifted south to the Hill of Tara, the eat of the High Kings of Ireland and the Celts' spiritual and political capital. Tara's heyday came in the 3rd century AD, but it etained its importance until the Normans nvaded in the 1100s.

Norman castles, such as the immense ortress at Trim in County Meath, attest to the shifting frontiers around the region of English influence known as the Pale *(see p136)*. By the end of the 16th century, this area incorporated nearly all the counties in the Midlands.

The Boyne Valley returned to prominence in 1690, when the Battle of the Boyne ended in a landmark Protestant victory over the Catholics *(see pp42–3)*.

Although part of the Republic since 1921, Monaghan and Cavan belong to the ancient province of Ulster, and the former retains strong links with Northern Ireland. The rounded hills called drumlins, found in both counties, are typical of the border region between the Republic and Northern Ireland.

Grassland and bog dotted with lakes are most characteristic of the Midlands, but the Slieve Bloom Mountains and the Cooley Peninsula provide good walking country. In addition to Meath's ancient sites, the historical highlights of the region are monasteries like Fore Abbey and Clonmacnoise, this last ranking among Europe's greatest early Christian centres.

Carlingford village and harbour, with the hills of the Cooley Peninsula rising behind

◀ Aerial view of Lough Oughter, County Cavan

Exploring the Midlands

Drogheda is the obvious base from which to explore the Boyne Valley and neighbouring monastic sites, such as Monasterboice. Trim and Mullingar, to the southwest, are less convenient but make pleasanter places in which to stay. The northern counties of Monaghan, Cavan and Longford are quiet backwaters with a patchwork of lakes that attract many anglers. To the south, Offaly and Laois are dominated by dark expanses of bog, though there is a cluster of sights around the attractive Georgian town of Birr. For a break by the sea, head for the picturesque village of Carlingford on the Cooley Peninsula.

West doorway of Nuns' Church at Clonmacnoise

Key

- Motorway
- Major road
- Secondary road
- Minor road
- Scenic route
- Main railway
- Minor railway
- International border
- County border
- Summit

Getting Around

In the Midlands, there is an extensive network of roads and rail lines fanning out across the country from Dublin. As a result, getting around on public transport is easier than in most other areas. The Dublin–Belfast railway serves Dundalk and Drogheda, while Mullingar and Longford town lie on the Dublin–Sligo route. The railway and M7 road between Dublin and Limerick give good access to Laois and Offaly.

For additional map symbols *see back flap*

Statue in Birr Castle's formal gardens

Sights at a Glance

0 kilometres 20

0 miles 20

View of Trim across the River Boyne

For hotels and restaurants in this region see p302 and pp321–3

Ruins of the monastery in Drumlane

❶ Monaghan

Road map D2. Co Monaghan. 6,000. Clones Rd (047 81122). **monaghantourism.com**

The spruce and thriving town of Monaghan is the urban highlight of the northern Midlands. Planted by James I in 1613 *(see p43)*, it developed into a prosperous industrial centre, thanks mainly to the local manufacture of linen. A crannog *(see p37)* off Glen Road is the sole trace of the town's Celtic beginnings.

Monaghan centres on three almost contiguous squares. The main attraction in Market Square is the 18th-century **Market House** (now an arts centre), a squat but charming building with the original oak beams still visible. To the east lies Church Square, very much the heart of modern Monaghan and lined with dignified 19th-century buildings, such as the Classical-style courthouse. The third square, which is known as the Diamond, was the original marketplace. It contains the **Rossmore Memorial**, a large Victorian drinking fountain with an ornate stone canopy supported by marble columns.

Do not miss the award-winning **County Museum**, which tells the story of Monaghan's linen and lace-making industries. The pride of the museum's historical collection is the Cross of Clogher, an ornate bronze altar cross which dates from around 1400.

The Gothic Revival Cathedral of St Macartan perches on a hilltop south of the town, with fine views over Monaghan.

County Museum
Hill St. **Tel** 047 82928. **Open** 11am–5pm Mon–Fri, noon–5pm Sat. **Closed** public hols. limited.

❷ Drumlane

Road map C3. 1 km (0.5 miles) S of Milltown, Co Cavan. to Belturbet.

Standing alone by the River Erne, the medieval church and round tower of Drumlane merit a visit as much for their delightful setting as for the ruins themselves. The abbey church, founded in the early 13th century but significantly altered about 200 years later, features fine Romanesque carvings. The nearby round tower has lost its cap but is unusual for the well-finished stonework, with carvings of birds on the north side.

❸ Corlea Trackway

Road map C3. Kenagh, Co Longford. **Tel** 043 322 2386. to Longford. **Open** mid-Apr–Oct: 10am–6pm daily (last adm: 45 mins before closing). limited.

The Corlea Trackway Visitor Centre interprets an Iron Age bog road built in the year 148 BC. The oak road is the longest of its kind in Europe. An 18 m (60 ft) length of preserved road is on permanent display in a specially designed hall to prevent the ancient wood cracking in the heat.

Corlea Trackway

Authentic Victorian kitchen in Tullynally Castle

Environs
Just 10 km (6 miles) north of Corlea Trackway, **Ardagh** is considered the most attractive village in Longford, with pretty stone cottages gathered around a green. The River Shannon, Lough Ree, River Inny and Lough Gowna make Longford an angler's paradise. The "hot water" stretch at Lanesboro is famous for attracting coarse fish, and canoeists head for the white-water rush at Ballymahon.

❹ Tullynally Castle

Road map C3. Castle Pollard, Co Westmeath. **Tel** 044 966 1159. to Mullingar. Castle: **Open** to pre-booked groups only. obligatory. Tea rooms & gardens: **Open** mid-Apr–Sep: 11am–6pm Thu–Sun only. ltd. **tullynallycastle.com**

This huge structure, adorned with numerous turrets and battlements, is one of Ireland's largest castles. The original 17th-century tower house was given a Georgian gloss, but this was all but submerged under later Gothic Revival changes. The Pakenham family have lived at Tullynally since 1655. Thomas Pakenham now manages the estate.

The imposing great hall leads to a fine panelled dining room hung with family portraits. Of equal interest are the Victorian kitchen, laundry room and the adjacent drying room.

The 8,000-volume library looks out on to rolling wooded parkland, much of which was landscaped in the 1760s. The grounds include Victorian terraces, walled kitchen and flower gardens, two small lakes, a Chinese and a Tibetan garden.

❺ Fore Abbey

Road map C3. Fore, Castle Pollard, Co Westmeath. **Tel** 044 966 1780. to Castle Pollard. **Open** daily.

The ruins of Fore Abbey lie in glorious rolling countryside about 8 km (5 miles) east of Tullynally Castle. St Fechin set up a monastery here in 630, but what you see now are the remains of the only Benedictine abbey founded around 1200. Located on the northern border of the Pale *(see p136)*, Fore Abbey was heavily fortified in the 15th century as protection against the native Irish.

The ruined church was part of the original Norman priory, but the cloister and refectory date from the 1400s. On the hill opposite lies St Fechin's Church, a Norman building said to mark the site of the first monastery. The tiny church nearby incorporates a 15th-century anchorite's cell.

❻ Kells

Road map D3. Co Meath. 5,500. 046 924 8856. **Open** 9:30am–5pm Mon–Fri. **discover ireland.ie/eastcoast**

Signposted by its Irish name, Ceanannus Mór, this modest town provides an unlikely backdrop to the monastery for which it is so famous.

Kells Monastery was set up by St Columba in the 6th century, but its heyday came after 806, when monks fled here from Iona. They may have been the scribes who illuminated the superb *Book of Kells,* now kept at Trinity College, Dublin *(see p68)*.

The monastery centres on a rather gloomy 18th-century church beside which stands a decapitated round tower. There are several 9th-century High Crosses; the South Cross is in the best condition.

Just north of the enclosure is **St Columba's House**, a tiny steep-roofed stone oratory, similar to St Kevin's Kitchen at Glendalough *(see p144)*.

The Market Cross, a High Cross that once served to mark the entrance to the monastery, now stands outside the Old Courthouse. It was used as a gallows during the uprising in 1798 *(see p45)*. The battle scene on the base is a subject rarely used in High Cross art.

Ruins of Fore Abbey, a medieval Benedictine priory

A fisherman's cottage on the Cooley Peninsula

7 Dundalk

Road map D3. Co Louth. 32,000. Jocelyn St (042 933 5484). Fri. **dundalk.ie**

Dundalk once marked the northernmost point of the Pale, the area controlled by the English during the Middle Ages *(see p136)*. Now it is the last major town before the Northern Irish border.

Dundalk is also a gateway to the magnificent countryside of the Cooley Peninsula. The **County Museum** is housed in an 18th-century distillery in the town. In three exhibition galleries it gives an imaginative history of the county, from the Stone Age to the present day.

County Museum
Jocelyn St. **Tel** 042 932 7056.
Open 10am–5pm Tue–Sat.
Closed 1 Jan, 25 & 26 Dec.

8 Carlingford

Road map D3. Co Louth. 1,500. Old Railway Station (042 937 3033). Carlingford Heritage Centre: Dundalk St (042 937 3454).
Open 10am–12:30pm, 2–4:30pm Mon–Fri. Carlingford Adventure Centre: Tholsel St (042 937 3100).
Open 9am–6pm Mon–Fri.
carlingfordheritagecentre.com

This is a picturesque fishing village, located between the mountains of the Cooley Peninsula and Carlingford Lough. The border with Northern Ireland runs through the centre of this drowned river valley, and from the village you can look across to the Mountains of Mourne on the Northern Irish side *(see pp288–9)*.

Carlingford is an interesting place to explore, with its pretty whitewashed cottages and ancient buildings clustered along medieval alleyways. The ruins of **King John's Castle**, built by the Normans to protect the entrance to the lough, still dominate the village. The **Holy Trinity Heritage Centre**, which is housed in a medieval church, traces the history of the port from Anglo-Norman times.

Carlingford is the country's oyster capital, and often holds an oyster festival in August. The lough is a popular water-sports centre too, and in summer you can go on cruises around the lough from the quayside where there is a marina.

The **Carlingford Adventure Centre** organizes walking tours, plus sailing, kayaking, canoeing and windsurfing.

Environs

A scenic route weaves around the **Cooley Peninsula**, skirting the coast and then cutting right through the mountains. The section along the north coast is dramatic: just 3 km (1.8 miles) northwest of Carlingford, in the **Slieve Foye Forest Park**, a corkscrew road climbs to give a gorgeous panoramic view.

The Tain Trail, which you can join at Carlingford, is a 30-km (19-mile) circuit through some of the peninsula's most rugged scenery, with cairns and other prehistoric sites scattered over the moorland. Keen hikers will be able to walk it in a day.

9 Monasterboice

Road map D3. Co Louth. to Drogheda. 041 983 7070.
Open daily.

Founded in the 5th century by an obscure disciple of St Patrick called St Buite, this monastic settlement is one of the most famous religious sites in the country. The ruins of the medieval monastery are enclosed within a graveyard in a lovely secluded spot north of Drogheda. The site includes a roofless round tower and two churches, but Monasterboice's greatest treasures are its 10th-century High Crosses.

Muiredach's High Cross is the finest of its kind in Ireland, and its sculpted biblical scenes are still remarkably fresh. They depict the life of Christ on the west face, while the east face, described in detail opposite, features mainly Old Testament scenes. The cross is named after an inscription on the base – "A prayer for Muiredach by whom this cross was made" – which is perhaps a reference to the abbot of Monasterboice. The 6.5-m (21-ft) West Cross, also known as the Tall Cross, is one of the largest in Ireland. The carving has not lasted as well as on Muiredach's Cross, but you can make out scenes from the Death of Christ. The North Cross, features a Crucifixion and a carved spiral pattern.

Detail from a tomb in Monasterboice graveyard

Round tower and West High Cross at Monasterboice

Ireland's High Crosses

High crosses exist in Celtic parts of both Britain and Ireland. Yet in their profusion and craftsmanship, Irish High Crosses are exceptional. The distinctive ringed cross has become a symbol of Irish Christianity and is still imitated today. The beautiful High Crosses associated with medieval monasteries were carved between the 8th and 12th centuries. The early crosses bore only geometric motifs, but in the 9th to 10th centuries a new style emerged when sculpted scenes from the Bible were introduced. Referred to as "sermons in stone", these later versions may have been used to educate the masses. In essence, though, the High Cross was a status symbol for the monastery or a local patron.

Pillar stones, inscribed with crosses, like this 6th-century example at Riasc *(see p162)*, were precursors of the High Cross.

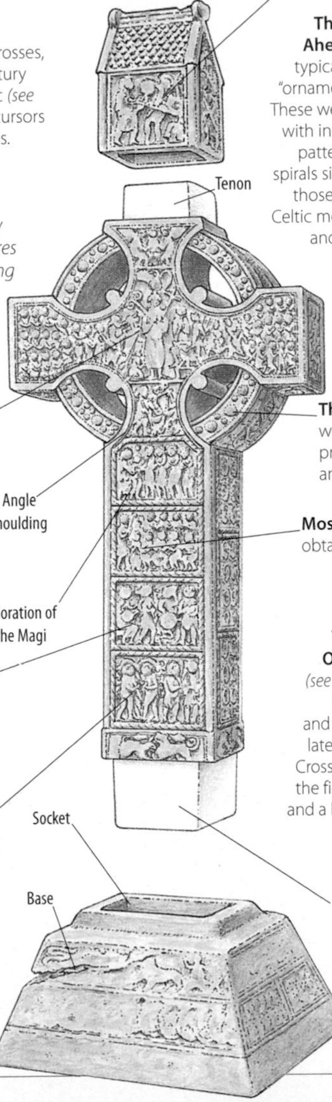

Muiredach's Cross

Each face of this 10th-century cross at Monasterboice features scenes from the Bible, including the east face seen here. The 5.8-m (19-ft) cross consists of three blocks of sandstone fitted together by means of tenons and sockets.

The Last Judgment shows Christ in Glory surrounded by a crowd of resurrected souls. The devil stands on his right clutching a pitchfork, ready to chase the damned souls into Hell.

The ring served a functional as well as a decorative purpose, providing support for the head and arms of the stone cross.

Moses smites the rock to obtain water for the Israelites.

The High Cross at Ahenny *(see p203)* is typical of 8th-century "ornamental" crosses. These were carved with interlacing patterns and spirals similar to those used in Celtic metalwork and jewellery.

The Dysert O'Dea Cross *(see p193)* dates from the 1100s and represents the late phase of High Cross art. It features the figures of Christ and a bishop carved in high relief.

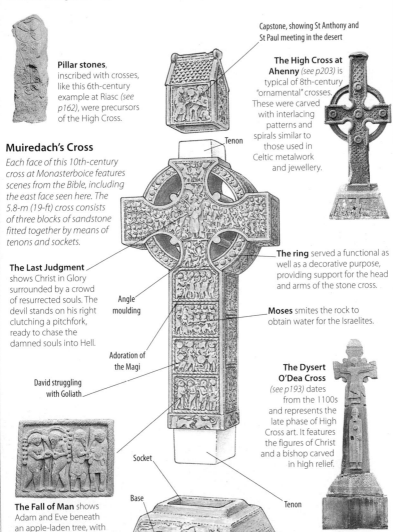

The Fall of Man shows Adam and Eve beneath an apple-laden tree, with Cain slaying Abel alongside. Both scenes are frequently depicted on Irish High Crosses.

⑩ Drogheda

Road map D3. Co Louth. 30,000. Mayoralty St (041 983 7070). Sat. **drogheda.ie**

In the 12th century, this Norman port near the mouth of the River Boyne was one of Ireland's most important towns. However, the place seems never to have recovered from the trauma of a vicious attack by Cromwell in 1649 *(see p43)*, in which 2,000 citizens were killed. The town still has its original street plan and has a rich medieval heritage.

Little remains of Drogheda's medieval defences but **St Lawrence Gate**, a fine 13th-century barbican, has survived. Nearby, there are two churches called **St Peter's**. The one belonging to the Church of Ireland, built in 1753, is the more striking and has some splendid grave slabs. The Catholic church is worth visiting to see the embalmed head of Oliver Plunkett, an archbishop martyred in 1681.

South of the river you can climb Millmount, a Norman motte topped by a Martello tower. It provides a good view and is the site of the **Drogheda Museum**, which contains interesting historical artifacts, including guns used in the War of Independence.

View of Drogheda from across the River Boyne and the De Lacy Bridge

Drogheda Museum
Millmount Square. **Tel** 041 983 3097. **Open** 10am–5:30pm Mon–Sat, 2–5pm Sun. **Closed** 7 days at Christmas. limited. **droghedamuseum.ie**

⑪ Newgrange and the Boyne Valley

Road map D3. Co Meath. to Drogheda. to Slane or Drogheda. Brú na Bóinne Interpretative Centre (041 988 0300). **Closed** 24–28 Dec.

Known as Brú na Bóinne, the "Palace of the Boyne", this river valley was the cradle of Irish civilization. The fertile soil supported a sophisticated society in Neolithic times. Much evidence survives, in the form of ring forts, passage graves and sacred enclosures. The most important Neolithic monuments in the valley are three passage graves: supreme among these is **Newgrange** *(see pp250–51)*, but **Dowth** and **Knowth** are significant too. The Boyne Valley also encompasses the Hill of Slane and the Hill of Tara *(see p252)*, both of which are major sites in Celtic mythology. Indeed, this whole region is rich in associations with Ireland's prehistory.

River Boyne near the site of the Battle of the Boyne

The Battle of the Boyne

In 1688, the Catholic King of England, James II, was deposed from his throne, to be replaced by his Protestant daughter, Mary, and her husband, William of Orange. Determined to win back the crown, James sought the support of Irish Catholics, and challenged William at Oldbridge by the River Boyne west of Drogheda. The Battle of the Boyne took place on 1 July 1690, with James's poorly trained force of 25,000 French and Irish Catholics facing William's hardened army of 36,000 French Huguenots, Dutch, English and Scots. The Protestants triumphed and James fled to France, after a battle that signalled the beginning of total Protestant power over Ireland. It ushered in the confiscation of Catholic lands and the suppression of Catholic interests, sealing the country's fate for the next 300 years.

William of Orange leading his troops at the Battle of the Boyne, 1 July 1690

With monuments predating Egypt's pyramids, the Boyne Valley is marketed as the Irish "Valley of the Kings".

Newgrange and Knowth can only be seen on a tour run by **Brú na Bóinne Interpretative Centre** near Newgrange. The centre has displays on the area's Stone Age heritage and a reconstruction of Newgrange.

Dowth

Off N51, 3 km (2 miles) E of Newgrange. **Closed** to the public.

The passage grave at Dowth was plundered by Victorian souvenir hunters and has not been fully excavated. You cannot approach the tomb, but it can be seen from the road.

Knowth

1.5 km (1 mile) NW of Newgrange. **Open** as Newgrange *(see pp250–51)*.

Knowth outdoes Newgrange in several respects, above all in the quantity of its treasures, which form the greatest concentration of megalithic art in Europe. Also, the site was occupied for a much longer period – from Neolithic times right up until about 1400.

Unusually, Knowth has two passage tombs rather than one. The excavations begun in 1962 are now complete and the site is open. The tombs can only be viewed externally to prevent further decay. Keep a lookout for the finely carved kerbstones. Visitors sign up for tours via Brú na Bóinne.

Ruined lavabo at Mellifont Abbey

Slane Castle in grounds landscaped by Capability Brown

⓬ Old Mellifont Abbey

Road map D3. Tullyallen, Cullen, Co Louth. **Tel** 041 982 6459. to Drogheda. to Drogheda or Slane. **Open** May–Sep: 10am–6pm daily (last adm: 45 mins before closing). mellifontabbey.ie

On the banks of the River Mattock, 10 km (6 miles) west of Drogheda, lies the first Cistercian monastery to have been built in Ireland. Mellifont was founded in 1142 on the orders of St Malachy, the Archbishop of Armagh. He was greatly influenced by St Bernard who, based at his monastery at Clairvaux in France, was behind the success of the Cistercian Order in Europe. The archbishop introduced not only Cistercian rigour to Mellifont, but also the formal style of monastic architecture used on the Continent. His new monastery became a model for other Cistercian centres built in Ireland, retaining its supremacy over them until 1539, when the abbey was closed and turned into a fortified house. William of Orange used Mellifont as his headquarters during the Battle of the Boyne in 1690. The abbey is now a ruin, but it is still possible to appreciate the scale and ground plan of the original complex. Little survives of the abbey church, but to the south of it, enclosed by what remains of the Romanesque cloister, is the most interesting building at Mellifont: a unique 13th-century octagonal lavabo where monks washed their hands in a fountain before meals. Four of the building's eight sides survive, each with a Romanesque arch. To the east of the cloister stands the 14th-century chapter house, with its impressive vaulted ceiling and medieval tiled floor.

Glazed medieval tiles at Mellifont Abbey

⓭ Slane

Road map D3. Co Meath. 950.

Slane is an attractive estate village, centred on a quartet of Georgian houses. The Boyne flows through it and skirts **Slane Castle Demesne**, which is set in glorious grounds laid out in the 18th century by Capability Brown. The castle was damaged by fire in 1991 but reopened in 2001.

Just to the north rises the **Hill of Slane** where, in 433, St Patrick is said to have lit a Paschal (Easter) fire as a challenge to the pagan High King of Tara *(see p252)*. The event symbolized the triumph of Christianity over paganism.

Newgrange

The origins of Newgrange, one of the most important passage graves in Europe, are steeped in mystery. According to Celtic lore, the legendary Kings of Tara *(see p252)* were buried here, but Newgrange predates them. Built in around 3200 BC, the grave was left untouched by all invaders until it was rediscovered in 1699. When it was excavated in the 1960s, archaeologists discovered that on the winter solstice (21 December), rays of sun enter the tomb and light up the burial chamber – making it the world's oldest solar observatory. All visitors to Newgrange and Knowth *(see pp248–9)* are admitted through the visitors' centre from where tours of the historic site are taken. Long queues are expected in summer and access is not always guaranteed.

Basin Stone
The chiselled stones in each recess would have contained funerary offerings and cremated human remains.

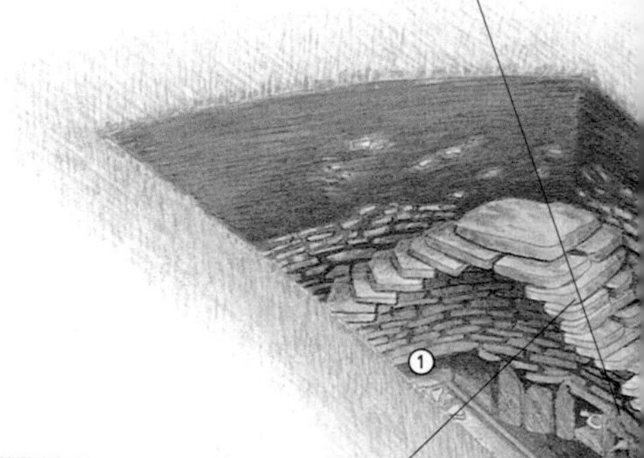

KEY

① **The chamber** has three recesses or side chambers: the north recess is the one struck by sunlight on the winter solstice.

② **The standing stones** in the passage are slabs of slate which would have been collected locally.

③ **Roof box**

④ **The retaining wall** around the front of the cairn was rebuilt using the white quartz and granite stones found scattered around the site during excavations.

Chamber Ceiling
The burial chamber's intricate corbelled ceiling, which reaches a height of 6 m (20 ft) above the floor, has survived intact. The overlapping slabs form a conical hollow, topped by a single capstone.

Construction of Newgrange

The tomb at Newgrange was designed by people with clearly exceptional artistic and engineering skills, who had use of neither the wheel nor metal tools. About 200,000 tonnes of loose stones were transported to build the mound, or cairn, which protects the passage grave. Larger slabs were used to make the circle around the cairn (12 out of a probable 35 stones have survived), the kerb and the tomb itself. Many of the kerbstones and the slabs lining the passage, the chamber and its recesses are decorated with zigzags, spirals and other geometric motifs. The grave's corbelled ceiling consists of smaller, unadorned slabs and has proved completely waterproof for the last 5,000 years.

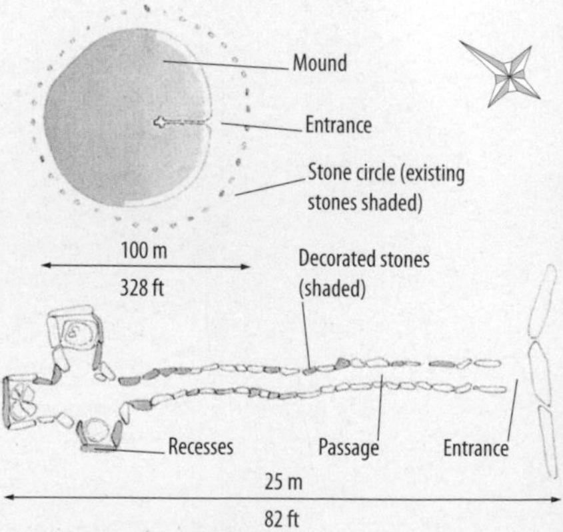

Plan of passage and burial chamber

Restoration of Newgrange
Located on a low ridge north of the Boyne, Newgrange took more than 70 years to build. Between 1962 and 1975 the passage grave and mound were restored as closely as possible to their original state.

VISITORS' CHECKLIST

Practical Information
Road map D3. 8 km (5 miles) E of Slane, Co. Meath. **Tel** 041 988 0300. **Open** May–Sep: 9am–6:30pm (Jun–mid-Sep: 7pm) daily; Oct–Apr: 9:30am–5:30pm (Nov–Jan: 9am–4:15pm) daily; last tour: 1 hr 45 mins before closing. **Closed** 24–27 Dec. inside tomb. Brú na Boinne visitors' centre only.
newgrange.com

Transport
to Drogheda. to Drogheda & Drogheda to Brú na Boinne visitors' centre.

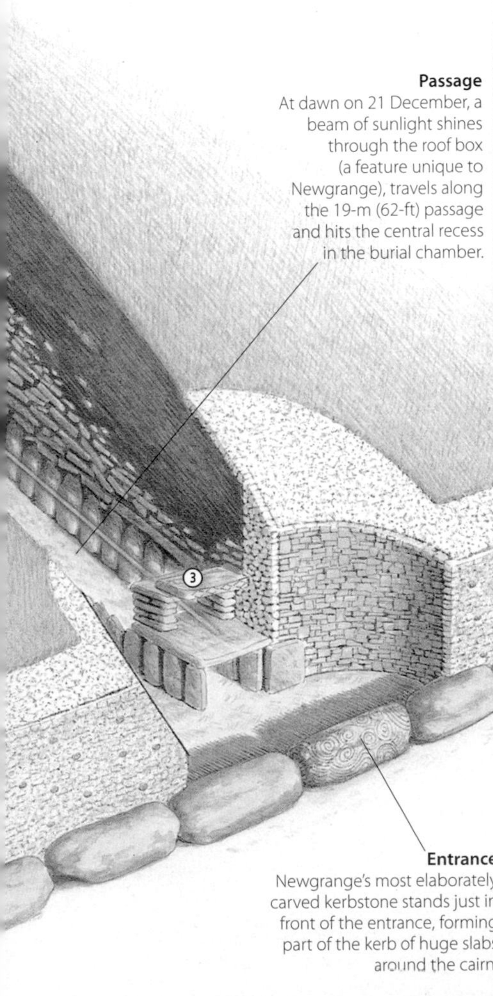

Passage
At dawn on 21 December, a beam of sunlight shines through the roof box (a feature unique to Newgrange), travels along the 19-m (62-ft) passage and hits the central recess in the burial chamber.

Entrance
Newgrange's most elaborately carved kerbstone stands just in front of the entrance, forming part of the kerb of huge slabs around the cairn.

Trim Castle set in water meadows beside the River Boyne

⓮ Hill of Tara

Road map D3. Nr Killmessan Village, Co Meath. **Tel** 046 902 5903. to Navan. **Open** mid-May–mid-Sep:10am–6pm daily (last adm 1hr before closing). Interpretative Centre. **hilloftara.org**

A site of mythical importance, Tara was the political and spiritual centre of Celtic Ireland and the seat of the High Kings until the 11th century. The spread of Christianity, which eroded the importance of Tara, is marked by a statue of St Patrick. The symbolism of the site was not lost on Daniel O'Connell *(see p46)*, who chose Tara for a rally in 1843, attended by over one million people.

Tours from the Interpretative Centre take in a Stone Age passage grave and Iron Age hill forts, which, to the untutored eye, look like mere hollows and grassy mounds. Clearest is the Royal Enclosure, an oval fort, in the centre of which is Cormac's House containing the "stone of destiny" *(Liath Fáil)*, fertility symbol and inauguration stone of the High Kings. Most moving, however, is the poignant atmosphere and views over the Boyne Valley.

⓯ Trim

Road map D3. Co Meath. 6,500. Castle St (046 943 7227). Fri. **meath.ie**

Trim is one of the most pleasing Midlands market towns. A Norman stronghold on the River Boyne, it marked a boundary of the Pale *(see p136)*.

The **Trim Visitor Centre** houses a multimedia exhibition on the town's history. It is also the starting point for a heritage trail, which takes in eight sites, including the town's two castles and two cathedrals.

The dramatic **Trim Castle** was founded in the 12th century by Hugh de Lacy, a Norman knight, and is one of the largest medieval castles in Europe. It makes a spectacular backdrop for films and was used in Mel Gibson's film *Braveheart* in 1995.

Over the river is **Talbot Castle**, an Augustinian abbey converted to a manor house in the 15th century. Just north of the abbey is **St Patrick's Cathedral**, which incorporates part of a medieval church with a 15th-century tower and sections of the original chancel. From here the trail leads to the Saints Peter and Paul Cathedral further east.

A lovely walk leads from the castle along the River Boyne to Newtown Abbey.

Trim Castle
Tel 046 943 8619. **Open** mid-Mar–Oct: 10am–6pm daily; Nov–mid-Mar: 9am–5pm Sat & Sun. obligatory. **heritageireland.ie**

⓰ Mullingar

Road map C3. Co Westmeath. 25,000. Market Square (044 934 8650). **mullingar.ie**

The county town of Westmeath is a prosperous but unremarkable market town encircled by the Royal Canal, which with its 46 locks links

Aerial view of Iron Age forts on the Hill of Tara

Dublin with the River Shannon. The cost of building the canal bankrupted its investors and it was never profitable. Mullingar's main appeal is as a base to explore the surrounding area, but pubs such as Canton Casey's and Con's are a pleasant interlude.

Environs

The Dublin to Mullingar stretch of the Royal Canal has attractive towpaths for walkers, and fishing.

Just off the Kilbeggan road from Mullingar stands **Belvedere House**, a romantic Palladian villa overlooking Lough Ennel. The house, built in 1740 by Richard Cassels, is decorated with Rococo plasterwork and set in beautiful grounds.

Shortly after the house was built, the first Earl of Belvedere accused his wife of having an affair with his brother, and imprisoned her for 31 years in a nearby house. In 1760, the Earl built a Gothic folly – the Jealous Wall – to block the view of his second brother's more opulent mansion across the way. The Jealous Wall remains as does an octagonal gazebo and follies.

Charming terraces descend to the lake. On the other side of the house is a picturesque walled garden, enclosed by an arboretum and parkland.

Belvedere House
6.5 km (4 miles) S of Mullingar. **Tel** 044 934 9060. **Open** May–Aug: 9:30am–5pm (house), 9:30am–8pm (garden) daily; Mar–Apr & Sep–Oct: 9:30am–7pm (house), 9:30am–5pm (garden) daily; Nov–Feb: 9:30am–4pm (house), 9:30am–4:30pm (garden). centre. **belvedere-house.ie**

The Jealous Wall at Belvedere House, near Mullingar

Athlone Castle below the towers of the church of St Peter and St Paul

⑰ Kilbeggan

Road map C4. Co Westmeath. 1,000.

Situated between Mullingar and Tullamore, this pleasant village has a small harbour on the Grand Canal. However the main point of interest is **Kilbeggan Distillery Experience**. Founded in 1757, it claims to be the oldest licensed pot still distillery in the world to be still producing whiskey. Unable to compete with Scotch whisky manufacturers, the company went bankrupt in 1954, but the aroma hung in the warehouses for years and was known as "the angel's share". The distillery reopened as a museum in 1987. The building is authentic, a solid structure complete with waterwheel and steam engine. A tour traces the process of Irish whiskey-making, from the mash tuns to the vast fermentation vats and creation of wash (rough beer) to the distillation and maturation stages. At the tasting stage, workers would sample the whiskey in the can pit room. Visitors can still taste whiskeys in the bar. Prod-uction restarted in 2007, with the results on sale from 2014 onwards.

Miniature whiskey bottles at Kilbeggan Distillery Experience

Kilbeggan Distillery Experience
Lower Main St. **Tel** 057 933 2134. **Open** Apr–Oct: 9am–6pm; Nov–Mar: 10am–4pm daily. **kilbeggandistillery.com**

⑱ Athlone

Road map C3. Co Westmeath. 16,000. Market Square (090 649 4630). Sat.

The town owes its historical importance to its position by a natural ford on the River Shannon. **Athlone Castle** is a 13th-century fortress, which was badly damaged in the Jacobite Wars *(see pp42–3)*. It lies in the shadow of the 19th-century church of St Peter and St Paul. The neighbouring streets offer several good pubs. Across the river from the castle, boats depart for Clonmacnoise *(see pp254–5)* or Lough Ree.

Athlone Castle
Visitors' Centre **Tel** 090 644 2130. **Open** 11am–5pm Tue–Sat; 12pm–5pm Sun. limited.

Environs

The **Lough Ree Trail** starts 8 km (5 miles) northeast of Athlone, at Glasson, and is a popular cycling tour that runs around the shores and into County Longford.

⑲ Clonmacnoise

This medieval monastery, in a remote spot by the River Shannon, was founded by St Ciarán in 545–548. Clonmacnoise lay at a crossroads of medieval routes, linking all parts of Ireland. Known for its scholarship and piety, it thrived from the 7th to the 12th century. Many kings of Tara and of Connaught were buried here. Plundered by the Vikings and Anglo-Normans, it fell to the English in 1552. Today, a group of stone churches (temples), a cathedral, two round towers and three High Crosses remain.

Last Circuit of Pilgrims at Clonmacnoise
This painting (1838), by George Petrie, shows pilgrims walking the traditional route three times around the site. Pilgrims still do this every year on 9 September, St Ciarán's Day.

Cross of the Scriptures
This copy of the original 9th-century cross (now in the museum) is decorated with biblical scenes, but the identity of most of the figures is uncertain.

KEY

① **The Pope's Shelter** was where John Paul II conducted Mass during his visit in 1979.

② **The Round Tower** *(see p24)* is over 19 m (62 ft) high with its doorway above ground level.

Visiting Clonmacnoise

The Visitors' Centre is housed in three buildings modelled on beehive huts *(see p25)*. The museum section contains early grave slabs and the three remaining High Crosses, replicas of which now stand in their original locations. The Nuns' Church, northeast of the main site, has a Romanesque doorway and chancel arch.

Key

1 South Cross
2 Temple Dowling
3 Temple Hurpan
4 Temple Melaghlin
5 Temple Ciarán
6 Temple Kelly
7 Cathedral
8 North Cross
9 Cross of the Scriptures
10 Round Tower
11 Temple Connor
12 Temple Finghin

0 metres 50
0 yards 50

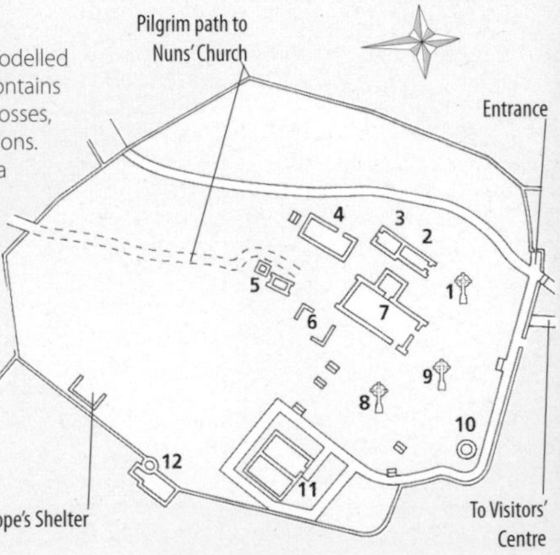

VISITORS' CHECKLIST

Practical Information
Road map C4. 7 km (4 miles) N of Shannonbridge, Co Offaly. **Tel** 090 967 4195. **Open** daily. Groups pre-book. **Closed** 25 & 26 Dec. in summer.
W **heritageireland.ie**

Transport
to Athlone, then minibus (090 647 4839/ 087 240 7706).
from Athlone.

Whispering Door
Above the cathedral's 15th-century north doorway are carvings of saints Francis, Patrick and Dominic. The acoustics of the doorway are such that even a whisper is carried inside the building.

Temples Dowling, Hurpan and Melaghlin
Built as a family crypt, Temple Hurpan was a 17th-century addition to the early Romanesque Temple Dowling. The 13th-century Temple Melaghlin has two fine round-headed windows.

The Tullamore Dew Heritage Centre, Co Offaly

⓴ Tullamore Dew Heritage Centre

Road map C4. Bury Quay, Tullamore, Co Offaly – access from Dublin Galway N6 & Dublin–Cork N7 roads. **Tel** 057 932 5015. **Open** 9:30am–6pm Mon–Sat, 11:30am–5pm Sun. **Closed** 24 Dec–1 Jan.
W **tullamoredew.com**

The town of Tullamore and its most famous export, Tullamore Dew Whiskey, are intrinsically linked. It makes sense, therefore, that the Tullamore Dew Heritage Centre should attempt to explore not only the history of the Tullamore Dew brand but also that of the town itself.

The refurbished centre is housed in the original Tullamore Dew distillery, dating back to 1897. Visitors can wander through the fascinating re-created working stations of the distillery, such as the malting, bottling, corking and cooperage areas as well as the warehouse where the old oak barrels filled with whiskey were left to mature.

The history of Tullamore town itself starts 9,000 years ago with the formation of the bog. The centre explains raised bogs and the different uses of peat. Here, too, visitors can chain themselves to stocks, a public punishment of the day, fill a whiskey bottle by hand and see and touch various artifacts for themselves.

The tour ends in the on-site bar with a complimentary glass of whiskey or Irish Mist Liqueur, both of which are on sale in the gift shop.

The Raised Bogs of the Midlands

Peatland or bog, which covers about 15 per cent of the Irish landscape, exists in two principal forms. Most extensive is the thin blanket bog found chiefly in the west, while the dome-shaped raised bogs are more characteristic of the Midlands – notably in an area known as the Bog of Allen. Although Irish boglands are some of the largest in Europe, the use of peat for fuel and fertilizer has greatly reduced their extent, threatening not only the shape of the Irish landscape but also the survival of a unique habitat and the unusual plants and insects it supports.

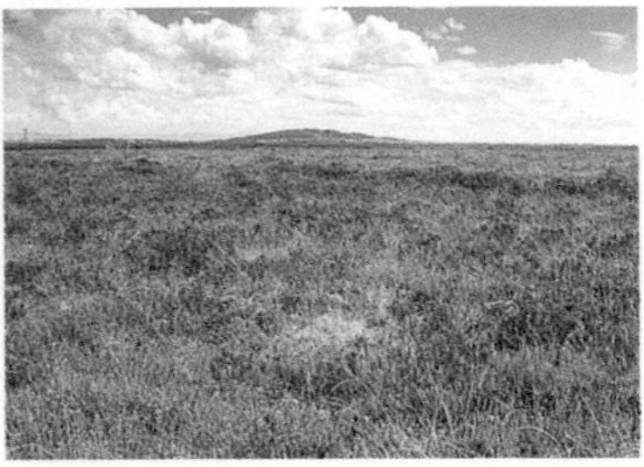

Unspoiled expanse of the Bog of Allen

Peat cutters still gather turf (as peat is known locally) by hand in parts of Ireland. It is then set in stacks to dry. Peat makes a good fuel, because it is rich in partially decayed vegetation, laid down over thousands of years.

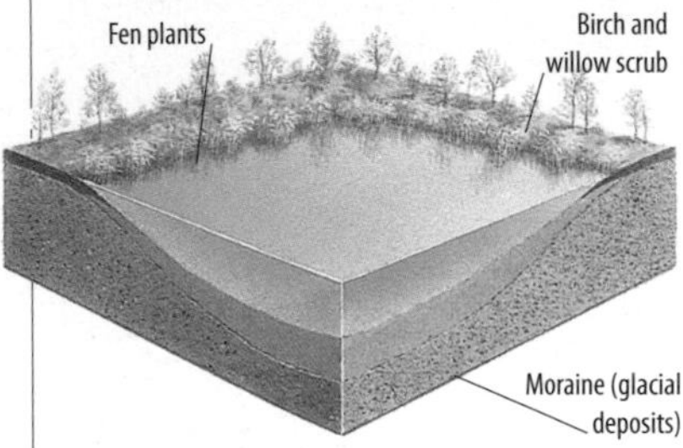

8000 BC: Shallow meltwater lakes that formed after the Ice Age gradually filled with mud. Reeds, sedges and other fen plants began to dominate in the marshy conditions which resulted.

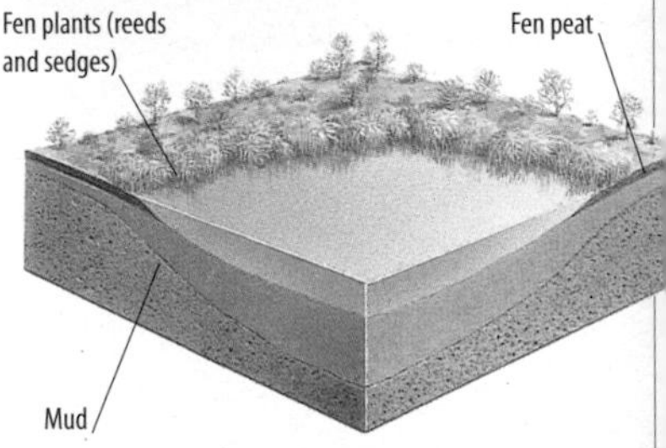

6000 BC: As the fen vegetation died, it sank to the lake bed but did not decompose fully in the waterlogged conditions, forming a layer of peat. This slowly built up and also spread outwards.

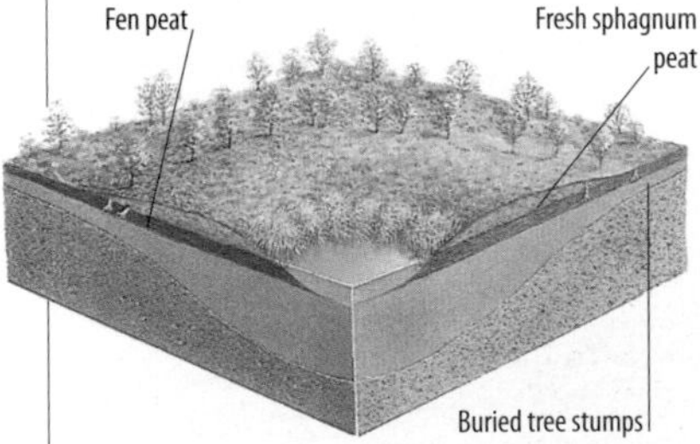

3000 BC: As the peat built up and the lake slowly disappeared, plant life in the developing bog had to rely almost exclusively on rainwater, which is acid. Fen plants could not survive in these acidic conditions and gave way to bog mosses, mainly species of sphagnum. As these mosses died, they formed a layer of sphagnum peat on the surface of the bog which, over the centuries, attained a distinctive domed shape.

Present day: Few raised bogs are actively growing today. Those that remain contain a fascinating historical record of the landscape. The survival of ancient tree stumps shows how well plants are preserved in peat.

Sphagnum moss

㉑ Birr

Road map 4C. Co Offaly. 4,100. May–Sep: Rosse Row (05791 20110). **Open** Mon–Fri.

Birr, a gentrified estate town, grew up in the shadow of the castle where the Earls of Rosse have resided for almost four centuries. It is famous for its authentic Georgian layout, with houses displaying original fanlights, door panelling and iron railings. Two particularly elegant streets are Oxmantown Mall, designed by the 2nd Earl of Rosse, and John's Mall.

Emmet Square may have sold its Georgian soul to commerce, but Dooley's Hotel is still a fine example of an old coaching inn. Foster's bar, in nearby Connaught Street, is one of many traditional shopfronts to have been restored in Birr.

Birr Castle Demesne
Rosse Row. **Tel** 05791 20336. Gardens **Open** mid-Mar–Oct: 9am– 6pm; Nov–mid-Mar: 10am–4pm.
birrcastle.com

Birr Castle was founded in 1620 by the Parsons, later Earls of Rosse, and is still the family seat. They are most noted for their contribution to astronomy – a telescope named the Leviathan, built by the 3rd Earl in 1845, was the largest in the world at the time. The 17-m (56-ft) wooden tube, supported by two walls, can be seen in the grounds, fully restored. The Historic Science Centre traces the family's work.

The castle is closed to the public, but the glory of Birr lies in its grounds, which are open. First landscaped in the 18th century, these are famous for their 9-m (30-ft), 200-year-old box hedges and for the exotic trees and shrubs from foreign expeditions sponsored by the 6th Earl. The magnolias and maples are particularly striking. The gardens overlook the meeting of two rivers.

An alcove in the front hall of Emo Court with a trompe l'oeil ceiling

㉒ Slieve Bloom Mountains

Road map D4. Co Offaly and Co Laois. to Mountmellick. May–Sep: Rosse Row, Birr (05791 20110).

This low range of mountains rises unexpectedly from the bogs and plains of Offaly and Laois, providing a welcome change in the predominantly flat Midlands. You can walk along the **Slieve Bloom Way**, a 30-km (19-mile) circular trail through an unspoiled area of open vistas, deep wooded glens and mountain streams. There are other marked paths too. Good starting points are **Cadamstown**, with an attractive old mill, and the pretty village of **Kinnitty** – both in the northern foothills.

㉓ Emo Court

Road map D4. 13 km (8 miles) NE of Portlaoise, Co Laois. **Tel** 05786 26573. to Monasterevin or Portlaoise. House: **Open** Easter–Sep: 10am–6pm daily (last adm: 1hr before closing). Gardens: **Open** daily. limited.

Emo Court, commissioned by the Earl of Portarlington in 1790, represents the only foray into domestic architecture by James Gandon, designer of the Custom House in Dublin *(see p92)*. The monumental Neo-Classical mansion has a splendid façade featuring an Ionic portico. Inside are a magnificent gilded rotunda and fine stuccowork ceilings.

Emo Court became the property of the Office of Public Works in 1994 but the previous owner is still resident on the grounds. These are adorned with fine statuary and include a lakeside walk.

㉔ Rock of Dunamase

Road map D4. 5 km (3 miles) E of Portlaoise, Co Laois. to Portlaoise.

The Rock of Dunamase, which looms dramatically above the plains east of Portlaoise, has long been a military site. Originally crowned by an Iron Age ring fort, the 13th-century castle which succeeded it is now more prominent – though it was virtually destroyed by Cromwellian forces in 1651. You can reach the battered keep by climbing up banks and ditches through two gateways and a fortified courtyard.

Rock of Dunamase viewed from Stradbally to the east

NORTHERN IRELAND

Londonderry · Antrim · Tyrone · Fermanagh
Armagh · Down

Northern Ireland has sights from every era of Ireland's history as well as magnificently varied coastal and lakeland scenery. During the years of the "Troubles", it received fewer visitors than the Republic, however, now that there is a movement towards peace it is attracting the attention it deserves.

The area constituted as of Northern Ireland was created after partition of the island in 1921. Its six counties (plus Donegal, Monaghan and Cavan) are part of Ulster, one of Ireland's four traditional kingdoms. It was most probably in Ulster that Christianity first ousted the old Celtic pagan beliefs. In 432 St Patrick landed at Saul in County Down, later founding a church at Armagh, which is still the spiritual capital of Ireland.

The dominant political force in early Christian times was the Uí Néill clan. Their descendants, the O'Neills, put up fierce resistance to English conquest in the late 16th century. Hugh O'Neill, Earl of Tyrone, had some notable successes against the armies of Elizabeth I, but was defeated and in 1607 fled to Europe with other Irish lords from Ulster, in what became known as the "Flight of the Earls". Vacant estates were granted to individuals and companies, who planted them with English and Scottish Protestants *(see p43)*. Many Plantation towns, such as Londonderry, preserve their 17th-century layout around a central square or "diamond". The arrival of new settlers meant that Irish Catholics were increasingly marginalized, thereby sowing the seeds of 400 years of conflict.

In the relative tranquillity of the 18th century, the Anglo-Irish nobility built stately homes, such as Mount Stewart House on the Ards Peninsula and Castle Coole near Enniskillen. Ulster also enjoyed prosperity in the 19th century through its linen, rope-making and ship-building industries.

Though densely populated and industrialized around Belfast, away from the capital the region is primarily agricultural. It also has areas of outstanding natural beauty, notably the rugged Antrim coastline around the Giant's Causeway, the Mountains of Mourne in County Down and the Fermanagh lakelands in the southwest.

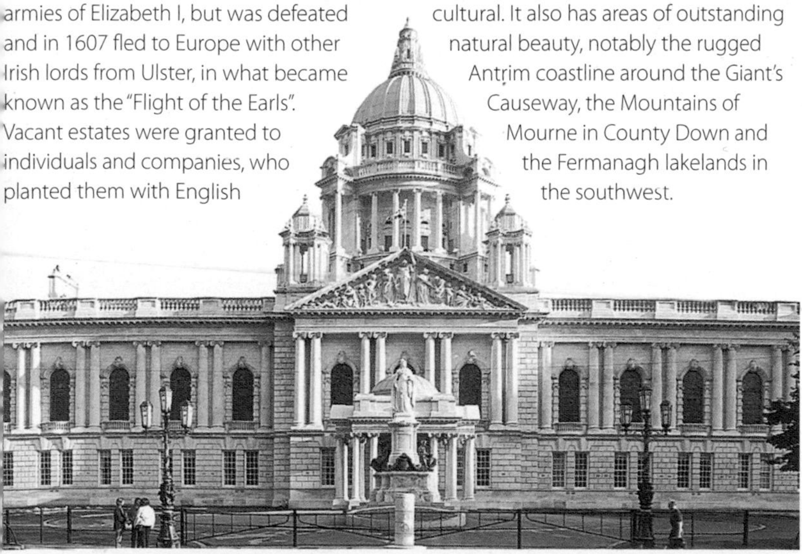

Belfast's City Hall (1906), symbol of the city's civic pride

◀ The striking stained-glass Famine Window in Belfast City Hall

Exploring Northern Ireland

The starting point for most visitors to the Province is its capital city, Belfast, with its grand Victorian buildings, good pubs and the excellent Ulster Museum. However, Northern Ireland's greatest attractions lie along its coast. These range from the extraordinary volcanic landscape of the Giant's Causeway to Carrickfergus, Ireland's best-preserved Norman castle. There are also Victorian resorts, like Portstewart, tiny fishing villages and unspoiled sandy beaches, such as Benone Strand. Ramblers are drawn to the Mountains of Mourne, while anglers and boating enthusiasts can enjoy the Fermanagh lakelands of Lower Lough Erne.

Harbour and promenade at the seaside resort of Portstewart

Key

- Motorway
- Motorway under construction
- Major road
- Secondary road
- Minor road
- Scenic route
- Main railway
- Minor railway
- International border
- County border
- △ Summit

Getting Around

Belfast is the transport hub of Northern Ireland. From here the train network runs northwest to Londonderry and south to Dublin. Buses serve rural areas in most parts of the Province and are frequent and punctual. However, a car is essential if you want to go off the beaten track in search of ancient monuments or tour the coast at leisure.

For additional map symbols *see back flap*

Sights at a Glance

Tours

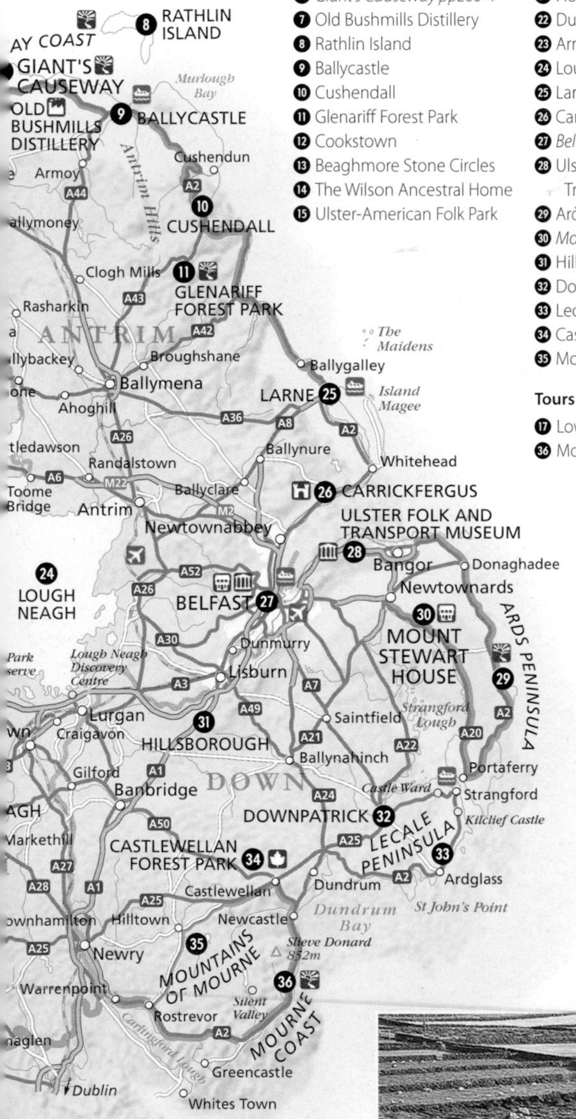

Dry-stone walls on slopes of the Mountains of Mourne

For hotels and restaurants in this region see pp302–3 and pp323–5

❶ Londonderry

St Columba founded a monastery here beside the River Foyle in 546. He called the place Doire or "oak grove", later anglicized as Derry. In 1613, the city was selected as a major Plantation project *(see pp42–3)*, organized by London livery companies. As a result, it acquired the prefix London, though it is equally popular as Derry. Although Derry suffered during the "Troubles", there have been a number of admirable heritage projects undertaken in the city, leading to it being named the 2013 UK City of Culture.

★ Tower Museum
The excellent displays on local history in this museum include one on the mapping of the area during the reign of Elizabeth I.

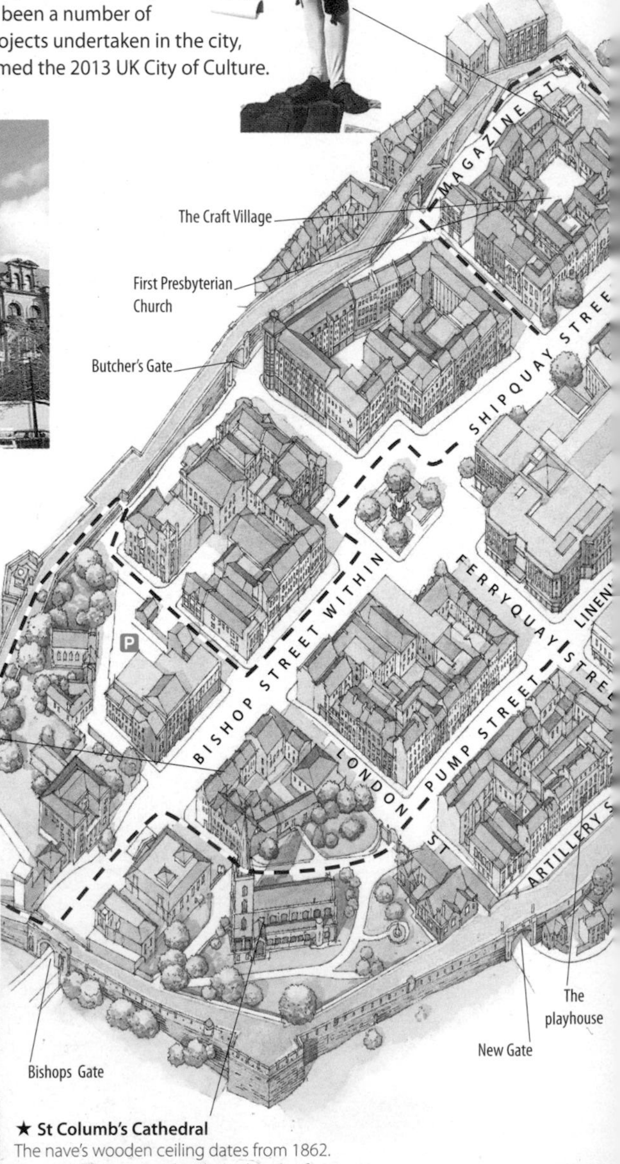

The Diamond
the war memorial in the Diamond or main square was erected in 1927. It was originally made for the city of Sheffield in England.

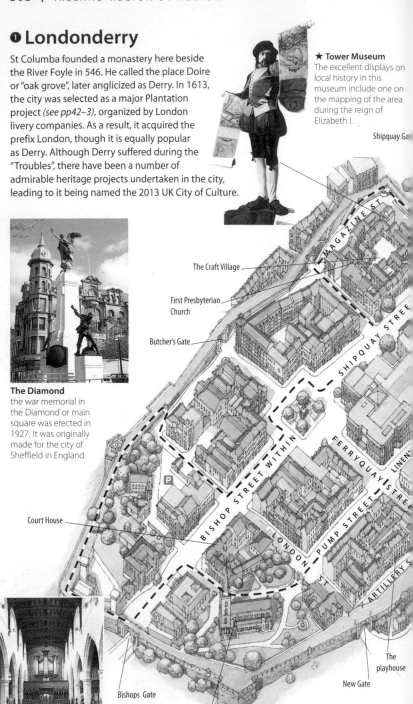

★ St Columb's Cathedral
The nave's wooden ceiling dates from 1862. The corbels are carved with the heads of former bishops and deans.

VISITORS' CHECKLIST

Practical Information
Road map C1. Co Londonderry. 107,000. 44 Foyle St (028 7137 7577). Hallowe'en Festival (Oct). Sat.

Transport
11 km (7 miles) E. Waterside, Duke St (028 7134 2228). Foyle St (028 7126 2261).

★ The Guildhall
This stained-glass window shows St Columba. Others feature incidents from the siege of Derry, including the Apprentice Boys shutting the city gates in 1688.

0 metres 100
0 yards 100

Key
Suggested route

St Columb's Cathedral

London St. **Tel** 028 7126 7313. **Open** Mon–Sat. on request. **stcolumbscathedral.org**

Built between 1628 and 1633, in "Planters' Gothic" style, St Columb's was the first cathedral to be founded in the British Isles after the Reformation.The interior was extensively restored in the 19th century. A small museum in the Chapter House has relics from the siege of 1689 *(see pp42–3)*, including the17th-century locks and keys of the city. In the vestibule is a hollow mortar cannonball that was fired into the city by James II's army. It carried terms for capitulation, but the reply of the Protestants within the walls was a defiant "No surrender".

Tower Museum

Union Hall Place. **Tel** 028 7137 2411. **Open** Nov–Mar: 10am–5pm Tue–Sat; Apr–Oct: 10am–6pm Mon–Sat, noon–4pm Sun.

Housed in O'Doherty Tower (a replica of the original 16th-century building on this site), the museum traces the history of the city from its foundation to the "Troubles" using multimedia displays. Upstairs, an exhibition about the 1588 Spanish Armada includes artifacts from the *Trinidad Valencera*, wrecked in nearby Kinnagoe Bay.

The City Walls of Derry

Access from Magazine Street.

Derry is the only remaining completely walled city in Ireland and its fortifications are among the best preserved in Europe. The city walls rise to a height of 8 m (26 ft) and in places are 9 m (30 ft) wide. Completed in 1618 to defend the new merchant city from Gaelic chieftains in Donegal, the walls have never been breached, not even during the siege of 1689, when 7,000 out of a population of 20,000 perished from disease or starvation. Restoration work means that it is possible to walk right around the walls. Just outside the old fortifications, beyond Butcher's Gate, is the Bogside, a Catholic area with famous murals that depict recent events in Northern Ireland's history.

The Guildhall

Guildhall St. **Tel** 028 7136 5151. **Open** 10am–5:30pm daily.

Standing between the walled city and the River Foyle, this Neo-Gothic building was constructed in 1890, but a fire in 1908 and a bomb in 1972 both necessitated substantial repairs. Stained-glass windows recount the history of Derry. To the rear is Derry Quay, from where Irish emigrants sailed to America in the 18th and 19th centuries.

Environs

The Peace Bridge, which opened in 2011, provides foot and cycle access across the River Foyle. The bridge links the city walls of Derry and the Ebrington Centre, which is being developed into an arts and culture centre and includes a 14,000-capacity outdoor performance plaza and a cinema.

The Derry Peace Bridge, linking Derry with Ebrington Centre

Spectacular view of the seashore at Portstewart

❷ Benone Strand

Road map. D1. Co Londonderry. Benone Tourist Complex, 53 Benone Ave, Limavady (028 7775 0555). **Open** Easter–Sep: daily.

The wide, golden sands of one of Ireland's longest beaches, also known as Magilligan Strand, sweep along the Londonderry coastline for more than 10 km (6 miles). The magnificent beach has been granted EU Blue Flag status for its cleanliness. At the western extremity of the beach is **Magilligan Point** where a Martello tower, built during the Napoleonic wars, stands guard over the entrance to Lough Foyle. To get to the point, renowned for its rare shellfish and sea birds, you have to drive past a military training ground. There are great views across to Donegal from the Strand.

❸ Mussenden Temple

Road map D1. Co Londonderry. **Tel** 028 708 48728. Grounds: **Open** dawn–dusk daily (last adm: 30 mins before closing). Temple: **Open** Mar–Oct: 10am–5pm daily. limited. **nationaltrust.org.uk**

The oddest sight along the Londonderry coast is this small, domed rotunda perched precariously on a windswept headland outside the family resort of Castlerock. The temple was built in 1785 by Frederick Augustus Hervey, the eccentric Earl of Bristol and Protestant Bishop of Derry, as a memorial to his cousin Mrs Frideswide Mussenden. The design was based on the Temple of Vesta at Tivoli outside Rome.

The walls, made of basalt faced with sandstone, open out at the four points of the compass to three windows and an entrance. Originally designed for use as a library (or, as some stories go, an elaborate boudoir for the bishop's mistress), the structure is now maintained by the National Trust and remains in excellent condition.

The bishop allowed the local priest to say Mass for his Roman Catholic tenants in the basement. The bishop's former residence, the nearby Downhill Castle, was gutted by fire and is now little more than an impressive shell.

The surrounding area offers some good glen and cliff walks and there are some magnificent views of the Londonderry and Antrim coastline. Below the temple is Downhill Strand, where the bishop sponsored horseback races between his clergy.

❹ Portstewart

Road map D1. Co Londonderry. 8,000. to Coleraine or Portrush. Coleraine (028 7034 4723). **northcoastni.com**

A popular holiday destination for Victorian middle-class families, Portstewart is still a family favourite today. Its long, crescent-shaped seafront promenade is sheltered by rocky headlands. Just west of town, and accessible by road or by a cliffside walk, stretches **Portstewart Strand**, a magnificent, long, sandy beach, protected by the National Trust.

On Ramore Head, just to the east, lies **Portrush**, a brasher resort with an abundance of souvenir shops and amusement arcades. The East Strand is backed by sand dunes and runs parallel with the world-class **Royal Portrush Golf Club**. You can stroll along the beach to White Rocks – limestone cliffs carved by the wind and waves into caves and arches.

To the south is **Coleraine**. Every May, the North West 200 *(see p32)*, the world's fastest motorcycle road race, is run between Portstewart, Coleraine and Portrush, in front of 100,000 people.

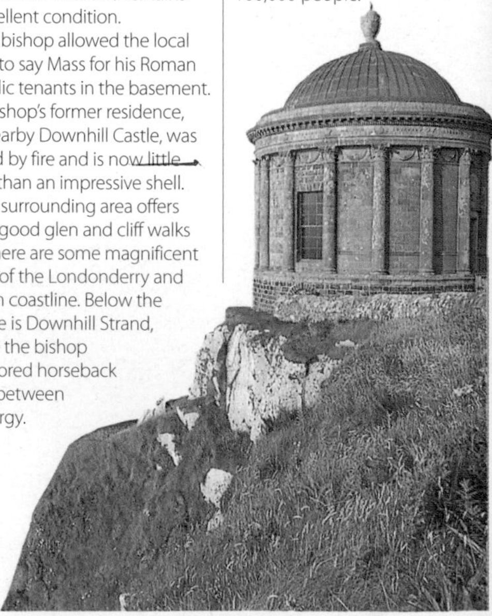

Mussenden Temple set on a clifftop on the Londonderry coast

5 Causeway Coast

Road map D1. Co Antrim. Giant's Causeway (028 2073 1855). Carrick-a-rede Rope Bridge **Tel** 028 2076 9839. **Open** 10:30am–3:30pm. **Closed** 25 & 26 Dec. limited. **nationaltrust.org.uk**

The renown of the **Giant's Causeway** *(see pp266–7)*, Northern Ireland's only World Heritage Site, overshadows the other attractions of this stretch of North Antrim coast. When visiting the Causeway, it is well worth investigating the sandy bays, craggy headlands and dramatic ruins that punctuate the rest of this inspirational coastline.

Approaching the Causeway from the west, you pass the eerie ruins of **Dunluce Castle** perched on a steep crag. Dating back to the 13th century, it was the main fortress of the MacDonnells, chiefs of Antrim. Although the roof has gone, it is still well preserved, with its twin towers, gateway and some cobbling intact.

Dunseverick Castle can be reached by road or a lengthy hike from the Causeway. It is a much earlier fortification than Dunluce and only one massive wall remains. Once the capital of the kingdom of Dalriada, it was linked to Tara *(see p252)* by a great road and was the departure point for 5th-century Irish raids on Scotland.

Just past the attractive, sandy **White Park Bay,** a tight switchback road leads down to the picturesque harbour of **Ballintoy**, reminiscent – on a good day – of an Aegean fishing village. **Sheep Island**, a rocky outcrop just offshore, is a cormorant colony. Boat trips run past it in the summer.

Just east of Ballintoy is one of the most unusual and scary tourist attractions in Ireland, the **Carrick-a-rede Rope Bridge**. The bridge hangs 25 m (80 ft) above the sea and wobbles and twists as soon as you stand on it. Made of planks strung between wires, it provides access to the salmon fishery on the tiny island across the 20-m (65-ft) chasm. There are strong hand-rails and safety nets, but it's definitely not for those with vertigo. Further east along the coast lies **Kinbane Castle**, a 16th-century ruin with spectacular views.

The roofless ruins of 13th-century Dunluce Castle

Carrick-a-rede Rope Bridge

Dunluce Castle
Tel 028 2073 1938. **Open** daily.
in summer and by appt.
discovernorthernireland.com

Fishing boats moored in the shelter of Ballintoy Harbour

The North Antrim Coastline

Key

Minor road

Major road

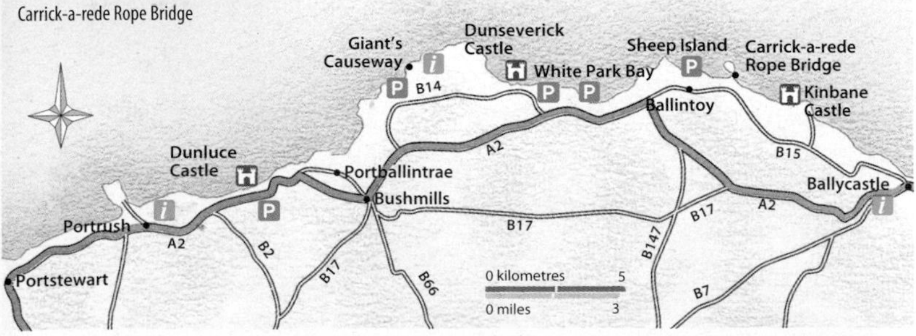

For additional map symbols *see back flap*

6 Giant's Causeway

The sheer strangeness of this place and the bizarre regularity of its basalt columns have made the Giant's Causeway the subject of numerous legends. The most popular tells how the giant, Finn MacCool *(see pp30–31)*, laid the causeway to provide a path across the sea to Scotland to engage in battle with a rival Scottish giant by the name of Benandonner. The Giant's Causeway attracts many tourists, who are taken by the busload from the visitors' centre down to the shore. Nothing, however, can destroy the magic of this place, with its looming grey cliffs and shrieking gulls; paths along the coast allow you to escape the crowds.

Aird's Snout
This nose-shaped promontory juts out from the 120-m (395-ft) basalt cliffs that soar above the Giant's Causeway.

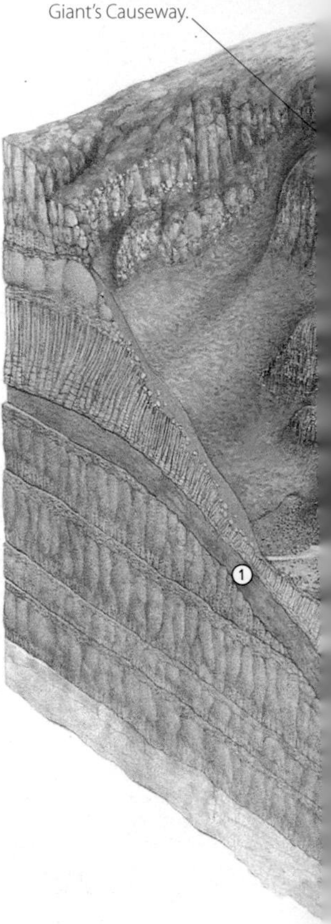

The Formation of the Causeway

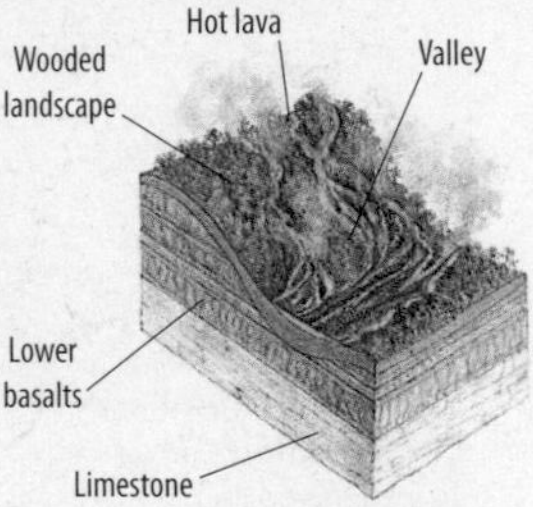

61 million years ago: In a series of massive volcanic eruptions molten lava poured from narrow fissures in the ground, filling in the valleys and burning the vegetation that grew there.

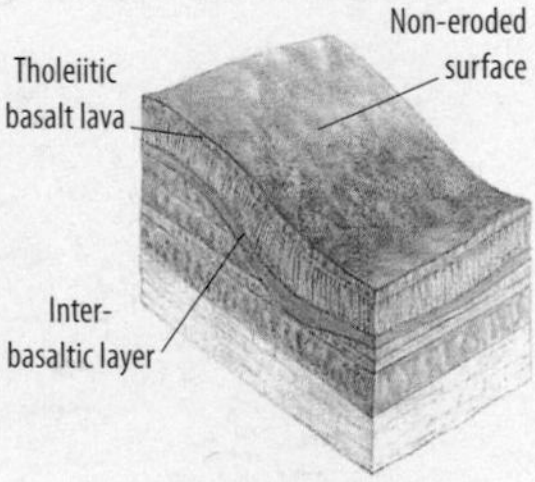

60 million years ago: This layer of tholeiitic basalt lava cooled rapidly. In the process it shrank and cracked evenly into polygonal-shaped blocks, forming columnar jointing beneath the surface.

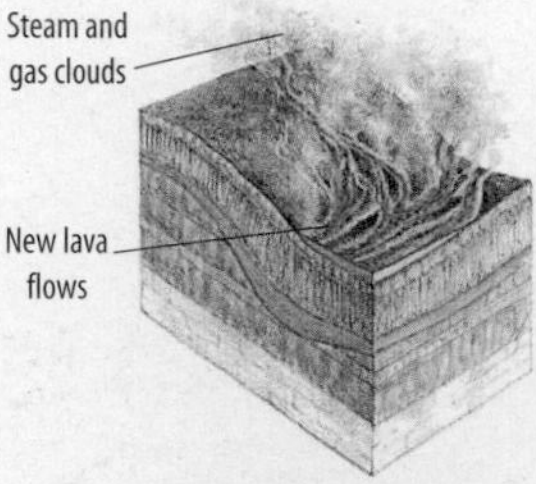

58 million years ago: New volcanic eruptions produced further lava flows. These had a slightly different chemical composition from earlier flows and, once cool, did not form such well defined columns.

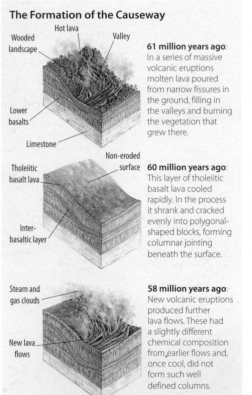

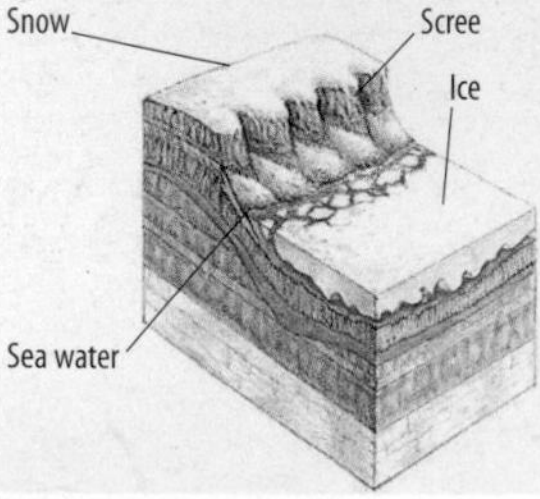

15,000 years ago: At the end of the Ice Age, when the land was still frozen, sea ice ground its way slowly past the high basalt cliffs, eroding the foreshore and helping to form the Giant's Causeway.

KEY

① **Inter-basaltic layer**

② **Road**

③ **Little Causeway**

④ **Plant debris** is trapped between the lava flows.

⑤ **Grand Causeway**

⑥ **Lower basalts**

Giant's Causeway and the North Antrim Coast
Millions of years of geological activity can be witnessed in the eroded cliffs flanking the Causeway. The striking band of reddish rock is the inter-basaltic layer, which formed during a long period of temperate climatic conditions. The high iron content explains the rock's rich ochre colour.

VISITORS' CHECKLIST

Practical Information
Road map D1. Co Antrim. Visitors' Centre Causeway Head (028 2073 1855).
W **nationaltrust.org.uk**
Open daily. **Closed** 24–26 Dec. limited. on request.
Giant's Causeway Bushmills Railway heritage steam trains: **Tel** 028 2073 2844.
Open call for times.

Transport
to Portrush. from Portrush, Bushmills or Coleraine.

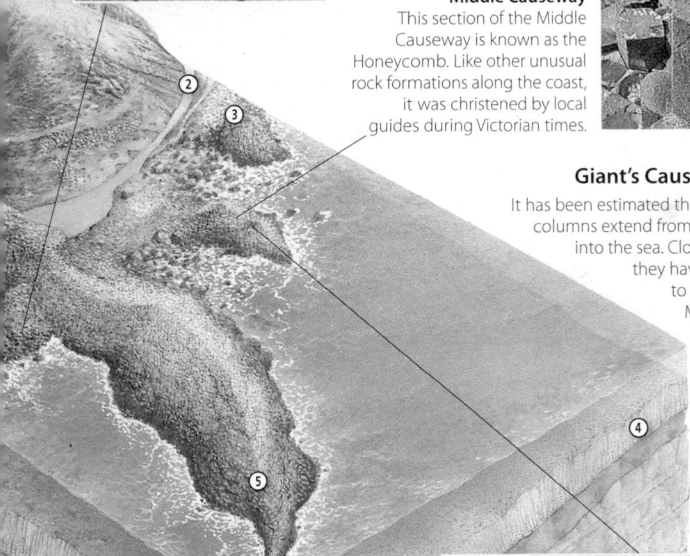

Shape of the Columns
Most columns are hexagonal, but some have four, five, eight or even ten sides. They generally measure about 30 cm (12 in) across.

Middle Causeway
This section of the Middle Causeway is known as the Honeycomb. Like other unusual rock formations along the coast, it was christened by local guides during Victorian times.

Giant's Causeway Today

It has been estimated that 40,000 basalt columns extend from the cliffs down into the sea. Close to the shore, they have been eroded to form the Grand, Middle and Little Causeways.

Wishing Chair
Myth has it that this rocky seat was made for Finn MacCool when he was a boy, and that wishes made here will come true.

Sun setting over the spectacular Giant's Causeway ▶

7 Old Bushmills Distillery

Road map D1. Bushmills, Co Antrim. **Tel** 028 2073 3272. from Giant's Causeway & Coleraine. **Open** daily. **Closed** 2 weeks at Christmas, Sun am. obligatory. limited. **bushmills.com**

The small town of Bushmills has an attractive square and a great river for salmon and trout fishing, but its main claim to fame is whiskey. The Old Bushmills plant on the edge of town prides itself on being the world's oldest distillery. Its Grant to Distil dates from 1608, but the spirit was probably made here at least 200 years before that.

In 2005 Bushmills became part of the Diageo Group, but its products have retained their own character. Most are a blend of different whiskeys; Old Bushmills, in contrast, is made from a combined blend of a single malt and grain.

The tour of the distillery ends with a whiskey sampling session in the 1608 Bar in the former malt kilns, which are also home to a small museum with old distilling equipment on display.

Murlough Bay, on the coast facing Scotland to the east of Ballycastle

8 Rathlin Island

Road map D1. Co Antrim. 90. daily from Ballycastle (028 2076 9299). Giant's Causeway (028 2073 1855). **rathlin-island.co.uk**

Rathlin is shaped rather like a boomerang – 11 km (7 miles) in length and at no point more than 1.6 km (1 mile) wide. The island is just a 50-minute boat ride from Ballycastle. About 90 people live on Rathlin Island, making a living from fishing, farming and tourism. Facilities are limited to a café, a pub, a guest-house and a hostel. The fierce, salty Atlantic winds ensure that the landscape on Rathlin is virtually treeless.

Whiskey barrel at Bushmills Distillery

High white cliffs encircle much of the island, and at craggy **Bull Point** on the westerly tip, tens of thousands of sea birds, including kittiwakes, puffins and razorbills, make their home. A local minibus service will take visitors to view the birds. At the opposite end of the island is **Bruce's Cave**, where, in 1306, Robert Bruce, King of Scotland, supposedly watched a spider climbing a thread. The spider's perseverance inspired the dejected Bruce to return and win back his kingdom.

9 Ballycastle

Road map D1. Co Antrim. 6,000. to Campbeltown (Scotland). Sheskburn House, 7 Mary St (028 2076 2024). Ould Lammas Fair (end Aug), Apple Fair (end Oct). **moyle-council.org**

A medium-sized resort town, Ballycastle boasts a pretty harbour and a sandy beach. Near the seafront is a memorial to Guglielmo Marconi, whose assistant sent the first wireless message across water from here to Rathlin Island in 1898.

Ballycastle's Ould Lammas Fair, held for nearly 400 years now, is one of the oldest traditional fairs in Ireland. Held in late August, it features stalls selling dulce (dried, salted seaweed) and yellowman (honeycomb toffee).

On the outskirts of town, the ruined 15th-century **Bonamargy Friary** houses the remains of Sorley Boy MacDonnell, former chieftain of this part of Antrim. Sections of the church, gatehouse and cloisters are well preserved.

Irish Whiskey

The word whiskey comes from the Gaelic *uisce beatha*, meaning water of life. Distillation was probably introduced to Ireland by monks from Asia over 1,000 years ago. Small-scale production became part of the Irish way of life, but in the 17th century, the English introduced a licensing system and started to close down stills. In the 19th century, post-famine poverty and the Temperance movement combined to lower demand. The result was that Scotch whisky (with no "e") stole an export march on the Irish, but thanks to lower production costs, improved marketing and the rise in popularity of Irish coffee, sales have increased around the world.

Poster showing the Old Bushmills Distillery beside the River Bush

For hotels and restaurants in this region see pp302–3 and pp323–5

Environs

Off the A2, 5 km (3 miles) east of town, a narrow scenic road starts to wind its way along the coast to Cushendall. First stop is **Fair Head**, where a poorly marked path meanders across heathery marshland to towering cliffs 200 m (650 ft) above the sea. From here there are stunning views of Rathlin and the islands off the Scottish coast.

To the lee side of the headland lies **Murlough Bay**, the prettiest inlet along the coast. This can be reached by road. Further to the southeast stands **Torr Head**, a peninsula that reaches to within 21 km (13 miles) of the Mull of Kintyre, making it the closest point in Ireland to Scotland.

⑩ Cushendall

Road map D1. Co Antrim. 2,400. 25 Mill St (028 2177 1180). **Open** Jun–Sep: 10am–5pm Tue–Sat; Oct–May: 10am–1pm Tue–Sat. **moyle-council.org**

Three of the nine Glens of Antrim converge towards Cushendall, earning it the unofficial title of "Capital of the Glens". This attractive village has brightly painted houses and an edifice known as Curfew Tower, built in the early 19th century as a lock-up for thieves and idlers.

Carnlough Harbour, a popular stop south of Cushendall

Environs

About 1.5 km (1 mile) north of the village stands **Layde Old** Church. It can be reached by a pretty walk along the cliffs. Founded by the Franciscans, it was a parish church from 1306 to 1790 and contains many monuments to the local chieftains, the MacDonnells.

Just over 3 km (2 miles) west of Cushendall, on the slopes of Tievebulliagh Mountain, lies **Ossian's Grave**, named after the legendary warrior-poet and son of the giant Finn MacCool *(see pp30–31)*. It is in fact a Neolithic court tomb: the area was a major centre of Stone Age tool-making and axeheads made of Tievebulliagh's hard porcellanite rock have been found at a wide range of sites all over the British Isles.

Other attractive villages further south along the coast road include **Carnlough**, which has a fine sandy beach and a delightful harbour, and **Ballygally**, whose supposedly haunted 1625 castle is now a hotel *(see p302)*.

Glenariff Forest Park

⑪ Glenariff Forest Park

Road map D1. Co Antrim. **Tel** 028 2955 6000. **Open** daily. for car park. limited. **nidirect.gov.uk/ forests**

Nine rivers have carved deep valleys through the Antrim Mountains to the sea. Celebrated in song and verse, the Glens of Antrim used to be the wildest and most remote part of Ulster. This region was not "planted" with English and Scots settlers in the 17th century and was the last place in Northern Ireland where Gaelic was spoken.

Today the Antrim coast road brings all the glens within easy reach of the tourist. Glenariff Forest Park contains some of the most spectacular scenery. The main scenic path runs through thick woodland and wild-flower meadows and round the sheer sides of a gorge, past three waterfalls. There are also optional trails to distant mountain viewpoints. William Makepeace Thackeray, the 19th-century English novelist, called the landscape "Switzerland in miniature".

Stone circle and stone rows at Beaghmore

⓬ Cookstown

Road map D2. Co Tyrone. 11,000. Burnavon, Burn Road (028 8676 9949). Sat.
cookstown.gov.uk

Cookstown sticks in the memory for its grand central thoroughfare – 2 km (1 mile) long and perfectly straight. The road is about 40 m (130 ft) wide and, as you look to the north, it frames the bulky outline of Slieve Gallion, a prominent mountain in the Sperrin Mountains. A 17th-century Plantation town *(see pp42–3)*, Cookstown takes its name from its founder Alan Cook.

Environs

The countryside around Cookstown is rich in Neolithic and early Christian monuments. To the east, on a desolate stretch of Lough Neagh shoreline, the **Ardboe Old Cross** stands on the site of a 6th-century monastery. Although eroded, the 10th-century cross is one of the best examples of a High Cross *(see p246)* in Ulster: its 22 sculpted panels depict Old Testament scenes on the east side and New Testament ones on the west. The **Wellbrook Beetling Mill**, west of Cookstown, is a relic of Ulster's old linen industry. "Beetling" was the process of hammering the cloth to give it a sheen. Set amid trees beside the Ballinderry River, the mill dates from 1768 and is a popular tourist attraction. The National Trust has restored the whitewashed two-storey building and its water-wheel. Inside, working displays demonstrate just how loud "beetling" could be. From the mill, there are pleasant walks along the river banks.

Ardboe old Cross

Ardboe Old Cross
Off B73, 16 km (10 miles) E of Cookstown.

Wellbrook Beetling Mill
Off A505, 6.5 km (4 miles) W of Cookstown. **Tel** 028 8674 8210. **Open** mid-Mar–Jun & Sep: Sat & Sun pm; Jul–Aug: Thu–Sun pm. **Closed** Sep–Mar. **nationaltrust.org.uk**

⓭ Beaghmore Stone Circles

Road map D2. Co Tyrone. Off A505, 14 km (9 miles) NW of Cookstown.

On a stretch of open moorland in the foothills of the Sperrin Mountains lies a vast collection of stone monuments, dating from between 2000 and 1200 BC. There are seven stone circles, several stone rows and a number of less prominent features, possibly collapsed field walls of an earlier period. Their exact purpose remains unknown, though in some cases their alignment correlates with movements of the sun, moon and stars. Three of the rows, for example, are clearly aligned with the point where the sun rises at the summer solstice.

The individual circle stones are small – none is more than 1.20 m (4 ft) in height – but their sheer numbers make them a truly impressive sight. As well as the circles and rows, there are a dozen round cairns (burial mounds). Up until 1945, the whole complex, one of Ulster's major archaeological finds, had lain buried beneath a thick layer of peat.

Ulster's Historic Linen Industry

The rise in Ulster's importance as a linen producer was spurred on by the arrival from France of refugee Huguenot weavers at the end of the 17th century. Linen remained a flourishing industry for a further two centuries, but today it is produced only in small quantities for the luxury goods market. Hundreds of abandoned mills dot the former "Linen Triangle" bounded by Belfast, Armagh and Dungannon. One of the reasons why the material diminished in popularity was the expensive production process: after cutting, the flax had to be retted, or soaked, in large artificial ponds so that scutching – the separation of the fibres – could begin. After combing, the linen was spun and woven before being bleached in the sun, typically in fields along riverbanks. The final stage was "beetling", the process whereby the cloth was hammered to give it a sheen.

18th-century print, showing flax being prepared for spinning

⓮ The Wilson Ancestral Home

Road map C2. 28 Spout Road, Dergalt, Strabane, Co Tyrone. **Tel** 028 7138 4444. **Open** Jul–Aug: 2–5pm Tue–Sun (guided tour only). Visits at other times by arrangement. **strabanedc.com**

Located 3 km (2 miles) south-east of Strabane, off the road to Plumbridge, is the ancestral home of US President Thomas Woodrow Wilson (1856–1924). Woodrow's grandfather, Judge James Wilson, left this house for America in 1807 at the age of 20. Today, a visit to the thatched whitewashed house on the slopes of the Sperrin Mountains provides valuable insight into the history behind Ulster-American ties. The carefully conserved rooms contain original furniture including curtained beds, kitchen utensils and farm implements. A portrait of James Wilson hangs over the traditional hearth fire.

Environs

Just outside the village of Newtownstewart, 12 km (7 miles) south of Strabane, is the medieval ruin of Harry Avery's Castle. This 14th-century Gaelic stone castle consisted of two storeys fronted by vast rectangular twin towers. These towers are still visible today.

⓯ Ulster-American Folk Park

Road map C2. Co Tyrone. **Tel** 028 8224 3292. from Omagh. **Closed** Mon & public hols. **nmni.com/uafp**

One of the best open-air museums of its kind, the Folk Park grew up around the restored boyhood home of Judge Thomas Mellon (founder of the Pittsburgh banking dynasty). The Park's permanent exhibition, called "Emigrants", examines why two million people left Ulster for America during the 18th and 19th centuries. It also shows what became of them, with stories of both fortune and failure, including the grim lives of indentured servants and the 15,000 Irish vagrants and convicts sent to North America in the mid-18th century.

The park has more than 30 historic buildings, some of them original, some replicas. There are settler homesteads (including that of John Joseph Hughes, the first Catholic Archbishop of New York), churches, a schoolhouse and a forge, some with craft displays, all with costumed interpretative guides. There's also an Ulster streetscape, a reconstructed emigrant ship and a Pennsylvania farmstead. The farmhouse is based on one built by Thomas Mellon and his father in the early years of their life in America.

The Centre for Migration Studies assists descendants of emigrants to trace their family roots. Popular American festivals such as Independence Day and Hallowe'en are celebrated here and there is an Appalachian-Bluegrass music festival in early September.

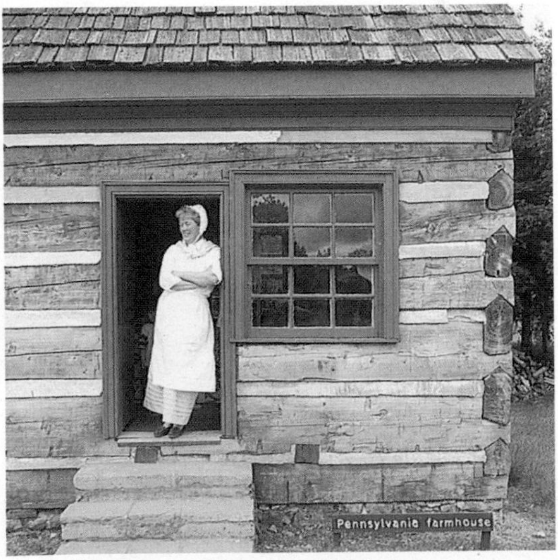

Pennsylvania log farmhouse at the Ulster-American Folk Park

Worker at the Belleek factory making a Parian ware figurine

⓰ Belleek Pottery

Road map C2. Belleek, Co Fermanagh. **Tel** 028 6865 9300. **Open** Jan–Feb: Mon–Fri; Mar–Dec: daily. **Closed** 1 week at Christmas. **belleek.com**

The little border village of Belleek would attract few visitors other than anglers were it not for the world-famous Belleek Pottery, founded in 1857. The company's pearly coloured china is known as Parian ware. Developed in the 19th century, it was supposed to resemble the famous Parian marble of Ancient Greece.

Belleek is now best known for its ornamental pieces of fragile latticework decorated with pastel-coloured flowers. These are especially popular in the USA. Several elaborate showpieces stand on display in the visitors' centre and small museum. There's also a 20-minute audiovisual presentation on the company's history, a gift shop and ample parking space for tour buses.

⑰ A Tour of Lower Lough Erne

Fermanagh lakelands around Lower Lough Erne boasts a rich combination of both natural and historic sights. From pre-Christian times, settlers sought the security offered by the lough's forests and inlets. Monasteries were founded on several of its many islands in the Middle Ages, and a ring of castles recalls the Plantation era *(see p43)*. The lake is a haven for waterbirds such as ducks, grebes and kingfishers, and the trout-rich waters attract many anglers. Lough Erne is a delight to explore by land or by boat. In summer, ferries serve several islands, and cruisers are available for hire.

View across Lower Lough Erne

⑤ Boa Island
Two curious double-faced figures stand in Caldragh cemetery, a Christian graveyard on Boa Island. While little is known about the stone idols, they are certainly pre-Christian.

⑥ Castle Caldwell Forest
Castle Caldwell's wooded peninsulas are a sanctuary for birds, and you can watch waterfowl from hides on the shore. You may see great crested grebes, the common scoter duck and perhaps even otters.

⑦ Belleek
Northern Ireland's most westerly village, Belleek is famous for its pottery *(see p273)*.

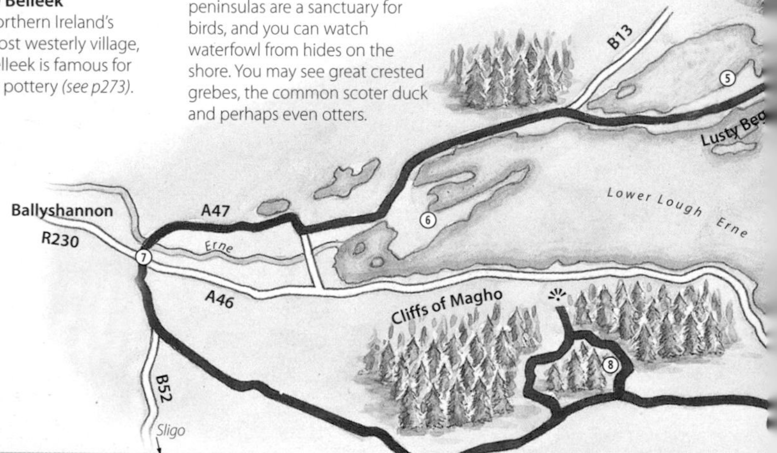

⑧ Lough Navar Forest Drive
An 11-km (7-mile) drive through pine forest leads to a viewpoint atop the Cliffs of Magho, with a magnificent panorama over Lough Erne and beyond. Trails weave through the woods.

Key

▬ Tour route

═ Other roads

Tips for Walkers

Length: 110 km (68 miles).
Stopping-off points: Outside Enniskillen, the best places to eat are the pubs in Kesh and Belleek; in summer, a café opens in Castle Archdale Country Park. There are good picnic places all along the route of this tour, including at the Cliffs of Magho viewpoint *(see also pp365–7)*.

⑨ Tully Castle
A delightful 17th-century-style herb garden has been planted and is maturing well alongside this fortified Plantation house.

④ **White Island**
The Romanesque church on White Island has bizarre pagan-looking figures set into one wall. Of uncertain origin, they probably adorned an earlier monastery on this site. Ferries to the island leave from Castle Archdale Marina in summer.

Boats moored at Castle Archdale Marina

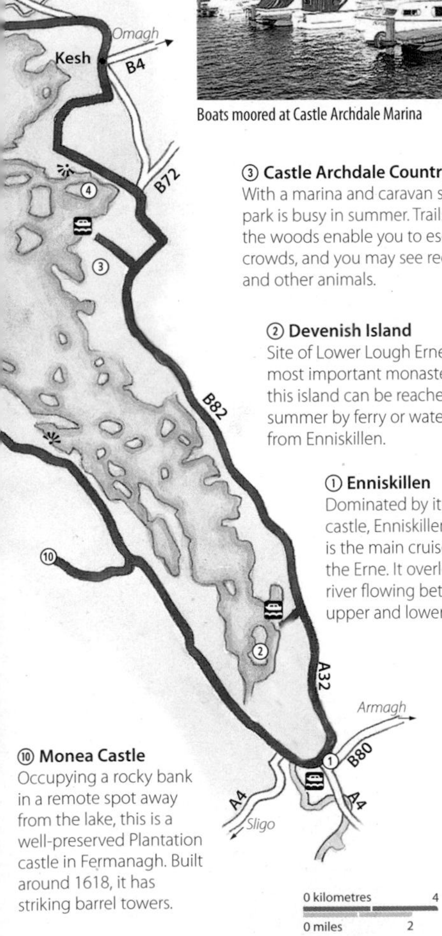

③ **Castle Archdale Country Park**
With a marina and caravan site, the park is busy in summer. Trails through the woods enable you to escape the crowds, and you may see red deer and other animals.

② **Devenish Island**
Site of Lower Lough Erne's most important monastery, this island can be reached in summer by ferry or water-bus from Enniskillen.

① **Enniskillen**
Dominated by its famous castle, Enniskillen *(see p276)* is the main cruiser base on the Erne. It overlooks the river flowing between the upper and lower loughs.

⑩ **Monea Castle**
Occupying a rocky bank in a remote spot away from the lake, this is a well-preserved Plantation castle in Fermanagh. Built around 1618, it has striking barrel towers.

Beautifully constructed round tower on Devenish Island

⑱ Devenish Island

Road map C2. Co Fermanagh. 028 6862 1588. Devenish Ferry (077 0205 2873) from Trory Point, 5 km (3 miles) N of Enniskillen: Easter–Sep: daily. for museum and tower.
discovernorthernireland.com

St Molaise III, who had 1,500 scholars under his tutelage, founded a monastery on this tiny windswept island in the 6th century. Though raided by Vikings in the 9th century and burned in 1157, it remained an important religious centre up to the early 17th century.

Several fine buildings have survived, including **Teampall Mor** near the jetty. Built in 1225, this church displays the transition between Romanesque and Gothic styles. On the highest ground stands **St Mary's Priory**, an Augustinian church that was erected in the 15th century. An intricately carved stone cross close by dates from the same period.

The most spectacular sight, however, is the 12th-century round tower, which stands some 25 m (82 ft) tall. From the high windows the monks could spot approaching strangers. It is perfectly preserved, and the five floors can be reached by internal ladders. Supporting the roof is an elaborate cornice with a human face carved above each of the four windows; this is a unique feature in an Irish round tower. A small museum covers both the history and architecture of the island, and contains a collection of antiquities discovered at the site.

⑲ Enniskillen

Road map C2. Co Fermanagh. 15,000. Wellington Road (028 6632 3110). Thu.
fermanaghlakelands.com

The busy tourist centre of Enniskillen occupies an island between Upper and Lower Lough Erne. The town gained fame for the wrong reason in 1987, when 11 people died in an IRA bomb attack, but it deserves a visit for its setting and sights.

At the west end of town stands **Enniskillen Castle**, dating from the 15th century. It houses **Fermanagh County Museum** and the Inniskilling Regimental Museum. Its most stunning feature, however, is the Watergate, a fairy-tale twin-turreted tower, best admired from the far bank of the river. Further west, **Portora Royal School**, founded in 1618, counts among its old boys the play-wrights Oscar Wilde and Samuel Beckett *(see pp26–7)*.

The **Cole Monument** stands in a pretty Victorian park on the east side of town. It is a tall Doric column with a spiral staircase that can be climbed for views of the lake country.

Enniskillen Castle seen from across the River Erne

Enniskillen Castle
Tel 028 6632 5000. **Open** Jul & Aug: 10am–5pm Tue–Fri, 2–5pm Sat–Mon; Apr–Jun & Sep-Oct: 10am–5pm Tue–Fri, 2–5pm Mon & Sat; Nov–Mar: 10am–5pm Tue–Fri, 2–5pm Mon. **Closed** 23 Dec–2 Jan. limited. **enniskillencastle.co.uk**

Environs

Just outside town, set in a park with mature oak woodland overlooking a lake, is **Castle Coole**, one of the finest Neo-Classical homes in Ireland. It has a long Portland stone façade, with a central portico and small pavilions at each end. The stone was shipped from Dorset to Ballyshannon. The first Earl of Belmore, who commissioned the house in the 1790s, was almost bankrupted by the cost of it. The original design was by Irish architect Richard Johnston, but the Earl then commissioned a second set of drawings by the fashionable English architect James Wyatt. The extravagant Earl died, deep in debt, in 1802 and it was left to his son to complete during the 1820s.

The glory of Castle Coole is that almost all the house's original furniture is still in place. Family portraits from the 18th century line the walls of the dining room. In the lavish State Bedroom there is a bed made specially for King George IV on the occasion of his visit to Ireland in 1821, though in the end he never came here to sleep in it. One of the finest rooms is the oval saloon (or ballroom) at the back of the house. The furnishings may not be to everyone's taste, but the spacious oak-floored room produces a magnificent effect of unostentatious luxury.

The saloon at Castle Coole, with original Regency furnishings

Castle Coole
Off A4, 2.4 km (1.5 miles) SE of Enniskillen. **Tel** 028 6632 2690. House: **Open** mid-Mar–end May & Sep: 11am–5pm Sat & Sun; Jun–Aug: 11am–5pm daily. **Closed** Sep–Mar. mandatory for house. Park: **Open** Mar–Oct: 10am–7pm daily; Nov–Feb: 10am–4pm daily.
nationaltrust.org.uk

⑳ Marble Arch Caves Global Geopark

Road map C2. Marlbank Scenic Loop, Florencecourt, Co Fermanagh. **Tel** 028 6634 8855. **Open** end Mar–Jun & Sep–Oct: 10am–4:30pm, Jul–Aug: 10am–5pm daily (phone first as bad weather can cause closure). obligatory.
marblearchcavesgeopark.com

The marble arch caves are cut by three streams which flow down the slopes of Cuilcagh Mountain, unite underground and emerge as the Cladagh River. Tours lasting 75 minutes consist of a boat ride into the depths of the cave complex and a guided walk that leads past stalagmites, calcite cascades and other curious limestone formations. The 9-m (30-ft) "Marble Arch" itself stands outside the cave system in the glen where the river gushes out from below ground.

The caves are very popular, so book ahead. It is best to ring to check the local weather conditions before setting out; the caves may be closed because of rain. Whatever the weather, bring a sweater and sensible walking shoes.

Boat trip through Marble Arch Caves Global Geopark

㉑ Florence Court

Road map C2. Co Fermanagh. **Tel** 028 6634 8249. House: **Open** times vary: check National Trust website. obligatory. Grounds: **Open** daily. for car park.
nationaltrust.org.uk

This three-storey Palladian mansion was built for the Cole family in the mid-18th century. The arcades and pavilions, which are of a later date than the main house, were added around 1770 by William Cole, first Earl of Enniskillen. The house features flamboyant Rococo plasterwork said to be by the Dublin stuccodore Robert West. Sadly, however, not much of what you see today is original as most of the central block was seriously damaged by fire in 1955. Much of the furniture was lost, but the plasterwork was painstakingly recreated from photographs. The finest examples are in the dining room, the staircase and the small Venetian room.

Perhaps more spectacular than the mansion are the grounds, which occupy a natural mountain-ringed amphitheatre. There are many enjoyable walks around the house. One woodland trail leads to the famous Florence Court yew tree, whose descendants are to be found all over Ireland. Closer to the house is a walled garden where pink and white roses make an attractive sight in summer.

㉒ Dungannon

Road map D2. Co Tyrone. 11,000. Ranfurly House, 26 Market Sq, Dungannon (028 8772 8600). Thu.
flavouroftyrone.com

Dungannon's hilly location made an ideal site for the seat of government of the O'Neill dynasty from the 14th century until Plantation *(see pp42–3)*, when their castle was razed. The town's **Royal School** is one of the oldest in Northern Ireland; it was chartered in 1608 by James I. Opened in 1614, it moved to its present site in 1789.

Once a major linen centre, this busy market town was also known for its glass-making, as it was the base of the famous Tyrone crystal factory. The factory closed in 2010, however.

The Linen Green shopping centre in nearby Moygashel offers factory outlet shopping from brands such as Newbridge Silverwear and Ulster Weavers.

Florence Court, the former seat of the Earls of Enniskillen

View of Armagh dominated by St Patrick's Roman Catholic Cathedral

23 Armagh

Road map D2. Co Armagh. 15,000. 40 English St (028 3752 1800). Tue & Fri. **armagh.co.uk**

One of Ireland's oldest cities, Armagh dates back to the age of St Patrick *(see p285)* and the advent of Christianity. The narrow streets in the city centre follow the ditches that once ringed the church, founded by the saint in 455. Two cathedrals, both called **St Patrick's**, sit on opposing hills. The huge Roman Catholic one is a twin-spired Neo-Gothic building with seemingly every inch of wall covered in mosaic. The older Anglican Cathedral dates back to medieval times. It boasts the bones of Brian Ború, the King of Ireland who defeated the Vikings in 1014 *(see pp38–9)*, and an 11th-century High Cross.

Armagh's gorgeous oval, tree-lined Mall, where cricket is played in summer, is surrounded by dignified Georgian buildings. One of these houses the small **Armagh County Museum**, which has a good exhibition on local history. Off the Mall, **St Patrick's Trian** is a heritage centre telling the story of the city. It also has a "Land of Lilliput" fantasy centre for children, based on *Gulliver's Travels* by Jonathan Swift *(see p86)*. The Armagh Planetarium is on College Hill in the **Observatory Grounds**, from where there are splendid views over the city.

Armagh County Museum
The Mall East. **Tel** 028 3752 3070. **Open** Mon–Sat. **Closed** some public hols. by arrangement. **nmni.com/acm**

Craftswirl
40 Upper English St. **Tel** 028 3752 1800. **Open** daily. **armagh.co.uk/place/craftswirl**

Observatory Grounds
College Hill. **Tel** 028 3752 3689. **Open** by appt only. Grounds: open Mon–Fri. Planetarium: **Tel** 028 3752 3689. **Open** varies; check website. for shows. **armaghplanet.com**

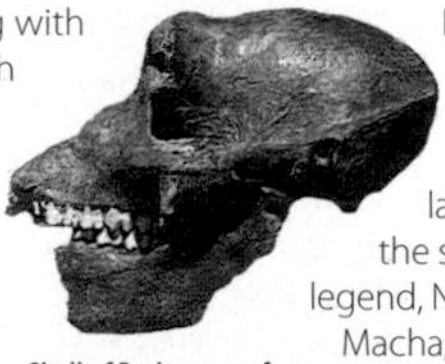

Skull of Barbary ape from Navan Fort

Environs

To the west of Armagh stands **Navan Fort**, a large earthwork on the summit of a hill. In legend, Navan was Emain Macha, ceremonial and spiritual capital of ancient Ulster, associated with tales of the warrior Cúchulainn *(see p30)*. The site may have been in use as much as 4,000 years ago, but seems to have been most active around 100 BC when a huge timber building, 40 m (130 ft) across, was erected over a giant cairn. The whole thing was then burned and the remains covered with soil. Archaeological evidence indicates that this was not an act of war, but a solemn ritual performed by the inhabitants of Emain Macha themselves.

Below the fort, the grass-roofed **Navan Centre** interprets the site. It is open to groups outside of the main summer season. One unexpected exhibit is the skull of a Barbary ape, found in the remains of a Bronze Age house. The animal must come from Spain or North Africa, evidence that by 500 BC Emain Macha was already a place with far-flung trading links.

Navan Centre
On A28 4 km (2.5 miles) W of Armagh. **Tel** 028 3752 9644. **Open** daily.

24 Lough Neagh

Road map D2. Co Armagh, Co Tyrone, Co Londonderry, Co Antrim.

Legend has it that the giant Finn MacCool *(see pp30–31)* created Lough Neagh by picking up a piece of turf and hurling it into the Irish Sea, thus forming the Isle of Man in the process. At 400 sq km (153 sq miles), the lake is the largest in Britain.

Bordered by sedgy marshland, it has few roads along its shore. The best recreational areas lie in the south: Oxford Island, actually a peninsula, has walking trails, bird lookouts and the informative **Lough Neagh Discovery Centre**. In the southwest corner, a narrow-gauge railway runs through the bogs of **Peatlands Park**. Salmon and

Navan Fort, the site of Emain Macha, legendary capital of Ulster

Hide for bird-watchers at Oxford Island on the southern shore of Lough Neagh

trout swim in the rivers that flow from Lough Neagh. The lake is famous for its eels, with one of the world's largest eel fisheries at **Toome**.

Lough Neagh Discovery Centre
Oxford Island. Exit 10 off M1.
Tel 028 3832 2205. **Open** daily.
Closed 24–26 Dec.
oxfordisland.com

Peatlands Park
Exit 13 off M1. **Tel** 028 3885 1102.
Park: **Open** daily. **Closed** 24 & 25 Dec.
Visitors' centre: **Open** Apr–mid-Sep: 1–7pm daily; Sep–Mar: noon–4pm Sat & Sun **doeni.gov.uk/niea**

25 Larne

Road map D1. Co Antrim. 20,000. Narrow Gauge Rd (028 2826 0088). **larne.gov.uk**

Industrial Larne is the arrival point for ferries from Scotland *(see pp362–4)*. The town is not the finest introduction to Ulster scenery, but it lies on the threshold of the magnificent Antrim coastline *(see p271)*.

The sheltered waters of Larne Lough have been a landing point since Mesolithic times – flint flakes found here provide some of the earliest evidence of human presence on the island – nearly 9,000 years ago. Since then, Norsemen used the lough as a base in the 10th century, Edward Bruce landed his Scottish troops in the area in 1315, and in 1914 the Ulster Volunteer Force landed a huge cache of German arms here during its campaign against Home Rule *(see pp48–9)*.

26 Carrickfergus

Road map E2. Co Antrim. 42,000. Antrim St (028 9335 8049). **Open** Apr–Sep: 10am–6pm, Oct–Mar: 10am–5pm. **Closed** Sun. Thu.
carrickfergus.org

Carrickfergus grew up around the massive castle begun in 1180 by John de Courcy to guard the entrance to Belfast Lough. De Courcy was the leader of the Anglo-Norman force which invaded Ulster following Strongbow's conquest of Leinster in the south *(see pp40–41)*.

Carrickfergus Castle was shaped to fit the crag on which it stands overlooking the harbour. The finest and best-preserved Norman castle in Ireland, it even has its original portcullis *(see pp40–41)*. Many changes have been made since the 12th century, including wide ramparts to accommodate the castle's cannons. Life-size model soldiers are posed along the ramparts. In continuous use up to 1928, the castle has changed hands several times over the years. Under Edward Bruce, the Scots took it in 1315, holding it for three years. James II's army was in control of the castle from 1688 until General Schomberg took it for William III in 1690. William himself stayed here before the Battle of the Boyne *(see p248)* in 1690.

De Courcy also founded the pretty **St Nicholas' Church**. Inside are rare stained-glass work and a "leper window", through which the afflicted received the sacraments. Other attractions include the **Andrew Jackson Centre**, the ancestral home of the seventh president of the USA, and **Flame**, a museum based around a Victorian coal gasworks.

Carrickfergus Castle
Tel 028 9335 1273. **Open** daily.
Closed 24–26 Dec, 1 Jan. limited. **discovernorthernireland.com**

Andrew Jackson Centre
2 Boneybefore. **Tel** 028 9335 8049.
Open by appt only.

The massive Norman keep of Carrickfergus Castle

27 Belfast

Belfast was the only city in Ireland to experience the full force of the Industrial Revolution. Its ship-building, linen, rope-making and tobacco industries caused the population to rise to almost 400,000 by the end of World War I. The "Troubles" and the decline of heavy industry have somewhat hampered economic life, but regeneration projects, such as Laganside, the Titanic Quarter, Victoria Square and the Cathedral Quarter, are breathing new life into run-down areas and Belfast remains a friendly, handsome city.

Mosaic in St Anne's Cathedral, showing St Patrick's journey to Ireland *(see p285)*

Interior of the Grand Opera House

Belfast City Hall

Donegall Square. **Tel** 028 9027 0456. call ahead for tour details.

Most of Belfast's main streets radiate out from the hub of Donegall Square. In the centre of the square stands the vast rectangular Portland stone bulk of the 1906 City Hall. It has an elaborate tower at each corner and a central copper dome that rises to a height of 53 m (173 ft). Highlight of the tour of the interior is the sumptuous oak-panelled council chamber.

Statues around the building include a glum-looking Queen Victoria outside the main entrance and, on the east side, Sir Edward Harland, founder of the Harland and Wolff shipyard, which built the *Titanic*. A memorial to those who died when the *Titanic* sank in 1912 stands close by.

Grand Opera House

Great Victoria St. **Tel** 028 9024 1919.
goh.co.uk

Designed by Frank Matcham, the renowned theatre architect, this exuberant late Victorian building opened its doors in 1894. The sumptuous interior, with its gilt, red plush and intricate plasterwork, was restored to its full glory in 1980. On occasions, bombings of the adjacent Europa Hotel disrupted business at the theatre, but it survives as a major venue for plays and theatre.

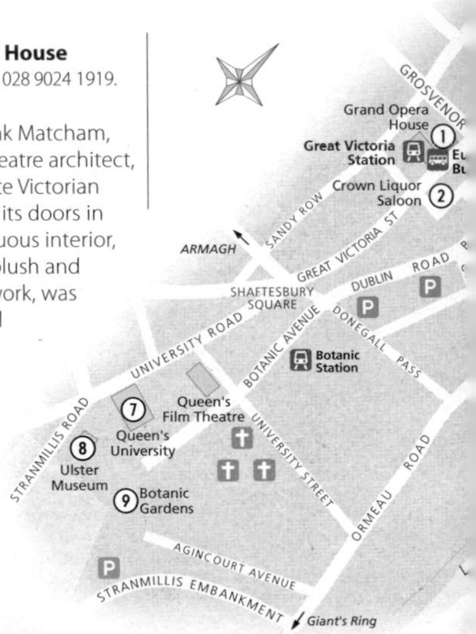

Key to Symbols *see back flap*

Sights at a Glance

1. Grand Opera House
2. Crown Liquor Saloon
3. Belfast City Hall
4. Linen Hall Library
5. The Entries
6. St Anne's Cathedral
7. Queen's University
8. Ulster Museum
9. Botanic Gardens
10. Albert Memorial Clock Tower
11. W5
12. Titanic Belfast

0 metres 500
0 yards 500

St Anne's Cathedral

Donegall St. **Tel** 028 9032 8332.
belfastcathedral.org

Consecrated in 1904, this Anglican cathedral took over 100 years to be completed. The impressive interior includes mosaics executed by the two Misses Martin in the 1930s. The one covering the baptistry ceiling contains over 150,000 pieces. The wide nave is paved with Canadian maple and the aisles with Irish marble. Lord Carson (1854–1935), leader of the campaign against Home Rule *(see p48)*, is buried in the south aisle.

Detail of *Titanic* Memorial outside Belfast City Hall

For hotels and restaurants in this region see pp302–3 and pp323–5

Linen Hall Library

17 Donegall Square North. **Tel** 028 9032 1707. **Open** Mon–Sat. **W** **linenhall.com**

Founded as the Belfast Society for Promoting Knowledge in 1788, Belfast's oldest library has thousands of rare, old books and is Ireland's last subscribing library. It is renowned for its unparalleled

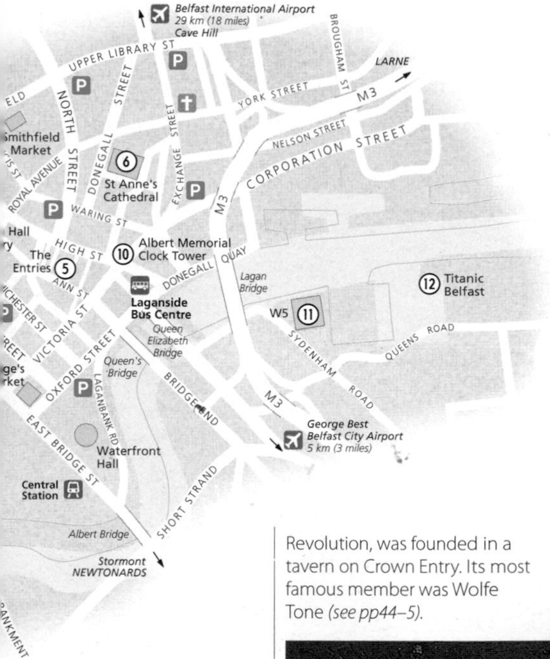

Irish and Local Studies Collection, ranging from comprehensive holdings of printed books to the 250,000 items in the Northern Ireland Political Collection, the definitive archive of the recent troubles. There is also a vast database of genealogical information as well as regular exhibitions. Above the library door you will see the Red Hand of Ulster, the emblem of the province. It is the subject of a gory legend about two Celtic heroes racing to see who would touch the land of Ulster first. In his determination to win, one cut off his own hand and threw it to the shore.

The Entries

The Entries are a series of narrow alleys just off High Street, dating from at least 1630 and marking the oldest part of the city. They feature some of the oldest pubs in the city, including White's Tavern *(see p331)*. McCracken's in Joy's Entry and the Morning Star on Pottinger's Entry both serve excellent lunches. In 1791, the United Irishmen, a radical movement inspired by the new ideas of the French Revolution, was founded in a tavern on Crown Entry. Its most famous member was Wolfe Tone *(see pp44–5)*.

VISITORS' CHECKLIST

Practical Information

Road map D2. Co Antrim. 500,000. 9 Donegall Square North (028 9024 6609). **W** **visit-belfast.com** Balmoral Show (May) & Belfast City Carnival (Jun).

Transport

George Best City Airport, 6.5 km (4 miles) E; Belfast International, 29 km (18 miles) NW. Central Station, East Bridge St (028 9066 6630); Great Victoria St Station (028 9066 6630). Europa Bus Centre, Great Victoria St; Laganside Bus Centre, Oxford St (028 9066 6630).

Crown Liquor Saloon

Great Victoria St. **Tel** 028 9024 3187. **Open** daily. **W** **nationaltrust.gov.uk**

Even teetotallers should make a detour to the tiled façade of this Victorian drinking palace. The Crown, which dates back to the 1880s, is the most famous pub in Belfast; today, it is a Grade A building and treasured landmark. The lovingly restored interior features stained glass, marbling, mosaics and a splendid ceiling with scrolled plasterwork. The wooden snugs facing the bar have their original gas lamps: the perfect place for a pint of Guinness and some Strangford Lough mussels.

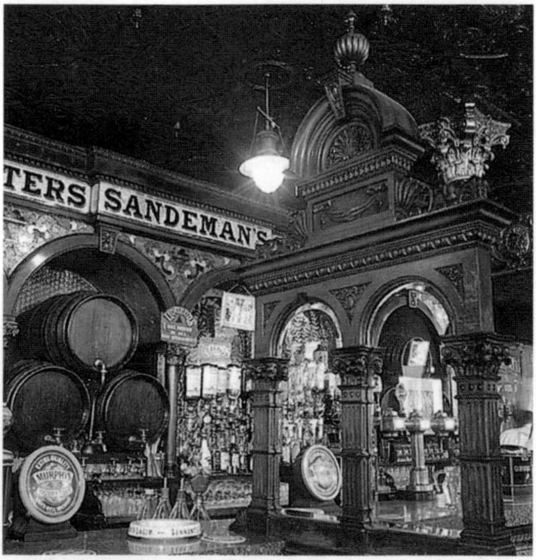

The ornate Victorian interior of the Crown Liquor Saloon

Exploring Belfast

Away from the city centre, Belfast has many pleasant suburbs to explore. The Queen's Quarter around Queen's University to the south of the city has two major attractions in the Ulster Museum and the Botanic Gardens. To the north, there are splendid views to be enjoyed from the heights of Cave Hill, while visitors interested in Belfast's industrial heritage will be keen to visit the Titanic Quarter, the old docks and the Harland and Wolff working shipyards.

Interior of the Victorian Palm House at the Botanic Gardens

Ulster Museum

Botanic Gardens. **Tel** 0845 608 0000. **Open** 10am–5pm Tue–Sun & bank hols on Mon. **nmni.com/um**

Founded in 1929 as the Belfast Municipal Museum and Art Gallery, the Ulster Museum reopened in 2009 following a £17 million refurbishment. Its galleries house rich collections of art, local history, natural sciences and archaeology. Modern Irish art is particularly well represented, while the 6 m- (20 ft-) long Edmontosaurus dinosaur skeleton in the Window On Our World display tower is one of Ulster's most popular exhibits along with Takabuti, the Egyptian mummy. In addition to its permanent collection, the museum has a changing programme of temporary exhibitions and events, several learning zones and plenty of opportunities for hands-on activities, including interactive areas where visitors can try on Victorian costumes and handle the skull of a two-headed calf.

Botanic Gardens

Botanic Ave. **Tel** 028 9032 4902. **Open** daily. **belfastcity.gov.uk**

Backing on to the university, the Botanic Gardens provide a quiet refuge from the bustle of campus. The 1839 Palm House is a superb example of curvilinear glass and cast-iron work. The Tropical Ravine, or Fernery, is another fine piece of Victorian garden architecture. Visitors can look down from the balcony to a sunken glen of exotic plants.

Large-scale metal sculpture outside the Ulster Museum

Queen's University

University Rd. **Tel** 028 9024 5133 **qub.ac.uk**

A 15-minute stroll south from Donegall Square, through the lively entertainment district known as the Golden Mile, leads to Northern Ireland's most prestigious university. The main building, designed by Charles Lanyon in 1849, bears similarities to Magdalene College, Oxford. A towered gateway leads to a colonnaded quadrangle.

W5

Odyssey, 2 Queen's Quay. **Tel** 028 9046 7700. **Open** daily (Sun: pm only). **w5online.co.uk**

W5, short for "whowhatwhere whenwhy", is an award-winning interactive museum, which presents science as an exciting process of discovery.

The Political Murals of West Belfast

Republican mural in the Falls Road

During the period of the "Troubles" (1968–1998), popular art played a conspicuous role in proclaiming the loyalties of Belfast's two most intransigent working-class communities, on the Protestant Shankill Road and the Catholic Falls Road. The gable walls of dozens of houses in these areas have been decorated with vivid murals expressing local political and paramilitary affiliations. Likewise, kerbstones on certain streets are painted either in the red, white and blue of the United Kingdom or the green, white and gold of Ireland. Even with the successes of the current peace process, many are likely to remain. Some tourists make the journey out to West Belfast just to see the murals. The simplest way to do this is to pre-book a "Black Cab Tour" through the Belfast Welcome Centre. Call 028 9024 6609.

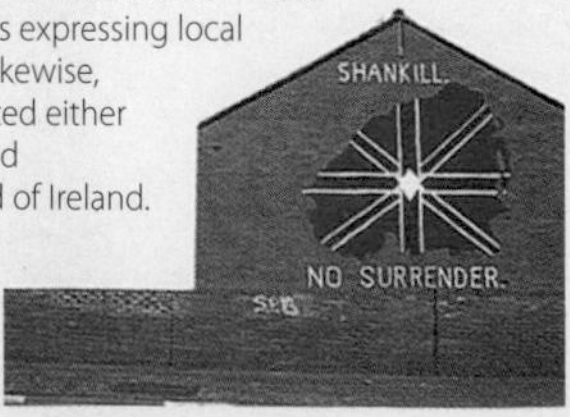

Protestant Loyalist mural

It has over 200 hands-on exhibits and experiments. Among many fascinating activities on offer, visitors can try working a replica of a Port of Belfast crane, sneak up on a butterfly, lift themselves up with pulleys, create an animated film or compose music on a laser harp.

Titanic Quarter

Queen's Road, Queen's Island. **Tel** 028 9076 6300. Titanic Belfast: **Tel** 028 9076 6386. **Open** Apr, Jun–Aug: 9am–7pm daily; May & Sep: 9am–6pm daily; Oct–Mar: 10am–5pm daily. **Closed** 24–26 Dec. **W titanicbelfast.com**

The doomed RMS *Titanic*, struck by an iceberg on its maiden voyage in 1912, was built in Belfast's docklands, and this area is now called the Titanic Quarter. The waterfront is being redeveloped, and space has been created for shops, restaurants, hotels and offices.

Titanic Belfast, a tourist attraction which opened in 2012 to mark the centenary of the fateful voyage, now sits above the ship's slipway. Boat, bus and walking tours, led by a descendant of one of the crew members, explore this vibrant area.

Inside the centre, there are nine galleries with interactive exhibits that guide visitors through the construction of the *Titanic* and its recovery. There is also an underwater exploration theatre. The restored SS *Nomadic*, the last remaining vessel of the White Star Line, is also worth a visit.

The Visitor's Centre at the Edwardian pump house next to the Titanic dry dock is an excellent way to get a sense of the maritime history that stretches back to the 1600s; the restaurant and café here make for a good pit stop. Elsewhere in the Quarter, visitors can trace their roots at the Public Record Office of Northern Ireland.

Albert Memorial Clock Tower

Queen's Square.

One of Belfast's best-known monuments, today the clock tower leans slightly as a result of subsidence. Beyond it, facing the river, stands the Custom House (1854) by Charles Lanyon, architect of Queen's University.

The Titanic Belfast, located in the Titanic Quarter

Cave Hill

Antrim Rd, 6.5 km (4 miles) N of city. Belfast Castle **Tel** 028 9077 6925. **Open** daily. **Closed** 25 Dec. **W belfastcity.gov.uk** Belfast Zoo: **Tel** 028 9077 6277. **Open** daily. **Closed** 25 & 26 Dec. **W belfastzoo.co.uk**

It was on Cave Hill, next to MacArt's Fort (named after an Iron Age chieftain), that Wolfe Tone *(see p45)* and the northern leaders of the United Irishmen met in 1795 to pledge themselves to rebellion. The five artificial caves near the fort were carved out during the Neolithic period.

On the wooded eastern slopes of the hill stands the baronial pile of Belfast Castle, built in 1870. Previously home to the Earl of Shaftesbury, the castle now belongs to the city and houses a restaurant and a visitors' centre that interprets the area's history. A little further along the road past the castle is Belfast Zoo. The zoo is home to over 1,200 animals and 140 species, including African wild dogs and Barbary lions.

Giant's Ring

Off B23, 5 km (3 miles) S of city centre.

Little is known about this awe-inspiring prehistoric enclosure almost 200 m (660 ft) in diameter. It is surrounded by a grassy bank averaging almost 6 m (20 ft) in width and 4.5 m (15 ft) in height. Bones from a Stone Age burial were found under the dolmen in the centre. During the 18th century the ring was a popular venue for horse races.

Stormont

Newtownards Rd, 8 km (5 miles) SE of city centre. **Closed** to the public. by arrangement only.

Built between 1928 and 1932, at a cost of £1,250,000, Stormont was designed to house the Northern Ireland Parliament. The huge Anglo-Palladian mass of Portland stone and Mourne granite stands at the end of a majestic avenue, 1.6 km (1 mile) long, bordered by parkland. A statue of Lord Carson *(see p48)* stands near the front entrance.

Since the parliament was disbanded in 1972, the building has been used as government offices. Although it has been suspended on several occasions, the devolved Northern Ireland Assembly has sat here since the 1998 Agreement.

Stormont in its parkland setting outside Belfast

28 Ulster Folk and Transport Museum

Road map E2. Cultra, near Holywood, Co Down. **Tel** 028 9042 8428. **Open** Tue–Sun & bank hols on Mon. **Closed** Christmas period. free for the disabled. **nmni.com/uftm**

This museum was set up following an act of parliament in 1958, to show the life and traditions of people in Northern Ireland. Demonstrations of traditional crafts, industries and farming methods are given.

The A2 road splits the folk museum from the transport section. This is dominated by a hangar that houses the Irish Railway Collection. The smaller Transport Gallery exhibits machinery made in Ulster, including a saloon carriage from the tram service that ran from Portrush to Giant's Causeway *(see pp266–7)*. Of particular note is a test model of the unsuccessful De Lorean car, made in Northern Ireland in the early 1980s with a huge government subsidy. There's also a popular exhibit on another ill-fated construction – the *Titanic*. It's best to allow half a day to take in most of the attractions.

Scrabo Tower, a prominent landmark of the Ards Peninsula

1883 tram carriage at the Ulster Folk and Transport Museum

29 Ards Peninsula

Road map E2. Co Down. to Bangor. Newtownards (028 9182 6846). **ards-council.gov.uk**

The peninsula – and some of Northern Ireland's finest scenery – begins east of Belfast at **Bangor**. This resort town has a modern marina and some well-known yacht clubs. A little way south is **Donaghadee**, from where boats sail to the three **Copeland Islands**, inhabited only by sea birds since the departure of the last human residents in the 1940s. The **Ballycopeland Windmill** (1784) is Northern Ireland's only working windmill and stands on the top of a small hill a little further south, near the town of Millisle.

Just across the peninsula is **Newtownards**. On a hill above the town is the pleasant and shady **Scrabo Country Park**. In the park stands the **Scrabo Tower**, built in 1857 as a memorial to the third Marquess of Londonderry.

Past the grounds of **Mount Stewart House** *(see pp286–7)* is the hamlet of Greyabbey, with its antique shops and Cistercian abbey ruins. Founded in 1193, **Grey Abbey** was used as a parish church until the 17th century. It is idyllically set in lush meadows by a stream and some of its features, particularly the finely carved west doorway, are well preserved.

On the tip of the peninsula, **Portaferry** overlooks the Strangford Narrows across from the Lecale Peninsula *(see p288)*. Portaferry's large aquarium, **Exploris**, displays the diversity of life in the Irish Sea and Strangford Lough.

Ballycopeland Windmill
On B172 1.6 km (1 mile) W of Millisle. **Tel** 028 9181 1491. **Open** Jul–Aug: 10am–5pm daily. limited.

Scrabo Country Park
Near Newtownards. **Tel** 028 918 1491. **Open** daily. Tower: **Open** Apr–May, Oct & Mar: weekends; Jun–Sep: daily; Nov–Feb: Sun.

Grey Abbey
Greyabbey. **Tel** 028 9181 1491. **Open** varies, call ahead.

Exploris
Castle Street, Portaferry. **Tel** 028 4272 8062. **Open** daily. **Closed** 24–26 Dec. **exploris.org.uk**

Ballycopeland Windmill, which dates back to 1784

30 Mount Stewart House

See pp286–7.

31 Hillsborough

Road map D2. Co Down. 4,000. The Square (028 9268 9717).
discovernorthernireland.com

Dotted with craft shops and restaurants, this Georgian town lies less than 16 km (10 miles) from Belfast. **Hillsborough Castle**, with its wrought-iron gates and coat of arms, is where visiting dignitaries to Northern Ireland normally stay.

Across from the 18th-century Market House in the town square is **Hillsborough Fort**. An artillery fort dating from 1650, it was remodelled in the 18th century for feasts held by the descendants of Arthur Hill, founder of the town.

Hillsborough Castle
Tel 028 9268 9406. **Open** Apr–Sep: 10:30am–5pm daily.

Hillsborough Fort
Access from town square or car park at Forest Park. **Tel** 028 9054 3030. **Closed** Mon. by arrangement.
visitlisburn.com

32 Downpatrick

Road map E2. Co Down. 19,000. 53a Market St (028 4461 2233). **Open** Sep–Jun: Mon–Sat; Jul–Aug: daily (Sun pm only). Sat.

Were it not for its strong links with St Patrick, Downpatrick would attract few visitors. The Anglican **Down Cathedral**, high on the Hill of Down, dates in its present form from the early 19th century – previous incarnations have been razed. In the churchyard is a well-worn 10th-century cross and the reputed burial place of St Patrick, marked by a 20th-century granite slab with the inscription "Patric".

Down County Museum, which is housed in the 18th-century Old County Gaol, features refurbished cells and exhibits relating to St Patrick, while close by is the **Mound of Down**, a large Norman motte and bailey.

Terraced houses in the town of Hillsborough

Down County Museum
English Street, The Mall. **Tel** 028 4461 5218. **Open** daily. **Closed** Christmas; Sat & Sun am.
downcountymuseum.com

Environs

There are several sights linked to St Patrick on the outskirts of Downpatrick. **Struell Wells**, believed to be a former pagan place of worship that the saint blessed, has a ruined church and 17th-century bathhouses. Further out and to the north at **Saul**, near where St Patrick landed and began his Irish mission in 432, is a small memorial church.

The nearby hill of **Slieve Patrick** is an important place of pilgrimage and has a granite figure of the saint at its summit.

Not far from the banks of the River Quoile is the Cistercian **Inch Abbey**, founded by John de Courcy in about 1180. Its attractive marshland setting is more memorable than its remains, but it's worth a visit.

Inch Abbey
5 km (3 miles) NW of Downpatrick.
Tel 028 9181 1491. **Open** daily.
doeni.gov.uk/niea

The Life of St Patrick

Little hard information is known about St Patrick, the patron saint of Ireland, but he was probably not the first missionary to visit the country – a certain Palladius was sent by Pope Celestine in 431. Most stories tell that Patrick was kidnapped from Britain by pirates and brought to Ireland to tend sheep. From here he escaped to France to study Christianity. In 432, he sailed back to Ireland and in Saul, County Down, he quickly converted the local chieftain. He then travelled throughout the island convincing many other Celtic tribes of the truth of the new religion. The fact that Ireland has no snakes is explained by a legend that St Patrick drove them all into the sea.

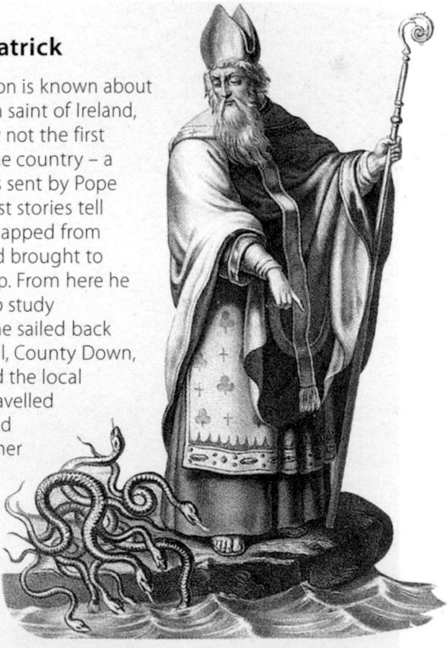
19th-century engraving showing St Patrick banishing all snakes from Ireland

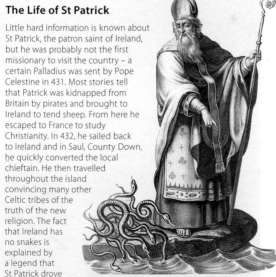

㉚ Mount Stewart House

This grand 19th-century house has a splendid interior, and the magnificent gardens are the main attraction. These were planted only in the 1920s, but the exotic plants and trees have thrived in the area's subtropical microclimate. Now owned by the National Trust, Mount Stewart used to belong to the Londonderry family, the most famous of whom was Lord Castlereagh, British Foreign Secretary from 1812 until his death in 1822. The house and it's treasures have recently benefited from a major restoration project by the National Trust.

★ Shamrock Garden
A yew hedge in the shape of a shamrock encloses this topiary Irish harp and a striking flower- bed designed in the form of a red hand, emblem of Ulster.

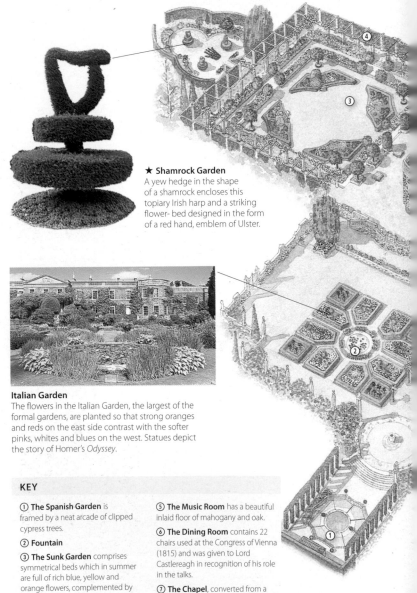

Italian Garden
The flowers in the Italian Garden, the largest of the formal gardens, are planted so that strong oranges and reds on the east side contrast with the softer pinks, whites and blues on the west. Statues depict the story of Homer's *Odyssey*.

KEY

① **The Spanish Garden** is framed by a neat arcade of clipped cypress trees.

② **Fountain**

③ **The Sunk Garden** comprises symmetrical beds which in summer are full of rich blue, yellow and orange flowers, complemented by purple foliage.

④ **Stone pergola**

⑤ **The Music Room** has a beautiful inlaid floor of mahogany and oak.

⑥ **The Dining Room** contains 22 chairs used at the Congress of Vienna (1815) and was given to Lord Castlereagh in recognition of his role in the talks.

⑦ **The Chapel**, converted from a sitting room in 1884, is still used by the Londonderry family.

★ **Hambletonian by George Stubbs**
This picture of the celebrated racehorse at Newmarket, painted in 1799, hangs halfway up the main staircase.

VISITORS' CHECKLIST

Practical Information
Road map E2. 3 km (2 miles) N of Greyabbey, Co Down. **Tel** 028 4278 8387. **W nationaltrust.org** House: **Open** call before visiting; undergoing renovations. Temple: **Open** Apr–Oct: 2–5pm Sun & public hols. Gardens: **Open** Mar–Oct: daily. Lake: **Open** all year. in house.

Transport
from Belfast.

Entrance Hall
The most austere room in the house, this hall features Ionic stone pillars which have been painted to resemble green marble. It is lit by an impressive glass dome.

The Temple of the Winds

This banqueting pavilion offers fantastic views over Strangford Lough and the Mourne Mountains beyond. It was built in 1785 by James "Athenian" Stuart, a renowned pioneer of Neo-Classical architecture, who took his inspiration from the Tower of the Winds in Athens. Restored in the 1960s, the building's finest features are the spiral staircase and the upper room's plasterwork ceiling and exquisite inlaid floor.

★ **Dodo Terrace**
The stone dodos and ark on this terrace relate to the Ark Club, a social circle set up by Lady Londonderry in London during World War I. Each member was given an animal nickname.

Lady Bangor's Gothic boudoir in Castle Ward on the Lecale Peninsula

33 Lecale Peninsula

Road map E2 Co Down. to Ardglass. Downpatrick (028 4461 2233). **discovernorthernireland.com**

A good way to get to this part of County Down is to take a car ferry from Portaferry on the Ards Peninsula to Strangford. Just outside this tiny port is **Castle Ward**, the estate of Lord and Lady Bangor, who seemed to argue about everything – including the design of their 18th-century mansion. His choice, Palladian, can be seen at the front, while her favourite Gothic style influences the garden façade. Likewise, interiors are a mix of Classical and Gothic fantasy. Look out for Lady Bangor's cluttered boudoir, with its extravagant fan-vaulted ceiling based on Henry VIII's chapel in Westminster Abbey. Around the grounds are trails, gardens, play areas and a farm-yard with a working corn mill.

About 4 km (2.5 miles) south of Strangford, the A2 passes **Kilclief Castle**, dating from the 15th century, one of the oldest tower houses *(see p24)* in Ireland. The road continues to **Ardglass**, now a small fishing village but once Ulster's busiest harbour. A cluster of castles was erected between the 14th and 16th centuries to protect the port, of which six remain. **St John's Point**, 6 km (3.5 miles) southwest of Ardglass, offers a sweeping panorama over Dundrum Bay.

Castle Ward

On A25, 2.5 km (1.5 miles) W of Strangford. **Tel** 028 4488 1204. House: **Open** Easter, Jul & Aug: noon–5pm daily; Apr–Jun: noon–5pm Wed–Sun; Sep & Oct: noon–5pm weekends. Grounds: **Open** Oct–Mar: 10am–4pm daily; Apr–Sep: 10am–8pm daily. **nationaltrust.org.uk**

34 Castlewellan Forest Park

Road map D2. Main St, Castlewellan, Co Down. **Tel** 028 4377 8664. **Open** 10am–sunset daily. for car park.

The outstanding feature of Castlewellan Forest Park, in the foothills of the Mourne Mountains, is its magnificent arboretum. This has grown far beyond the original walled garden, begun in 1740, and now comprises hothouses, dwarf conifer beds and a rhododendron wood.

Elsewhere in the park are a 19th-century Scottish baronial-style castle (now a conference centre), a lake and pleasant woodlands; these are at their most colourful in autumn.

35 Mountains of Mourne

Road map D2. Co Down. to Newry. to Newcastle. 10–14 Central Promenade, Newcastle (028 4372 2222). **downdc.gov.uk**

These mountains occupy just a small corner of County Down, with no more than a dozen peaks surpassing 600 m (2,000 ft), and yet they attract thousands of visitors each year.

Only one road of any size, the B27 between Kilkeel and Hilltown, crosses the Mournes, making this ideal territory for walkers. A popular but tough trail runs from **Newcastle**, the main gateway to the area, up to the peak of **Slieve Donard**: at 848 m (2,781 ft), this is the highest mountain in the range. Part of the route follows the **Mourne Wall**, which was erected in 1904–22 to enclose the catchment area of the two reservoirs in the **Silent Valley**.

Over 20 short hikes are to be enjoyed in the area. These range from easy strolls around Rostrevor Forest to rather more arduous treks up Slieve Muck and other Mourne peaks. Tourist information centres will have details.

Some 35 km (22 miles) north of Newcastle, the **Legananny Dolmen** *(see p36)* is one of the finest and most photographed ancient sites in the country.

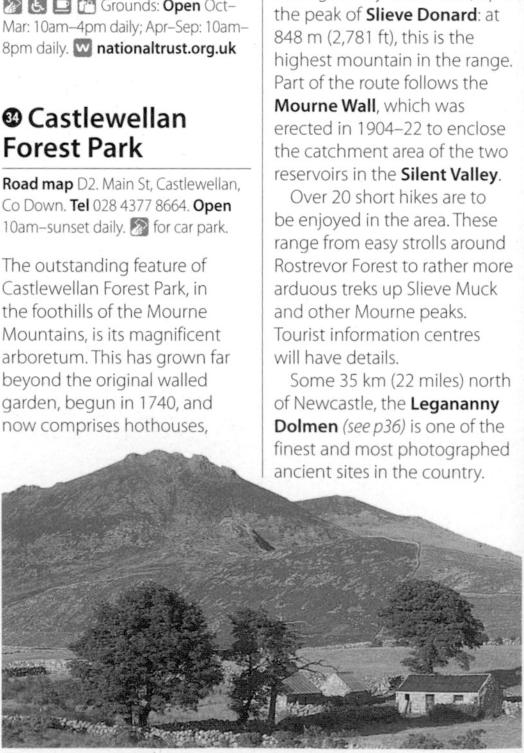

Rounded peaks of the Mountains of Mourne

36 A Tour of the Mourne Coast

Newcastle, where, in the words of the 19th-century songwriter Percy French, "the Mountains of Mourne sweep down to the sea", makes a good base from which to explore this area. Driving up and down the dipping roads of the Mournes is one of the highlights of a trip to Northern Ireland. Along the coast, the Mourne Coastal Route drive skirts between the foothills and the Irish Sea, providing lovely views and linking a variety of fishing villages and historic castles. Heading inland, you pass through an emptier landscape of moorland, purple with heather. The Silent Valley, with a visitors' centre and well-marked paths, is one of the areas that have been developed especially for tourists.

② Dundrum
The town is overlooked by the ruins of a Norman castle, and from the nearby bay you can see the mountains rising in the distance.

③ Tollymore Forest Park
This attractive park is dotted with follies like the Gothic Gate that formed part of the original 18th-century estate.

④ Spelga Dam
There are stunning views north from the Spelga Dam over the Mourne foothills.

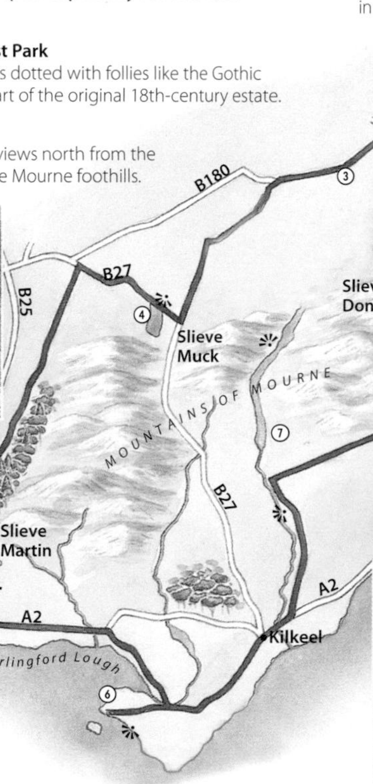

① Newcastle
A popular resort since the early 19th century, Newcastle has a promenade overlooking a sweeping, sandy beach.

Rostrevor with Slieve Martin behind

⑤ Rostrevor
This tranquil and leafy Victorian resort nestles below the peak of Slieve Martin, on the shores of Carlingford Lough.

⑦ Silent Valley
The valley is closed to traffic, but you can walk to the top of Ben Crom Mountain from the car park, or in summer go by bus.

Tips for Drivers

Length: 85 km (53 miles).
Stopping-off points: Newcastle has the biggest choice of pubs and restaurants. Dundrum, Annalong, Kilkeel and Rostrevor all have pubs, and a café opens in the Silent Valley in summer. The Spelga Dam and Tollymore Forest Park are good picnic spots *(see also pp365–7)*.

⑥ Green Castle
Erected in the 13th century, Green Castle lies at the end of a single track road on a rocky outcrop at the entrance to Carlingford Lough.

0 kilometres 5
0 miles 3

Key
Tour route
Other roads
Viewpoint

TRAVELLERS' NEEDS

WHERE TO STAY

Whether you are staying in exclusive luxury or modest self-catering accommodation, you can be sure of a warm welcome. The Irish are renowned for their friendliness. Even in big corporate hotels, where you might expect the reception to be more impersonal, the staff go out of their way to be hospitable. The choice is enormous: you can stay in an 18th-century country house, a luxurious (or slightly run-down) castle, a Victorian town house, a commercial hotel, a cosy village inn, or on a working farm. For the hardier visitor there are good hostels, trailer and camping sites, or even your own horse-drawn caravan. We give details here of the types of accommodation available, tourist board ratings and the choices for house or apartment rental. Our listings on pages 296–303 recommend hotels around the country, ranging from simple bed-and-breakfast to luxury accommodation. Fáilte Ireland (the Irish Tourist Board) and the Northern Ireland Tourist Board both publish comprehensive guides.

Luxurious spa at the Hayfield Manor Hotel *(see p298)*

Hotels

At the top of the price range there are a handful of expensive, luxury hotels in castles and stately country houses. Magnificently furnished and run, they offer maximum comfort, delicious food and a wide range of sports facilities – either owned by the hotel or available close by. Salmon fishing, fox-hunting and shooting can be arranged as well as riding, golf, sailing and cycling.

If your priority is a full range of indoor facilities, such as a gym, sauna and pool, the modern hotel chains will best cater to your needs. **The Doyle Collection** and **Carlton Hotel Group** offer this standard of accommodation in the Republic, as does **Hastings Hotels** in Northern Ireland.

Coastal resort hotels usually offer a range of sports activities or can advise you on the best places to go. In smaller towns, the main hotel is often the social centre of the area.

The shamrock symbols of both the Northern Ireland Tourist Board and Fáilte Ireland are displayed by hotels (and other forms of accommodation) that have been inspected and officially approved.

Country House Accommodation

Visitors wishing to stay in a period country home and sample authentic Irish country life can contact a specialist organization called **Hidden Ireland**. However, this type of accommodation may not suit everybody, as the houses are not guesthouses or hotels, but something quite different. You should therefore not expect modern hotel-style facilities and services. Instead the experience is an intimate one; guests dine together with their hosts as if at a private dinner party. Many of the houses have been in the same family for hundreds of years and the stories attached to them can be fascinating.

Prices reflect the type of house and standard of accommodation, but all offer excellent value and an experience of an old world grandeur that forms one aspect of Irish life and history.

There are many other private residences that also take paying guests, some of which include luxury spas. *Ireland's Blue Book* (Irelands-blue-book.ie) provides information on these homes, and reservations can be made through their website.

Guesthouses

Most guesthouses are found in cities and large towns. They are usually converted family homes and have an atmosphere all of their own. Most offer a good-value evening meal and all give you a delicious full Irish breakfast *(see p306)*. Top-of-the-range guesthouses can be just as good, and sometimes even better, than hotels. You will see a much more personal side of a town or city while staying at

The entrance to the Shelbourne Dublin *(see p296)*

◀ Powerscourt Hotel Spa *(see p297)*, Powerscourt, County Wicklow

A bed-and-breakfast on the River Corrib in Galway

a guesthouse. If you are looking for anonymity, however, a guesthouse may not suit you – both the proprietor and your fellow guests are likely to try to draw you into conversation.

There are plenty of good guesthouses to choose from in the Dublin area and the prices are usually reasonable. The **Irish Hotels Federation** website has over 600 hotels and guesthouses covering the whole of Ireland and bookings can be made directly through the site. The Northern Ireland Tourist Board 's website (discovernorthernireland.com) also has a comprehensive list of approved accommodation options and a booking engine.

Bed-and-Breakfast Accommodation

Ireland has the reputation for the best B&Bs in Europe. You will never be far from a place to stay, even in the remotest spots. Your welcome will always be friendly and the food and company excellent. Even if the house is no architectural beauty, the comfort and atmosphere will more than compensate. The **Ireland Bed and Breakfast Network** and **B&B Ireland** provide details of accommodation throughout Ireland.

Farmhouses

Farmhouse vacations are a popular tradition in Ireland. **Irish Farmhouse Holidays** has a list of farmhouses in the Republic that take paying guests. You can stay for one night or longer and they make an excellent base for touring the countryside. As with most things in Ireland, it is the hospitality and friendliness of the people that makes staying on a farm so memorable. You get a feel of rural Ireland with its rich agricultural heritage, and the families are determined you will enjoy every moment of your stay.

House and Apartment Rentals

Rental houses are an increasingly popular option in Ireland and there are properties to rent all over the country. You are likely to have more choice in the south and west as these areas have traditionally attracted the majority of tourists. Fáilte Ireland has a small section in its accommodation guide, but local tourist offices can provide area-specific lists. Accommodation can range from quaint, stone cottages and converted barns to more modern, purpose-built bungalows. All will generally have adequate facilities, with simple but comfortable furnishings, modern kitchen equipment and televisions.

The properties available through **Rent An Irish Cottage** are built in traditional style with whitewashed walls and painted roofs and windows; the decor is also traditional, simple and attractive. Locations are generally superb; the only possible criticism is for those that want to be "away from it all", they are built in clusters of about ten.

At the other end of the scale, you could rent a castle or country house, furnished with paintings and antiques. In some cases, the properties are fully staffed. **Elegant Ireland** has a selection of such properties. **Irish Landmark Trust** has a range of stunning accommodation in castles, lighthouses and gate lodges. The popularity of **Airbnb**, which allows owners to rent out their properties directly, is growing rapidly in Ireland. The thousands of options available range from rooms in sleek city-centre apartments (or the entire place) to treehouses, castles and converted churches.

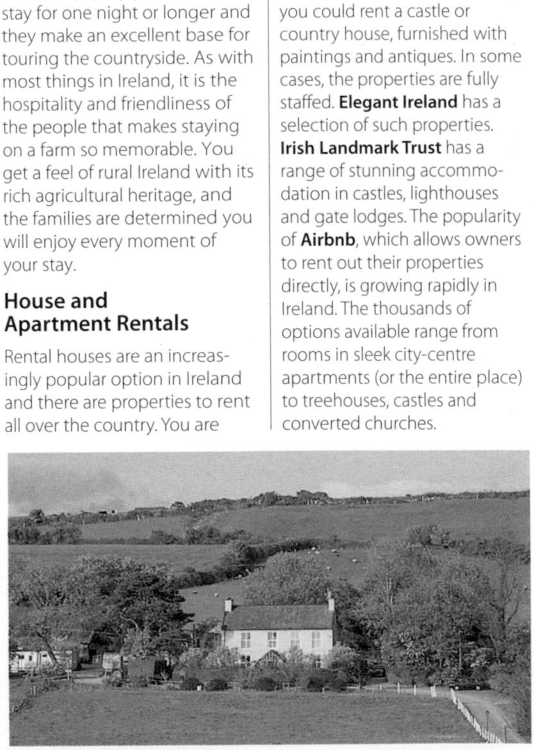

A farmhouse in Clonakilty, County Cork

A traditional painted horse-drawn caravan

Camping, Trailers and Motor Homes

A list of Fáilte Ireland approved camping and trailer parks can be found at camping-ireland.ie. Many campsites and parks offer additional facilities such as a shop, restaurant, games room, laundry, tennis court and mini-golf. The standard and condition of these facilities will vary but you can be reliably guided by the tourist board's star ratings: four-star graded parks have an extensive range of facilities with a high standard of management and there's a descending scale to one-star parks, which have the minimum facilities required for registration with Fáilte Ireland. A complete list of approved camping sites in the North can be found at discover northernireland.com/camping.

For a boutique camping experience, "glamping" sites are an emerging trend around Ireland. Visitors can book to stay in a tepee or yurt. **Boutique Camping** in Castletown Geoghegan in the Midlands, is one such facility.

If you want to experience the Irish countryside at a more leisurely and relaxing pace, it is possible to hire a traditional horse-drawn caravan. One company that specializes in this type of trip is **Kilvahan Horsedrawn Caravans**, based at Coolrain in Laois.

Youth Hostels

There are 22 youth hostels registered with **An Óige** (the Irish Youth Hostel Association), set in some wonderfully scenic areas in buildings ranging from castles to military barracks. Accommodation is generally provided in simple dormitories with comfortable beds and basic cooking facilities. There are discounts for members of An Óige or of organizations affiliated to the International Youth Hostel Federation. Charges vary according to the standard of accommodation, location and season. Northern Ireland is covered by the **Hostelling International Northern Ireland (HINI)**, which has three registered hostels.

Independent Holiday Hostels of Ireland publishes a guide to a host of independent hostels, and places such as universities offer similar inexpensive accommodation. Tourist boards have recommendations or check booking websites such as www.hostelworld.com

Prices

Room rates advertised in both Northern Ireland and the Republic are inclusive of tax and service. In general, prices in the Republic are on a par with the North. Hotel rates can vary by as much as 40 per cent depending on the time of year, and rates can more than double during festivals. Prices can also vary significantly between weekends and weekdays. Many hotels often have large discounts. Country house rates also vary a great deal according to the season. Prices are also influenced by their proximity to tourist sights and public transport. For those on a tight budget, farmhouse accommodation represents excellent value, though the cheapest option is self-catering in a rented cottage *(see p293)*.

Tipping

Tipping is not a common practice in Ireland, even at the larger hotels. Tasks performed by staff are considered part of the service. Tipping is not expected, for example, for carrying bags to your room. However, it is usual to tip the waiting staff in hotel restaurants: the standard tip is around 10 per cent and anything over 15 per cent of the bill would be considered generous.

Booking

It is wise to reserve your accommodation during the peak season and public holidays *(see p55)*, particularly if your visit coincides with a local festival or major sporting event *(see pp32–3)*. Fáilte Ireland can offer advice and make reservations through its nationwide accommodation service; the Northern Ireland Tourist Board runs a similar service. Central reservation facilities are available at the hotel chains that have been listed here.

Disabled Travellers

A fact sheet for disabled visitors can be obtained from tourist offices, Dublin Tourism, and Fáilte Ireland, and in their main accommodation

Façade of the Londonderry Arms in Carnlough, County Antrim

The Grace Kelly Suite at the Gresham Hotel *(see p296)* in Dublin

guide there is a symbol for wheelchair accessibility. A similar symbol is used in the accommodation listings in this book *(see pp296–303)*. The Citizens Information Board *(see p352)* is another body that offers information on accommodation for the disabled.

The annual publication *Holidays in the British Isles* caters specifically for the disabled traveller and covers Northern Ireland. There is also a guide, with comprehensive listings, available from the Northern Ireland Tourist Board entitled *Accessible Accommodation*.

Recommended Hotels

Our hotels are divided into eight geographical areas: Dublin, Southeast Ireland, Cork and Kerry, The Lower Shannon, the West of Ireland, Northwest Ireland, the Midlands and Northern Ireland. They are then subsequently organized by town. The hotels have been chosen as the best of what their region has to offer and based on a variety of factors, such as service, welcome, family-friendly approach, idyllic locations and comfort.

There is a huge variety of places to stay in Ireland – from guesthouses and castles that ooze character to hotels that have rooms with beautitful views. We have given each of our hotels a theme as guidance. Luxury establishments are at the top end of the price bracket and offer an exclusive service with high levels of comfort. They are often landmark properties, set on rolling green acres with lakes and forests. Hotels listed as Budget are at the other end of the scale and are competitive on price.

Throughout our listings, we've marked recommended hotels as DK Choice. We've chosen these hotels because they offer a special experience – either for superlative service, beautiful interiors and rooms, top-notch amenities and gadgets, the thought given to families, rooms that overlook stunning scenery, an excellent on-site restaurant, or a combination of these.

DIRECTORY

Hotels

Carlton Hotel Group
Parkway House, Cloghran, Dublin Airport, Co Dublin.
Tel 01 866 7555.
W carlton.ie

The Doyle Collection
156 Pembroke Rd, Dublin 4.
Tel 01 607 0070.
W doylecollection.com

Hastings Hotels
1066 House, Upper Newtownards Rd, Belfast.
Tel 028 9047 1066.
W hastingshotels.com

Country House Accommodation

Hidden Ireland
P. O. Box 31, Westport, Co Mayo. **Tel** 01 662 7166 or 098 66650.
W hiddenireland.com

Guesthouses

Irish Hotels Federation
13 Northbrook Rd, Dublin 6. **Tel** 01 497 6459.
W irelandhotels.com

Bed-and-Breakfast Accommodation

B&B Ireland
W bandbireland.com

Ireland Bed and Breakfast Network
W ireland-bnb.com

Farmhouses

Irish Farmhouse Holidays
Belleek Rd, Ballyshannon, Co Donegal.
Tel 071 982 2222.
W irishfarmholidays.com

House and Apartment Rentals

Airbnb
W airbnb.ie

Elegant Ireland
Box No 10871, Dublin 8.
Tel 01 473 2505.
W elegant.ie

Irish Landmark Trust
11 Parnell St Sq, Dublin 1.
Tel 01 670 4733.
W irishlandmark.com

Rent an Irish Cottage
51 O'Connell St, Limerick.
Tel 061 411109.
W rentacottage.ie

Camping, Trailers & Motor Homes

Boutique Camping
Castletown Geoghegan, Co Westmeath.
Tel 087 987 5277.
W Boutiquecamping.ie

Kilvahan Horsedrawn Caravans
Coolrain, Co Laois.
Tel 05787 35178.
W horsedrawn caravans.com

Youth Hostels

An Óige (Irish YHA)
61 Mountjoy St, Dublin 7.
Tel 01 830 4555.
W anoige.ie

Independent Holiday Hostels of Ireland
PO Box 11772, Fairview, Dublin 3.
Tel 01 836 4700.
W hostels-ireland.com

HI Northern Ireland
22–32 Donegall Rd, Belfast.
Tel 028 9031 5435.
W hini.org.uk

Where to Stay

Dublin

Southeast Dublin

The Davenport €€
Luxury **Map** F4
8–10 Merrion Street Lower, Dublin 2
Tel *01 607 3500*
W davenporthotel.ie
Behind a Neo-Classical façade dating from 1863. Mahogany and brass finishings give this hotel a gentleman's club feel.

Kilronan House €€
Guesthouse **Map** D5
70 Adelaide Road, Dublin 2
Tel *01 475 5266*
W kilronanhouse.com
In a listed town house dating from 1854. Georgian charm is coupled with modern comforts, including orthopaedic beds.

Stauntons on the Green €€
Rooms with views **Map** D5
83 St Stephen's Green, Dublin 2
Tel *01 478 2300*
W stauntonsonthegreen.ie
Cosy and modest. Bedrooms at the back are quieter and have views of Iveagh Gardens.

Buswells €€€
Hotel with character **Map** E4
23–27 Molesworth Street, Dublin 2
Tel *01 614 6500*
W buswells.ie
One of the first hotels in Dublin, established in 1882. Old-fashioned Georgian building, with a classy interior.

DK Choice

The Merrion €€€
Luxury **Map** D5
Upper Merrion Street, Dublin 2
Tel *01 603 0600*
W merrionhotel.com
Four elegant 18th-century town houses in the heart of Georgian Dublin have been converted into this luxury hotel. The walls are hung with Irish artworks, and there's a spa and two restaurants.

Number 31 €€€
Hotel with character **Map** E5
31 Leeson Close, Dublin 2
Tel *01 676 5011*
W number31.ie
Boutique guesthouse housed in an elegant and classical Georgian building. Luxurious and individually decorated bedrooms. Known for it's unique hospitality.

The Shelbourne Dublin €€€
Luxury **Map** E4/5
27 St Stephen's Green, Dublin 2
Tel *01 663 4500*
W marriott.com
Landmark hotel with uniformed doormen, a grand lobby and a stylish bar. Plush bedrooms too.

The Westin €€€
Luxury **Map** D3
35–39 Westmoreland Street, Dublin 2
Tel *01 645 1000*
W westin.com/dublin
Housed in a beautiful former bank overlooking Trinity College. The well-appointed bedrooms are furnished to a high standard.

Southwest Dublin

Avalon House €
Hostel **Map** C4
55 Aungier Street, Dublin 2
Tel *01 475 0001*
W avalon-house.ie
Cheap and cheerful accommodation in a restored red-brick Victorian building. Clean dorms have pine floors and high ceilings.

Brooks Hotel €€€
Luxury **Map** D4
59–62 Drury Street, Dublin 2
Tel *01 670 4000*
W brookshotel.ie
Immaculately maintained boutique hotel with a great reputation. Contemporary flourishes accompany the tastefully traditional decor.

Central Hotel €€€
Hotel with character **Map** D5
1–5 Exchequer Street, Dublin 2
Tel *01 679 7302*
W centralhoteldublin.com
Built in 1887. Functional, neat rooms and modern facilities in an old-fashioned atmosphere.

Luxurious living room in the Presidential Suite, The Westin

Price Guide
Prices are based on one night's stay in high season for a standard double room, inclusive of service charges and taxes.

€	up to €80
€€	€80–€180
€€€	over €180

Radisson Blu Royal Hotel €€€
Chain hotel **Map** C4
Golden Lane, Dublin 8
Tel *01 898 2900*
W radissonblu.ie/royalhotel-dublin
This hotel on a quiet street has spacious rooms. Guests can use a fitness centre and pool nearby.

North of the Liffey

Cassidys €€
Budget **Map** D2
8–9 Cavendish Row, Upper O'Connell Street, Dublin 1
Tel *01 878 0555*
W cassidyshotel.com
Modern en suite rooms with features of the Georgian age. Great city centre location.

The Gresham €€€
Hotel with character **Map** D1
23 Upper O'Connell Street, Dublin 1
Tel *01 874 6881*
W gresham-hotels.com
One of Dublin's oldest and best-known hotels. Cheerful, well-equipped rooms.

The Morrison €€€
Boutique **Map** C3
Ormond Quay, Dublin 1
Tel *01 887 2400*
W morrisonhotel.ie
This hip and vibrant hotel is in the heart of the city. Rooms are stylish with a range of amenities.

Further Afield

DK Choice

Ariel House €€
Guesthouse with character
Road map D4
50–54 Landsdowne Road, Dublin 4
Tel *01 668 5512*
W ariel-house.net
Built in 1850, this Victorian house is located in a suburb close to the city centre. Tasteful period decor. The guesthouse is a short walk from the Aviva stadium.

Clayton Hotel €€
Budget **Road map** D4
Merrion Road, Ballsbridge, Dublin 4
Tel *01 668 1111*
W claytonhotelballsbridge.com

Elegant suite at Cliff House Hotel in Ardmore

Housed in a magnificent red-brick former masonic school. Big rooms have comfortable, contemporary furnishings.

Clontarf Castle €€
Hotel with character **Road map** D3
Castle Avenue, Clontarf, Dublin 3
Tel *01 833 2321*
W clontarfcastle.ie
A 12th-century castle with 21st-century comforts and amenities. Warm and cosy atmosphere.

Fitzpatrick Castle €€
Hotel with character **Road map** D4
Killiney, Co Dublin
Tel *01 230 5400*
W fitzpatrickcastle.com
Old-style luxury in this family-owned 18th-century castle hotel located high above Dublin Bay.

Herbert Park €€
Luxury **Road map** D4
Ballsbridge, Dublin 4
Tel *01 667 2200*
W herbertparkhotel.ie
Big, bright and airy, with well-appointed and stylishly designed bedrooms. Irish abstract art and furniture throughout.

Portmarnock Hotel and Golf Links €€
Hotel with character **Road map** *D3*
Strand Rd, Portmarnock, Co. Dublin
Tel *01 846 0611*
W portmarnock.com
This grand Victorian beachside house was originally home to the famous Jameson (whiskey) family. It has well-furnished rooms views of the bay.

The Dylan €€€
Luxury **Road map** D4
Eastmoreland Place, Dublin 4
Tel *01 660 3000*
W dylan.ie
A plush boutique hotel with sumptuous individually designed rooms and an award winning, elegant restaurant along with a popular cocktail bar.

InterContinental Hotel €€€
Luxury **Road map** D4
Simmonscourt Road, Ballsbridge, Dublin 4
Tel *01 665 4000*
W ihg.com
Period-style elegance combined with contemporary comforts. Lavish bedrooms and exceptional service.

Southeast Ireland

DK Choice

ARDMORE:
Cliff House Hotel €€€
Luxury **Road map** C5
Ardmore, Co Waterford
Tel *024 87800*
W thecliffhousehotel.com
This hotel boasts a stunning cliff-side setting. The spacious rooms, most with private balconies or terraces, overlook Ardmore Bay and are decorated with Irish art. Michelin-starred restaurant that serves Irish and international cuisine, a luxury spa with an indoor infinity and an outdoor rock pool are on site.

ASHFORD: Ballyknocken House €€
Farmhouse **Road map** D4
Glenealy, Ashford, Co Wicklow
Tel *0404 44627*
W ballyknocken.com
Romantic Victorian farmhouse and cookery school managed by celebrity Irish chef and food writer Catherine Fulvio.

DK Choice

BALLINAKILL:
Waterford Castle €€€
Luxury hotel with character
Road map D5
The Island, Ballinakill, Waterford
Tel *051 878 203*
W waterfordcastleresort.com
Dating from the 15th century, this luxury castle on a private island is reached by car ferry. Inside, old-world elegance meets modern comforts, with good fine-dining choices, an 18-hole golf course and tennis courts. There are also 48 luxury holiday lodges on the island.

ENNISKERRY:
Powerscourt Hotel €€€
Luxury **Road map** D4
Powerscourt Estate, Enniskerry, Co Wicklow
Tel *01 274 8888*
W powerscourthotel.com
Luxury hotel within the historic Powerscourt Estate. Rooms are spacious and elegant, and some have open fireplaces.

GOREY: Marlfield House €€€
Luxury hotel with character
Road map D5
Gorey, Co Wexford
Tel *053 942 1124*
W marlfieldhouse.ie
This Regency-style mansion is luxuriously furnished with fine art, antiques, crystal chandeliers and marble fireplaces.

INISTIOGE: Cullintra House €€
Farmhouse with character
Road map D5
The Rower, Inistioge, Co Kilkenny
Tel *051 423 614 (call to book)*
W cullintrahouse.com
A historic farmhouse with cosy, romantic rooms, log fires and home-cooked candlelit dinners.

KILKENNY:
Langton House Hotel €€
Boutique **Road map** C4
69 John Street, Kilkenny, Co Kilkenny
Tel *056 776 5133*
W langtons.ie
A friendly boutique-style hotel full of character and charm. Food and service are both excellent.

MACREDDIN: The BrookLodge Hotel & Wells Spa €€
Boutique **Road map** D4
Macreddin Village, Co Wicklow
Tel *0402 36444*
W brooklodge.com
Set amid the pretty Wicklow countryside, this hotel boasts Ireland's only certified organic restaurant, the Strawberry Tree.

For more information on types of hotels *see p295*

NEWTOWNMOUNTKENNEDY: Druids Glen Resort €€
Rooms with views **Road map** D4
Newtownmountkennedy, Co Wicklow
Tel *01 287 0800*
W druidsglenresort.com
Large resort hotel in a woodland location. Well-appointed rooms, a spa, leisure facilities and two golf courses.

RATHNEW: Tinakilly Country House & Restaurant €€
Hotel with character **Road map** D4
Main St, Rathnew, Co Wicklow
Tel *0404 69274*
W tinakilly.ie
A classical Victorian-Italianate mansion with modern comforts and true Irish hospitality and charm. Bedrooms are individually decorated with antique furniture.

ROSSLARE: Kelly's Resort Hotel & Spa €€€
Resort **Road map** D5
Rosslare, Co Wexford
Tel *053 913 2114*
W kellys.ie
Family-friendly seaside resort hotel with a leisure centre and crèche. Superb facilities such as tennis courts and a spa.

STRAFFAN: Kildare Hotel & Country Club (K Club) €€€
Luxury **Road map** D4
Straffan, Co Kildare
Tel *01 601 7200*
W kclub.ie
Dating from 1832, the hotel retains it's original art work and antiques. French elegance is abound with excellent restaurants and leisure facilities.

THOMASTOWN: Mount Juliet Estate €€€
Luxury **Road Map** D5
Thomastown, Co Kilkenny
Tel *056 777 3000*
W mountjuliet.ie
Luxury hotel in a country estate – a nature and golf lovers' paradise. Indulge in the stylish treatments at their award-winning spa.

Cork and Kerry

BALTIMORE: Casey's €€
Rooms with views **Road map** B6
Baltimore, Co Cork
Tel *028 20197*
W caseysofbaltimore.com
Along the Wild Atlantic Way this hotel has stunning views and a cosy bar with excellent seafood.

Bantry House, set in a stunning location overlooking Bantry Bay

DK Choice

BANTRY: Bantry House €€
Hotel with character **Road map** B6
Bantry, Co Cork
Tel *027 50047*
W bantryhouse.com
This 17th-century stately home is a special place to stay, with wonderful period rooms, many of which overlook the beautiful gardens. Climb the monumental stone Stairway to the Sky for superb views over Bantry Bay. Open from March to October.

CLONAKILTY: Inchydoney Island Lodge & Spa €€€
Luxury **Road map** B6
Clonakilty, West Cork, Co Cork
Tel *023 883 3143*
W inchydoneyisland.com
Ireland's first sea-water spa. Many rooms have balconies overlooking the Atlantic Ocean and a fantastic Blue Flag beach.

DK Choice

CORK: Hayfield Manor €€€
Luxury hotel with character **Road map** C5
Perrott Avenue, College Road, Cork
Tel *021 484 5900*
W hayfieldmanor.ie
This small, elegant hotel is located within its own grounds. Although it opened in 1996, it has the feel of a period house, with generously sized bedrooms, elegant furnishings and impeccable service. There are excellent leisure facilities too, including a spa and indoor pool.

CORK: Maryborough Hotel & Spa €€€
Hotel with character **Road map** C5
Maryborough Hill, Douglas, Cork
Tel *021 436 5555*
W maryborough.com
Modern rooms in a handsome 18th-century mansion. Ornate 300 year old listed gardens.

DINGLE: Dingle Benners Hotel €€
Hotel with character **Road map** A5
Main Street, Dingle, Co Kerry
Tel *066 915 1638*
W dinglebenners.com
Dingle's oldest hotel. Great setting, a rustic feel, excellent breakfast and friendly service.

DINGLE: Dingle Skellig Hotel & Peninsula Spa €€
Spa hotel **Road map** A5
Dingle, Co Kerry
Tel *066 915 0200*
W dingleskellig.com
Ideal for families with crèche services, kids club and children's menu.

DINGLE PENINSULA: Gorman's Clifftop House & Restaurant €€
Guesthouse **Road map** A5
Glaise Bheag, Ballydavid, Co Kerry
Tel *066 915 5162*
W gormans-clifftophouse.com
Cosy hotel at the heart of the stunning Dingle Peninsula with sea views and open turf fires.

FOTA ISLAND: Fota Island Resort €€
Luxury **Road map** C6
Fota Island, Co Cork
Tel *021 488 3700*
W fotaisland.ie
Stunning contemporary resort with a golf course and spa, plus an adjacent wildlife resort.

KENMARE: Sea Shore Farm Guesthouse €€
Guesthouse **Road map** B5
Tubrid, Kenmare, Co Kerry
Tel *064 664 1270*
W seashore-kenmare.com
At the head of the Ring of Kerry with beautiful views of Kenmare Bay and the Beara Peninsula.

Key to prices *see p296*

DK Choice

KENMARE: Sheen Falls Lodge €€€
Luxury **Road map** B5
Kenmare, Co Kerry
Tel *064 664 1600*
W sheenfallslodge.ie
In a waterside location overlooking Sheen Falls and across the river from town, this five-star hotel set in 120 ha (300 acres) of land is said to be one of the best in the country. It is lavishly decorated in classic style. Highlights include clay-pigeon shooting and wild-salmon fishing. The perfect base from which to explore the Wild Atlantic Way.

KILLARNEY: The Europe Hotel and Resort €€€
Luxury **Road map** B5
Fossa, Killarney, Co Kerry
Tel *064 667 1300*
W theeurope.com
An award-winning resort hotel overlooking the famous Lakes of Killarney. Home to a premium spa and leisure centre.

KILLARNEY: The Malton €€€
Hotel with character **Road map** B5
Town Centre, Killarney, Co Kerry
Tel *064 663 8000*
W themalton.com
Retaining original Victorian features and architecture, this is a charming retreat with pretty landscaped gardens.

KILLORGLIN: Carrig Country House €€
Guesthouse **Road map** A5
Caragh Lake, Killorglin, Co Kerry
Tel *066 976 9100*
W carrighouse.com
Open fires and antiques create a warm, peaceful atmosphere. Beautifully appointed rooms and an excellent restaurant overlooking Caragh Lake.

KINSALE: Carlton Hotel Kinsale €€
Rooms with views **Road map** B6
Rathmore Road, Kinsale, Co Cork
Tel *021 470 6000*
W carltonkinsalehotel.com
A tranquil and contemporary hotel with sea views, in addition to a pool, kids' club and spa.

LITTLE ISLAND: Radisson Blu Hotel & Spa Cork €€
Chain hotel **Road map** C6
Ditchley House, Little Island, Cork
Tel *021 429 7000*
W radissonblu.ie/hotel-cork
A chic, elegant spa hotel with a mix of old-world charm and contemporary design. Hydrotherapy pool and gym available.

SNEEM: Parknasilla Hotel Resort & Spa €€€
Hotel with character **Road map** A6
Sneem, Co Kerry
Tel *064 6675600*
W parknasillahotel.ie
Victorian hotel overlooking Kenmare Bay. On-site spa and a 12-hole golf course.

TRALEE: Ballyseede Castle Hotel €€
Hotel with character **Road map** B5
Ballyseede, Tralee, Co Kerry
Tel *066 712 5799*
W ballyseedecastle.com
Dating back to the 1590s, this family-run castle hotel is set in woodland. Elegant rooms.

The Lower Shannon

ADARE: Dunraven Arms €€
Hotel with character **Road map** B5
Adare, Co Limerick
Tel *061 605 900*
W dunravenhotel.com
Luxurious country house famed for its hospitality. Spacious rooms feature beautiful furnishings.

Elegantly furnished bedroom at Moy House

DK Choice

ADARE: Adare Manor Hotel & Golf Resort €€€
Luxury hotel with character **Road map** B5
Adare, Co Limerick
Tel *061 605 200*
W adaremanor.com
This Neo-Gothic mansion, on the banks of the River Maigue, was the former home of the Earls of Dunraven. Elegant, high-ceilinged rooms with period features are luxuriously furnished and overlook formal gardens. There is also a pool and steam room.

BALLYVAUGHAN: Gregans Castle Hotel €€€
Hotel with character **Road map** B4
Ballyvaughan, Co Clare
Tel *065 707 7005*
W gregans.ie
Boasting a superb location in the Burren this manor house is nestled within beautifully attended gardens. Rooms are decorated in a contemporary country-house style.

DOOLIN: Ballinalacken Castle Country House Hotel €€
Country house **Road map** B4
Doolin, Co Clare
Tel *065 707 4025*
W ballinalackencastle.com
Welcoming rooms await at this 15th-century hotel along with warm fires, sea views and a renowned restaurant.

KILMALLOCK: Flemingstown House €€€
Farmhouse **Road map** B5
Kilmallock, Co Limerick
Tel *063 98093*
W flemingstown.com
A 250-year-old farmhouse on a working farm with a tranquil setting. Perfect for families and large groups.

LAHINCH: Moy House €€€
Luxury **Road map** B4
Lahinch, Co Clare
Tel *065 708 2800*
W moyhouse.com
An 18th-century hotel with elegant furnishings, as well as an orchard and vegetable gardens.

LIMERICK: Savoy Hotel €€
Boutique Hotel **Road map** C3
Henry St, Limerick
Tel *061 448 700*
W savoylimerick.com
This hotel offers luxury rooms and relaxation treatments. Perfect base to explore attractions such as the Cliffs of Moher and King John's Castle.

For more information on types of hotels *see p295*

The plush drawing room of Ashford Castle looks out over beautiful gardens

LIMERICK: No.1 Pery Square €€€
Hotel with character **Road map** B4
1 Pery Square, Limerick
Tel *061 402 402*
oneperysquare.com
A glamourous Georgian town house with spacious, tastefully decorated bedrooms and a spa.

DK Choice

NEWMARKET-ON-FERGUS: Dromoland Castle €€€
Luxury hotel with character **Road map** B4
Newmarket-on-Fergus, Co Clare
Tel *061 368 144*
dromoland.ie
This is one of Ireland's finest hotels. Its grand elegance – antiques, high-end furnishings and crystal chandeliers – is enhanced by the scenery of the surrounding estate. Bedrooms are utterly luxurious.

THURLES: Inch House €€
Country house **Road map** C4
Nenagh Rd, Thurles, Co Tipperary
Tel *0504 51348*
inchhouse.ie
Stately Georgian house with spacious, high-ceilinged rooms and award-winning restaurant.

The West of Ireland

ACHILL ISLAND: Grays Guest House €
Guesthouse **Road map** A3
Dugort, Achill Island, Co Mayo
Tel *098 43244*
grays-guesthouse.ie
Old-fashioned but comfortable accommodation in the pretty village of Dugort.

ACHILL ISLAND: Bervie Guesthouse €€
Guesthouse **Road map** A3
The Strand, Keel, Achill Island, Co Mayo
Tel *098 43114*
bervie-guesthouse-achill.com
A former coastguard station with warm hospitality, a turf fire and direct access to Keel Beach.

ARAN ISLANDS: An Dún Guest House €€
Guesthouse **Road map** B4
Inis Meain, Aran Islands, Co Galway
Tel *099 73047*
inismeainaccommodation.com
Comfortable and friendly place surrounded by culture and scenic views. Great, wholesome food.

ARAN ISLANDS: Kilmurvey House €€
Rooms with views **Road map** B4
Inis Mór, Aran Islands, Co Galway
Tel *099 61218*
kilmurveyhouse.com
An 18th-century stone house with comfortable sitting rooms. Bedrooms have great views.

DK Choice

BALLINA: Ice House Hotel €€
Luxury **Road map** B2
The Quay, Ballina, Co Mayo
Tel *096 23500*
icehousehotel.ie
An iconic design hotel in a restored ice house with floor-to-ceiling windows allowing for riverside views. Relax in the steam room or the hot tub, then enjoy fine modern Irish cuisine in the award-winning restaurant.

CARRICK-ON-SHANNON: The Landmark Hotel €€
Luxury **Road map** C3
Carrick-on-Shannon, Co Leitrim
Tel *071 962 2222*
thelandmarkhotel.com
Centrally located hotel with lovely views of the Shannon.

CASTLEBAR: Breaffy House Resort €€
Country house **Road map** B3
Castlebar, Co Mayo
Tel *094 902 2033*
breaffyhouseresort.com
Well-appointed bedrooms with a kids' room and leisure facilities, including a spa.

CASTLEREA: Clonalis House €€€
Luxury **Road map** C3
Castlerea, Co Roscommon
Tel *094 962 0014*
clonalis.com
Historic mansion built in 1878, set within a large estate. Rooms have period decor.

CLIFDEN: Dolphin Beach House €€
Rooms with views **Road map** A3
Lower Sky Road, Clifden, Co Galway
Tel *095 21204*
dolphinbeachhouse.com
In the heart of Connemara. Stylish beachside house. Spacious rooms boast antique furniture.

CONG: Ashford Castle €€€
Luxury **Road map** B3
Cong, Co Mayo
Tel *094 954 6003*
ashford.ie
Ireland's most luxurious castle (1228) hotel is set in 350 acres (140 ha) of parkland, lakes and gardens.

GALWAY: Hotel Meyrick €€
Elegant **Road map** B4
Eyre Square, Galway, Co Galway
Tel *091 564 041*
hotelmeyrick.ie
This historic railway hotel has a mahogany-and-brass interior, ornate rooms and a health spa.

GALWAY: Jurys Inn €€
Chain hotel **Road map** B4
Quay Street, Galway, Co Galway
Tel *091 566 444*
jurysinns.com
A centrally located hotel with functional bedrooms. Breakfast and Internet access are extras.

GALWAY: The Twelve Hotel €€
Luxury **Road map** B4
Barna Village, Galway, Co Galway
Tel *091 597 000*
thetwelvehotel.ie
Stylish boutique hotel near the beach. Pizza kitchen, bakery and treatment rooms on-site.

INISHBOFIN: Doonmore Hotel €€
Budget **Road map** A3
Inishbofin Island, Co Galway
Tel *095 45804*
doonmorehotel.com
Traditional family-run hotel. The bar has an open fire and holds regular live music sessions.

NEWPORT: Newport House €€
Luxury **Road map** B3
Newport, Co Mayo
Tel *098 41222*
newporthouse.ie
Historic Georgian mansion offering refined comfort, gracious hospitality and an internationally renowned wine cellar.

RENVYLE: Renvyle House Hotel €€
Country house **Road map** A3
Renvyle, Connemara, Co Galway
Tel *095 46100*
renvyle.com
Atmospheric and historic house

Key to prices *see p296*

on the shores of the Atlantic with a private lake and a 9-hole golf club.

ROSCOMMON: Abbey Hotel €€
Country house **Road map** C3
Galway Road, Roscommon
Tel *090 662 6240*
W abbeyhotel.ie
En-suite bedrooms are appealingly furnished with modern facilities.

DK Choice

WESTPORT: Ardmore Country House €€
Country house **Road map** B3
The Quay, Westport, Co Mayo
Tel *098 25994*
W ardmorecountryhouse.com
Overlooking Clew Bay, Ardmore is a peaceful haven, yet it is only a short stroll from the bustle of Westport's 18th-century harbour. This family-run hotel is famed for its fabulous breakfasts.

WESTPORT: Knockranny House Hotel €€
Country house **Road map** B3
Westport, Co Mayo
Tel *098 28600*
W knockrannyhousehotel.ie
Inviting hotel with log fires and antique furniture. Bright, airy rooms.

Northwest Ireland

ARDARA: The Green Gate €€
Guesthouse **Road map** C2
Ardvally, Ardara, Co Donegal
Tel *074 954 1546*
W thegreengate.eu
Accommodation is spread over two low, thatched-roof cottages with simple but pleasant rooms.

BUNDORAN: Great Northern Hotel €€
Luxury **Road map** C2
Sea Road, Bundoran, Co Donegal
Tel *071 984 1204*
W greatnorthernhotel.com
With its leisure facilities and 18-hole golf course, this hotel is ideal for relaxed family holidays.

DONEGAL TOWN: Ard Na Breatha €€
Guesthouse **Road map** C2
Drumrooske Middle, Donegal Town, Co Donegal
Tel *074 972 2288*
W ardnabreatha.com
Spearheading the Irish eco-tourism movement, this guesthouse has stunning views of the Bluestack Mountains.

DOWNINGS: Rosapenna Hotel €€
Rooms with views **Road map** C1
Downings, Co Donegal
Tel *074 915 5301*
W rosapenna.ie
Tastefully decorated rooms, many with private balconies and sea views, and two golf courses.

DUNFANAGHY: Arnolds Hotel €€
Rooms with views **Road map** C1
Dunfanaghy, Co Donegal
Tel *074 913 6208*
W arnoldshotel.com
Family-run hotel with en-suite rooms overlooking Sheephaven Bay. The lounge has an open fire.

DK Choice

LOUGH ESKE: Lough Eske Castle Hotel & Spa €€
Luxury **Road map** C2
Lough Eske, Donegal Town, Co Donegal
Tel *074 972 5100*
W solishotels.com
Nestled on the shores of Lough Eske this beautiful castle-hotel combines its historic past with contemporary elegance. The only five-star hotel in the county, it boasts a spa, fine dining restaurant and bar, splendid afternoon teas and lavishly decorated rooms, all surrounded by acres of unspoiled woodland.

LOUGH ESKE: Harvey's Point €€€
Luxury **Road map** C2
Lough Eske, Donegal Town, Co Donegal
Tel *074 972 2208*
W harveyspoint.com
This Swiss-style hotel features palatial bedrooms with views of the lake and a few pet-friendly rooms. The restaurant, offering fine dining, is the heart and soul of the hotel.

DK Choice

MALIN TOWN: The Malin Hotel €€
Hotel with character **Road map** C1
Malin Town, Inishowen, Co Donegal
Tel *074 937 0606*
W malinhotel.ie
French-themed boutique hotel with a warm welcome, a lively bar and individually designed, sumptuous boudoirs. Rooms feature designer wallpaper and Egyptian cotton sheets.

MOHILL: Lough Rynn Castle €€
Luxury **Road map** C3
Mohill, Co Leitrim
Tel *071 963 2700*
W loughrynn.ie
Elegant castle hotel on a 150-acre (60-ha) estate. Old-world charm and elegance aplenty.

RIVERSTOWN: Coopershill House €€€
Luxury **Road map** C2
Riverstown, Co Sligo
Tel *071 916 5108*
W coopershill.com
Elegant 17th-century house. The spacious bedrooms are decorated with tasteful antiques.

ROSSES POINT: Yeats Country Hotel €€
Resort **Road map** B2
Rosses Point, Co Sligo
Tel *071 917 7211*
W yeatscountryhotel.com
This hotel offers warm, cosy and stylish en-suite rooms, as well as a swimming pool and spa.

ROSSNOWLAGH: Sand House Hotel €€
Rooms with views **Road map** C2
Rossnowlagh, Co Donegal
Tel *071 985 1777*
W sandhouse.ie
Imposing castellated hotel. Well-decorated rooms and beachside views.

Exterior of the grand 19th-century Lough Rynn Castle in Mohill

For more information on types of hotels *see p295*

SLIGO: Clarion Hotel €€
Chain hotel **Road map** C2
Clarion Rd, Sligo, Co Sligo
Tel *071 911 9000*
W clarionhotelsligo.com
Impressive, family-friendly hotel, set on beautiful grounds and with great views of Ben Bulben.

The Midlands

ATHLONE: Hodson Bay €€
Rooms with views **Road map** C3
Hodson Bay, Athlone, Co Westmeath
Tel *090 644 2000*
W hodsonbayhotel.com
Many of the cheerfully decorated rooms have views of Lough Ree. Shannon cruises available.

CARLINGFORD: Beaufort House €€
Guesthouse **Road map** D3
Ghan Road, Carlingford, Co Louth
Tel *042 937 3879*
W beauforthouse.net
The shoreside location ensures great views. There are beautifully appointed rooms and a sailing school run by the hotel owners.

CAVAN: Radisson Blu Farnham Estate €€€
Chain hotel **Road map** C3
Farnham Estate, Cavan, Co Cavan
Tel *049 4377700*
W farnhamestate.ie
A contemporary glass atrium links to a grand 18th-century house with sumptuous rooms.

CLONES: Hilton Park €€
Luxury hotel with character **Road map** C2
Clones, Co Monaghan
Tel *047 56007*
W hiltonpark.ie
Period-style accommodation in a country house owned by the Madden family since 1734.

Superb views of Lough Ree from the spa's balcony, Hodson Bay

Key to prices *see p296*

CLOVERHILL: The Olde Post Inn €€
Hotel with character **Road map** C3
Cloverhill, Co Cavan
Tel *047 55555*
W theoldepostinn.com
Housed in the former post office, the inn has rustic ambience, cosy rooms and a superb restaurant.

DROGHEDA: Boyne Valley Hotel & Country Club €€
Country house **Road map** D3
Stameen, Drogheda, Co Louth
Tel *041 983 7737*
W boyne-valley-hotel.ie
Family-friendly historic house. Rooms in the old part of the building have more character; the others have better facilities.

KILLENARD: The Heritage Golf & Spa Resort €€
Luxury **Road map** C4
Killenard, Co Laois
Tel *057 864 5500*
W theheritage.com
Impressive public spaces, exceptional leisure facilities and three restaurants can be found here.

KILMESSAN: Station House Hotel €€
Hotel with character **Road map** D3
Kilmessan, Co Meath
Tel *046 902 5239*
W stationhousehotel.ie
Victorian train station turned cosy hotel. The well-equipped rooms have a pleasant decor, and there is also an award-winning restaurant.

KINNITTY: Ardmore House €
Guesthouse **Road map** C4
The Walk, Kinnitty, Co Offaly
Tel *05791 37009*
W kinnitty.com
The place to experience the real Old Ireland, with a turf fire, home cooking and a relaxed atmosphere. Warm welcome.

LONGFORD: Viewmount House €€
Country house **Road map** C3
Dublin Road, Longford
Tel *043 334 1919*
W viewmounthouse.com
This Georgian house previously owned by the Earl of Longford has bright, stylish rooms.

MOUNTRATH: Roundwood House €€
Hotel with character **Road map** C4
Mountrath, Co Laois
Tel *05787 32120*
W roundwoodhouse.com
Enjoy a truly unique experience staying at the Flynn family's gracious Palladian home, which is set in a delightful mountainside location.

MULLINGAR: Greville Arms €
Budget **Road map** C3
Pearse Street, Mullingar, Co Westmeath
Tel *044 934 8563*
W grevillearmshotel.ie
Traditional country town hotel with comfortable bedrooms, a large bar and a nightclub.

DK Choice

SLANE: Tankardstown House €€€
Luxury **Road map** D3
Slane, Co Meath
Tel *041 9824621*
W tankardstown.ie
Lime trees line the avenue leading to this 18th-century manor. Inside, there are exquisite rooms with fine antiques and beautiful bathrooms, as well as excellent dining. Guests can explore the orangery and gardens.

TRIM: Trim Castle Hotel €€
Hotel with character **Road map** D3
Castle Street, Trim, Co Meath
Tel *046 948 3000*
W trimcastlehotel.com
Bright, spacious rooms, some with views of the castle. Guests can enjoy the off-site leisure facilities at a reduced rate.

TULLAMORE: Anna Harvey House €
Farmhouse **Road map** C4
Tullamore, Co Offaly
Tel *05793 43544*
W annaharveyfarm.ie
A rural idyll – open fires, pine floors and cosy bedrooms in a restored grain barn. Equestrian activities are a major draw.

Northern Ireland

ARMAGH: Armagh City Hotel ££
Leisure club hotel **Road map** D2
2 Friary Road, Armagh
Tel *028 375 18888*
W armaghcityhotel.com
Look beyond the charmless exterior. This hotel has clean, well-equipped rooms, and facilities include a gym and pool.

BALLYCASTLE: Whitepark House ££
Guesthouse **Road map** D1
150 Whitepark Rd, Ballintoy, Ballycastle, Co Antrim
Tel *028 2073 1482*
W whiteparkhouse.com
Elegant country living in a house dating from 1730. Breakfast is served in a lovely conservatory.

Price Guide
Prices are based on one night's stay in high season for a standard double room, inclusive of service charges and taxes.

£	up to £85
££	£85–£180
£££	over £180

BALLYGALLY:
Hastings Ballygally Castle ££
Hotel with character **Road map** D1
274 Coast Road, Ballygally, Co Antrim
Tel *028 2858 1066*
W hastingshotels.com
These rooms with beamed ceilings and antiques, have modern facilities. Stay in the Ghost Room, in the 17th-century tower.

BALLYMENA:
Galgorm Resort and Spa ££
Luxury **Road map** D1
136 Fenaghy Road, Ballymena, Co Antrim
Tel *028 2588 1001*
W galgorm.com
Luxurious rooms, many with river views, and excellent service. Self-catering cottages and log cabins are also available.

BANGOR: Cairn Bay Lodge ££
Guesthouse **Road map** E2
278 Seacliff Road, Bangor, Co Down
Tel *02891 467 636*
W cairnbaylodge.com
Edwardian-style B&B by the bay. The elegant dining room looks out on beautiful gardens.

BELFAST: An Old Rectory £
Guesthouse **Road map** D2
148 Malone Road, Belfast, Co Antrim
Tel *028 9066 7882*
W anoldrectory.co.uk
A former Church of Ireland rectory boasting many original features. Each room is uniquely decorated. Excellent organic breakfasts.

BELFAST: Europa Hotel ££
Business hotel **Road map** D2
Great Victoria Street, Belfast, Co Antrim
Tel *028 9027 1066*
W hastingshotels.com
Classic hotel in an imposing building. There is a bar and a lounge, while fitness facilities are available nearby.

BELFAST: Merchant Hotel £££
Luxury **Road map** D2
16 Skipper Street, Belfast, Co Antrim
Tel *028 9023 4888*
W themerchanthotel.com
Housed in a listed building in the Cathedral Quarter. Facilities include a spa and a rooftop gym.

Patio and garden area at the entrance to Bushmills Inn

DK Choice

BUSHMILLS: Bushmills Inn ££
Hotel with character **Road map** D1
9 Dunluce Road, Bushmills, Co Antrim
Tel *028 2073 3000*
W bushmillsinn.com
This charming coaching inn has turf fires and cosy nooks. It is said to date back to 1608, the same year the neighbouring distillery gained the world's first-ever licence to distil whiskey. There are excellent dining facilities, too, plus live Irish music on Saturdays in the Gas Bar.

CRAWFORDSBURN:
The Old Inn at Crawfordsburn ££
Hotel with character **Road map** E2
Main St, Crawfordsburn, Co Down
Tel *028 9185 3255*
W theoldinn.com
Thatched 17th-century inn. Each individually decorated room features a plush four-poster bed.

DOWNHILL: Downhill Hostel £
Hostel **Road map** D1
12 Mussenden Road, Downhill, Co Londonderry
Tel *028 7084 9077*
W downhillhostel.com
Located beneath cliffs, facing a beach. Dorms and private rooms, kitchen and laundry facilities.

DUNGANNON: Grange Lodge ££
Guesthouse **Road map** D2
7 Grange Road, Dungannon, Co Tyrone
Tel *028 8778 4212*
W grangelodgecountryhouse.com
Tranquil country house dating from 1698. Pretty rooms, warm hospitality and great food.

ENNISKILLEN: Killyhevlin Hotel £
Resort **Road map** C2
Killyhevlin, Enniskillen, Co Fermanagh
Tel *028 6632 3481*
W killyhevlin.com
This hotel is situated on the shores of Lough Erne. Pay extra to have a room with an outstanding waterside view.

HOLYWOOD:
Hastings Culloden Hotel ££
Luxury **Road map** E2
Bangor Road, Holywood, Co Antrim
Tel *028 9042 1066*
W hastingshotels.com
This opulent hotel by Belfast Lough was once the palace of the Bishop of Down. Pleasant rooms, some with great views.

LONDONDERRY: Beech Hill Country House ££
Luxury **Road map** C1
32 Ardmore Road, Londonderry
Tel *028 7134 9279*
W beech-hill.com
Grand country house hotel with comfortable rooms, antique furniture and good service.

LONDONDERRY:
Everglades Hotel ££
Business hotel **Road map** C1
Prehen Road, Londonderry
Tel *028 7132 1066*
W hastingshotels.com
Imposing riverside hotel with spacious rooms. The Grill Room restaurant uses local ingredients.

NEWCASTLE:
Hastings Slieve Donard £££
Leisure club and spa hotel **Road map** E2
Downs Road, Newcastle, Co Down
Tel *028 4372 1066*
W hastingshotels.com
Majestic red-brick hotel in a spectacular location where the Mountains of Mourne sweep down to the sea. Comfy rooms, great spa and world-class golf.

PORTAFERRY: Ardbrae Country House ££
Guesthouse **Road map** E2
Dunevly Rd, Portaferry, County Down
Tel *02842772914*
W ardbrae.co.uk
Comfortable rooms and excellent hospitable service, all surrounded by wonderful countryside views.

For more information on types of hotels *see p295*

WHERE TO EAT AND DRINK

Although the highest concentration of top gourmet restaurants is in Ireland's main cities, equally fine cuisine can be found in some very unlikely, remote locations around the country. Good, plain cooking is on offer at moderately priced, family-style restaurants all over Ireland. The restaurants listed on pages 308–25 are recommended for their high standards of service, quality of food and value for money. To supplement these listings, look out for the *Dining in Ireland* booklet published by Fáilte Ireland, the Irish Tourist Board. Pub lunches are one of Ireland's top travel bargains, offering generous portions of fresh vegetables and prime meats, and can often serve as the main meal of the day for a very reasonable price. Light meals, bar food and a variety of takeaway dishes are also widely available.

Irish Eating Patterns

Traditional Irish breakfasts feature bacon, sausages, black pudding, eggs, tomatoes and brown bread. In Northern Ireland this, plus potato cakes and soda farls *(see p306)*, is known as an "Ulster Fry". These hearty plates often appear on menus as 'all day breakfast' options and coincide with the popularity in brunch fare that has now become part of the Irish dining out culture.

Continental breakfasts are easily available, along with the traditional breakfast, both of which are included in most hotel and bed-and-breakfast rates, as well as porridge, meat, cheese, cereals and fruits. Lunchtime menus offer lighter options such as salads or soup and sandwiches and main meals are served in the evening. Vestiges of the old eating patterns remain in the huge midday platefuls still served in pubs.

Lunch menu at Farmgate Café *(see p314)*

Tips on Eating Out

Elegant dining becomes considerably more affordable when you make lunch your main meal of the day. In many of the top restaurants, the fixed-price lunch and dinner menus are similar, but lunch comes at half the price. House wines are quite drinkable in most restaurants and can reduce the total cost of your bill. If you are travelling with children, look for one of the restaurants that provide a less expensive children's menu.

Lunch is usually served between noon and 2:30pm, with dinner between 6:30 and 10pm, although many ethnic and city-centre restaurants stay open later, particularly in Temple Bar in Dublin's city centre. Bed-and-breakfast hosts will often provide an ample home-cooked evening meal, and many will serve tea and scones in the late evening at no extra charge.

In top restaurants, men are expected to wear a jacket, though not necessarily a tie, and women to wear a dress or suit. Elsewhere, the dress code is pretty informal.

Visa and MasterCard are the most commonly accepted credit cards, and debit cards are also widely accepted. In rural areas, especially in small cafés and pubs, be prepared to pay with cash. Many restaurants have early-bird menus, allowing you to eat in a more expensive place at a cheaper rate.

Gourmet dining at Hayfield Manor Hotel *(see p298)*

Gourmet and Ethnic Dining

This once gourmet-poor land now sports restaurants that rank among Europe's very best, with chefs trained in outstanding domestic and continental institutions. There is a choice of Irish, French, Italian, Chinese, Indonesian and even Russian and Cuban cuisines, with styles ranging from traditional to regional to *nouvelle cuisine*. Locations vary as widely as the cuisine, from hotel dining rooms, town-house basements and city mansions to castle hotels and village cafés. The small County Cork town of Kinsale has established itself as the "Gourmet Capital of Ireland". Outstanding chefs also reign over the gracious houses listed in *Ireland's Blue Book of Country Houses and Restaurants*, available from tourist offices.

Budget Dining

It is quite possible to eat well on a small budget wherever you are in Ireland. In both city and rural locations, there are small cafés, tea rooms and family-style restaurants with inexpensive meals. Even if a café or tea room is at a main tourist attraction, such as Bantry House, you can still expect good, home-made food and freshly baked bread and cakes. Sandwiches are made with thick slices of cheese or meat (not processed); salad plates feature smoked salmon and cold meats; and hot meals usually come with large helpings of vegetables and potatoes cooked every which way.

Pub Food

Ireland's pubs have moved into the food field with a vengeance. In addition to bar snacks (soup, sandwiches and so on), available from noon until late, salads and hot meals are served from midday to 2:30pm. Hot plates all come heaped with mounds of fresh vegetables, potatoes in one or more versions, and good portions of local fish or meat. Particularly good bargains are the pub carveries that offer a choice of joints, sliced to your preference. International staples such as spaghetti, lasagne and quiche also appear on pub menus. For a list of recommended pubs, see pages 326–31.

Fish and Chips and Other Fast Foods

The Irish, from peasant to parliamentarian, love their "chippers", immortalized in Roddy Doyle's novel *The Van*, and any good pub night will end with a visit to the nearest fast-food shop. At any time of day, however, if you pass by Leo Burdock's in Dublin, there will be a long queue for this international institution *(see p309)*. With Ireland's long coastline, wherever you choose, the fish will usually be the freshest catch of the day – plaice, cod, haddock, whiting or ray. The many other fast-food outlets include a host of familiar international chains, as well as a wide variety of burger and kebab shops. There are several good pasta and pizza chains, such as Pizza Express, which is called Milano in the Republic.

Sign at Leo Burdock's *(see p309)*

Picnics

Ireland is a glorious picnic country. Farmhouse cheeses and thick pâtés are picnic treats, or stop by one of the small delis or shops that sell freshly made sandwiches. The coast is ringed with sandy beaches and over 400 forest areas, many with picnic tables; great views add to the pleasure of mountainside picnics, and there are often places to pull off the road in scenic spots.

Recommended Restaurants

Ireland offers a wealth of styles of cooking and a great spread of international flavours – from Italian and Moroccan to Asian street food (often Chinese and Thai fresh noodle or rice dishes, plus skewers of marinated meats and spring rolls). Modern Irish cooking extends far beyond meat and potatoes and takes on a variety of influences to create a fresh and often imaginative use of classic local ingredients, such as salmon, lamb, oysters and beef.

The restaurants are divided into eight geographical areas: Dublin, Southeast Ireland, Cork and Kerry, The Lower Shannon, the West of Ireland, Northwest Ireland, the Midlands and Northern Ireland. They are then subsequently organized by town. The restaurants have been chosen based on a variety of factors. Some offer fantastic Irish cuisine, others are friendly spots with hearty food suitable for families, others provide unrivalled atmosphere, while still others offer excellent choices for ethnic cuisine.

Throughout our listings, we've marked recommended restaurants as DK Choice. We've chosen these because they offer a special experience – either for the superb cuisine, for enjoying a uniquely Irish meal out surrounded by locals, for the excellent value, or a combination of these.

Beachside picnic at Rathmullan House

The Flavours of Ireland

Boxty, barm brack, champ, coddle, cruibins, colcannon – the basic dishes that have nourished Ireland are spiced with fancy names. But the secret of their success is their ingredients, which are nurtured in a warm, damp climate on lush hills that brings them flavour. Beef and dairy cattle can stay out all year and they make abundant butter, cheese and cream. Pork and pork products, such as ham and bacon, are a mainstay, though lamb is traditional, too. Potatoes, the king of vegetables, turn up in soup, pies, cakes, bread and scones that are piled on breakfast and tea tables. And the rivers, lakes and shores are rich in seafood.

Oysters

A chef in Connemara displays traditional Irish cuisine

The Basic Dishes

Irish stews are thick and tasty, traditionally featuring lamb or mutton, onion and potatoes, while beef and Guinness make a darker casserole, sometimes with the addition of oysters. Carrots and turnips are the first choice of vegetables for the pot. Pork is the basis of many dishes. Trotters, called cruibins or crubeens, are sometimes pickled, while bacon can be especially meaty. Dublin coddle, a fill-me-up after the pub on a Saturday night, relies on sausages and potatoes as well as bacon. Ham is sometimes smoked over peat and, for special occasions, it is baked with cloves and brown sugar and served with buttered cabbage. Colcannon is made with cabbage, cooked and chopped with mashed potato and onions, sometimes with the addition of butter and some milk. Boxty is a bake of raw and cooked potato mashed with butter, buttermilk and flour; champ is potatoes mashed with milk, butter and onions.

Fish and Seafood

The Atlantic Ocean and Irish Sea have a rich variety of shellfish, from lobsters and Dublin Bay prawns to mussels

Selection of the many traditional Irish breads

Irish Traditional Food

Gubbeen cheese

If your heart is up to it, start the day with an Ulster Fry. This breakfast fry-up includes thick, tasty bacon, plus black pudding, soda farls and potato cake. A "lady's breakfast" will have one egg, a "gentleman's" two. Gooseberry jam will be spread on fried bread, and mugs of tea will wash it down. Irish stews traditionally use mutton, not so common today, while Spiced Beef uses up brisket, which is covered in a various spices then left for a week before being cooked slowly with Guinness and vegetables. A high tea in the early evening is the major meal in many homes; a main course will be followed by a succession of breads and cakes.

Irish Stew Traditionally, neck of mutton, potatoes, carrots and onions are slowly cooked together for hours.

Fruit and vegetable stall at Moore Street Market, Dublin

and oysters, scallops, clams and razorshells. Herring, mackerel, plaice and skate are brought in from the sea, while the rivers and lakes offer up salmon, trout and eels, which are often smoked. Galway salmon has the best reputation and its oyster festival is famous. Salmon is usually smoked in oak wood kilns. Along the shore, a red seaweed called dulse is collected and mixed with potatoes mashed in their skins to make dulse champ.

Baked Goods

Freshly baked breads make up a large percentage of the Irish diet. Unleaven soda bread is ubiquitous (it's great with Irish cheeses). In Northern Ireland, brown soda bread is called wheaten bread. Potato bread is fried or eaten cold, as cake. Farls ("quarters") are made with wheat flour or oats, bicarbonate of soda and butter-milk, which goes into many recipes. Fruit breads include barm brack, traditionally eaten at Hallowe'en and on All Saint's Day, while rich porter cake is made with Guinness or other stout. White, brown and fruit scones will never be far from tea and breakfast tables.

Sea trout, plucked fresh from the Atlantic Ocean

Dairy Products

Butter, usually salted, is used generously, on vegetables and in sauces as well as in puddings and on bread. Cream, too, is used in cooking, stirred into soups and whipped for puddings. The variety and quality of Irish farmhouse cheeses is impressive, although a medium Cheddar produced by a large manufacturer was hailed "Best Irish Cheese" at the 2005 World Cheese Awards.

Irish Cheeses

Carrigaline Nutty-tasting, Gouda-like cheese from Cork.

Cashel Blue The first Irish blue cheese. Soft and creamy. Unpasteurized; from Tipperary.

Cooleeny Small, Camembert-style unpasteurized cheese from Tipperary.

Durrus Creamy, natural-rind unpasteurized cheese from West Cork. May be smoked.

Gubbeen Semi-soft washed rind cheese. Rich, milky taste.

Milleens Soft, rich rind-washed cheese. Unpasteurized; from the Beara peninsula, Cork.

St Killian Hexagonal Brie-like creamy cheese from Wexford.

Dublin Coddle This is a comforting mixture of sausages, bacon, potatoes and onions, stewed in ham stock.

Galway Salmon Top quality fish can be simply served with an Irish butter sauce, watercress and colcannon.

Brown Bread Ice Cream Considered a luxury in the19th century and now a modern classic in Irish restaurants.

Where to Eat and Drink

Dublin

Southeast Dublin

Hatch & Sons €
Irish **Map** D4
15 St Stephen's Green, Dublin 2
Tel *01 661 0075*
Housed in an elegant, light-filled basement in the Little Museum of Dublin, this restaurant serves traditional Irish food. The blaas, a soft white roll, with a selection of fillings is recommended.

Steps of Rome €
Italian **Map** D4
1 Chatham Street, Dublin 2
Tel *01 670 5630*
A tiny, buzzing café serving tasty pizza slices, bruschetta, and pasta dishes, as well as fine coffee. Open into the evening.

37 Dawson St €€
European **Map** D4
37 Dawson Street, Dublin 2
Tel *01 902 2908*
Expect delicious dishes and tempting cocktails in this hip restaurant bar. Whiskey-lovers are in for a treat with a fantastic selection from across the world.

DK Choice

Avoca Restaurant €€
Irish **Map** D3
11–13 Suffolk Street, Dublin 2
Tel *01 672 6019*
This bright loft restaurant atop the eponymous Irish crafts shop is always busy. Imaginative salads, generous sandwiches, hot dishes and irresistible desserts make the wait worthwhile. Daytime opening hours only. There's a cheaper deli with a few tables in the basement.

Cornucopia €€
Vegetarian **Map** D3
19 Wicklow Street, Dublin 2
Tel *01 677 7583*
Diners can choose from a wide range of tasty and wholesome vegetarian and vegan dishes at the counter – hot plates, wraps, salads and guilt-free desserts.

Dada €€
Moroccan **Map** D4
45 South William Street, Dublin 2
Tel *01 617 0777*
Atmospheric, sumptuously decorated restaurant. The fantastic tagines and couscous dishes are all authentically presented.

Dunne & Crescenzi €€
Italian **Map** E4
14–16 South Frederick Street, Dublin 2
Tel *01 675 9892/01 677 3815*
Open day and night, this *enoteca* offers a warm atmosphere and a lively terrace, along with its range of delicious platters and pasta dishes. The coffee is said to be among the best in town.

Fallon & Byrne €€
Bistro-Irish **Map** D3
11–17 Exchequer Street, Dublin 2
Tel *01 472 1010*
An elegant dining room above F&B's fantastic food hall and cellar wine bar. Top-notch classic cuisine; try the Oysters Bienville or the stuffed loin of rabbit.

The Green Hen €€
French-Irish **Map** D4
33 Exchequer Street, Dublin 2
Tel *01 670 7238*
The authentic Parisian-café vibe here is the perfect accompaniment to the terrific food and cocktails. Duck confit and assiette of pork are among the highlights.

The bright dining room of Avoca Restaurant, southeast Dublin

Price Guide
For a three-course meal per person, with a half-bottle of house wine, including tax and service.

€	under €25
€€	€25 to 50
€€€	over €50

L'Gueuleton €€
French **Map** C4
1 Fade Street, Dublin 2
Tel *01 675 3708*
This charming bistro offers a menu featuring French specialities such as snails in garlic, pastis butter and Corleggy goat's cheese.

The Woollen Mills €€
Modern Irish **Map** D3
42 Lower Ormond Quay, Dublin 1
Tel *01 828 0835*
A sprawling "eating house" spread over four floors of an old haberdashery, with a huge terrace overlooking the Ha'penny Bridge. The food is fresh with a focus on freshly baked cakes, salads and hearty dinners.

Avenue By Nick Munier €€€
Modern Irish **Map** D3
1 Crow Street, Dublin 2
Tel *01 645 5102*
The restaurant offers a unique gastronomic experience with high-protein, low carbohydrate dishes. At the Eclair De Luxe Bar, diners can enjoy delicious comfort food in custom built train booths. Excellent cocktail lounge.

L'Écrivain €€€
French-Irish **Map** F5
109a Lower Baggot Street, Dublin 2
Tel *01 661 1919* **Closed** *Sun*
The menu at this Michelin-starred restaurant mixes French cuisine with Irish delicacies and features scallops, venison and foie gras. Impeccable service.

Peploe's Wine Bistro €€€
Bistro **Map** D4
16 St Stephen's Green, Dublin 2
Tel *01 676 3144*
This place in the basement of an elegant Georgian town house serves excellent steaks and quality wines. Advance booking highly recommended.

Pichet €€€
Bistro **Map** D3
14–15 Trinity Street, Dublin 2
Tel *01 677 1060*
Exquisite food and perfect service in a relaxed atmosphere. Try the pork cheek, crispy belly and the frozen Espresson Bombe to finish.

Restaurant Patrick Guilbaud €€€
French fine dining **Map** E5
21 Upper Merrion Street, Dublin 2
Tel *01 676 4192* **Closed** *Sun, Mon, bank hols; Christmas wk*
Diners come to this restaurant boasting two Michelin stars for the imaginative, contemporary French menu. Book a table in advance.

Shanahans on The Green €€€
Steakhouse **Map** D5
119 St Stephen's Green, Dublin 2
Tel *01 407 0939* **Closed** *Sun*
Dublin's biggest, juiciest, finest American-style steaks are served in a splendid Georgian dining room. Excellent seafood, too.

Trocadero €€€
Bistro **Map** F5
4 Andrew Street, Dublin 2
Tel *01 677 5545*
This has been Dublin's hallowed theatre restaurant since 1956. Famed for its steaks, it also serves savoury pâtés, fresh fish and classic desserts.

Unicorn €€€
Italian **Map** F5
12b Merrion Court, Merrion Row, Dublin 2
Tel *01 676 2182* **Closed** *Sun*
Mediterranean-inspired food – home-made gnocchi, rigatoni, Irish lobster and truffle risotto. Children are welcome until 9pm.

Southwest Dublin

Leo Burdock's €
Fish and chips **Map** B4
2 Werburgh Street, Christchurch, Dublin 8
Tel *01 454 0306*
Good, honest fish and chips – tasty ray, lemon sole, cod. There are branches of Leo Burdock's, Dublin's oldest chipper, on Liffey Street and in Phibsboro, too.

Neon €
Asian street food **Map** C5
17 Camden Street, Dublin 2
Tel *01 405 2222*
This is a great place for groups and children. Try the Pad Thai or one of the curries, which range from mild to extra hot. Pour your own free whipped ice-cream cone for dessert.

Pitt Bros €
American **Map** C3
Unit 1, Wicklow House, South Great George's Street, Dublin 2
Tel *01 677 8777*
Extremely popular with meat-lovers, Pitt Bros' signature style is slow cooked meat. The brisket and pulled pork are favourites.

The cosy interior of The Queen of Tarts café, southwest Dublin

The Queen of Tarts €
Irish baking **Map** C3
4 Cork Hill, Dame Street, Dublin 2
Tel *01 670 7499*
Great brunches, soups, savoury dishes and, most importantly, magnificent cakes can be enjoyed at this quaint café opposite City Hall.

The Chameleon Restaurant €€
Asian **Map** C3
1 Lower Fownes Street, Temple Bar, Dublin 2
Tel *01 671 0362* **Closed** *Mon*
The menu here offers Asian tapas, Indonesian cuisine, and Irish beef, chicken and seafood. Javanese short rib of beef served in a star-anise-infused Kecap Manis is a must-try.

Chez Max €€
French **Map** C3
1 Palace Street, Dublin 2
Tel *01 633 7215*
Enjoy classic French favourites – *moules frites*, rabbit rillettes and mousse au chocolat – right by the gates of Dublin Castle. A fantastic early-bird menu is available 5:30–7pm (Sun–Thu).

Cleaver East €€
European **Map** C3
East Essex Street, Temple Bar, Dublin 2
Tel *01 531 3500*
This popular eatery serves sharing plates of lobster dumplings, oriental mushrooms and lemon-grass broth, cushion of venison with braised red cabbage and wild mushrooms and much more.

Delahunt €€
Irish **Map** C5
39 Camden Street Lwr, Dublin 2
Tel *01 598 4880*
Set in a lovely Victorian building, the restaurant uses traditional cooking techniques to create a unique Irish menu. The specialities include home curing and smoking, slow cooked braises, pickles, preserves and bread making.

Elephant and Castle €€
American brasserie **Map** D3
19 Temple Bar, Dublin 2
Tel *01 679 3121*
There is no need to pre-book at this lively eatery. California salads, generous burgers and omelettes are all good, and the chicken wings are a definite winner. Great for weekend brunch.

Jules €€
French **Map** C3
74 Dame Street, Dublin 2
Tel *01 679 4555*
This upscale French restaurant specializes in fresh seafood. The crab linguine is highly recommended. They also have a good wine list.

The Lord Edward €€
Seafood **Map** B4
23 Christ Church Place, Dublin 8
Tel *01 454 2420* **Closed** *Sun–Tue*
Located above a traditional pub, offering charming service and classic fish dishes such as dressed crab and Galway bay oysters. There are also steak and chicken options.

Monty's of Kathmandu €€
Nepalese **Map** C3
28 Eustace Street, Dublin 2
Tel *01 670 4911*
Friendly, popular restaurant with interesting fish, chicken and lamb dishes in fragrant, creamy sauces. Full coeliac menu and extensive vegetarian selection, too.

Odessa €€
American bistro **Map** D3
13–14 Dame Court, Dublin 2
Tel *01 670 7634*
With a chic retro vibe, Odessa is renowned for its fancy weekend brunches – decadent fry-ups, eggs Benedict, Bellinis. The menu has a decent selection of dishes for vegetarians too.

For more information on types of restaurants *see page 305*

The Porthouse €€
Tapas **Map** D4
64A South William Street, Dublin 2
Tel *01 677 0298*
Spanish heaven in the heart of Dublin, this restaurant serves a wide selection of tasty tapas like deep-fried Tetilla cheese, served with tomato salad and honey.

Rustic Stone €€
Irish **Map** C4
17 South Great George's Street, Dublin 2
Tel *01 707 9596*
Chef Dylan McGrath's restaurant puts great emphasis on nutrition, seasonality and local ingredients. Meat and fish are served on a hot volcanic stone, so diners can cook them to their liking.

Soder + Ko €€
Asian **Map** C4
64 South Great George's Street, Dublin 2
Tel *01 478 1590*
An eclectic menu offering dim sum, Korean steamed buns, platters of crispy duck pancakes and chicken Yakitori. Live music on selected evenings (Thu–Sat).

Yamamori Izakaya €€
Japanese-Chinese **Map** C3
12–13 South Great George's Street, Dublin 2
Tel *01 645 8001*
Housed in the old Bewley's building, this café boasts grand Oriental decor with a laid-back vibe. The menu includes sushi and dim sum. There is a lively Japanese cocktail bar downstairs.

Sabor Brazil €€€
Brazilian **Map** C5
50 Pleasants Street, off Camden St, Dublin 8
Tel *01 475 0304* **Closed** *Mon*
Baroque decor, impeccable service and fine cuisine, with prosecco and olives on arrival. Try the remarkable seven-course tasting menu (booking required).

Historic Beshoff's, serving fantastic fish and chips

The stylish booths of Chapter One, north of the Liffey

North of the Liffey

Beshoff's €
Fish and chips **Map** D2
6 Upper O'Connell Street, Dublin 1
Tel *01 872 4400*
Delicious catch of the day, plus non-fish options and a children's menu. Founded in 1913 by a Russian immigrant who came from a long line of fishermen.

Fish Shop €
Seafood **Map** A2
No. 6 Queen Street, Smithfield, Dublin 7
W fish-shop.ie **Closed** *Mon*
A quirky restaurant with an intimate walled and roofed garden. Try fried oysters, wood-roasted mackerel or beer-battered catch of the day.

Lovinspoon €
Irish **Map** C1
15 North Frederick Street, Dublin 1
Tel *01 804 7604* **Closed** *Sun*
Generous all-day breakfasts and creative lunches can be enjoyed at this friendly café.

Panem €
Italian **Map** C3
21 Lower Ormond Quay, Dublin 1
Tel *01 872 8510* **Closed** *Sun, 24 Dec–8 Jan*
Quayside café/bakery serving sweet brioche, savoury focaccia, almond biscuits, great coffee and a deliciously dark hot chocolate. Open only during the day.

Le Bon Crubeen €€
Irish-French **Map** E2
81–82 Talbot Street, Dublin 1
Tel *01 704 0126*
Classic fare – scallops, Kerry lamb, pork belly – in cosy surroundings. There are also great weekend brunches and a good-value pre-theatre menu. Jazz on Saturdays.

The Church €€
Irish **Map** C2
Jervis Street, Dublin 1
Tel *01 828 0102*
A four-storey venue in a historic building with a huge terrace. Bar food is available, or try the Gallery Restaurant for hearty dishes such as beef and Guinness pie.

Jo Burger Town €€
Irish **Map** D4
4–5 Castle Market, Dublin 2
W joburger.ie
Gravity-defying burgers piled high with delicious combinations of cheeses, relishes and other tasty ingredients.

L. Mulligan. Grocer €€
Irish **Map** A2
18 Stoneybatter, Dublin 7
Tel *01 670 9889* **Closed** *Mon*
Set in a former grocer's shop, this gastro pub has a delectable menu featuring spiced potted crab, wild venison burger and slow roasted pork belly. Excellent selection of beers.

Musashi Noodle & Sushi Bar €€
Sushi **Map** C3
15 Capel Street, Dublin 1
Tel *01 532 8068*
Fresh sushi is served in this bustling and friendly restaurant. Noodle dishes are also recommended and you can bring your own alcohol.

Chapter One €€€
European **Map** C1
18–19 Parnell Square North, Dublin 1
Tel *01 873 2266* **Closed** *Sun & Mon; 1–14 Aug & 24 Dec–7 Jan*
This Michelin-starred eatery in the cosy and characterful cellar of the Dublin Writers Museum offers a creative menu. The pre-theatre deal is quite popular.

Key to price guide *see page 308*

The Winding Stair €€€
Irish **Map** C3
40 Lower Ormond Quay, Dublin 1
Tel *01 872 7320*
Overlooking the iconic Ha'penny Bridge, this charming restaurant also has a bookshop/gallery. The simple dishes include potted crab claws and calf's liver with mustard mash. Craft beers and wines from boutique makers.

Further Afield

Olive €
Irish **Road map** D3
86a Strand Street, Skerries, Co Dublin
Tel *01 849 0310*
A good stop for an informal alfresco lunch near the beach. Fresh soups, paninis and delectable home-baked cookies.

Caviston's Seafood Restaurant €€
Seafood **Road map** D4
Glasthule, Sandycove, Co Dublin
Tel *01 280 9245* **Closed** *Sun & Mon*
Stunning seafood, prepared with flair; try the pan-fried haddock or the chargrilled sardines. Advance booking recommended. The adjoining delicatessen sells artisanal foods great for a picnic.

Forest Avenue €€
Modern Irish **Road map** D4
8 Sussex Terrace, Ballsbridge
Tel *01 667 8337*
This exciting addition to the Dublin restaurant scene offers a five-course tasting menu which changes frequently in order to incorporate the freshest seasonal ingredients with a Nordic twist.

Johnnie Fox's €€
Irish **Road map** D4
Glencullen, Co Dublin
Tel *01 295 5647*
Located 30 minutes south of the city, on top of the Dublin Mountains, this friendly pub has hearty Irish food and traditional music.

Juniors Deli & Café €€
Irish-Italian **Road map** D4
2 Bath Avenue, Dublin 4
Tel *01 664 3648*
Swing by this informal deli, which serves the best chargrilled chicken sandwich in Dublin. Open for brunch and dinner. If you feel like a slice, then visit Paulie's Pizza, their pizzeria next door.

Ouzo's €€
Seafood **Road map** D4
22 Castle Street, Dalkey, Co Dublin
Tel *01 285 1890*
A cosy neighbourhood favourite, with fabulous local seafood and sumptuous, cut-to-order steaks. Specialities include the Great Crab and Lobster Feast. Barrel wines and satisfying desserts.

Rasam €€
Indian **Road map** D4
18–19 Glasthule Road, Sandycove, Dun Laoghaire, Co Dublin
Tel *01 230 0600*
Plush Indian restaurant boasting chefs from all across the South Asian subcontinent – Bengal, Orissa, Rajasthan. Fine, fragrant specialities include beetroot chicken, *barrah nalli* (lamb shank marinated in onions, cardamom, cloves and yoghurt) and *phirni* (broken rice and saffron pudding).

DK Choice

Aqua €€€
Californian-Italian
Road map D3
1 West Pier, Howth, Co Dublin
Tel *01 832 0690* **Closed** *Mon & Tue*
A former yacht club, this contemporary restaurant boasts incredible views – from both the first-floor vantage point and the full-length windows on all sides – on to the choppy seas and vast sunsets at Howth Harbour. Service is attentive, and the food is elegantly presented. Specialities include lobster and crayfish salad, seafood chowder and fillet of beef.

Bon Appetit €€€
French **Road map** D4
9 St James Terrace, Malahide, Co Dublin
Tel *01 845 0314* **Closed** *Mon*
Michelin-starred fine dining in an elegant Georgian town house near the marina. Menu favourites include seafood, and rump of Wicklow lamb. The basement houses a more informal brasserie.

Warm, intimate interiors of The Lobster Pot, Dublin

Hartley's €€€
Irish **Road map** D4
1 Harbour Road, Dun Laoghaire, Co Dublin
Tel *01 280 6767* **Closed** *Mon*
Housed in the old Kingstown train station, by Dun Laoghaire Harbour, specialities here include Hereford beef steaks, salt and pepper squid and roast spiced pears. Beautiful decor and ambience.

King Sitric €€€
Seafood **Road map** D3
East Pier, Howth, Co Dublin
Tel *01 832 5235* **Closed** *Mon & Tue in winter*
Award-winning restaurant named after the medieval Norse king of Dublin. In a stylish room, diners enjoy such specialities as crab mornay, and black sole meunière.

The Lobster Pot €€€
Seafood **Road map** D4
9 Ballsbridge Terrace, Ballsbridge, Dublin 4
Tel *01 668 0025* **Closed** *Sun*
This sophisticated restaurant tantalizes with Kilmore crab and Dublin Bay prawns. Steaks and roast duckling flamed with Grand Marnier are also on the menu.

Roly's €€€
Bistro **Road map** D4
7 Ballsbridge Terrace, Ballsbridge, Dublin 4
Tel *01 668 2611*
Come to this lively bistro in the heart of Ballsbridge for colourful, aromatic food – Kerry lamb pie, roast monkfish, Dublin Bay prawns. The downstairs café is the place to buy freshly baked bread to take away.

Southeast Ireland

BALLYMACARBRY: Hanora's Cottage €€€
Modern Irish **Road map** C5
Nire Valley, Ballymacarbry, Co Waterford
Tel *052 613 6134* **Closed** *Sun; 7 days at Christmas*
Pleasant restaurant aimed chiefly at residents of the guesthouse, but open to all. Tuck into the pan-fried hake fillet with celeriac puree as you enjoy the lovely views of the garden and riverscape. Reservations essential.

For more information on types of restaurants *see page 305*

BLESSINGTON: Grangecon Café €
Modern Irish **Road map** D4
Lake Road, Blessington, Co Wicklow
Tel *045 857 892* **Closed** *Sun & Mon*
An excellent lunchtime venue serving a small range of dishes prepared with locally sourced and largely organic ingredients. Bring your own wine.

CAMPILE: Georgian Tea Rooms €
Home cooking **Road map** D5
Great Island, Campile, Co Wexford
Tel *051 388 109* **Closed** *winter*
Enjoy a range of hearty soups, stuffed paninis and more in the beautiful Georgian conservatory or alfresco, and then spend some time wandering the gardens.

CARLOW: Lennons @ Visual €€
Irish **Road map** D4
Visual Centre for Contemporary Art, Old Dublin Road, Carlow, Co Carlow
Tel *59 917 9245*
Good, locally sourced food, great cakes and pastries are on the menu here. Silverhill Irish duck breast is a speciality.

CARNE: Lobster Pot Seafood Bar €€
Modern European **Road map** D5
Ballyfane, Carne, Co Wexford
Tel *053 913 1110* **Closed** *Mon; Jan*
Though it is mainly seafood at this cute old pub, the menu has plenty of variety. Children are allowed only at lunchtimes.

CELBRIDGE: La Serre €€€
Modern Irish **Road map** D4
Village Lyons Demesne, Co Kildare
Tel *01 630 3500* **Closed** *Mon & Tue*
Conservatory restaurant serving freshly cooked fare in an informal environment. Eat inside, or out in the pretty courtyard.

Canopied entrance of the beautiful Marfield House, Gorey

Key to price guide *see page 308*

DK Choice

DUNGARVAN: The Tannery €€€
Modern Irish **Road map** 5C
10 Quay Street, Dungarvan, Co Waterford
Tel *058 454 20* **Closed** *Mon*
Well-known chef/proprietor Paul Flynn cooks up a storm in this converted tannery building, now a restaurant and cookery school. His menus change with the seasons and use locally caught fish, local cheeses and organic meats; the vegetables travel no further than from the kitchen garden across the road. The set menu offers good value for money.

ENNISKERRY: Poppies €
Traditional Irish **Road map** D4
The Square, Enniskerry, Co Wicklow
Tel *01 282 8869*
Village eatery serving quiches, tartiflette, beef and Guinness pie, as well as gorgeous cakes and breads. There are a few tables inside, and more on the street.

GOREY: Marlfield House €€€
Modern European **Road map** D4
Courtdown Road, Co Wexford
Tel *053 942 1124*
White tablecloths, silver service and a marvellous atmosphere. Much of the veg on your plate is grown in the restaurant's own garden. Reservations required.

GREYSTONES: The Three Q's €
International **Road map** D4
Church Road, Greystones, Co Wicklow
Tel *01 287 5477* **Closed** *dinner Mon*
This award-winning restaurant is considered to be an institution in Wicklow. Try their lemon sole with prawn and crabmeat filling.

GREYSTONES: The Happy Pear €€
Vegetarian **Road map** D4
Church Road, Greystones, Co Wicklow
Tel *01 287 3655*
A family-run restaurant, The Happy Pear serves scrumptious, healthy dishes. There is also a grocery store next door which sells fresh, organic and seasonal produce.

KILDARE: Silken Thomas Chapter 16 €€
Modern Irish **Road map** D4
The Square, Kildare, Co Kildare
Tel *045 522 232*
Pub-restaurant serving big portions of family favourites in a comfortable setting. Check out the weekend lunch offers.

KILKENNY: Ristorante Rinuccini €€
Italian **Road map** C4
1 The Parade, Kilkenny, Co Kilkenny
Tel *056 776 575*
They offer a range of classic Italian dishes with an inventive Irish spin, an extensive wine list and white tablecloths. No pizzas.

KILKENNY: Zuni €€
Modern European **Road map** C4
26 Patrick Street, Kilkenny, Co Kilkenny
Tel *056 772 3999* **Closed** *25 & 26 Dec*
Imaginary fusion cooking served in a boutique hotel with sleek rooms. Food locally sourced.

DK Choice

KILKENNY: Campagne €€€
French **Road map** C4
5 Gas House Lane, Kilkenny, Co Kilkenny
Tel *056 777 2858* **Closed** *dinner Sun, Mon & Tue (after bank hols)*
A stylish place with oak flooring, banquette seating and artworks on the walls. Locally sourced ingredients are used to create excellent French dishes with an Irish twist at this Michelin-starred restaurant. Try the wood pigeon or the spring lamb. A thoughtful wine list and attentive staff complete the experience.

DK Choice

KILMACANOGUE: Sugar Tree Café €€
Home cooking **Road map** D2
Kilmacanogue, Bray, Co Wicklow
Tel *01 274 6939*
Excellent self-service restaurant in a renovated pavilion in the former Jameson distillery, now part of the Avoca complex. The convivial atmosphere and huge portions of traditional Irish home-cooked meals make this place a must-visit destination and perfect for children.

KILMACOW: The Thatch €
Pub food **Road map** D5
Grannagh, Kilmacow, Co Kilkenny
Tel *051 872 876*
Better-than-average pub food – juicy burgers, fresh seafood, and salads – served in a friendly environment. Live music on Weds.

KILMORE QUAY: The Silver Fox €€
European-Asian **Road map** D5
Kilmore Quay, Co Wexford
Tel *053 912 9888* **Closed** *Mon–Thu (Nov–Feb)*
The simple dishes – mainly locally caught fish and seafood,

Sophisticated dining at La Boheme, Waterford

though there is something for everyone – are enlivened by a taste of the Orient. Artworks by Ivan Sutton decorate the room.

LEIGHLINBRIDGE: Lord Bagenal Restaurant €€
Traditional Irish **Road map** D4
Main St, Leighlinbridge, Co Carlow
Tel *059 977 4000*
Tuck into a good-value meal in this well-regarded restaurant. More informal fare is served daily in the traditional bar.

MACREDDIN VILLAGE: The Strawberry Tree at Brook Lodge €€€
Organic **Road map** D4
The Brooke Lodge, Macreddin Village, Co Wicklow
Tel *090 236 444* **Closed** *Mon (except Aug)*
Ireland's only certified organic restaurant serves simply cooked, good-quality organic and foraged food. Try the baked wild Hake with Rainbow chard or the homemade Arancini with wild garlic pesto.

NAAS: Brown Bear €€
Modern European **Road map** D4
Two Mile House, Naas, Co Kildare
Tel *045 883 561* **Closed** *Mon & Tue*
High-quality food at down-to-earth prices. The menu is vegetarian- and coeliac-friendly, and most ingredients are sourced locally – many are even grown in the restaurant's own garden. Booking advised at weekends.

ROUNDWOOD: The Roundwood Inn €€
European **Road map** D4
Main Street, Roundwood, Co Wicklow
Tel *01 281 8107* **Closed** *Mon–Thu*
An extensive wine list biased towards European offerings complements the home-cooked food at this traditional pub with open log fires. Booking essential.

TRAMORE: The Copper Hen €€
Modern European **Road map** C5
Fenor, Tramore, Co Waterford
Tel *051 330 300* **Closed** *Mon & Tue (summer), Mon–Wed (winter)*
This place serves big portions of simple, well-cooked food. Great value for money, it also offers lots of room, which makes it popular with families at Sunday lunchtime.

THOMASTOWN: Blackberry Café €
Home cooking **Road map** C4
Market Street, Thomastown, Co Kilkenny
Tel *086 775 303* **Closed** *Sun*
Home-made soups, sandwiches and salads, plus an array of cakes and pastries, in a pleasant all-day eatery that is popular with the local community. Friendly service.

THOMASTOWN: The Lady Helen €€€
International **Road map** C4
Mount Juliet, Thomastown, Co Kilkenny
Tel *056 777 3000 (ext. 1113)*
Closed *Sun, Tue*
This Michelin-starred restaurant is perfect for a special occasion, with gorgeous plasterwork and views out over the estate. Classic dishes with a modern twist.

WATERFORD: The Ginger Man €
Pub food **Road map** D5
6–7 Arundel Lane, Waterford, Co Waterford
Tel *051 879 522*
Better-than-average pub food – wraps, paninis, soups, steak sandwiches and more. A busy place offering large portions.

WATERFORD: Bodega €€
Mediterranean **Road map** D5
54 John St, Waterford, Co Waterford
Tel *051 844 177* **Closed** *Sun*
Sunny, friendly place serving locally sourced food – mainly fish and seafood, but there is something to satisfy all palates. The early-bird menu is great value for money.

WATERFORD: La Boheme €€
French **Road map** D5
2 George's Street, Waterford, Co Waterford
Tel *051 875 645* **Closed** *Mon; 25–27 Dec*
Elegant restaurant with stone floors, mood lighting and vaulted ceilings. Classic French cuisine is given an Irish twist. As well as being vegetarian- and coeliac-friendly, the menu is MSG-free.

WEXFORD: Cistin Eile €
Modern Irish **Road map** D5
80 Sth Main St, Wexford, Co Wexford
Tel *053 912 1616* **Closed** *Sun*
Imaginative fare in no-nonsense surroundings. Choosing the set menu brings this smart place into the budget range. There is a small but intelligent wine list.

WEXFORD: La Dolce Vita €
Italian **Road map** D5
6–7 Trimmers Lane, Wexford, Co Wexford
Tel *053 917 0806* **Closed** *Sun, bank hols; lunch Fri & Sat; 4 days at Christmas*
An authentic Italian restaurant located in a light, airy room, with pavement seating for sunny days. A great place for the entire family.

WEXFORD: Greenacres €€
Modern Irish **Road map** D5
Selskar, Wexford, Co Wexford
Tel *053 912 2975*
The airy dining room is lined with bottles of wine, which you can enjoy with your meal or purchase to take home. The set menu is fantastic value.

Cork and Kerry

BALLYBUNION: Kilcooly's Country House €€€
Traditional Irish **Road map** A5
Ballybunion, Co Kerry
Tel *068 27112* **Closed** *Mon & Tue (Nov–Mar)*
Victorian guesthouse offering both bar food and fine dining (Apr–Oct). The restaurant has live piano music at summer weekends. Good children's menu.

BALLYCOTTON: Capriccio €€€
Modern Irish **Road map** C6
The Bayview Hotel, Ballycotton, Co Cork
Tel *021 464 6746* **Closed** *Nov–Mar*
Expect some serious cooking at this family-owned and-run eatery serving predominantly seafood. There is also a vegetarian menu.

For more information on types of restaurants *see page 305*

Sample inventive vegetarian dishes at Café Paradiso, Cork City

BALLYDEHOB: Antonio's €€
Italian **Road map** B6
Main Street, Ballydehob, Co Cork
Tel *028 37139* **Closed** *Mon (summer); call for winter hours*
Authentic pizzeria in a lovely old stone building. Pasta dishes, steaks and seafood. Reservations recommended in the summer.

BALTIMORE: Casey's of Baltimore €€
Seafood **Road map** B6
Baltimore, Co Cork
Tel *028 20197*
Organic vegetables straight from their kitchen garden, paired with the freshest black sole, monkfish, lobster and prawns make this a must stop for any food lover.

BALTIMORE: The Lookout €€
Modern Irish **Road map** B6
The Waterfront Hotel, Baltimore, Co Cork
Tel *028 20600* **Closed** *Sun–Thu (early and late summer); Oct–Easter (except a few days at Christmas)*
Airy first-floor restaurant with huge windows and views over the harbour. Limited opening hours; however, simple food is available daily from La Jolie Brise, a pizzeria in the same hotel.

BANDON: Blue Geranium Café €
Irish **Road map** B6
Hosford's Garden Centre, Enniskeane, Co Cork
Tel *023 883 9159* **Closed** *Mon*
Good café-style food – quiches, sandwiches and some cooked meals. Ideal for families, as there is a children's area and lots of space.

BANTRY: O'Connor's Seafood Restaurant €€
Seafood **Road map** B6
Wolf Tone Square, Bantry, Co Cork
Tel *027 55664*
Long-established place serving delicious and affordable fare – fish and chips, seafood pie and monkfish and smoked venison risotto. It gets very busy with locals at lunchtime, so it is best to book a table, especially in the summer.

BLARNEY: Blair's Inn €€€
Traditional Irish **Road map** B5
Cloghroe, Blarney, Co Cork
Tel *021 438 1470*
Award-winning pub serving excellent home-cooked food, either in the bar or the restaurant. Classic traditional dishes – lemon sole in butter, shepherd's pie, sausages and mash – sit alongside more unusual offerings.

CASTLETOWNSHEND: Mary Ann's Bar €€
European **Road map** B6
Main St, Castletownshend, Co Cork
Tel *028 36146* **Closed** *Mon & Tue (winter); 3 wks Jan*
A well-loved pub with a restaurant upstairs and lots of outside tables for alfresco dining in the summer. The seafood menu changes according to the daily catch, and portions are generous. Also on the menu are poultry, steaks and roasts.

CORK CITY: Crawford Gallery Café €
Irish **Road map** C6
Emmet Place, Cork City
Tel *021 427 4415* **Closed** *Sun, bank hols; 10 days Dec–Jan*
From soups and sandwiches to more substantial lunches, there is plenty on the menu at this art-gallery café to satisfy all palates.

CORK CITY: Farmgate Café €
Traditional Irish **Road map** C6
English Market, Princes Street, Cork City
Tel *021 427 8134* **Closed** *Sun, bank hols; 10 days Dec–Jan*
Traditional local dishes – sausage and mash, shepherd's pie – made with fresh ingredients from the bustling market downstairs.

CORK CITY: Jacob's on the Mall €€
Modern European **Road map** C6
30 Sth Mall, Cork City
Tel *021 425 1530* **Closed** *Sun, bank hols; 2 days at Christmas*
A former Turkish bathhouse provides the atmospheric setting for stylish, modern food. Set-price menus are available all evening for the budget-conscious.

CORK CITY: Café Paradiso €€€
Vegetarian **Road map** C6
16 Lancaster Quay, Cork City
Tel *021 427 7939* **Closed** *Sun & Mon; 7 days at Christmas*
Ireland's most famous vegetarian restaurant serves inventive and complex dishes, such as kale and smoked Ardrahan cheese ravioli, feta and pistachio couscous.

CORK CITY: Greene's Restaurant €€€
Modern European **Road map** C6
48 MacCurtain Street, Cork City
Tel *021 455 2279* **Closed** *3 days at Christmas*
Come to this art-filled restaurant for an interesting, modern take on traditional Irish cooking. Ask for a seat overlooking the pretty courtyard waterfall.

CORK CITY: The Ivory Tower €€€
Asian fusion **Road map** C6
1st Floor, 35 Princes Street, Cork City
Tel *021 427 4665* **Closed** *Sun–Wed*
This is as eclectic as it gets, from the food – a mix of Japanese, Mexican and traditional Irish dishes – to the bric-a-brac and artwork decorating the room.

DINGLE: The Half Door €€
Traditional Irish **Road map** A5
John Street, Dingle, Co Kerry
Tel *066 915 1600* **Closed** *Sun*
Housed in a country cottage-style building. The menu is predominantly seafood, simply cooked and served in generous portions. Book in the summer.

DK Choice

DINGLE: Lord Baker's Restaurant and Bar €€
Traditional Irish **Road map** A5
Main Street, Dingle, Co Kerry
Tel *066 915 1277* **Closed** *Thu*
This ancient pub – with its stone walls, open fires and country-inn decorations – has a warm and welcoming atmosphere, whether you eat in the bar or the restaurant. A pretty conservatory opens out into a walled garden. Dishes include sirloin steak with pepper sauce and Dingle Bay crab claws.

DINGLE: Out of the Blue €€
Seafood **Road map** A5
Waterside, Dingle, Co Kerry
Tel *066 915 0811* **Closed** *Nov–Mar*
Small bar cooking freshly caught fish in classical style. Book ahead, especially in the summer.

DINGLE: The Chart House €€€
Modern Irish **Road map** A5
The Mall, Dingle, Co Kerry
Tel *066 915 2255*
Closed *2 Jan–12 Feb*
Innovative dishes are made with the finest locally sourced ingredients, such as Annascaul black pudding, Cromane mussels and Skeaghanore duck.

DURRUS: Good Things Café €€
Modern Irish **Road map** B6
Durrus, near Bantry, Co Cork
Tel *027 61426* **Closed** *Nov–Mar*
Inventive seasonal fare based on local ingredients is served in an airy room with a view of the kitchen.

DURRUS: Blairscove €€€
Modern European **Road map** B6
Durrus, near Bantry, Co Cork
Tel *027 61127* **Closed** *Mon; Nov–mid-Mar*
Booking is essential for this eatery with a long-established reputation. Lovely desserts.

GOLEEN: Heron's Cove €€
Modern Irish **Road map** B6
Harbour Road, Goleen, Co Cork
Tel *028 352 25* **Closed** *limited hours Nov–Mar; call for details.*
A long-established place in a pretty shoreside location. Local seafood and meats are cooked simply. Reservations essential.

KENMARE: Purple Heather €
Home cooking **Road map** B6
Henry Street, Kenmare, Co Kerry
Tel *064 664 1016* **Closed** *Sun, bank hols; 1 wk at Christmas*
At the back of a dark, 1970s-style bar is a restaurant serving simple café food – open sandwiches, tasty pâtés and local cheeses. Free Wi-Fi.

KENMARE: Lime Tree Restaurant €€
Modern Irish **Road map** B6
Shelbourne Street, Kenmare, Co Kerry
Tel *064 664 1225* **Closed** *Mon–Fri (Oct–Mar), Sun*
Housed in a lovely stone building, this restaurant offers classic dishes with a twist. Vegetarian options are available.

KENMARE: Mulcahy's €€
Modern Irish **Road map** B6
Henry Street, Kenmare, Co Kerry
Tel *064 664 2383* **Closed** *Mon*
This place draws diners with it's fusion of Irish ingredients and Asian flavours. There is a pleasant bar area and welcoming staff.

KENMARE: Packie's €€
Modern Irish **Road map** B6
35 Henry Street, Kenmare, Co Kerry
Tel *064 664 1508* **Closed** *Sun; mid-Jan–mid-Feb*
Fresh seafood dominates the menu here, but there is also Irish stew and rack of lamb.

KILLARNEY: Jam €
Café food **Road map** B5
Old Market Lane, Killarney, Co Kerry
Tel *064 663 7716* **Closed** *Sun; 4 days at Christmas*
Roomy café serving sandwiches, quiches, lasagne and other home-cooked staples. Desserts include banoffee pie, bread-and-butter pudding and a delicious lemon meringue.

KILLARNEY: Lord Kenmare's Restaurant €€
Modern Irish **Road map** B5
College Street, Killarney, Co Kerry
Tel *064 663 1294* **Closed** *Mon & Tue (Jan); 3 days at Christmas*
Classic dishes with a modern twist. Try the pork belly cooked in whiskey, Calvados and honey, or the ox tongue and quail salad.

Elegant dining hall at Blairscove, Durrus

Tempting cakes and pastries on offer at Jam, Killarney

KILLARNEY: Treyvaud's €€
International **Road map** B5
62 High Street, Killarney, Co Kerry
Tel *064 663 3062* **Closed** *Mon (Sep–May)*
Well-respected menu featuring game in season, as well as more unusual offerings, such as guinea fowl. Vegetarian and seafood options, too.

KILLARNEY: Gaby's Seafood Restaurant €€€
French-Irish **Road map** B5
27 High Street, Killarney, Co Kerry
Tel *064 663 2519* **Closed** *Sun; 7 days at Christmas & New Year*
It is mainly seafood at this long-established restaurant. The signature dish of lobster is cooked in Cognac, wine and cream.

KILLARNEY: The Garden Room €€€
International **Road map** B5
The Malton Hotel, Killarney, Co Kerry
Tel *064 663 800*
A grand dining room in an old railway hotel, with elegant furnishings and domed ceilings. Classic, well-cooked dishes.

KILLORGLIN: Nick's Seafood Restaurant €€€
Seafood **Road map** A5
Lower Bridge Street, Killorglin, Co Kerry
Tel *066 976 1219* **Closed** *Mon & Tue (summer), Sun–Wed (winter); 2 days at Christmas*
Both the early bird and the bar menu offer great value, and there is plenty for vegetarians, too. In a spacious room above a piano bar.

For more information on types of restaurants *see page 305*

KINSALE: Crackpots €€
European **Road map** B6
3 Cork Street, Kinsale, Co Cork
Tel *021 477 2847*
Seafood dominates the menu here, but there are also tasty vegetarian and meat options. Imaginative and carefully prepared food is served on crockery made by the owner; if you like it, you can buy it. A pleasant garden area allows outside dining in the summer.

KINSALE: Fishy Fishy €€
Modern seafood **Road map** B6
Crowleys Quay, Kinsale, Co Cork
Tel *021 470 0415*
Smart seafood restaurant spread over two floors and offering simple, freshly cooked dishes. Booking is advised during peak season.

KINSALE: Spaniard Inn €€
European **Road map** B6
Scilly, Kinsale, Co Cork
Tel *021 477 2436*
An old pub and dining room serving simple but well-loved dishes – seafood chowder, rack of lamb, steaks. Open fires, beamed ceilings and traditional music.

DK Choice

KINSALE:
Man Friday €€€
European **Road map** B6
Scilly, Kinsale, Co Cork
Tel *021 477 2260*
Seafood dominates, but there are many other carnivore-friendly options at this eatery and nice views of the harbour. The food is consistently good, and there are often queues; a reservation is essential.

KINSALE: Max's Wine Bar €€€
Traditional French **Road map** B6
48 Main Street, Kinsale, Co Cork
Tel *021477 2443* **Closed** *bank hols; mid-Nov–mid-Mar*
A popular place with lots of light. The menu is heavily biased towards seafood; vegetarians might struggle.

LISTOWEL:
Allo's Restaurant €€
Modern Irish **Road map** B5
41 Church Street, Listowel, Co Kerry
Tel *068 22880* **Closed** *Sun & Mon; 3 days at Christmas*
This pub/restaurant decorated with salvaged items serves good, inventive food. Thursdays are theme nights, featuring a different style of cuisine each week.

MALLOW:
President's Restaurant €€€
Traditional French **Road map** B5
Longueville House, Mallow, Co Cork
Tel *022 471 56* **Closed** *Mon & Tue*
Enjoy a grand dining experience in a stunning Georgian mansion. Advance booking is necessary. Afternoon tea is served 2–5pm.

MITCHELSTOWN:
O'Callaghan's €
Café food **Road map** C5
Lower Cork Street, Mitchelstown, Co Cork
Tel *025 24657* **Closed** *Sun*
Sandwiches, paninis, soups and a small range of hot meals. Lunch alfresco in the covered area at the back, or purchase goods from the deli shop for a picnic.

MONKSTOWN: The Bosun €€€
Traditional Irish **Road map** C6
The Pier, Monkstown, Co Cork
Tel *021 484 2172*
A busy place with a large and simple seafood-dominated menu that also features dishes such as leek and potato soup, roast duckling and steaks.

PORTMAGEE: The Moorings €€
Modern Irish **Road map** A5
Portmagee, Co Kerry
Tel *066 947 7108*
Located beside the harbour. The daily catch is always super-fresh – it only has to travel across the road before reaching the kitchen!

SHANAGARRY:
Ballymaloe House €€€
Home cooking **Road map** C6
Shanagarry, Co Cork
Tel *021 465 2531*
A famous country house where traditions are maintained. Much of the produce is grown on the estate. Reservations are essential.

TRALEE:
The Oyster Tavern €€
Seafood **Road map** A5
The Spa, Tralee, Co Kerry
Tel *066 713 6102* **Closed** *Good Fri, 25 Dec*
This large, modern eatery with lovely views over the bay serves superb-quality seafood and more. Vegetarians will fare well here.

YOUGHAL:
Aherne's Seafood Bar €€€
Seafood **Road map** C5
163 N Main Street, Youghal, Co Cork
Tel *024 92424*
Seafood dominates, but there are other options, too – local cheeses, heavenly desserts and excellent home-made breads.

The Lower Shannon

ADARE: The Wild Geese €€
Modern Irish **Road map** B5
Rose Cottage, Adare, Co Limerick
Tel *061 396451* **Closed** *1 wk Oct*
A picture-postcard cottage with several small, tastefully decorated dining rooms. Luxurious fare includes pan-seared scallops with chorizo, roast breast of duck, rack of lamb and a few veggie choices.

BALLINDERRY:
Brocka-on-the-Water €€€
Modern Irish **Road map** C4
Kilgarvan Quay, Ballinderry, Co Tipperary
Tel *067 220 38* **Closed** *Sun; summer; call for winter hours*
Simply cooked seasonal food in a family home with open fires and a reception area for aperitifs. The restaurant operates only if bookings are made, so call in advance.

Ballymaloe country house, Shanagarry

Key to price guide *see page 308*

The enticing patio at Burren Perfumery Tea Rooms, Carron

DK Choice

BALLINGARRY: The Mustard Seed €€€
Modern Irish **Road map** B5
Echo Lodge, Ballingarry, Co Limerick
Tel *069 68508* **Closed** *Mon & Tue (winter); 3 days at Christmas*
This long-established restaurant is famous for its hospitality and the quality of its food. Select from the menu while enjoying aperitifs and *amuse-bouches* in the library, then move to the spacious dining room and enjoy four courses (three if you choose the early-bird menu) of imaginative food.

BALLYVAUGHAN: An Fear Gorta €
Café food **Road map** B4
Coast Road, Ballyvaughan, Co Clare
Tel *085 726 1315* **Closed** *Mon–Thu (Dec); Nov, Jan–Mar*
A pretty tea room set in beautiful gardens. Lovely cakes, savoury tarts, sandwiches, fish pies, and home-made soups using produce from their own kitchen garden.

BALLYVAUGHAN: Monks €
Seafood **Road map** B4
Ballyvaughan, Co Clare
Tel *065 707 7059* **Closed** *25 Dec*
Homely old pub with open fires, specializing in seafood. Favoured by tour bus groups, so it gets busy at lunchtime in the summer.

CARRON: Burren Perfumery Tea Rooms €
Café food **Road map** B4
Fahee North, Carron, Co Clare
Tel *065 708 9102* **Closed** *Oct–Apr*
Soups, quiches, home-baked goods, sandwiches and salads. Many of the teas are made from plants grown in the gardens.

CASHEL: Café Hans €
Modern Irish **Road map** C5
Moor Lane, Cashel, Co Tipperary
Tel *062 63660* **Closed** *Sun & Mon; 2 wks end Jan*
Busy café serving better-than-average snacks: salads, fishcakes, soups and sandwiches. Cash only.

CASHEL: Chez Hans €€€
Modern Irish **Road map** C5
Moor Lane, Cashel, Co Tipperary
Tel *062 611 77* **Closed** *Sun & Mon; last 2 wks Sep, last 2 wks Jan*
Classic, award-winning food such as local lamb and quail in a beautifully converted old synod building. The wine list includes offerings from both Europe and the New World. Reservations essential.

CLOGHEEN: The Old Convent Gourmet Hideaway €€€
Modern Irish **Road map** C5
Mount Anglesby, Clogheen, Co Tipperary
Tel *052 746 5565* **Closed** *Mon–Thu; Jan, 3 wks Dec*
An Irish artisan menu including local buffalo ricotta and rare breed pork is offered nightly in a beautiful room with stained-glass windows. A vegetarian option is available. Booking is essential.

DOOLIN: Cullinan's Seafood €€
Modern Irish **Road map** B4
Doolin, Co Clare
Tel *065 707 4183* **Closed** *Sun & Wed; Nov–Apr*
The modern Irish menu at this place overlooking the river leans towards local seafood – wild monkfish, pan-seared Castletownbere scallops. Lovely home-made desserts. Reservations recommended.

DOOLIN: Riverside Bistro €€
Pub food **Road map** B4
Roadford, Doolin, Co Clare
Tel *065 707 5604* **Closed** *Mon & Tue (Nov–Feb); timings vary in summer*
Tasty, café-style fare served in a cheerful room with an open fire; in summer, the action moves outdoors, to the pretty garden terrace. This friendly restaurant is sandwiched between two pubs, and there is music – here or next door – most nights in summer.

DOONBEG: Morrisseys Seafood Bar & Grill €€
Pub food **Road map** B4
Doonbeg, Co Clare
Tel *065 905 5304* **Closed** *Mon; Nov, Jan & Feb*
This pub with a contemporary interior and views over the river serves simple dishes – Doonbeg crab claws, Cajun chicken salad, steaks and burgers – in generous portions. No bookings are taken, which means queues in summer.

ENNIS: Town Hall Bistro €€
Modern Irish **Road map** B4
O'Connell Street, Ennis, Co Clare
Tel *065 682 8127* **Closed** *25 Dec*
By day a pretty café serving snacks, sandwiches and more substantial meals, at night this place becomes a candlelit bistro. Reservations recommended.

KILLALOE: Cherry Tree Restaurant €€€
Modern Irish **Road map** C4
Lakeside, Ballina, Killaloe, Co Clare
Tel *061 375688* **Closed** *Mon; 2 wks Jan–Feb, 24 & 25 Dec*
Contemporary Irish food is served with great finesse in a room overlooking the River Shannon. The menu also features a few exotic options, such as crab spring rolls with chilli jam.

For more information on types of restaurants *see page 305*

LAHINCH: Barrtra Seafood Restaurant €€
Modern Irish **Road map** B4
Lahinch, Co Clare
Tel *065 708 1280* **Closed** *Sun–Thu (Jan & Feb); timings vary in summer*
In a stone cottage with a large conservatory dining room. The menu is biased towards seafood, with lobster a relatively affordable signature dish.

LIMERICK: Sage Café €
Café food **Road map** B4
67–68 Catherine Street, Limerick
Tel *061 409458* **Closed** *Sun, bank hols; 1 wk at Christmas*
Light, airy café serving snacks, baked goods and sandwiches, as well as more substantial dishes. Try the courgette and basil tagliatelle.

LIMERICK: Copper and Spice €€
Asian **Road map** B4
2 Cornmarket Row, Limerick
Tel *061 313620* **Closed** *25 Dec*
Popular restaurant with a modern decor. Early-bird and à la carte menus, and takeaway service.

LIMERICK: The Cornstore €€
Steaks and seafood **Road map** B4
19 Thomas Street, Limerick
Tel *061 609000* **Closed** *25 Dec*
Come here for a decadent dining experience, including a cocktail bar and a smoking area. Mains include a delicious 21-day aged fillet steak.

LIMERICK: Hamptons Grill €€
Traditional Irish **Road map** B4
Henry Street, Limerick
Tel *061 609325*
A sleek place with lots of mirrors, low lighting and banquette seating. Famous for its grills, but the menu will please all tastes.

LISDOONVARNA: The Wild Honey Inn €€
Modern Irish **Road map** B4
Kincora Road, Lisdoonvarna, Co Clare
Tel *065 707 4300* **Closed** *Tue; Jan–mid-Feb*
Food – steaks, wild game in season, organic vegetables, local seafood – is cooked to order. Stone walls and open fires in winter create a cosy atmosphere. No reservations, so first come, first served.

NENAGH: Pepper Mill €€
Modern Irish **Road map** C4
27 Kenyon Street, Nenagh, Co Tipperary
Tel *067 34598* **Closed** *Mon; Good Fri, 24 & 25 Dec*
Romantically decorated in warm shades of brown and cream. The bistro-style menu includes locally sourced beef and seafood.

Derg Inn, Terryglass

DK Choice

NEW QUAY: Linnane's Lobster Bar €€
Seafood **Road map** B4
The Pier, New Quay, Co Clare
Tel *065 707 8120* **Closed** *Mon–Thu (winter); Good Fri, 25 Dec*
Set on the rocky shoreline, with stunning seascapes behind and the dramatic Burren in front. On the menu is simple, classic Irish seafood – poached salmon with chive cream sauce, seafood platter – but also steak in pepper sauce. Open fire in winter and outdoor seating in summer.

NEWMARKET ON FERGUS: Earl of Thomond €€€
Modern Irish-French **Road map** B4
Dromoland Castle Hotel, Newmarket on Fergus, Co Clare
Tel *061 368144* **Closed** *25 Dec*
Opulent dining room with views over the lake and woods. Choose between the five-course *table d'hote* and the à la carte menu.

TERRYGLASS: Derg Inn €€
Modern Irish **Road map** C4
Terryglass, Co Tipperary
Tel *067 22037* **Closed** *Good Fri, 25 Dec*
Pretty lakeside inn serving good pub food and an excellent Sunday lunch. The daily specials depend on what is in season.

The West of Ireland

ACHILL ISLAND: The Beehive €
Home cooking **Road map** A3
Keel, Achill Island, Co Mayo
Tel *098 43134* **Closed** *Nov–Feb*
Self-service daytime restaurant with high-quality, home-made, traditional fare. Try their cakes, scones, tea bracks and fruit tarts.

ACHILL ISLAND: Ferndale Restaurant & Guest Accommodation €€
International **Road map** A3
Keel, Achill Island, Co Mayo
Tel *098 43908* **Closed** *Mon–Wed; Nov–Easter*
Exciting menu, from Marco Polo's Adventure Platter (venison, kangaroo, bison and crocodile steaks) to the Medieval Fish Platter (tiger prawns, scallops and monkfish).

BALLINASLOE: Kariba's €
Home cooking **Road map** B3
Society Street, Ballinasloe, Co Galway
Tel *090 964 4830* **Closed** *Sun*
This place offers a menu of local and international favourites and home-made desserts.

BALLYCASTLE: Mary's Cottage Kitchen €
Home cooking **Road map** B2
Main Street, Ballycastle, Co Mayo
Tel *096 43361*
Charming restaurant offering traditional home-cooked food. Sit outside on good days and by the roaring fire in winter.

BARNA: O'Gradys on the Pier €€
Seafood **Road map** B4
Seapoint, Barna, Co Galway
Tel *091 592223*
A two-storey restaurant a few metres from the beach and with instant access to the freshest fish. Steak, lamb and rabbit is also available.

CASTLEBAR: Café Rua €
Irish **Road map** B3
New Antrim Street, Castlebar, Co Mayo
Tel *094 9023376*
Breakfast and lunch specials change daily. The home-baked sweet treats are not to be missed.

Key to price guide *see page 308*

CLEGGAN: Oliver's Bar €€
Seafood **Road map** A3
Cleggan, Co Galway
Tel *095 44640*
A very popular haunt for both locals and visitors, who come to sample the ultra-fresh seafood.

CLIFDEN:
Mitchells Restaurant €€
Seafood **Road map** A3
Market Street, Clifden, Co Galway
Tel *095 21867* **Closed** *Nov–Feb*
This family-run restaurant offers good and keenly priced food. Try the monkfish with colcannon and bacon potato cake.

CLIFDEN:
Ardagh Hotel & Restaurant €€€
Irish **Road map** A3
Ballyconneely Road, Clifden, Co Galway
Tel *095 21384* **Closed** *Nov–Easter*
Award-winning restaurant with spectacular views at sunset. It specializes in lobster and oysters, as well as steaks.

DK Choice

CONG:
George V Dining Room €€€
European **Road map** B3
Ashford Castle, Cong, Co Mayo
Tel *094 954 6003*
Dine under 11 Waterford crystal chandeliers while listening to the resident pianist. Highlights of the menu include Monkfish tail with fennel and Fivemiletown goat's cheese panacotta.

CONNEMARA:
Owenmore Restaurant €€€
Irish **Road map** B3
Ballynahinch Castle Hotel, Recess, Co Galway
Tel *095 31006*
Elegant dining in a stunning location. The seasonal menus rely on locally sourced meats, game, fish and oysters. Reservations essential.

GALWAY: Ard Bia at Nimmos €€
Home cooking **Road map** B4
Spanish Arch, Galway City
Tel *091 561114*
Café by day and restaurant by night, Ard Bia serves great local food with influences from Europe and the Middle East.

GALWAY: McDonagh's €€
Seafood **Road map** B4
22 Quay Street, Galway City
Tel *091 565001* **Closed** *Sun*
This renowned institution is said to have the widest selection of fish in the county and is the place in Galway for high-quality fish and chips and fresh seafood.

GALWAY:
The Seafood Bar @ Kirwans €€
Seafood **Road map** B4
Kirwans Lane, Galway City
Tel *091 568266*
The tasteful furnishings create a warm, friendly ambience, while the menu offers bistro-style dishes with meat and vegetarian options.

GALWAY: Kai Cafe + Restaurant €€€
Modern Irish **Road map** B4
20 Sea Road, Galway City
Tel *091 526 003*
Fresh, organic dishes bursting with the flavours of the west coast. Try their homemade fish fingers, crab salad, ox tongue and pumpkin jam, or Monkfish and sea spaghetti.

INIS MEAIN:
Inis Meain Restaurant €€€
Irish **Road map** B4
Inis Meain, Aran Islands, Co Galway
Tel *086 826 6026* **Closed** *Oct–Apr*
The menu offers delicious dishes made with freshly caught or locally grown ingredients. Enjoy panoramic sea views from the contemporary dining room. Open for dinner only; menu changes every night.

INISHMORE:
Pier House Restaurant €€
Country kitchen **Road map** B4
Inishmore Island, Co Galway
Tel *099 61417* **Closed** *winter*
The contemporary, modern Irish menu here features local fresh seafood and lamb. Ingredients are sourced from local producers.

KILCOLGAN:
Morans Oyster Cottage €€
Seafood **Road map** B4
The Weir, Kilcolgan, Co Galway
Tel *091 796113*
In the same family for seven generations, this restaurant in a thatched cottage has a seafood-heavy menu – crab, oysters, lobster, mussels and prawns.

KINVARA:
Pier Head Restaurant €€
Irish **Road map** B4
Kinvara, Co Galway
Tel *091 638188*
Live music and great views of the bay await at this restaurant. On the menu are prime steaks, seafood and a small vegetarian choice.

LEENANE: Blackberry Café €€
Home cooking **Road map** B3
Leenane, Co Galway
Tel *095 42240* **Closed** *Oct–Easter*
A charming café with excellent and hearty meals – oysters, stews, fishcakes and chowders.

LETTERFRACK:
Kylemore Abbey Restaurant €
Home cooking **Road map** A3
Kylemore, Co Galway
Tel *095 52001*
Self-service restaurant in a stunning mountainside setting. Benedictine nuns run the gardens that yield many vegetables on the menu.

George V Dining Room, Cong

LOUGHREA: Taste Matters €€
European **Road map** A3
Westbridge, Loughrea, Co Galway
Tel *091 880010* **Closed** *Mon*
This cosy, relaxed bistro offers innovative dishes that have their roots in Ireland, France and Italy. Good value for money.

MOYCULLEN: White Gables €€
Seafood **Road map** B4
Moycullen, Co Galway
Tel *091 555744* **Closed** *Mon & Tue*
This 1920s stone cottage houses an intimate restaurant. Seafood is the mainstay of the menu, with a range of classic dishes alongside some imaginative creations.

PORTUMNA: The Modena €€
European **Road map** C4
Portumna, Co Galway
Tel *0909 759568*
Family-run restaurant with an eclectic menu featuring Irish, Italian and Indian dishes – from traditional roasts to jalfrezi.

ROSCOMMON:
Gleesons Townhouse €€
Home cooking **Road map** C3
Market Square, Roscommon, Co Roscommon
Tel *0906 626954*
Traditional fare prepared with locally sourced ingredients. This restaurant, in a restored 19th-century house overlooking the town square, offers great value.

DK Choice

ROUNDSTONE:
O'Dowd's Restaurant €€
Home cooking **Road map** A3
Roundstone, Co Galway
Tel *095 35809*
Serving locals and visitors since 1840, this traditional wood-panelled restaurant offers great fish – delivered daily from the nearby harbour – and indulgent desserts. The seafood platter is the star attraction.

TUAM:
Finns Bar & Restaurant €€
European **Road map** B3
Milltown, Tuam, Co Galway
Tel *093 51327* **Closed** *Mon & Tue*
Come to this relaxed restaurant for generous portions of Irish and international fare at a reasonable price.

WESTPORT:
McCormack's €
Home cooking **Road map** B3
Bridge Street, Westport, Co Mayo
Tel *098 25619*
This small, family-run restaurant has a selection of delicious home-made dishes and mouthwatering desserts.

WESTPORT:
An Port Mor €€
European **Road map** B3
Westport, Co Mayo
Tel *098 26730* **Closed** *Mon*
The award-winning chef here uses the best local ingredients to create a classic, seafood-led menu. Excellent value for money.

Northwest Ireland

ARDARA:
Nancy's €€
Bar snacks **Road map** C1
Ardara, Co Donegal
Tel *074 954 1187*
Nancy's has a reputation for great-quality fish and seafood, and is especially renowned for its seafood chowder. Casual atmosphere; no need to book.

ANNAGRY:
Danny Minnies Restaurant €€€
Seafood **Road map** C1
Annagry, The Rosses, Co Donegal
Tel *074 954 8201* **Closed** *Sun*
Prints, tapestries and paintings adorn the walls of this elegant restaurant. Irish meat and locally caught seafood feature prominently on the menu.

O'Dowd's Restaurant, Roundstone

BALLYSHANNON: Nirvana €€
European **Road map** C2
The Mall, Ballyshannon, Co Donegal
Tel *071 982 2369*
Contemporary restaurant and wine bar. Food is prepared using good-quality and often locally sourced ingredients.

CARRICK-ON-SHANNON:
The Oarsman Restaurant €€
Irish **Road map** C3
Bridge Street, Carrick-on-Shannon, Co Leitrim
Tel *071 962 1733* **Closed** *Sun*
Renowned in the local area for the superb quality of its slow-cooked food. Relaxed ambience.

DK Choice

CASTLEBALDWIN:
Cromleach Lodge Country House €€€
Irish **Road map** C3
Castlebaldwin, Co Sligo
Tel *071 916 5155* **Closed** *Mon & Tue*
Gourmet dining in a hilltop country house. The award-winning executive chef creates innovative Irish dishes with a modern twist. Diners can choose from more than 100 wines, from cheap and cheerful bottles to rare French vintages.

DONEGAL TOWN:
The Blueberry Tearoom €
Irish **Road map** C2
Castle Street, The Diamond, Donegal Town, Co Donegal
Tel *074 972 2933*
Cosy café serving a hearty menu of breakfast and lunch options. The incredible desserts, in particular the delectable chocolate steam pudding, have made this spot a local favourite.

DONEGAL TOWN:
Olde Castle Restaurant €€
Irish **Road map** C1
Tirconnell Street, Donegal Town, Co Donegal
Tel *074 972 1262*
A modern Irish menu that relies on locally sourced ingredients. Seafood is a speciality – Donegal Bay mussels and oysters, Bruckless Bay crabs.

DUNKINEELY:
Castle Murray House €€€
French **Road map** C2
St Johns Point, Dunkineely, Co Donegal
Tel *074 973 7022*
Classic French dishes made with high-quality local produce. Start with the cream of salsify soup, and follow that with seafood, or

Key to price guide *see page 308*

red meats, which feature prominently in the winter. The house special of St Johns Point langoustine and Killybegs monkfish is a must.

GLENTIES: Highlands Hotel €€
European **Road map** C1
Main Street, Glenties, Co Donegal
Tel *074 955 1111*
This acclaimed restaurant offers great hospitality, friendly staff and a varied menu, from locally caught seafood to juicy steaks. Famed for its huge portions.

GREENCASTLE:
Kealys Seafood Bar €€
Seafood **Road map** C1
The Harbour, Greencastle, Co Donegal
Tel *074 938 1010* **Closed** *Mon–Wed*
Award-winning food made with organic local produce. The kitchen is barely 6 metres (20 ft) from the harbour, so the freshness of the seafood is never in doubt.

INISHOWEN: Harry's Bar and Restaurant €€
Irish **Road map** C1
Bridgend, Inishowen, Co Donegal
Tel *074 936 8544*
This restaurant serves the finest local food in Inishowen. The steaks are quite popular and highly recommended.

KINCASSLAGH: Iggy's Bar €
Bar snacks **Road map** C2
Main Street, Kincasslagh, Co Donegal
Tel *074 954 3112* **Closed** *Mon*
Popular with locals and visitors alike, including a remarkable number of celebrities. Simple pub fare with a slant towards seafood is served during the summer months.

LETTERKENNY: Castle Grove €€
French **Road map** C1
Ballymaleel, Letterkenny, Co Donegal
Tel *074 915 1118* **Closed** *Mon*
A stylish restaurant, in keeping with the rest of this stunning 300-year-old house. The chef uses produce from the garden and local ingredients to create beautiful dishes with Gallic flair.

LETTERKENNY:
The Lemon Tree €€
French-Irish **Road map** C1
Lower Main Street, Letterkenny, Co Donegal
Tel *074 912 5788*
Family-run and a firm favourite with both locals and visitors. The food combines the best aspects of traditional Irish fare and classic French cuisine.

Weeping Elm on the Rathmullan Estate, Rathmullan

RATHMULLAN:
Weeping Elm €€€
Seafood **Road map** C1
Rathmullan House, Rathmullan, Co Donegal
Tel *074 915 8188*
Gourmet restaurant offering award-winning food prepared with the finest ingredients. Try the delicious selection of local cheeses. The wine list specializes in small, independent producers.

SLIGO TOWN: Bella Vista €€
European **Road map** C2
Shore Road, Strand Hill, Co Sligo
Tel *071 912 2222*
Simple but good-quality food during the day, and an emphasis on seafood and steaks at night.

SLIGO TOWN:
Coach Lane Restaurant €€
European **Road map** C2
1 Lord Edward Street, Sligo Town, Co Sligo
Tel *071 916 2417*
This restaurant has a reputation for innovative cuisine. Try the seafood platter – salmon, shrimp, scallops, cod, halibut, and crab claws grilled with lemon, Chardonnay and butter.

SLIGO TOWN:
Davis's Restaurant €€
International **Road map** C2
Drumcliff, Co Sligo
Tel *071 916 3117*
Award-winning eatery featuring an extensive à la carte menu – from burgers to crab claws – suits all budgets and tastes. The desserts are well-paired with a selection of fine wines

SLIGO TOWN: Montmartre €€
French **Road map** C2
Market Yard, Sligo Town, Co Sligo
Tel *071 916 9901* **Closed** *Mon & Sun*
Owned and staffed by French nationals, this popular restaurant has an imaginative menu; the guinea fowl with a cabbage and bacon fondue is a highlight. Advance booking recommended.

STRANDHILL: Shells Café and Little Shop €
Irish **Road map** B2
Strandhill, Co Sligo
Tel *071 912 2938*
Overlooking the sea, this popular restaurant serves homemade breads and cakes and is a perfect spot for brunch.

DK Choice

TUBBERCURRY:
Killoran's Restaurant €€
Irish **Road map** B3
Teeling Street, Tubbercurry, Co Sligo
Tel *071 918 5679* **Closed** *Sun*
Modern living has made little impact on this traditional eatery. Killoran's offers a genuinely warm welcome and service with a smile. The quality of the food is second to none.

The Midlands

ATHLONE: Kin Khao Thai €€
Thai **Road map** C3
1 Abbey Lane, Athlone, Co Westmeath
Tel *090 649 8805*
A yellow- and red- building houses one of Ireland's best Thai restaurants. Delightful staff and a wide selection of regional specialities. Booking advised.

ATHLONE:
The Left Bank Bistro €€
Bistro **Road map** C3
Fry Place, Athlone, Co Westmeath
Tel *090 649 4446* **Closed** *Sun & Mon*
Stylish restaurant in the old town serving delicious, creative food in a relaxed atmosphere. Great fish and steaks. Lunchtime offerings include focaccias and fajitas.

For more information on types of restaurants *see page 305*

ATHLONE: Thyme €€
Irish **Road map** C3
Custume Place, Athlone, Co Westmeath
Tel *090 647 8850*
Delicious, well-priced food made with local produce. Try the salt baked celeriac or pan-roasted fillet of Kilmore Quay Hake. Booking recommended.

ATHLONE: Wineport Lodge €€€
Bistro **Road map** C3
Glasson, Athlone, Co Westmeath
Tel *090 643 9010*
Award-winning restaurant in a pretty lakeside lodge. Try the pickled mackerel and fennel salad, followed by the steamed lemon pudding. Arrive by boat for added romance.

BATTERSTOWN: Caffrey's €€
Irish **Road map** D3
Batterstown, Dunboyne, Co Meath
Tel *01 825 8479*
A traditional country-style pub with antique furnishings, open fires and live music on Thursdays. Try the garlic rope mussels or the succulent steaks.

BIRR:
The Thatch Bar & Restaurant €€
Irish **Road map** D2
Crinkill, Birr, Co Offaly
Tel *057 912 0682*
This old-fashioned thatched, whitewashed pub decked in flowers has a warm ambience and great countryside cuisine – chowder, chicken, steaks.

DK Choice

BLACKLION:
MacNean House & Bistro €€€
Irish **Road map** D2
Main Street, Blacklion, Co Cavan
Tel *071 985 3022* **Closed** *Mon & Tue*
Weekends tend to be booked out months in advance at this culinary gem. Delicacies include seared quail and Thornhill duck breast with wild mushroom polenta. There is also a full vegetarian menu. Named after the nearby lakes, MacNean is the place for an utterly romantic experience.

CARLINGFORD:
Kingfisher Bistro €€
Bistro **Road map** D3
Darcy McGee Court, Dundalk Street, Carlingford, Co Louth
Tel *042 937 3716*
Arguably the best restaurant in town. Fantastic seafood – salmon, lobster, Carlingford mussels and oysters. Desserts include chocolate and hazelnut brownies.

Ghan House, Carlingford

CARLINGFORD:
The Oystercatcher Bistro €€
Irish **Road map** D3
Market Square, Carlingford, Co Louth
Tel *042 937 3989* **Closed** *Mon & Tue (winter)*
Warm hospitality in pretty surroundings. Try the *cataplana* (a spicy fish and chorizo stew), the black pudding and muesli mousse or the Carlingford oysters.

CARLINGFORD:
Ghan House €€€
Irish **Road map** D3
Carlingford, Co Louth
Tel *042 937 3682*
In a grand 18th-century country house with views over the lake. Though the emphasis is on seafood – lobster, oysters, mussels – the menu also features Cooley lamb and beef.

CARRICKMACROSS:
Nuremore
Hotel & Country Club €€
Irish **Road map** D3
Carrickmacross, Co Monaghan
Tel *042 966 1438*
Housed in a scenic country hotel, this restaurant attracts visitors from far and wide. Try the pigeon or the Annagassan white crab.

CLOVERHILL:
The Olde Post Inn €€€
French-Irish **Road map** C3
Cloverhill, Co Cavan
Tel *047 55555* **Closed** *Mon*
Award-winning restaurant and guesthouse in a quaint former post office. Try the loin of spring lamb, then cleanse your palate with the champagne sorbet.

COLLON:
Forge Gallery Restaurant €€
French-Irish **Road map** D3
Collon, Co Louth
Tel *041 982 6272* **Closed** *Mon & Tue*
Friendly environment, full of character, art and imagination. The menu is strong on seafood, but there are also great fillet steaks and roast duckling.

DUNDALK: Fahrenheit Rooftop Restaurant €€
Seafood **Road map** D3
Crowne Plaza Dundalk, Inner Relief Road, Dundalk, Co Louth
Tel *042 939 4900*
Feast on locally sourced food in this restaurant with panoramic views of the Cooley Mountains and Peninsula and the Irish Sea. Do not miss their signature chocolate fondue.

GLASLOUGH:
The Lodge at Castle Leslie €€€
Irish **Road map** D3
Castle Leslie Estate, Glaslough, Co Monaghan
Tel *047 88100* **Closed** *call to check*
Located in a fabulous castle. Diners can enjoy simple food in the convivial bar, or dine in style in the oak-beamed restaurant. The terrine of rabbit with wild mushrooms and the pan-seared river trout are sure-fire winners.

KELLS: The Vanilla Pod €€
Bistro **Road map** D3
Headfort Arms Hotel, Kells, Co Meath
Tel *046 924 0084*
Stylish, contemporary bistro. Try the creamy seafood chowder or the rack of lamb. A tapas menu is served 5–7:30pm on weekdays; children eat free 5:30–6:45pm.

LONGFORD:
Aubergine Gallery Café €
Irish-Mediterranean
Road map C3
1st Floor, The White House, 17 Ballymahon Street, Longford, Co Longford
Tel *043 334 8633* **Closed** *23 Dec–2 Jan*
Lively restaurant offering steaks, quesadillas and buttermilk fried chicken. Vegetarians are well looked after, too. Good craft beers menu.

Key to price guide *see page 308*

MONAGHAN:
Andy's Restaurant €€
Irish **Road map** D2
12 Market Street, Monaghan, Co Monaghan
Tel *047 82277* **Closed** *Mon*
Award-winning gastropub in a lovely white-washed building. Specialities include chicken Monaghan, served with a tangy mushroom and onion sauce.

MULLINGAR:
Brioche Café & Delicatessen €
Spanish-Irish **Road map** C3
11 Mount Street, Mullingar, Co Westmeath
Tel *044 934 7650* **Closed** *Fri*
This little lunchtime gem offering soups and snacks becomes a tapas bar in the evening – tortillas, *gambas*, *calamares*. Good wine list.

MULLINGAR:
JP's Steakhouse €€
Italian-Steakhouse **Road map** C3
28 Dominic Street, Mullingar, Co Westmeath
Tel *044 933 3620* **Closed** *Mon*
Friendly service and unpretentious decor. On the menu are hearty Italian favourites and delicious steaks served with a special Jack Daniel's sauce.

NAVAN: Earl's Kitchen €
Irish **Road map** D3
Old Corn Market, Navan, Co Meath
Tel *046 905 9678* **Closed** *Sun*
The place for a pleasant lunch – salads, savouries and desserts. Closed in the evening.

NAVAN:
Eden at Bellinter House €€€
Irish **Road map** D3
Bellinter House, Navan, Co Meath
Tel *046 903 0900*
Atmospheric restaurant in a Palladian-style country hotel. Try the rump of lamb with colcannon, pan-seared sea-bream or roasted squash parcels with marinated feta. Good wine list.

PORTLAOISE: Seasons Bistro €€
Bistro **Road map** C4
24a Market Square, Portlaoise, Co Laois
Tel *057 868 0809*
A popular and welcoming family bistro serving modern European dishes made with locally sourced ingredients. Try the scallops and prawns in white wine and cream.

TRIM: Franzinis O'Brien's €€
International **Road map** D3
French's Lane, Trim, Co Meath
Tel *046 943 1002* **Closed** *Mon (winter)*
In addition to the lovely views of Trim Castle, diners here will find an easy-going atmosphere, friendly service and affordable fare such as fajitas and pizzas.

Northern Ireland

ARMAGH:
Manor Park Steak House ££
Steakhouse **Road map** D2
2 College Hill, The Mall, Armagh
Tel *028 3751 5353* **Closed** *Mon*
Modern, inventive fare – lemon sole with cockles, delicious monkfish, beef on the bone – in a grand Georgian house.

ARDGLASS: Aldo's ££
Italian **Road map** E2
7 Castle Place, Ardglass, Downpatrick, Co Down
Tel *028 4484 1315* **Closed** *Mon–Wed (winter)*
Delightful, friendly restaurant run by the same family since 1973. Aldo's serves antipasti, pasta dishes, locally sourced seafood and meats, and a great vegetarian selection.

BALLYCASTLE:
The Cellar Restaurant ££
Irish **Road map** D1
11b The Diamond, Ballycastle, Co Antrim
Tel *028 2076 3037*
A cosy haven with friendly staff and hearty portions. Steaks are cooked to perfection, or try the Surf and Turf, featuring half a Rathlin lobster. Great value.

BELFAST: Archana ££
Indian **Road map** D2
53 Dublin Road, Belfast, Co Antrim
Tel *028 9032 3713*
Gracious service and a relaxed ambience at this place famed for its Northern Indian vegetarian and vegan options. The *thali* (platter) lunch is great value.

Price Guide
For a three-course meal per person, with a half-bottle of house wine, including tax and service.

£	under £25
££	£25 to 50
£££	over £50

BELFAST: Barnett Restaurant ££
Brasserie **Road map** D2
Malone House, Barnett Demesne, Belfast
Tel *028 9068 1246*
An elegant dining room in a late Georgian mansion. Excellent food made with fine local produce. There are some good-value lunch menus.

BELFAST: Belfast Castle Cellar Restaurant ££
Brasserie **Road map** D2
Antrim Road, Belfast, Co Antrim
Tel *028 9077 6925*
Closed *Sun & Mon*
A strikingly romantic setting in an ornate hilltop castle. Try the peppered fillet of venison or the pan-fried salmon. The gardens offer some of Belfast's best views.

BELFAST: Coppi ££
Italian **Road map** D2
St Anne's Square, Cathedral Quarter, Belfast
Tel *028 9031 1959*
Considered as one of the best Italian eateries in Northern Ireland, the menu includes freshly made pasta, risotto, pizzette and cichetti.

BELFAST:
Crown Liquor Saloon ££
Irish **Road map** D2
46 Great Victoria Street, Belfast, Co Antrim
Tel *028 902 43187*
A Belfast landmark, established in 1849. Enjoy the traditional atmosphere while tucking into Irish stew and champ, a local speciality of mashed potatoes with spring onions and butter.

Crown Liquor Saloon, Belfast

For more information on types of restaurants *see page 305*

BELFAST: Deane's ££
French-Irish **Road map** D2
36–40 Howard Street, Belfast, Co Antrim
Tel *028 9033 1134* **Closed** *Sun*
Eat in the seafood bar on the first floor, or in the French brasserie at the entrance. The scallops and potted crab are great choices.

BELFAST: Ginger Bistro ££
Bistro **Road map** D2
7–8 Hope Street, Belfast, Co Antrim
Tel *028 9024 4421* **Closed** *Sun*
Chic but friendly local favourite. Signature dishes include crispy-skin hake fillet on a creamy celeriac and crayfish casserole.

BELFAST: Hakka Noodle ££
Asian **Road map** D2
51 Adelaide Street, Belfast, Co Antrim
Tel *028 9031 3270*
Stylish, lively eatery serving dumplings, noodles, stir-friess and soups in a converted Victorian warehouse. Great cocktails.

BELFAST: James Street South ££
French **Road map** D2
21 James Street South, Belfast, Co Antrim
Tel *028 9043 4310* **Closed** *Sun*
Classic dining in a refurbished old linen mill. Try the wild turbot with green tomato, Rathlin Island kelp linguine and ginger.

BELFAST: Metro Brasserie ££
Brasserie **Road map** D2
13 Lower Crescent, Belfast, Co Antrim
Tel *028 9032 3349*
Try the duck breast with celeriac and thyme rosti or the pan-fried hake wrapped in Serrano ham in this eatery with a sophisticated yet relaxed ambience.

DK Choice

BELFAST: Mourne Seafood Bar ££
Irish **Road map** D2
34–36 Bank Street, Belfast, Co Antrim
Tel *028 9024 8544* **Closed** *24, 25 & 26 Dec*
A gem in the city centre, next to the 16th-century tavern where Henry Joy McCracken and the United Irishmen planned the 1798 Rising. Pass through the old-style fish shop into a cosy bar-restaurant. The food is terrific – fish from the morning's catch and shellfish from Mourne's own beds in Carlingford Lough. Reservations are highly recommended.

BELFAST: Neill's Hill Brasserie ££
Brasserie **Road map** D2
229 Upper Newtownards Road, Belfast, Co Antrim
Tel *028 9065 0079*
A local favourite with tasty dishes. Try the Guinness and honey glazed chicked, or the wood pigeon crostini.

BELFAST: The Potted Hen ££
Bistro **Road map** D2
Edward Street, Belfast, Co Antrim
Tel *028 9023 4554*
Chic restaurant with a pretty terrace. Highlights include spiced monkfish fritters and ribeye steak. On Lazy Sundays, children eat for free between noon and 9pm.

BELFAST: Ox Belfast £££
Irish **Road map** D2
1 Oxford Sreet, Belfast, Co Antrim
Tel *028 903 14121* **Closed** *Sun & Mon*
One of the most talked about joints in Belfast, Ox focuses on sustainable, locally sourced ingredients with a particular emphasis on vegetables.

BUSHMILLS: The Bushmills Inn ££
Irish **Road map** D1
9 Dunluce Road, Bushmills, Co Antrim
Tel *028 2073 3000*
Popular hostelry near the Giant's Causeway. On the menu are wholesome Irish specialities – such as onion and Guinness soup and roast venison.

CARRICKFERGUS: Maud's Ice Cream Parlour £
Ice-cream parlour **Road map** E2
52 Scotch Quarter, Carrickfergus
Tel *028 9336 7428*
Coffees and snacks are served here alongside delicious home-made ice cream, including long-time favourite, Pooh Bear.

DUNDRUM: The Buck's Head ££
Irish **Road map** E2
77 Main Street, Dundrum, Co Down
Tel *028 4375 1868* **Closed** *Mon (winter)*
The main draw here is the top-quality local seafood – for example, Dundrum Bay oysters with garlic and Cheddar crust.

DUNGANNON: Viscount's Restaurant ££
Irish **Road map** D2
10 Northland Row, Dungannon, Co Tyrone
Tel *028 8775 3800* **Closed** *Mon*
A Victorian church refashioned as a medieval-style banqueting hall. There is a good carvery, or try the Portavogie pan-seared scallops.

ENNISKILLEN: The Sheelin Tea Shop £
Irish **Road map** C2
178b Derrylin Road, Bellanaleck, Enniskillen, Co Fermanagh
Tel *028 6634 8232*
Thatched cottage on the shore of Lough Erne. Great traditional home cooking – T-bone steak and Guinness beef pie. Daytime hours only; no alcohol served.

ENNISKILLEN: Café Merlot at Blakes of the Hollow ££
Bistro **Road map** C2
Blakes of the Hollow, 6 Church Street, Enniskillen, Co Fermanagh
Tel *028 6632 0918*
Located in the basement of a pub. From the creative menu, try the dry-aged Irish beef, pork belly or halibut. Booking is advised.

ENNISKILLEN: Dollakis ££
Greek **Road map** C2
2b Cross Street, Enniskillen, Co Fermanagh
Tel *028 6634 2616* **Closed** *Sun & Mon*
Excellent restaurant with a warm welcome. Try the grilled chicken

The Bushmill's Inn, Bushmills

souvlaki, the pork gyro or the creamy vegetarian moussaka. There is also a Cuban cigar menu.

ENNISKILLEN:
The Belleek Restaurant £££
Irish **Road map** C2
Manor House Country Hotel, Killadeas, Enniskillen, Co Fermanagh
Tel *028 6862 2200*
Lake views accompany delicious traditional fare. The roast rack of Fermanagh spring lamb with lemon-glazed sweetbreads and kale colcannon cake is a highlight.

HILLSBOROUGH:
Hillside Bar & Bistro ££
Bistro **Road map** D2
21 Main Street, Hillsborough, Co Down
Tel *028 9268 9233*
Attractive country-style pub and restaurant with a good seasonal menu. Start with the beef shin pie and end with the delicious ice cream from nearby Glastry Farm.

HOLYWOOD: The Bay Tree ££
Irish **Road map** E2
118 High Street, Holywood, Co Down
Tel *028 9042 1419* **Closed** *dinner (except Fri); Sun*
A café/bakery renowned for its cinnamon scones. The bacon and banana toasted sandwich with maple syrup is delicious for breakfast. Also on the menu are fresh fish and organic salads.

LIMAVADY: The Lime Tree ££
Irish **Road map** D1
60 Catherine Street, Limavady, Co Londonderry
Tel *028 7776 4300* **Closed** *Sun & Mon*
Small and simply decorated restaurant with an ambitious menu that includes a Galician fish stew.

LONDONDERRY:
Badger's Bar £
Irish **Road map** C1
16–18 Orchard Street, Co Londonderry
Tel *028 7136 0763*
This wood-panelled Victorian pub gets packed for lunch but is calmer in the evenings. Try the baked smoked haddock.

LONDONDERRY:
The Metro Bar £
Irish **Road map** C1
3–4 Bank Place, Londonderry
Tel *028 7126 7401*
A local favourite beneath Derry's walls. First-rate, hearty lunches include Guinness beef stew, as well as lighter soups and sandwiches.

Brown's Restaurant & Champagne Lounge, Londonderry

LONDONDERRY:
Brown's Restaurant & Champagne Lounge ££
European **Road map** C1
1 Bonds Hill, Co Londonderry
Tel *028 7136 5180* **Closed** *lunch Sat, dinner Sun, Mon*
An unremarkable façade hides a gastronomic treasure. Gracious service, a fine wine list and, on the menu, great steaks and scallops. Also delicious is the pan-seared fillet of Greencastle monkfish.

LONDONDERRY: Quaywest Wine Bar & Restaurant ££
Bistro **Road map** C1
Boating Club Lane, Co Londonderry
Tel *028 7137 0977*
Cool and smart urban dining. Try the Cajun salmon with spicy rice and lemon and lime salsa. Great wine list. Booking essential.

PORTBALLINTRAE: The Porthole Bar & Restaurant ££
Irish **Road map** D1
Bay View Hotel, 2 Bayhead Road, Portballintrae, Co Antrim
Tel *028 2073 4100*
Stunning views, a relaxed vibe and tasty food prepared with local produce. Try the venison sausage or the baked fishcake.

PORTRUSH:
The Harbour Bistro ££
Irish **Road map** D1
The Harbour, Portrush, Co Antrim
Tel *028 7082 2430*
The best restaurant in town, with roaring fires and a cosy, friendly atmosphere. On the menu is delicious Irish food with a twist.

PORTSTEWART: Harry's Shack £
Seafood **Road map** D1
116 Strand Road, Portstewart, Co Londonderry
Tel *028 7083 01783*
The fresh fish and meat dishes served at this restaurant are popular with visitors. The idyllic setting overlooking the sea affords some of the best views in the town.

OMAGH:
Grant's Restaurant ££
Irish **Road map** C2
29 George's Street, Omagh, Co Tyrone
Tel *028 8225 0900*
Named after US president Ulysses S. Grant, this place, popular with locals, offers a hearty and varied menu – seafood, steaks and vegetarian options available.

RICHHILL:
Stonebridge Brasserie ££
Irish **Road map** D2
74 Legacorry Road, Richhill, Co Armagh
Tel *028 3833 7232*
Housed in an atmospheric building, this family-run eatery offers an excellent all-day menu of locally sourced food. The Armagh pork belly is a speciality.

STRANGFORD: The Cuan ££
Irish **Road map** E2
4 The Square, Strangford, Downpatrick
Tel *028 4488 1222*
Warm, family-run hostelry on the shore of Strangford Lough. Seafood dominates the menu, and the delicious chowder is particularly memorable.

WARRENPOINT:
Restaurant 23 ££
Irish **Road map** D2
The Balmoral Hotel, 13 Seaview, Warrenpoint, Co Down
Tel *028 4175 3222*
Imaginative food created by top chef Raymond McArdle. The seafood is superb, or try the slow cooked dry-aged beef from Dromara. Great value lunch menu.

For more information on types of restaurants *see page 305*

Pubs in Ireland

The archetypal Irish pub is celebrated for its convivial atmosphere, friendly locals, genial bar staff and the "craic" – the Irish expression for fun. Wit is washed down with whiskey or Guinness, the national drinks. Irish pubs date back to medieval taverns, coaching inns and shebeens, illegal drinking dens which flourished under colonial rule. In Victorian times, brewing and distilling were major industries. The sumptuous Edwardian or Victorian interiors of some city pubs are a testament to these times. Snugs, partitioned-off booths, are another typical feature of Irish pubs. Traditional pubs can be boldly painted, thatched or "black-and-white" – beamed with a white façade and black trim. Some rural pubs double as grocers' shops. All pubs across Ireland are now smoke-free, but many have beer gardens where smoking is permitted.

Good pubs are not evenly distributed throughout the country: in the Southeast, Kilkenny is paradise for pub-lovers, while Cork and Kerry possess some of the most picturesque pubs. The Lower Shannon region is noted for its boisterous pubs, especially in County Clare where spontaneous music sessions are common. The West has an abundance of typical Irish pubs, and the many tourists and students guarantee a profusion of good pubs in Galway. The listings below cover a selection of pubs throughout Ireland; for Dublin pubs, see pages 114–15.

Southeast Ireland

BRITTAS BAY: Jack White's Inn
Jack White's Cross, Co Wicklow.
Road map D4. **Tel** 0404 47106.

A typical Irish country pub perfectly situated off the N11, which runs from Dublin to the Southeast. Simple but tasty pub fare is served until 9pm. A real local legend, this pub is mired in controversy, due to a murder committed here in 1996.

CARLOW: Teach Dolmain
Tullow St, Co Carlow.
Road map D4. **Tel** 059 913 0911.

This multi-award winning pub, in Carlow's town centre, has a curious collection of unique pottery and ancient artifacts from the town's and Ireland's history. This pub has an excellent menu and is ideally suited for large groups.

DUNGARVAN: Merry's Gastro Pub
Lower Main St, Co Waterford.
Road map D5. **Tel** 058 24488.

Established in 1868, this is a relaxed, friendly and popular pub on Dungarvan's main street. The kitchen offers excellent pub grub (the steaks are excellent), using locally sourced organic ingredients where possible. There's a good selection of craft beers and wines, and occasionally live music.

ENNISCORTHY: The Antique Tavern
14 Slaney St, Co Wexford.
Road map D5. **Tel** 053 923 3428.

This traditional, timbered, black-and-white pub is charming. The dark, intimate bar contains relics such as pikestaffs from Vinegar Hill, the decisive battle in the 1798 uprising that was fought outside town. Pub lunches and local chat are on offer. In good weather, you can sit on the balcony and enjoy the pleasant views of the River Slaney.

ENNISCORTHY: Holohan
Slaney Place, Co Wexford.
Road map D5. **Tel** 053 923 5743.

At the back of the Castle Museum, this is essentially an evening-only pub with few pretensions. Its unusual location makes it worth a visit for a pint or two – it is built right into the base of an old quarry and a vertical cliff forms part of the back wall of the bar.

KILKENNY: Hibernian
1 Ormonde St, Co Kilkenny.
Road map C4. **Tel** 056 777 1888.

Sited in an old bank and part of the Hibernian Hotel, this rather formal pub, popular with a mixed age crowd, still has its original decor. Modern Irish food is available and live Irish music every Tuesday year-round.

KILKENNY: Kyteler's Inn
27 St Kieran's St, Co Kilkenny.
Road map C4. **Tel** 056 772 1064.

In good weather you can sit in the courtyard of this historic coaching inn and cellar bar. Food is available all day, and meals are served daily until 9pm (last orders). Traditional music is played from Friday to Sunday. An effigy of a witch sits in the window frame, a reminder of the story of a former resident, Dame Alice Kyteler. In 1324, Alice and her maid were pronounced guilty of witchcraft after four of Alice's husbands had died in mysterious circumstances; although pardoned, Alice was again accused but escaped, leaving her maid Petronella to burn at the stake.

KILKENNY: Langton's
69 John St, Co Kilkenny.
Road map C4. **Tel** 056 776 5133.

Langton's is noted for its black-and-white exterior, Edwardian ambience and the stylish glass interior at the back. The front bar is cosy with a low ceiling. Pub food is on offer, and there's music and dancing at least one night a week during the summer; Tuesday, Thursday and Saturday are club nights.

KILKENNY: The Left Bank
High St, Co Kilkenny.
Road map C4. **Tel** 056 775 0016.

Encompassing a sports' bar, an outdoor bar and a cocktail bar, this venue in an impressive old city centre bank is vast yet hospitable. There are plenty of nooks for quiet chat, as well as every option to be in the thick of it with room to dance and a sociable smoking area.

KILKENNY: Marble City Bar
66 High St, Co Kilkenny.
Road map C4. **Tel** 056 776 1143.

Marble City Bar, the most famous pub in town, is named after the local limestone, which becomes black when polished. This four-storey building has an Art Deco façade. A busy café-bar with no reservations. Bar food till 9pm.

KILKENNY: Tynan's Bridge House Bar
2 John's Bridge, Co Kilkenny.
Road map C4. **Tel** 056 772 1291.

This is the most genuine old-world pub in town, with an intimate interior lit by charming lamps. Quaint relics of the former grocery store and pharmacy are on display, from a set of old scales to the drawers labelled with names of nuts and spices. Live music from Monday to Thursday. An outdoor smoking area has been added.

KILMORE QUAY: The Strand Inn
Dunmore East, Co Wexford.
Road map D5. **Tel** 051 383 174.
Once a renowned haunt for smugglers, this hotel pub has cosy snugs and open fires for winter, and a sunny seaside patio overlooking Hook Head Lighthouse for the summer months.

LEIGHLINBRIDGE: The Lord Bagenal Inn
Co Carlow. **Road map** D5.
Tel 059 972 1668.
This pub is a well-known stop-off point for those travelling south from Dublin. Set in a small, peaceful village in County Carlow, the Lord Bagenal overlooks a picturesque marina on the River Barrow. It boasts award-winning food and has a children's crèche. Accommodation is available in the hotel here.

NEW ROSS: Corcoran's Pub
Irishtown, Co Wexford.
Road map D5. **Tel** 051 425920.
Head here if you crave fresh, home-made food. Having had five generations of continuous ownership, Corcoran's is one of the oldest pubs in town and has a friendly atmosphere. Card games are played every Monday with music sessions on weekends, including Irish music, singing and dancing.

WATERFORD: Henry Downes
8–10 Thomas St, Co Waterford.
Road map D5. **Tel** 051 874118.
Dating from 1759, this unusual pub located in County Waterford bottles its own whiskey. It is dark and cavernous with a chequered history. This makes it a fine stop for a good pint and a chat with the locals.

WATERFORD: Jack Meade's Pub
Dunmore Rd, Co Waterford.
Road map D5. **Tel** 051 850950.
Situated under an old stone bridge 7 km (4 miles) south of town, Jack Meade's provides a quiet and quaint atmosphere. In the summer, musicians play outdoors and children can amuse themselves in the playground. Drop by for the setting and some lunch.

WATERFORD: T & H Doolan
George's St, Co Waterford.
Road map D5. **Tel** 051 841504.
Set in the city's most charming pedestrianized street, this traditional, 18th-century black-and-white pub offers an intimate atmosphere and good "craic". Traditional folk music sessions are held every night.

WEXFORD: Centenary Stores
Charlotte St, Co Wexford.
Road map D5. **Tel** 053 912 2303.
Tucked away in a converted warehouse, this dimly lit pub is the most popular in Wexford. The friendly bar staff and a mixed local and bohemian crowd chat in the wood-panelled bar. Drinkers are entertained with sessions of traditional music every Sunday morning, and it's open until late on Friday and Saturday nights.

WEXFORD: Macken's
Bull Ring, Co Wexford.
Road map D5. **Tel** 053 912 2949.
This pub has a prime location on one of the corners of the historic bull ring. It's an excellent place to stop for a pint or two and watch the world go by. If you're lucky, there might even be some live music.

Cork and Kerry

BALTIMORE: Bushes
Co Cork.
Road map B6. **Tel** 028 20125.
Famous in County Cork, this pub serves the best ales and pints in the village and is well used to visitors dropping by. Sit outside in the summer and gaze out onto the islands or watch the beautiful sunset.

CAHIRCIVEEN: The Point Bar
Renard Pt, Valentia Harbour, Co Kerry.
Road map A5. **Tel** 066 947 2165.
Best to save this one for the summer months. With its variety of ultra-fresh seafood dishes and stunning view of Valentia Island, the Point Bar is considered by many to be one of Kerry's greatest.

CASTLETOWNSHEND: Mary Ann's
Co Cork.
Road map B6. **Tel** 028 36146.
Since opening in 1846, Mary Ann's has maintained excellent service and a great reputation for quality home-made food. Full of interesting antiques, this is one of the best examples of a traditional pub in Ireland.

CLONAKILTY: De Barra's
55 Pearse St, Co Cork.
Road map B6. **Tel** 023 883 3381.
This is one of the best-known pubs in West Cork, with a traditional folk club open most nights; many musicians come from the Gaeltacht *(see p233)*. The bar is true to its origins, with hand-painted signs and traditional whiskey jars. Simple snacks and full lunches are served from noon to 4pm.

CORK: Bodega
St Peter's Market, Cornmarket St, Co Cork.
Road map C5. **Tel** 021 427 3756.
This bright, modern pub and restaurant was once a warehouse. The high ceilings create a feeling of openness; the huge wall-spaces are taken up by art, much of it for sale. Soup and sandwiches in the afternoon give way to an international menu in the evening. On Saturdays, the open-air market outside adds to the hustle and bustle.

CORK: Chateau Bar
93 St Patrick's St, Co Cork.
Road map C5. **Tel** 021 427 0370.
This bar in the heart of the city occupies a striking building that was once on the quayside. Founded in 1793, this elegant pub has a stylish Victorian interior and offers good-quality bar fare.

CORK: Clancy's
15–16 Princes St, Co Cork.
Road map C5. **Tel** 021 427 6097.
One of Cork's oldest pubs, Clancy's has been open since 1824. It has one of the longest continuous bars in Ireland and has live music performances from May to September. Food is available in the Lunchtime Carvery or Steak Restaurant where the emphasis is on quality Irish cuisine.

CORK: Henchy's
40 St Luke's, Co Cork. **Road map** C5.
Tel 021 450 7833.
This traditional pub dates from 1884 and has retained much of its Victorian ambience, enhanced by the mahogany bar and stained glass. It has long been associated with artists and is where young hopefuls come to show their work to a largely sympathetic audience.

CORK: The Long Valley
10 Winthrop St, Co Cork.
Road map C5. **Tel** 021 427 2144.
Located just off Patrick Street, this pub has a sense of the unexpected. It attracts all sorts of characters from chancers to professionals. It is well known for its smooth pints of Murphy's, which any self-respecting local will choose over Guinness.

CORK: Sin É
8 Coburg St, Co Cork.
Road map C5. **Tel** 021 450 2266.
This is one of Cork's cosiest and most popular pubs, famous for its traditional music sessions and the eclectic collection of bric-a-brac adorning the walls.

DINGLE: Ashes
Main St, Co Kerry.
Road map A5. **Tel** 066 915 0989.
An old-world style-bar dating back to 1849. The charming traditional frontage sets the tone for the cosy and inviting atmosphere found within. Pop in for a casual drink or light snack in the day or an informal and good-value seafood meal in the evening.

DINGLE: Dick Mack's
Greene St, Co Kerry.
Road map A5. **Tel** 066 915 1787.
This individualistic spot is part shoe shop, part pub, and retains the original shop and drinking counters. The pub is a haunt of local artists, eccentrics and extroverts. In the evening, regulars often congregate around the piano.

DUNQUIN: Krugers
Annadale Rd, Ballyferriter, Co Kerry.
Road map A5. **Tel** 066 915 6127.
Situated close to the quays for the Blasket Islands, this well-known family pub is also a guesthouse from April to August. The pub is decorated with family memorabilia and stills from the famous films made in the area, such as *Ryan's Daughter* and *Far and Away*.

GLENCAR: The Climber's Inn
Co Kerry.
Road map B5. **Tel** 066 976 0101.
This family-run pub is a famous land-markonthewaytotheKerryhigh-lands. It boasts an open fire and serves up great home-cooked meals with interesting vegetarian options. Chat with other hikers and climbers after a day's trekking. Live Irish music

KILLARNEY: Buckley's Bar
College St, Co Kerry.
Road map B5. **Tel** 064 663 1037.
This oak-panelled bar is noted for its regular traditional music sessions and its filling meals. The pub was opened in 1926 when Tom Buckley, a homesick emigrant, returned from New York. Bar food is served until 4pm.

KILLARNEY: The Laurels
Main St, Co Kerry.
Road map B5. **Tel** 064 643 1149.
This claims to be Killarney's liveliest pub and is popular with young locals and tourists. It has been run by the O'Leary family for almost a century and provides excellent bar snacks and meals (steak, mussels, oysters, fish) in a separate restaurant area.

KILLORGLIN: The Bianconi
Lower Bridge St, Ring of Kerry, Co Kerry.
Road map A5. **Tel** 066 976 1146.
If it is hospitality you are after, this renowned bar is the place for you. This award-winning restaurant, hotel and modern bar offers excellent-quality local produce at an affordable price.

KINSALE: Kieran's Folk House Inn
Guardwell, Co Cork. **Road map** B6.
Tel 021 477 2382.
This convivial corner of old Kinsale draws locals and visitors alike. The interior is snug and welcoming, with live music every night during the season. The inn also houses a pleasant guesthouse and a noted restaurant – the Shrimps Seafood Bistro, open for lunch and dinner all year.

KINSALE: The Lord Kingsale
Main St, Co Cork. **Road map** B6.
Tel 021 477 2371.
This beamed, old-fashioned pub attracts a quiet, genteel crowd. It is several hundred years old but the interior is, in part, a clever fake. In summer, live music is performed every night. Bar food is served from noon to 3pm.

SCILLY: The Spaniard Inn
Kinsale, Co Cork.
Road map B6. **Tel** 021 477 2436.
Set on a hairpin bend in the village of Scilly, this popular fishermen's pub has the air of a smugglers' inn. There is live traditional music in one of the bars most nights during the summer and it is particularly popular at weekends. The restaurant and bar offer simple, but excellent fare.

SHERKIN ISLAND: The Jolly Roger
Co Cork.
Road map B6. **Tel** 028 20379.
Island atmosphere pervades this cosy pub, which serves outstand-ingly good-value lunches. In summer you can sit outside and admire the view of Baltimore Harbour and the bay. Delicious chowder.

The Lower Shannon

ANNACOTTY: Finnegan's
Co Limerick.
Road map B5. **Tel** 061 337338.
Originally a 17th-century coach stop, history and folklore permeate this renowned establishment in County Limerick. Finnegan's specializes in steaks and freshly caught seafood. Cosy and extremely friendly.

BALLYVAUGHAN: Monk's Pub
Old Pier, Co Clare.
Road map B4. **Tel** 065 707 7059.
This quaint pub is situated beside the pier, overlooking Galway Bay. Inside, country furniture and peat fires are matched by local seafood including chowder. There's also traditional Irish music performed. Ring for details.

BUNRATTY: Durty Nelly's
Co Clare.
Road map B4. **Tel** 061 364861.
Set beside Bunratty Castle, this extremely commercialized pub appeals to locals as well as tourists. The 17th-century atmosphere is sustained by the warren of rooms, inglenook fireplaces and historical portraits. Traditional music is performed most evenings, and wholesome food is available both from the bar and from the two restaurants.

DOOLIN: Gus O'Connor's
Clare Coast, Doolin.
Road map B4. **Tel** 065 707 4168.
This famous pub is known to lovers of traditional music the world over. The pub has been in the O'Connor family for over 150 years and combines an authentic grocery store with a lively pub. This is the place for spontaneous music, simple bar food, young company and great "craic".

DOOLIN: McDermott's
Roadfoard, Co Clare.
Road map B4.
Tel 065 707 4328 or 707 4700.
No Clare pub is complete without a traditional music session and McDermott's does not disappoint. It has live music every night from St Patrick's Day until late October. A warm welcome and a cold pint are guaranteed by the staff. The original 1867 tiled floor is still in place.

ENNIS: The Cloister
Abbey St, Co Clare.
Road map B4. **Tel** 065 686 8198.
This historic pub is situated by the famous Ennis Friary *(see p193)*. The pub's cosy, atmospheric interior is complemented by a patio in summer, and by traditional music on some nights.

ENNIS: Queen's Front Bar
Abbey St, Co Clare.
Road map B4. **Tel** 065 682 8963.
This historical pub lies beside the impressive ruins of Ennis Friary *(see p193)*. It serves superb, traditional Irish food. Good for families, the Queen's welcomes all ages.

KILLALOE: Goosers
Ballina Rd, Co Clare.
Road map C4. **Tel** 061 376791.
This delightfully picturesque waterfront pub on the Ballina side of the river has a thatched roof, traditional interior and a welcoming atmosphere. Noted for its cuisine, Goosers serves reasonably priced seafood in the restaurant and satisfying "pub grub" in the rustic bar.

KILRUSH: Crotty's Pub
Market Square, Co Clare.
Road map B4. **Tel** 065 905 2470.
This popular and award-winning pub was once run by one of the foremost exponents of the concertina, Lizzie Crotty (1885–1960). Today it hosts live traditional music three nights of the week in summer. Tasty bar food is available all day Monday to Saturday.

LIMERICK: The Locke
3 George's Quay, Co Limerick.
Road map B4. **Tel** 061 413733.
Overlooking the Abbey river, this is a typical black-and-white pub. In summer, it is a favourite port of call for riverside strollers. In winter, blazing fires and snugs make it a cosy spot. Traditional music is played from Sunday to Thursday nights. The restaurant is open all day.

LIMERICK: Nancy Blake's
19 Upper Denmark St, Co Limerick.
Road map B4. **Tel** 061 416443.
Limerick's best-known bar, Nancy Blake's has much to offer in the way of good "craic" and traditional music. If you prefer rhythm and blues, try the adjoining Outback Bar. The cosy main bar serves soup and sandwiches at lunchtime. Music is played on Monday, Wednesday, and Saturday.

The West of Ireland

ARAN ISLANDS: Ti Joe Macs
Kilronan, Inishmore, Co Galway.
Road map B2. **Tel** 099 61248.
This pub stands straight in front of visitors as they leave the boat. It serves soup and sandwiches.

CLARINBRIDGE: Moran's Oyster Cottage
The Weir, Kilcolgan, Co Galway.
Road map B4. **Tel** 091 796113.
This bar, set in a thatched cottage, was a regular port of call for crews from passing "hookers" (traditional ships). Nowadays, you can sample all kinds of seafood here, though Moran's is best known as the most famous oyster bar in Ireland – the owner holds the local speed record for shelling oysters.

CLARINBRIDGE: Paddy Burke's Oyster Inn
Co Galway. **Road map** B4.
Tel 091 796226.
Founded in 1835, this authentic thatched pub has leaded window-panes and a charming beamed interior. Apart from the renowned Clarinbridge oysters and buffet lunches, gourmet menus are also available at lunch and dinner.

CLIFDEN: E J Kings
The Square, Co Galway.
Road map A3. **Tel** 095 21330.
This spacious, bustling pub is situated on several floors, with the ground floor the most appealing. Seafood platters or varied pub fare can be enjoyed by the peat fire. In summer, live music is often on offer, especially folk and ballads. The staff are exceptionally friendly.

GALWAY: Busker Brownes
Cross St Upper, Co Galway.
Road map B4. **Tel** 091 563377.
This barn-like city pub occupies several storeys, including the shell of a 16th-century convent on the top floor. The Slate House, the pub next door, is under the same management, and both are popular with local students. There are jazz sessions on Sundays.

GALWAY: Cookes Thatch Bar
Cooke's Corner, 2 Newcastle Rd, Co Galway.
Road map B4. **Tel** 091 582959.
Situated on the outskirts of Galway, this traditional thatched inn is one of the city's oldest pubs and is still renowned for its live music (traditional sessions are on Wednes-days and Sundays) and friendliness. The pub includes an off-licence.

GALWAY: Dew Drop Inn
Mainguard St, Co Galway.
Road map B4. **Tel** 091 561070.
Locally known as Myles Lee, this is an intimate, vintage pub that encapsulates Galway's Bohemian traditions. The authentic low-level lighting makes this pub a comfy place, especially on cold nights when the log fire is crackling. The Dew Drop serves one of the best pints of Guinness in town.

GALWAY: The King's Head
15 High St, Co Galway.
Road map B4. **Tel** 091 566630.
Founded in 1649, this historic pub is adorned with a bow-fronted façade. The homely interior contains 17th-century fireplaces. Simple lunch snacks are served in the main bar. In the back bar, various live bands playing in the evenings attract a youthful crowd.

GALWAY: McSwiggan's
3 Eyre St, Wood Quay,
Co Galway. **Road map** B4.
Tel 091 568917.
In the centre of the city, this snug, relaxing café-bar has terracotta floors and comfortable seats.

GALWAY: The Quays
11 Quay St, Co Galway.
Road map B4. **Tel** 091 568347.
The Quays was originally a small thatched cottage but the building was knocked down to make way for this three-storyed bar. The top floor is a circular mezzanine that overlooks the rest of the bar. A good venue for music, the traditional music nights are Friday and Sunday evenings. Hearty lunches are served daily. Outside seating during the summer months.

GALWAY: Ti Neachtain
17 Cross St, Co Galway.
Road map B4. **Tel** 091 568820.
Set in the "Latin Quarter", this 18th-century town house boasts a distinctive oriel window. Inside, a musty wood interior is home to old-world snugs and friendly service. Traditional music can often be heard here, and upstairs is Ard Bia restaurant.

KILLALA: Golden Acres Co Mayo.
Road map B2. **Tel** 096 32183.
This comfortable pub is located near the major activity centres of the area. Deep-sea fishing, golf and boat trips are all within walking distance of this homely country bar. It features good pub food.

OUGHTERARD: The Boat Inn
Main St, Connemara, Co Galway.
Road map B3. **Tel** 091 552196.
This hotel, bar and restaurant is located next to Lough Corrib on the edge of Connemara. The lively boat-shaped bar serves bar food and snacks. Local musicians perform at weekends and on weekdays during the summer.

WESTPORT: The Asgard Tavern
The Quay, Co Mayo.
Road map B3. **Tel** 098 25319.
This old inn facing the pier and Clew Bay is decorated with a nautical theme. Both the main downstairs back bar and the upstairs restaurant provide excellent seafood and salads. The small downstairs front bar, known as the snug, is the most atmospheric.

WESTPORT: Matt Molloy's
Bridge St, Co Mayo.
Road map B3. **Tel** 098 26655.
Founded by the flautist from the traditional Irish folk band The Chieftains, this deceptively spacious pub is designed along equally traditional lines. There is live music in the back room every evening, when the pub is packed.

Northwest Ireland

BURTONPORT: The Lobster Pot
Co Donegal.
Road map C1. **Tel** 074 954 2012.
This cosy pub lies near the pier. The old timber surrounds of the interior are used as a backdrop to an incredible selection of Gaelic sporting memorabilia. The seafood is renowned as the best, but other good dishes are served as well.

CROLLY: Leo's Tavern
Meenaleck, Co Donegal.
Road map C1. **Tel** 074 954 8143.
Owned by the father of modern folk musicians Clannad and of the singer Enya, this friendly pub attracts locals and tourists for its sing-songs round the accordion, ceili and traditional music nights.

CULDAFF: McGrory's
Co Donegal.
Road map C1. **Tel** 074 937 9696.
On the idyllic Inishowen Peninsula *(see pp230–31)*, this is a place of quality food and drink. McGrory's restaurant caters for up to 60 diners in a comfortable yet stylish setting. The Backroom Bar, also located in the pub, is a top music venue, featuring live music of all kinds.

DONEGAL: O'Donnell's
The Diamond, Co Donegal.
Road map C2. **Tel** 074 972 1049.
This middle-of-the-road venue has a small bar. A larger lounge in the back is used for live performances and karaoke nights. Local musicians entertain here on any given night.

DROMAHAIR: Stanford Village Inn
Main St, Co Leitrim.
Road map C2. **Tel** 071 916 4140.
Set in a picturesque village, this traditional pub has been in the same family for generations. The tiny, quaint Biddy's Bar remains unchanged, adorned with family portraits and old grocery jars. The main bar has mellow brickwork and flagstones from a ruined castle. Delicious food is on offer all day in the summer and there are often impromptu evening music sessions.

SLIGO: Hargadons
5 O'Connell St, Co Sligo.
Road map C2. **Tel** 071 915 3714
This is an old world pub that sports an authentic interior to match. Tasty bar food is available along with a warm atmosphere. Take advantage of the popular summer beer garden on balmy nights.

SLIGO: Osta
Stephen St, Sligo.
Road map C2. **Tel** 071 914 4639.
This airy wine bar is located on the bank of the Garavogue river. The wines have been hand-picked by those in the know. It's also a good stop for a bite to eat.

SLIGO: Shoot the Crows
Grattan St, Co Sligo.
Road map C2. **Tel** 071 916 2554.
This authentic, old-world pub attracts all kinds of colourful characters and has a great atmosphere. Music is ambient jazz and traditional Irish.

STRANDHILL: Strand House Bar
Strandhill, Co Sligo.
Road map C2. **Tel** 071 916 8140.
The turf fire here warms the surfers from the nearby beach, while the snugs make for perfect one-to-one conversations over a pint or some food.

The Midlands

ABBEYLEIX: Morrissey's
Main St, Co Laois.
Road map C4. **Tel** 057 873 1281.
If driving through County Laois, it is worth stopping at this genuinely traditional pub. The 18th-century inn was remodelled in the Victorian era and has stayed the same ever since. The grocery section survives while the plain and unpretentious bar serves simple bar snacks.

CARLINGFORD: PJ O'Hare's Anchor Bar
Tholsel St, Co Louth.
Road map D3. **Tel** 042 937 3106.
Known locally as PJ's, this atmospheric pub and grocery store is popular with sailors and locals alike. A friendly and often eccentric welcome is matched by bar food such as oysters and sandwiches. Music is played in the summer.

CRINKILL: The Thatch
Birr, Co Offaly.
Road map C4. **Tel** 05791 20682.
Mooted as *the* traditional pub, the Thatch is one of the oldest pubs in South Offaly and, as its name suggests, has always been thatched. It has won All Ireland Pub of the Year five times and certainly lives up to its reputation. Children are welcome.

DUNDALK: The Jockeys
47 Anne St, Co Louth.
Road map D3. **Tel** 042 933 4621.
This friendly pub offers home-cooked lunches daily at very reasonable prices. The walls are covered in Gaelic Athletic Association mementos *(see p33)*, portraying its proud Gaelic sports' tradition. This pub has been in existence, in one guise or another, since 1799. Live music on Friday and Saturday nights.

KILBEGGAN: Kilbeggan Distillery Experience
Mullingar, Co Westmeath.
Road map C3. **Tel** 057 933 2132.
As well as being the oldest licensed pot still distillery in the world (established in 1757), this historic complex has a whiskey bar – the ideal place to sample a few brands before buying *(see p253)*. There is an adjoining restaurant.

KILNALECK: The Copper Kettle
Co Cavan.
Road map C3. **Tel** 0494 336223.
This lively family-run pub has a wonderful atmosphere. It is well known for its wholesome, home-cooked meals, served all day. There's entertainment every Saturday night all year round.

KINNITTY: The Dungeon Bar
Birr, Co Offaly.
Road map C4. **Tel** 05791 37318.
Sited in the basement of medieval Kinnitty Castle, less than a mile from Kinnitty village, this candlelit bar is not quite as spooky as it sounds. Historic Irish memorabilia covers the walls and the food and drinks are well presented. There's traditional Irish music every Friday and Saturday night.

LONGFORD: Edward J Valentine's
Main St, Co Longford.
Road map C3. **Tel** 043 334 5509.
Relax in Edward Valentine's wonderful, warm, old-world atmosphere. There is a lively atmosphere at the weekends in what is otherwise a home away from home.

PORTLAOISE: O'Donoghues
Market Sq, Co Laois.
Road map C4. **Tel** 057 862 1199.
Leave the modern world behind and enjoy the traditional atmosphere of this award-winning, old-style pub. This is the perfect spot for a quiet pint or a snack. The Seasons Restaurant is located overhead.

PORTLAOISE: Treacy's Bar and Restaurant
The Heath, Co Laois.
Road map C4. **Tel** 057 864 6538.
This charming thatched cottage pub and restaurant is 6 km (3 miles) outside of the town, but is well worth the journey. It is the oldest family-run pub in these parts, and there is a good range of pub grub (roasts, fish, salads) as well as prime steak at reasonable prices.

Northern Ireland

ARDGLASS: Curran's Bar & Seafood Steakhouse
83 Strangford Rd, Chapeltown, Co Down. **Road map** E2.
Tel 028 4484 1332.
This charming pub and restaurant is in the Curran ancestral home, which dates from 1791. Expect warm service and the freshest catch. A good choice for families, with its play area and beer garden.

BANGOR: Jenny Watt's
41 High St, Co Down.
Road map E2. **Tel** 028 9127 0401.
Likeable and very popular, this bar with Victoriana trimmings is found in the centre of town. The walls are adorned with local photos and memorabilia. There's live jazz at Sunday lunchtime, and more music on Tuesdays, Wednesdays and Thursdays. Bar food is served, and there's a beer garden.

BELFAST: Crown Liquor Saloon
46 Great Victoria St, Co Antrim.
Road map D2. **Tel** 028 902 43187.
This Victorian gin palace ranks as one of the most gorgeous bars in Ireland *(see p281)*. Lunch includes several local specialities, such as Irish stew and champ, but the Strangford Lough oysters really do stand out. Robinson's, the pub next door, is particularly lively in the evening.

BELFAST: Lavery's
12–18 Bradbury Place, Co Antrim.
Road map D2. **Tel** 028 9087 1106.
Yet another of Belfast's fine old gin palaces. Bar food served at lunch and discos in the evenings. It is popular with students from Queen's University.

BELFAST: White's Tavern
Winecellar Entry, Co Antrim.
Road map D2. **Tel** 028 9024 3080.
Just one of several daylight-free pubs tucked away in the Entries *(see p281)* sector of Belfast city that are best at lunchtime when decent, reasonably priced pub food is served. White's lays claim to be the oldest tavern (1630) in the city. Other pubs in this series of alleys that are worth a look include the Morning Star.

BROUGHSHANE: The Thatch Inn
57 Main St, Co Antrim.
Road map D2. **Tel** 028 258 61366.
This old thatched pub in the ancient village of Broughshane exudes charm, character and warmth. The Thatch Inn is well known for great food, warm welcomes and live music.

BUSHMILLS: Bushmills Inn
9 Dunluce Rd, Co Antrim.
Road map D1. **Tel** 028 207 33000.
Set in an old coaching inn, this cosy bar is lit by gaslights. There is also a restaurant on the premises.

ENNISKILLEN: Blake's of the Hollow
6 Church St, Co Fermanagh.
Road map C2. **Tel** 028 663 25388.
One of a number of popular town-centre pubs, Blake's dates back to Victorian days and has many of its original fittings.

HILLSBOROUGH: Plough Inn
The Square, Co Down.
Road map D2. **Tel** 028 9268 2985.
This typical village pub, dating from the 1750s, has wooden ceiling beams and a selection of crockery, china and other ornaments on the walls. There's a bistro upstairs open during the day, serving international dishes. The Hillside, just down the main street, is also worth a visit.

KILLYLEA: Digby's Bar & Restaurant
53 Main St, Co Armagh.
Road map D2. **Tel** 028 3756 8330.
This friendly, traditional village inn, decorated with old photographs of local places and people, is family-run. It boasts an extensive menu with some good wines and is a relaxed, enjoyable venue for families.

LONDONDERRY: The Park Bar
35 Francis St, Co Londonderry.
Road map C1. **Tel** 028 7126 4674.
A family-run bar close to the city centre and adjacent to St Eugene's Cathedral. The European lagers and Guinness are on tap.

OMAGH: The Mellon Country Hotel
134 Beltany Rd, Co Tyrone.
Road map C2. **Tel** 028 816 61891.
Just 1 mile from the Ulster American Folk Park, this country inn is a popular stopping-off point. Set in the foothills of the Sperrin mountains, the inn overlooks the Strule River. A comfortable place with friendly service.

SHOPPING IN IRELAND

Ireland offers a wide range of handmade goods, usually regionally based and highly individual. Its most renowned products include chunky Aran sweaters, Waterford crystal, Irish linen, hand-loomed Donegal tweed and tasty farmhouse cheeses. The thriving crafts industry is based on traditional products with an innovative twist. Typical of contemporary Irish crafts are good design, quality craftsmanship and a range spanning Celtic brooches, bone china, knitwear and designer fashion, carved bogwood and books of Irish poetry. Kitsch souvenirs also abound, from leprechauns and shamrock emblems to Guinness tankards and garish religious memorabilia. In the directory on page 335, a map reference is given for each address. Dublin shopping is covered in detail on pages 108–109. Road map references are to the towns and cities on the inside back cover.

Fruit and vegetable market in Moore Street, Dublin

Where to Shop

The choice of places to shop in Ireland ranges from tiny workshops to large factory outlets, and from elegant boutiques to high-street chain stores. Bargains can often be had at bric-a-brac shops and local markets, although the banter is sometimes the best thing on offer. This guide lists market days for every town featured. Sometimes the best produce or products are to be found off the beaten track; locals are always happy to let you know where.

When to Shop

Most shops are open from Monday to Saturday, 10am to 5:30 or 6pm. In shopping centres and large towns, shops tend to have at least one late-night opening, usually on Thursday or Friday (Thursday in Dublin). In tourist areas, craft shops are generally open on Sundays too. Shops are closed at Easter and Christmas and on St Patrick's Day but are open on most other public holidays. In Killarney, Ireland's tourist capital, most shops are open until 10pm in summer.

How to Pay

Major credit and debit cards are generally accepted in department stores and larger retail outlets, but smaller shops prefer cash. Most traveller's cheques are accepted in major stores with a passport as identification.

Sales Tax and Refunds

Most purchases are subject to VAT (sales tax) at 23 per cent, included in the sales price. However, visitors from outside the European Union (EU) can reclaim VAT prior to departure. When shipping goods overseas, refunds can be claimed at the point of purchase. If taking your goods with you, look for the CashBack logo in shops, fill in the special voucher, then visit CashBack offices at Dublin or Shannon Airport.

Books

Reading is a national passion in Ireland, so bookshops are generally very good. In bigger shops expect solid sections on Irish archaeology and architecture, folklore, history, politics and cuisine. **Eason and Son** is one of the country's most widespread bookstore chains with a large collection of Irish literature and newspapers. Seek out the smaller, "Irish Interest" shops too. In Galway, **Kenny's Books**, hidden away in an industrial area, is packed with both new and second-hand books.

Music

Traditional musical instruments *(see pp28–9)* are made in many regions, especially County Clare, also known as the "singing county". Handmade harps are a speciality in Mayo and Dublin. Instruments such as handcrafted *bodhráns*, uilleann pipes, tin whistles and fiddles are on sale throughout Ireland. There are

A traditional fiddle maker in his workshop in Dingle

Colourful bric-a-brac shop in Kilkenny

several specialist record shops that sell traditional Irish recordings. **Golden Discs** is a chain of music stores, and stocks a good selection of traditional Irish music.

Food and Drink

Kylemore Abbey teapot

Markets have become a popular way to shop for food in Irish cities. Most of what's on offer is produced locally under organic conditions. Smoked salmon, home-cured bacon, farmhouse cheeses, soda bread, preserves and handmade chocolates make perfect last-minute gifts.

Guinness travels less well and is best drunk in Ireland. Irish whiskey is hard to beat as a gift or souvenir. Apart from the cheaper Power's and Paddy brands, the big names are Bushmills *(see p270)* and Jameson *(see p183)* . Rich Irish liqueurs include Irish Mist and Baileys Irish Cream.

Crafts

Crafts are a flourishing way of life in rural Ireland, and the distinctive products can be purchased from either city department stores or work-shops and individual vendors. The **Crafts Council of Ireland** has branches in Dublin and Kilkenny, and can recommend good small-scale outlets in the country. Tourist offices also provide lists of local workshops, where you can watch the production process. Craft shops, such as the **Kilkenny Design Centre** and **Bricín**, sell good examples of different crafts. In Cork and Kerry there is an abundance of workshops, mainly in Kinsale and Dingle. The *Guide to Craft Outlets* is available at local tourist offices.

Distinctive products from this area are traditional tiles based on designs found in Kilkenny Cathedral and nearby medieval abbeys. Further west, green Connemara marble is made into "worry stones", small charms traditionally exchanged between families as marks of long-lasting friendship. Also in Connemara, **Roundstone Music** makes *bodhrans* in front of interested tourists.

Other crafts include metal-work, leatherwork and carpentry. Local woods are used for ash or beech furniture, blackthorn walking sticks and sculptures made of 1,000-year-old bogwood – petrified wood salvaged from Ireland's unique boglands during turf cutting.

Pottery display in Kilkenny Design Centre

Crystal and Glassware

In the wake of Waterford Crystal *(see p151)*, the brand leader, come countless followers. The price depends on reputation, the quantity of lead used in the glass and the labour-intensiveness of the design. **Tipperary Crystal** offers a range of lines, and **Galway Irish Crystal** is another elegant brand.

In Kilkenny, the famous Jerpoint Abbey inspires local designs by **Jerpoint Glass**. Decorated with simple yet stylish motifs, the small vases, candlesticks, jugs and bowls make pleasing gifts. Most stores will pack and send glassware overseas for you.

Crystal from around Ireland can be found in most craft and design shops, but if you want to see how glass is made it's best to visit a factory.

Ceramics and China

Although more renowned for crystal, Ireland also has many reputable producers of ceramics and china. Established in 19th-century Ulster, Belleek Pottery *(see p273)* produces creamy china with a lustrous sheen and subtle decorative motifs, including shamrocks and flowers. In Galway, **Royal Tara China** is Ireland's leading fine bone china manufacturer, with Celtic-influenced designs, while Kylemore Abbey *(see p212)* specializes in exquisite hand-painted pottery. **Louis Mulcahy's Pottery**, in Ballyferriter, is noted for fine decorative glazes, while in Bennettsbridge, **Nicholas Mosse Pottery** produces hand-painted designs. Enniscorthy in Wexford is another centre for ceramics.

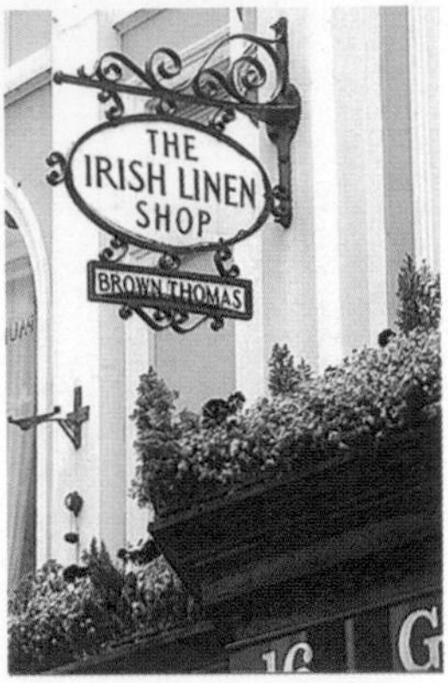

Old sign for the linen department at a former Brown Thomas store

Linen

Damask linen was brought to Armagh by Huguenot refugees fleeing French persecution during the late 17th century. As a result, Belfast became the world's linen capital. Ulster is still the place for linen, with sheets and double-damask table linen on sale in Belfast – at **Smyth's Irish Linen**, for example – and in other towns. Linen, embroidered by hand, is made in Donegal. Linen-making can be seen at Wellbrook Beetling Mill *(see p272)*.

Knitwear and Tweed

Aran sweaters are sold all over Ireland, particularly in County Galway and on the Aran Islands themselves. One of Ireland's best buys, these oiled, off-white sweaters used to be handed down through generations of Aran fishermen. Legend has it that each family used its own motifs. If a fisherman died at sea and his body was unidentifiable, his family could recognize him by his sweater.

Given the Irish experience of wet weather, warm and waterproof clothes are generally of good quality, from waxed jackets and duffel coats to sheepskin jackets. Knitwear is on sale all over Ireland. **Avoca Handweavers** and **Blarney Woollen Mills** are the best-known outlets. Good buys include embroidered sweaters and waistcoats as well as hand-woven shawls, hats, caps and scarves.

Donegal tweed is a byword for quality, and is noted for its texture, tension and subtle colours (originally produced by dyes made from lichens and minerals). Tweed caps, scarves, ties and suits are sold in outlets such as **Magee of Donegal**.

Interior of Avoca Handweavers in Kilmacanogue

Jewellery

In its golden age, Celtic metalwork was the pride of Ireland *(see pp36–9)*, and many contemporary craftspeople are still inspired by traditional Celtic designs. Handcrafted or factory-made silver, gold and ceramic jewellery is produced in a variety of designs. The Claddagh ring from Galway is the most famous Celtic design – the lovers' symbol of two hands cradling a crowned heart. **Cahalan Jewellers** in County Galway is one of the most renowned and has a huge range of unique Irish and antique jewellery. For heraldic jewellery, try **James Murtagh Jewellers** in County Mayo.

Fashion

Inspired by a predominantly young population, Ireland is fast acquiring a name for fashion. Conservatively cut tweed and linen suits continue to be models of classic good taste, though young designers are increasingly experimental, using bold lines and mixing traditional fabrics. Irish design has seen enormous success across the world.

At **Brown Thomas** on Grafton Street and in many small boutiques, you will find clothes designed by the best Irish designers, including J. W. Anderson, Heidi Higgins and Mary Grant. The **Kilkenny** shops located around the country stock a range of ladies' fashion by Irish designers.

Some designers, such as Simone Rocha and Una Burke, have eschewed traditional Irish textiles and forged fresh styles in new materials.

Ladies' fashion and the hottest trends can be found in **O'Donnell's** in Limerick, while up north, there are many outlets of **Clockwork Orange** and **Fosters Clothing**.

For budget clothing, Dunnes Stores and Penneys have branches throughout the Republic and Northern Ireland. Clothing and shoe sizes are identical to British fittings. The main streets of the big cities are lined with British and European fashion outlets, including H&M, Zara, Warehouse and Topshop.

Selection of hand-knitted sweaters at a craft shop in Dingle

DIRECTORY

Books

Eason and Son
113 Patrick's St, Cork, Co Cork.
Road map C5.
Tel 021 427 0477.
W easons.com

Kenmare Bookshop
Shelbourne St, Kenmare, Co Kerry.
Road map B6. **Tel** 064 664 1578.

Kenny Bookshop & Art Gallery
Líosban Retail Park, Tuam Rd, Galway, Co Galway.
Road map B4.
Tel 091 709 350.
W kennys.ie

McLoughlin's Books
Shop Street, Westport, Co Mayo. **Road map** B3.
Tel 098 27777.

Music

The Dingle Record Shop
Green St, Dingle, Co Kerry.
Road map A5.
Tel 087 298 4550.
W dinglerecordshop.com

Golden Discs
Unit 16, Harbour Place, Mullingar, Co Westmeath.
Road map B4.
Tel 044 934 5499.

Plugd Records
Triskel Arts Centre, Tobin St, Cork, Co Cork.
Road map C5.
Tel 021 427 6300.

Food and Drink

McCambridges
38–39 Shop St, Galway, Co Galway.
Road map B4. **Tel** 091 562259.

Spillane Seafoods
Lackabane, Killarney, Co Kerry. **Road map** B5.
Tel 064 31320.

Crafts

Bricín
26 High St, Killarney, Co Kerry. **Road map** B5.
Tel 064 66 34902.

Crafts Council of Ireland
Castle Yard, Kilkenny, Co Kilkenny.
Road map C4.
Tel 056 776 1804.

Doolin Crafts Gallery
Doolin, Co Clare.
Road map B4.
Tel 065 707 4309.
W doolincrafts.com

Geoffrey Healy Pottery
Rocky Valley, Kilmacanaogue, Co Wicklow. **Road map** D4.
Tel 01 282 9270.
W healy-pottery.com

Kilkenny Design Centre
Castle Yard, Kilkenny, Co Kilkenny. **Road map** C4.
Tel 056 772 2118.
W kilkennydesign.com

Roundstone Music
Roundstone, Connemara.
Road map B4. **Tel** 095 35808. **W** bodhran.com

West Cork Crafts
61 Townsend St, Skibbereen, Co Cork.
Road map B6.
Tel 028 22555.
W westcorkcrafts.ie

The Wicker Man
44–46 High St, Belfast, Co Antrim. **Road map** D2.
Tel 028 9024 3550.

Crystal and Glassware

Connemara Marble Factory
Moycullen, Co Galway.
Road map B4.
Tel 091 555102.

Galway Irish Crystal
Merlin Park, Galway, Co Galway. **Road map** B4.
Tel 091 757311.
W galwaycrystal.ie

Jerpoint Glass
Stoneyford, Co Kilkenny.
Road map D5.
Tel 056 772 4350.
W jerpointglass.com

Sligo Crystal
Hyde Bridge, Sligo, Co Sligo. **Road map** C2.
Tel 071 914 3440.

Tipperary Crystal
Barrynoran, Carrick-on-Suir, Co Tipperary.
Road map C5.
Tel 051 640543.

Ceramics and China

Louis Mulcahy's Pottery
Clother, Ballyferriter, Dingle, Co Kerry.
Road map A5.
Tel 066 915 6229.
W louismulcahy.com

Michael Kennedy Ceramics
Bolands Lane, Gort, Co Galway. **Road map** B4.
Tel 091 632245.

Nicholas Mosse Pottery
Bennettsbridge, Co Kilkenny.
Road map D5.
Tel 056 772 7505.
W nicholasmosse.com

Royal Tara China
Tara Hall, Mervue, Galway, Co Galway. **Road map** B4.
Tel 091 705602.
W royal-tara.com

Treasure Chest
31–33 William St, Galway, Co Galway. **Road map** B4.
Tel 091 567237.

Linen

Forgotten Cotton
Savoy Centre, St Patrick's St, Cork, Co Cork.
Road map C5.
Tel 021 427 6098.

Irish Linen & Gift Centre
65 Royal Ave, Belfast, Co Antrim. **Road map** D2.
Tel 028 9031 4272.

Knitwear and Tweed

Avoca Handweavers
Kilmacanogue, Co Wicklow.
Road map D4.
Tel 01 274 6900.

Blarney Woollen Mills
Blarney, Co Cork.
Road map B5.
Tel 021 438 5280.

Magee of Donegal
The Diamond, Donegal, Co Donegal. **Road map** C2. **Tel** 074 972 2660.

Quills Woollen Market
High St, Killarney, Co Kerry. **Road map** B5.
Tel 064 663 2277.

Studio Donegal
The Glebe Mill, Kilcar, Co Donegal. **Road map** B2.
Tel 074 973 8194.

Jewellery

Cahalan Jewellers
Main St, Ballinasloe, Co Galway. **Road map** B2.
Tel 09096 42513.

Hilser Bros
Grand Parade, Cork, Co Cork. **Road map** C5.
Tel 021 427 0382.

James Murtagh Jewellers
14 Bridge St, Westport, Co Mayo. **Road map** B3.
Tel 098 25322.

O'Shea's Jewellers
24 Main St, Killarney, Co Kerry. **Road map** B5.
Tel 064 663 2720.

Fashion

Brown Thomas
88–95 Grafton St, Dublin 2. **Road map** D3.
Tel 01 605 6666.
W brownthomas.com

Clockwork Orange
Victoria Square, Belfast, Co Antrim. **Road map** D2.
Tel 028 9032 0298.

Kilkenny
6–15 Nassau St, Dublin 2.
Road map D3.
Tel 01 677 7066.
W kilkennyshop.com

O'Donnell's
11 Catherine St, Limerick, Co Limerick.
Road map B4.
Tel 061 415932.

What to Buy in Ireland

Hundreds of gift and craft shops scattered throughout Ireland make it easy to find Irish specialities to suit all budgets. The best buys include linen, tweeds and crystal from factory shops which invariably offer an extensive choice of good-quality products. Local crafts make unique souvenirs, from handmade jewellery and ceramics to traditional musical instruments. Religious artifacts are also widely available. Irish food and drink are evocative reminders of your trip.

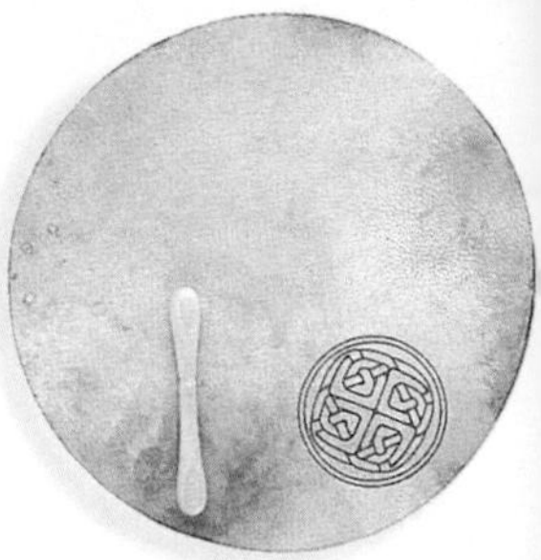

Traditional hand-held drum *(bodhrán)* and beater

Connemara marble "worry stone"

Traditional Claddagh ring

Modern jewellery and metalwork draw on a long and varied tradition. Craftspeople continue to base their designs on sources such as the *Book of Kells* *(see p68)* and Celtic myths. Local plants and wildlife are also an inspiration. County Galway produces Claddagh rings – traditional betrothal rings – in gold and silver as well as "worry stones".

Fuchsia earring from Dingle

Enamel brooch

Celtic-design enamel brooch

Bronzed resin Celtic figurine

Donegal tweed jacket and waistcoat

Tweed skirt and jacket

Clothing made in Ireland is usually of excellent quality. Tweed-making still flourishes in Donegal where tweed can be bought ready-made as clothing and hats or as lengths of cloth. Knitwear is widely available all over the country in large factory outlets and local craft shops. The many hand-knitted items on sale, including Aran sweaters, are not cheap but should give years of wear.

Tweed cap

Tweed fisherman's hat

Aran sweater

Irish linen is world-famous and the range unparalleled. There is a huge choice of table and bed linen, including extravagant bedspreads and crisp, formal tablecloths. On a smaller scale, tiny, intricately embroidered handkerchiefs make lovely gifts as do linen table napkins. Tea towels printed with colourful designs are widely available. You can also buy linen goods trimmed with fine lace, which is still handmade in Ireland, mainly in Limerick and Kenmare.

Set of linen placemats and napkins

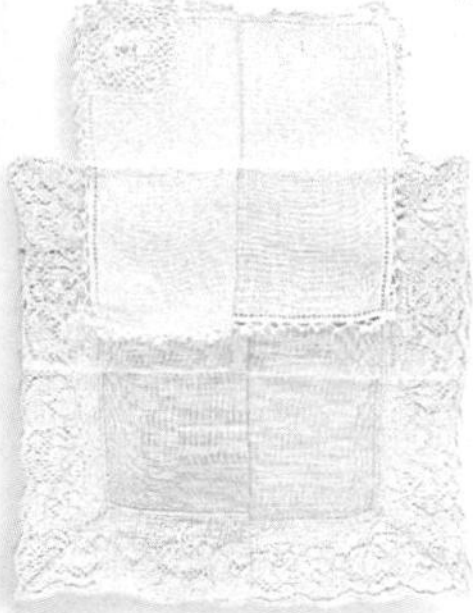

Fine linen handkerchiefs

Irish ceramics come in traditional and modern designs. You can buy anything from a full dinner service by established factories, such as Royal Tara China or the Belleek Pottery, to a one-off contemporary piece from a local potter's studio.

Book of Irish Proverbs

Books and stationery are often beautifully illustrated. Museums and bookshops stock a wide range.

Celtic-design cards

Irish crystal, hand-blown and hand-cut, can be ordered or bought in many shops in Ireland. Visit the outlets of the principal manufacturers, such as Waterford Crystal and Jerpoint Glass, to see the full range – from glasses and decanters to elaborate chandeliers.

Waterford crystal tumbler and decanter

Food and drink will keep the distinctive tastes of Ireland fresh long after you arrive home. Whiskey connoisseurs should visit the Old Bushmills Distillery *(see p270)* or the Jameson Heritage Centre *(see p183)* to sample their choice of whiskeys. Good regional food can be found at local shops all over Ireland. Try the dried seaweed, which is eaten raw or added to cooked dishes.

Jameson whiskey

Bushmills whiskey

Fruit cake made with Guinness

Jar of Irish marmalade

Packet of dried seaweed

ENTERTAINMENT IN IRELAND

If there is one sphere in which Ireland shines, it is entertainment. For details about entertainment in Dublin, see pages 112–19. Elsewhere in Ireland, nightclubs and concerts by international entertainers tend to be concentrated in large cities, but many other events including theatre, arts festivals, traditional music and dance, cultural holidays and even medieval banquets take place all over the country. Most towns and cities also have one or two cinemas showing the latest movies on release. Not to be overlooked is the free entertainment (planned or spontaneous) provided by a night in a pub. For more active forms of entertainment, covered on pages 342–7, the list is even longer, from golf to pony trekking and cycling to scuba diving. Those who prefer their sports sitting down can go along as spectators to Ireland's famous horse race meetings, as well as Gaelic football, hurling, soccer and rugby matches. A happy mix of these activities can easily be put together with almost any itinerary.

Ulster Symphony Orchestra at the Ulster Hall in Belfast

Information Sources

The tourist board for the Republic, **Fáilte Ireland**, and the **Northern Ireland Tourist Board** *(see p351)* both publish a yearly *Calendar of Events* that lists major fixtures around the country, and all the regional tourist offices have information about happenings in each locality. To supplement these listings, check regional newspapers and enquire locally.

Booking Tickets

Tickets can usually be bought at the door on the day or evening of most events. Advance booking is a must, however, for popular concerts and plays. Many cultural and arts festivals require tickets only for the key performances, but for internationally famous festivals, such as the Wexford Opera Festival, you will need to book well in advance through the festival office for all performances. Credit-card bookings for plays, concerts and other events around Ireland can be made by telephone through **Keith Prowse Travel (IRL) Ltd** and **Ticketmaster** in Dublin.

Major Venues

In many Irish cities, the main theatres host a huge variety of events. In Cork, the **Opera House** presents predominantly Irish plays during the summer, with musical comedy, opera and ballet at other times of year. The city's **Everyman Palace Theatre** stages plays by local and visiting companies interspersed with concerts of both classical and popular music. Sligo's **Hawks Well Theatre**, Limerick's **Belltable Arts Centre** and Carlow's **George Bernard Shaw Theatre** are venues for drama and concerts. In Belfast, the **Grand Opera House, Waterfront Hall** and **Lyric Theatre** present Irish and international plays, experimental drama, pantomime and opera.

Theatre

From international tours to amateur productions, there is excellent theatre to be seen in virtually every location in Ireland. In Galway, the **Druid Theatre** specializes in avant-garde plays, new Irish plays and Anglo-Irish classics, with frequent lunchtime and late-night performances, while Gaelic drama, Irish music, singing and dancing have all thrived at the **Taibhdhearc Theatre** since 1928. Waterford boasts its resident Red Kettle Theatre Company which performs at the **Garter Lane Theatre**, while the **Theatre Royal** brings amateur drama and musicals to the city. In Limerick, the **Lime Tree Theatre** on the grounds of Mary Immaculate College hosts a diverse programme of drama, comedy and dance.

Keep an eye out for small theatre groups performing

Home of the Druid Theatre Company in Galway *(see p214)*

The Moscow Ballet at Belfast's Grand Opera House *(see p280)*

in local halls around the country. Many of them are superb and they have spawned several of Ireland's leading actors.

Classical Music, Opera and Dance

Major venues for classical music include the **Crawford Art Gallery**, Opera House and Everyman Palace in Cork; the Theatre Royal in Waterford and the Hawks Well Theatre in Sligo. Belfast's **Ulster Hall** hosts concerts from rock bands to the Ulster Symphony Orchestra.

Opera lovers from around the world come to Ireland for the **Wexford Festival of Opera** in October and November, where rare or forgotten operatic works are revived. Elsewhere, opera is performed in Cork's Opera House and in Belfast's Grand Opera House.

Ireland has no resident ballet or avant-garde dance companies, but leading international companies perform occasionally at the major venues around the country.

Rock, Jazz and Country

When international music stars tour Ireland, concerts outside Dublin are held at large outdoor sites. RDS and 3Arena in Dublin, **Semple Stadium** in County Tipperary and Slane Castle *(see p249)* in County Meath are popular venues. Tickets and information are available from Ticketmaster.

Musical pubs *(see pp326–31)* are your best bet for good rock and jazz performed by Irish groups. Check local tourist offices and newspapers for rock and jazz nights, which usually take place midweek, with country and traditional music at weekends. For some of Ireland's "big band" jazz music, keep an eye out for Waterford's Brass and Co who play at dances around the country. Jazz lovers have a field day at the **Cork Jazz Festival** in late October, when international jazz greats play in the city's theatres.

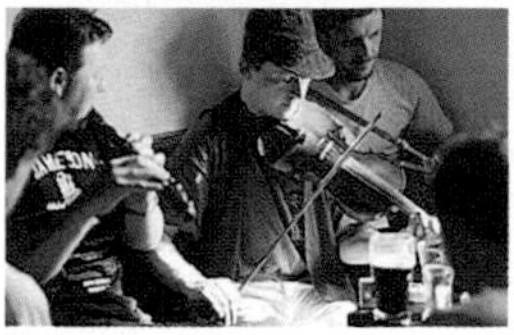

Pub scene, with musicians playing at the Feakle Festival, County Clare

Traditional Music and Dance

The country pub has helped keep Irish music alive and provided the setting for the musical revival that began in the 1960s. Today, sessions of informal or impromptu music are still commonplace. In pubs, traditional music embraces ballads and rebel songs, as well as the older *sean-nós* – unaccompanied, understated stories, often sung in Irish.

Nights of Irish music and song are scheduled in many pubs, such as The Laurels and the Danny Mann in Killarney, the Yeats Tavern in Drumcliff, near Sligo, and An Brog in Cork. In Derry, the Gweedore Bar, Castle Bar and Dungloe Bar are among the cluster of musical pubs along Waterloo Street. Wherever you are, a query to the locals will send you off to the nearest musical pub. For more pub listings, *see pp 326–31*.

In Tralee, **Siamsa Tíre**, the National Folk Theatre, stages marvellous folk drama incorporating traditional music, singing and dance. The Barn, in Bunratty Folk Park, is the setting for a traditional Irish night during the summer months.

Comhaltas Ceoltóirí Éireann, in Monkstown *(see p341)* has branches around the country and organizes traditional music and dance nights all year. Traditional Irish dancing can be stylish step dancing or joyous set dancing. Visitors are usually encouraged to join in the fun.

The Fleadh Cheoil (national traditional music festival) is a weekend of music, dance, song and stage shows that spill over into colourful street entertainment. It takes place at the end of August in a different town each year and attracts large crowds. Earlier in August, the **Feakle Festival** in County Clare is a more intimate celebration of traditional music, song and dance.

The Opera House adjoining the Crawford Art Gallery in Cork

Acrobats perform at the annual Galway Arts Festival

Festivals

The Irish are experts at organizing festivals, staging a week of street entertainment, theatre, music and dance to celebrate almost everything under the sun *(see pp52–5)*.

In mid-July the lively town of Galway is host to the **Galway Arts Festival**, one of the largest festivals in Ireland. Here you will find Irish and international theatre and music, street entertainment and events for children. Taking place over one week in late July and early August is the **Boyle Arts Festival**. The events here include art exhibitions, poetry and drama performances as well as classical, traditional, folk and jazz concerts. Creative workshops are run for both adults and children.

Kilkenny Arts Festival in August, another major festival, features poetry, classical music concerts, movies and a range of crafts. The **Cork Film Festival** takes place either in October or November when international feature, documentary and short films are screened at venues all over the city. The **Belfast Festival at Queen's** is held for two weeks in October to late November. The lively and cosmopolitan programme includes a mixture of drama, ballet, comedy, cabaret, music and film. These take over the Queen's University campus plus theatres and other venues throughout Belfast.

In May, June and July the **County Wicklow Gardens Festival** entices gardening enthusiasts to wander around the county's most beautiful gardens. In mid-June, the **Music in Great Irish Houses** festival opens the doors to many of Ireland's historic homes to which the public seldom has access, with classical music performed by top-rate musicians. Venues include Killruddery House *(see p137)* and Christ Church Cathedral *(see pp84–5)*.

Kilkenny Arts Week street theatre

Traditional Banquets with Entertainment

Ireland's banquets have gained international fame and are great fun. Each of the banquets features costumed waiters and performers, as well as traditional food and drink of the chosen period. Most famous are the medieval banquets – the one at Bunratty Castle *(see pp196–7)* was the first and is the liveliest, with year-round performances. From April to October, there is a medieval banquet at Knappogue Castle *(see p193)*, and at Dunguaire Castle *(see p218)* there is a quieter, more intimate programme of music and poetry. From March until November, the highly enjoyable Killarney Manor Banquet, held at the stately manor on the Loreto road just south of Killarney, creates an early 19th-century atmosphere.

Cultural Breaks

A break in Ireland focused on any one of the cultural aspects of Irish life is enriching as well as fun. Choose from a variety of cultural topics and study courses: Irish music and literature, great houses and gardens, Irish language and folklore, crafts and cookery.

One of the most fascinating possibilities is the exploration of Ireland's 5,000-year history as revealed in the many relics strewn across the landscape. The **Achill Archaeological Field School** in County Mayo, for example, runs a course that includes the active excavation of ancient sites.

To learn the secret of Irish cooking, there is no better place than the **Ballymaloe School of Cookery** in County Cork; it is run by Darina Allen, Ireland's most famous cook.

For literature enthusiasts, the **Yeats International Summer School** studies the works of Yeats and his contemporaries, while **Listowel Writers' Week** brings together leading writers for lectures and workshops.

Folk dancers in traditional Irish costume

DIRECTORY

Booking Tickets

Keith Prowse Travel (IRL) Ltd
9 Marlborough Court, Marlborough St, Dublin 1.
Tel 01 878 3500.
W keithprowse.ie

Ticketmaster
Ticketron, St Stephen's Green S/C, Dublin 2.
Tel 01 648 6060.
W ticketmaster.ie

Major Venues

Belfast Waterfront
2 Lanyon Place, Belfast.
Tel 028 9033 4400.
W waterfront.co.uk

Cork Opera House
Emmet Place, Cork.
Tel 021 427 0022.
W corkoperahouse.ie

Everyman Palace Theatre
15 MacCurtain St, Cork.
Tel 021 450 1673.
W everymancork.com

George Bernard Shaw Theatre
Old Dublin Rd, Carlow, Co Carlow. **Tel** 059 917 2400.
W visualcarlow.ie

Grand Opera House
Great Victoria St, Belfast.
Tel 028 9024 1919.
W goh.co.uk

Hawks Well Theatre
Temple St, Sligo.
Tel 071 916 1518.
W hawkswell.com

Lime Tree Theatre
69 O'Connell St, Limerick.
Tel 061 774774.
W imetreetheatre.ie

Lyric Theatre
55 Ridgeway St, Belfast.
Tel 028 9038 1081.
W lyrictheatre.co.uk

Theatre

Druid Theatre
Druid Lane, Galway.
Tel 091 568660.
W druid.ie

Garter Lane Theatre
O'Connell St, Waterford.
Tel 051 855038.
W garterlane.ie

Taibhdhearc Theatre
Middle St, Galway.
Tel 091 563600.
W antaibhdhearc.com

Theatre Royal
The Mall, Waterford.
Tel 051 874402.
W theatreroyal.ie

Classical Music, Opera and Dance

Crawford Art Gallery
Emmet Place, Cork.
Tel 021 480 5042.
W crawfordartgallery.ie

Town Hall Theatre
Courthouse Square, Galway.
Tel 091 569755.
W tht.ie

Ulster Hall
Bedford St, Belfast.
Tel 028 9033 4455.
W ulsterhall.co.uk

Wexford Festival Opera
Theatre Royal, High St, Wexford.
Tel 053 912 2144.
W wexfordopera.com

Rock, Jazz and Country

Cork Jazz Festival
20 South Mall, Cork.
Tel 021 427 0463.
W guinnessjazz festival.com

Semple Stadium
Thurles, Co Tipperary.
Tel 0504 22702.

Traditional Music and Dance

Comhaltas Ceoltóirí Éireann
32 Belgrave Sq, Monkstown, Co Dublin.
Tel 01 280 0295.
W comhaltas.com

Feakle Festival
Feakle, Co Clare.
Tel 061 924 3885.
W feaklefestival.ie

Siamsa Tíre
Siamsa Tire Theatre, The Town Park, Tralee, Co Kerry.
Tel 066 712 3055.
W siamsatire.com

The Traditional Irish Night
Bunratty Castle and Folk Park, Bunratty, Co Clare.
Tel 061 360788.
W shannon heritage.com

Festivals

Belfast Festival at Queen's
Festival House, 25 College Gardens, Belfast.
Tel 028 9097 1197.
W belfastfestival.com

Boyle Arts Festival
King House, Main St, Boyle, Co Roscommon.
Tel 071 966 3085.
W boylearts.com

Cork Film Festival
Emmet House, Emmet Place, Cork.
Tel 021 427 1711.
W corkfilmfest.org

County Wicklow Gardens Festival
St Manntan's House, Kilmantin Hill, Wicklow.
Tel 0404 20070.

Galway Arts Festival
Black Box Theatre, Dyke Rd, Terryland, Galway.
Tel 091 509700.
W giaf.ie

Great Music in Irish Houses
65 Sandymount Road, Sandymount.
Tel 01 660 4492.
W greatmusicinirish houses.com

Kilkenny Arts Festival
11 St Patrick's Court, Patrick St, Kilkenny.
Tel 056 7763 663.
W kilkennyarts.ie

Cultural Breaks

Archaeology

Achill Archaeological Summer School
Folk Life Centre, Dooagh, Achill Island, Co. Mayo.
Tel 098 43564.
W achill-field school.com

Cookery

Ballymaloe School of Cookery
Shanagarry, Co Cork.
Tel 021 464 6785.
W cookingisfun.ie

Great Houses and Gardens

Houses, Castles & Gardens of Ireland
Tel 087 777 6428.
W hcgi.ie

National Trust
Rowallane House, Saintfield, Ballynahinch, Co Down.
Tel 028 9751 0721.
W nationaltrust.org.uk

Irish Language

Conversation Classes Oidhreacht Chorca
Dhuibhne, Ballyferriter, Co Kerry.
Tel 066 915 6100.
W oidhreacht.ie

Irish Music

Willie Clancy Summer School
Miltown Malbay, Co Clare. **Tel** 065 708 4281.

Literary

Goldsmith International Literary Festival
Terlicken, Ballymahon, Co Longford.
Tel (087) 923 6983.
W goldsmithfestival.ie

James Joyce Summer School
University College Dublin, Belfield, Dublin 4.
Tel 01 716 8159.
W joycesummer school.ie

Listowel Writers' Week
24 The Square, Listowel, Co Kerry. **Tel** 068 21074.
W writersweek.ie

William Carleton Summer School
Dungannon District Council, Circular Rd, Dungannon, Co Tyrone.
Tel 028 8772 0300.

Yeats International Summer School
Yeats Society, Yeats Memorial Building, Hyde Bridge, Sligo.
Tel 071 914 2693.
W yeatssociety.com

Sports and Outdoor Activities

Even in the largest Irish cities, the countryside is never far away, and it beckons alluringly to every lover of the great outdoors. Spectator sports in Ireland are focused on horse racing, followed by hurling, Gaelic football and soccer, which make for very exciting viewing. Those who want to do more than just watch, can choose between fishing, golf, horse riding, sailing, cycling, walking and water sports all of which can be enjoyed throughout the country or via designated routes along the coastline on the Wild Atlantic Way. In addition to the contacts on pages 346–7, Fáilte Ireland in the Republic, the Northern Ireland Tourist Board and all local tourist offices have information on spectator and participant sports. For details of main events in the sporting calendar, see pages 32–3.

Steeplechase at Fairyhouse Racecourse

Wild Atlantic Way

The world's longest defined coastal touring route, the **Wild Atlantic Way** stretches from the Inishowen Peninsula in County Donegal to Kinsale in County Cork. The driving route passes through nine counties along the coast and is considered the ultimate way to explore one of the most dramatic coastlines in the world. Road signs are marked with the Wild Atlantic Way symbol to guide visitors driving around the region and ideas for pre-planned itineraries, attractions and sights along the route are comprehensively detailed on the Wild Atlantic Way website or can be obtained from tourist information centres.

Spectator Sports

The Irish passion for horse racing is legendary. **The Curragh** *(see p135)*, where the Irish Derby is held, is a leading racecourse. **Fairyhouse**, the venue for Ireland's Grand National, is a popular spot year-round, but especially around Christmas when punters descend to lay bets on the annual races. **Punchestown**, in County Kildare, has been a fixture of the racing scene since 1824 and has a capacity of 80,000 people. **Leopardstown** in Dublin has year-round racing.

Galway Race Week in late July is a great social event. A racing calendar for the whole of Ireland, available from **Horse Racing Ireland**, lists National Hunt and flat race meets, which occur on 230 days of the year.

There are also 19 greyhound stadia operating in the Republic. The best known are Dublin's **Shelbourne Park** and **Harold's Cross Stadium**, both of which have excellent dining facilities. **Croke Park** hosts Gaelic football and hurling matches. International rugby and soccer matches are usually held at the **Aviva Stadium**, Ireland's most impressive sports stadium. For soccer tickets, contact the **Football Association of Ireland**. Rugby enthusiasts should get in touch with the **Irish Rugby Football Union**.

For golfers, the annual highlight is the Irish Open Golf Championship in July. The venue varies from year to year. For tickets, contact the **European Tour**.

Fishing

With some of the cleanest stretches of freshwater found in all of Europe, Ireland is a paradise for anglers. Coarse, game and sea fishing are all very popular. The lakes and rivers are home to bream, pike, perch and roach. Coastal rivers yield the famous Irish salmon, along with other game fish. Sea trout and brown trout also offer anglers a challenge. Flounder, whiting, mullet, bass and coalfish will tempt the sea angler, while deep-sea excursions chase abundant supplies of dogfish, shark, skate and ling. The Cork and Kerry coastline is a highly favoured starting point for sea-angling trips.

Clonanav Fly Fishing Centre near Clonmel, County Waterford,

Fishing in the canal at Robertstown, County Kildare *(see p134)*

Walking in the Gap of Dunloe, Killarney *(see p167)*

is popular with both novice and experienced anglers as it has superb accommodation, as well as reliable, experienced staff. Regarded as the best fishing river in the east, River Slaney has many fisheries along its banks. **Ballintemple Fishery** offers angling equipment for hire, and instruction if needed. **Rory's Fishing Tackle** in central Dublin is also a good place to buy tackle and live bait.

Information on the required permits can be obtained from the **Central Fisheries Board** in the Republic, and from **Inland Fisheries**, Department of Culture, Arts and Leisure, Northern Ireland. Contact the **Irish Federation of Sea Anglers** for useful tips, or in order to book sea-fishing trips or courses.

Maps and other information on fishing locations can be obtained from Fáilte Ireland in the Republic, and from the Northern Ireland Tourist Board *(see pp350–51)*. Also, consult the **Irish Angling Update** website, which posts regularly updated reports on angling conditions.

Walking and Mountaineering

The network of waymarked trails all over the country cut through some of the most glorious Irish landscape. Information on long-distance walks is available from Fáilte Ireland and the Northern Ireland Tourist Board. The loveliest routes include Wicklow Way *(see p143)*, Dingle Way, Kerry Way, Munster Way and Barrow Towpath. Each of these may be split into shorter sections for less experienced walkers or those short of time. The 800-km (500-mile) Ulster Way encircles Northern Ireland, taking in the spectacular scenery around Giant's Causeway *(see pp266–7)* and the peaks of the mountains of Mourne *(see pp288–9)*.

Sign for the Ulster Way, the trail around Northern Ireland

Irish Ways offers walking holidays in the Republic. To find out about organized walks in Northern Ireland, contact the **Ulster Federation of Rambling Clubs**. **An Óige Hill Walkers Club** organizes a hike each Sunday on the Wicklow and Dublin mountains for experienced walkers. Once a month, the club's programme includes an introductory hard hike which allows novices to try out more rigorous hiking.

The award-winning **Michael Gibbons' Walking Ireland Centre** specializes in half-day walks and full-day tours in summer that guide walkers through the landscape and heritage of Connemara.

Skibbereen Historical Walks enables visitors to learn about Ireland's past via Skibbereen, a small town largely associated with the Great Famine.

Contact the **Mountaineering Council of Ireland** for more details about mountaineering and rock-climbing holidays. For any hike, remember to go well-equipped for the highly changeable Irish weather.

Cycling

Several organizations such as **Celtic Trails** offer planned cycling itineraries as well as accommodation. **Cycling Ireland** is the governing body of cycling in Ireland, and its website provides information on cycling routes and amenities. The Off-Road Commission organizes events and provides information on the country's off-road trails and terrain routes.

You can transport your bike fairly cheaply by train or bus. For bike rental, try **Neill's Wheels** or **Cycleways**, both in central Dublin, or **Phoenix Park Bike Hire** to explore Europe's largest urban park.

Cycling through the Muckross House estate near Killarney *(see p163)*

Golfers at Portstewart in Northern Ireland *(see p264)*

Golf

There are more than 300 golf courses spread throughout Ireland, and over 50 are championship class. Many of the most beautiful greens verge on spectacular stretches of coast, and are kept in top condition.

In County Kilkenny, the internationally acclaimed golf course **Mount Juliet** was designed by golfing legend Jack Nicklaus. County Kildare's **K Club** is home to two superb 18-hole championship golf courses. Arnold Palmer designed both, but each has its own characteristics and special set of challenges. Champion golfer Christy O'Connor Junior designed **Galway Bay Golf Club**. This difficult course, a must for all keen golfers, is dotted with historic ruins dating back to the 16th century.

Acknowledged as one of the truly great links courses, **Portmarnock Golf Club** is situated to the north of Dublin, about 19 km (12 miles) from the city centre. Its quality and location have made it a splendid venue for some of the game's most celebrated events. On the Atlantic coast, **Lahinch Golf Club** in County Clare is a must for devoted golfers, and is a recognized Mackenzie course.

Northern Ireland's best-known courses are **Royal Portrush Golf Club** and **Royal County Down Golf Club**. The **Golfing Union of Ireland**, the **Irish Ladies Golfing Union** and the tourist boards have information on courses, conditions and green fees all over the country. Equipment can be hired at most clubs.

Horse Riding and Pony Trekking

The Irish are rightly proud of their fine horses. Many riding centres, both residential and non-residential, offer trail riding and trekking along woodland trails, deserted beaches, country lanes and mountain routes. Dingle, Donegal, Connemara and Killarney are all renowned areas for trail riding – post-to-post and based. Post-to-post trails follow a series of routes with accommodation in a different place each night. Based trail rides follow different routes in one area, but riders return to stay at the same location each night.

Horse riding in Killarney

Aille Cross Equestrian Centre in Connemara offers horseback trail riding for both experienced and novice riders. Riders spend four to six hours a day on Connemara ponies or hunting horses. Further south, **Killarney Riding Stables** is located just 2 km (1 mile) from the heart of Killarney town. Adventurous riders can start the four- or six-day Killarney Reeks Trail here.

The **Mountpleasant Trekking and Riding Centre** can be found within 2,000 acres of forestry and rolling countryside around Castlewellan in County Down. The centre caters for both novice and experienced riders.

Five Counties Holidays provides vacations that include horse riding in different areas of the northwest of Ireland. Also, many riding centres, such as **Equestrian Holidays Ireland** based in Co Cork, offer guidance and lessons to beginners as well as to more advanced riders and lessons in show jumping.

Water Sports

With a coastline of over 4,800 km (3,000 miles), Ireland is the perfect venue for water sports. Surfing, windsurfing, scuba diving and canoeing are the most popular activities.

Conditions in Sligo are the best in Ireland for surfing, but many other coastal locations offer good conditions. The **Irish Surfing Association**, the national governing body for surfing and related activities such as knee-boarding and body-surfing, has plenty of information about surfing in all 32 Irish counties. Windsurfing centres in Ireland are

Surfing at Bundoran, Donegal Bay *(see p234)*

mainly found near Dublin, Cork and Westport.

Diving conditions are variable but visibility is particularly good on the west coast. The **Irish Underwater Council** will put you in touch with courses and facilities. **DV Diving** organizes scuba-diving courses and offers accommodation near Belfast Lough and the Irish Sea where there are a number of historic wrecks to be explored.

Inland, Lower Lough Erne *(see pp274–5)* and Killaloe by Lough Derg *(see p194)* are popular holiday centres. The **Lakeland Canoe Centre** between Upper and Lower Lough Erne gives canoeing courses and also organizes canoeing holidays (with overnight camping), including one down the charming Shannon-Erne Waterway *(see p239)*. From March, **Atlantic Sea Kayaking** organizes one-day outings, as well as two- to eight-day trips around Castlehaven, Baltimore and beyond.

There are several areas all around the coast that are safe for experienced swimmers. Ask locally for details. In Dublin, the popular 40 Foot in Sandycove is a favourite haunt of dedicated sea swimmers. Children are quite safe in the sandy waters inside the harbour while adults can enjoy the deeper waters on the seaward side of the harbour wall. Contact the **Dublin Tourist Office** for more details.

Cruising and Sailing

A tranquil cruising holiday is an ideal alternative to the stress and strain of driving, and Ireland's 14,000 km (900 miles) of rivers and some 800 lakes offer a huge variety of conditions for those who want a tranquil waterborne holiday. Stopping over at waterside towns and villages puts you in touch with the Irish on their home ground. Whether you opt for Lough Derg or elsewhere on the Shannon, or the Grand Canal from Dublin to the Shannon, a unique view of the Irish countryside opens up all along the way.

Yachting off Rosslare, County Wexford *(see p155)*

Running between Carrick-on-Shannon in Country Leitrim and Upper Lough Erne in Fermanagh, is the **Shannon-Erne Waterway** *(see p239)*, a disused canal reopened in 1993. From here it is simple to continue through Upper and Lower Lough Erne *(see pp274–5)* to Belleek. **Emerald Star** has a fleet of cruisers for use on the waterway.

Shannon Castle Line runs a modern and high-quality fleet of cruisers on the Shannon. **Silver Line Cruisers**, which also operates on the Shannon, is barely 2 kms (1 mile) from the grand canal, and promises relaxed, uncrowded cruises.

The coast between Cork and the Dingle Peninsula is a popular sailing area. The **International Sailing Centre** near Cork offers tuition. The **Irish National Sailing School** in County Dublin provides lessons at all levels.

More experienced sailors can charter a yacht and sail up the dramatic Irish shore to the western coast of Scotland.

Hunting and Shooting

Ireland's hunting season runs from October to March, and although fox-hunting tends to predominate, stag and hare hunts also take place. Contact **The Irish Master of Foxhounds Association** in the Republic, and the **Countryside Alliance** in Northern Ireland.

Duck shooting is also available. The shooting season is from September to the end of January. Clay-pigeon (year-round) and pheasant shooting (November to January) are also popular. **Mount Juliet Estate** offers guns for hire and supplies cartridges. **Colebrook Park** in County Fermanagh offers deer-stalking outings and lodging. Northern Ireland's **National Countrysports Fair**, usually held in May, is a major attraction for game enthusiasts.

The **National Association of Regional Game Councils** provides details of permits required for hunting.

Sports for the Disabled

Sports enthusiasts with a disability can obtain details of facilities for the disabled from the **Irish Wheelchair Association**. Central and local tourist boards and many of the organizations listed in the directory also advise on available facilities. The **Share Village** provides a range of activity holidays for both disabled and able-bodied people.

Boats moored at Carnlough Harbour on the Antrim coast *(see p271)*

DIRECTORY

Wild Atlantic Way

W wildatlanticway.com

Spectator Sports

Aviva Stadium
Lansdowne Rd, Dublin 4.
Tel 01 238 2300.
W **avivastadium.ie**

Croke Park
Jone's Rd, Dublin 3.
Tel 01 819 2300.
W **crokepark.ie**

Curragh Racecourse
The Curragh, Co Kildare.
Road map D4.
Tel 045 441205.
W **curragh.ie**

European Tour
W **europeantour.com**

Fairyhouse
Rataoth, Co Meath.
Road map D3.
Tel 01 825 6167.
W **fairyhouse.ie**

Football Association of Ireland
National Sports Campus, Abbotstown, Dublin 15.
Dublin map F4.
Tel 01 899 9500.
W **fai.ie**

Harold's Cross Stadium
Harold's Cross Rd, Dublin 6.
Tel 01 497 1081.
W **igb.ie**

Horse Racing Ireland
Ballymany, The Curragh, Co Kildare.
Road map D4.
Tel 045 455455.
W **goracing.ie**

Irish Rugby Football Union
10–12 Lansdowne Road, Dublin 4. **Tel** 01 647 3800.
W **irishrugby.ie**

Leopardstown Racecourse
Leopardstown, Dublin 18.
Tel 01 289 0500.
W **leopardstown.com**

Punchestown Racecourse
Naas, Co Kildare.
Road map D4.
Tel 045 897704.
W **punchestown.com**

Shelbourne Park
South Lotts Rd, Dublin 4.
Tel 01 668 3502.
W **igb.ie**

Fishing

Ballintemple Fishery
Ardattin, Co Carlow.
Road map D4.
Tel 059 915 5037.
W **ballintemple.com**

Central Fisheries Board
Swords. **Tel** 01 884 2600.
W **cfb.ie**

Clonanav Fly Fishing Centre
Ballymacarbry, Co Waterford. **Road map** C5.
Tel 613 6765.
W **flyfishingireland.com**

Inland Fisheries Ireland
Causeway Exchange, 1–7 Bedford St, Belfast.
Road map D2.
Tel 028 9151 3101.
W **dcalni.gov.uk**

Irish Angling Update
Tel 01 884 2600.
W **cfb.ie**

Irish Federation of Sea Anglers
Brian Reidy, Ballydavid, Athenry, Co Galway.
Tel 01 085 733 9040.
W **ifsa.ie**

Rory's Fishing Tackle
17a Temple Bar, Dublin 2.
Road map D3.
Tel 01 677 2351.
W **rorys.ie**

Walking and Mountaineering

An Óige Hill Walkers Club
Dublin map C1.
Tel 086 356 3843.
W **hillwalkers club.com**

Michael Gibbons' Walking Ireland Centre
Market Street, Clifden, Co Galway.
Road map A3.
Tel 095 21379.
W **walkingireland.com**

Mountaineering Council of Ireland
Irish Sport HQ, National Sports Campus, Blanchardstown, Dublin 15.
Tel 01 625 1115.
W **mountaineering.ie**

Skibbereen Historical Walks
Skibbereen Heritage Ctr, Skibbereen, Co Cork.
Road map B6.
Tel 028 40900.
W **skibbheritage.com**

Ulster Federation of Rambling Clubs
23 Innisfayle Park, Bangor, Co Down
Road map D2.
Tel 0780 151 5232.
W **ufrc-online.co.uk**

Cycling

Ardclinis Activity Centre
High St, Cushendall, Co Antrim.
Road map D1.
Tel 028 2177 1340.
W **ardclinis.com**

Celtic Trails
1 Gordon Villas, Portobello Harbour, Dublin 8. **Road map** D4.
Tel 086 265 6258.
W **celtictrails.com**

Cycleways
185–6 Parnell St, Dublin 1.
Dublin map C3.
Tel 01 873 4748.
W **cycleways.com**

Cycling Ireland
619 North Circular Rd, Dublin 1.
Tel 01 855 1522.
W **cyclingireland.ie**

Neill's Wheels
Cow's Lane, Temple Bar, Dublin 2. **Road map** C3.
Tel 087 933 8312.
W **rentabikedublin.com**

Phoenix Park Bike Hire
Phoenix Park, Dublin.
Road map D4.
Tel 086 265 6258.
W **phoenixparkbike hire.com**

Golf

Galway Bay Golf Club
Renville, Oranmore, Co Galway.
Road map B4.
Tel 091 790711.
W **galwaybaygolf resort.com**

Golfing Union of Ireland
Carton Demesne, Maynooth, Co Kildare.
Road map D3.
Tel 01 505 4000.
W **gui.ie**

Irish Ladies Golfing Union
Q House, 76 Furze House, Sandyford Industrial Estate, Dublin 18.
Tel 01 293 4833.
W **ilgu.ie**

The K Club
Straffan, Co Kildare.
Road map D4.
Tel 01 601 7200.
W **kclub.com**

Lahinch Golf Club
Lahinch, Co Clare.
Road map B4.
Tel 065 708 1003.
W **lahinchgolf.com**

Mount Juliet
Thomastown, Co Kilkenny.
Road map D5.
Tel 056 777 3000.
W **mountjuliet.ie**

Portmarnock Golf Club
Portmarnock, Co Dublin.
Road map D3.
Tel 01 846 2968.
W **portmarnock golfclub.ie**

Professional Golf Association
Dundalk Golf Club, Blackrock, Dundalk, Co Louth.
Road map D3.
Tel 042 932 1193.
W **pga.info**

Royal County Down Golf Club
36 Golf Links Rd, Newcastle, Co Down.
Road map E2.
Tel 028 4372 3314.
W **royalcounty down.org**

DIRECTORY

Royal Portrush Golf Club
Dunluce Rd, Portrush, Co Antrim.
Road map D1.
Tel 028 7082 2311.
W royalportrushgolfclub.com

Horse Riding and Pony Trekking

Aille Cross Equestrian Centre
Loughrea, Co Galway.
Road map B4.
Tel 091 843968.
W connemara-trails.com

Association of Irish Riding Establishments
Millennium Park, Naas, Co Kildare.
Road map D4.
Tel 045 854518.
W aire.ie

British Horse Society
120 Main St, Greyabbey, Newtownards, Co Down
Road map D2.
Tel 028 4278 8681.
W bhsireland.com

Equestrian Holidays Ireland
Road map C6.
W ehi.ie

Five Counties Holidays
Ardmourne House, 36 Corgary Rd, Castlederg, Co Tyrone. **Road map** C2.
Tel 028 8167 0291.
W five-counties-holidays.com

Killarney Riding Stables
Ballydowney, Killarney, Co Kerry.
Road map B5.
Tel 064 663 1686.
W killarney-riding-stables.com

Mountpleasant Trekking and Horse Riding Centre
Bannonstown Rd, Castlewellan, Co Down.
Road map D2.
Tel 028 4377 8651.
W mountpleasantcentre.com

Water Sports

Atlantic Sea Kayaking
Reen Pier, West Cork
Road map B6.
Tel 028 21058.
W atlanticseakayaking.com

Baltimore Diving
Baltimore, Co Cork.
Road map B6.
Tel 028 20300.
W baltimorediving.com

Dublin Tourist Office
W visitdublin.com

DV Diving
138 Mount Stewart Rd, Newtownards, Co Down.
Road map E2.
Tel 028 9186 1686.
W dvdiving.co.uk

Irish Surfing Association
Easkey Surf and Information Centre, Easkey, Co Sligo.
Road map B2.
Tel 096 49428.
W isasurf.ie

Irish Underwater Council
78a Patrick St, Dun Laoghaire, Co Dublin.
Road map D4.
Tel 01 284 4601.
W diving.ie

Fermanagh Lakelands
Wellington Road, Enniskillen.
Road map C2.
Tel (028) 6632 3110.
W fermanaghlakelands.com

Cruising and Sailing

Athlone Cruisers
Jolly Marina, Coosan, Athlone, Co Westmeath.
Road map C3.
Tel 090 647 2892.
W iwai.ie

Carrick Craft
Unit 1, Fairgreen Rd, Markethill, Co Armagh
Tel 01 278 1666.
W cruise-ireland.com

Charter Ireland
Radharc an Chlair, Grattan Rd, Salthill, Co Galway
Road map B4.
Tel 089 442 3699.
W charterireland.ie

Emerald Star
The Marina, Carrick-on-Shannon, Co Leitrim.
Road map C3.
Tel 071 962 7633.
W leboat.ie

International Sailing Centre
East Beach, Cobh, Co Cork.
Road map C6.
Tel 021 481 1237.
W sailcork.com

Irish National Sailing School
Dun Laoghaire, Co Dublin.
Tel 01 284 4195.
W inss.ie

Lough Melvin Holiday Centre
Garrison, Co Fermanagh.
Road map C2.
Tel 028 6865 8142.
W melvinholidaycentre.com

Shannon Castle Line
Williamstown Harbour, Whitegate, Co Clare.
Road map C4.
Tel 061 927042.
W shannon-river.com

Silver Line Cruisers
The Marina, Banagher, Co Offaly.
Road map C4.
Tel 05791 51112.
W silverlinecruisers. com

Hunting and Shooting

Colebrooke Park
Brookeborough, Co Fermanagh.
Road map C2.
Tel 028 8953 1402.
W colebrooke.info

Countryside Alliance
Larchfield Estate, Bailliesmills Road, Lisburn, Co Antrim.
Road map D2.
Tel 028 9263 9911.
W caireland.org

The Irish Master of Foxhounds Association
W imfha.com

Mount Juliet Estate
Thomastown, Co Kilkenny.
Road map D5.
Tel 056 777 3000.
W mountjuliet.ie

National Association of Regional Game Councils
Brosna Way, Ferbane Business Park, Ballycumber Rd, Ferbane, Co Offaly.
Tel 090 645 3623.
W nargc.ie

National Countrysports Fair
Balmoral Park, Maze, Lisburn, Co Antrim.
Road map D4.
Tel 077 3067 8701.
W countrysidefestivals.com

Sports for the Disabled

Irish Wheelchair Association
Blackheath Dr, Clontarf, Dublin 3.
Tel 01 818 6400.
W iwa.ie

Share Village
Smith's Strand, Lisnaskea, Co Fermanagh.
Road map C2.
Tel 028 6772 2122.
W sharevillage.org

SURVIVAL GUIDE

PRACTICAL INFORMATION

Although Ireland is quite a small island, visitors should not expect to see everything in a short space of time, since many of the country's most magnificent attractions are in rural areas. In remote parts of the island the roads are narrow and winding, the pace of life is very slow and public transport tends to be infrequent. However, although the Republic of Ireland remains one of Europe's most unspoiled destinations, it has a very well-developed economy. Any decent-sized town in the Republic is likely to have a tourist information centre which offers a full range of facilities to help the visitor, including maps and leaflets to take away, as well as staff on hand to offer advice. Northern Ireland has its own tourist board which also has offices in most towns. The level of hospitality is first-rate across the whole of the country.

The Irish Whiskey Collection at Terminal 2, Dublin Airport

Visas and Passports

Visitors from the EU, US, Canada, Australia and New Zealand require a valid passport but not a visa for entry into the Republic or Northern Ireland. All others, including those wanting to study or work, should check with their local Irish or British embassy first. UK nationals born in Britain or Northern Ireland do not need a passport to enter the Republic of Ireland but should take one with them for car rental, medical services, cashing of traveller's cheques or if travelling by air.

Travel Safety Advice

Visitors can get up-to-date travel safety information from the **State Department** in the US, the **Foreign and Commonwealth Office** in the UK, and the **Department of Foreign Affairs and Trade** in Australia.

Customs Information

When you arrive at any of Ireland's airports you will find three queues for immigration. Since Ireland is a member of the European Union, any citizen from other EU countries can pass directly through the blue channel – but random checks are still carried out to detect any prohibited goods. Travellers entering from countries outside of the EU, as well as those coming from the Channel Islands and Canary Islands, are required to pass through customs. Go through the green channel if you have nothing to declare and use the red channel if you have goods to declare or are uncertain of the allowances.

Tourist Information

Both the Republic and Northern Ireland have an impressive network of tourist information offices. In addition to providing lots of free local information, the tourist offices in large towns sell maps and guide books and can reserve accommodation for a nominal charge. There are also tourist information points in some of the smaller towns

Language

The Republic of Ireland is officially bilingual – almost all road signs have place names in both English and Irish. English is the spoken language everywhere apart from a few parts of the far west, called Gaeltachts *(see p233)*, but from time to time you may find signs written only in Irish. Here are some of the words you are most likely to come across from the ancient language.

Sign using old form of Gaelic

Useful Words

an banc – **bank**
an lár – **town centre**
an trá – **beach**
ar aghaidh – **go**
bád – **boat**
bealach amach – **exit**
bealach isteach – **entrance**
bus – **bus**
dúnta – **closed**
fáilte – **welcome**
fir – **men**
gardaí – **police**
leithreas – **toilet**
mná – **women**
oifig an phoist – **post office**
oscailte – **open**
óstán – **hotel**
siopa – **shop**
ticéad – **ticket**
traein – **train**

◄ Scenic coastal road in County Kerry

The Heritage Service-run Parke's Castle in County Leitrim *(see p237)*

and villages. Opening hours can be somewhat erratic and many are open only during the summer season. Local museums and libraries can be another useful source for a selection of tourist literature.

Before leaving for Ireland you can get brochures and advice from **Tourism Ireland.** Their Discover Ireland offices can be found in major cities all over the world. **Fáilte Ireland** (the Irish Tourist Board) and the **Northern Ireland Tourist Board** (NITB) can also supply you with maps and leaflets. For more local information on sights, accommodation and car rental, it's worth contacting the regional tourist offices in Dublin, Cork, Galway and Limerick.

If you pick up a list of places to stay in a tourist office, it's worth noting that not every local hotel and guesthouse will be included – these lists recommend only those establishments that have been approved by the Tourist Board.

The Irish **Heritage Service** maintains national parks, museums, monuments and gardens. The Heritage Card, allows unlimited, free admission to all sites managed by the service for a year. At €21 for adults, €16 for senior citizens, €8 for children and students, and €55 for a family ticket, the card is good value. Popular Heritage Service sites include Céide Fields *(see p208)*, Cahir Castle *(see p202)* and the Blasket Centre *(see p162)*.

Entrance fees in Northern Ireland are about the same, also with discounts offered to students and senior citizens. North of the border the **National Trust** has a membership scheme, but is more expensive (£48.50 per year per person or £84.50 for a family ticket). The card can be used at sights like Mount Stewart House *(see p286–7)* and Carrickfergus Castle *(see p279)*. The card only represents good value for money if you are also planning to visit National Trust sites elsewhere in Great Britain.

Heritage Card giving access to historic sites

Admission Charges

Most of Ireland's major sights, including ancient monuments, museums and national parks, have an admission fee. For each place of interest in this guide, we specify whether or not there is a charge. The entrance fees in the Republic of Ireland are normally between €3 and €8, with some offering discounts for students and seniors.

Opening times

Opening hours are usually between 10am and 5pm. Some sights close for lunch. Few places are open on Sunday morning and some museums shut on Mondays.

From June to September all the sights are open but crowds peak. July is the marching season in the North *(see p53)* but tensions have eased in peacetime Belfast and Derry; many shops and restaurants still choose to close at this time. Some attractions close for winter, while others keep shorter hours. Many places open for public holidays, such as Easter, and then close again until summer.

DIRECTORY

Tourism Ireland Offices Abroad

United Kingdom
For the whole of Ireland: Tourism Ireland UK, Nations House, 103 Wigmore St, London W1U 1QS.
Tel 0800 039 7000.
W **tourismireland.com**
W **discoverireland.com**

United States
345 Park Avenue, New York, NY 10154. **Tel** 1 800 223 6470.
W **tourismireland.com**

Tourist Board Offices in Ireland

Fáilte Ireland
Baggot St Bridge, Dublin 2.
Tel 01 602 4000.
W **failteireland.ie**

Northern Ireland Tourist Board
59 North St, Belfast BT1 1NB.
Tel 028 9023 1221.
Belfast Welcome Centre:
47 Donegall Place.
Tel 028 9024 6609.
W **discovernorthern ireland.com**

Other Contacts

National Trust
Tel 028 9751 0721.
W **nationaltrust.org.uk**

The Heritage Service
Tel 01 647 6000.
W **heritageireland.ie**

Travel Safety Advice

Australia
Department of Foreign Affairs and Trade
W **dfat.gov.au**
W **smartraveller.gov.au**

UK
Foreign and Commonwealth Office W **gov.uk/foreign-travel-advice**

US
US Department of State
W **travel.state.gov**

Interpretative centre at Connemara National Park *(see p212)*

Interpretative Centres

Many of Ireland's major sights are ruins or Stone Age archaeological sites, which can be difficult to fully appreciate. However, interpretative or visitors' centres, which explain the historical significance of sites, are widely available. Entry to the site may be free, but you have to pay to visit the interpretative centre.

In areas of natural beauty, such as Connemara National Park *(see p212)*, an interpretative centre acts as a useful focal point. The centre provides information leaflets and has reconstructions of sites. There are 3-D models and displays, as well as an interesting audiovisual presentation on the development of the local landscape over the last 10,000 years. There is also a shop selling postcards, books and posters.

Religious Services

Ireland has always been a deeply religious country and churchgoing is still an important way of life for many. The Republic of Ireland is 87 per cent Roman Catholic, which means that finding a non-Catholic church may sometimes be difficult. In the Republic and Northern Ireland, the tourist offices, hotels and B&Bs all have a list of local church service times available.

Student Travellers

Students with a valid ISIC card (International Student Identity Card) benefit from reduced admission to museums, concerts and other forms of entertainment. It also procures over 15 per cent reduction on the Bus Éireann network. ISIC cards can be obtained from branches of **USIT** travel in Dublin, Belfast and other college towns. To find out where your nearest issuing office is, visit www.isic.org. USIT will also supply under-30s with an EYC (European Youth Card) for discounts on airfares, and in restaurants, museums, shops and theatres. The card is recognized in over 20 European states.

International Student Identity Card

An ISIC card no longer obtains rail travel reductions in Ireland. In the Republic, Irish Rail produces its own Student Travelcard for a good discount on Irish Rail (also known as Iarnród Éireann), DART, Dublin Bus and Luas fares. Cards cost €12 and are issued by post or in person at one of the listed card centres at www.studenttravelcard.ie. Bring along the completed online form and a signed letter from your university. Similarly in the North, discounts on NI Railways, Ulsterbus and Metro (the Belfast bus service) are available with the Translink Student Discount Card. See www.translink.co.uk for further details.

Facilities for the Disabled

Most sights in Ireland have access for wheelchairs. This book gives basic information about disabled access for each sight, but it's worth phoning to check details. The **Citizens Information Board** provides information for the Republic, publishing county guides to accommodation, restaurants and amenities. In the North, **Disability Action** can advise on accessibility, while **ADAPT** provides information and a book on disabled access to over 400 venues in the cultural sector. Both tourist boards also have guides to accommodation and amenities.

Travelling with Children

Ireland has a large young population, and children are made welcome in hotels and restaurants. However, note that in the Republic those under the age of 18 can visit a pub only if accompanied by a parent or guardian, and then only until 9pm. There are often great deals or discounts available to families. Many sights offer a discount admission to children and under-5s usually get in free. School holidays are obviously peak times for travelling with children, and there are many activities available to cater for families. Some hotels offer a special family deal, which includes horse riding and fishing, among other things.

Familes relaxing, Kinsale Harbour, County Cork

Black Abbey in Kilkenny has disabled access

Electricity

The standard electricity voltage in both parts of Ireland is 230 volts AC, 50 Hz. The standard plug is the three-pin IS 411 (BS 1363), as used throughout Great Britain. Adaptors are readily available in airport shops. Before using appliances from other countries, always make sure that they are compatible with the Irish system; it might be that you need to use a power converter or power transformer.

Irish Time

The whole of Ireland is in the Western European Time zone, the same as Great Britain, that is five hours ahead of New York and Toronto, one hour behind Germany and France, and ten hours behind Sydney. In both the North and the South, clocks go forward one hour for summertime.

Conversion Chart

Imperial to Metric

1 inch = 2.5 centimetres
1 foot = 30 centimetres
1 mile = 1.6 kilometres
1 ounce = 28 grams
1 pound = 454 grams
1 pint = 0.6 litres
1 gallon = 4.6 litres

Metric to Imperial

1 millimetre = 0.04 inches
1 centimetre = 0.4 inches
1 metre = 3 feet 3 inches
1 kilometre = 0.6 miles
1 gram = 0.04 ounces
1 kilogram = 2.2 pounds
1 litre = 1.8 pints

Green Ireland

Ireland has long been known as the Emerald Isle, but this has more to do with the small population and a lack of industrialization than any official environmental initiatives. However, the Green Party joined a coalition government in the Republic in 2007, and building standards have been tightened; motor tax favours cars with lower emissions; second homes are now taxed, and a carbon tax was introduced in 2010, followed by water charges in 2014.

The land of Ireland is still predominantly in agricultural use. Organic food produce is becoming popular and farmers' markets are held regularly in most large towns. There are vast areas of unspoiled coastline, lakes, mountains and forests. Pollution from agriculture and sewage can be a problem, but the situation is improving and the water quality in coastal bathing areas is good.

Ecotourism is on the increase and organizations such as **The Organic Centre** and the **Centre for Environmental Living and Training (CELT)** run courses on such topics as beekeeping, sustainable house design, and organic gardening. Agritourism is also more widespread with working farms offering guestrooms throughout the country; these can be booked through **Irish Farmhouse Holidays**.

For more information on green issues, the Sustainable Ireland website (www.sustainable.ie) is an indispensible resource.

DIRECTORY

Embassies

Australia
Fitzwilton House,
Wilton Terrace, Dublin 2.
Tel 01 664 5300.
W ireland.embassy.gov.au

Canada
7–8 Wilton Terrace, Dublin 2.
Tel 01 234 4000.
W **canada.ie**

UK
29 Merrion Rd, Dublin 4.
Tel 01 205 8777.
W **britishembassy.gov**

US
42 Elgin Rd, Ballsbridge, Dublin 4.
Tel 01 668 7122.
W **dublin.usembassy.gov**

Useful Contacts

ADAPT
109–113 Royal Avenue, Belfast.
Tel 028 9023 1211.
W **adaptni.org**

Centre for Environmental Living and Training (CELT)
East Clare Community Co-op,
Main Street, Scariff,
Co Clare.
Tel 061 640765.
W **celtnet.org**

Citizens Information Board
43 Townsend St, Dublin 2.
Tel 01 605 9000.
W **citizensinformation.ie**

Disability Action
189 Airport Rd West, Belfast.
Tel 028 9029 7880.
W **disabilityaction.org**

Irish Farmhouse Holidays
Tel 071 982 2222.
W **irishfarmholidays.com**

The Organic Centre
Tel 071 985 4338.
W **theorganiccentre.ie**

USIT
19/21 Aston Quay, Dublin 2.
Tel 01 602 1906.
Fountain Centre, College St,
Belfast BT1 6ET.
Tel 028 9032 7111.
W **usit.ie**

Personal Security and Health

Ireland is probably one of the safest places to travel in Europe. Petty theft, such as pickpocketing, is seldom a problem outside certain parts of Dublin and a few other large towns. Tourist offices and hoteliers gladly point out the areas to be avoided. In Northern Ireland security measures have been relaxed in the light of the peace accord. In the Republic, however, crimes against the individual are on the increase, but rates still tend to be lower than in other parts of the UK and Europe.

Pearse Street Garda Station, Dublin

Police

The police, should you ever need them, are called the Garda Síochána (Gardaí, for short) in the Republic of Ireland and the Police Service of Northern Ireland (PSNI) in the North. The PSNI is the only territorial police force in the UK that is routinely armed.

Both police forces are working together to tackle the issue of organized cross-border crime.

Garda PSNI policeman

Personal Safety in the Republic

Violent street crime is relatively rare but it is still advisable to take suitable precautions, such as avoiding poorly lit streets in the cities and larger towns. Poverty and a degree of drug addiction in central Dublin have been known to cause a few problems, and Limerick isn't the most inviting of places after dark. But if you take sensible precautions, avoiding back-streets at night and keeping to the popular and busy areas, there should be little cause for concern.

In some of the larger towns you may be approached in the street by people asking for money. This rarely develops into a troublesome situation, but it is best to politely refuse and walk away.

Personal Safety in Northern Ireland

Even at the height of the Troubles in Northern Ireland, there was never a significant threat to the tourist, and travelling around the Province was deemed to be as safe as in the Republic. As long as peace prevails, no extra precautions need to be taken here but first-time visitors should be prepared for certain unfamiliar situations, no better or worse than in the South. When driving, if you see a sign that indicates you are approaching a checkpoint, slow down and use dipped headlights. To keep fuss down to a minimum in these situations, it is a good idea to keep a passport or some other form of identification close at hand. If you are walking around the city centres of Belfast and Londonderry, you may notice a strong police or military presence. This is unlikely to inconvenience you.

During July, visitors may find themselves in slow-moving traffic behind an Orange march *(see p53)*. Tensions between local communities can be higher at this time, but the affected areas are easily avoided.

Personal Property

As pickpocketing and bag-snatching can be a problem in the larger towns, it's best not to carry around your passport or large amounts of cash. Most hotels have a safe; or consider using traveller's cheques *(see p356)*. When out and about, use a bag that can be held securely, and be alert in crowded places and restaurants. A money belt may be a good investment. If travelling by car, ensure that all valuables are locked in the boot and always lock the car, even when leaving it for just a few minutes. In Northern Ireland, do not leave any bags or packages unattended, as they may result in a security scare.

Garda station

PSNI badge

Lost Property and Baggage Rooms

Report all lost or stolen items at once to the police. In order to make a claim against your insurance company you need to send in a copy of the police report. Most train and bus stations in the Republic operate a lost-property service but there is no equivalent available in Northern Ireland.

If you wish to do a day's sightseeing unencumbered by baggage, most hotels and some main city tourist offices, both in the Republic and Northern Ireland, offer baggage storage facilities. Ensure all luggage is locked.

In an Emergency

In the Republic and Northern Ireland, the emergency phone number for Police, Ambulance or Fire Brigade is 999 or 112 from a mobile, which should only be used if really necessary. In a medical emergency which does not require an ambulance, you should visit a general practitioner (GP) or the out-patients, accident and emergency or casualty department of the nearest public hospital. In the Republic, if you are not referred to the hospital by a GP you may be asked to pay a fee of about €85.

If you find yourself in difficulties, with no money, or unwell and not speaking the language, call the nearest police station for practical advice. Tourist offices will also be able to help. Public hospitals are used to providing translation for patients of many nationalities. The Irish Tourist Assistance Service (ITAS) provides practical assistance to victims of crime, and can liaise with embassies, organize money transfers and cancel credit cards.

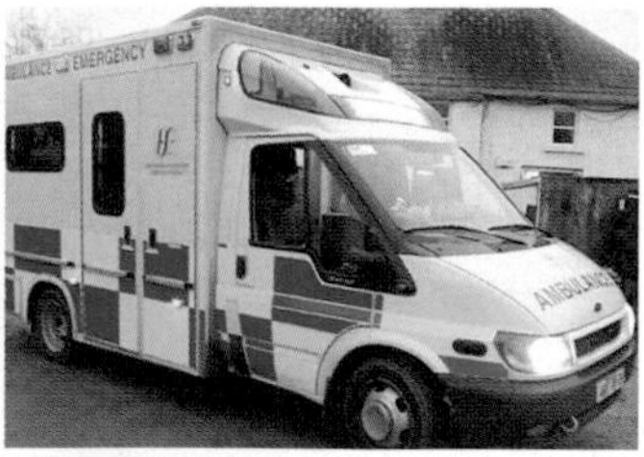

Dublin ambulance

Dublin fire engine

Garda patrol car

Hospitals and Pharmacies

Residents of countries in the European Union, the European Economic Area and Switzerland can claim free medical treatment in Ireland with a European Health Insurance Card (EHIC) *(see below)*. Cards can be applied for online, are free of charge and are valid for five years. Also, be sure to let the doctor know that you want treatment under the EU's social security regulations. In Northern Ireland, British citizens need no documentation.

Non-EU travellers should either have their own travel insurance or be prepared to pay up front for treatment.

A wide range of medical supplies is available over the counter at pharmacies. However, many medicines are available only with a prescription authorized by a local doctor. If you are likely to require specialized drugs during your stay, ensure you bring your own supplies and a copy of the original prescription. You can also ask your doctor to write a letter with the generic name of the medicine you require. Always obtain a receipt for insurance claims.

Small rural health centre in County Donegal

Travel and Health Insurance

Before travelling, make sure that your possessions are insured; it might be difficult and more expensive to get insurance in Ireland. It is also worth noting that travel insurance for the UK may not cover you in the Republic, so make sure you have an adequate policy.

Private health insurance policies may include a certain level of travel coverage. US visitors especially should check before leaving home whether they are covered by their insurance company for medical care abroad. They may have to pay first and reclaim costs later; if so, be sure to get an itemized bill.

DIRECTORY

Useful Addresses

Police, Fire, Ambulance and Coastguard Services
Tel Dial 999 or 112 in both the Republic and Northern Ireland.

Police Exchange
For non-emergency police assistance in Northern Ireland.
Tel 028 9065 0222.

Beaumont Hospital
Beaumont Road, Dublin 9.
Tel 01 809 3000.

City Hospital
Lisburn Road, Belfast BT9 7AB. (also emergency dental treatment).
Tel 028 9032 9241.

Dublin Dental Hospital
Lincoln Place, Dublin 2.
Tel 01 612 7200.

European Health Insurance Card
W ehic.org

Hickey's Pharmacy
55 Lr O'Connell St, Dublin 1.
Tel 01 873 0427.

Irish Tourist Assistance Service
6-7 Hanover St East, Dublin 2.
Tel 1 890 365 700.

Royal Victoria Hospital
Grosvenor Road, Belfast BT12 6BA. **Tel** 028 9024 0503.

Banking and Local Currency

The Republic and Northern Ireland have different currencies. The euro is the currency in the Republic and the pound sterling is the currency in Northern Ireland, the same as in Great Britain. When travelling between Northern Ireland and the Republic, there's no shortage of money-changers in towns near the border. Check online or in the daily newspapers for the standard rate of exchange to give yourself a guideline. Some tourist attractions offer money-changing facilities but for the best exchange rates use the banks or *bureaux de change*.

Banks and Bureaux de Change

Banks throughout Ireland generally provide a very good service, although opening times can vary significantly. Both north and south of the border, there are fewer bank branches in small towns than there once were, so it's advisable to do your banking in the bigger towns if possible.

In the Republic of Ireland, retail banks include the Bank of Ireland, the Allied Irish Bank (AIB), the Ulster Bank, and the Permanent tsb. The usual banking hours are Monday to Friday from 10am to 12:30pm and from 1:30 to 4pm, but most branches now stay open during lunchtime. There is extended opening (until 5pm) on one day of the week. In Dublin, Cork and most other cities and towns, late opening is on Thursdays. Branches of the Permanent tsb remain open at lunchtime and up to 5pm on weekdays. Some rural areas are visited once or twice a week by a mobile bank. Check locally for days and times.

In Northern Ireland there are three retail banks: the Ulster Bank, the Bank of Ireland, and the First Trust Bank, along with Danske Bank, which was formerly known as Northern Bank. Most are open from 10am till 4pm, though a few close for a lunch hour at 12:30pm.

In both the Republic and in Northern Ireland, all banks close on public holidays, some of which differ from North to South *(see p55)*. In addition to the foreign exchange counters at the main banks, there are some private *bureaux de change* in large towns and cities. As with most other exchange facilities, *bureaux de change* stay open later than banks. Check their rates first before undertaking any transactions.

Northern Bank

Danske Bank logo

ATMs

ATMs or cash dispensers, are common in most towns in Ireland, in and outside of banks on main streets, in large shops and at shopping centres. Using these machines is the fastest and most convenient way to manage your money while on holiday, and exchange rates are good. Cards in the Plus, Link, Cirrus and Maestro networks, and Visa and MasterCard credit cards, can be used in most ATMs.

Be careful to protect your PIN at all times and avoid using ATMs that appear to have been tampered with.

Credit Cards and Traveller's Cheques

Throughout Ireland you can pay by credit card in most hotels, petrol (gas) stations and large shops. Keep in mind that you will need your PIN. VISA and MasterCard are the most commonly accepted; fewer businesses take American Express and Diners Club cards. Traveller's cheques are the safest way to carry large amounts of money. These can be bought before setting out at American Express, Travelex, or your own bank. In Ireland, they can be purchased and exchanged at banks and *bureaux de change*.

Wiring Money

The cheapest way to get money from home is to have your own bank wire funds to a bank in Ireland. This process is very slow, often taking several days; it's much faster, though expensive, to get money sent through a company such as Western Union (tel: 1 800 395395).

DIRECTORY

Bureaux de Change

Joe Walsh Tours
69 Upper O'Connell St, Dublin 1.
Tel 01 872 2555.
W joewalshtours.ie

Thomas Cook
Belfast Park S.C.
Tel 084 4335 7068.
W thomascook.com

Travelex
Belfast International Airport.
Tel 028 9444 7500.
W travelex.com

Ornate post office and *bureau de change* in Ventry, County Kerry

Currency in Northern Ireland

Northern Ireland uses British currency – the pound sterling (£), which is divided into 100 pence (p). As there are no exchange controls in the UK, there is no limit to the amount of cash you can take into and out of Northern Ireland. In addition to the British currency, four provincial banks issue their own banknotes (bills), worth the same as their counterparts. To tell them apart, look for the words "Bank of England" on British notes. It is best to use the provincial banknotes in Northern Ireland rather than in Britain – some shops may be reluctant to accept notes that are unfamiliar to them.

Banknotes

British banknotes are issued in the denominations £50, £20, £10 and £5. Always carry small denominations as some shops may refuse the £50 note.

£50 note

£20 note

£10 note

£5 note

Coins

Coins come in the following denominations: £2, £1, 50p, 20p, 10p, 5p, 2p and 1p. All have the Queen's head on one side and are the same as those elsewhere in the UK, except that the pound coin has a different detail – a flax plant – on the reverse side.

£2 £1 50p 20p 10p

The Euro

The Republic of Ireland was one of 12 countries which adopted the euro in 2002. EU members using the euro as sole currency are known as the eurozone. Several EU members have opted out of joining this common currency.

Euro notes are identical throughout the eurozone, each featuring designs of fictional architectural structures and monuments. The coins have one side identical (the value side), and one side with an image unique to each country. Notes and coins are exchangeable in each of the participating euro countries.

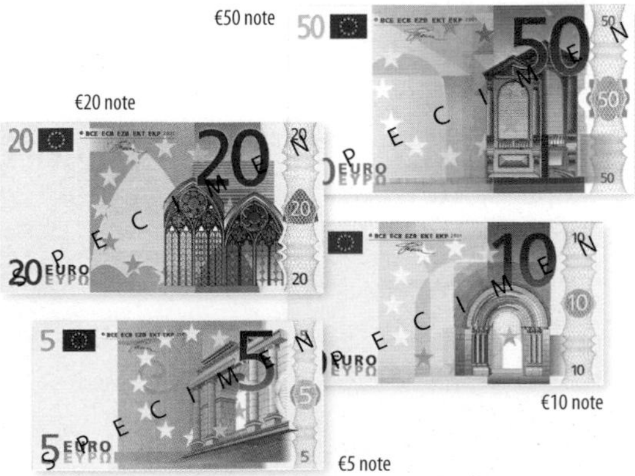

€50 note

€20 note

€10 note

€5 note

Banknotes

Euro banknotes, each a different colour and size, have seven denominations. The €5 note (grey in colour) is the smallest, followed by the €10 note (pink), €20 note (blue), €50 note (orange), €100 note (green), €200 note (yellow) and €500 note (purple).

€2 coin €1 coin 50 cents 20 cents 10 cents

Coins

The euro has eight coin denominations: €2 and €1 (gold and silver); 50 cents, 20 cents, 10 cents (gold); 5 cents, 2 cents and 1 cent (bronze).

Communications and Media

Both parts of Ireland are well served for national daily and Sunday newspapers, and there are many Irish magazines. The TV and radio are dominated by the state broadcasters RTE and BBC, but independent local radio thrives all over Ireland. The postal system is reliable and there are post offices in every small town. The Irish are big users of mobile phones, and as a result, public telephones are less used now. Prepaid phonecards, however, remain good value. Most large towns have an Internet café, and Wi-Fi points are becoming more common.

Public Telephones

The Republic's national telephone company, eircom, once ran all the telephone services in the country, but other companies now also provide public phones. Eircom's service includes coin, card and credit-card telephones that provide an efficient service. For those intending to spend more than €5 on calls during their stay, it is worth using a phonecard, as these offer discounts.

Northern Ireland uses British Telecom (BT) public phones, which accept either coins, cards or credit cards. Both BT and eircom phonecards are available from post offices, supermarkets and other retail outlets.

Phoning from the Republic of Ireland

Cheap call rates within the Republic and to the UK are from 6pm to 8am on weekdays and all day at weekends. Off-peak times for international calls vary depending on the country you call, but are generally as above.

- To call Northern Ireland: dial 048, followed by the 8-digit number.
- To call the UK: dial 00 44, the area code (minus the leading 0), then the number.
- To call other countries: dial 00, followed by the country code (for example, 1 for the USA, 61 for Australia), the area code (minus the leading 0), then the number.
- Credit cards issued in certain countries including the USA, Australia and Canada are accepted as payment for calls to the country in which the card was issued.

Phoning from Northern Ireland

Cheap call rates within and from the Province are the same as for the Republic.

- For calls within Great Britain and Northern Ireland: dial the area code and the number required.
- For calls to the Republic of Ireland: dial 00 353, then the area code minus the first 0, then the number.
- For international calls: dial 00, then the country code (for example, 1 for Canada, 64 for New Zealand), then the area code minus the first 0, then the number.

All phone numbers in Northern Ireland have an area code of 028, followed by an 8-digit local number.

Mobile Phones

Vodafone, 3 Mobile and Meteor are the main service providers. Before travelling, activate your phone for use abroad but also check on your provider's roaming charges for making and receiving calls. It may work out more economical to buy an Irish SIM card if your phone is not locked (or get your phone unlocked before you go away). Alternatively, you could consider buying a cheap pre-pay phone with its own SIM card. The Irish network uses the 900 or 1800 GSM system, so visitors from the US (where the system is 800 or 1900 MHz band) will need to acquire a tri- or quad-band set.

Radio and Television

Ireland has three state-controlled television channels, RTÉ One, RTÉ Two and Irish-language TG4, as well as two privately run channels, TV3 and 3e. Other channels, including five British terrestrial ones, are available. There are six national radio stations.

Irish Independent
OBAMA: 24-PAGE SPECIAL INSIDE
SCHOOLS RUGBY
I'm ready to lead
THE IRISH TIMES
HOME & AWAY
GETTING BY
NewsDigest
Taoiseach willing to push back deadline on cutbacks
Regulator investigates Quinn disposal of 10% stake in Anglo

Daily newspapers of the Republic

Newspapers and Magazines

The Republic of Ireland has eight national daily papers and seven Sunday papers. Quality dailies include the *Irish Independent*, the *Examiner* and *The Irish Times*, the latter being well known for its journalistic excellence. The North's top local paper is the *Belfast Telegraph*, which has morning, afternoon and late editions. The Province's morning papers, the *Belfast News Letter* and *Irish News*, are less rewarding. Ireland's daily tabloids are the *Star*, *Irish Sun*, *Irish Daily Mirror*, *Irish Daily Mail* and *The Herald*.

To find out what's on and where, the broadsheets are a useful source of information and most towns have a local or regional paper with listings.

In larger towns, British newspapers (including *The Times*) are on sale, as well as US publications *Newsweek*, *USA Today* and *Time* magazine.

Coffee and computers at the Central Cyber Café in Dublin

The Internet

The main cities in the Republic and Northern Ireland have plenty of access to the Internet. Almost all hotels and guesthouses offer Wi-Fi, usually for no extra charge. Public facilities are available free of charge from public libraries, but you may have to book in advance. Most cafés now have free Wi-Fi. As a public service, free Wi-Fi hotspots are provided throughout Dublin. Check out www.dublincity.ie for more information and details.

Northern Ireland Post Office sign

Republic of Ireland Post Office logo

Postal Services

Main post offices in the Republic and Northern Ireland are usually open from 9am to 5:30pm during the week and from 9am to around 1pm on Saturdays, although times do vary. Some smaller offices close for lunch on weekdays and do not open on Saturdays. Standard letter and postcard stamps can also be bought from some newsagents.

The Republic of Ireland does not have a first- and second-class system, but sending a postcard is a few cents cheaper than a letter. Though it is improving all the time, the postal service in the Republic is still quite slow – allow three to four days when sending a letter to Great Britain and at least six days for the United States.

In Northern Ireland, letters to other parts of the UK can be sent either first- or second-class, with most first-class letters reaching their UK destination the next day. The cost of a letter from Northern Ireland is the same to all EU countries.

Both postal services offer the faster option of couriers, which offer delivery from the next working day for the UK and Europe.

Postboxes

Postboxes in Ireland come in two colours – green in the Republic and red in the North. Many of Ireland's postboxes are quite historic. Some of those in the Republic even carry Queen Victoria's monogram on the front, a relic from the days of British rule. Most towns and villages have a postbox, from which the mail is collected regularly. All postal offices are shut on Saturdays.

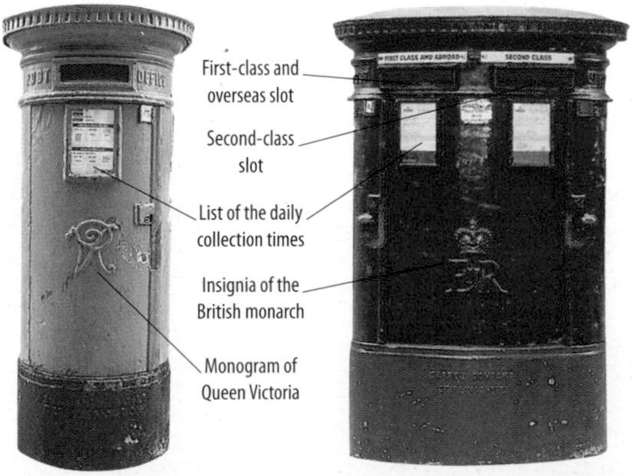

Postbox in the Republic

Northern Ireland double postbox

DIRECTORY

Useful Numbers Republic of Ireland

Emergency Calls
Tel 999.

Directory Enquiries
Tel 11811 (Republic and Northern Ireland). **Tel** 11818 (all other countries).

Operator Assistance
Tel 10 (Ireland and Great Britain).
Tel 114 (international calls).

Useful Numbers Northern Ireland

Emergency Calls
Tel 999.

Directory Enquiries
Tel 118118 (UK, Republic of Ireland and all other countries).
Tel 153 (all other countries).

Operator Assistance
Tel 100 (UK).
Tel 114 (all other countries).

Internet Cafés

Claude's Café
4 Shipquay St, Derry.
Tel 028 7127 9379.
W claudescafe.co.uk

Central Internet Café
6 Grafton Street, Dublin.
Tel 01 677 8298.
W centralinternetcafe.com

Browsers Internet Café
77 Dublin Road, Belfast.
Tel 028 9032 2272.

Post Offices

General Post Office (Dublin)
O'Connell Street, Dublin 1.
Tel 01 705 7600 (customer services).

Bridge Street Post Office (Belfast)
Bridge Street, Belfast.
Tel 08457 223 344.

TRAVEL INFORMATION

Ireland's three main airports, Dublin, Shannon and Belfast, are well served by flights from Britain, the United States and an increasing number of countries around the world. If you are travelling by sea from the UK, there is a very good choice of ferry routes from ports in Britain to both the Republic and Northern Ireland. Instead of buying separate tickets, you can purchase combined coach/ferry and rail/ferry tickets from almost all of the towns in mainland Britain. The slowly improving public transport systems in both the North and South reflect the rural nature of the island. With this in mind, travelling around Ireland is probably best enjoyed if you embrace the Irish way of thinking and just take your time.

Green Travel

There is a relatively well-established railway infrastructure covering some parts of Ireland, and train travel is a good option, particularly on the Dublin–Cork and Dublin–Belfast routes. The rail network may have received little funding in recent years, with greater investment in the national system of motorways, but there have been improvements in the rolling stock and the frequency of services. The bus network is also good, offering comfortable services to all parts of the country *(see pp370–71)*.

If you are interested in car sharing, note that the Northern Ireland Roads Service operates a scheme. Their website (www.carshareni.com) can provide you with further information.

In the cities, public transport is plentiful but hampered by the abundant use of private cars. There are discussions underway regarding the introduction of a congestion charge in Dublin and Belfast. Elsewhere, walkers are well catered for with waymarked trails. There is also good cycling on an extensive network of minor roads.

Flying to the Republic of Ireland

Flights from most of the major European cities arrive at **Dublin Airport**, which is Ireland's busiest airport. Regular services to the Republic depart from London's five airports (Heathrow, City, Gatwick, Luton and Stansted) and other cities in Britain, plus the Channel Islands and the Isle of Man.

The exterior of Dublin International Airport

The major airline operating scheduled flights between Britain and the Republic is **Aer Lingus**. However, **Ryanair** is a fierce rival, with cheap fares from several airports in Britain and all over Europe. **Aer Arann** offers flights within Ireland and to the UK.

Aer Lingus and **United Airlines** fly direct from the US to Dublin Airport and **Shannon Airport**, ten miles outside Limerick. **Delta Air Lines** fly direct to Shannon and then on to Dublin.

Cork Airport is served by flights from London (Heathrow and Stansted), Birmingham, Manchester, Bristol, Plymouth, Cardiff, Leeds, Glasgow, Paris, Amsterdam and Dublin. No airlines fly direct to Ireland from Australia or New Zealand, but there are plenty of connections via London and other capitals.

The Republic's other airports have fewer flights. There are many charter flights for pilgrims to **Ireland West Airport Knock** in Co Mayo, which also has flights from Dublin, London (Stansted) and Manchester. There are flights into Kerry from Dublin, Luton and Stansted airports, and Waterford Airport has flights from both Manchester and Luton. Galway is well served with five daily flights from Dublin.

Airport sign in English and Gaelic

Airport Connections in the Republic

The Republic's three main airports are all served by regular bus services. Dublin Airport is accessible by over 700 buses and coaches daily, including direct services between the airport, the city's main rail and bus stations and the city centre every 15 to 20 minutes, from early morning to around midnight. The trip takes 30 minutes to an hour. At Cork, the Bus Éireann service takes 25 minutes from the airport into the city. Buses run every 45 minutes on weekdays and hourly at the weekends. At Shannon Airport, Bus Éireann runs a regular service into Limerick which takes

30 to 45 minutes to the city centre. In addition, several buses a day go to the town of Ennis, about 20 km (12 miles) away. The Republic's smaller airports depend mainly on local taxi services.

All airports in the Republic have both long- and short-stay parking facilities.

Flying to Northern Ireland

Aer Lingus operates flights from Heathrow as well as regional UK airports to **Belfast International Airport**. There are also flights every two hours, operated by **British Midland**, from London Heathrow to **George Best Belfast City Airport**.

This airport is used by smaller aircraft, but is favoured by many because of its location just 6.5 km (4 miles) from the city centre. The airport also has more flights from the UK – around 15 cities plus London Gatwick, Stansted and Luton – than Belfast International. The City of Derry Airport is Northern Ireland's smallest and handles flights from Stansted, Manchester and Glasgow.

Airport Connections in Northern Ireland

The airports in Northern Ireland are generally well served with transport links. The Belfast International Airbus service will take you from the airport to the Europa Buscentre. This runs every half-hour and takes about 40 minutes from end to end. The Airport Express 300 runs from Belfast International to the city centre every 15 minutes. At Belfast City Airport the Airport Express 600 runs every 20 minutes throughout the day.

One of the Airlink buses which take passengers from Dublin Airport into the city centre

Check-in desks at Cork Airport

There are also trains from the airport to Central Station about every 30 minutes. Derry's airport is on local bus route number 143, which goes into the city centre once an hour (less frequently at weekends). All airports in Northern Ireland have taxi ranks and both long- and short-term parking facilities.

Tickets and Fares

Airline options between the United States and Ireland have increased in the last few years, with frequent flights now from both the East and West coasts. It's quite easy to get a round-trip flight to Shannon from the East Coast for under US$700. The best bargains are on flights with fixed dates. Airfares from the US are at their highest in the peak season which runs from July to September.

Many UK airports serve Ireland and airlines offer a host of options on fares. It's not difficult to get a round-trip flight from mainland UK to Dublin for well under £100. The cheapest place to fly from is usually London, especially Luton and Stansted airports. Prices are fairly constant all year except at Christmas, during summer and on public holidays, when there are few discounted fares.

Many airlines offer discounts to under-25s, while USIT *(see p352)*, Campus Travel and specialist travel agents often have cheaper rates for students and under-26s.

DIRECTORY

Major Airports

Belfast International
Tel 028 9448 4848.

Cork Airport
Tel 021 431 3131.

Dublin Airport
Tel 01 814 1111.

George Best Belfast City Airport
Tel 028 9093 9093.

Ireland West Airport Knock
Tel 094 936 8100.

Shannon Airport
Tel 061 712000.

Airlines

Aer Lingus
Tel 081 836 5000 (Ireland).
Tel 1 800 474 7424 (US).
Tel 0870 876 5000 (UK).
W **aerlingus.com**

Aer Arann
Tel 0818 210210 (Ireland).
Tel 020 474 7747 (Netherlands).
Tel 0870 876 7676 (UK).
W **aerarann.ie**

British Midland (bmi)
Tel 01 407 3036 (Ireland).
Tel 0870 607 0555 (UK).
W **flybmi.com**

Cityjet
Tel 01 870 0100 (Ireland).
W **cityjet.com**

Delta Air Lines
Tel 01 407 3165 (Ireland).
Tel 1 800 241 4141 (US).
Tel 0845 600 0950 (UK).
W **delta.com**

easyJet
Tel 0870 600 0000 (UK).
W **easyjet.com**

Qantas
Tel 01 407 3278 (Ireland).
Tel 13 13 13 (Aus). **Tel** 1 800 227 4500 (US). **W** **qantas.com.au**

Ryanair
Tel 01 812 1212 (Ireland).
W **ryanair.com**

United Airlines
Tel 1 800 864 8331 (US).
W **united.com**

Arriving by Sea

Travelling by ferry is a popular way of getting to Ireland, especially for groups or families intending to tour the country by car. Nine ports in Great Britain and two in France provide ferry crossings to Ireland's six ports. Nowadays, all ferries are of the modern drive-on/drive-off variety with lounges, restaurants and shops. There are also a greater number of crossings and shorter journey times available. Prices vary largely depending on the time of year.

Stena HSS on the Dun Laoghaire to Holyhead crossing

Ferries to Dublin and Dun Laoghaire

There is a good choice of ferry services running between Holyhead in Wales and Ireland. **Irish Ferries**, the country's largest shipping company, operates on the Holyhead–Dublin Port route and has up to five crossings a day. The high-speed service takes 1 hour 49 minutes, while the conventional ferry takes about 3¼ hours. **Stena Line** also operates four ferry crossings each day on the same route.

The service from Holyhead to the Dublin suburb of Dun Laoghaire is operated by Stena Line. This route is served by the Stena HSS (High-speed Sea Service) and takes 1 hour 49 minutes. As the largest ferry on the Irish Sea, the HSS has the same passenger and vehicle capacity as the conventional ferries but its jet-engine propulsion gives it twice the speed.

P&O Irish Sea offers an 8-hour crossing from Liverpool to Dublin. **Norfolkline** makes the same journey in approximately 7 hours, and offers one daytime and one night-time service daily. Note that on Sundays and Mondays there is only a night crossing available.

Vehicle loading and unloading times on the fast ferries are considerably shorter than with other ferries. Passengers requiring special assistance at ports or on board the ship should contact the company they are booked with at least 24 hours before the departure time. Passengers travelling with bicycles should mention this when booking – most ferry companies allow bicycles free of charge. Companies generally operate throughout the year with the exception of Christmas Day and Boxing Day.

Ferries to Rosslare

Rosslare, in County Wexford, is the main port for crossings

Irish Ferries ship loading up at Rosslare Harbour

Logo of Irish Ferries

from South Wales to Ireland. Stena Line runs a service from Fishguard in South Wales using both the conventional ferry and the speedier Sea Lynx catamaran-style ferries. Those intending to take a car on Sea Lynx should make sure the measurements of their vehicle, when fully loaded, are within those specified. The maximum dimensions allowable per vehicle are 3 m (10 ft) high by 6 m (20 ft) long and up to 3 tonnes.

Irish Ferries operates two daily crossings to Rosslare from Pembroke in South Wales (3 hrs 45 mins), with 14 crossings weekly, as well as a service from Roscoff in France (17 hrs 30 mins), with three crossings weekly. Irish Ferries and P&O also run regular services to Rosslare from Cherbourg (18 hours). Cabins and berths are available on all crossings to Rosslare and should be booked well in advance. **Celtic Link**, which is now owned by Stena Line, runs a budget service all year round from Rosslare to Cherbourg in France (18 hours), with three crossings per week. Amenities include bars, a cinema, inside and luxury suites.

Ferries to Cork

There is only one route per week direct to Cork from Roscoff in France operated by **Brittany Ferries**. The ferry leaves from Cork on a Saturday and from Roscoff on a Friday. The service is only available from April to October and the crossing time is 14 hours. Cabins and berths are available on routes to Cork but need to be booked well in advance in high season.

Dun Laoghaire terminal

Port Connections in the Republic

All Ireland's ports have adequate bus and train connections, as well as taxis waiting to meet arrivals.

At Dublin Port, Bus Éireann buses meet ferry arrivals and take passengers straight into the city centre.

From Dun Laoghaire, DART trains run into Dublin every 10 to 15 minutes calling at Pearse, Tara Street and Connolly Stations. These go from the railway station near the main passenger concourse. Buses also run to Eden Quay and Fleet Street in the city centre every 10 to 15 minutes.

For those requiring car hire, Hertz has a desk at Dun Laoghaire. However, anyone arriving at Dublin Port will have to rent from the city centre. There is an Avis office at Old Kilmainham and a Hertz office on South Circular Road, both in the city centre.

Train and Bus Through-Tickets

It is possible to travel from any train station in Great Britain to any specified destination in Ireland on a combined sea/rail ticket, available from train stations throughout Britain.

Eurolines, a subsidiary of Bus Eireann, runs a through-bus service from about 35 towns in Britain to over 100 destinations in the Republic. **Ulsterbus/Translink** offers the same service to destinations in Northern Ireland. Tickets for both these bus companies can be booked through **National Express**, which has over 2,000 agents in Great Britain. Travellers from North America, Australia, New Zealand and certain countries in Asia can buy a Brit Ireland pass. As well as including the return ferry crossing to Ireland, it allows unlimited rail travel throughout Great Britain and Ireland on any five or ten days during one month.

DIRECTORY

Ferry Companies

Brittany Ferries
Tel 021 427 7801 (Cork).
Tel 0870 907 6103 (UK).
W brittany-ferries.com

Celtic Link
Tel 053 916 2688.
W book.celticlinkferries.com

Irish Ferries
Tel 0818 300400 (ROI).
Tel 0870 517 1717 (UK).
W irishferries.com

Norfolkline Ferries
Tel 01 819 2999 (ROI).
Tel 0870 8701 020 (UK).
W norfolkline-ferries.co.uk

P&O Irish Sea
Tel 01 407 3434 (ROI).
Tel 0871 664 4999 (UK).
W poirishsea.com

Stena Line
Tel 01 204 7777 (Dublin).
Tel 0870 570 7070 (UK).
W stenaline.co.uk

Bus Companies

Eurolines
Tel 01 836 6111(Dublin).
Tel 0870 514 3219 (UK).
W buseireann.ie

National Express
Tel 08717 818 181 (UK).
W nationalexpress.com

Ulsterbus/Translink
Tel 028 9066 6630 (Belfast).
W translink.co.uk

Ferry Routes to the Republic of Ireland	Operator	Length of Journey
Roscoff–Rosslare	Irish Ferries	17hrs 30min (Oscar Wilde)
Fishguard–Rosslare	Stena Line Stena Line	3hrs 15min (Stena Europe) 1hr 50min (Fastcraft)
Holyhead–Dublin	Irish Ferries Stena Line	1hr 49min (Dublin Swift) 3hrs 15min (Stena Adventurer)
Holyhead–Dun Laoghaire	Stena Line	1hr 49min (Stena HSS)
Liverpool–Dublin	Norfolkline P&O Irish Sea	8hrs 8hrs (Norbay)
Cherbourg–Rosslare	P&O Irish Sea Irish Ferries	18hrs (Normandy) 18hrs (Normandy)
Pembroke–Rosslare	Irish Ferries	3hrs 45min (Isle of Inishmore)

The Stena Line ferry docked at Birkenhead

Ferries to Belfast and Larne

Stena Line offers two routes from Northern Ireland – Belfast to Cairnryan which runs up to six times daily, and Belfast to Liverpool with a choice of day or night sailings.

A Liverpool to Belfast service is run by Norfolkline, leaving Liverpool (Birkenhead) every evening and six mornings a week, and taking approximately 8 hours to reach Belfast. Note that on Mondays there is only a night crossing available. Crossing the Irish Sea with the Isle of Man Steam Packet Co lets you visit the Isle of Man en route. Leaving from Liverpool, this service provides the added advantage of allowing you to disembark at Dublin and return from Belfast or vice versa.

There are three routes from Britain to Larne (north of Belfast): from the Scottish ports of Cairnryan (1 hour 45 minutes) and Troon (1 hour 50 minutes); and from Fleetwood in Lancashire (8 hours). The services from Cairnryan and Troon are operated by P&O Irish Sea, who sail both conventional ferries and the high-speed Superstar Express on the Larne–Cairnryan route. This service runs from mid-March to early October and takes just under 2 hours. During the week there are up to seven sailings a day to Cairnryan. The services from Fleetwood to Larne, on the other hand, are run by Stena Line and run daily.

Port Connections in Northern Ireland

Belfast Port is located 1.5 km (1 mile) from the city centre, and can be easily reached by bus, taxi or on foot. Flexibus shuttles also operate to the city centre via the Europa Buscentre and Central Railway Station. From Larne Harbour, a regular bus service connects to the town's bus station, and from here, buses run every hour into Belfast city centre. There are also trains to take ferry passengers from Larne Port to Belfast's Yorkgate and Central train stations.

Fares and Concessions

Fares on ferry crossings to Ireland vary dramatically according to the season – prices on certain days during the peak period of mid-June to mid-September can be double those at other times of the year. Prices increase greatly during the Christmas and New Year period, too. It is advisable to book your journey both ways before setting out. Those travelling to ports without a reservation should always check availability before setting out. Check the ferries' websites for special offers and discounts.

Often, the cheapest way for families or groups of adults to travel is to buy a ticket that allows you to take a car plus a maximum number of passengers. At certain times of the year on particular routes, the return ticket for a car and two adults (two children count as one adult) can cost less than €120. The cheapest crossings are usually those where the passenger must depart and return within a specified period. Fares are normally reduced for mid-week travel and early-morning or late-night crossings. Ferry companies offer discounts for students with a student travel card *(see p352)* and some have cut-price deals for those with InterRail tickets *(see p369)*.

Ferry Routes to Northern Ireland	Operator	Length of Journey
Cairnryan–Larne	P&O Irish Sea P&O Irish Sea P&O Irish Sea	1hr 45min (European Causeway) 1hr (Superstar Express) 1hr 45min (European Highlander)
Fleetwood–Larne	Stena Line	8hrs (Stena Pioneer) 8hrs (Stena Leader)
Liverpool–Belfast	Norfolkline	9hrs
Stranraer–Belfast	Stena Line	1hr 45 (Stena HSS) 3hrs 15min (Stena Caledonia)
Troon–Larne	P&O Irish Sea	1hr 50 min (North Channel Fast Ferry)

On the Road

One of the best ways to see Ireland's magnificent scenery and ancient sites is by car. Driving on the narrow, twisting country roads can be a pleasure; often you don't see another vehicle for miles. It can also be frustrating, especially if you find yourself stuck behind a slow-moving tractor or a herd of cows. If you don't want to take your own vehicle, you'll find car rental in Ireland no problem. All the international car rental firms operate in the Republic and are also well represented in the North. Touring by bicycle is another enjoyable way of seeing the best parts of the island at your own leisurely pace.

Irish-language road sign instructing motorists to yield or give way

What You Need

If you intend to take your own car across on the ferry *(see pp362–4)* check your car insurance to find out how well you are covered. To prevent a fully comprehensive policy being downgraded to third-party coverage, ask your insurance company for a Green Card. Carry your insurance certificate, Green Card, proof of ownership of the car and, importantly, your driver's licence. If your licence was issued in Great Britain, you should also bring your passport with you for ID.

Membership of a reputable breakdown club like the **AA** or **Green Flag National Breakdown** is advisable unless you are undaunted by the prospect of breaking down in remote parts. Non-members can join up for just the duration of their trip. Depending on the type of coverage, automobile clubs may offer only limited services in Ireland.

Car Hire

Car rental firms do good business in Ireland, so in summer it's wise to book ahead. Rental – particularly in the Republic – is quite expensive and the best rates are often obtained by renting in advance. Broker companies, such as **Holiday Autos**, will shop around to get you the best deal. Savings can also be made by choosing a fly-drive or even a rail-sail-drive vacation, but always check for hidden extras.

Car rental usually includes unlimited mileage plus passenger indemnity insurance and coverage for third party, fire and theft, but not damage to the vehicle. If you plan to cross the border in either direction, however briefly, you must tell the rental company, as there may be a small insurance premium.

To rent a car, you must show a full driver's licence, held for two years without violation. US visitors are advised to obtain an international licence through AAA before leaving the States to facilitate dealing with traffic officials should problems occur.

Rural petrol pump

Petrol

Unleaded petrol (gas) and diesel fuel are available just about everywhere in Ireland. Although prices vary from station to station, fuel in the Republic and in Northern Ireland is expensive. Almost all the stations accept VISA and MasterCard, although it is worth checking before filling up, particularly in rural areas.

Road Maps

The road map on the inside back cover shows virtually all the towns and villages mentioned in this guide. In addition, each chapter starts with a map of the region showing all the major sights and tips on getting around. If you plan to do much driving or cycling, you should obtain a more detailed map. Ordnance Survey Holiday Maps are among the best road maps. You can usually get town plans free from tourist offices *(see pp350–51)*. The tourist boards of the Republic and Northern Ireland both issue free lists of suggested routes for cyclists. **The National Trails Office** website is a good online resource.

The road signage outside Dublin Airport

The familiar sight of a farmer and cattle on an Irish country road

Rules of the Road

Driving in Ireland is unlikely to pose any great problems. For many, the most difficult aspect of it is getting used to overtaking on the right and giving way to traffic on the right at roundabouts (traffic circles). On both sides of the border, the wearing of seat belts is compulsory for drivers and all passengers. Children must have a suitable restraint system. Motorcyclists and passengers must wear helmets. Northern Ireland uses the same Highway Code as Great Britain. The Republic of Ireland's Highway Code is very similar – find copies of both at bookstores. In the Republic, learner drivers display an "L" plate, and in Northern Ireland, cars carrying a red "R" plate identify "restricted" drivers who have passed their driving test within the previous 12 months and have to keep to lower speeds. Random breath-testing is common, especially at Christmas and on bank holiday weekends.

Speed Limits

The maximum speeds are shown in miles in Northern Ireland and kilometres in the Republic, except in some rural areas where they are still in miles. They are much the same as those in Britain:

• 50 km/h (30 mph) in built-up areas.
• 100 km/h (60 mph) on national roads and dual carriageways.
• 120 km/h (70 mph) on motorways.

In inner-city Dublin the speed limit is 30km/h (20 mph). On certain roads, which are clearly marked, the speed limits are either 65 km/h (40 mph) or 80 km/h (50 mph). Where there is no indication, the limit is 95 km/h (60 mph). In the Republic, vehicles towing caravans (trailers) must not exceed 90 km/h (55 mph).

A rural road, Dingle Peninsula

Directions and Road Signs

Road signs in the Republic are in both English and Irish, and distances are shown in kilometres. In the North distances are shown in miles.

One sign that is unique to the Republic is the regulatory traffic sign "Yield" ("Géill Slí" in Irish-speaking areas) – in the UK this is worded "Give Way". Throughout the Republic and Northern Ireland, brown signs with white lettering indicate places of historic, cultural or leisure interest.

Signs in the Republic

Unprotected quay or river ahead

Junction ahead

Children or school ahead

Dangerous bends ahead

Signs In Northern Ireland

Motorway direction sign

Primary route sign

Road Conditions

Roads in Northern Ireland and the Republic are well surfaced and generally in good condition, although both have many winding stretches requiring extra caution. The volume of traffic, particularly in the South, is much lower than in rural parts of Britain. On some of the more isolated rural roads you may not come across another driver for miles.

Many sections of Ireland's national roads have been upgraded to motorways, and there has been extensive construction of two-lane carriageways across the country, including in remote areas such as County Donegal.

Parking

Finding parking in Ireland used to be easy, but this is no longer the case. Due to increased congestion, the majority of towns now have paid parking on and off street. Dublin, Belfast and a few other cities have either parking meters or (fairly expensive) parking lots. Parking on the street is allowed, though a single yellow line along the edge of the road means there are some restrictions (there should be a sign nearby showing the permitted parking times). Double yellow lines indicate that no parking is allowed at any time.

Parking disc sign

Disc parking – a version of "pay & display" – operates in most large towns and cities in the Republic and the North. Discs can be purchased from fuel stations, roadside machines, tourist offices and many shops.

In Northern Ireland, almost all towns and villages have Control Zones, which are indicated by large yellow or pink signs. For security reasons, unattended parking in a Control Zone is not permitted at any time of the day.

Cycling

The quiet roads of Ireland make touring by bicycle a real joy. The unreliable weather, however, can be something of a hindrance. Shops such as **Kearney** in Galway, rent bikes to tourists and are usually open at least six or seven days a week. It is often possible to rent a bike in one town and drop it off at another for a small charge. You can also take bikes on buses and trains, usually for a small surcharge.

Many dealers can provide safety helmets, but it is always best to bring your own lightweight waterproof clothing to help cope with the unpredictable weather.

Security Roadblocks in Northern Ireland

Control Zone
NO VEHICLE TO BE LEFT UNATTENDED
at any time

Warning sign in Northern Ireland

In the late 1960s, when the Northern Ireland Troubles began, roadblocks were introduced on to the roads, with checkpoints staffed by the army or the police. These days, the peace agreement has led to a much more relaxed attitude and if you are travelling by road, whether in the centre of Londonderry or the remote Sperrin Mountains, you are very unlikely to come across a roadblock.

In the unlikely event of your being stopped, show your driver's licence and insurance certificate or rental agreement when asked.

Cyclists checking their directions in Ballyvaughan, County Clare

DIRECTORY

Car-Rental Companies

Alamo
Tel 0870 599 4000 (UK).
Tel 877 222 9075 (US).
W alamo.com

Argus Rent-a-Car
Tel (0) 23 83002 (Ireland).
W argusrentals.com

Avis
Tel 021 432 7460 (Cork).
Tel 08445 818181 (UK).
Tel 800 331 1084 (US). **W** avis.com

Budget
Tel 01 844 5150 (Dublin).
Tel 800 793159 (US). **W** budget.ie

Dan Dooley
Tel 062 53103 (Dublin).
W dan-dooley.ie

Hertz
Tel 01 844 5466 (Dublin).
Tel 0207 026 007 (UK).
Tel 800 654 3001 (US).
W hertz.com

Holiday Autos
Tel 0871 472 5229 (UK).
W holidayautos.co.uk

Irish Car Rentals
Tel 1850 206088 (ROI).
Tel 0800 4747 4227 (UK).
W irishcarrentals.com

Murrays/Europcar
Tel 01 614 2888 (Dublin).
W europcar.ie

National Car Rental
Tel 061 206025 (Limerick).
W carhire.ie

Breakdown Services

Automobile Association
Tel 01 617 9999 (ROI).
Tel Rescue No. 1800 667788.
W aaireland.ie

Green Flag National Breakdown
Tel 0800 000111 (to enrol in UK).
W greenflag.com

Trails and Routes

The National Trails Office
W irishtrails.ie

Bicycle-Rental Shops

Kearney Cycles
Tel 091 563356.
W kearneycycles.com

Travelling by Train

The Republic of Ireland's rail network is run by **Irish Rail** (Iarnród Éireann) and is state-controlled. The rail network is far from comprehensive and quite expensive, but the trains are generally reliable and comfortable and can be a good way of covering long distances. The service provided by **Northern Ireland Railways** (NIR) is more limited but fares are slightly cheaper. There is an excellent train service between Dublin and Belfast, with a journey time of approximately two hours. Fares can be as little as €36 round trip, with substantial discounts for online bookings.

The DART at Bray railway station, County Wicklow

Train Services in the Republic of Ireland

Although the more rural areas in the Republic of Ireland are not served by train, Irish Rail operates a satisfactory service to most of the large cities and towns. Taking the train is probably the fastest and most convenient way of going from Dublin to places like Cork, Limerick, Galway, Waterford and Sligo. However, there are glaring gaps in the network; for example, Donegal is totally devoid of train services, so if you are planning to explore the west coast of Ireland using public transport, you will have to continue westward from towns such as Sligo, Westport, Galway and Limerick using the local bus services.

The two main train stations in Dublin are Connolly Station, for trains to the north, northwest and Rosslare, and Heuston Station, which serves the west, midlands and southwest. These two stations are connected to the city centre by the No. 90 bus service and the Luas which run every 10 to 15 minutes and take a quarter of an hour – traffic permitting. All trains in the Republic of Ireland have standard and super-standard (first-class) compartments. Bicycles can be taken on inter-city trains for a small fee.

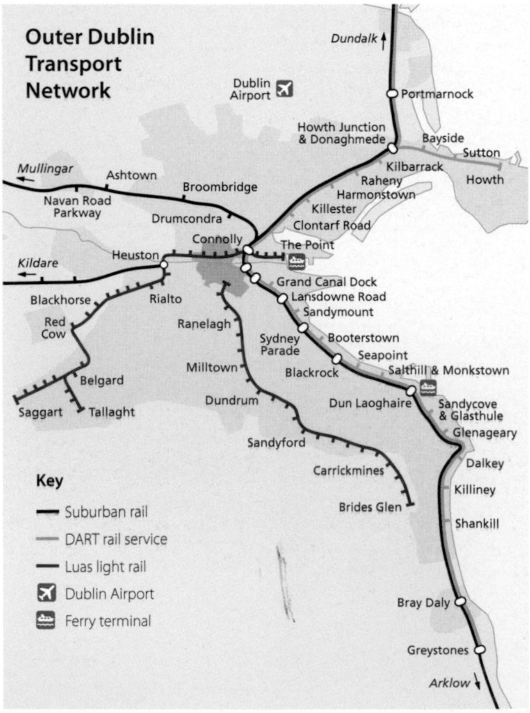

Outer Dublin Rail Services

The handy electric rail service known as DART (Dublin Area Rapid Transit) serves 30 stations between Malahide and Greystones with several stops in Dublin city centre. A Rail/Bus ticket allows three consecutive days' travel on DART trains as well as Dublin Bus services. Tickets can be purchased at any of the DART stations. The Luas light rail service connects central Dublin with the suburbs. The first lines were completed in 2004, and interconnect with the DART *(see also p372)*.

Train Services in Northern Ireland

The rail network in Northern Ireland is sparse, with only two main routes out of Belfast. One line travels west to Londonderry via Coleraine (for the Giant's Causeway) and the other provides Ireland's only cross-border service, operating a high-speed link between Belfast and Dublin eight times a day. There is also an express service out to Larne Harbour and a commuter line to Bangor.

All trains leave from Central Station, which is not in fact in the centre, but has regular links to Great Victoria Street station in the heart of the city's business and shopping district. There are no baggage rooms at any of Northern Ireland's train or bus stations.

Tickets and Fares

Throughout Ireland, train tickets are generally quite expensive, but discounts are available for students and there are lots of bargain incentives and concessionary passes. Most of these include bus travel, so you can get virtually anywhere in Ireland on one ticket.

One of the best tickets available is the Open-Road Pass which allows unlimited travel on all Bus Éireann services from periods of three days (€57) to 15 days (€249). An 8-day Irish Explorer ticket, which costs €245, is valid on all Irish Rail and Bus Éireann services throughout the Republic; travel in Northern Ireland is not included.

Both passes cover many local services, including transport in Cork, Waterford, Limerick and Galway.

Passengers in a queue at the ticket office at Belfast's Central Station

Concessions

Good concessions for students are available with cards issued by Irish Rail and Translink for use in the South and Northern Ireland respectively *(see p352)*.

An InterRail Youth Global Pass allows unlimited travel for a continuous period of 22 days or one month, or for a flexible duration of 5 or 10 days in the Republic and 30 other European countries. It is available for European citizens only. Older travellers can get InterRail Adult passes costing slightly more. Similar passes are offered by Eurail for non-Europeans.

Ireland's Rail Network

Irish Rail (Iarnród Éireann)
35 Abbey St Lower, Dublin 1.
Tel 01 836 6222. **irishrail.ie**

Northern Ireland Railways
Central Station, East Bridge St, Belfast BT1 3PB.
Tel 028 9066 6630. **translink.co.uk**

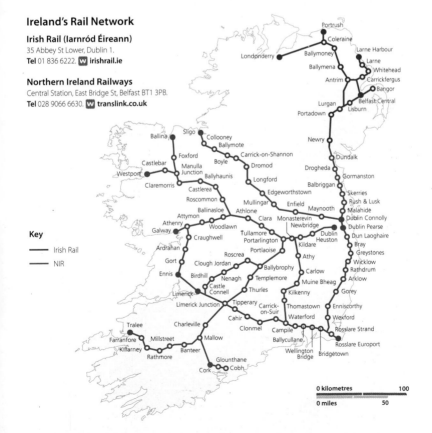

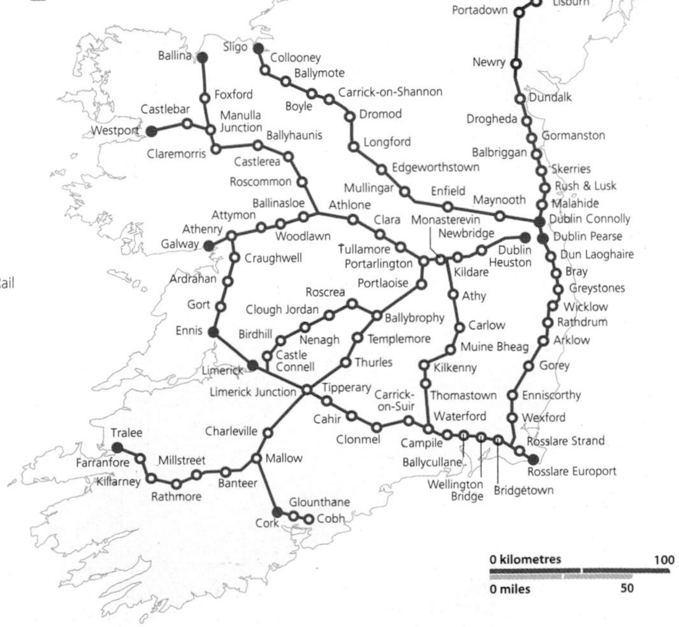

Key

Irish Rail

NIR

Travelling by Bus and Taxi

The bus services throughout Ireland are generally quite good, for such a rural island. However, longer journeys often involve changing buses en route so extra travelling time should be allowed. Touring by bus is also a good way to see Ireland – local tourist offices have details and prices of the numerous tours available and they often take bookings. Taxi services are available in all major cities and towns in Ireland. In the Republic, taxis are identified by a yellow light on the roof. In the North, cities like Belfast and Londonderry have both mini-cabs and London-style black cabs.

A typical passenger bus used for public transport in Dublin

Getting Around by Bus

The Republic of Ireland's national bus company, **Bus Éireann,** operates a countrywide network of buses serving all the cities and most of the towns. In Dublin, the main bus station is the Busáras on Store Street, a short walk from O'Connell Street.

There are a number of private bus companies which either compete with the national network or provide services on routes not covered by Bus Éireann. In rural Donegal, for example, there are several private bus services. Some are not fully licensed, so check whether you would be covered in the event of an accident. Local tourist offices should be able to point out the most reputable firms.

Ulsterbus runs an excellent service throughout Northern Ireland including express links between all the major towns. Belfast has two main bus stations – the Europa Buscentre off Great Victoria Street and Laganside Station. Check before setting out that you are going to the right one. Note that for reasons of security, there are no baggage rooms at any of the stations in Northern Ireland.

Tickets and Fares

In the Republic, long-distance buses are about half the price of the equivalent train trip. If you are making the return trip on the same day, ask for a day-return ticket, which is much cheaper than the normal round-trip fare. Under-16s pay approximately half the adult fare and student travelcard holders also get a healthy reduction. For those intending to do a lot of travelling it is cheaper to buy a "Rambler" ticket. This allows unlimited bus travel throughout the Republic for a certain number of days in a set period, for example, 15 days' travel out of 30 consecutive days. A variety of other tickets are also available.

A "Freedom of Northern Ireland" ticket gives you unlimited travel on all Ulsterbus routes for either a day, three days or a week. Ulsterbus also offers cheap day-return tickets. Students are eligible for a 15 per cent discount by showing a Translink Student Discount Card. There are also a number of period passes available that combine bus and rail travel *(see p369)*.

Bus Tours

While the bus services in Ireland are generally adequate for getting from town to town, using public transport isn't a very practical way of exploring specific areas or regions in great detail, unless you have a lot of time on your hands. If you find yourself in a remote area like Connemara *(see pp210–12)* but have only a very limited amount of time in which to see its main

Express service bus in Northern Ireland

attractions, a local guided tour of the area is a good idea. For about €25 per adult you can do the picturesque "figure of eight" circuit by bus, starting from Galway and taking in Spiddal, Kylemore, Letterfrack, Oughterard and then returning to Galway (summer only). The bus sets out at 10am and returns at about 5:30pm, making regular stops at places of interest. The price does not include admission fees or lunch. Book in advance or on the day at Galway Tourist Information Centre. Four-hour or one-day tours such as this are available in many of Ireland's main tourist areas. Other popular tours of rural Ireland include Glendalough *(see pp144–5)*, Donegal *(see pp228–35)* and the Ring of Kerry *(see pp168–9)*.

In Dublin and other cities in the Republic, Bus Éireann and some local companies run half- and one-day excursions. **Dublin Bus** (Bus Átha Cliath) runs a Dublin City tour, which leaves from O'Connell Street Upper. This guided tour takes in the city's most famous sights.

In Northern Ireland, Ulsterbus operates tours from the Europa Buscentre in Belfast to all the major places of interest. These tours include the Causeway Coast *(see p265)*, the Glens of Antrim *(see p271)* and the Ulster-American Folk Park *(see p273)* near Omagh. Ulsterbus prefers bookings to be made in person at their Belfast office. In summer, **Translink** operates up to two guided bus tours per day around Belfast; in winter tours run on Thursday and Saturday only.

Local Transport

Local bus services throughout the Republic are generally well run and reasonably priced. **Dublin Bus** runs the bus services in the Greater Dublin area *(see p372)*. The on-street light rail service, **Luas** *(see p372)*, provides an easy way to reach suburban areas previously only accessible by bus. The Luas lines connect with the DART rail service *(see p372)* at Connolly Station.

In the rest of the Republic the bus services, including city buses in Galway, Limerick, Waterford and Cork, are operated mainly by Bus Éireann; a timetable is available at tourist offices and bus stations. Some bus routes connecting towns and villages are served by private companies as well as Bus Éireann. For bus times (and stops) in more remote areas, try asking the locals.

Northern Ireland's bus network is run by **Ulsterbus/ Translink**, including in Belfast where the local service is called **Metro** *(see p373)*. Regional timetables are available at bus stations.

Cars wait in line at a Dublin taxi rank

Taxis in the Republic

With the exception of the Republic's most rural places, there is usually a local taxi service. Apart from in Dublin, where they are plentiful, cruising taxis are a rarity and the best places to find taxis are at train or bus stations, hotels and taxi ranks – your hotel or B&B will also be able to provide details. Four- or eight-seater taxis are available and prices are usually based on metered mileage; if not, it is always best to confirm the fare to your destination before travelling.

Taxis in Northern Ireland

Taxis in Northern Ireland are reasonably priced; journeys within the centre of Belfast will usually cost no more than £10 by mini-cab or black cab. In most decent-sized towns in the North you will find at least one taxi office or a rank where you can wait for a cab. Other- wise, ask for the number of a taxi firm at a local hotel or B&B. A taxi plating scheme is in place, with large plates front and rear of the vehicle, which helps identify legal taxis. Tipping taxi drivers is customary but not obligatory.

DIRECTORY

National Bus Companies

Bus Éireann
Tel 01 836 6111. **W buseireann.ie**

Ulsterbus/Translink
Tel 028 9066 6630.
W translink.co.uk

Bus Tours

Irish City Tours and Gray Line
Tel 01 898 0700.
W irishcitytours.com

McGeehan Coaches
Fintown PO, Co Donegal.
Tel 074 954 6150.
W mcgeehancoaches.com

Dublin Bus
Tel 01 873 4222. **W dublinbus.ie**

Translink
Tel 028 9045 8484.
W translink.co.uk

Travelling within Cities

The historic centres of Dublin and Belfast are compact and very easy to navigate. Both are well served by public transport, whether by bus, commuter train or, in the case of Dublin, tram. Each city can be explored in a leisurely fashion on foot – a little less so by bicycle. Both cities offer plenty to see in a small area, as well as easy access to the mountains.

Travelling within Dublin

Bus

A Dublin Bus double-decker is still the best way to see the city. You can buy prepaid tickets (including a one-day pass for €6.90) in newsagents, or pay as you board. It is best to have the correct fare, otherwise you will be given a receipt for the excess amount, which can only be cashed in at Dublin Bus HQ in O'Connell Street. Fares start at €1.65 and depend on how far you travel. Buses run from about 6am to 11.30pm; Nitelink buses run through the night at weekends. Bus routes and timetables are displayed at each bus stop. For bus tours *see p370.*

LUAS

The Luas (luas is the Irish word for speed) light rail system, completed in 2004, is a comfortable and speedy way to get around. There are two on-street lines, the Red line and the Green line. A Luas line connecting both these lines is under construction and is scheduled to be completed by 2017. The Red line connects with the railway stations Heuston and Connolly, and with the DART at Connolly. Payment is made at ticket machines at Luas stops, and a return fare starts from €3.20.

DART and Luas tickets

DART

The electric rail commuter system DART (Dublin Area Rapid Transit) serves 30 stations along the coast from Malahide and Howth on the north side to Greystones on the south, with several stops in the city centre. DART stations have ticket machines and booking offices. They also sell the rail timetable (€3) which contains maps and schedules for DART and mainline rail services. Avoid rush hour for great views of the bay.

Luas light rail station, Dublin

Tickets and Fares

The new pre-paid Leap Card can be purchased and topped up at newsagents, and used on Luas, DART and commuter rail services, as well as on Dublin Bus.

Fares are discounted by about 15 per cent when compared to buying single tickets. A three-day Rambler ticket for Dublin Bus costs €15; a five-day-ticket costs €25. Tickets are on sale from newsagents, the Dublin Bus office in O'Connell Street, and machines at Luas stops and DART stations.

Driving in Dublin

Driving a car in Dublin's congested city centre is best avoided. The short distances are more easily covered on foot, or by bus or Luas. If you do need to drive, there are plenty of multistorey car parks, and a system of pay-and-display on-street parking which costs €2–€5 per hour, depending on the zone. Costs are shown on the ticket machines in the street. Make sure you return to your car on time as clamping is common.

The M50 ring road around Dublin is a barrier-free, no-cash toll road. Tolls must be paid online within 48 hours (www.eflow.ie).

Cycling in Dublin

Dublin has many cycle lanes, and ever more people travel to work by bike. **Dublinbikes** is a self-service bike rental scheme with 40 hire stations around the city. The first 30 minutes of hire are free.

A good place for the uninitiated cyclist is along the paths on either side of the River Liffey below the Custom House. Local shops, such as **Cycle Ways**, rent bikes to tourists. Alternatively, try **Neill's Wheels** in Dublin, which offers city cycle tours with a local guide.

Walking in Dublin

The outer suburbs of Dublin may sprawl for miles, but the city centre is very small and makes for a pleasant amble on foot. A walk east along the river from stately Heuston Station to the far end of the south quays near the sea will take less than an hour, and a walk between Dublin's two Georgian squares, Parnell Square on the north side to St Stephen's Green on the south, takes little more than half an hour. St Stephen's Green itself is pleasant for a relaxed stroll.

Travelling within Belfast

Belfast Metro Bus

Bus

Metro, Belfast's local bus service, is a great way to see the city and its environs. Prepaid tickets are on sale in shops displaying the Metro sign or at the Metro kiosk in Donegall Square West. These need to be placed on the electronic reader next to the driver when you board. Alternatively, pay the driver in coins. The fare depends on how far you travel, starting at £1.40. Maps showing the bus routes are available on www.translink.co.uk.

Tickets and Fares

The handy Metro Day Ticket (£3.20 or £3.70, depending on the time), allows unlimited travel all day on the Metro bus system. There are multi-journey tickets from £6 for people staying more than a few days.

Metro prepay ticket

Driving in Belfast

As with any other small city centre, there is no great advantage in driving a car in Belfast. Public transport is good, the distances are easily covered on foot and the black taxis are cheap. There is even a black taxi tour of the city.

Those who do wish to drive around the city will find that there is little traffic congestion. Ample car parking can be found in the centre of the city with multistorey car parks and on-street pay-and-display parking *(see p367)*. Make sure you get back to your car on time to avoid a fine.

Cycling in Belfast

Belfast is becoming more cycle-friendly, with a good network of cycle lanes and tracks. The many parks are ideal for cycling and walking, and a number of traffic-free cycleways connect Belfast with other towns. For further details, visit www.sustrans.org.uk.

All bicycles are carried free of charge on Translink (the overall transport authority) buses and trains, and there is covered bicycle parking at many stations. Bikes are available for hire from local shops such as **McConvey Cycles**.

Walking in Belfast

Belfast is a peaceful city these days, and visitors can walk around without need for concern. The city centre is small and easily negotiated on foot. It's a 20-minute walk from the centre to Queen's University, the Titanic Quarter or West Belfast. Walking tours leave from the Belfast Welcome Centre at Donegall Place. These include the general tour, **Historic Belfast**, and the **Blackstaff Way**, which visits the streets around the city centre. Both of these tours cost £6.

Sign for cycle and pedestrian path

DIRECTORY

Cycling

Cycle Ways (Dublin)
Tel 01 873 4748.
W **cycleways.com**

Dublinbikes
W **dublinbikes.ie**

Neill's Wheels (Dublin)
Tel 087 933 8312.
W **rentabikedublin.com**

McConvey Cycles (Belfast)
Tel 028 9033 0322.
W **mcconveycycles.com**

City Transport

DART (Dublin)
Tel 01 836 6222. **W** **irishrail.ie**

Luas (Dublin)
Tel 1 800 300604. **W** **luas.ie**

Taxis & Taxi Tours

National Radio Cabs (Dublin)
Tel 01 677 2222.

Black Taxi Tours of Belfast
Tel 028 9064 2264.

Walking Tours

Blackstaff Way (Belfast)
Tel 028 9029 2631.

Historic Belfast
Tel 028 9024 6609.

General Index

Page numbers in **bold** refer to main entries.

M

Q

R

Acknowledgments

Dorling Kindersley would like to thank the following people whose contributions and assistance have made the preparation of this book possible.

Main Contributors

Lisa Gerard-Sharp is a writer and broadcaster who has contributed to numerous travel books, including the *Eyewitness Travel Guide to France*. She is of Irish extraction, with roots in County Sligo and County Galway, and a regular visitor to Ireland.

Tim Perry, from Dungannon, County Tyrone, writes on travel and popular music for various publishers in North America and the British Isles.

Additional Contributors

Cian Hallinan, Eoin Higgins, Douglas Palmer, Audrey Ryan, Trevor White, Roger Williams.

Additional Photography

Peter Anderson, Jonathan Buckley, Joe Cornish, Andy Crawford, Brian Daughton, Michael Diggin, Steve Gorton, Anthony Haughey, Nigel Hicks, Mike Linley, Ian O'Leary, Stephen Oliver, Stephen Power, Magnus Rew, Clive Streeter, Rough Guides/Michelle Bhatia, Rough Guides/Roger Mapp, Rough Guides/Mark Thomas, Matthew Ward, Alan Williams.

Additional Illustrations

Richard Bonson, Brian Craker, John Fox, Paul Guest, Stephan Gyapay, Ian Henderson, Claire Littlejohn, Gillie Newman, Chris Orr, Kevin Robinson, John Woodcock, Martin Woodward.

Additional Picture Research

Miriam Sharland.

Editorial and Design

Managing Editors Vivien Crump, Helen Partington
Managing Art Editor Steve Knowlden
Deputy Editorial Director Douglas Amrine
Deputy Art Director Gaye Allen
Production David Proffit, Hilary Stephens
Picture Research Sue Mennell, Christine Rista
DTP Designer Adam Moore
Maps Gary Bowes, Margaret Slowey, Richard Toomey (Era-Maptec, Dublin, Ireland)
Map Co-Ordinators Michael Ellis, David Pugh
Marion Broderick, Margaret Chang, Martin Cropper, Guy Dimond, Fay Franklin, Yael Freudmann, Sally Ann Hibbard, Annette Jacobs, Erika Lang, Michael Osborn, Polly Phillimore, Caroline Radula-Scott.

Relaunch – Editorial and Design

Editorial Claire Baranowski, Fay Franklin, Anna Freiberger, Bhaswati Ghosh, Susanne Hillen, Claire Jones, Ciara Kenny, Sumita Khatwani, Rahul Kumar, Kathryn Lane, Alison McGill, Susan Millership, Mani Ramaswamy, Lucy Richards,
Alka Thakur, Aine Toner, Asavari Singh
Factcheck Des Berry
Design Maite Lantaron, Baishakhee Sengupta, Shruti Singhi
Picture Research Ellen Root
DTP Vinod Harish, Jason Little, Shailesh Sharma
Cartography Uma Bhattacharya, Casper Morris, Kunal Singh.

Index

Hilary Bird.

Special Assistance

Dorling Kindersley would like to thank all the regional and local tourist offices in the Republic and Northern Ireland for their valuable help. Particular thanks also to: Ralph Doak and Egerton Shelswell-White at Bantry House, Bantry, Co Cork; Vera Greif at the Chester Beatty Library and Gallery of Oriental Art, Dublin; Alan Figgis at Christ Church Cathedral, Dublin; Labhras Ó Murchu at Comhaltas Ceoltóirí Éireann; Catherine O'Connor at Derry City Council; Patsy O'Connell at Dublin Tourism; Tanya Cathcart at Fermanagh Tourism, Enniskillen; Peter Walsh at the Guinness Storehouse, Dublin; Gerard Collet at the Irish Shop, Covent Garden, London; Dónall P Ó Baoill at ITE, Dublin; Pat Cooke at Kilmainham Gaol, Dublin; Angela Shanahan at the Kinsale Tourist Office; Bill Maxwell, Adrian Le Harivel and Marie McFeely at the National Gallery of Ireland, Dublin; Philip McCann at the National Library of Ireland, Dublin; Willy Cumming at the National Monuments Divison, Office of Public Works, Dublin; Eileen Dunne and Sharon Fogarty at the National Museum of Ireland, Dublin; Joris Minne at the Northern Ireland Tourist Office, Belfast; Dr Tom MacNeil at Queen's University, Belfast; Sheila Crowley at St Mary's Pro-Cathedral, Dublin; Paul Brock at the Shannon Development Centre; Tom Sheedy at Shannon Heritage and Banquets, Bunratty Castle, Co Clare; Angela Sutherland at the Shannon-Erne Waterway, Co Leitrim; Máire Ní Bháin at Trinity College, Dublin; Anne-Marie Diffley at Trinity College Library, Dublin; Pat Maclean at the Ulster Museum, Belfast; Harry Hughes at the Willie Clancy School of Traditional Music, Miltown Malbay, Co Clare.

Revisions Team

Namrata Adhwaryu, Emma Anacootee, Parnika Bagla, Shruti Bahl, Meghna Baruah, Claire Baranowski, Des Berry, Subhashree Bharati, Nadia Bonomally, Emma Brady, Roisin Cameron, Louise Cleghorn, Tara Corristine, Kathleen Crowley, Karen D'Souza, Neha Dhingra, Rory Doyle, Vidushi Duggal, Sylvia Earley, Nicola Erdpresser, Anna Freiberger, Rhiannon Furbear, Darragh Geraghty, David Gordon, Yvonne Gordon, Lydia Halliday, Kaberi Hazarika, Peter Hynes, Claire Jones, Bharti Karakoti, Rupanki Arora Kaushik, Ciara Kenny, Sumita Khatwani, Rahul Kumar, Rakesh Kumar Pal, Delphine Lawrance, Jude Ledger/Pure Content, Anwesha Madhukalya, Therese McKenna, Alison McGill, Caroline Mead, Kate Molan, Vikki Nousiainen, David O'Grady, Mary O'Grady, Susie Peachey, Madge Perry, Marianne Petrou, Tom Prentice, Pete Quinlan, Rada Radojicic, Sands Publishing Solutions, Sean Sheehan, Azeem Siddiqui, Rituraj Singh, Beverly Smart, Sadie Smith, Susana Smith, Tracy Smith, Scott Stickland, Avantika Sukhia, Áine Toner, Zafar ul-Islam Khan, Conrad Van Dyke, Vinita Venugopal, Ajay Verma, Deepika Verma, Dora Whitaker, Debra Wolter.

Photography Permissions

The publisher would like to thank all those who gave permission to photograph at various cathedrals, churches, museums, restaurants, hotels, shops, galleries and other sights too numerous to list individually.

Picture Credits

a - above; b - below/bottom; c - centre; f - far; l - left; r - right; t - top.

The publisher would like to thank the following individuals, companies and picture libraries for permission to reproduce their photographs:

Abbey Theatre: Ros Kavanagh 119tl; **Aer Lingus/Airbus Industrie:** 360tc; **AKG, London:** National Museum, Copenhagen/Erich Lessing 30cl; **Alamy Images:** AntipasM 339br; AU Photos 28-29c; Caro/Sorge 355clb; David Cordner 373cla; Phil Crean A 332cl; De Luan 150cl; Michael Diggin 15tr; FMD Stock Photography 82bl; Peter Forsberg 119cr; fstop2/Keith Pritchard 246tl; Robert Harding Picture Library 306cla; Robert Harding Picture Library Ltd/Pearl Bucknall 368tr; imagebroker/Dr. Wilfried Bahnmüller 164-5; incamerastock 12crb, 290–1, 312bl; David Lyons 224, 352br; Barry Mason 363tl, 372bl; Daryl Mulvihill 307tl; David Newton 371bl; rumal 12tc; Radharc Images 90bl, 369tr; Stephen Saks Photography 353tl; Picturamic 309tr; Ian Shipley ARC 119tr; Striking Image 308bl; Tetra Images 76; Peter Titmus 361bl; Transport/© Stephen Barnes 373cra; **Allsport:** David Rogers 32c; Steve Powell 51tl; Appletree Press Ltd, Belfast (*Irish Proverbs* © illustrations Karen Bailey) 337cl; **Ashford Castle:** 300tc, 319b.

Bantry House and Garden: 298tl; **Beshoff Restaurants:** 310bl; **Blairscove House & Restaurant**: 315bl;
The Bridgeman Art Library: Yale Center for British Art, Paul Mellon Collection, USA- View of Powerscourt County Wicklow, c.1760–2 (oil on canvas) by George Barret the Elder (c.1728–84) 8–9; **La Boheme**: 313t; **Patrick Brady**: 107tl, 107br, 226cl, 234tl; © **Bristol City Museums and Art Gallery:** 36bl; © **British Library:** *Richard II's Campaigns in Ireland* Ms.Harl.41tl; © **British Museum:** 37bl; **Browns Restaurant & Champagne Lounge:** 325tr; **Burren Perfumery Tea Rooms:** 317t; **Bus Éirieann:** 371tr;
© **Bushmills Ltd:** 270bl; **Bushmills Inn Hotel:** 303tr, 324br.

Café Paradiso: 314tl; © **Central Bank of Ireland:** 357 all; **Central Cyber Café, Dublin:** Finbarr Clarkson 359tr; **Chapter One Restaurant:** 310tr; © **Chester Beatty Library, Dublin:** 81tr; **Christ Church Cathedral:** 84cl, 85tl ; © **Classic Designs/Ij Young Ltd, Blarney:** 337c; **The Cliff House Hotel:** 297tl; **Clo Iar-chonnachta:** publishers of *Litríocht agus Pobal* by Gearóid Denvir 51cb; **Bruce Coleman Ltd:** Mark Boulton 22tr; Adrian Davies 22br; Rodney Dawson 23cl; Pekka Helo 23cr; Jan Van de Kam 191tr; Gordon Langsbury 22cl, 191tc; MR Phicon 22crb; Kim Taylor 23tc; R Wanscheidt 23crb; Uwe Walz 22cr; **Corbis:** Richard Cummins 18; Demotix / Brendan Donnelly 33br; Demotix/Art Widak 33cr; Design Pics 13tr; Destinations 2–3, 137t, 240; EPA / Maxwells; Eurasia Press / Steven Vidler 323br; Oscar Elias 15bc; Jack Fields 307c; Irish Government Pool 51crb; Alen MacWeeney 220–1; Jean-Pierre De Mann 11tl; National Geographic Society/Chris Hill 231cla; Jeanne Rynhart 1; SOPA/ Stefano Torrione 13bc; Paul Thompson 14tr; © **Cork Examiner:** 33tl; © **Cork Public Museum:** 39cla; **Joe Cornish:** 23cla,274tr;
Crawford Municipal Art Gallery: *The Meeting of St Brendan and the Unhappy Judas*, Harry Clarke 178bl.

Danske Bank Group, Ireland: 356c; **Davison & Associates, Ltd, Ireland:** 85cra; © **The Department of the Environment, Heritage and Local Government, Ireland:** 176bl, 181tc, 250c, 251tl, 251cr, 252br; **The Derg Inn:** 318tr; **Derry City Council:** 262tr; **Michael Diggin:** 157b, 167cr, 168cla, 169tr, 189tl, 210bl, 229t, 230tr, 230cl, 343tl, 343b, 344c, 350bc, 355tl, 356br; **Dreamstime.com:** Agabek 60; Leonid Andronov 264tl; Arsty 180bl, Asteri77 23fcrb, Atgimages 364tl; Banner25 209bc; Bartkowski 23tl; Christian Bertrand 28bl; Bred2k8 108bl; Gunold Brunbauer 301br; Alain Cezard 213bl; Daniel M. Cisilino 131br; Darkbird77 340br; Datacode66 248tr; Dbeatson 23ca; Digitalimagined 256br; Dublinuser 20tl; Linda Duncan 21t; Fr3ank33 59tl; 370tr; Siobhan Fraser 23fclb; Antonio Guillem 23clb; 23cb; Hdanne 23tc; Jeans550 23bc; Patryk Kosmider 124–5; 198b; Kristýna Lipenská 263br; Littleny 214bl; Patricia Lock 213bc; Lucacom 28br; Menno67 191tc (1); Lucian Milasan 21br; Danilo Mongiello 32cb, David Morrison 183tr; Steve Morris 283tr; Mps197 22fcrb; Natursports 22clb; Nhtg 19b; Notcatherinezeta 23tr; Uwe Ohse 22cb, Umit Ozgur 212bc; Pajda83 106tl; Pattdug 189cb; Sean Pavone 65tl; Rihardzz 340tl; Richard Semik 244tl; Thruthelensphotos 10cl; Scattosel vaggio 191tc; Whiskybottle 22fclb, 23bl, Ian Whitworth 97tr; Ykkaa 11tc, 112cl, 113tl; **Dublin Airport Authority:** 360cra, 361tc, 365br; **The Dubliner Magazine:** Jennifer Philips 108cr, 109br; **G A Duncan:** 50bc, 50bl; **Dublin Tourism Image Library:** DRTA 52cla; **Dundee Art Gallery:** *The Children of Lir*, John Duncan 31tc.

Empics Ltd: Hayden West 342cl; **ET Archive**: 31bl; **Mary Evans Picture Library:** 30tr, 30bl, 30br, 31cla, 38bl, 41bc, 42bl; 48bl, 81cl, 93bl, 285br, 291,

Fáilte Ireland/irish Tourist Board: 206cl; Brian Lynch 28–9, 29tl, 250tr, Pat Odea 340c; © **Stephen Faller Ltd, Galway:** 336cla; © **Famine Museum Co Roscommon:** 223cra; **J Farmgate Café:** 304cr; **Jim Fitzpatrick:** 83bl.

Getty Images: Design Pics/Gareth McCormack 156, /Peter Zoeller 204; Flickr/Tony Garcia 140–1; Richard I'Anson 93tr, The Image Bank/Terry Williams 114bl; Brian Lawrence 268–9; National Geographic/Jim Richardson 217bl; Donald Nausbaum 366bl; Panoramic Images 193tr; Steve Powell 51tl; Slow images 14bl; **Ghan House:** 322tr; **Gill and Macmillan Publishers, Dublin:** 49bl; **Glasnevin Trust:** 105br; **Ronald Grant Archive:** *The Commitments*, Twentieth Century Fox 27br; **Gresham Hotel Dublin:** 295tl © **Guinness Ireland Ltd:** 102bl, 102br, 102tl, 103br, 103crb,103tl, 103tr, 103bl.

Hayfield Manor Hotel: 292cl, 304bl; **Hodson Bay Hotel:** 302bc; **Hulton Deutsch Collection:** 26cb, 27tr, 43tl, 46br, 46clb, 50br, 67br.

Images Colour Library: 52bl; **Inpho, Dublin:** 32cla, Billy Stickland 32br; **Irish Picture Library, Dublin:** 42cla, 45tl; © **Irish Times:** 138br; © **Irish Traditional Music Archive, Dublin:** 29bl; **ISIC:** 352c; **iStockphoto.com:** Phil Crean A 64cr

Jam Killarney: 315tr; **Jarrold Colour Publications:** Ja Brooks 66bc; **Michael Jenner:** 247cr.

© Lambeth Palace Library, London: Plan of the London Vintners' Company Township of Bellaghy, Ulster, 1622 (ms. Carew 634 f.34) (detail) 43cra; **Frank Lane Picture Agency:** Roger Wilmshurst 191ftr; **© Leeds City Art Gallery:** *The Irish House of Commons*, Francis Wheatley 44cla; Left Bank Bistro: 322bl; **Pat Liddy:** 109tl; The Lobster Pot, Dublin: 311bc; **Londonderry Arms Hotel:** 294br.

Mander and Mitcheson Theatre Collection: 28cl; **Mansell Collection:** 44bl, 49cra, 85bl, 272bc; **Archie Miles:** 212br; **Moy House:** 299br; **John Murray:** 55bl, 134c; **© Museum of the City of New York:** Gift of Mrs Robert M Littlejohn, *The Bay and Harbor of New York 1855*, Samuel B Waugh 46–7.

National Botanic Gardens, Dublin: 104tl. **Reproduction Courtesy of © National Gallery of Ireland, Dublin:** *WB Yeats and the Irish Theatre*, Edmund Dulac 26tr, *George Bernard Shaw*, John Collier 26br, *Carolan the Harper*, Francis Bindon 28tr, *Leixlip Castle*, Irish School 45cla, *The Custom House, Dublin*, James Malton 45bc, *Pierrot*, Juan Gris 74tr, *A Landscape*, Thomas Roberts 74bl, *The Taking of Christ*, Caravaggio 75tc, *Judith with the Head of Holofernes, Andrea* Mantegna 75cr, *The Sick Call*, Matthew James Lawless 75br, *Jonathan Swift, Satirist*, Charles Jerval 86bc, *James Joyce*, Jacques Emile Blanche 94tr, *Interior with Members of a Family*, P Hussey 136br, *William Butler Yeats, Poet*, J B Yeats 237tl, *The Last Circuit of Pilgrims at Clonmacnoise*, George Petrie 254tr; **© National Gallery, London:** *Beach Scene*, Edgar Degas 95br; **© National Library of Ireland, Dublin:** 27cla, 27cb, 35b, 38clb, 40bc, 42clb, 44clb, 46bl, 47crb, 47tl, 48clb, 49tl, 49crb, 145tr, 182cra, 248b; **© National Museum of Ireland, Dublin:** 3, 36clb, 36cb, 36crb, 36–7, 37c, 37clb, 37br, 38cla, 39cb, 39br, 59bl, 63crb, 70–1 all; **The National Trust, Northern Ireland:** *Hambletonian*, George Stubbs 287tl, 287cra; **The National Trust Photographic Library:** Mathew Antrobus 277b, John Bethell 288tl, Patrick Pendergast 276bl, Will Webster 281br, 291; **National Wax Museum Plus:** 72clb; **Nature Photographers:** B Burbridge 191bc, Paul Sterry 191tl; **Northern Ireland Tourist Board:** 32tr, 277tr, 338cl, 339tl; **Norton Associates:** 78clb.

O'Dowds of Roundstone: 320bl; **Courtesy of the OPW:** 351clb.

Pacemaker Press International, Ltd: 354bc, 354cb; **Walter Pfeiffer Studios, Dublin:** 29 all in panel; **Photo Flora:** Andrew N Gagg 190bc; **Photolibrary:** The Irish Image Collection 188bc; **Photostage:** Donald Cooper 118tr; **Popperfoto:** 50cla, Reuter/ Crispin Rodwell 51tr.

Range Pictures: 47cra; Rathmullan House: 305br, 321tr; **The Reform Club London:** 46cla; **Report/Derek Spiers, Dublin:** 282bl, 282br; **Retrogpraph Archive, London:** © Martin Ranicar-Breese 69br; **Rex Features:** Sipa Press 51bl; **Robert Harding Picture Library:** Patrick Dieudonne 170tl;
F & K Schorr: 244br.; **Shannon-Erne Waterway:** 239bc; **The Slide File, Dublin:**, 22cla, 22cra, 26cla, 32crb, 33clb, 36cla, 53cb, 54cla, 54cra, 54cb, 55cra, 81br, 118bc, 126cla, 135br, 142cl 142br, 155br, 189br, 215tl, 216cb, 216bc, 217cr, 219tr, 228br, 231tr, 234b, 236tr, 241b, 252t, 254–5, 256cra, 274clb; **Sportsfile, Dublin:** 33tc; **Stena Line:** 362cl; **SuperStock:** Richard Cummins 98; Eye Ubiquitous 88; imagebroker.net/Martin Siepmann 258; The Irish Image Collection 128, 184, 348–9, Photononstop 56–7; Tips Images 124–5; **Don Sutton International Photo Library:** 293br.

© Tate Gallery Publications: *Captain Thomas Lee*, Marcus Gheeraedts 42br; **Tipperaryphotos.com:** 355bl, 355cl; **Topham Picture Source:** 45br; **Tourism Ireland:** 334c; **Translink:** 370bl; **© Trinity College, Dublin:** Ms.1440 (Book of Burgos) f 41cb; Ms. 58 (Book of Kells) f 4tr, *The Marriage of Princess Aoife and the Earl of Pembroke*, Daniel Maclise 40cla, (Book of Durrow), 59cr, (Book of Durrow) 67cr, (Book of Kells) f.129v 68cra, Ms.58 (Book of Kells) f.36r 68cl, Ms.58 (Book of Kells) f.28v 68crb, Ms.58 (Book of Kells) f.200r 68b; **Trip:** R Drury 144c; **Tullamore Dew Heritage Centre:** 255tr.

© Ulster Museum, Belfast: bAscona by Philip King 282clb; *The Festival of St Kevin at the Seven Churches, Glendalough*, Joseph Peacock 34, *The Relief of Derry*, William Sadler II 42–3, 43crb, 48cla.

Viking Ship Museum, Strandengen, Denmark: watercolour by Flemming Bau 39tl.

© Waterford Corporation: 39bl, 40clb, 41bl; **The Westin Dublin:** 296bl.

Peter Zöller: 23cra, 52cr, 53cra, 53bl, 150br, 223bl, 253tr, 344br.

Front endpaper:
Alamy Images: David Lyons Ltr; Tetra Images Rcb; **Corbis:** Destinations Rbc; **Dreamstime.com:** Agabek Rcrb; **Getty Images:** Design Pics/Gareth McCormack Lbl; Design Pics/Peter Zoeller Lcla; **SuperStock:** Eye Ubiquitous Rtr; imagebroker.net / Martin Siepmann Rtc; The Irish Image Collection Rbl, Lclb.

Jacket
Front main and spine: AWL Images: Shaun Egan.

All other images © Dorling Kindersley. For further information see www.DKimages.com

Road Map of Ireland

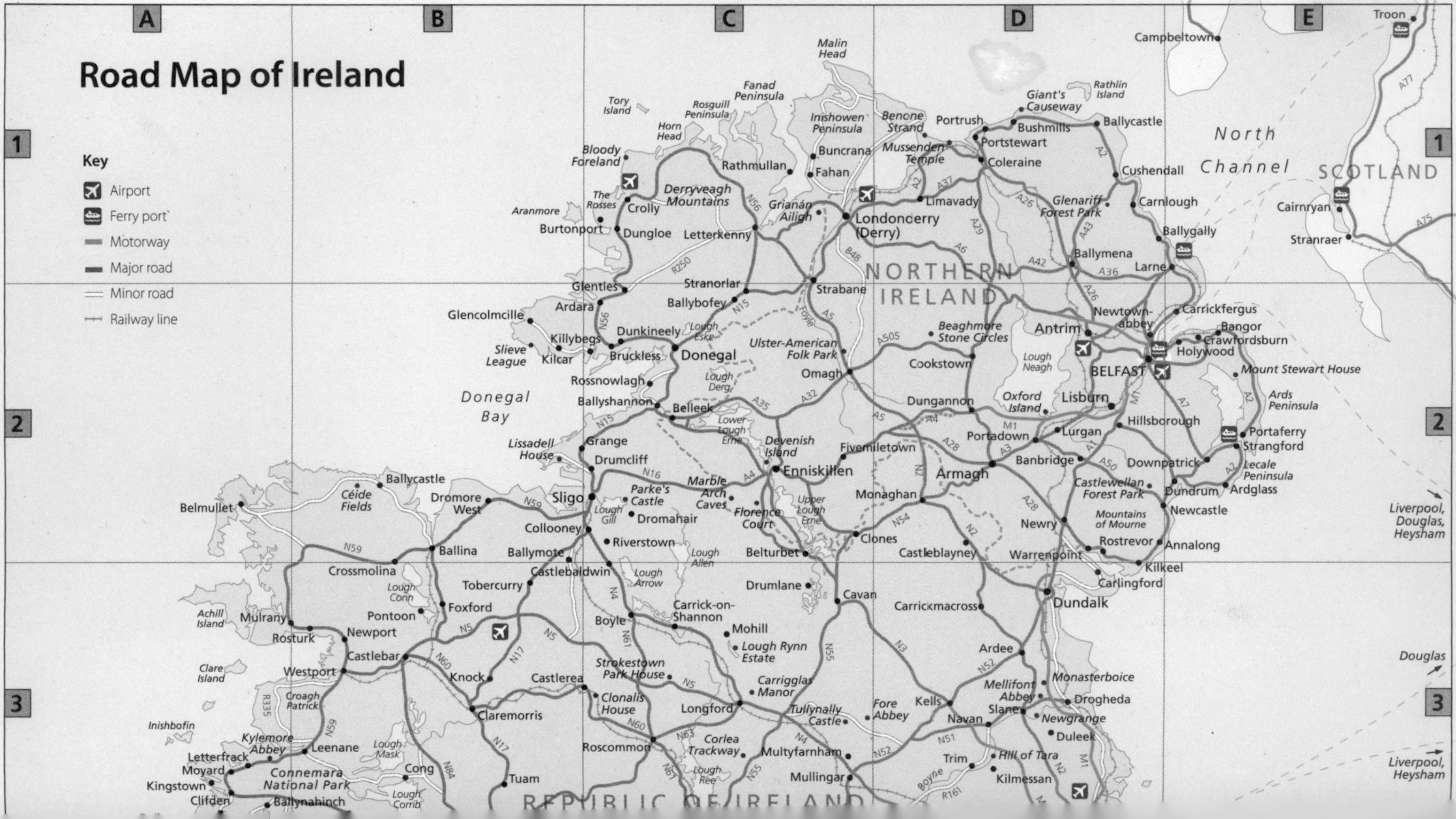